EAKINS REVEALED

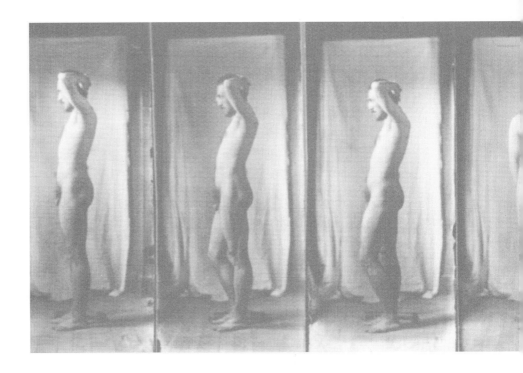

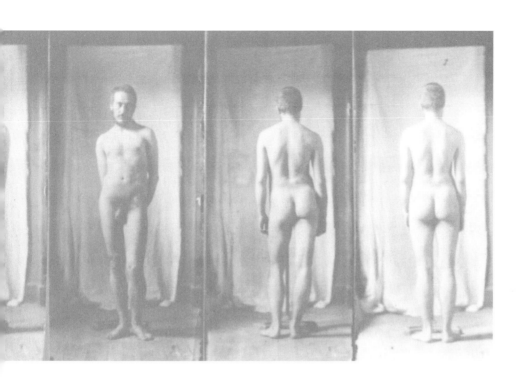

EAKINS REVEALED

The Secret Life of an American Artist

HENRY ADAMS

OXFORD
UNIVERSITY PRESS

2005

OXFORD
UNIVERSITY PRESS

Oxford University Press, Inc., publishes works that further
Oxford University's objective of excellence in research, scholarship,
and education.

Oxford New York
Auckland Cape Town Dar es Salaam Hong Kong Karachi
Kuala Lumpur Madrid Melbourne Mexico City Nairobi
New Delhi Shanghai Taipei Toronto

With offices in
Argentina Austria Brazil Chile Czech Republic France Greece
Guatemala Hungary Italy Japan Poland Portugal Singapore
South Korea Switzerland Thailand Turkey Ukraine Vietnam

Published by Oxford University Press, Inc.
198 Madison Avenue, New York, New York, 10016
http://www.oup-usa.org

Oxford is a registered trademark of Oxford University Press

Library of Congress Cataloging-in-Publication Data
Adams, Henry, 1949–
Eakins revealed : the secret life of an American artist / Henry Adams.
p. cm.
Includes bibliographical references and index.
ISBN 019-515668-4
1. Eakins, Thomas, 1844–1916. 2. Artists—United States—Biography
I. Eakins, Thomas, 1844–1916. II. Title.
N6537.E3A84   2005
759.13—dc22   2004023284

Book design by Mark McGarry, Texas Type & Book Works
Set in Monotype Dante

9 8 7 6 5 4 3 2 1

Printed in the United States of America
on acid-free paper

*For Sandra Dijkstra with boundless gratitude
and to the memory of John Caldwell,
who died too young.*

One must say everything—then no one will know.

CHARLES DEMUTH

CONTENTS

Preface: Riddles   xiii

PART ONE: The Eakins Legacy

1.   Within the Walls   3
2.   The Perfect Crime   11
3.   The Loin Cloth Scandal   49
4.   Family Quarrels   61
5.   The Death of Ella Crowell   69
6.   The Insanity of Lillian Hammitt   85
7.   Explanations and Enigmas   105
8.   Analyzing Eakins   125

PART TWO: Life and Art

9.   An American in Paris   133
10. All in the Family   165
11. Turning the Stake   193
12. The Gross Clinic   215
13. William Rush and His Model   243
14. A Fine Old Row   257
15. Naked in Arcadia   271
16. Swimming   305
17. Conversations with the Dead   333
18. Inflicting Pain   383

PART THREE: The Case of Thomas Eakins

| 19. | Love of Looking | 415 |
| 20. | The Greatest American Artist | 463 |

Acknowledgements	478
Biographical Key	481
Notes	487
Bibliography	537
Index	559

Portrait of Eakins. *Silver gelatin developed out print. Samuel Murray Archival Collection, Hirshhorn Museum and Sculpture Garden, Smithsonian Institution.*

PREFACE: RIDDLES

THIS STUDY began as a popular article and evolved into a serious piece of research. For many years I felt dissatisfied by what has been written on Thomas Eakins, but could not quite pinpoint the reason. The accounts of this artist's life have always contained an element of optimistic boosterism, and something about this, and about the way he was portrayed as a heroic and moral figure, did not quite jibe with the troubled mood that I sensed in his paintings. While one can hardly fail to admire Eakins's technical skill and power of emotional expression, there is something in his work that has always struck me as brutal and unpleasant. I felt this even as a child when I first looked at reproductions of Eakins's work, but over the years I could never quite put my finger on what bothered me.

What finally inspired me to grapple with this question was the discovery in 1984 of the Bregler papers, a group of long-lost documents from Eakins's studio, and their purchase in 1985 by the Pennsylvania Academy of the Fine Arts. The uncovering of hidden treasure always makes a good story; and I thought that I could write this discovery up in journalistic fashion for *Smithsonian*, a popular magazine aimed at a family audience.

Lying behind my effort was a certain sense of guilt. I had never responded to Eakins's work with the intense national pride and moralistic fervor that is expected of Americanists, and that serves as a kind of familial tie—a sort of badge of belonging, like a Masonic handshake—for those in the American art field. I thought that this project would enable me to remedy this fault. If I got to know Eakins better, so I thought, I would learn to empathize with him, and come to admire his artistic and moral framework.

As I began to read through the Bregler materials, however, I realized there was a much richer story here, as well as a much darker one. In fact, the papers seemed to me to provide the elements necessary for a complete reinterpretation of Eakins and a deeper understanding of the inner forces that drove him.

By the time I was finished, my essay was much too long for *Smithsonian,* and its content not appropriate for such a publication. Consequently, *Smithsonian* published only a small portion of what I had written, presenting my ideas in abbreviated and softened form. I put forth my thoughts here for the first time at full length, including those that would have been unsuitable for a family magazine, but are essential to anyone who wants to come to grips with Eakins's paintings.[1]

At the heart of my investigation is a relatively simple notion: that Eakins's paintings, which invariably portray somber or depressed people, and which often portray disturbing subjects, represent a tragic outlook that must have had some basis in his own life experience. The failure of most scholars to pursue this avenue of inquiry suggests to me some fundamental inhibition in the practice of art history. To cite a simple instance, it would raise no eyebrows among literary scholars to propose that Eugene O'Neill's tragic play *Long Day's Journey Into Night* was based on his own family experience, and indeed is a form of thinly disguised autobiography. In writing about Eakins, however, all but a few brave souls have steered away from the troubling new discoveries about his private life, as if they had no bearing on his art. Indeed, some reviews of the massive recent Eakins exhibition at the Philadelphia Museum of Art have praised the catalogue precisely because it avoided discussing this scandalous material.[2]

Perhaps the roots of this idealization lie in ancient theories of the visual arts. Whereas literary criticism traces its origins back to Aristotle's *Poetics*—a work that proposed that horrible and tragic events could create an emotional catharsis, and thus could be morally uplifting—visual art criticism has cherished the Platonic notion that art should imitate an ideal, and thus should perfect the world rather than explore its horrors. To a distressing degree, the art critics have never developed a viable conception of tragedy. In dealing with artists such as Eakins, who possessed a profoundly tragic vision, art historians have always tended to impose idealizing notions that have little bearing or relevance. Their practice of polishing the artist's biography goes along with a tendency to prettify the art itself. But neither Eakins's art nor his life offers an ideal. The lessons they teach us are of a very different kind.

To some the structure of this book may be difficult to grasp, since it is unfamiliar, at least for a work of art history, coming closer to the structure of some novels, by figures such as Henry James, or to Akira Kurosawa's film *Rashomon*. The narrative does not always move forward in a purely chronological fashion; or to put things more precisely, it does move chronologically but tells the story twice. The pattern is one often used in music, of voices in counterpoint. Essentially, a set of opening chapters lay out the enigmas and controversies of Eakins's life. Then, armed with awareness that there is a mystery to be solved, we review Eakins's biography and artistic accomplishment, probing for clues to its meaning. Essentially the chapters can be seen as a series of themes, like voices in a fugue, which establish more and more complex relationships with each other as the story develops.

At the same time, however, the chapters may be read as discrete, individual, seemingly disconnected mysteries—some of them quite complicated and confusing in their own right. Each chapter lays out a riddle or series of riddles about Eakins: either about his behavior, which clearly baffled his contemporaries, or about his paintings, whose subjects and emotional undercurrents are so unusual that they almost suggest a letter written in secret code.

At a deep level, however, all these mysteries are connected. Those readers who can solve one can solve them all, for disparate as these puzzles sometimes seem, the solution to all of them, at its fundamental level, is the same. Taken together they reinforce each other, all providing useful clues for understanding Eakins. When we put these clues together, as I have done in the last chapter, we can move forward to a new way of understanding Eakins's behavior and of decoding his secret language of expression.

Although readers will see that I am often critical of Eakins's behavior, and sometimes of his work, my purpose is not simply to tear down his reputation. Nor is my goal a "revisionist" portrait of Eakins that corrects the errors of those who have praised him by disparaging him instead. Rather, this book is an attempt to explore the complex relationship between one artist's life and his work, and what it is that makes them both so troubling. By doing so, I believe we can arrive at a new realization of the intensity and emotional desperation of Eakins's art, and recognize how hard-won were his achievements.

PART ONE

THE EAKINS LEGACY

Home of Thomas Eakins, 1729 Mount Vernon Street, Philadelphia, ca. 1936. *Society Photo Collection, Residences, Thomas Eakins, The Historical Society of Pennsylvania.* Eakins lived most of his life under his father's roof and died there in 1916. After his father's death he constructed a studio on the fourth floor. One can still discern the original roofline in the wall.

Chapter 1

WITHIN THE WALLS

IN A PHYSICAL SENSE, the world of Thomas Eakins—whom many scholars now rank as the greatest nineteenth-century American painter—was surprisingly limited, even claustrophobic. It was a world dominated by his father's house, a home he never truly left. In 1857, when Eakins was thirteen years old, his father, Benjamin, purchased a three-story brick home at 1729 Mount Vernon Street in Philadelphia. This building remained the center of Eakins's world for the remainder of his life and he drew his last breath within its walls.

Aside from three and a half years of study in Europe, mostly in Paris, Eakins established a residence outside this home only once.[1] Fifteen years after returning from Paris, Eakins married Susan MacDowell, and for about a year he and his wife lived in a studio on Chestnut Street, just a short walk from the Pennsylvania Academy of the Fine Arts, where he was then teaching. In 1886, however, the artist was fired from the Academy amid acrimonious rumors and controversy about his lifestyle and his treatment of female students. At his father's invitation, and "for propriety's sake," that is, to dispel gossip about his living arrangements, he moved back into the family home with his wife.[2] After that, he never left the shelter of the family roof. For fourteen years Eakins maintained a studio downtown, but after his father's death in 1900, he abandoned it and remodeled the upper floor of the family home—a space directly over the room where his parents had slept—to serve as his studio.[3] After a stroke in 1910, Eakins hardly left the house. He died on June 25, 1916, a month before his seventy-second birthday, in his father's bedroom.[4]

One of the extraordinary things about Eakins's paintings, which today strike so many viewers as immensely rich and expansive in their expressive qualities and transcendent in their meaning, is the narrow geography that inspired them, and the equally narrow interpersonal landscape they document. Indeed, as his career progressed, Eakins gradually abandoned outdoor scenes. By the end of his life, all his paintings were set in a shadowy interior space like that of the house he lived in.

Visiting the family home is a good way to cross the threshold into Eakins's world. The building still stands, saved from the wrecking ball by the efforts of one of Eakins's admirers, Seymour Adelman. It now serves as a community art center, and when I first visited, it was being renovated for such use. A portable toilet for the workmen stood on the sidewalk out in front, and a brooding photograph of Eakins, with bloodshot eyes, stared out in a strangely sinister fashion from one of the downstairs windows.

Many things have changed from how they were when Eakins lived. The dark mahogany furniture and clutter of bric-a-brac, paintings, papers, tools, and other objects that once filled the rooms have disappeared. The interiors are now painted white, rather than the dull chocolate shades of the nineteenth century, and most of the original hardware and architectural detail has been lost in the course of repairs and renovations. The windows now let in light from the outside. Throughout Eakins's lifetime, the shutters were drawn both in summer and winter—in the words of his biographer Lloyd Goodrich, they were "kept closed against the heat of summer or the winter snow." [5] The house has also been equipped with modern conveniences. During Eakins's lifetime the house had no electricity. For most of his life there was no plumbing and the only water came from a pump in the backyard.[6]

Given the lack of plumbing, the place was probably aromatic, particularly in summer. Judging from the many references to Susan Eakins's poor housekeeping, it was probably also very dusty. To visualize the house as it was when Eakins lived there we must imagine a place that was much more dimly lit, more gloomy, more smelly, more dusty, more cluttered and more claustrophobic than it is now. Nonetheless, for all the changes, it is strangely moving to visit the house and stand within the walls that inspired or enclosed so many of Eakins's major works.

The house is really two dwellings, both fairly large—one in front, one in back—set against each other, with a staircase set between them that connects but also separates the two. In concept, the front section was clearly designed as the family apartments and the back as the servant wing. In practice, however, this division was surely not a neat one, since children probably also slept and played in the rooms at the back.

In spatial terms, the experience is difficult to grasp, for the house feels both very small and very large. From the street it looks not only gloomy, with its factory-like brick, but also cramped, because its proportions are pinched and narrow in relation to its height. But as you enter the front door the main corridor extends a considerable length before you—almost a street or back alley in its own right. A moment later, as you step inside, the width of the house becomes apparent, for there is a sizable front parlor to the left, the likely setting of Eakins's early paintings of his family.[7]

While the paint color and ornamental details have changed, the basic room arrangement has not. Downstairs are larger rooms, such as the parlor and kitchen, whose functions are not difficult to understand. But upstairs, the house is confusing and mazelike. The rooms often have odd angles, with doorways that lead off in strange directions, and the original purpose of some rooms is difficult to guess. One of the odd things about the design is that the floors of the front and back halves are on slightly different levels, with landings of still different heights in between. As a result, the architectural relationships are difficult to grasp, and even rooms that are reasonably close to each other do not feel harmonious or connected . Strolling through, it is interesting to speculate what happened in each space.

Over the course of Eakins's lifetime, the building housed not simply a "nuclear family," but a haphazard, ever-shifting collection of relatives, friends, and servants. Eakins's father, a writing master and landlord, had his office in the front room on the third floor, and Eakins's parents had their bedroom on the second floor, in the room just below. But it is not clear which bedrooms held which children—Thomas and his three younger sisters, Frances, Margaret, and Caroline. No doubt the arrangement changed over time, as they aged and as relationships shifted. At one point or another not only Eakins but Frances and Caroline all brought their spouses to live in the house, and there were often small children who came to visit (Frances had ten children, Caroline had three). When Goodrich interviewed those who had known Eakins, they often mentioned naked nephews and nieces running around the place.

Other occupants of the home included Aunt Ella, the sister of Eakins's mother; a family friend and distant relative, Addie Williams, who came to live in the house after the death of Eakins's father; and Eakins's nieces Ella and Margaret Crowell, who came to live with Eakins when they were teenagers—before he broke off his relationship with their parents, his sister Frances and her husband, Will Crowell. During Eakins's childhood there were probably cooks, cleaning ladies, babysitters and other servants, apparently including some African Americans.[8] After Eakins's marriage, his wife, Susan, abandoned her art career and spent her days doing housework, but in addition, until the early 1890s there was an Irish maid, Tuffy, who cooked and cleaned, and may even have lived on the premises.[9] Add to this a small menagerie of animals, including not only the dog, Harry, but more exotic species, such as Eakins's ill-tempered monkey, Bobby, who fought with the cat and tried to bite Susan's hand whenever she reached into the cage to feed it.[10]

Over time, however, the house became emptier, as family members died or became so estranged that they would no longer visit. To save money, most if not all of the domestic help was dismissed after the death of his father, since Eakins inherited only a third of his father's estate.

Trying to position these characters within this maze makes one imagine the place as one of those transparent cut-away houses in a Jo Mielziner stage set—a place with multiple rooms and levels, each one the setting for its own private world of experience and sorrow. One can hardly refrain from the mental game of attempting to match memorable episodes from Eakins's life with their physical location. There is the front door, where Eakins's student Lillian Hammitt, appeared one day, hopelessly insane, believing that she was married to Eakins; the front parlor where Eakins probably sat with his mother during her final illness; his parents' bedroom, which is most likely where his mother finally died of mania or starvation; the third floor room, where his father patiently kept accounts from the slum housing he owned, and transcribed documents with a neat, unwavering hand; the third floor bedroom where Eakins made a practice of strolling around with no pants on, much to the horror of his sister Caroline's husband, Frank Stephens; another upstairs bedroom, where a bell on the door warned the family if Aunt Ella, who suffered from senile dementia, escaped; the back garden, where Eakins shot his sister Caroline's cat; and of course the studio that Eakins added on the fourth floor, after his father's death, where Eakins painted his somber late portraits, often dressed only in underwear as he worked, and sometimes completely nude.

A good many of these goings-on can be visualized in their physical settings, either exact or approximate, but it is anyone's guess where other events occurred. For example, we do not know whether Will Crowell, the husband of Eakins's sister Frances, threatened to kill Eakins in the living room, the dining room, or somewhere in the labyrinth of the upper floors; and it is not clear which bedroom belonged to Eakins's sister Margaret, to whom biographers agree the artist was unusually "close," and with whom brother-in-law Frank Stephens claimed the painter had an incestuous relationship. Before her suicide, the artist's niece Ella claimed that Eakins sexually molested her.

While her accusation of indecent advances is well documented, we have no information about where she said it took place.

Many of Eakins's most notable canvases depict the family home and were painted there. Those that opened his career—his early portraits of his sisters, his fiancée, and his father—were set in the front parlor and appear to have been largely executed in a third floor studio in the back of the house. Those that he produced around 1900—such as the late portraits of his dying father, himself, and his suffering wife—very likely were also executed in the family home. After 1900 all his paintings were produced in the new fourth-floor studio. The series portraying William Rush with his nude model, in which Rush bears a pronounced resemblance to Eakins, seem, with a few modest liberties, to portray that room.

Eakins did not bother to display many of his works, whether in public or on the walls of the family home. A great many of his paintings—particularly the portraits that were returned by unhappy sitters—were stacked against the walls in the studio and rooms upstairs. We can make out dozens of such paintings in the one surviving photograph of Eakins at work in his studio. In certain instances, however, Eakins placed works on display in the home in a fashion that suggests that they had some meaning specifically related to their location.

Photographer unknown, Thomas Eakins in the Mount Vernon Street Studio, *ca. 1909. Gelatin silver print, 4 ¾ x 7 ¹⁵⁄₁₆ in., Bryn Mawr College Library, Seymour Adelman Collection, photograph by Will Brown.* **The only photograph of Eakins in his home studio shows him at work with a group of completed canvases stacked against the wall.**

The Crucifixion. *Oil on canvas, 96 x 54 in., Philadelphia Museum of Art, gift of Mrs. Thomas Eakins and Miss Mary Adeline Williams.* Eakins hung his *Crucifixion* by the front door of the family home, where it was the first thing visitors encountered.

For example, Eakins's nearly lifesize *Crucifixion* hung by the entryway and was the first thing a visitor saw after coming through the front door. The painting portrays Jesus' body with straightforward naturalism, as if it were a corpse in a morgue. As we look, however, we realize that the body must still be alive, since it does not yet have a wound in its side. Thus, the painting records not death but a kind of death within life. Most nineteenth-century viewers were shocked by the painting's absence of hopefulness or religious sentiment. Surely it was no accident that Eakins chose to greet his visitors with this brutal and surprising subject.

The prominent position over the mantelpiece of the living room, just a few yards away, seems to have been reserved, by contrast, for more romantic pictures. For years, *Elizabeth at the Piano*, a radiant rendering of the beautiful young Elizabeth Crowell, hung in this spot. Goodrich and Eakins's other biographers have always conjectured that Eakins was in love with her, although he was engaged for years not to her but to her sister, Kathrin. Toward the end of his life Eakins replaced this canvas with *The Concert Singer*, a painting that also represents music and also seems to have expressed feelings of desire or romantic longing. For some reason Eakins did not choose to place a portrait of his wife, Susan, in this spot, but seems to have preferred having her look at likenesses of other women he had loved. He did paint two small portraits of Susan, which I will discuss in their place, both extremely unflattering. But there is no record of where or whether they were displayed.

It is always fascinating to wonder what walls and rooms have witnessed, and even to imagine that they have kept a memory of what transpired within their confines, as if their surface was a sensitive film, like the interior of a camera. This is silly no doubt, but when I visited the home, despite the sunshine coming in through the windows, and the overlay of new white paint, from time to time, as I walked through, I had the sensation that dark and unpleasant things had happened there. Perhaps even unmentionable things, too horrible to discuss. This is hardly scientific, of course. No one has yet found a way to get walls to talk, at least not in clear language. The intimations we get from rooms come to us through some sixth sense that is hard to convey in words. I cannot deny, however, that I had troubling feelings when I visited the place and that in some way these feelings permeated my thoughts when I sat down to examine the Eakins story, and to search for an answer to its mysteries.

Elizabeth at the Piano, 1875. *Oil on canvas, 72 ⅛ x 48 ²⁄₁₆ in. © Addison Gallery of American Art, Phillips Academy, Andover, Massachusetts, all rights reserved, gift of an anonymous donor.* **Even after his marriage, Eakins hung his romantic portrait of Elizabeth Crowell in the place of honor over the mantelpiece in the living room.**

Sidney Wainthrob of Budd Studios, Lloyd Goodrich with the Painting Human Pool Tables, 1938, by Reginald Marsh at the Whitney Museum of American Art in 1955. *Frances Mulhall Achilles Library Archive, Whitney Museum of American Art, New York.* For fifty years, Lloyd Goodrich's biography of Eakins remained unchallenged, in part because the documents it was based on had disappeared.

Chapter 2

THE PERFECT CRIME

THE FIRST STEP in unraveling a mystery is to recognize that there is a mystery to solve. In the case of Eakins this means recognizing that a century of accumulated scholarship, widely praised for its insight and truthfulness, contains fabrications. When we investigate, we soon discover that Eakins has been so swathed in the mantle of praise that he has become all but invisible—like a figure so covered in bulky coats and scarves that his actual shape and individual features can no longer be distinguished. If we wish to get down to the naked truth and the bare facts, we must begin by investigating how the prevailing readings of his work and character came to be accepted. When we do so, we immediately stumble upon two peculiar things.

The first is that the current interpretation of Eakins and his art is radically different from how he was viewed in his lifetime. His character, now touted as praiseworthy, honest and moral, was seen as shifty, disreputable, and tainted with unmentionable vices. His paintings, now viewed as honest and probing, were viewed as slanderous and untrue. In short, the currently accepted views of both Eakins's work and his character are nearly a complete inversion of how he was regarded in his lifetime.

The second is that the currently standard view of Eakins comes almost entirely from the claims of a single scholar, Lloyd Goodrich, who in 1933 published *Thomas Eakins, His Life and Work*, the first book-length study of the artist. Goodrich was a compelling writer, but his dominance over the literature on Eakins—the fact that his account stood unchallenged for half a century—was due to a highly unusual circumstance. In writing his text, Goodrich had access to extensive documents in the Eakins home. These materials disappeared shortly after his book was published. Thus, subsequent scholars had access to primary data on Eakins only through Goodrich's narrative. By the time these materials—the Bregler papers—reappeared, Goodrich's views of Eakins had been repeated, essentially unchallenged, in dozens of books on the artist as well as in every general textbook and survey of American art. Now that these documents have again become accessible (along with the notes that Goodrich made for his book), it becomes evident that Goodrich deliberately suppressed large quantities of material that were unflattering to Eakins and made many statements that he surely knew were untrue. But by this time reverence for Eakins had become so deeply ingrained in the American field that these revelations have had surprisingly little impact. So far, no writer has challenged the fundamental substance of Goodrich's narrative.

Yet to an exceptional degree, Goodrich's account of Eakins was clearly a fiction. The first step toward understanding Eakins is to understand this concoction—one deliberate enough to call a cover-up. Goodrich's misunderstandings and deceptions have permeated every aspect of the literature on Eakins—and have cast their shadow on every page of this book. To get to the real Thomas Eakins we need to understand how this deceit occurred and why it was carried out.

Thomas Eakins has always been singled out as unusual. His contemporaries thought that he was psychologically disturbed, and viewed him as a pariah, even a criminal. More recent artists, writers, and art critics have eulogized him as a paragon of ethical insight and an artistic genius. How should we reconcile these two views? Certainly, if Eakins was a criminal he committed the perfect crime, not only escaping punishment, but being transformed by his supporters into a role model, a moral exemplar.

The Revival of Eakins's Reputation

Narratives of Eakins's life have always revolved around a nasty public scandal. In 1886, while teaching a class at the Pennsylvania Academy of the Fine Arts, Eakins removed the loincloth from a male model, whose genitals were thus exposed to a class of female students. Within a few days, after a chain of events that has never fully been documented or explained, he was dismissed from his teaching position. For the rest of his life, he remained a social pariah. People would cross the street to avoid encountering him; young women would leave the room to avoid speaking with him.[1] Even those who continued to associate with him seem to have felt misgivings. His paintings were frequently excluded from exhibitions, and while he continued to paint portraits, many of the individuals who sat for him either failed to retrieve the unflattering likenesses he made of them—or else took them home and quietly burned them.

The extent to which Eakins was ostracized is suggested by an anecdote. When the society portraitist John Singer Sargent visited Philadelphia, his hostess asked him if there was anyone he would like to see. "Well, there's Eakins for instance," Sargent commented diffidently. "And who is Eakins?" his hostess replied, her tone of voice indicating that Eakins was beyond the pale.[2]

The low point of Eakins's career seems to have occurred in the early 1890s, when he was shunned by Philadelphia society and his work was frequently rejected from exhibitions. In 1892, for example, Eakins resigned from the Society of American Artists in New York after his paintings had been excluded from the annual exhibition for three consecutive years. Among the paintings rejected was *The Agnew Clinic*, one of his largest and most important works. In addition, in 1894–1895 Eakins was dismissed from his post at the Drexel Institute in Philadelphia and in 1897 he was dropped from the National Academy of Design in New York, effectively ending his teaching career. A modest turning point occurred in 1894, when a new director of the Pennsylvania Academy, Harrison Morris, invited Eakins to submit his paintings to the institution's annual exhibitions, which he did for many years thereafter.[3] But overall the 1890s were unsuccessful for Eakins—he had difficulty showing his work, had no real following, and enjoyed little critical support.[4]

A change occurred around 1900, with the dawn of a new century. Somewhat mysteriously, Eakins began to find favor among his peers, winning prizes and serving on juries of award. In 1899 he served for the first time on the jury of the Carnegie International Exhibition at the Carnegie Institute in Pittsburgh, which invited him back four more times. In 1901 he served on the jury of the Pennsylvania Academy's Annual Exhibition. During the early years of the twentieth century he won a series of prizes, including the Temple Gold Medal at the Pennsylvania Academy, a gold medal at the Universal Exposition in St. Louis, a bronze medal at the Exposition Universelle in Paris, the Proctor Prize of the National Academy of Design, the gold medal of the American Art Society of Philadelphia, and a second class medal at the Carnegie Institute. In 1902, within the space of a few months, and after being ignored for more than thirty years, he was elected first an associate and then a full member of the National Academy of Design. In 1914 his work received headlines when Dr. Albert Barnes purchased a study of Dr. Agnew for $4,000— a noteworthy price for the period and more than double the amount paid for any other painting by Eakins in his lifetime.[5]

Eakins also began to figure in critical discussion, such as the columns of Helen Henderson in the *Philadelphia Inquirer*, who made a point of featuring his work. The most significant breakthrough came in 1902, when Sadakichi Hartmann discussed Eakins's work in his two-volume *History of American Art*, boldly ranking him with one of the most famous American artists of the time, Winslow Homer, and declaring that the two were the most powerful and "masculine" of American painters.[6] Five years later, Charles Caffin repeated many of the same themes in his *Story of American Painting*, again comparing Eakins with Homer.[7]

Thus, by the time of his death in 1916, Eakins's work was beginning to be admired among young artists and critics of advanced taste. Nonetheless, throughout this period it must have been difficult to get a sense of Eakins's achievement. At the time of his death his work was represented in only three American museums: those of Smith College and the Pennsylvania Academy (each of which owned one picture), and of the Metropolitan Museum of Art in New York (which owned two). The only place where Eakins's paintings could be seen in quantity was in his own home, and even there it was difficult to make out the character of his work, since most of his paintings were stacked up back to back against the wall, in no particular order. It was not easy to get to them, and difficult to make sense of his artistic development.

Bryson Burroughs

The key figure in consolidating Eakins's reputation at this critical stage was Bryson Burroughs, one of the most fascinating and multitalented figures in the art world of the time. Burroughs was born outside of Boston, but grew up in Cincinnati. His original goal was to be a bicycle racer, but shortly after winning the state championship in Ohio he entered the Cincinnati School of Art and shifted his ambitions to painting. He subsequently studied at the Art Students League in New York and at the École des Beaux-Arts in Paris. After returning to the United States, Burroughs won several medals when he sent his paintings to exhibitions. He also unintentionally caused a scandal when one of his depictions of his five nude children wading in a New Hampshire stream was publicly condemned by the powerful self-appointed guardian of public morals, Anthony Comstock, the leader of the New York Society for the Suppression of Vice.[8]

Regrettably, neither medals nor scandal created a steady flow of income. Consequently, in 1906 Burroughs went to work for the Metropolitan Museum of Art, as assistant to Roger Fry, the famous writer on modern art, with the understanding that he would be allowed to paint in the morning and do his curatorial work in the afternoon. He maintained this unusual arrangement even after Fry was fired in 1909 following a run-in with the tyrannical financier J. P. Morgan. After that event, Burroughs replaced Fry as curator of paintings.

Henry Caro-Delvaille, Portrait of Bryson Burroughs, *1917. Oil on canvas, 39 x 40 ½ in., photograph courtesy of Hirschl & Adler Galleries, New York.* **Painter in the morning, curator in the afternoon, Bryson Burroughs staged the first major exhibition of Eakins's work in 1917.**

The work that Burroughs made as a painter is somewhat difficult to appreciate today. Burroughs's first love in art was the romantic work of the English Pre-Raphaelites, and he was much influenced by the muralist Puvis de Chavannes, with whom he associated when he was an art student in Paris. Burroughs's own paintings present timeworn religious and mythological themes of a sort similar to those found in the work of the artists he admired, but placed in modern settings in a fashion that often seems highly incongruous. In one picture, for example, he portrayed Saint Ursula in a flapper dress, embarking from a pier with a steamer trunk marked "U." Works such as these are somehow too classical and carefully composed to function as a cartoon, but too humorous to make sense as ideal figure paintings. What is curious is that Burrough's own creations are utterly different from the works he acquired for the Metropolitan Museum of Art. From his own idealizing, sweet-tempered, backward-looking paintings, one would never guess that Burroughs would become an advocate of modernism, let alone that he would champion the tough-minded realism of figures such as Eakins.

But while his work as an artist remains problematic, as a curator Burroughs exhibited unarguable genius in a range of fields. He acquired major works by old masters for a pittance—including a priceless Pieter Bruegel landscape that he picked up for a few thousand dollars, and one of Michelangelo's greatest drawings, *The Libyan Sibyl,* which he purchased on the recommendation of John Singer Sargent. He startled the trustees by acquiring modern works as well, including the Metropolitan's first painting by Cézanne. Finally, Burroughs organized pioneering exhibitions of American art, including the first major retrospectives of Eakins, Winslow Homer, and Albert Pinkham Ryder.

The Eakins retrospective—which opened at the Metropolitan Museum of Art in November of 1917, the year after the artist's death, and then toured a month later to the Pennsylvania Academy—established Eakins, in a single stroke, as a major figure. It represented the first time that Eakins's paintings had been gathered as a group, and thus the first time that the full extent of his artistic accomplishment became apparent. Even for his small circle of admirers, the show proved a revelation. While it took some time for Eakins to become popular with the general public, Burroughs's exhibition had an extraordinary impact in artistic circles, particularly among the younger generation of critics and painters.

During the 1920s, a dozen or more serious articles on Eakins appeared, most of them by writers in one way or another friendly with Burroughs.[9] The most important was a three-part series in *The Arts* by Alan Burroughs, Bryson's son, accompanied by photographs taken by the painter Yasuo Kuniyoshi, reproducing works that had never been seen before. The first two articles presented the first significant biography of Eakins; the third provided a checklist of 343 paintings, compiled with the help of Susan Eakins.[10] Over the course of the 1920s, paintings by Eakins were also purchased by half a dozen major American museums, as well as by several astute private collectors, including the painter Reginald Marsh, who purchased two paintings as a result of a visit to Mrs. Eakins in 1928.[11]

In the early 1930s, major institutions and writers climbed onto the Eakins bandwagon. In March 1930, the Philadelphia Museum of Art accepted fifty oil paintings, as well as other works, donated by Mrs. Eakins and Addie Williams. The energetic director the museum, Fiske Kimball, had met with the two women to arrange the gift. As a consequence, for the first time a large group of Eakins's major works went on permanent public view. The next month the newly formed Museum of Modern Art, on the initiative of its young new director, Alfred H. Barr, held an exhibition of the work of Homer, Ryder, and Eakins, whom it identified as the three most significant American artists of the nineteenth century. A year later, in his influential study of American culture, *The Brown Decades*, Lewis Mumford pointed to Eakins and Ryder as the foremost American artists of their period.[12]

Although Burroughs was the main catalyst for this Eakins revival, he confessed that he was astonished by the resurgence of Eakins's reputation. As he wrote in an article written just a few weeks before his death:

> The contrast between our present rating of Eakins and the neglect he suffered
> from our forerunners is astounding. What change has come about so sud-

denly? The pictures are the same as they have always been (only a little darker perhaps with the lapse of time) but the best judgment of the last generation passed them by, while the best judgment of this generation hails them as masterpieces. It is very perplexing.

As Burroughs noted, this new admiration for Eakins corresponded with a move away from the kind of painting that had been most admired in the nineteenth century.

> An acquaintance, a painter of international distinction since 1895, said to me, while looking at pictures in the Metropolitan museum a few years ago, "Why is it that the enormous attraction which Sargent's portrait of Marquand had for me in the old days is now weakened? Then it was one of the greatest of contemporary portraits; now Eakins's *Thinker* or his *Writing Master* appeals to me with far greater force."[13]

Several themes dominated writing on Eakins in this period: that his works were homely but honest, that they were intensely masculine, and that they reflected qualities that were uniquely American. Moreover, during this period several writers (including Henry McBride and Lewis Mumford) asserted that Eakins was one of the greatest painters this country ever produced—or even, the single greatest American artist. Eakins became a key figure for those who advocated a new way of looking at American culture—one that was scornful of the rigidity and hypocrisy of Victorian society, and that condemned the extravagance and venality of the Gilded Age. In short, by 1930, when Goodrich wrote his monograph, a revival of interest in Eakins's work was already in full force and the main themes of interpreting his work had already been identified. Goodrich's task was to find facts that would support these interpretations and organize them into a compelling narrative.

Lloyd Goodrich: The Father of Eakins Scholarship

When I was in graduate school in the late 1970s, Lloyd Goodrich was still a vital presence in the American art field, and despite his age, an impressively dashing character. Then about eighty, he had a husky voice that suggested a life of hard and intense living. Nonetheless, his eyes twinkled and he retained a dynamic, emphatic, enthusiastic, even boyish quality. At the parties where I met him, he always had a martini glass in his hand. I was by no means the only person who found him intensely charismatic—a model of what a real man should be like, a kind of archetypal father figure. The art historian William Gerdts, for example, a writer hardly given to flattery, has described Goodrich as "the finest scholar and art historian, and the most gallant man, I have ever known."[14]

Goodrich combined scholarly activities with active engagement in the art life of his time. As David Huntington has noted, Goodrich's writings on nineteenth-century American art "established Homer and Eakins as monumental figures who were deserving of monumental scholarship."[15] But Goodrich also actively supported living artists. He became not only the biographer and critical champion, but also the close friend of such notable American painters as Reginald Marsh, John Sloan, Raphael Soyer, Charles Burchfield, and Edward Hopper. Finally, Goodrich was an able administrator and museum director, who played a major role in raising the Whitney Museum from an informal club of artists into a major cultural institution.

To the generation of Americanists who came after him, Goodrich exemplified honesty and passionate dedication to the deep inner truths of great art. Words and phrases like "integrity," "high standards," and "an inspiration" have been regularly applied to his work. The art historian John Wilmerding has described Lloyd Goodrich not simply as one of "the Founding Fathers" of American art history, but as "our Department of Truth, and our National Bureau of Standards."[16]

Goodrich's 1933 monograph on Eakins remains at the center of his reputation as a scholar. Its importance to the American field is suggested by Helen Cooper's remarkable claim that it represents "the earliest comprehensive biography of any American artist."[17] Taken literally, this description is hardly true, for there are many nineteenth-century biographies of American artists that are just as solidly researched, and arguably more accurate.[18] Nonetheless, Cooper's statement conveys the uncanny, mesmeric power that Goodrich's book has exerted over the American field, from the date of its writing up to the present, some three-quarters of a century later.

Goodrich's Background

While of different generations, Burroughs and Goodrich had somewhat similar backgrounds. Like Burroughs, Goodrich lacked any formal training as an art historian, and never attended college. His avenue to art writing came through the study of painting.

Goodrich grew up in Nutley, New Jersey, just outside New York City. It was an artistic community, with a separate enclave known as "The Enclosure," which was entirely inhabited by artists, including the muralist Fred Dana Marsh. Marsh's son, Reginald (who went on to become one of the most famous painters of his generation) became Lloyd's best friend almost from the time they were born. "We were only a few months apart in age," Goodrich later recalled.

> A memorable part of my childhood was the Marsh home: the big studio with his father's paintings in progress; Fred's ingenious maquettes of skyscrapers in construction with little wax figures of the workmen; living models from the city (if they were nude, we were not allowed to see them); on the walls, reproductions of Titian, Tintoretto, Rubens, Rembrandt, the Pre-Raphaelites, Franz Stuck; many art books; bound volumes of *Jugend* and *Fliegende Blätter* with their strong graphic work—a house in which everything had to do with art.[19]

With the encouragement of his parents, Goodrich decided to become a painter and as a consequence was the only member of his family who did not attend college. Instead, he enrolled in the Art Students League. There his most inspiring teacher was Kenneth Hayes Miller, who was also the teacher of Reginald Marsh and other notable realists of the period, such as Isabel Bishop, Peggy Bacon, and Alexander Brook.[20]

In the fall of 1918, however, Goodrich had a searing crisis of confidence about his abilities as a painter. In an abrupt about-face, he went into the steel business, but perhaps fortunately, was not successful. After several businesses folded under him, he drifted into publishing, taking a job at Macmillan's, where he worked in the religious division, editing volumes of sermons.

At this time, one of his painter friends, Alexander Brook, mentioned that Forbes Watson at *The Arts* needed someone to write a few reviews. Goodrich began writing freelance pieces, which he composed on nights and weekends, since he was still working full-time for Macmillan. Watson was pleased with his work and in 1925 hired him to become associate editor, which entailed most of the work of designing and publishing the magazine. This job in turn brought Goodrich into contact with the Whitney Studio Club, which supported up-and-coming young artists, since Juliana Force, who ran the club for Gertrude Vanderbilt Whitney, was Watson's lover and a financial supporter of his projects. Goodrich began to do occasional writing for her and, when the Whitney Museum was formed, became her assistant. Goodrich spent the rest of his career at the Whitney, where he gradually made his way up through the ranks until he attained the position of director.[21]

Goodrich thus found himself at the center of a group of remarkable American realist painters, including Edward Hopper, Charles Burchfield, Reginald Marsh, Raphael Soyer, and Thomas Hart Benton, who soberly portrayed the "ugly" side of American life—such subjects as gas stations, bowery bums, strippers, and the dilapidated buildings of American cities and small towns. All these artists belonged to the Whitney Studio Club, and Goodrich persuaded them to write articles for *The Arts*.[22]

Today these figures are celebrated. At the time, however, their work lacked patronage and support. Most American collectors focused on European art, whether by the old masters or the moderns. The most energetic figure promoting American work, the dealer Alfred Stieglitz, represented only five artists (John Marin, Marsden Hartley, Arthur Dove, Charles Demuth and Georgia O'Keeffe), all of whom worked in a modernist vein.[23]

Almost by accident, Goodrich found himself in the role of advocate for the new group of realists, and as moral crusader for their cause. On the one hand, this made it necessary to distinguish the work of the young realists from the stale formulas of academic painting and commercial illustration. On the other, it entailed defending a realist approach against the new modern "isms" that had gained attention in Europe, such as Cubism and Fauvism, which made the work of American painters seem old-fashioned. Goodrich's work on Eakins must be understood in this context. In extolling Eakins, he was finding a father figure for the living realist painters he admired.

Goodrich knew Bryson Burroughs well, for his friend Reginald Marsh had married Burroughs's daughter, the sculptor Betty Burroughs. Thus, Goodrich was in the ideal position to learn about Eakins before his work had become widely known. The opportunity to write on Eakins came in 1930 through a series of fortunate events. First, Reginald Marsh, agreed to lend Goodrich $500 to start the project. Shortly afterward, in an offer of unprecedented generosity, Juliana Force agreed to provide him with a full salary for three years to complete the project.

Goodrich's Monograph on Eakins

Goodrich's book was published in 1933, during the depths of the Depression. Its reassessment of American values struck a deep chord at a time of national self-examination. In this bleak period the cheerful, sun-splattered pictures of the American Impressionists seemed superficial, even false, while the dark sobriety of Eakins's paintings appeared "honest," "authentic," and congenial.

In keeping with the character of his subject, Goodrich's prose had a self-conscious simplicity. Barbara Novak and Brian O'Doherty have described it as "clear, direct, efficient, and spare" and have noted that it "always gave one the sense of a man working with unpretentious dignity."[24] David Tatham has perceptively noted that Goodrich's style was modern in the sense that Hemingway and the *New Yorker* were modern in the 1920s."[25] Goodrich achieved his lean prose through much hard work and endless revision. He once told me that it was his practice to read every word of his books aloud to his wife, an exercise that quickly revealed any wording that was flowery, unnecessary, or pretentious.

In his biography of Eakins, Goodrich built his story around the idea of a "neglected genius," an image that was often employed by art historians of the period to champion the work of modern artists, such as the Impressionists, Van Gogh, or even Picasso, who rebelled against conventional values. Through clever shifts of emphasis, however, and twists in the treatment of value-laden words, Goodrich reconfigured the elements of this formula to make them suit a very different sort of painter.

The difficulty that faced Goodrich in presenting this theme was that Eakins did not challenge academic practices, but defended academic realism against the incursion of new approaches. As a young man Eakins dismissed the work of the romantic French rebel Eugene Delacroix as "abominable," and as a mature painter and teacher, he stolidly resisted the new directions that transformed nineteenth-century pictorial practice, such as *plein-air* painting and Impressionism.[26] Amazingly, Eakins lived well into the age of Futurism and Cubism, although his own work looks a hundred years older. Not surprisingly he dismissed such new-fangled modes of painting out of hand. "They are all nonsense, and no serious student should occupy his time with them," he told a reporter in 1915.[27] Thus, Goodrich was placed in the odd position of making a modernist hero out of a figure whose artistic approach, in all its outward aspects, remained fundamentally backward looking and reactionary. Goodrich's solution to this dilemma was to argue that Eakins's art represented a pragmatically American alternative to the "superficial" qualities of innovative European styles, such as Impressionism.

Goodrich carefully structured his narrative so that every seeming flaw of Eakins's personality, such as his well-documented rudeness and social ineptitude, his disinterest in artistic innovation, and his mistreatment of women, was pictured as the reflection of a deeper, more important quality of moral character. While the book was intended as a salvo against the falseness of

Victorian values, in fact its language and storyline were profoundly sentimental. Throughout, Goodrich portrayed Eakins's supporters as moral paragons, whereas those who played a role in his downfall, however subsidiary, he cast as heinous villains.

Goodrich's Life of Eakins

Goodrich's first chapter established the setting for the drama, rooting Eakins's greatness as an artist in his solid middle-class identity and family values. But it explained that to achieve really sound artistic training he needed to look beyond Philadelphia and go to study in Paris.

According to Goodrich, Eakins grew up on a "quiet, tree-lined street of red brick houses," and "his childhood was that of any normal American boy of the period." His father, a writing master, was "kindly, sociable, of absolute integrity," and "beloved by all who knew him." His mother had "a face full of character, in which one divines a capacity for strong feeling." Along with leading "a healthy outdoor life," Eakins was "an excellent student... always near the head of his class." He also showed marked mechanical ability and an early love of drawing. After graduating from high school, Eakins received some "desultory teaching" at the dusty, antiquated Pennsylvania Academy of the Fine Arts. To supplement this, however, he attended anatomical courses at Jefferson Medical College under the famous surgeon Joseph Pancoast. After four or five years of such study, he realized that it was necessary to go abroad to receive more systematic training, and his father agreed to help him financially. Consequently, in September 1866, at the age of twenty-two, he set off for Paris.

The second chapter explored Eakins's artistic training in Europe, a delicate matter, since as Goodrich noted, the art that Eakins admired in Paris was thoroughly conservative and academic in character. After describing the practical obstacles of enrolling in the studio of Jean-Léon Gérôme, Goodrich recounted the young American's struggles to master Gérôme's techniques, which proved difficult since Eakins had come to art through drawing, and had painted very little before leaving the United States. With a certain pride, Goodrich noted that Eakins showed little interest in aesthetic issues, and dressed with the same informal casualness that he had in the United States. By the end of three years of study, however, he had developed self-confidence as a painter, along with an ability to speak French. To conclude his art training, he made a journey to Spain, where the work of the great Spaniards, such as Velázquez, revealed to him the possibilities of sober, realistic painting of a sort quite different from the frivolous work of the French. While in Spain, Eakins produced his first painting that attempted to be more than a classroom study, a composition of some gypsy children that Goodrich confessed was "a little awkward in handling," but which showed "courage" and "a genuinely original vision."

On his return to the United States, Eakins began painting "the life he had known before he went abroad," a series of pictures of his own family, such as a group showing his sisters at the piano. He also "resumed his vigorous outdoor life" and recorded it in paintings of hunting, sailing, and rowing. Goodrich noted that to construct his paintings, Eakins made careful, measured mechanical drawings. According to Goodrich, however, "in spite of these seemingly cold scientific methods, there was no lack of vitality or warmth in the finished pictures."

The most ambitious painting by Eakins of this period showed Dr. Samuel Gross—"one of the greatest surgeons in the country" and "a magnetic teacher"—conducting an operation in a medical amphitheater. Unfortunately, it was rejected from the Centennial Exposition and severely criticized in the newspapers. Nonetheless, Eakins "showed no signs of discouragement, or any attempt to compromise with popular taste." By the middle of the 1870s his reputation was gradually growing, although sales and commissions were still few.

The next chapter, which opened with the claim that "Eakins was a born teacher," provided a kind of fulcrum for the drama of the book. The chapter was neatly divided into two halves. The first half deals with Eakins's teaching methods, which according to Goodrich were a radical contrast with the "conservative program" of his predecessor, Christian Schuessele. Whereas Schuessele believed in drawing from plaster casts, Eakins stressed painting from the living model, and also insisted on rigorous study of animal and human anatomy. He also provided lucid lectures on perspective.

The second half dealt with the most mysterious episode of Eakins's career, his forced resignation from his teaching position. According to Goodrich, under Eakins's leadership, the Academy became widely known as "the most progressive in the country." But opposition to his ascendancy grew because he was "too energetic, too full of new ideas." Moreover, "women were entering art in increasing numbers," and "Eakins made art too strenuous for them." A series of incidents involving Eakins's use of the nude caused complaints. The culminating incident occurred when he removed the loin cloth from a male model in front of a class of female students. A special committee was formed to investigate the affair, and shortly afterwards Eakins proffered his resignation. "The whole affair," Goodrich notes, "was one of the severest blows of his career."

Goodrich's account of Eakins's rise and fall from power formed the dramatic center of his account. From this point on, his narrative began to drift, and he shifted from a framework that deals with events chronologically to one which organized material by theme.

According to Goodrich, Eakins's middle years were "quiet externally." After being dismissed from the Academy, Eakins moved back into the old home on Mount Vernon Street, where he lived for the remainder of his life. Nonetheless, Eakins "had a gift for friendship, being interested in all kinds of people," and "the house was always full of nephews and nieces." He and his wife "lived simply and frugally," and seldom left home. Hard working and abstemious, Eakins paid little attention to dress or appearances and focused intently on his work. In his search for character he disregarded conventional beauty, and because of this many of his subjects discontinued their sittings, or rejected the finished paintings. In 1910 his health began to decline, and after this he did little painting. He died in 1916, attended by his friend Samuel Murray. Hardly had he died, however, than his work began to receive wider recognition, beginning with a major exhibition at the Metropolitan Museum of Art.

Goodrich's book brought together three potent themes that have dominated subsequent writing on Eakins. One was that his work was fundamentally realistic and expressed a moral viewpoint of absolute and unflinching integrity. ("Seldom has there been so consistent a realist as Eakins," Goodrich maintained.)[28] Another was that such a realistic, pragmatic, down-to-earth viewpoint was characteristically American, and a healthy antidote to the facile sophistication of European art. Third was the notion that Eakins was "the greatest American artist." While Goodrich did not put the matter in such simple words, he made the point quite clearly by a process of elimination: he ended his book by comparing Eakins in turn with the other great masters of his time—Sargent, Whistler, La Farge, Homer, and Ryder—making it clear in each case that Eakins was the more significant figure. Sargent for example, was more brilliant, but more superficial; Whistler more sophisticated but more superficial; La Farge more "learned" but more superficial; and Homer more "picturesque" (a not altogether flattering adjective), but presumably also more superficial. By Goodrich's reckoning, only the mystic, Albert Pinkham Ryder, produced work as deep and profoundly haunting as that of Eakins. But Ryder could not compare in the overall richness of his achievement. Goodrich concluded his list with the comment that "Among American artists of the latter part of the nineteenth century, he [Eakins] emerges as one of those whose work has the most enduring qualities."[29]

Eakins's Rise to Glory

Looking back on it late in life, Goodrich confessed that his book was "too laudatory," but within a few decades his praise was surpassed by a host of other writers. Today Eakins is widely regarded as the greatest nineteenth-century American painter, while his large, dark, grim canvas of surgery, *The Gross Clinic*, which was greeted with distaste in the artist's lifetime, has been elevated to the stature of "the greatest American painting."[30] In Philadelphia, Eakins has been transformed from a pariah to a local hero. Jefferson Medical Center now houses an "Eakins Room" where the artist's medical paintings are enshrined in a dark chapel-like interior where spotlights pick out each portrait; the Philadelphia Museum of Art devotes a room to his work; and the prominent traffic circle in front of the museum carries the name Eakins Circle in his memory.

A fundamental assumption of most writing on Eakins became that Eakins was not simply a great painter but an exceptionally moral human being. In notable contrast to contemporary reactions, Eakins's name became a byword for honesty and moral probity. Robert Henri declared that "His quality was honesty. 'Integrity' is the word which seems best to fit him."[31] Alfred H. Barr Jr., the director of the Museum of Modern Art, wrote of Eakins's "passion for truth."[32] Similarly, Fairfield Porter, in a short monograph on Eakins, insisted that the artist's "supreme qualities" were "high-mindedness" and "conscientiousness." According to Porter, Eakins's work was an expression of "moral force," of "high moral standards and a strict conscience."[33] Continuing this interpretive tradition, in the mid 1960s, Leslie Katz, a New York philanthropist who had studied art history with Meyer Schapiro at Columbia University, attached Eakins's name to a private press and foundation to symbolize the goal of "human excellence."[34]

After Goodrich's book, scholarship on Eakins took on some of the aspects of a cult. Sylvan Schendler, in his book *Eakins* of 1967, put forward the Eakins myth in its simplest and most sentimental form.[35] He presented Eakins as an utterly sincere, honest craftsman, uninterested in affectation, who saw through the social fakery of his sitters and was punished with neglect and social ostracism. Throughout his account, Eakins did battle with the pompous hypocrites of Philadelphia society. Even more upbeat in approach was

Elizabeth Johns's book of 1983, *Thomas Eakins: The Heroism of Modern Life* which portrayed Eakins as a simple-hearted idealist who loved sports, medicine, and modern advances, and whose paintings celebrate the triumphs of the modern age. In Johns's account, nothing dark or unpleasant was explored. The controversies he created moved out of the spotlight into the shadows. She declared that Eakins perfectly embodied the ideals of the nineteenth century, and was "Carlyle's poet," "Baudelaire's painter," and "Emerson's artist." She proposed that we use the term "The Age of Eakins" to acknowledge his role in celebrating "the moral, disciplined, self-made man." "The heroism Eakins found in modern life," she wrote, "he lived in his own life."[36]

Writers for the popular press parroted these views and trumpeted them to a mass audience. Thus, for example, John Russell, the art critic for the *New York Times*, wrote of Eakins that: "We prize him above all for a new dimension of moral awareness that he brought to American painting." In case we could not fully grasp the point, he went on to declare that Eakins's paintings exhibit "a steadiness of moral purpose," and characterized Eakins as "one of the great American moralists." He concluded with the thought: "We ask ourselves whether Thomas Eakins was not the greatest American painter who ever lived."[37]

Similarly, in an echo of Parson Weems's notoriously untruthful biography of George Washington, *Time* magazine's art critic, Robert Hughes, has termed Eakins "an artist who refused to tell a lie."[38]

Notably, in biographies of Eakins, very often the discussion of specific paintings shifts abruptly to praise of the moral values supposedly exemplified by his art. No other American artist seems to inspire this sort of moral fervor, at least not to a comparable degree.

Along with winning over scholars and art critics, Eakins became the darling of painters. Indeed, artists played a major role in the revival of Eakins's reputation. Robert Henri, for instance, the charismatic leader of the so-called Ash Can School, hailed Eakins as "one of the very great men in all American art," and his admiration was shared by two of his famous students, George Bellows and Edward Hopper, both of whom looked back to Eakins as a model.[39] Another great American painter, Reginald Marsh, visited the artist's widow and acquired two paintings by the artist. As has been noted, he also subsidized the first serious monograph on Eakins, written by his boyhood friend Lloyd Goodrich.[40]

Perhaps the single most striking tribute to Eakins is not a written statement but a painting—a large group portrait executed in his honor by the noted social

Raphael Soyer, Homage to Thomas Eakins, 1963–1965. *Oil on canvas, 88 ⅛ x 80 ¼ in., Hirshhorn Museum and Sculpture Garden, Smithsonian Institution, Gift of the Joseph H. Hirshhorn Foundation, 1966.* At a time when representational painting was being supplanted by abstract expressionism, Raphael Soyer portrayed Lloyd Goodrich and a group of realist painters gathered around their touchstone of artistic excellence, Eakins's *The Gross Clinic*.

realist painter Raphael Soyer. Modeled on Henri Fantin-Latour's famous *Homage to Eugene Delacroix*, which pictured a group of the adventurous French painters gathered around a portrait of Delacroix, Soyer's *Homage to Thomas Eakins* (1965) showed ten admirers of Eakins in front of *The Gross Clinic* and two other Eakins masterworks.[41] Each of the figures was a noted American realist painter influenced by Eakins—Leonard Baskin, Moses Soyer, Jack Levine, Henry Varnum Poor, Edward Hopper, Reginald Marsh (who had died by this time, but was included posthumously), John Koch, Edwin Dickinson, and John Dobbs. Lloyd Goodrich stood at the center of the group, the only art historian to be included.

Being placed in the painting was viewed as a considerable honor, and as Edward Hopper anticipated grumpily, when Soyer first asked him to pose, some people with only a remote connection to Eakins sought to be included as a token of their status and importance in the art world.[42] The art historian John Rewald, for example, a scholar of French art known for his *The History of Impressionism*, unsuccessfully tried to be included on the grounds that he had once persuaded a collector to purchase a painting by Eakins.[43]

Although it purported to be idealistic, Soyer's project can also be viewed as a thoroughly self-serving venture, concocted by a realist painter who deeply resented the fact that he had just been pushed out of the spotlight of critical attention by a more radical group, the Abstract Expressionists. Nonetheless, it is noteworthy that of all American painters, Soyer unhesitatingly chose Eakins to represent what was most admirable in the American realist tradition. Even if we see Soyer's painting as self-serving and reactionary—a last-ditch effort to preserve an outmoded realistic style—his homage points toward some quality in Eakins's work that makes him stand apart, and that separates him from any other figure in nineteenth-century American art. No other American artist of the nineteenth century has ever been accorded such reverence. Something about Eakins's work seems to have a force, a toughness, unlike that of any other American painter.

Some Oddities of the Literature on Eakins

At the risk of being blunt, and of offending scholars who in some cases are my friends, several things strike me as unusual about the literature on Eakins. One is the value accorded to unremarkable insights. In 1996, for example, Helen Cooper at the Yale University Art Gallery organized an exhibition of Eakins's rowing pictures that traveled to some of America's most distinguished museums, such as the National Gallery, and was universally praised by reviewers in distinguished magazines and journals, including the *New York Times*.[44] The interpretive framework employed in the exhibition was curiously simple: that Eakins's paintings portray real people and real places, and refer to rowing races that actually occurred. Hardly original, this approach was borrowed from the work of Elizabeth Johns, who had already specifically identified all the same places and races in her widely praised book on *Thomas Eakins and the Heroism of Modern Life*.

In the work of other painters of equal or possibly greater technical skill, such as Andrew Wyeth or Norman Rockwell, such meticulous recreation of actual events and people would be viewed as a negative—as evidence that they do not deserve the title of artists. "Slavish realism," in fact, has been a derogatory term in art writing since the 1950s. Scholars who study Norman Rockwell's renditions of restaurants and doctor's offices in Stockbridge, Massachusetts, and who discover that he devoted great care to the rendering of the wallpaper, are relegated to the lunatic fringe of serious art history, and do not gain critical acclaim.[45] Clearly there is something about Eakins's work that makes seemingly ordinary insights appear profound or emotionally reassuring. But the praise is so exaggerated that it makes one wonder what deeper motive lies behind the accolades.

Linked with this phenomenon is the fact that Eakins's abilities outside the sphere of paintings are often described as altogether extraordinary, when that does not appear to have been the case. John Singer Sargent, for example, not only painted with remarkable flair, but also spoke five or six languages, most of them fluently and with no trace of accent, played the piano with professional skill, and composed music. These accomplishments, however, are generally treated as unsurprising and even as signs of decadence, presumably because they are seen as reflections of Sargent's socially privileged background. (Anyone who has spent time with children of the idle rich would argue the reverse: these facts are all the more amazing given Sargent's affluent and aimless social milieu.) Eakins, on the contrary, is praised as a master linguist on the basis of the fact that he could speak some French after spending several years in France (notably, the claims that his French was fluent are based on statements by individuals, such as Samuel Murray, who did not speak French); he is extolled as a mathematical genius, because he mastered basic calculus (although he had no interest in mathematics of a more creative sort); and he is even described as an expert rower because he is recorded to have rowed a boat (although he never joined a rowing team or entered a race). The enthusiasm with which quite ordinary accomplishments have been treated as if they were unparalleled achievements suggests that something not quite honest is being pushed across.

Still more peculiar is that descriptions of Eakins's paintings frequently avoid mentioning their most obvious visual characteristics. A striking case is *Portrait of the Artist's Wife with a Setter Dog*. Eakins showed his wife Susan in a state of lassitude and dejection. Nonetheless, Goodrich declares that Susan's dress "is in fine taste, befitting an artist and the wife of an artist"; Schendler observes that Susan is "forcefully conscious" of the "coercive force" of her environment; and Leslie Katz goes so far as to describe Susan's neck as "alert" and "graceful in its naiveté," while her hand, with its limp, forlorn gesture, is "power recumbent."[46] All three writers studiously avoided mentioning the most obvious thing about the painting, namely that Susan looks profoundly depressed and careworn. Almost as if they were in league with one another, Goodrich and Schendler both pass over this fact, while Leslie Katz (taking a hint from Schendler) does something even more peculiar. In a remarkable turnabout, he verbally transforms a portrait of lethargy, inelegance, and weakness into an expression of alertness, grace, and power.

Finally, standards of evidence seem to work differently with Eakins than with other American artists. Perhaps this is already evident from the examples I have cited, but let me also mention another instance. One of the odder articles in the American field is an essay by Elizabeth Johns, "Thomas Eakins and 'Pure Art' Education," which purports to explain why Eakins was fired from the Pennsylvania Academy.[47] I use the word "odd" because of the way that Johns treats a hypothesis as if it were a fact. She argues from a premise that is fundamentally flawed: the never-questioned assumption that Eakins's motives must have been idealistic and moral. The proof of statements is that they are in accord with this doctrine. The comments of past writers about the scandals surrounding Eakins are cavalierly dismissed, and no new evidence is provided to support her conclusions.

Johns insists that Eakins's only fault at the Pennsylvania Academy was the rigor of his interest in such subjects as anatomy and perspective. Consequently, he instituted a pattern of teaching that was too professional and too demanding to meet with social approval. Even taken on it own terms, her argument seems far-fetched. But what is most disturbing is her amazing disregard of evidence—her systematic omission of the many other complaints that were made against Eakins as a teacher, or even of any mention of the loin cloth incident, which had always played a large role in earlier narratives. Johns presents an essentially imaginary reconstruction of Eakins's ideals and motives, one which transforms him into a moral paragon.

In fact, a good deal of evidence exists to counter many of Johns's assertions, but in her article, *a priori* assumptions about the fundamental virtuousness of Eakins's character serve as a substitute for any sort of pragmatic test. This neglect of contradictory evidence is even treated as a proof of moral superiority, since it demonstrates support of Eakins and of the virtuous qualities which have been attributed to him. Implicitly, the reader is invited to become morally superior also, by joining the Eakins team.

Perhaps what is most interesting, is not simply the shortcomings of the article but the degree to which Johns's approach has been embraced by others in the American field. Johns's article has been widely reprinted, and it is often assigned to classes on American art, presumably as a model of what students should aspire to achieve.[48]

Falsifying the Record

We now know that Goodrich suppressed a good deal of material in his monograph of 1933, and even made statements that he must have known were false. Goodrich's notes from his interviews with people who knew Eakins have become available since his death, and they reveal that he withheld any material that did not fit into a comfortable pattern of interpretation.

Could this suppression and falsification have been detected in the 1930s, even without the evidence that has since become available? This is a delicate question. Hindsight, of course, always makes things easier to recognize, but in fact many of Goodrich's statements went quite far in twisting the facts, and should have been questioned even in the 1930s. To be sure, in most cases these points were seemingly minor ones, concerning such matters as the artist's appearance and personal behavior. Nonetheless, such details helped to build up the image of Eakins as an honorable, straightforward, heroically moral figure, and thus had larger implications. Today, as we struggle to discover the real Eakins, and to cut through the pious rhetoric that has surrounded his work, a good place to start is with these points. In important ways, they provide clues about deeper aspects of Eakins's art and personality, as well as a foundation that will be useful when we explore more significant and terrible questions.

The fashion in which Goodrich took creative liberties is evident from his physical description of Eakins. One of Goodrich's favorite literary devices, which he borrowed from Victorian novelists, was that of describing physical traits that purport to provide clues about an individual's character. According to Goodrich's account, Eakins was strong, tall, supple and light-footed, with heavy eyebrows, high cheekbones, and a prominent mouth with full firm lips.[49]

As in a romantic novel, each of these physical attributes clearly serves as a kind of shorthand for some supposedly positive, even heroic, aspect of Eakins's personality. The strength, height, and suppleness assert his alleged athletic ability and love of exercise, the heavy eyebrows stand for moody thoughtfulness, the high cheekbones evoke a romantic quality, and the full lips suggest a passionate and powerfully sensual temperament. According to Goodrich, even Eakins's hands were remarkable. "His hands . . . were not large, but extremely vital and sensitive."[50] As one would expect in a painter whose forte was the ability to see the world with peculiar intensity of vision, Goodrich found something particularly remarkable about Eakins's eyes. Thus Goodrich writes: "His most expressive features were his eyes: alive, direct, observing."[51]

All of this sounds wonderfully precise and observant until we take the trouble to compare Goodrich's description with photographs of Eakins or with contemporary accounts. In fact, Eakins was by no means classically handsome, and by early middle life he had become obese and flatulent. In photographs he tends to look morose. While Goodrich maintains that Eakins had intensely observant eyes, this is not born out by photographs, for his eyes never seem to engage the viewer or the camera directly. In early photographs his eyes tend to look haunted or shifty, and in later photographs they look increasingly vacant, and take on a glassy quality.

Contemporary descriptions emphasize the lack of sparkle in Eakins's eyes rather than their intensity. Eakins's acquaintance Harrison Morris, for example, noted that when Eakins painted him, the artist had "lack-luster eyes, with listless lids."[52] In another account he stated that the artist "looked back with a rather listless attention."[53]

The truth of Morris's statements is well documented in photographs of Eakins, from all phases of his life. In most of them he looks emotionally troubled, if not emotionally disturbed. For example, when I showed a photograph of Eakins to a class of graduate students, I received responses such as these:

"He looks threatening."
"He looks conniving."
"He looks like a murderer."
"He looks like he's contemplating something that satisfies him—but something terrible."

These are very subjective responses, of course, and words are admittedly clumsy in describing the shifting nuances of human glances and expressions. A skeptic might argue that I was prejudiced against Eakins, and therefore encouraged my students to come up with negative reactions. Surely, however, anyone who takes a moment to study the photographs of Eakins can easily see that his appearance and demeanor were unusual—and in a way that often seems to relate closely to what was unusual about his paintings. For example, one of the peculiarities of Eakins's portraits is that the eyes of the sitters often look unfocused and vacant. Was there a connection between their appearance and that of Eakins himself? While it would be dangerous to jump to conclusions about the reasons for this glassy-eyed look, we should at least note the parallels between the appearance of the artist and his sitters, and file it away as an interesting clue.

Disregarding the evidence, Goodrich insisted on picturing Eakins according to the standard formulas of the romantic artist. His one concession to the facts was to admit that Eakins did not dress in velveteen, but even here he seems to have softened the reality a good deal. According to Goodrich's account, Eakins dressed in soft, comfortable clothes. He avoided mentioning the fact that Eakins's untidiness and frequent state of near undress often appears to have been a calculated social affront.

Circle of Thomas Eakins, Thomas Eakins at Age 35 to 40 in a Heavy Wool Jacket, ca. 1882. *Dry-plate negative, 4 x 5 in., courtesy of The Pennsylvania Academy of the Fine Arts, Philadelphia, Charles Bregler's Thomas Eakins Collection, purchased with the partial support of the Pew Memorial Trust.* **Photographs of Eakins often reveal a hunted or haunted look. His brother-in-law Frank Stephens described his gaze as "wolf-like."**

Goodrich's published descriptions of Eakins imply that the artist possessed a whole roster of positive and perhaps even heroic qualities, such as athletic ability, romantic intensity, and intellectual rectitude. The attributes mentioned by Goodrich's informants, however, were very different. They stressed that he looked dirty, was heavy and physically out of shape, that his eyes seemed "listless" (to repeat that word one more time), that he had a sagging lip, and that he often drooled saliva when he was painting.[54]

At one point, in his unpublished notes, Goodrich summed up what people had told him about Eakins and came up with the following list (transcribed directly from his notes):

Soft spoken. High-pitched voice.
   Issues of propriety
   Sloppy dress.
   Sexual stories.

Undressing.

Crude language.

Dirty jokes.[55]

Admittedly, this list of attributes does not consist of purely physical traits, although in many cases it implies them. Such a list certainly provides a very different picture of Eakins than the one that Goodrich published.

One of the most interesting facts, which runs against the conventional view that Eakins was intensely masculine, is that several people noted that his manner was feminine, if not effeminate. His high voice sounded like a woman, and even his gait is said to have been womanlike: he walked in short, rapid steps, hardly lifting his feet from the ground.[56] One of the women who posed for him, Mrs. Lavell, commented that in her opinion "the feminine in his character dominated over the masculine."[57]

Goodrich's notes also contain many cryptic references that he never ampli-fied into fully understandable statements. Even in their abbreviated form, however, many of these jottings appear to be unflattering to Eakins. Thus, for example, a section from his notes with Mrs. Addicks, the former Weda Cook, reads as follows:

Didn't like Jews. Mrs. Douty. Bad manners. Max Weil.

Boy riding at Avondale—urinating. Always used the word—never "go to wash hands."

Liked risqué stories that were artistic.[58]

From the context we can deduce that the phrase "didn't like Jews" refers to Eakins, since he is clearly the referent in other instances. According to Goodrich's notes, Mrs. Douty was Jewish, and "Max Weil" is probably a Jew-ish name. The words "bad manners" clearly refer to Eakins and seem to allude to an incident that involved a Max Weil and some sort of anti-Semitism. One cannot help wondering whether Goodrich deliberately avoided leaving a clear account of the episode, since he knew that anti-Semitism would be a sensitive issue in the New York art world.[59]

The reference to "Boy riding at Avondale—urinating" could refer to an off-color story, of the sort that Eakins is known to have enjoyed. It might also refer to a photograph, since a good many photographs survive showing naked boys with animals at Avondale. No photograph of a boy urinating has yet been located, but we know that Goodrich's widow and relatives destroyed many of Eakins's photographs, particularly those that portrayed nudes.

As with the anti-Semitism, Goodrich did not mention this urinating boy in any of his publications, quite possibly because it seemed psychologically strange. In his monograph of 1982, Goodrich did cite Walt Whitman's statement that Eakins was "quite a Rabelaisian," but he did so in a way that implies that Eakins was simply honest and forthright. In fact, many of those who knew Eakins saw the matter differently, and thought that he was psychologically fixated on bathroom functions.[60] It is hard to blame Goodrich for his evasions, since it is often embarrassing to describe Eakins's speech and behavior. We can understand why Eakins's contemporaries, particularly women, felt uncomfortable in his presence; and we get a glimpse of something troubled about Eakins that deserves deeper explanation.

A Passive-Aggressive Figure

I do not wish to imply, of course, that all of Goodrich's information was inaccurate. He researched Eakins's life assiduously. The problem is that he reported information very selectively, suppressing things that seemed inconsistent or odd about Eakins's behavior, and even deliberately altering facts to support his view of Eakins's character.[61]

Indeed, one of the key points that emerges when one goes back to the uncensored descriptions of Eakins in Goodrich's notes is a sense of unresolved tension in his personality—the sort of tension that modern psychologists would characterize as passive-aggressive. Many of those who encountered Eakins commented on his exceptional gentleness, which had an almost feminine quality. Mrs. Adicks noted that Eakins was never sharp. She only saw him lose his temper once, with the journalist Francis Ziegler, after Ziegler published an account of the mental breakdown of one of Eakins's students, Lillian Hammitt. Adolph Burie, another acquaintance, also noted that Eakins "was very gentle" and had "a sweet voice." Elizabeth Burton, who posed for him, spoke of his "gentle simplicity."[62]

Yet Eakins could suddenly shift from gentleness to brutality. James L. Wood, the son of Eakins's personal physician, noted that Eakins once angrily demolished a statue made by a student, which he thought was too carefully finished. Similarly, when he objected to the bracelet of one of his models, he snatched it off her wrist and smashed it on the floor. Wood noted that while

Eakins was "ordinarily very gentle," he could be "both gentle and brutal." If he was crossed in some way, Wood testified, Eakins would become so emotionally agitated that the spittle would trickle out of the corner of his mouth."[63] Mr. and Mrs. Douty both spoke of how "gentle" Eakins was, but both also noted that he was unforgiving of any slight. "He was never bitter or sharp, but simply absolutely determined—nothing would stand in his way. He did not quarrel with people, but if anyone did him what he thought was an unfair injury, he would never forgive them—would simply have no more to do with them."[64] Goodrich's account systematically omitted statements such as this, which suggest the real depth and complexity of Eakins's personality.

Can We Trust Susan?

Not only did Goodrich twist what people told him, but the nature of his informants also deserves scrutiny. A fundamental premise of Goodrich's research was the notion that what most people in Philadelphia thought about Eakins was incorrect, and that Eakins's behavior was not morally tainted in any significant respect. The people he chose to interview were generally biased in favor of Eakins, and he gave greatest weight to those who were most favorable. Those who had posed for Eakins generally had mixed reactions, which Goodrich reported only in part. The bulk of his book was drawn from the accounts of just three people, all of whom idolized Eakins: his wife Susan, and his students Charles Bregler and Samuel Murray. Of the three, Susan played by far the largest role in shaping Goodrich's account and it is her personal bias that seems to explain many of his most notable omissions.[65]

Most writers on Eakins, following Goodrich, have seen Susan Macdowell as the ideal soul mate for her husband and their marriage as a melding of passionate love and perfectly matched interests. Kathleen Foster, for example, seems to view Susan as an almost infallible authority on matters about Eakins. In Foster's various writings, Susan's support is frequently cited as proof of Eakins's high moral standards, and her statements are invoked to settle controversies of fact or dating.[66]

It does not take much investigation, however, to discover that Susan's statements were often inaccurate and misinformed. To cite a typical instance, in a letter of 1923 to the art dealer William Macbeth, Susan stated:

> I never knew Mr. Eakins to sign his pictures in any place but the lower right-hand corner—the usual way with most artists, and always with dark paint.[67]

In fact, Eakins signed at least thirty paintings elsewhere than the lower right-hand corner—including *A May Morning in the Park* and *The Concert Singer*, which at the time of the letter were in Susan's possession, and *The Pathetic Song*, in which she appears. At best this indicates that Susan was not terribly observant. But it also suggests that she may not have played a large role in her husband's artistic activities, and may not have been a perfect soul mate after all.

In fact, even by the standards of the time, the marriage seems to have been lacking in signs of affection or sexual interest. After Eakins was fired from the Pennsylvania Academy, his enemies circulated the rumor that he was not married. This proved to be untrue, and Eakins produced his marriage certificate to squelch the attack. But the fact that the rumor circulated makes it clear that Eakins's marriage was a strangely private affair. Foster does suggest that the couple probably lived together before their marriage—definite fodder for scandal in the nineteenth century.[68]

While a great many photographs exist of Eakins, at a time when photog-

Photographer unknown, Susan Macdowell Eakins with Daisies in Buttonhole, *1875–1880. Tintype, 3 7/16 x 2 1/16 in., The Pennsylvania Academy of the Fine Arts, Philadelphia, Charles Bregler's Thomas Eakins Collection, purchased with the partial support of the Pew Memorial Trust.* **After her marriage, Susan Eakins abandoned her professional career and devoted herself to caring for and defending her husband.**

raphy was not yet common, he never made photographs of his marriage, or of his married life, the one thing that most couples in the nineteenth century, as today, took trouble to record. In all the hundreds of photographs taken by Eakins and his students, I know of only one, taken very late in life, which shows him and his wife together, and in that they are standing apart, looking in opposite directions.[69] But many photographs show him with other people, including several that show him naked and touching a naked woman.

Eakins married on the late side, at the age of forty. From the early 1870s until 1879, he was engaged to Kathrin Crowell, but took no steps to consummate

*Attributed to
Samuel Murray,*
Thomas Eakins
and His Wife with
a Dog, *1910–1914.
Gelatin silver print,
5 ½ x 3 ½ in.,
collection of Daniel
W. Dietrich II.*
**Only one
photograph
shows Eakins and
his wife together,
this casual
snapshot taken in
their old age.**

their courtship. The relationship appears to have been pressed upon him by his father, and Eakins may well have been relieved when Kathrin died of meningitis at the age of twenty-eight. He married Susan Macdowell five years later, in 1884. One may ask why he chose to marry at this time, a question which curiously enough, none of Eakins's many biographers have ever posed.

The only occasion on which Eakins set forth his views on love and marriage are in two letters from Paris that he wrote to his friend Will Crowell and to his sister Frances. Like many of Eakins's letters, these contain abrupt shifts of direction. He opened his letter to Crowell by noting that "I look upon love & marriage as two very different things," a statement that he never fully explained in the passages that follow. He did make it clear, however, that the goal of marriage is to have children. "If ever I marry," he stated, "it will be only for the delight of raising children for the love of children grows on me not to leave a natural void." In his letter to his sister Frances, he expressed similar thoughts—sometimes using almost the same language—but elaborated on certain points. He noted that he was not interested in an intellectual spouse and would not pursue a "New England she doctor" but would look favorably upon "an Italian or Jersey farmer's daughter." "If ever I marry it will likely be with a girl of Southern feeling good impulses & heart healthy & able to bear strong beautiful children."[70] While the exact train of thought is not easy to follow, Eakins clearly felt that marriage should not be a matter of romantic passion but of good sense. He also made it clear that he did not wish a woman of intellect, who would challenge his authority, but a woman with a healthy body to bear his children.

Curious on their own, Eakins's statements become even more so when we consider their discrepancy with the course he actually followed. Admittedly, Susan was not well-educated, and she always docilely followed his lead. But she was not sensual and physically strong, nor capable in handling practical affairs. She was tiny, quite the opposite of a healthy Italian peasant, weighing less than one hundred pounds. One of Eakins's sitters, the educator Lucy Langdon W. Wilson, described Mrs. Eakins as "undersexed," and her marriage with Eakins was childless.

Eakins and his wife came from similar social backgrounds, both being part of a network of printmakers and scribes that functioned almost like an extended family. Susan's father, William Macdowell, was an engraver of diplomas, certificates, invitations, and banknotes, a trade very similar to that of Eakins's father, except that he worked with gravers and printing plates rather than with a pen. He and Benjamin Eakins moved in similar social circles. Despite this precise, exacting work, however, William Macdowell was a fierce individualist, freethinker, and admirer of the atheist Thomas Paine, author of *Common Sense*. Susan was the fifth of eight children in this large, disorderly, unconventional family.

With her father's encouragement, Susan learned to paint and attended the Pennsylvania Academy. Eakins never seems to have liked treating women as equals, and in his first encounter with Susan he was overbearing. She later recalled that when she first asked for his advice that "his criticism crushed me for a while."[71] Nonetheless, she was the leader of the group that protested when Eakins was asked to stop teaching his life class, and she lobbied to have him recalled. By this time she already seems to have become one of his confidantes. When he was later rehired by the Academy, one of his first acts was to write a note telling her of the news, and boasting of his triumph against John Sartain, his principal adversary on the board.

Although Susan had shown some promise as an artist, after their marriage Eakins pressed her into service as a cook and housekeeper—fields in which she had no experience. One of the artist's former students, Charles Bregler, later noted that "Mrs. Eakins was kinda killed when she married."[72] Shortly after the wedding, Bregler once came upon her in tears in the kitchen, where she was supposed to cook a meal for Eakins although she had no idea how to do so. From all accounts Susan was a poor housekeeper, and indeed, this was one of the complaints lodged against her by her brother- and sister-in-law, Will and Frances Crowell, who not only considered the house untidy, but believed that she neglected Eakins's father, and his mother's sister, Aunt Ella.[73]

Contemporary accounts make it clear that Susan did not share in most of her husband's social activities. Whether because of the pressure of housekeeping, or because Eakins did not want her company, she remained largely tied to the family home.[74] In the latter part of his career, Eakins's constant social companion was Samuel Murray, who shared his studio and accompanied him on outings and social junkets.

Why then did Eakins marry? The simplest explanation seems to be that in 1882, when Eakins started up his relationship with Susan, he had just lost his sister Margaret, who died of typhoid fever. For some time Margaret had been acting as his secretary, bookkeeper, and personal servant. Eakins needed another woman to play that role and turned to the one nearest to him, his dedicated student Susan Macdowell. Susan's role as a companion seems to have started immediately after Margaret's death. Margaret Eakins died on Christmas Eve, 1882; he married Susan Macdowell on January 19, 1884, almost exactly a year later.[75]

Close reading of Goodrich's account suggests that there was some tension between Susan and Samuel Murray as to which of them was more closely "married" to Eakins. Murray stated that he was with Eakins for the last two weeks of his life, night and day. During that time he spent most of his time holding the artist's hand—"He didn't seem to want me to leave," Murray wrote to the art critic Henry McBride.[76] Murray also reported that Eakins would only take food or medicine from his hand, and refused to take anything from Susan or Addie Williams, the two women in the household.

Goodrich repeated this account in his 1933 biography (and it has subsequently been repeated by other biographers).[77] Susan Eakins, however, took issue with Murray's report. As she wrote to Lloyd Goodrich on October 16, 1932, shortly before his book appeared: "I would correct your account of the period when my husband was an invalid. Murray was not the nurse. A constant visitor, always helpful, anxious to be of service to us, Miss Williams and I [were] the nurses."[78]

Unfortunately, there is no way to know who was telling the truth. Perhaps what is most interesting is that Samuel Murray and Susan Eakins told two mutually incompatible stories, and both were eager to press their own position as Eakins's most loyal friend and confidant. Here we find an instance of a common pattern of Eakins's life: radically divergent accounts and interpretations of the same event, even by those who actually witnessed it.

What was Susan's bias? Susan's role as Goodrich's central informant has certainly contributed much misleading information about Eakins, such as altered titles for paintings and inaccurate dates for many works.[79] More profoundly, however, it has obscured one of the central issues of Eakins's career—his fascination with the nude—by shrouding the issue under a cloak of prudery.

Eakins stirred up the controversy that ended his teaching career at the Pennsylvania Academy by removing the loin cloth from a male model. Throughout his life he showed a compulsive interest in the nude. Susan Eakins, however, avoided any discussion of such matters. When Goodrich spoke to her about individuals such as J. Laurie Wallace, who had posed nude for Eakins, Susan commented that this was not generally known, and quickly changed the subject. She spoke critically about the figure of the woman, Nannie Williams, who posed for Eakins's famous painting of William Rush, disparaging her good looks in a way that suggests an undercurrent of sexual jealousy. "She was still nervous about such incidents," Goodrich recalled, noting that she seemed fearful of the specter of past scandals.[80] Goodrich later confessed that he withheld material from his 1933 monograph in cases where he felt that Susan would disapprove of it. For example, he did not mention the suicide of Eakins's niece, Ella Crowell, although he heard about this matter in detail from several of the people he interviewed.

Later Scholarship on Eakins

Despite the seemingly obvious errors in his account, for forty years after the publication of his monograph, Goodrich enjoyed a near monopoly on Eakins scholarship, in part because he would not share his source material with other scholars. In the years following the publication of Goodrich's study, only one book appeared with new documentary information: a small, privately printed volume by Margaret McHenry titled *Thomas Eakins Who Painted* (Philadelphia, 1946). While distinctly amateurish from the literary standpoint, McHenry carried out extensive interviews with both Samuel Murray and Charles Bregler, and as a consequence her account is full of fascinating insights into Eakins and the workings of his household. Though less well organized than Goodrich's monograph, it is also less censored.

The first major challenge to Goodrich's preeminence as an authority on Eakins came from Gordon Hendricks, a self-taught art historian whom many in the field regarded as an obnoxious upstart. Nonetheless, Hendricks uncovered a wealth of new information about Eakins, and demonstrated that scholars need not work solely from the information provided by Goodrich. In *The Photographs of Thomas Eakins* (1972), Hendricks revealed an aspect of Eakins's artistic activity that Goodrich had ignored, indeed suppressed. Shortly afterward, in *The Life and Work of Thomas Eakins* (1974), Hendricks presented a wealth of visual and documentary material not included in Goodrich's monograph.[81]

Hendricks's book marked the beginning of a new era of Eakins research, during which the pace of new publications exploded. Indeed, Goodrich himself responded to the challenge of Hendricks's work with a two-volume study, *Thomas Eakins* (1982), which was clearly intended to be the final and definitive word on the subject. Though timid in its interpretations, and consequently quite dull to read, this hefty monograph presented a great deal of new documentary material, much of it drawn from the interviews that Goodrich had conducted in the 1930s with people who had known Eakins.[82]

The Bregler Hoard

Until the mid-1980s, however, the foundation of fact that could be brought to bear upon Eakins was fairly limited. Bit by bit, scholars expanded the knowledge of Eakins's life through background research, study of old newspapers, and inquiry into the lives of his sitters. On the whole, however, they were confined to recycling the same fairly limited body of basic biographical information—as it were, to rearranging a fixed set of dominos.[83]

This situation dramatically changed with the discovery in the spring of 1984 of a huge trove of Eakins material, which provided completely new information about the artist's life, his working process, and the scandals that plagued his professional career. Probably never before has the understanding of a major American artist been so completely revamped by the discovery of new biographical material. Sorting through this huge and diverse body of information will probably take decades, but already it is apparent that a major revision of scholarship is in order. What is this cache? Nothing less than Eakins's own collection of papers, sketches, and artistic paraphernalia. For fifty years, this material lay hidden, its existence rumored but unconfirmed.[84]

During the 1930s, when Lloyd Goodrich visited the Eakins home and rummaged through the fourth-floor attic studio, the place was filled with sketches, photographs, manuscripts and early letters, some of which he dutifully copied and worked into his biography. After the death of Eakins's widow in 1939, however, most of this material disappeared. Over the years, a few photographs and letters surfaced from time to time, but the bulk of the studio material was simply unaccounted for, and most scholars believed that it had been destroyed.

We now know that almost the entire contents of Eakins's studio were rescued by his pupil Charles Bregler, who befriended Susan Eakins after her husband's death and who often performed odd jobs for her. The two beneficiaries of Susan's will—her sister Elizabeth Kenton, and Addie Williams, had little interest in Eakins's art, and quarreled bitterly with each other over the value and allocation of the household furniture and other objects. After art dealers had selected a few of the more significant paintings, furniture movers were called in to clear out the home, and when Bregler arrived a little later he found a scene of total devastation. Bregler described what he found as:

> The most tragic and pitiful sight I ever saw. Every room was cluttered with debris as all the contents of the various drawers, closets, etc., were thrown upon the floor as they removed the furniture. All the life casts, etc. were smashed. One of the horse Clinker I saved and gave to the Graphic Sketch Club, as Mrs. Eakins wished. The frames and other things she wanted me to give to students. But I could find no one who wanted them. So they were carted away. I never want to see anything like this again.[85]

Shortly afterward, with or without permission—it is not clear—Bregler cleared out Eakins's studio, taking everything to his home at 4935 North Eleventh Street in the Logan section of Philadelphia. The marvelous thing about Bregler's collecting was that he was aesthetically indiscriminate. He valued the master's armchair quite as much as his paintings, and he preserved letters, note-books, sketchbooks, plaster casts, broken camera equip-ment, oil sketches, old photographs, and old receipts—a total of some 4,500 items. To improve his desperate financial situation, Bregler sold a few scraps of this pot-pourri through Knoedler's—a few letters and Eakins's cowboy costume, for example—most of which found their way to the Hirshhorn Museum in Washington, D.C. The bulk of the material, however, he kept hidden, showing it to no one, and refusing to share it with Eakins scholars.

In the late 1940s, Bregler met Mary Louise Picozzi, a young woman from South Philadelphia. According to her own account, shortly after their first meeting she had a dream or vision that he needed help, and went to his apartment to find him ill and without food. Taking pity on his helplessness, she became first his cook and house-keeper, then his common-law wife. Mary somewhat resented Bregler's preoccupation with Eakins, which she felt had prevented him from promoting his own work. But when Bregler died in 1958 at the age of ninety-three, she inherited his hoard of Eakins memorabilia; she took

Charles Bregler, ca. 1887. *Albumen print, 3 ⁹⁄₁₆ x 2 ⅝ in., courtesy of The Pennsylvania Academy of the Fine Arts, Philadelphia, Charles Bregler's Thomas Eakins Collection, purchased with the partial support of the Pew Memorial Trust.* **After Susan Eakins died, Charles Bregler took Eakins's papers and hid them. Twenty-seven years after Bregler's death, they were discovered in the possession of his widow.**

it with her when she moved back to her mother's row house on South Warnock Street in South Philadelphia.

Rumors circulated about this body of material, but Mary Picozzi kept scholars at bay, and over the years skepticism set in as to whether it really existed. As she grew older and her health began to fail, however, Mary Picozzi grew anxious about the fate of her husband's trove. In May 1984, she finally agreed to lend her collection to the Pennsylvania Academy of the Fine Arts for safekeeping, and, almost immediately, a crew of movers and curators descended on her home and removed the material.[86] After a year of appraisal and negotiation, aided by Mrs. Bregler's lawyer, William J. Kelly, the Academy arranged to purchase the collection. Five years of work by a team of scholars followed, and in 1989 the Academy presented the first fruits of this labor by publishing the major manuscripts from the Bregler papers, organized and transcribed by Cheryl Leibold, with commentary by Kathleen Foster.

Oddly enough, the artistic contents—the student notebooks, the anatomical diagrams, the clay models, and the elaborate perspective drawings—though often highly technical in nature, have proved fairly easy to interpret. What is noteworthy about them, in fact, is the literalness, the exactitude of Eakins's method, which bears little relation to conventional notions of artistic inspiration.[87] The personal papers, however, have proved to be more challenging, since they are filled with surprising revelations. Until recently scholars depended largely on guesswork in evaluating the scandals of Eakins's career. The Bregler papers shed new light on these matters.

Admittedly, the record they provide remains incomplete. Eakins seems to have destroyed many personal items that one would have expected him to save, such as all his father's papers, his wife's letters, and the letters of his fiancée, Kathrin Crowell.[88] With regard to the controversies that surrounded him, Eakins generally destroyed the accusatory documents, keeping only the papers he used in his own defense. Key pieces of the story are still missing, and the motivations of Eakins's opponents must often be reconstructed from circumstantial evidence. Nonetheless, even this biased account, containing only the evidence on Eakins's behalf, provides a chilling picture of his behavior, and particularly of his psychological manipulation of women. The notion that Eakins was an innocent victim of misunderstanding becomes almost untenable. The Bregler papers suggest that our view of Eakins's personality needs to be completely revised, and that our understanding of the deeper motives of his art has been heavily sugarcoated.

Now that this collection has been published, the most important source materials for reinterpreting Eakins are fully accessible. However, a warning is in order. Kathleen Foster, who summarized the contents of the Bregler papers, has done a fine job of gathering facts and references, but her editorial comments often inhibit comprehension rather than aiding it. Throughout, she presents Eakins as abused and maligned, and when the evidence does strongly line up against him, she expresses bewilderment, or comments that we will never know what actually occurred.[89] To make sense of the material, we need to be willing to follow the clues it provides, according to the dictates of common sense, rather than to blindly follow the road map offered by Foster.

Eakins Scholarship Today

Today, the time seems ripe for a fundamental reappraisal of Eakins. While Goodrich's view of Eakins as a highly moral figure remains the dominant one, it has been seriously eroded over the last two decades, not simply among scholars but for the public at large. The exact point at which it began to collapse is difficult to pinpoint, although some general markers can be indicated. The discovery of the Bregler papers has undoubtedly contributed to this shift. But in fact, the change also seems to be due to some larger alteration in how we look at artists and paintings. Some of the boldest new interpretations of Eakins have been made by scholars who made no use of the Bregler material.

As late as 1983, when Elizabeth Johns wrote her book on *Thomas Eakins and the Heroism of Modern Life*, it was still plausible to view Eakins as a model of virtue. Indeed, no book I can recall in the American field has been so enthusiastically received. Even the Marxist art historian Alan Wallach, well known for his harsh criticism of other scholars, praised the book as a splendid achievement.[90] Johns's book in turn served as the basis for Helen Cooper's exhibition of Eakins's rowing pictures in 1997. Again, the subtext of the narrative was that Eakins's art was founded on moral principles and again the project was warmly received.

By this time, however, a countertradition had begun to develop that viewed Eakins not as a bastion of solid male values, but as psychologically troubled, even disturbed. The first step in this direction was taken by David Lubin, who presented bizarre, erotic readings of *The Agnew Clinic* in his book *Act of Portrayal: Eakins, Sargent, James* (1985). Shortly afterward, in 1987, Michael Fried wrote an extended essay on Eakins's *Gross Clinic* titled *Realism, Writing, Disfiguration,* which even more effectively set aside the idealizing mode that had been the norm in Eakins scholarship up to that time. Fried's argument was centered on an obvious point that had somehow escaped the attention of previous writers on *The Gross Clinic*—that the painting deliberately does violence to our sensibilities. With its cringing mother, oozing wound, and the bloody hand of Dr. Gross holding a scalpel, the painting presents a scene that is both painful to look at and yet impossible not to be drawn to. As Fried observed, the artist clearly drew pleasure from inflicting pain on his viewers.

Shortly after Fried's challenging essay, a group of revisionist studies on Eakins began to appear by writers such as Marcia Pointon (1990), Michael Hatt (1993), Whitney Davis (1994), Randall Griffin (1995), Kathleen Spies (1998), Jennifer Doyle (1999), and Martin A. Berger (2000). These viewed Eakins as troubled about his masculine identity. Many of these writers were homosexual and involved in establishing gay studies as a legitimate discipline. This interest undoubtedly influenced the tone of many of these presentations, which tended to take Eakins's attraction to naked men as their point of departure. Several seem to have adopted Eakins as some sort of homosexual role model, although at least one (Marcia Pointon) criticized him for his hostility toward women. As will be seen, while I sometimes have disagreements, and write in quite a different manner, my own investigation has benefited greatly from the work of this revisionist camp.

Oddly, most of these revisionists did not make much use of the Bregler papers. The principal writer to do so has been William Inness Homer, whose Eakins biography (1992) balances the traditional hagiography of Lloyd Goodrich with episodes of a more disturbing nature, drawn from this source.

Curiously, also, to a large degree this new approach has existed in a world of its own and has had little influence on mainstream Eakins scholarship. Significantly, when Darrell Sewell organized a major Eakins retrospective for the Philadelphia Museum in 2002–2003—an exhibition that traveled to both the Musee d'Orsay in Paris and the Metropolitan Museum in New York—he systematically excluded revisionist writers both from the catalogue and the lectures that accompanied the show. All thirteen of the writers included in the Philadelphia catalogue avoided probing into the scandals of Eakins's life, and, with modest variations, followed the traditional line of interpreting his work set seventy years earlier by Lloyd Goodrich. To have their voices heard, the revisionist group was forced to create its own symposium outside the official proceedings—a kind of a *salon des réfusés*.[91]

Nonetheless, the exhibition lacked the self-righteousness and moral fervor of previous displays of Eakins's work, and the critics, even the general public, seem to have sensed this fact. For one thing, the exhibition and its catalogue necessarily included materials that seem to demand some new form of explanation—whether Eakins's extensive photographs of his students in the nude, or various disturbing episodes in his personal life recorded in the Bregler papers, which the catalogue could hardly avoid mentioning, at least in passing. The failure of the catalogue to come to terms with these things was widely noted. More profoundly, we seem to have moved from a modern to a postmodern age, in which issues of good and bad have become less clear, and the notion that the art of a figure like Eakins is morally pure can no longer be accepted without question. When we see works of art that express a tragic vision, we sense that they were based on the experience of terrible things and want to know what they were.

Can we take it as an omen that the critical response to the exhibition was quite different from that awarded to earlier ventures of a similar nature? Even those critics who essentially parroted the traditional phrases of praise for Eakins and the moral qualities of his realistic style seem to have sensed something dark and peculiar about his outlook, and to have felt that the exhibition did not probe very deeply into the reasons. As David Lubin perceptively noted in an essay in the *Art Bulletin*, "Eakins's oeuvre possesses much more of a night side, a dark, gothic, pre-, post-, or anti-Enlightenment dimension, than the exhibition acknowledged."[92]

Eakins scholarship thus stands at an odd moment. The old interpretations of Lloyd Goodrich still serve as the foundation for most accounts of his work, and are routinely repeated. But they no longer seem quite believable.

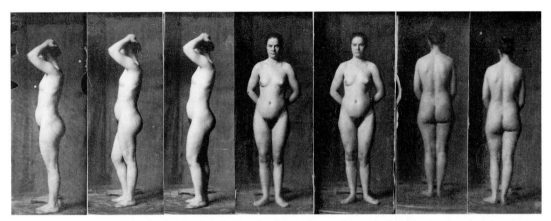

Naked Series: Female Model (sometimes identified as Blanche Hurlbert, who studied with Eakins), 1883. *Seven albumen prints mounted on card, 3 ⅟₁₆ x 8 ¹³⁄₁₆ in., The J. Paul Getty Museum, Los Angeles.* **While teaching at The Pennsylvania Academy, Eakins photographed nude figures in seven standing positions. Many of the models were his students.**

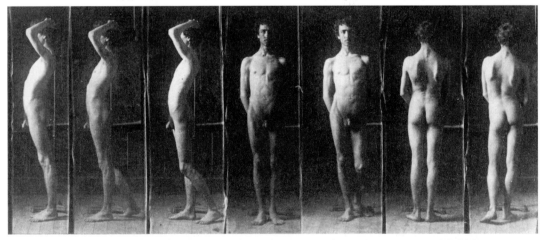

Naked Series: John Laurie Wallace, ca. 1883. *Seven albumen prints, mounted on card, 3 ³⁄₁₆ x 7 ⅝ in., Philadelphia Museum of Art, purchased with the Smith Kline Beckman Corporation Fund, 1984.* **J. Laurie Wallace also posed in the nude for Eakins's *Crucifixion.***

Chapter 3

THE LOIN CLOTH SCANDAL

THROUGHOUT HIS LIFE, Eakins was involved in feuds and quarrels. These often contained an element of conspiracy, with individuals shifting sides and plotting against one another. Because these scandals were so numerous and the charges against Eakins so serious, it becomes far-fetched to suppose that he was completely faultless and innocent. But if we simply take the role of prosecuting attorney and seek to pin the blame on Eakins, we run the risk of oversimplifying and misrepresenting both his actions and his intentions. Eakins's contemporaries were clearly bewildered about both his behavior and his motivations, and seem to have shifted sides because they often found that their initial explanations for his actions did not hold up. In short, the first step toward understanding Eakins is to recognize that his behavior was truly puzzling and that something by no means simple or straightforward was taking place.

An understanding of Eakins is made difficult by the fact that his behavior touched on an area of life, namely sex, which most nineteenth-century Philadelphians did not like to discuss in public.[1] Moreover, the Victorian vocabulary for describing or analyzing sexual activity was quite limited. It was possible to judge whether sexual behavior was "moral" or "immoral," but all "immoral" sexual behavior tended to be grouped in a single category. The highly specific character of certain sexual aberrations and obsessions was not understood, and sexual motivations were not clearly distinguished. As a consequence of this fact, every accusation against Eakins needs to be weighed and analyzed carefully. On the one hand we can often fill in what was left unsaid for reasons of prudery or embarrassment. On the other, we need to consider that many statements were probably misleading, since they were based on supposition about Eakins's motives rather than solid evidence. Eakins's contemporaries seem to have been confused about whether Eakins's behavior was "moral" or "immoral" because something about it did not make sense to them.

Reducing these conflicts to a linear narrative is not easy, since the episodes often overlap and run together. Later disputes would often raise issues and complaints from some previous one, which would then be replayed, often in a fashion slightly twisted from the first occurrence. In many instances the disturbances that Eakins created are not well documented, and consequently are susceptible to more than one explanation. But as we run through the various episodes, certain patterns recur. Indeed, events that are puzzling viewed by themselves, begin to make sense when we match them up with other similar incidents. To start with, it seems to me, the best approach for making sense of Eakins is not to cast judgment, but simply to look for patterns that repeat themselves. Given that none of the existing explanations seems satisfactory, even small details are worth attending to, since they may point toward a different way of viewing things. At the risk of being tedious or confusing, it is worth looking at these scandals in detail, going back to the primary sources.

Since the story has as many characters as a novel by Tolstoy, I have added a biographical key at the back of the book, which summarizes the lives of the key figures and clarifies their relationship to each other.

The best-known scandal of Eakins's career—his dismissal from the Pennsylvania Academy of the Fine Arts—is one of the least well documented. The directors of the Academy provided no explanation for their decision and left no report or transcript of the investigation of Eakins that they conducted. While he made occasional references to the episode, Eakins never made a detailed statement in his defense, either at the time of the firing or afterwards. The Bregler papers contain useful information about this event, but the references are often cryptic and for the most part made in connection with later controversies. When all the available evidence is assembled, however, we can piece together roughly what happened.

At the time the Bregler papers were acquired, Elizabeth Johns conjectured that they would demonstrate that Eakins was fired from the Pennsylvania Academy because of disputes over the curriculum he imposed and its excessively rigorous approach.[2] In fact, this guess could not have been more wrong. What the papers reveal instead is that the complaints against Eakins were bitter and personal, rather than professional, and that many of those who were closest to him, including members of his immediate family, had grave doubts about his moral character.

As has already been mentioned, Eakins was fired from the Pennsylvania

Academy after undraping a male model in front of a class of female students. This precipitated complaints that led to his resignation about a month later. The classic account of Eakins's firing was given by Goodrich in four crisp sentences:

> A few proper females complained to the directors. A special committee was formed, which upon hearing both sides ruled that Eakins must exercise restrictions in posing the model, or resign. His reply was that he would remain only on condition that he was not hampered in his teaching. On February 13, 1886, his resignation was presented to the directors and accepted.[3]

Goodrich's summary remains the basis of most subsequent accounts, but every sentence of his paragraph is incorrect or misleading except the last phrase indicating that Eakins resigned, which did indeed occur. Goodrich implies that the directors of the Academy fired Eakins because of the loin cloth episode. In fact, the directors of the Academy initially came to Eakins's defense. At the time the first scandal broke, one trustee even told a journalist that the loin cloth matter was simply "a tempest in a teapot."[4] It seems clear that something of a more serious nature surfaced shortly afterwards, and led the directors to reverse their earlier position. In other words, the loin cloth incident was significant only because it led to the disclosure of more serious problems.

Goodrich states that the attacks against Eakins came from a few prudish individuals. In his account of Eakins's resignation he reduces this group to "a few proper females," although elsewhere in his book he mentions that the opposition came from "a small group of Eakins's own staff and students." In fact, Eakins's entire teaching staff sided against him. His most vigorous enemy was his main teaching assistant and second-in-command, Thomas Anshutz, but Anshutz was backed by the other instructors, James Kelly and Colin Campbell Cooper, as well as by the anatomy demonstrators, Mary Searle, Charlotte Connard, and Jesse Godley.[5] There is no evidence that any of these figures was a prude. The student body seems to have been about evenly divided between those who supported Eakins and those who advocated his ouster. The group advocating Eakins's ouster, however, included many of his most talented students, as well as members of his extended family. Among the members of this group were Alice Barber, one of his two most gifted female students, who went on to become a successful illustrator; his brother-in-law Frank Stevens; and Elizabeth Macdowell, the sister of Eakins's wife.

Goodrich and other writers have always implied that resistance to Eakins came from "proper Philadelphia society," and was led by individuals opposed to the use of nude models. This does not seem to have been the case. Eakins's opponents were artistic colleagues and former friends, most of whom accepted the use of nude models as a matter of course.

Possibly personality factors contributed to the conflict. There is ample evidence that Eakins imposed his way on people, without much regard for their feelings. Even his nickname suggests a stubborn and authoritarian quality: his students knew him as "The Boss." Nonetheless, the extent of the opposition to Eakins, and the fact that this group was successful in persuading the directors to push Eakins out, strongly suggests that Eakins had done something either quite shocking or unarguably out of line with guidelines that had been laid down by the board.

Goodrich also implies that Eakins's resignation was a calculated moral decision—that he was given the choice of staying if he changed his manner of teaching, but that he refused to do so. In fact, there is no evidence that Eakins was given the choice of retaining his post if he agreed to relinquish study of the nude model. On the contrary, the trustees were apparently so distressed by what their inquiry turned up that they insisted Eakins submit his resignation.

It appears that there were four general complaints. First, Eakins was undoubtedly criticized for his seemingly excessive emphasis on the nude. When he became director of the art school of the Academy, he eliminated all the courses in design, still-life painting and landscape. Except for training in perspective, every class in his program was devoted to some aspect of rendering the nude. While men and women worked separately from each other, he insisted on using models of both sexes for both male and female classes.

This seems to have been considered particularly shocking for women, since in the nineteenth century most women led protected lives, within the confines of the home. As early as 1882, a certain R. S. (who seems to have been the mother of a student or prospective student) wrote to James Claghorn, the president of the Academy, to complain about the emphasis on the nude, which she felt was morally offensive. As she protested:

> Would you be willing . . . to know [your daughter] was sitting there with a dozen others, *studying* a nude figure, while the professor walked around criticizing the nudity, as to her *roundness in this part*, and swell of the muscles in another? That daughter at home had been shielded from every thought that might lead her young mind from the most rigid chastity. Her mother had

never allowed her to see her young naked brothers, hardly her sisters after their babyhood & yet at the age of eighteen or nineteen, for the culture of *high Art*, she has entered a class where both male & female figures stood before her in their horrid nakedness. This is no imaginary picture.[6]

This statement has often been used to vindicate Eakins, yet we can also read it as an assertion of the prevailing social norm in Philadelphia, where young girls might come to study art having never seen a naked figure, either male or female. While this letter has been widely ridiculed, it indicates how radically Eakins's procedures violated the social conventions of the times, at least for Philadelphia.[7] No doubt the directors of the Academy were aware of this tension.

Nonetheless, Eakins's use of nude models, by itself, can hardly have led to his departure, for it was a recognized part of professional artistic training. Eakins's emphasis on the nude was already known to the board, and they had gone along with his curricular changes, although perhaps reluctantly. After Eakins's departure the teachers at the school continued to use nude models, just as they had when Eakins was director.[8]

Second and more serious was student complaints that Eakins's behavior was often coarse. He employed crude language, was fond of dirty jokes, and often seemed to take delight in drawing attention to matters usually not discussed, such as male genitals and excrement. When dissecting male cadavers, for example, Eakins did not remove the penis, as was apparently the practice at the time. When he presented the cadaver to the class he not only exposed the penis but also discussed his decision at great length. When discussing bodily functions he did not use polite euphemisms, but, as several students complained, made a point of loudly asking his female pupils if they needed to "pee." He also told dirty jokes, including one about plums that presumably dealt with diarrhea.[9] Indeed, his fascination with anal matters was noted by several of his students. Around the time of the Eakins memorial exhibition, one student wrote a letter to Bryson Burroughs about Eakins's personality that contained the following story:

One day in the woman's modeling class (they had a live cow as model) the cow started to answer a call of nature. Eakins was criticizing one of the young ladies and when he saw this he jumped up and fairly yelled to Anshutz. "Get the camera, Tommy, I have discovered a new muscle! You can imagine the effect. Eakins was full of stories and jokes.[10]

Surely some of Eakins's pupils must have been less than delighted by such emphasis on the anus of a defecating cow. This sort of behavior would be shocking today, let alone in a society that draped piano legs, so that they would not be seen in public undressed. Clearly this issue of coarse behavior represented a legitimate matter of concern.

However, issues of tone and propriety are open to wide variations of interpretation, and it was often a matter of dispute whether Eakins had been offensive or simply excessively frank. If this issue of verbal propriety had been the only matter raised against Eakins, it seems likely that he would have escaped with a reprimand, rather than insistence that he resign.

Third, and more serious, Eakins had defied the normal boundaries between student, instructor and model: he had pressured students to pose in the nude and he had taken his own clothes off in front of students. Many accounts indicate that he coaxed and badgered his female students to pose nude, whether or not they were willing to do so. When they resisted, he did not back off, but continued to pressure them to undress. He seems to have applied similar coercive tactics to his male students as well.[11]

This practice stirred up a good deal of gossip, and stories about his behavior were still circulating fifty years later, when Goodrich began collecting material for his biography. In his 1933 monograph, Goodrich mentioned one such incident:

> Once when a model in the women's class had not appeared, and he was explaining an anatomical point about the female back, he asked one of the young ladies to take off her clothes so that they could see her back; but instead she burst into tears and went home, and told her father, who caused a commotion which was with difficulty smoothed over.[12]

As so often happens with Goodrich's accounts, the episode is reported in a way that seems to justify Eakins's behavior but is evasive about key points. Thus, Goodrich implies that Eakins was acting from necessity, but does not specify whether the model was just a few minutes late or completely failed to appear. He also does not clarify a key point, that is, whether Eakins asked the young woman to undress completely or simply to show her back. The one thing that we know for sure is that the student was distressed by his behavior.

Goodrich was also told about a young woman who had an unusual talent for catching a likeness. Supposedly, she carelessly left her sketchbook of drawings of naked fellow students in the classroom, where it was found by the incoming men's class, to their scandal and enjoyment. As Goodrich notes, this story has the quality of a fiction.[13] Nonetheless, it may contain at least a grain of truth, since in one of his letters Eakins himself blamed a female student for the circulation of the names of his models. With characteristically awkward grammar and poor punctuation he noted:

> One of the women pupils, some years ago gave to her lover who communi-cated it to Mr. Frank Stephens a list of these pupils [who had posed in the nude] as far as she knew them.[14]

While Eakins does not provide the name of this female pupil, he was prob-ably referring to Alice Barber, one of his most talented students, who became a successful illustrator. Alice Barber married Charles Stephens, who played a major role in the campaign against Eakins, and she was undoubtedly a key source for the stories that Stephens circulated.

In fact, Barber seems to have suffered from malicious gossip because she had posed nude. As Eakins's sister Frances recalled in 1890, four years after he was fired:

> Take Alice Barber, for instance. Her crime was having posed for her professor, yet when discovered her name was made subject of coarse jest among low New York students.[15]

Eakins also had undressed in front of his students. It is unclear exactly what the directors of the Academy discovered during their inquiry, but eight months after Eakins was fired, in September 1886, Eakins freely admitted to Edward Horner Coates, the president of the board, that he had invited one of his female students, Amelia Van Buren, to come to his studio so that he could explain an anatomical point about the pelvis. "There stripping myself, I gave her the explanation as I could not have done by words only."[16]

In addition to the somewhat fragmentary written evidence, we also have another form of testimony—Eakins's own photographs. Around 1976 a group of twenty-one prints, most of them of nudes, were discovered in the safe deposit box of Edward Coates. Evidently he had confiscated them at the time of the Academy scandal, both as evidence and to prevent them from falling into the wrong hands.[17] Additional photographs have also surfaced in other places, including many in the Bregler collection. While we do not have Coates's letter, Eakins later mentoned that Coates had complained that

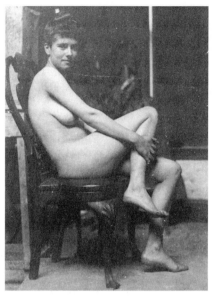

Male Nude Sitting on Modeling Stand, Holding Small Sculpture of Horse, in Pennsylvania Academy Studio, ca. 1885. *Albumen print, 3 ¹³⁄₁₆ x 4 ¾ in., courtesy of The Pennsylvania Academy of the Fine Arts, Philadelphia, Charles Bregler's Thomas Eakins Collection, purchased with the partial support of the Pew Memorial Trust.*

Female Nude Sitting on Queen Anne Chair, ca. 1885. *Platinum print, 4 ¹³⁄₁₆ x 3 in., courtesy of The Pennsylvania Academy of the Fine Arts, Philadelphia, Charles Bregler's Thomas Eakins Collection, purchased with the partial support of the Pew Memorial Trust.*

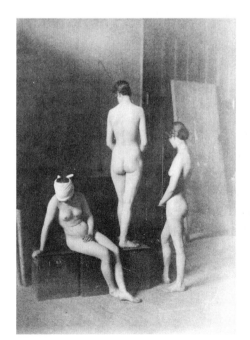

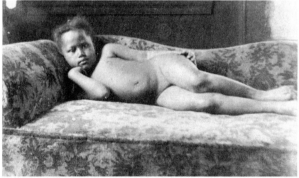

African-American Girl Nude, Reclining on Couch, ca. 1882. *Albumen print, ¹⁷⁄₁₆ x ²⁷⁄₁₆ in., courtesy of The Pennsylvania Academy of the Fine Arts, Philadelphia, Charles Bregler's Thomas Eakins Collection, purchased with the partial support of the Pew Memorial Trust.* **Eakins photographed not only naked adults but children as well.** LEFT *Three Female Nudes, Pennsylvania Academy of the Fine Arts, ca. 1883, albumen print, 5 x 3 ⅝ in., Founders Society Purchase, Robert H. Tannahill Foundation Fund, photograph © 1984 The Detroit Institute of Arts.* **This photograph confiscated by Edward Coates showed three female students posing nude in a classroom at The Pennsylvania Academy.**

Eakins "had made photographs of female pupils naked," so there can be little doubt that this issue surfaced at this time.[18]

Since I will discuss these photographs later in relation to Eakins's paintings there is no need to analyze them in detail here. But two points should be mentioned: first, many of these photographs portray students who are nude, often in full frontal nudity; and second, many of these photographs contain indications that the models were not comfortable, such as averted gazes or other signs of embarrassment. The photographs thus appear to confirm what is indicated in written accounts—that Eakins's students posed in the nude for him, and that some were reluctant but complied because of intense pressure or coercion from their teacher. In his teaching and demonstrations of anatomy, Eakins also regularly placed his hands on the model, which must have made his breach of the usual standards of decorum even more distressing.[19]

Photographs of Eakins himself in the nude have also come to light. These fall into two categories. A first group shows Eakins standing nude in front, back, and side views. These shots were allegedly taken to demonstrate something about human posture. A second group shows him standing beside a nude woman or carrying this woman in his arms. It is not clear what purpose this second group served. Taken together, the photographs securely document both that Eakins posed his students in the nude and that he himself undressed in front of them.

This charge of using students as models was surely the most damaging of the allegations against Eakins, and the photographs that Coates collected left no doubt that this charge was true. For one thing, the board had specifically requested that Eakins not engage in this practice. Thus, in purely legalistic terms, they were justified in firing him for failing to obey their directives. In addition, such conduct clearly went against normal artistic practice and the customary professional standards of artists and art schools. Many American and European art teachers used nude models, but they allowed their students to retain their clothes, indeed, insisted that they do so. The fact that Eakins had also undressed in front of his students surely added significantly to the case against him. Although Eakins maintained that his reasons were "professional," there was no professional precedent, either in Europe or America, for such a practice.

The fourth and final accusation was that Eakins had engaged in sexual misconduct, including not only improper advances on students, but more shocking practices, including sodomy, bestiality, and incest. Such stories were apparently still circulating about Eakins at the time that Goodrich began his research, although because of Goodrich's circumspection we will probably never know what they were. With his usual tendency to dismiss evidence that did not place Eakins in a favorable light, Goodrich noted, "Another conservative pupil told wilder tales, which were made unreliable by his inaccuracy in other matters."[20]

Since the witnesses against Eakins testified behind closed doors, and no record of their statements was made, we do not know specifically what charges were made against him at the time of the Academy scandal. Shortly afterwards, however, public allegations about Eakins's misbehavior began to surface. Eakins's brother-in-law, Frank Stephens, was particularly active in pushing forward charges of sexual misconduct, and he was supported by other witnesses, such as Alice Barber and Thomas Anshutz.

Such charges of sexual immorality surely must have been disturbing to the directors of the Academy, who were concerned about the school's good reputation. Yet these charges were difficult to prove and in many cases may have appeared implausible. In fact, one of the arguments frequently raised in Eakins's defense was that there was no solid evidence (such as an illegitimate child, an estranged mistress, or a clear accusation of rape) that he had ever seduced a female student. He himself maintained that his motives were purely professional in nature. In short, while Eakins's behavior toward students clearly violated normal social boundaries and art school practices, his motives were far from clear.

Paradoxically, the scandalous nature of Eakins's behavior provided him with protection, since neither the students involved nor the directors of the Academy wished these matters to be widely known. Female students were naturally embarrassed that they had been pressured into posing in the nude, while the Academy did not wish it to be publicly revealed that such activities had occurred. As a consequence, during the inquiry into Eakins's activities, students made their accusations orally rather than in writing, and the Academy did not preserve its report on their investigation, if indeed it was ever written. When the Academy dismissed Eakins, it gave no reasons other beyond a general need for "a change of management of the school."[21]

Newspaper articles of the time also used evasive language to describe what happened, although they hinted at something scandalous. Thus, for example, an article in the *Philadelphia Evening Bulletin* stated:

> With a few abnormal exceptions the women at the Life School recognized the
> fact that much as they might risk in coming in conflict with the Academy

authorities, they would risk infinitely more by accepting the conditions that Mr. Eakins proposed to force upon them.[22]

The phrasing of the article strongly suggests that the writer knew that Eakins had pressured his students to undress, but significantly, he alluded to this through discrete hints rather than direct statements.

While Eakins's troubles have generally been blamed on Victorian prudery, his behavior would be considered even more inappropriate today. The Victorians had only vague standards of "morality" and "proper conduct" with which to regulate Eakins, and they tended to support male authority. Today we have a legal concept—sexual harassment—that could be applied against him, and a long series of legal precedents defining the nature of such behavior. In today's world, Eakins would not only be fired, but would be subject to lawsuits by the women he pressured to undress. Thus, for example, Anne McCauley has noted of Eakins:

> His reported loose language and telling of off-color stories to his female students (to say nothing of the famous episode of dropping his trousers to make an anatomical point) could by modern standards be considered sexual harassment.[23]

Surprisingly, opposition to Eakins did not end when he was dismissed. Instead, it simply moved on to other arenas, where the conflict simmered on for the remainder of Eakins's life. The ensuing feuds and conflicts were so numerous, and such a mix of public and private, that it is difficult to reduce them to a linear narrative. But what is most startling about the revelations of the Bregler papers is that they show that much of the opposition to Eakins came not from professional colleagues, but from within his own family.

At the risk of oversimplification, it is convenient to divide this thirty-year war into two major battles, the first setting Eakins against his youngest sister Caroline and her husband Frank Stephens, and the other pitting Eakins against his only other surviving sister, Frances, and her husband, Will Crowell. Siblings, in-laws, cousins, pupils, and acquaintances were progressively drawn into both conflicts, creating a mud-slinging melee of accusations and recriminations.

LEFT *Potter and Co.,* George Frank Stephens, 1881. *Albumen cabinet card, courtesy of The Pennsylvania Academy of the Fine Arts, Philadelphia, purchased with funds donated by The Pennsylvania Academy Women's Committee.* **George Frank Stephens, who married Eakins's sister Caroline, campaigned vigorously against Eakins, accusing him of indecent behavior with his students, as well as incest with his sister Margaret.** RIGHT *Schreiber and Sons,* Caroline Eakins, June 15, 1878. *Albumen carte-de-visite, 3 ⁷⁄₁₆ x 2 ⁵⁄₁₆ in., courtesy of The Pennsylvania Academy of the Fine Arts, Philadelphia, purchased with funds donated by The Pennsylvania Academy Women's Committee.* **Eakins's sister Caroline disliked him intensely, and never forgave him for murdering her cat.**

Chapter 4

FAMILY QUARRELS

SHORTLY AFTER Eakins was fired from the Academy, procedures were started to expel him from the Philadelphia Sketch Club. The Sketch Club had been created in 1860, when life classes were not held at the Academy. When Eakins instituted such classes, he was invited to join the club. It was located at 1328 Chestnut Street, practically next door to Eakins's studio at 1330 Chestnut Street. Many of the members of the Sketch Club were also members of the Philadelphia Art Club, which also set in motion charges to expel Eakins.[1]

Not a single member of the Sketch Club was among the fifty-five male students who signed a petition to retain Eakins at the Pennsylvania Academy. What is more, the leaders of the action against him at the Sketch Club were all individuals who had worked closely with Eakins at the Academy. They included his second-in-command, Thomas Anshutz, as well as Frank Stephens, Charles Stephens, James Kelly, and Collin Campbell Cooper. Remarkably, Eakins's most active opponent within this group, Frank Stephens, was married to Eakins's sister Caroline. In short, the students at the Pennsylvania Academy who defended Eakins were all newcomers. His attackers were people who knew him well, including members of his family.

The person at the center of this attack remained partly hidden, since women were not allowed to speak for themselves. In all the Academy and art club controversies, Eakins's sister Caroline, known in the family as Caddy, was represented by her husband, Frank Stephens. Caroline, the youngest child in the Eakins family, was twenty-one years younger than her brother. She evidently disliked him intensely, finding him brutish and overbearing. Will Crowell later recalled that she expressed "an extravagance of hostility" when Eakins's name came up.[2] Kathleen Foster has alleged that they possessed very different personalities: whereas Eakins was casual about nudity and enjoyed dirty jokes, Caroline appears to have been demure, dainty, and ladylike.[3]

Her husband, Frank Stephens, was known as "Kid Stephens," since he was four years younger than his cousin Charles, who also joined the campaign against Eakins. Frank Stephens had studied at the Pennsylvania Academy and served as Eakins's teaching assistant in 1880. After he left the Academy he worked on the sculpture of the Philadelphia City Hall, and taught at several art schools, including the Drexel Institute. He married Eakins's sister in 1885, only shortly before Eakins became embroiled in scandal. What he discovered when he thus gained privileged access into the Eakins household clearly was a major factor in turning him against the artist, as is evident from the statements he made. In 1886, at the time of the Academy controversy, he was twenty-five years old.

Margaret Eakins and Thomas Eakins's Setter Harry on Doorstep of the Family Home at 1729 Mount Vernon Street, Philadelphia, ca. 1881. *Albumen print, 2 ¹³/₁₆ x 3 ¼ in., courtesy of The Pennsylvania Academy of the Fine Arts, Philadelphia, Charles Bregler's Thomas Eakins Collection, purchased with the partial support of the Pew Memorial Trust.* Eakins was particularly close to his middle sister, Margaret, who never married. After her death, Frank Stevens accused the two of incest.

Elizabeth Macdowell in Print Dress, Sitting, Hands Behind Head, ca. 1889. *Collodoin printing-out-paper print, 4 ¼ x 3 ¹³⁄₁₆ in., courtesy of The Pennsylvania Academy of the Fine Arts, Philadelphia, Charles Bregler's Thomas Eakins Collection, purchased with the partial support of the Pew Memorial Trust.* Elizabeth Macdowell, the sister of Eakins's wife, testified against Eakins when he was fired from The Pennsylvania Academy. She later recanted, resumed friendly relations, and often stayed in the Eakins home.

William G. Macdowell, Facing Left, ca. 1885. *Albumen print, 2 ¹³⁄₁₆ x 2 ⁹⁄₁₆ in., The Pennsylvania Academy of the Fine Arts, Philadelphia, Charles Bregler's Thomas Eakins Collection, purchased with the partial support of the Pew Memorial Trust.* Susan's brother William provided Eakins with legal advice during the Academy and art club scandals.

Several writers have described Stephens's hatred as a kind of mania, though apart from his animosity toward his brother-in-law, he seems to have shown no signed of mental imbalance. Indeed, aside from Eakins's father, Stephens was the only member of the extended Eakins family who ever held gainful employment for more than a short period. Stephens's charges against Eakins included not only nude posing and crude language, but also a series of other moral lapses, among them bestiality and incest.[4]

Stephens was joined in his attacks by his first cousin, Charles Stephens, a successful illustrator who specialized in Native American subjects and assembled an outstanding collection of Native American artifacts, now at the University of Pennsylvania Museum.[5] Stephens had once studied with Eakins and was engaged to Eakins's gifted female pupil, Alice Barber. He derived many of his accusations from his fiancée, who claimed that Eakins had made unwanted sexual overtures and attempted to seduce her. Evidently the tenor of these accusations was often heated. According to Susan Eakins, Charles Stephens burst into one meeting which Eakins had arranged to set forth his side of things and "with tragic air, disheveled hair and wild eyes" demanded that Eakins confess his misconduct.[6]

The dispute split the Eakins family down the middle. On one side, attacking Eakins, were his sister Caroline and her husband; on the other side, defending Eakins, were his sister Frances and her husband, Will Crowell, who for once made use of his legal training to come to the artist's defense. Even Eakins's favorite sister, Margaret, who had died four years earlier, was drawn into the fray when Stephens claimed that his knowledge of "domestic improprieties," including incestuous advances on Margaret, based on information that Margaret had confided to him or to his wife.[7]

The family of Eakins's wife Susan was also equally divided. William Macdowell, Susan's older brother, a practicing lawyer, helped the artist with his defense, but her younger sister, Elizabeth, who had studied with Eakins, sided against him and supported Alice Barber's assertions of his morally questionable behavior toward his female students.[8] Susan's other brother Walter stayed out of the conflict, but regarded Eakins with suspicion and distrust. He confided his feelings to his small daughter, whom he cautioned to watch out that Eakins did not paint her naked or entice her into bathing in front of him. Decades later she still viewed Eakins with hostility. "Oh, he was a rascal!" she stated of Eakins in her old age, in an interview with David Sellin.[9]

In the long document he drew up in defense of Eakins, Will Crowell took issue with some of Frank Stephens's assertions, and on the basis of one alleged discrepancy of fact, branded him as a liar. Objectively measuring the truth of Crowell's claim is no longer possible, since it hinges on a small detail. Crowell claimed that Stephens could not have known about Eakins's use of nude models as early as he claimed, since he was not told about it until a later date. Such issues of who told what to whom are difficult to pin down under the best of circumstances, and tend to become more confused when anger and conflict enter the picture. It seems quite possible that Stephens occasionally padded or exaggerated his case and that some of his statements may have been inaccurate. But this does not necessarily invalidate his contention that something about Eakins's behavior was peculiar, offensive, and perhaps even dangerous.

If we set aside the effort to determine the exact truth of all the charges and counter-charges, a larger pattern becomes apparent. One of the things that is striking not only about Eakins, but about other members of the family, is the fashion in which they consistently adopted extreme positions, with no middle ground. Not only was Eakins extreme in the way he denounced others as immoral, but we find that Will Crowell and Frank Stephens had the same tendency. Something about the general pattern of behavior in the Eakins family seems to have encouraged individuals to take an extreme approach, much as in war two opponents will tend to match the viciousness of each other's tactics. Years later, in 1946, in a letter to Eakins's biographer Margaret McHenry, Eakins's nephew, Will Crowell Jr., noted, "All our family have definite ideas, and are very hard to shift."[10] It is interesting to ask just how this pattern of violent denunciations originated in the Eakins family. While of course this cannot be established with certainty, it seems very likely that an example was set by Eakins's father, who appears to have been authoritarian and unbending in his views, and prone to moral denunciations of outsiders, or those who challenged his rules.[11]

As with the Academy controversy, the two art clubs seem to have taken care to misplace, and probably destroy, many of the documents pertinent to the case.[12] Meetings, arguments, procedural motions, and shouting matches were still taking place more than a year after the initial accusations. Once again, we are largely limited to the statements made in Eakins's defense. Much of the information these documents provide, however, is profoundly unsettling.

Will Crowell's written statement was intended to disprove Frank Stephens's accusations of incest and sexual impropriety, but the picture he drew of Eakins's character is hardly flattering. Crowell attributed Stephens's hatred to "slights or incivilities, some, no doubt real," and noted that long before Stephens knew that Eakins used nude models, he and his wife had spoken of Eakins with "an extravagance of hostility," complaining about his "wolfish looks," "his boorish manners," "his brutal talk," and so forth.[13] Crowell went on to suggest that some of this hostility was due to the fact that Eakins had shot a diseased cat that belonged to Caroline, without consulting her—allegedly at his father's request.[14]

The most remarkable revelation was that Crowell himself had once engaged in an extremely bitter feud with the artist, for reasons he did not specify. This episode "had bred in me such an intense hostility toward him that I confess having said to him, in the presence of his father, that if it were possible to confine the consequences of the act to our two selves, I would take his life."[15]

Crowell argued against the claims that Eakins had participated in incest or sexual impropriety, but he did note that Eakins "sometimes used coarse expressions in his talk," and that he was in the habit of walking around the house and in front of his sisters with no pants, and that this might have given rise to the allegations.[16]

Even if we credit Crowell's defense of Eakins, the picture that this document presents is by no means a pleasant one. It seems clear that Eakins belonged to a seriously dysfunctional family, in which sexual embarrassment, crude and threatening language, violent actions, and even death threats created terrible rifts between individuals. Eakins emerges as an unpleasant, even frightening personality.

In the course of this first full-scale battle, both Eakins and his enemies drew blood. Frank Stephens succeeded in his goal of getting Eakins thrown out of the two art clubs, and did lasting damage to his reputation. But Eakins won a victory when his father threw Frank Stephens and Caroline out of the family home, just after their first child was born, and broke off relations with them entirely. (The Stephens' child, Margaret, was apparently named for Eakins's middle sister, Margaret, who had died four years before, just three days before Christmas.)[17] Caroline died only two years after this expulsion. Neither her father nor Eakins ever spoke with her or visited her again, even during her final illness.[18]

If Eakins ever felt remorse for any of the actions that led him to be dismissed from the Academy, he never expressed it. Indeed, in March 1895, when he was invited to deliver an anatomy lecture at the Drexel Institute, about a mile from the scene of the earlier scandal, Eakins once again removed the loin cloth from a nude model and was once again dismissed. In an acid letter,

Clifford Grayson, the provost, noted that "the money for your course of lectures will be paid in full, although you have delivered only four of them. You will have no occasion therefore to sue the Institute. In view of your weakness for cheap notoriety, this, no doubt, will be a disappointment to you."[19] The comment is interesting since it suggests that some of Eakins's contemporaries believed that he deliberately staged episodes to stir up scandal. Eakins did, however, receive a letter of support from a certain J. R. Wilcroft, expressing approval of his actions among "all us Whitman fellows."[20] (It is not clear whether Wilcroft saw Walt Whitman as a general advocate of free lifestyles, or was celebrating his homosexuality.)

Ella Crowell, ca. 1897. *Silver print, 3 ⅞ × 2 ⅜ in., courtesy of The Pennsylvania Academy of the Fine Arts, Philadelphia, purchased with funds donated by The Pennsylvania Academy Woman's Committee.* Ella Crowell committed suicide in 1897, after complaining to her parents about her uncle's "degrading touch."

Chapter 5

THE DEATH OF ELLA CROWELL

FRANK STEPHENS'S claim that Eakins was in some way dangerous was seemingly borne out by subsequent events. The second phase of the battle, which was briefer and less public, but bloodier and even more tragic, pitted Eakins against his main defender at the time of the Academy controversy, William Crowell—his old friend, and former high school classmate, with whom he had once traveled in Europe. Will had married Eakins's oldest sister, Frances, and he was the brother of Kathrin Crowell, to whom Eakins was engaged until her premature death. The dispute culminated in the suicide of Will and Frances's daughter Ella.

A notably ineffectual man, Will Crowell never worked or provided income to support his family. Although he earned a law degree, he was unwilling to practice. His excuse for avoiding the profession was that he suffered from "a weak heart," but despite this alleged illness he lived to an advanced age. In fact, the heart problems may well have been imaginary.[1] Instead of working, Crowell moved out of the city to a farm named Avondale.[2] The place was not financially profitable, and Will bitterly missed the cultural distractions of the city. In photographs, Will always has a look of mild-mannered distraction, and he seems to have spent most of his time either gossiping at the country store or reading the newspaper.[3] His wife, Frances, their children, and a hired man seem to have performed the actual work of running the farm.

Apparently tension developed between Will Crowell and Benjamin Eakins, in part for financial reasons. Shortly after Will and Frances married, Benjamin Eakins lent Crowell $5,275 to purchase the house and property at Avondale, a very considerable sum at the time. Evidently he had promised the money if Will would finish law school. Doubtless he was irked when Will finished

LEFT *F. Gutekunst, Frances Eakins, 1880. Albumen cabinet card, courtesy of The Pennsylvania Academy of the Fine Arts, Philadelphia, purchased with funds donated by The Pennsylvania Academy Women's Committee.* Eakins's sister Frances publicly defended her brother, but family papers reveal that there was considerable tension between the two. After Ella's death she broke off all relations with him.   RIGHT *Photographer unknown,* Crowell Farmhouse, Avondale, Mr. and Mrs. Robert Trostle. Will Crowell never repaid Benjamin Eakins for the purchase of a farmhouse in Avondale, where he and his wife, Frances, raised nine children.

school but never practiced. The loan was never repaid, and in Benjamin's will, he deducted the amount from Frances's share of his estate. In addition, he took care to exclude Will from the bequest, specifying that the remaining sum left to Frances was to be held in trust, and the income paid "for her sole and separate use free from the debts, control and engagements of her present or any future husband."[4] While the unpaid debt was surely one reason for adding this clause, Benjamin Eakins was surely also distressed by Will Crowell's general failure to work or provide income for his family. For whatever reason, Eakins never painted Will Crowell, despite their long association.

Will fathered ten children, although supporting them was a challenge with the meager income from the farm. In a photograph of the family, probably taken by Eakins, the place looks unkempt and the children's clothes are shabby. Revealingly, Will sits off on the left side, reading his newspaper, seemingly only half aware of the others.[5]

Before he became estranged from his sister Frances and Will Crowell, Eakins often visited the farm at Avondale. There he took many photographs of naked children and young men, and skinned and dissected small animals that he shot while wandering around the farm. He even set up a small studio in the attic of the farmhouse, which included a human skeleton with which he enjoyed frightening the Crowell children. On several occasions, Eakins gave guns to the family as presents.[6]

Since the farm offered no future to the children, in April 1890 Will and Frances sent their daughters Ella and Maggie (who were respectively seventeen and fourteen years old) to live and study art with Eakins. They did so, however, with deep reluctance: the Bregler papers indicate that, although they had come to Eakins's defense earlier, Will and his wife had strong reservations about the artist's conduct. Both wrote him long letters begging him not to force the girls to pose in the nude. Noting that both children were "so innocent, and ignorant of the very existence of evil," Frances specifically pleaded that they never be asked "to pose nude or even to strip in any way." In a startling aside she added in her letter to her brother: "I almost feel as if we were sending them to probable destruction."[7] What is more, despite their defense of Eakins during the art club scandals, the Crowells had kept up a relationship

The William Crowell Family, ca. 1890. *Modern print from a film negative, courtesy of The Pennsylvania Academy of the Fine Arts, Philadelphia, Charles Bregler's Thomas Eakins Collection, purchased with the partial support of the Pew Memorial Trust.* Will Crowell distractedly reads a newspaper while his family gathers on the steps at Avondale. His daughter Ella (on the far right) and her sister Maggie (seated on the top step next to her mother), moved into Eakins's home the year this photograph was taken. Later they were joined by their brother Ben, who holds the family dog.

with Eakins's arch-enemy Frank Stephens. In other words, their feelings about Eakins seem to have been deeply ambivalent.

Possibly they also sensed that their daughter Ella was unusually vulnerable. Susan Eakins later complained of Ella's "poor self-government." According to Susan, after being refused permission to ride her horse to Philadelphia, Ella once "got on one of the horses and at a furious rate rode around the farm until the beast was exhausted, then betaking her self to the meadow stream remained in swimming until exhausted herself, this followed by sickness." Susan added: "This exhausting her strength as a vent to her passionate rebellion against restraint was a usual practice."[8] Such histrionic behavior raises the possibility that Ella may have been manic-depressive, like her grandmother, Eakins's mother, Caroline.

The forebodings of Will and Frances Crowell proved well founded. Allegedly, Eakins had high hopes that Ella would become an animal sculptor, but she found the emotional anxiety that resulted from studying under her uncle too much for her.

According to various informants, Ella posed in the nude for Eakins.[9] One cannot help wondering whether Frances's expression of concern about her brother's focus on the nude may not have triggered some unconscious reaction on his part, and led him to focus with increased intensity on getting Ella to undress for him. Apparently Eakins resorted to physical force to make Ella take her clothes off. Goodrich's unpublished notes from his interview with Ella's mother, contains the notation: "Spanking—making Ella Crowell pose."[10]

Ella also complained to her parents of Eakins's "degrading touch" and indicated to them that he had in some way touched her genitals and sexually molested her.[11] According to one of her siblings (unnamed) who was interviewed by Gordon Hendricks, Ella also stated that Eakins had invited her to touch his own "private parts."

In 1895, Ella abruptly shifted from art to nursing. Some of Eakins's unwanted advances seem to have come after she made this decision since Eakins is said to have justified his insistence that Ella touch his genitals by insisting that this would prepare her for the harsh realities of nursing.[12] His strange behavior, however, seems to have started earlier, when she was studying painting with him.

Around the time she shifted to nursing, Ella became emotionally unbalanced and began to exhibit behavior that was threatening to others or dangerous to herself. Weda Cook (later Mrs. Addicks), who was posing for Eakins's painting *The Concert Singer* around this time, told Goodrich that Ella came to see her and related that by mistake she had given a patient an overdose of a drug that almost killed him. This mistake had been so upsetting that Ella had decided to kill herself, but first she was going to kill Miss Cook. She then produced a loaded revolver. Cook told Goodrich she spent one of the worst hours of her life persuading Ella not to carry through with her threat. Ella then left and took the same overdose that she had given to the patient, which almost killed her.

According to Weda Cook, Ella later threatened to kill Eakins, presumably with the same revolver she used in the first episode. This fact was confirmed by Ella's sister, Frances. When Goodrich interviewed her at Avondale in 1931, she stated that Ella tried to kill Eakins. [13]

After a series of such disturbing incidents, Ella was placed in a mental hospital. Two months later, she was taken home to Avondale and kept in a locked room. On July 2, 1897, she broke out of her room and killed herself with a shotgun—probably a shotgun that Eakins had brought back from his trip to the Dakotas and given to the family.[14] She was just twenty-four years old.

From the coroner's report we know that Ella shot herself in the head, presumably at close range.[15] Thus, her death must have been an exceptionally messy affair, leaving her face an almost unrecognizable pulp and blowing bits of blood, flesh, brain and bone around the room. To grasp the full ghastliness of the event we need to imagine not simply the moment of death but the subsequent task of preparing the body for burial and cleaning up the gore. Ella's siblings were out in the fields when the tragedy occurred and more than one of them later recalled that they "heard the shot," but this phrasing of what they witnessed suggests that they did not see the body as it was found.[16] It seems probable that Ella's siblings were kept away from the corpse, although her parents must have seen it. Without much doubt, Will and Frances needed to supervise the process of clean-up, even if they did not do the work themselves. While it may seem gruesome to bring out these points, surely they are relevant to an understanding of Will and Frances' reaction. Nearly all of Eakins's biographers have condemned Will and France Crowell for being angry at Eakins, but surely this was quite natural in light of their daughter's statements about what Eakins had done to her as well as the horror they had witnessed.

Susan Eakins's Account of Ella Crowell

Ella's suicide raises many questions. Did she suffer from mental illness of some sort, such as manic-depression or schizophrenia? Was she sane but deeply distraught over some sort of sexual assault? Was Eakins in some way responsible? Did her distress reflect trouble within her family? Did it relate to some larger disturbance with the extended Eakins family? The dramatic violence of Ella's suicide is a further puzzle. The form of Ella's suicide was quite unusual: while men often commit suicide by hanging or shooting, women most commonly do so by methods that do not disfigure the body, such as poison or drowning. We need to ask why Ella chose to blow her head off with a gun.[17]

Unfortunately, like many of the figures associated with Eakins, we know of Ella largely through the distorted lens of accusations and recriminations. It is often difficult to reconcile the facts of the different accounts, let alone arrive at an understanding of reasons and motives for what occurred. In fact, the fullest account of Ella Crowell's breakdown is one that is strongly biased—a long memorandum written by Susan, Eakins's wife, by far the longest surviving document from her hand. It is not clear for whom this memorandum was intended: it could not have been intended for Will or Frances Crowell, since it repeatedly attacks their integrity. Whoever the intended reader, the central purpose of the document was clearly to defend and justify her husband's behavior (and implicitly her own as well).

Writing was clearly a struggle for Susan. As with her husband's letters, her spelling is often unconventional. Her text is also full of cross-outs and fractured, run-together sentences. More significantly, the information is disorganized, with many redundancies and ideas and anecdotes that break off abruptly, leaving their meanings unclear. Writers such as Lloyd Goodrich or Kathleen Foster have always presented Susan in a relentlessly positive light, as a fountain of wisdom, understanding, and compassionate insight. In her memo, however, she comes across as judgmental and narrow in her outlook. Moreover, her presentation is not very logical. She often provides mutually contradictory explanations for the same event, whose single common denominator is that they place no blame on herself or her husband.

According to Susan, Ella came to Philadelphia to live with Eakins and herself on September 2, 1894, having finished her course at the university the previous spring. (Ella had stayed at Mount Vernon Street two years earlier, but Susan left this out of her account.) Eager to move to the city, Ella agreed to help Susan with the housekeeping in return for permission to stay with them. During the summer, when Eakins was working at Avondale on a full-scale sculpture of a horse, she helped him with his work.

Even before Ella's arrival there were tensions between the Eakins and the

Crowell households. Susan reports that Eakins thought his sister and her husband were "narrow-minded and aggressively sure of their own perfections," and over the course of the 1890s he became convinced that they were "dishonorable" as well.[18] On the Crowell side, despite their support of Eakins during the Academy scandal, Will and Frances were clearly troubled by his behavior, and worried about how he would influence their two young daughters. Ella was thus placed in the middle of a simmering family conflict.

Rather than remaining neutral, which may well not have been possible, Ella provided both sides with ample gossip to support their point of view. In her conversations with Susan, Ella complained about the sad state of the farm at Avondale and spoke critically both of her mother and her father. Her mother, she reported, was often unreasonably touchy about things. She took offense, for instance, when Ella complained that the milk was often sour. What is more, her mother had no concern with "the honor of an act." For example, Frances had denounced Eakins's antagonist, Frank Stephens, yet decided to send her son Ben to work in his terracotta shop.

Ella described her father as "a melancholy, unhappy, and disappointed man," who led an idle life and did nothing to keep up the farm. He wasted every morning in the village reading the newspapers and then spent the afternoons "either at useless instruction of the younger children or despairing over their laziness." Since he never did any work himself, the children "had no respect for his complaints," and grew up without a role model or proper discipline. Despite his faults, however, Ella had a close bond with her father, and "knew his secret thoughts," which he confided to her rather than to his wife, who "could not understand him." "From childhood he had confided to her, and...after listening to his confessions she would be so exhausted that she could hardly drag herself from the room."[19]

Not only did Ella speak critically of her parents, but she made a point of reporting the negative things they had said about her uncle and his wife, or things they had done which would

Three Crowell Boys Nude, in Creek at Avondale, Pennsylvania, ca. 1885. *Platinum print, 3 ⅛ x 4 ¹/₁₆ in., The Pennsylvania Academy of the Fine Arts, Philadelphia, Charles Bregler's Thomas Eakins Collection, purchased with the partial support of the Pew Memorial Trust.* **During his visits to Avondale, Eakins took many photographs of the Crowell children in the nude.**

upset the Eakinses. For example, she confided that her parents were severely critical of Susan's housekeeping, felt that she was too extravagant, and believed that she neglected Aunt Eliza and Benjamin Eakins. As mentioned, she also made a point of telling Susan that her parents planned to send her brother Ben to live and work with Eakins's arch-enemy, Frank Stephens.[20]

Ella even told Susan that the Crowells hoped to move everyone out of 1729 Mount Vernon Street so that they could escape the farm in Avondale and move to the city.[21] When Susan confronted the Crowells with this story, however, Will and Frances wrote a letter stating that the alleged plan was entirely Ella's invention, and that they would never have even discussed such a change without consulting Eakins and his wife.

At the same time that Ella was feeding gossip to Eakins and his wife about her family, she complained to her parents and siblings about Eakins. These complaints seem to have included statements about Eakins's preoccupation with the nude as well as the claim that he had made unwanted advances of some sort toward her. But just what Ella said and when she said it became a matter of dispute, since Susan allowed no accusation against her husband to stand unchallenged. Will and Frances presented one version of events, Susan presented another.

In a letter of November 1, 1896 (cited by Susan), Will declared that nearly two years earlier he had experienced his "first excess of rage and grief" at Ella's disclosures. This suggests that very soon after she arrived at Mount Vernon Street, Ella began making allegations of a serious nature against her uncle. Susan Eakins, however, claimed that this was impossible, because Will and Frances continued to allow Ella to live in the Eakins home, and had also allowed their daughter Maggie and their son Ben to come live there.

In another letter, also dated November 1, 1896, Frances declared that Ella fled from Mount Vernon Street to the Presbyterian Hospital "to escape Tom's approaches." Susan noted, however, that Ella did not really flee at this time. According to Susan, while working at the hospital, Ella continued to spend her off-duty hours either at the house on Mount Vernon Street or at her uncle's studio, entirely of her own choice.

In Susan's version of events, the relationship between Ella and Eakins continued to be affectionate up to the point of Ella's final breakdown. As late as August 22, 1896, Ella visited Eakins's studio and declared, with tears running down her cheeks, "Oh Uncle Tom, I wish I was at work with you again like in old times."[22] Ella also took Eakins's side in the ongoing feud between Eakins and her parents, defending him against their accusations. Around this time, for example, Ella told Eakins and Susan that her father was trying to break up the friendship between Eakins and Samuel Murray by making scandalous allegations about Eakins's behavior.

Whatever the cause, by August 1896, Ella began to show symptoms of emotional imbalance and distress. On the twenty-first of the month, Susan wrote to Will that he should bring his daughter home, since "Tom & I could no longer control her and we feared she would carry out some of the wild plans she was forming." Susan insisted, however, that Ella's problems were not caused by Eakins, whom she declared was not only blameless but a "benefactor." The problem, she convinced herself, was the girl's relationships with her parents.

According to Susan, after Ella went home on August 22, 1896, there were "intense quarrels and excitements being kept up between Ella & her father."[23] Hardly more than a week after her homecoming, on August 31, Ella was committed to a hospital for the insane.[24]

Apparently at this point, rumors began to circulate that Eakins had done something indecent that had contributed to Ella's breakdown. Ella's siblings, Ben and Maggie, were both cited as the source of these stories, although in conversations with Susan they both denied any involvement. Thus, for example, Will and Frances accused Eakins of "trying to ruin their daughter Maggie's reputation" (these are Susan's words for what surely was a more specific accusation), and claimed that their information came from Maggie. When Susan confronted Maggie, however, she denied that she was the source of negative statements about Eakins. Shortly afterward, gossip about Eakins's behavior towards Ella was circulated throughout Philadelphia by students at the Pennsylvania Academy. Again, Maggie was cited as the source of the information, although again, according to Susan, Maggie denied being responsible and insisted that she had not started the rumors.

Similarly, Susan was told through a third party that Ben Crowell "had gone to Mr. Quinn, an old friend of Tom's, and had by his utterances insinuated that Ella had been seduced by her Uncle." However, when Susan confronted Ben with his actions, Ben declared that "he had not intended such information" and "had not meant that his Uncle injured Ella at all." According to Susan, Ben retracted his accusations in a letter. Susan, however, seems to have been skeptical of Ben's protestations of innocence. In a subsequent sentence, noting that Ben lived in the Eakins home until about a month before Ella's death, she described him as a "spy."[25]

Making sense of all these accusations and counter-accusations is not easy, since Susan's logic seems to run in two contradictory ways. On the one hand she attempts to prove that Maggie and Ben were not the source of negative rumors about her husband, and that consequently these slurs had no solid basis in fact. On the other hand, she seems to insinuate that both Maggie and Ben were deceitful and dishonest, and consequently that their stories should not be credited. (In fact, her account of the children's parents contains a similar contradiction. At one moment she constructs a case that provides "indisputable evidence of their trust in Tom," at the next she seeks to establish that they were "secretly desiring to injure him.")[26]

Significantly, Susan never deals directly with the issue of her husband's behavior, not even with the question of whether he pressured Ella to pose in the nude, which seems very plausible. Thus, the document that she clearly intended as a defense of Eakins becomes something different. Rather than exonerating Eakins, it leaves our questions about his character unanswered, while bringing to light troubling matters in addition to the original charges. Above all, it reveals that there were serious tensions among the members of the Eakins family, and that Ella's tragic death was part of a larger web of unhappiness and conflict. In addition, while Eakins has always been associated with honesty, it becomes clear that he stood at the center of a tangle of intrigue and dishonesty, and that something about him fed and encouraged this. A theme that surfaces time and time again is that of an individual who was said to have been the source of a story or rumor but who denied it when directly questioned. Clearly someone was lying—either the person who spread the story, or the person accused of starting it.

There are two ways of interpreting this phenomenon, both of which I believe have merit. One is to suppose that individuals such as Ben and Maggie Crowell—or for that matter Ella—were caught between groups that had different demands. When they moved from one group to another—particularly, when they moved back and forth between the Eakins and Crowell households—they were pressured to change their stories to fit their situation. This shift between the two families seems to have been particularly difficult, since both the Eakins and the Crowell households were firm and uncompromising in their positions, and intolerant toward dissent. Ella, Maggie and Ben were still children, and thus dependent on adults for support.

In addition, we can suppose that people were confused about what was happening around them—most significantly, puzzled by the motives for Eakins's behavior—and thus conveyed information in a confused fashion. Ben and Maggie, for example, seem to have sensed something wrong in Eakins's relationship with Ella, but not to have understood just what was going on. Because Eakins's behavior seemed to be both sexual and nonsexual, and both sinister and benevolent, it seems likely that at one moment they would voice suspicions that something indecent was taking place and at another that they would deny having done so. They seem to have observed things that were troubling about Eakins, but could not understand his motives.

Significantly, communication tended to operate not directly but through hearsay—and sometimes along such elaborate routes that the original source of allegations could no longer be identified. Thus, the accusations made by Maggie, Ben, and even Ella generally reached the Eakins household through third parties who, in turn, were held accountable for seeing things in a particular way. This piling up of rumors multiplied the possibilities of treachery. Not surprisingly then, the correspondence of both Eakins and his wife is filled with references to "spies," and to evil people who could not be trusted.

Susan's memorandum seems to circle around the question of why Ella had her mental breakdown. She places the blame for Ella's suicide on the "dishonor" of Ella's parents and the fact that they failed to properly discipline her as a child. But this is hardly sufficient explanation for a suicide, and in particular, it fails to explain why Ella arrived at the Eakins home in an apparently normal state and then began behaving irrationally.[27] In general, her accounts both of the accusations against Eakins, and of his defense against these charges, have a strangely exaggerated quality. Thus, for example, Susan notes that the Crowells pictured Eakins as "a wicked persecutor of innocence," yet she maintains that he was Ella's "benefactor and loving Uncle."[28] It never seems to occur to her to find a middle ground between two viewpoints.

In the end it is simply not possible to make judgments about the truth or falsehood of Susan's description of specific incidents, although much of what she describes seems to suggest psychological undercurrents that she did not understand and that demand some deeper form of explanation. What we do learn from her account, very clearly, is that there was considerable tension between Eakins and the other members of his family, and that this cast a shadow on the lives of Ella and her siblings.

So far as can be determined, Eakins made no response whatever to his niece's death. Ella killed herself on July 2 and by the third week of July Eakins was in Seal Harbor, Maine, working on his portrait of the physicist Henry Rowland. His twelve letters home to his wife detail the progress of the work but make no mention of Ella. His seven subsequent letters to Rowland also contain no reference to the event. Surely it would have been natural to at least mention that something upsetting had occurred. Eakins's failure to do so suggests that he was deliberately avoiding the subject, and implies an element of subterfuge. While Susan wrote up a long memorandum providing her side of the story, so far as is known Eakins never even alluded to Ella's death.[29] There is no record of Eakins expressing his condolences to Ella's parents.

Eakins's Portraits of Ella Crowell

While Eakins left no written statements about Ella, he did provide another form of evidence. He represented Ella twice—in a photograph made not long before her death, and in a painting, made when she was a baby. Both representations suggest disturbing undercurrents in his relationship with his niece.

The photograph relates most directly to the stories that Eakins sexually assaulted Ella. Ella's age seems to be in her early twenties, so they must have been made not so very long before Ella committed suicide. While the matter is sensitive, and inherently somewhat subjective, the photograph makes it clear that Ella was hardly a seductive siren, whether by modern or Victorian standards. Indeed, according to Samuel Murray, Ella Crowell's character was not feminine but strikingly masculine. He remembered her as "a tom-boy, mannish, restless."[30]

In the photograph, Ella looks miserable, in fact desperate. Indeed, as we study the photograph more closely we note an aspect of her distress that raises disturbing questions. Ella did not wish to be photographed. She was being hunted. Eakins had trapped her between him and a tree. The photograph catches her just as she was beginning to dodge to one side and for that reason it is slightly blurred. From what we can deduce, Eakins's behavior had a certain analogy to a lover's pursuit of a young woman, but judging from the photograph his pursuit had none of the playfulness nor even the erotic quality of a lover's. Instead, there is a hint of sadism: he appears to have been interested in obtaining a record of her discomfort. As we shall see, Eakins commonly did things to make his sitters uncomfortable while they posed for him. The photograph of Ella Crowell provides a particularly troubling instance of this practice.

Eakins was accused of a form of sexual assault—touching the genitals of his niece. If guilty, he must have violated one of the most basic of social barriers, the taboo of incest. The accusation becomes still stranger when we discover that Ella was not feminine but masculine in her qualities, and that Eakins was in some way interested in or attracted to an aspect of her personality that was emotionally distraught. However we choose to construe Eakins's motives, he does not seem to have followed a conventional pathway of sexual attraction.

The painting relates less directly to Ella's death, since it was made twenty-two years earlier. Nonetheless, it communicates important things about Eakins's expectations for Ella, and her important place within the extended Eakins family. Ella was the first grandchild of Benjamin Eakins. Perhaps in part for this reason, Eakins made a portrait of her, *Baby at Play* (1876), when she was two. She was the only one of his nieces or nephews that he ever painted. Many writers have commented on how the painting differs from most paintings of children in its somberness of mood.

The baby sits on a brick patio between a toy horse and cart (to our left) and a discarded rag doll (to our right). The horse and cart seem to represent boyish games, the rag doll female ones. However, she has cast aside these items in favor of a set of wooden blocks, with which she is constructing a two-story tower.

Baby at Play, 1876. *Oil on canvas, 32 ¼ x 48 ⅜ in., John Hay Whitney Collection, © Board of Trustees, National Gallery of Art, Washington, D.C.* Eakin's portrait of Ella as a baby shows her turning away from her doll (on the right) and other childish toys to build a structure from alphabet blocks.

Although Ella was a girl, the baby's strong features and cropped hair are sexually ambiguous, and the monumentality of the figure gives it a masculine feeling. As noted, Samuel Murray remembered Ella as a tomboy. What the painting suggests is that in some fashion Ella's sexual confusion was pushed upon her from babyhood, by a family that viewed men as superior to women and wanted Ella to be a male child.

In hindsight it is tempting to read certain elements of the painting as fore-shadowings of Ella's violent death. The cast-off female doll on the right looks like the victim of a murder or rape. Eakins placed his signature on the one brick that joins the child's body to the lifeless figure of the rag doll, as if he were the link that connected the living child to a corpse. The horse and cart are also dark in their implications, since they resemble a hearse. The block in the cart, which is long and narrow, resembles a coffin.

Admittedly, to read these elements in this way is to suppose that Eakins was predicting a future still decades ahead. Eakins probably intended these ele-ments in the painting to simply represent different choices that were available to Ella—female toys (the doll) and male toys (the cart). The message of the painting seems to be that she rejected both, and preferred toys of a more intel-lectual nature—alphabet blocks. Eakins was thus presenting an ideal of educa-tion. The painting expresses the hope that Ella would set aside childish toys and study letters and numbers—like her grandfather, the writing master.[31]

Yet even if we suppose that Eakins intended a positive message about edu-cation, the painting is both strangely cheerless in its overall feeling, and also filled with oddly violent elements, such as the discarded doll. Disturbingly, the tower of alphabet blocks that Ella is building appears unstable. A long shadow under one of the blocks informs us that it extends out from the structure and is likely to collapse.

Surely in some fashion the painting provides clues about Ella's unhappy fate. If nothing else it suggests the weight of family expectation that was placed on her, the confusion of male and female roles that this entailed, and the stress of growing up with such emotional pressures.[32]

Eakins's Break with the Crowells

Not surprisingly, in light of their initial misgivings about Eakins's morals as well as the sexually disturbing accusations that Ella made shortly before her death, Will and Frances blamed Eakins for their daughter's mental breakdown and subsequent suicide. From this point forward they refused to associate with Eakins, never again mentioned his name, and forbade their children to do so. Thus, by 1897, Eakins had become completely estranged from his last surviving sibling, just as he had from his sister Caroline a decade before.[33] Their response was natural in its way. Clearly the sheer horror of what they had experienced was too much for them and defied their powers of speech. In certain ways however, this approach played to Eakins's advantage since it is clear that even Will and Frances's children were confused about what had occurred.

Embarrassment was always one of Eakins's most effective weapons. His offenses were difficult to discuss, since even to speak of them was embarrassing and awkward. In Ella's case, this embarrassment had several layers. One was propriety. To even speak of Eakins's touching and spanking of Ella, her undressing in front of him, his touching of her private parts, and his inviting her to touch his genitals, violated normal standards of proper and decent discourse. Furthermore, it involved defiling Ella's memory, since Eakins's offense had tarnished the purity of his victim. Ella's messy suicide deepened the discomfort, as it was too horrible to describe.

Not surprisingly, this caused confusion. As with the Academy scandal, after Ella died there was disagreement about who was to blame. Indeed, some people first took one position, and then later shifted sides. Weda Cook told Lloyd Goodrich that she spoke to Benjamin Crowell about the event and that he told her that his uncle had driven Ella out of her mind. On that basis she broke off posing for Eakins and wrote to the artist saying that she never wanted to see him again. A year later, however, Benjamin came to see her and said he had been wrong, that his uncle was not to blame. Weda then wrote to Eakins asking to see him, and re-established their relationship. Other members of Benjamin's family, however, continued to blame Eakins. As late as 1931, Frances Crowell, Ella's next-to-youngest sibling, told Goodrich that her uncle had "contaminated her sister with his beastly ideas."[34]

Girl in a Big Hat (Lillian Hammitt), ca. 1888. *Oil on canvas, 24 ⅛ x 24 ⅛ in., Hirshhorn Museum and Sculpture Garden, Smithsonian Institution, gift of Joseph H. Hirshhorn, 1966.* Eakins's student Lillian Hammitt "went insane" in 1888 and was arrested on the streets of Philadelphia wearing a bathing suit, claiming that she was married to Eakins.

Chapter 6

THE INSANITY
OF LILLIAN HAMMITT

ELLA CROWELL'S suicide was not the only scandal that troubled Eakins in the 1890s. Almost simultaneously with the Ella Crowell tragedy, one of Eakins's students, Lillian Hammitt, lost her sanity. Somewhat perversely, Susan Eakins gathered together a group of papers related to the Hammitt case, including letters from Lillian herself, leaving a note to her friend Addie Williams to destroy them after her death. This request was not followed, and the packet survives among the Bregler papers, providing an intriguing although incomplete account of the Hammitt incident. While many questions remain, because of the survival of this packet we can piece together a general sequence of events.

Lillian Hammitt first attended the Pennsylvania Academy in 1883, when she was eighteen. After Eakins's ouster, she joined the loyal students who formed an Art Students League with him that spring. Her letters to Eakins from this period record frequent financial difficulties, since her father was dead, her mother frail, and her relatives unhelpful. In 1887 she seems to have spent a great deal of time with Eakins in his home, and Eakins started a portrait of her, which he stopped abruptly when he received an "inexpressibly" shocking letter on February 29, 1888. The letter is now lost, and was probably destroyed, but from later references it appears that Hammitt discussed her belief that Eakins would divorce Susan and marry her. Eakins replied in a letter of March 2, declaring that "you are laboring under false notions."[1] In fact, he accused her of insanity. As he stated: "That you should have consulted a lawyer as to my getting a divorce is so extravagant that I must excuse it on the suspicion of mental disorder."[2]

Events become vague at this point, but around 1890, Hammitt apparently returned home to Dothan, Alabama, to nurse her dying mother. After her mother's death, she moved to Atlanta, where she supported herself as a seamstress and domestic servant. During this period, Hammitt seems to have sent Eakins further marriage proposals and also asked his advice about whether she should turn to prostitution to support herself. At some point, Eakins provided her with money to cover some travel costs, an action that was later held against him.

Intriguing portions survive of a curious four-way correspondence between Eakins, Lillian, her brother Charles, and Mrs. L. B. Nelson, Hammitt's employer in Atlanta. Mrs. Nelson was convinced that Eakins had seduced Lillian, and had provided her with travel money to get her out of the way. Consequently, she wrote to Eakins, requesting that he take responsibility for his actions and provide Lillian with financial support. She also wrote to Hammitt's brother, providing a lurid picture of Eakins's emotional grip on Lillian. "I am sure he is the one responsible for her erroneous beliefs," she noted. "I think it is his purpose in order to vindicate himself to carry the idea of insanity . . . She [Lillian] seems completely in his power. Whenever she loses faith in this man there is some hope of getting her eyes to the truth."[3]

Charles Hammitt also assumed that Eakins had seduced her. "Your affair with Mr. Eakins—who claims to be a married man—is most astounding and ridiculous," he wrote. "This man has turned you *infidel*, and after *getting enough of you* now *casts you off* on the plea of insanity." Declaring that the bad reputation she had earned at home made it impossible for her to return to Alabama, he ended by closing his home to her and refusing to provide financial support. Even if we suppose that Eakins had not seduced Hammitt—though it is quite clear that both Mrs. Nelson and Charles Hammitt's believed he had done so—these letters show that Eakins exerted some strange psychological hold over her.

Shortly afterward, Hammitt wrote her last surviving letter to Eakins, speaking of her financial difficulties, denying that she had claimed that Eakins would marry her, and attributing the perception of her insanity to the fact that she was a woman. She was no more crazy than Eakins, she declared, but, being a woman was not allowed freedom of speech or action. "I wonder that I am not really insane," she concluded, in a poignant echo of Eakins's claim that she was.[4]

At this point documentation breaks off for two years until 1892, when a letter from Miss Maggie Unkle to Susan Eakins indicates that Hammitt was institutionalized in a hospital in Philadelphia. A few years later, she was briefly released and made her way to the Eakins home, demanding to see her "husband." She also visited Eakins's studio on Chestnut Street with the same demand, as Samuel Murray later reported. Not long afterward she was picked up by the police wandering the streets of Philadelphia in a bathing costume, attire that would have been extremely startling and provocative at the time. To achieve similar shock value today, one would probably have to go out on the street naked. When questioned, Hammitt claimed to be married to Thomas Eakins. She was institutionalized again, this time permanently.[5]

Eakins's Portrait of Lillian Hammitt

While no photographs of her have yet been found, we can put a face to this episode, for in 1888 Eakins started a portrait of Lillian Hammitt. Remarkably, despite its unfinished state and the scandal associated with the subject, Susan Eakins did not discard the canvas, although she would not divulge the subject of the painting to Lloyd Goodrich, describing it only as "The Girl in the Big Hat." The identity of the sitter was finally established in the 1960s, when the painting entered the collection of the Hirshhorn Museum. As has been mentioned, Eakins stopped work on the painting after he received the surprising letter, in which Hammitt expressed her belief that he would divorce Susan and marry her. This fact is documented by his return letter to her.[6] As a consequence, the artistic effect of the painting is quite crude. Even in its present rough form, however, the painting reveals interesting things about Hammitt's appearance and character.

Since Eakins painted few portraits of his female students, this act alone suggests that Hammitt occupied an unusually intimate place in his life. What is striking about the painting, however, is that it seems to contradict what little we know of their relationship. Two things are odd about the painting—the degree to which it conceals Hammitt's figure and flesh, and the degree to which it obscures her sexual identity.

Lillian Hammitt was in some sense a champion undresser. According to Weda Cook, she posed in the nude for Eakins and she also wore a bathing costume in public in such as way as to embarrass even Eakins, a man who seems to have delighted in creating embarrassing situations through states of nakedness or partial undress. Yet Eakins's portrait of Hammitt contains nothing in the way of exposed flesh. Not only is her torso completely covered, but her collar runs up so high that we do not even see her neck. Even her hair is covered by her large hat. The effect is strikingly proper and spinsterish.

There must have been sexual undercurrents in Hammitt's relationship with Eakins, although it is not clear how they were expressed. Even if Eakins had not seduced her, as many believed, she clearly had amorous feelings toward him, since she had plans to marry him and become his sexual partner. One would expect some of this sexual tension, and these feelings of desire on Hammitt's part, to be evident in Eakins's portrait. One would expect it to exhibit feminine or seductive qualities. Instead, it does just the reverse. Overall, the image is surprisingly androgynous, and not obviously sensual. Hammitt's face might almost be that of boy. At first glance one could mistake her for a young male art student—and, in fact, the style of her broad-brimmed hat matches that worn by male art students in Paris. With her dark garb and tight collar, she also brings to mind a young priest, sworn to celibacy. The spectacles, blotchy complexion, and serious expression seem to dull any implications of sensuality or romance.

It seems crude to deduce from such evidence that Hammitt was not sexually attractive. We like to avoid stating such sensitive matters so bluntly. As it happens, however, the painting's testimony on this point is supported by a letter from Susan Eakins to Hammitt, which discusses her shortcomings in making herself attractive to men. In an earlier missive to Susan that does not survive, Lillian seems to have proposed marrying someone old and unattractive in order to gain financial support. Troubled that Lillian might rush into a marriage "so out of the usual way," Susan suggested strategies that Lillian should use to find a proper mate—associating more with people her own age, reading less, and paying more attention to her appearance.[7]

Susan's remarks create a consistent picture of a woman who was lonely, lacked feminine skills, did not present herself well, and did not attract male suitors. Eakins also seems to have noted that there was something unfeminine, even manlike in Hammitt's character, although he viewed the matter more favorably. In one of his letters, Eakins declared that Hammitt possessed "an intellect unusual in a woman."[8] In other words, she was like a man.

Issues of feminine appearance are inherently sensitive. Nonetheless, when we look over the evidence, it is striking that one of the most notable sexual scandals of Eakins's career involved a woman who was boyish; who was careless, perhaps even slovenly about her appearance; and who was not considered particularly good-looking. As a target for seduction—if this was indeed what Eakins intended—Lillian Hammittt made an unusual choice. Notably, however, the same could also be said of Ella Crowell, the other woman with whom Eakins's behavior caused a major scandal.

Some Incidents in Paris

It is natural to ask whether Eakins's early life offered premonitions of these scandals. In fact, although the Academy controversy of 1886 was shockingly public, it was not the first time that Eakins had scandalized his friends and associates. Indeed, when Eakins was in Paris, his first known romance with Emily Sartain foundered because of her distress over his "immoral" activities. Emily was the daughter of John Sartain, Philadelphia's leading engraver and one of the most respected figures in Philadelphia's art world. Sartain moved in similar business circles to Eakins's father but was more financially successful and held higher social standing. Eakins's father seems to have encouraged the romance in part because it furthered his social and financial ambitions. After an encouraging start in Philadelphia, however, the romance faded after Eakins moved to Paris for artistic study. Emily laid out her concerns in an intriguing letter of July 8, 1868. In it she declared:

Naudin Studios, Emily Sartain, ca. 1880. *Photograph, Library Archives, Moore College of Art and Design, Philadelphia.* **Eakins's first girlfriend, Emily Sartain, broke off with him because of her distress over his "immoral" activities in Paris.**

> When you left home and people talked of the temptations of the great city you were going to, I smiled at their fears. I thought of your singleness and purity of heart, and believed too that the warm love you had for me would be a safeguard to you if any were needed. To my sorrow after only two years of absence, I find you laughing at things you ought to censure, excusing your companions for the vices—and even, I fear joining with them, making yourself like them.[9]

Emily's letter alludes to an encounter with certain women in the Palais Royale, a notorious Parisian gathering place for prostitutes, and declares that what Eakins told her caused her to cry "so much that night it made me sick for several days." Eakins also seems to have visited the Closerie de Lilas, a dance hall frequented by art students and promiscuous shop girls. References to the "closerie" are contained in Eakins's account books.[10] Emily concluded her letter by urging Eakins to abandon his "vicious companions," to stop reading Boccaccio and Rabelais, and to "come home and go to work at something else, rather than lose your power of distinguishing right from wrong."[11]

Unfortunately, information about what shocked Emily is incomplete. Did Eakins have sex with prostitutes, or did he just ogle them? Did he engage in sexual activities or did he simply revel in the smuttiness of bohemian Paris?[12] Still, it is striking that many years before the Academy scandal, Eakins's behavior was categorized as immoral by a close friend. Later in life Eakins enjoyed telling risqué stories about France. Eleanor Pue, for example, stated that when she posed for Eakins in 1907 he told "broad stories" of student days in Paris.[13] James L. Wood (the son of Eakins's personal physician, Horatio Wood), also reported that "Eakins was very loose sexually—went to France, where there are no morals, and the French morality suited him to a T."[14]

Eakins's Fixation on the Nude

After he was fired from the Academy, Eakins did little to dispel the troubling rumors that circulated about his conduct. Indeed, there are many accounts that suggest that he felt some powerful psychological compulsion both to undress women and to expose himself to them. In the 1930s, for example, of the eight women Lloyd Goodrich interviewed who had posed for Eakins, five told him that Eakins had asked to paint them in the nude. Other such requests have been noted by Gordon Hendricks.[15]

Weda Cook, for instance, reported that when she was posing for *The Concert Singer* Eakins kept after her to pose nude, even though she always refused. His manner then took on the quality of a seduction. His eyes, she said, would become soft and appealing, and he would drop into the Quaker "thee"— "gentleness combined with the persistence of a devil," she recalled. One day he got her down to her underclothes, although she never undressed any further. However, Cook believed that Eakins had succeeded in wearing down a number of other women, including his niece Ella.[16] Goodrich's notes report: "She felt that it was an obsession with him. He said that society was hypocritical, that he would like everybody to go nude." In summing up her reactions to Eakins, Cook noted that he inspired "love and fear."[17]

Mrs. James G. Carville, niece of Eakins's friend, the photographer Louis Husson, posed for Eakins in 1904, when she was about thirty. Her daughter, Elizabeth Carville, wrote to Goodrich in 1969:

> I remember Momma telling me that Mr. Eakins asked her to pose for him in the nude,—and even though this was over thirty years later, she blushed when telling me about it, and was still indignant and outraged as she was the day she refused,—muttering to herself,—"I just let him know I wasn't that kind of woman."[18]

Mary Hallock Greenewalt, whom Eakins painted at the age of thirty-two, told Goodrich that Eakins had wanted to paint her in the nude, but that she had not consented.[19] Helen Parker, who posed for *The Old-Fashioned Dress* reported the same thing, and also kept her clothes on. Elizabeth Dunbar, an art reporter for the *Philadelphia Press*, "was asked several times by the painter to run upstairs to the studio and pose for a life study."[20] She declined. Eleanor Pue (later Mrs. E. Farnum Lavell) recalled that Eakins kept urging her to pose nude. He even went to her mother and asked her to grant permission. But Pue never did undress for him. Although Eakins told some dirty stories while he painted her, "he made no advances."[21]

Weda Cook provided the names of several individuals whom she believed Eakins persuaded to pose nude, including Ella Crowell and Lillian Hammitt. She also noted that Eakins claimed that he had persuaded Alice Barber to pose for him, boasting to her: "Many's the time I've seen her ass." [22]

Eakins's letters sometimes gratuitously shift discussion toward the nude. A case in point is a letter he wrote to Elizabeth Burton, who posed for a portrait he made in 1906. Shortly after her marriage, which broke off the portrait sittings, Burton moved to British North Borneo. After opening the letter with social pleasantries, Eakins abruptly introduced the thought: "I suppose you might go in to swim without much of a bathing suit."[23]

Interestingly, Eakins's fixation on the nude applied to middle-aged and elderly women as well as young ones. Mrs. Nicholas Douty, whose portrait he painted in 1910, noted that Eakins "seemed starved for the nude." When Eakins asked her to pose nude she declined, protesting that her figure was not beautiful. He said that didn't matter, every figure was beautiful.[24] He also asked Mrs. Greenewalt to pose nude—although she didn't—and once told her: "How beautiful an old woman's skin is—all those wrinkles!"[25]

Goodrich also reports the testimony of Alice Kurtz:

"Mr. Eakins," she told him during one sitting, "my collar button has gone down my back and it hurts sitting there." He reached down to retrieve it, and told her, "your back is more like a boy's than a girl's." He told her he would like to paint her in the nude.[26]

An interesting aspect of this anecdote is that it reveals that Eakins found boyish women particularly appealing.

Even when he did not undress his sitters, Eakins often touched them in ways that were startling. For example, Eakins executed his portrait of Mrs. James Mapes Dodge in her home on McKean Avenue, facing an open window. During one sitting he came over and started to dig his fingers into her chest. She said, "Tom, for Heaven's sake what are you doing," and he said, "I'm feeling for bones." She commented that the neighbors must have thought it rather peculiar.[27]

Mrs. Dodge recalled that when she first visited Eakins's studio with her husband she was surprised to see a red-haired female model, completely nude. This was the first time that she had ever seen either a woman or a man completely undressed. Eakins insisted on taking them over to examine the model. He ran his hands down her side and said how fine it was ("He didn't need to do that," Mrs. Dodge commented); and he then took them around to admire her back. Several years later, after her husband had died, Eakins gave them some "lantern slides" that he had taken of himself and nude models, one of which showed him carrying a nude model in his arms. Mrs. Dodge later gave these slides to her son; they were "not the kind of thing for a respectable widow," she remarked.[28]

Even when he could not persuade women to undress, Eakins seems to have enjoyed creating moments of embarrassment when they posed for him. According to Margaret McHenry:

> John Wright brought Weda Cook to the Art Students League to sing at birthday parties and Eakins decided that he wanted to paint her. He brought her over and "dumped her in the life class" where, since she was only eighteen, she was very much embarrassed.[29]

It is not precisely clear from McHenry's account what embarrassed Cook, though presumably it was the exposure to nude models, an experience which must have been new to her. What is interesting is that Eakins seems to have derived pleasure not simply from the nude model, but from the embarrassment this model could provoke from onlookers.

Eakins's interest was not limited to female models. He also liked to study naked men, as is evident from his painting *Swimming* and the many photographs of nude men associated with it. His boxing pictures, also, entailed study of nude models. Eakins's preliminary studies for these paintings show models who are completely naked. Notably, this nude posing often had an impromptu character. For example, Margaret McHenry reports:

> One Sunday morning a German, Buntz, came to show his muscles to Eakins, who at the time was painting pictures of various sports. Buntz disrobed with some thoroughness and was going thru exercises when Benjamin Eakins walked in on the naked athlete performing.[30]

Again, McHenry's account is somewhat ambiguous, but it seems to imply that Buntz undressed not in the studio but in a room of the house used for everyday purposes, and that Benjamin Eakins was shocked when he encountered him.

Eakins seems to have enjoyed embarrassing men as well as women. When Francis Ziegler was posing for him in the nude, he invited a woman into his studio, to Ziegler's great embarrassment.[31] Indeed, the famous loin cloth incident has a psychological twist that has not been noted previously. Not only would it have been embarrassing to the class of female students, but it also must have been embarrassing to the male model, whose genitals were unexpectedly exposed.

Despite his interest in having men and women pose for him in the nude, very few paintings of the nude by Eakins survive. Martin Berger has calculated that he completed only fourteen paintings of nude or scantily clad figures over forty years. Goodrich attributed this small number to social pressures. As he wrote of Eakins: "In spite of his intense interest in [the nude], his realism and the prevailing prudery had combined to keep him from painting it more than a few times."[32] Similarly, he notes that after the mid-1880s, Eakins painted no more nudes, except for prizefighters, and seeks to provide an explanation. "This was undoubtedly due in large part to the affair at the Pennsylvania Academy and the repulse of his teaching of the nude."[33] In summing up Eakins's failure to paint the nude more often, Goodrich concludes: "His interest in the nude had come up against the prudery and meagerness of his environment and had been defeated."[34] Goodrich's explanation, however, raises more questions than it solves. Why would Eakins go out of the way to cause offense in his personal life with his demands that women pose for him nude and then give in to social pressure with his paintings?

Eakins's Self-Exposure

Along with looking at others who were undressed, Eakins enjoyed undressing in front of other people. For example, it is well documented that Eakins enjoyed swimming naked when spectators were present. Samuel Murray told Margaret McHenry that when he was staying at Benjamin Eakins's boathouse on Cohansey Creek, on hot summer nights Eakins would open the doors and sleep naked on a cocoa mat in full view of whoever might come along. Eakins also enjoyed discussing or proposing nude swimming, a practice that sometimes caused discomfort. Elizabeth Corless (who was the daughter of a close friend of Benjamin Eakins) noted that "Eakins once shocked them all terribly by wanting all of them to go in swimming nude." (Apparently Eakins wanted men and women to swim naked together, although Goodrich's notes are unclear on this point.)[35] Eakins also liked to "sail naked." Goodrich declares that he "cared little if others were shocked."[36] Although the evidence strongly suggests that he derived pleasure from shocking people.

As soon as photography became available, Eakins had photographs taken of himself in the nude, a practice he continued for the rest of his life. As he grew older, although he grew heavy and eventually quite obese, he continued to parade naked before the camera. Photographs taken late in his life, when he was about seventy, show him wading into the water naked, his genitals exposed, his belly protruding.

Eakins also seems to have derived pleasure from posing for other artists in the nude. In a letter to Frank Hamilton Cushing of July 14, 1895, Eakins noted that "Murray is just starting a statuette of me to go with that of my wife. He is modeling my naked figure before putting on the clothes and I wish you were modeling alongside of him."[37] Eakins's letter not only indicates his pleasure in posing nude, but also suggests that he derived further pleasure from describing it to Cushing, and from imagining Cushing seeing his nakedness too.

This yen for nudity seems to have been manifest by his early teens. Thus, for example, a portrait of Eakins by Charles Fussell, which was made before he went to study in Paris, shows him sitting stark naked at an easel, with no covering except brush and palette.[38]

A letter to Eakins from Will Crowell notes that Eakins made a practice of strolling into a bedroom occupied by his sisters Margaret and Caroline and his Aunt Eliza dressed only in his shirt, with no pants on, and that he often entered in such a state of near-undress when Margaret's friend Sallie Shaw was there as well. This was so distressing to Caroline that she arranged to move to a bedroom in another part of the house, which was not easily accessible to her brother. Margaret, however, remained with Aunt Eliza, apparently feeling that she needed someone to either protect or care for her.[39] Eakins shot Caroline's cat shortly after she changed bedrooms, possibly in retaliation for her move and her complaints against him.

Charles Lewis Fussell, Young Art Student *(sketch of Thomas Eakins), ca. 1860–1865. Oil on paper on canvas, 15 x 13 in., Philadelphia Museum of Art, gift of Seymour Adelman.* Shortly before Eakins left for Paris, his friend Charles Fussell portrayed him painting in the nude.

When painting portraits, Eakins went out of his way to shock those who posed for him, particularly women, both with coarse language and through his own state of undress. On one occasion, he greeted a proper society matron at the front door dressed only in his underwear.

Even more remarkable, James L. Wood reported that when Murray was doing a portrait of a Philadelphia girl, Eakins came in, went into the next room and reappeared stark naked. Walking in front of the sitter he declared: "I don't know whether you ever saw a naked man before; I thought you might like to see one."[40] (When Goodrich told Mrs. Addicks the story of Eakins coming in nude in front of a sitter "she said she thought it was in character.")[41]

Notably, members of Eakins's own family found his interest in the nude peculiar. Will Crowell accused him of setting up the "the worship of the nude as a kind of fetish."[42] In addition, Eakins's father, while he consistently supported his son when he became involved in public scandals, seems to have been troubled by his use of nude models. This at least is the implication of an odd contract which Eakins signed with his father in 1883, in which he specifically prohibited any family discussion of the models he brought for "professional purposes" to the third floor studio of the house on Mount Vernon Street. As the contract states:

> Thomas Eakins will have the right to bring to his studio his models, his pupils, his sitters, and whomsoever he will, and both Benjamin Eakins and Thomas Eakins recognizing the necessity and usage in a figure painter of professional secrecy it is understood that the coming of persons to the studio is not to be the subject of comment or question by the family."[43]

Eakins's obsession with undressing appears to have been part of a larger propensity to challenge sartorial convention. As Sylvan Schendler has noted: "At one time or another he wore his corduroy breeches, his flannel shirt, his pea jacket, and his carpet slippers upon inappropriate occasions."[44] Eakins also seems to have frequently stripped down to his underclothes when he painted, particularly in summer when it was hot. Harrison Morris, who posed for Eakins, wrote that the artist was "almost a study in the nude as he modeled or painted in his attentive way."[45] Not only was Eakins interested in displaying his body, but undergarments also seem to have appealed to him in some way. For example, his nephew noted that when at Avondale he often went around in long underwear rather than normal clothes.

Eakins also seems to have been fascinated by women's underwear. Thus, while Eakins was normally taciturn in social situations, Catherine A. Janvier, a friend for many years, also spoke of his "delightful friendly side . . . how full of fun he could be—like a boy—and what good company he was, and very lovable." She recalled:

> Once in Philadelphia I took him to see two dear old ladies who lived in an old house way downtown. The visit was rather formal at first but he made himself so charming that all became informal, and one of the old ladies actually brought her mother's stays to show him, first whispering to me to ask if I thought it could be done without impropriety, as he was an artist. He was really much interested.[46]

A striking element of this description is the transformation of Eakins's demeanor from formal to charming when a view of women's underwear was at stake. (The personality shift is similar to the one that Weda Cook observed when Eakins was coaxing her to undress.)

Mrs. Douty reported that Eakins loved dirty stories—as she evidently did also. She found him a collection of them and could never get the book away from him.[47] James L. Wood also reported that Eakins told ribald stories, and apparently repeated one to Goodrich "about an artist and a model on a painting trip outdoors."[48] Goodrich, unfortunately, was too prudish to describe the tale, even in his notes, and he omitted mention of it in his publications on Eakins.

We have just one example of the sort of off-color French humor that Eakins enjoyed, a little ditty that he copied into a notebook he used while visiting Spain in 1870. This runs:

> Si le mari doute
> Que sa femme foute
> Qu'il prenne un crayon
> Et qu'il margue au cou.

> La marque efface
> La femme est baise
> L'enfant est batard
> Et le mari cornard

> If a husband questions
> Whether his wife is fucking
> Let him take a pencil
> And mark her ass.

> The mark is erased,
> The woman is laid.
> The child is a bastard
> And the husband is a cuckold.[49]

Dirty jokes generally contain some undercurrent of anxiety. In this case, along with the vulgarity of the language, the humor revolves around the difficulty of keeping women under control.

Many of those who knew Eakins intimately believed that he engaged in sexual escapades. James L. Wood (who presumably derived this information from his father, Eakins's physician, Horatio Wood) reported that "Mrs. Eakins suffered from his affairs." Declaring that Eakins indulged in "sexual excesses," he said that "Eakins never tried to restrain himself; he said it was 'nature.'"[50] Clarence Cranmer, a sports reporter who often went to boxing matches with Eakins (and who became involved, after the artist's death, in selling Eakins's work for his widow), told Lloyd Goodrich that Eakins once boasted to him

Addie Williams, ca. 1899. *Albumen print, 4 ⅝ x 3 ¼ in.,
courtesy of The Pennsylvania Academy of the Fine Arts,
Philadelphia, Charles Bregler's Thomas Eakins Collection,
purchased with the partial support of the Pew Memorial
Trust.* **Many of Eakins's closest friends believed that
he maintained a sexual relationship with Addie
Williams, who moved in with Eakins and his wife
around 1900.**

that "he had had" one of his models—had sexual
intercourse with her—although he did not provide the name of the person in question.[51]

Rumors of other liaisons also circulated.
Around 1900, for example, when Eakins was in
his mid-sixties, a family friend named Addie
Williams moved into the household. Samuel
Murray, Eakins's closest companion in these
years, believed that the artist maintained a
ménage à trois with Addie Williams and Susan
Eakins, and imparted this information to Lloyd
Goodrich. According to the information in
Goodrich's unpublished notes, this supposition
seems to have been widely held by members of
Eakins's circle. Weda Cook described Addie
Williams as Eakins's "mistress."[52] Eakins's
nephew told Gordon Hendricks, "You know, of
course, that Uncle Tom made love to Addie
Williams."[53] Mr. Douty declared that Eakins
maintained a *ménage à trois*. (Douty's wife, however, challenged him on this claim, saying "Do
you actually know it was a *ménage à trois*?")

Significantly, however, other people who
knew Eakins questioned whether he actually had
affairs. Thus, for example, Lucy Langdon W. Wilson, a liberal educator and
feminist, provided a different assessment of Eakins's character and motives.
She told Goodrich that Eakins used crude language while painting two portraits of her in 1908 and 1909, apparently in an effort to shock her, but when he
saw she didn't mind his language, he stopped. He did not seem interested in
seduction. In her opinion, Eakins's sexuality was largely talk; she believed that
if a situation developed, "he would leave before the critical moment." In her
view, Eakins was filled with "physical inhibitions." She considered him an
utterly selfish man, especially toward his wife, who had sacrificed everything
for him. "He never loved anyone," she commented.[54]

Eakins himself seems to have been inconsistent in his statements. Shortly
after he was fired from the Pennsylvania Academy he declared in a letter to
Edward Coates, "I never in my life seduced a girl, nor tried to."[55] As we have

seen, however, he also boasted to Clarence Cranmer that he had seduced one of his models.

None of the women Goodrich interviewed found him physically appealing. They described him as "like a bear," "rough, like a St. Bernard dog," "like a gorilla," and "that thick, through." One woman noted that "when he sat down he sat down all of a heap."[56] Weda Cook described Eakins as "sallow, with stubby gray hair, a fat belly, ugly; he *looked* dirty, though he wasn't." She considered him "absolutely unmoral," and noted that "he was not attractive to women."[57]

Eakins's Attitude Toward Women

Many forms of evidence confirm that Eakins viewed women as physically and intellectually inferior to men, and felt some sort of deep-rooted loathing or anxiety about their female state. Throughout his life, Eakins reacted heatedly when women threatened to take over male prerogatives.

Eakins's insistence on the inferior role of women seems to have led to the breakup of his first romance, with Emily Sartain, who made the mistake of implying that a woman could think or act as an equal with a man. As he wrote to Emily at Christmastime in 1867:

> There is one thing though very funny in your letter "I insist that the duties and responsibilities of men & women are equal etc." Tell me truly how hard did you set down your pretty little foot after writing that. You never learned that from yourself Emily or my mother or your mother or next door at your sister Helen's.[58]

The issue clearly rankled, since he returned to it later in letters to both his sister Frances and his father. To Frances he complained (writing in French):

> There are women who wish to rule everything and to take the place of men, and only because they are foolish and incapable of directing themselves.[59]

He later repeated nearly the same words in a letter to his father. Benjamin Eakins had heard some negative gossip about his son from a New York friend of Emily Sartain. Eakins responded testily that the New Yorker was a "dirty crook" and then complained about Emily:

There are some women who want to rule over everything and especially over men and especially those who are weak and incapable of running themselves. And once a woman gets this notion, she knows no limits or modesty and sticks her nose into everything, interferes in other people's business, spreads family secrets, lays her plans and thinks of others as belonging to her, as her personal tools for her success and not as people who have a good idea.[60]

In short, in Eakins's view of the world, the consequences of letting a woman express her mind are disastrous, particularly for those with "family secrets" to hide. In still another letter to his father, defending himself against Emily's criticisms, Eakins sarcastically slipped into what he clearly regarded as female baby talk. He sneered:

I can't help thinking that Emily has been talking to you about my affairs. Perhaps she would like me to leave Gérôme & this naughty Paris & join their sweet little class & come & fetch her & see her home after it . . . We could drawery wawery after the nice little plaster busty wustys & have such a sweet timey wimey.[61]

In fact, Eakins's contempt for women served as his general organizing principle for distinguishing good from bad. Throughout his life he characterized things that he disliked as feminine. In a letter from Paris, for example, Eakins told his sister Frances that finishing his paintings was simply "lady's work," and was not significant.[62] Similarly, he used words like "beautiful" and "poetical" as terms of derision, apparently because of their feminine connotations. Thus, for example, when Cecilia Beaux showed Eakins one of her pictures he commented "that's beautiful" in an ironic tone that made it clear to her that the adjective was not intended as a compliment.[63]

Study of Eakins's letters and other statements provides many instances of his negative use of words like "beautiful" and "poetic." For example, in a letter describing his study with Gérôme he noted that "only once he told me that I was going backwards and that time I had made a poetical sort of outline."[64] Similarly, in describing his disgust with a painting of Hiawatha that he had abandoned because he felt it was too sentimental, he wrote to the art critic Earl Shinn, whom he had known as a student in Paris: "I used to write poetry when I was a grammar school boy all about sweethearts. I guess they were madrigals. When I had them bad my mother used to give me vermifuge [a strong intestinal purge]."[65] Still another letter about the Hiawatha project

blamed its failure on his long hair—presumably because long hair was feminine—but fortunately the problem was solved when he got a haircut.

> It got so poetic at last that when Maggy would see [the painting] she would
> make as if it turned her stomach. I got so sick of it myself soon that I gave it
> up. I guess maybe my hair was getting too long, for on having it cropped again
> I could not have been induced to finish it.[66]

The evidence seems plain, in short, that Eakins thought of women as inferior, and preferred the company of men. What is more, he actively took steps to
keep women in their place. When he was a young man, a family friend, Sallie
Shaw, remembered him as "very domineering" and also recalled that "Tom
didn't approve of higher education for women."[67] Indeed, Eakins prevented his
sister Frances from attending high school, since he maintained that education
was not necessary for women. As we have noted, while his wife had talent as a
painter, he forced her to abandon art and focus on housekeeping. While teaching at the Pennsylvania Academy, Eakins specifically stated that "I do not believe
that great painting or sculpture or surgery will ever be done by women."[68]
Although the view that women were inferior to men was common in the late
nineteenth century, Eakins's heated insistence on this point, and his professed
loathing of feminine traits, seems extreme even by Victorian standards.

Samuel Murray, Thomas Eakins, 1907. *Painted plaster with metal palette, 9 x 9 ½ x 8 ¾ in., The Pennsylvania Academy of the Fine Arts, Philadelphia, gift of Malcolm Sausser.* **Samuel Murray portrayed Eakins seated on the floor, painting** *The Agnew Clinic.*

Chapter 7

EXPLANATIONS AND ENIGMAS

JUST WHAT LED Eakins to behave as he did has caused much vexation to scholars, whose elaborate efforts to find excuses for the artist's conduct often resemble those "all for the best" philosophers of the eighteenth century whom Voltaire satirized in *Candide*. Two strategies have been taken up in Eakins's defense. The first is to disparage the motives of those who attacked him, even to the extent of declaring that they were mentally unbalanced. According to this view, Frank Stephens suffered from mania; Thomas Anshutz was an unscrupulous prude, who sought to topple Eakins to advance his own career; and Lillian Hammitt and Ella Crowell were mentally unstable, so one should not take them seriously. A major problem with this argument is that the motives ascribed to these individuals often do not make sense. We must assume that they acted in ways that have no convincing motive, and that fundamentally differ from how they behaved on other occasions.

Frank Stephens, for example, as has been mentioned, never showed any signs of mania apart from his attacks on his brother-in-law. He ran a successful business, producing decorative terracotta for buildings, and he maintained long-term business relationships with a number of Philadelphia artists, several of whom sided with him in the controversy about Eakins. He also raised a family and provided jobs for his Crowell nephews. He ended his career as a popular lecturer on artistic subjects. There is no evidence that he was a prude. In fact, later in life, he was accused of being a proponent of "free love," since after Caroline's death he lived unmarried with a woman for several years. By no means conservative in outlook, in 1900 Stephens founded the community of Arden, Delaware, which was a utopian single-tax community in which art, craft, labor, utility, and leisure were interwoven.[1]

Photographer unknown, Thomas Anshutz, ca. 1885. *Private collection.* **Eakins's entire teaching staff joined the campaign to have him fired, including his second-in-command, Thomas Anshutz.**

The attacks on Thomas Anshutz by Eakins's defenders also appear to be without solid foundation. Anshutz was anything but a prude. He made many drawings of nude models, and he produced a well-known series of watercolors that portray naked boys by the seashore. It is hard to believe that he would have been shocked by the exposure of a nude male figure. Indeed, he treated the nude in his paintings more frequently than Eakins did.

Nor does Anshutz appear to have been obsessed by career ambition, as Kathleen Foster, for example, has implied.[2] For one thing, battling with Eakins would have been an extremely risky strategy if there were nothing of real substance at stake and his statements were not supported by other members of the staff. Given the hierarchical structure of nineteenth-century society, it seems clear that Anshutz was placing his own career at risk.

In addition, this view does not accord with what we know of his personality. Anhutz never exhibited overweaning ambition or a tendency to push his career forward by unscrupulous means. On the contrary, later accounts by his students, such as Charles Demuth, present Anshutz as remarkably modest, even-tempered, open-minded, and judicious. Unlike most art teachers of his generation, he remained friendly with former students, even when they converted to modernism and moved along artistic paths very different from his own.[3]

In 1891, a few years after being placed in charge of the Academy, Anshutz resigned from his teaching position and made an extended trip to Paris to study at the Academie Julian and rejuvenate himself as an artist. Although he was invited to return to the Academy in 1893, Anshutz seems to have left Philadelphia with no guarantees that he would be rehired. Such an action is hardly consistent with the notion that he plotted nefariously to gain his teaching post.[4]

In short, for Anshutz to have launched self-interested attacks on Eakins would have been completely out of character. As with Frank Stephens, we are asked to believe that someone who was sane and good-natured under other circumstances developed a vicious or unbalanced motive—such as "mania" or "self-interest"—where Eakins was concerned.

Similarly, Goodrich and his followers have dismissed Ella Crowell and Lillian Hammitt as not worth considering because she was mentally ill. Goodrich, for example, shrugged off Ella's suicide with the comment that "by all accounts, she was mentally unbalanced."[5] Kathleen Foster has been even harsher in her judgments, describing Ella as flighty, immature, manipulative, unstable, a notorious liar, and mentally ill.[6]

Was Ella Crowell mentally unstable? The evidence is ambiguous. Perhaps she was indeed crazy, as Lloyd Goodrich and several of his followers have insisted. But when she first came to live with Eakins she was regarded as sane. Most troubling to consider, if Eakins did indeed sexually molest her, this would explain her emotional distress, even her suicide, quite as convincingly as an unspecified mental illness. One of the most chilling facts is that Ella's parents feared for her safety before they sent her to study with Eakins. Moreover, Susan Eakins's letter, while intended to exonerate her husband from blame, seems to suggest that Ella was caught in a web of family conflicts. If we seek the reasons why Ella became so psychologically distraught, there are strong reasons to believe Eakins played a role.

Lillian Hammitt may also have been crazy, as Lloyd Goodrich once again insists. But she sounds surprisingly sane in the surviving letters she wrote to Eakins, which are logical and clear and contain no discernible exaggerations or misrepresentations. Perhaps she just "went crazy," without reason or without warning. But it is natural to ask what could have pushed her over the edge, and if we ask this simple question we cannot help but ask what role Eakins played in her psychological problems. Those who knew Lillian, such as her brother and her employer, felt that Eakins played a sinister role in her life. In addition, Eakins played a central role in her mental delusions—she imagined that she was married to him. In fact, her "insane" behavior mirrored Eakins's own actions. We have many accounts of Eakins exhibiting his nakedness or appearing in scanty or inappropriate clothes. When Lillian appeared on the street in a bathing suit, she was engaging in a very similar sort of exhibitionism to Eakins himself.

Along with casting blame on figures such as Frank Stephens, Thomas Anshutz, Ella Crowell, and Lillian Hammitt, Goodrich did his best to divert attention from the fact that Eakins's siblings played a large role in the campaigns against him. With regard to the Academy and Art Club feuds, for example, Goodrich states as fact that Caroline's husband, Frank Stephens, "succeeded in turning her against her brother."[7]

It seems more likely, however, that Caroline disliked her brother before she married Stephens, and drew him into the conflict. Will Crowell's letter in Eakins's defense proposes that the trouble started with a conflict between Eakins and Caroline, because Eakins murdered Caroline's cat.[8] He also indicates that it was Caroline who first told Frank Stephens that female students were improperly posing in the nude for Eakins.[9] Even if we do suppose that Stephens was the source of the trouble—although the evidence suggests the contrary—the fact that Caroline was so thoroughly won over to her new husband's point of view suggests that something was already fractured in the family relationship, and needed only a slight jolt to break apart.

Similarly, when the Crowell family broke off contact with Eakins, Goodrich blamed it on Will rather than Frances. After reporting Ella's suicide, he commented that Ella's father "unjustly blamed Eakins's influence on her, and forbade his visiting the family and Avondale."[10] Once again, the logic of this statement is highly questionable. In fact, it seems to have been Frances quite as much as Will who insisted that the family break of relations with Eakins. She did not change her stance after Will's death, as would have been logical if he had been forcing it on her. When Goodrich visited her, during her final illness, she refused to speak to him about her brother. (Goodrich's smug assertion that Will Crowell blamed Eakins "unjustly" is also clearly his interpretation of what happened, not a secure fact).

Goodrich's statements conveniently place the blame on outsiders, and thus divert attention from possible conflicts within the Eakins family. Thus, he avoids the obvious question of whether the family itself was dysfunctional or emotionally troubled.

An interesting assumption of the standard defense of Eakins has never been mentioned or examined—its systematic disparagement or exclusion of the testimony of the many women who felt they were abused or mistreated by Eakins. While Susan Eakins has been praised for kneeling obediently at the shrine of her husband's genius, those who did not do so have been ridiculed or viewed as nullities. As I have already noted, both Ella Crowell and Lillian Hammitt have been dismissed as crazy, and thus irrelevant, but at least their distress has been recorded, whereas that of other women often has been entirely pushed out of consideration. Thus, for example, both Caroline Eakins, the artist's sister, and Alice Barber, his most talented pupil, have been left out of accounts of the quarrels around Eakins, on the assumption that they were entirely dominated by their husbands, and that consequently their thoughts and opinions did not matter. The qualms of Emily Sartain, the artist's first girlfriend, have been dismissed on the grounds that she was a Victorian prude—or perhaps worse, since several writers intimate that she might have been a lesbian. (The chief evidence for this insinuation is that Emily did not marry and pursued a professional career. No writer on Eakins has troubled to mention that Emily was a major pioneer in providing truly professional art instruction for women.)[11] The complaints of the dozens of women who felt that Eakins mistreated them when they were posing, or who objected to his behavior as a teacher, or who objected to his crude language, gauche behavior, or state of undress in some social situation, have been dismissed as mere symptoms of Victorian prudery, and frequently have been pictured as laughable. Or they have simply been deleted from the record. For example, no biography of Eakins mentions the fact that the outstandingly gifted illustrator, Jessie Willcox Smith, who studied with him for a year in 1885, later described him as "a madman."[12] Even the statements of those women who formed part of Eakins's intimate circle, such as Weda Cook, have been articulated without nuance to imply that they wholeheartedly adored Eakins, when in fact it is clear that many of them found something about him was extremely troubling, even frightening.

The psychological foundations for this exclusion and nullification of female testimony would themselves form a fascinating subject for study. Early writers on Eakins, nearly all of whom were male, often took an openly misogynistic stance, and this attitude was enshrined in Goodrich's classic account of the artist. Goodrich consistently blames women for the setbacks in Eakins's career (for example, proposing, quite contrary to the evidence, that "a few proper females" caused Eakins's troubles at the Pennsylvania Academy).[13] Throughout his account, feminine qualities in art are treated as a sign of weakness, and lapses of good manners are viewed as positive, since they demonstrate that Eakins was a manly fellow, and not a homosexual. Viewed in hindsight, Goodrich's misogynistic and homophobic statements often seem implicit confessions of male insecurity, and strikingly parallel the expressions of sexual anxiety that we also found in paintings of the same period, such as the burlesque paintings of his best friend, Reginald Marsh.

In recent years, however, the ground has shifted and expressions of bias toward Eakins have gone through a peculiar shift. Male writers, from William Inness Homer to Martin Berger, have raised thoughtful, provocative questions about Eakins's motives and behavior and have suggested that Eakins's treatment of women was peculiar. On the other hand, a group consisting primarily of women, such as Elizabeth Johns, Helen Cooper, Helene Barbara Weinberg, Kathleen Foster, and even Linda Nochlin, one of the founders of feminist art history, have taken over the role formerly occupied by Goodrich, of maintaining a hard-line defense of Eakins's motives. None of these female writers has thought it necessary to closely examine the testimony of the women in Eakins's life, with the exception of Foster, who has energetically attacked the character of both Hammitt and Ella Crowell, judging them both unreliable and hysterical. No attempt has been made to gather the testimony of Eakins's female students, such as Jessie Willcox Smith. Thus, we have a seeming paradox—a self-proclaimed feminist art history that largely excludes the voices of women.

The issue of listening to female testimony has many ramifications. One is simply to acknowledge that many statements made by women who knew Eakins do not fit into the traditional hagiography of the artist. In particular, we should look at the female testimony that Goodrich gathered but censored from his published accounts. Another is to develop a sympathetic ear to the testimony of nineteenth-century women, who often had psychological and social concerns different from those of women today. We should recognize that in the nineteenth-century women had few professions or means of livelihood open to them and that they were always liable to have their reputations and means of survival ruined by sexual scandal. Rather than simply mocking the prudery of nineteenth-century women, we should recognize that issues of decorum provided one of the few lines of defense available to women in challenging male dominance. Finally, we should recognize that writers on Eakins, from Lloyd Goodrich on, have often failed to record statements, particularly the statements of women, which did not fit their preconceptions. Due to their smug conviction that they knew Eakins's character better than his acquaintances and neighbors, a large body of valuable information has been lost forever. We should at least acknowledge that the testimony about Eakins is extremely biased, and that female voices have been excluded from the record with particular frequency.

Remarkably, scholars have never considered the possibility that Eakins might have been lying, or at least telling less than the entire truth, although this is one possibility that should be explored. The view that Eakins was interested in the honest disclosure of the facts is not borne out by the evidence. He vigorously protested when one of his students revealed that he had enticed a young woman to pose nude at his home. Similarly, when Francis Ziegler, who had been his secretary at the Art Students League and had become a newspaper reporter, came by to see the artist after publishing an entirely accurate account of Lillian Hammitt's affliction, Eakins slammed the door in his face and then had Susan send a note informing him that he was no longer welcome in the studio.[14] Certainly Eakins was not unusual in attempting to suppress information that did not show him in a favorable light. Surely, however, this does not fit with the notion, promulgated in so much of the literature on the artist, that he was an advocate of open, uninhibited behavior or a champion of complete frankness and honesty.

Despite Eakins's fascination with undressing in public and revealing the nude body, he was also extremely secretive, even evasive, about his life and practices. His letters are full of complaints about "professional" matters that someone had divulged. "For the public," he once wrote, "my life is all in my work."[15]

Lying, of course, can take different forms, as is evident in the requirement of law that witnesses not only tell "the truth" but also "the whole truth" and "nothing but the truth." As will be shown, there are several instances (some of them reported by Goodrich) in which it can be documented that Eakins made false statements or engaged in deceitful behavior. Thus, it seems quite possible that some of the statements Eakins made in his defense were not truthful. In most cases, however, it appears that Eakins did not so much lie as avoid answering questions, or make statements that were technically true but misleading.

Eakins's statements invariably avoid a direct answer to the charges laid against him, although the charges were often quite specific, and they do not address the deeper motives for his behavior. Instead, he resorted to more devious methods. Often he launched counteraccusations. Thus, for example, at the time of the Academy scandal, Eakins complained about "the infamous lies that were circulated and which imposed upon some people who should have known better."[16] However, he never specified which statements were lies, or seriously attempted to refute the charges with evidence. In other instances, he focused on procedural matters. For example, Eakins's letters about the Art Club focus on the claim that he could not be expelled because he was an honorary member, an argument of dubious logic and hardly a straightforward response to the accusations against him.

Attempts to Justify Eakins's Interest in the Nude

Scholars defending Eakins have also taken a second tack. In their desire to vindicate Eakins, writers have also gone to extreme lengths to argue that his
interest in the nude was strictly a professional matter, a reflection of his scientific interest in anatomy or of his artistic practice. According to this view, the
scandals were rooted not in Eakins's behavior, but in the fact that American
culture was prudish and unsophisticated in its attitudes. Many writers have
maintained that working from the nude was not customary in America at this
time. (Jennifer Doyle, for example, has written that "studying from living
naked models was unheard of in the United States.")[17] Thus they have implied
that if he had simply worked in Paris or some other European city he would
not have stirred up so much controversy. The view that other American artists
did not work from the nude, however, is clearly incorrect. Many artists of this
period worked regularly from the nude, among them a fellow Philadelphian,
Howard Roberts, who studied in Paris at the same time as Eakins and
returned to work in his native city at the same time also. In fact, some artists
roughly contemporary with Eakins, such as the painter Will Low or the sculptor Frederick McMonnies, specialized in producing paintings or sculpture that
portrayed the nude figure. Many of these artists also taught classes using nude
models.

Clearly the problem was not that Eakins used nude models but that he did
so in ways that were unusual. Indeed, Eakins used nude models differently
than any other artist of the nineteenth century, either in America or Europe.
Eakins was reluctant to use professionals, even when they were readily available, and he seldom if ever used his wife as a nude model after their marriage.
But he insisted on his right to undress his students and to undress in front of
them. What is more, he often manifested a desire to place himself and his students (or other individuals) in naked physical contact with one another, in
ways that have no obvious connection with any scientific or artistic purpose.
Surely, for example, there was no professional reason for the incident
described by Weda Cook, when he strode into a room unclothed while a
woman was posing for Samuel Murray and taunted her to look at his nakedness.

The degree to which Eakins's behavior was unusual becomes apparent
when we ask ourselves a simple question: what other nineteenth-century
American artist had himself photographed in full frontal nudity? The answer
is none—with the exception of the aspiring artists in Eakins's classes whom he

persuaded to pose. We have no nude photographs of Eakins's artistic contemporaries, such as Winslow Homer, John La Farge, William Merritt Chase, Kenyon Cox, and so forth, even in instances when these painters worked extensively from the nude. Only in a very few instances do we have nude photographs of major European painters of this period, despite the more permissive attitude toward nudity in Europe, particularly in Paris.[18]

Eakins also insisted on flaunting his use of nude models in instances when he encountered social resistance. Other artists who faced similar opposition responded more tactfully, as did the sculptor Augustus Saint-Gaudens, who was questioned in August 1891, when he was teaching at the Art Students League in New York, "as to the propriety of both sexes working from the same [nude] model." When the League's president interviewed the sculptor on this issue, Saint-Gaudens "expressed the hope that the present arrangement would not be changed, but if it was thought best as a matter of expediency to do so, he would not oppose the board."[19] In the end, Saint-Gaudens was allowed to go ahead and use nude models freely.

Goodrich notes:

> What strikes one about these incidents is not only Eakins' persistence in showing the completely nude model at certain lectures, but that in spite of his confrontations with the Pennsylvania Academy in 1886, and later with the Art Students' League and the National Academy in New York, he displayed innocent surprise each time the inevitable reaction occurred. To read his letter to Blashfield and his interviews about the Drexel Institute affair, one would think that the reaction had never happened before.[20]

Goodrich also notes that Eakins showed a similar disregard of public opinion with what he terms the "realism" of his paintings, that is to say, his unflattering representation of his sitters and the "brutality" of much of his subject matter, such as boxing matches and medical operations. In other words, Eakins's behavior seemed to form a repetitive pattern, in which he consistently courted hostility while denying that he was doing so.

One cannot help suspecting that Eakins often used arguments of professionalism as a shield, since a great deal of his behavior seems to have little relation to accepted artistic or scientific practice. In other words, one may ask whether Eakins studied the nude so that he could create art, or whether he became an artist so that he could look at people who were undressed and expose his own unclothed body to others. (As Kay Redfield Jamison has observed, in her study *Touched by Fire*: "Certain lifestyles provide cover for defiant and bizarre behavior. The arts have long given latitude to extremes of behavior and mood.")[21]

Even Goodrich recognized that this interest in the nude "did become an obsession and a self-defeating one."[22] He writes that Eakins's "continuing persistence in these importunities, in spite of rebuffs, is a curious psychological phenomenon, showing a complete disregard of his sitter, codes of behavior and the morals of his community . . . It was like his stubborn insistence on the entirely nude male model in certain anatomical lectures, and his ignoring of popular squeamishness in his two great clinic paintings. . . . In the end, this obsessive persistence may have had an element of conscious defiance of social conventions."[23]

One might argue that Eakins displayed a certain integrity in such determined disregard for the morals of his community. But it was not only Eakins who bore the cost of his behavior. For example, the women who were placed under Eakins's control at the Pennsylvania Academy were bound by the constraints and cultural practices of the nineteenth century, which ostracized women who were viewed as "immoral." A common theme of literature (and painting) of the time was that of the "woman with a past"—who was discarded as unworthy once her transgressions were discovered. Even the French, who were more permissive than Americans, considered this a morally proper way for a man to behave. Alexandre Dumas, the younger, for example, celebrated such a rejection of a woman in his single most popular and celebrated work, *La Dame Aux Camelias* (1848), later rewritten as the play *Camille* (1852).[24]

It is all very well for twentieth-century onlookers, who live in a very different cultural framework, to celebrate the fact that Eakins disregarded such strictures. But for the women who were his students, these concerns were no joking matter. Alice Barber, for example, was subjected to widespread gossip and ridicule because she had posed nude for Eakins. The women who allied themselves with Eakins generally forfeited a normal social life. They did not marry, they did not pursue viable careers, and they did not live socially engaged lives. Those who were closest to him often seem to have suffered from mental illness or depression.

Notably, Eakins's classroom difficulties appear related to other aspects of his daily behavior that violated or stood on the fringes of acceptable conduct. He was notorious for his obscenities and dirty jokes. He made a point of sleeping in the nude at his summer house, but of leaving the door open so that he would be visible to anyone coming along on the nearby creek.[25] He took evident delight in shocking Philadelphia society women when he painted their portraits, by using obscene language, by inviting them to pose nude for him, and even by greeting them at the door dressed only in his underwear.

The Rhetoric of Sodomy

The scandals that surrounded Eakins coincided with larger battles about morality and public decency. In 1873 Anthony Comstock founded the New England Society for the Suppression of Vice, which was financially supported by wealthy industrialists concerned about the decline of America's moral fabric. In the same year that he created his society, Comstock engineered the passage of the Comstock Law, which prohibited sending "obscene" materials through the U.S. mail. Comstock's supporters occasionally became involved in artistic issues. In 1891, for example, the Philadelphia branch of Comstock's society organized their supporters to write to Edward Horner Coates, requesting that he remove paintings of female nudes from the walls of the Pennsylvania Academy. Opposing Comstock was the National Liberal League, an assortment of atheists, communists, and advocates of free love, which held its founding convention in Philadelphia in 1876.[26]

The conflict between these two groups provides interesting insights into the sexual mores of the time. Above all, it shows that attitudes toward sexual matters were extremely varied in the nineteenth century, and that Victorian society contained not only stern moralists but supporters of nudism, free love, and other radical social views. There is no evidence, however, that Eakins ever took part in these larger public debates or that he ever made any attempt to defend other artists or free speech in general. Eakins's battles always concerned his personal behavior rather than larger moral positions.

As Jennifer Doyle has noted, controversies about art and artists often illuminate social attitudes about moral and immoral behavior. She notes that "the rhetoric of sodomy" was applied against Eakins.[27] What this term meant in the nineteenth century is far from clear. Generally, sodomy refers to oral or, more often, to anal sex with members of either gender. Bestiality, of which Eakins was also accused, may refer to sex with animals, but also to sex that is "beast-like" in nature, and thus to such transgressions as sodomy or incest. Recent theorists have argued that the distinguishing marker of sodomy was that it stood outside procreative sex and thus "stood outside of marriage and the boundaries of the family and the nation-state." According to this view, identifying Eakins as a sodomite served as a "fetishistic ritual of reassuring an audience of the sanctity and stability of a dominant ordering of sex and gender."[28]

In the long memorandum about Ella Crowell defending her husband, Susan Eakins cited a claim that Maggie Crowell had made against him, namely that "Ella's insanity was brought on by the wearing effect of unnatural sexual excitements practiced upon her in the manner of Oscar Wilde." Wilde was often cited in this period not only as an instance of the dangers of bohemianism, but with regard to a specific form of sexual misbehavior— homosexual sodomy. Given that Eakins was accused of sodomy, it is striking that Susan Eakins spontaneously selected this example.[29] Her use of this example was also in part incongruous, since while Eakins's behavior with Ella may conceivably have involved incest, it was obviously not homosexual.

Curiously, scholars commenting on this passage have not noted one of the most obvious aspects of Susan's statement: its willful exaggeration. Clearly the intent of Susan's statement was to express Maggie's assertions in such exaggerated terms that they would become unbelievable. Yet at the same time, jokes and exaggerations often carry unintended meanings. At the least, Susan's statement points toward some kind of preoccupation with sodomy either on the part of Eakins or of those who surrounded him.

The Riddle of Eakins's Motives

Goodrich writes that "Eakins's training in medical schools and his anatomical studies had given him an attitude toward the human body as uninhibited as a physician's."[30] Yet if we read Eakins's statements about the nude or about women, it is clear that this is not the case. Previous writers on Eakins have tried to argue that his motives were fundamentally wholesome, even normal, and thus have made two claims about his fixation on nude modeling that are not supported by the evidence: first, that it reflected a stance of openness and honesty about sexual matters, and second, that it expressed a drive toward sexual and emotional liberation. If we read Eakins's own statements, however, it becomes clear that something more peculiar was taking place. Rather than being open about sexual matters, or about his interest in the nude, Eakins was intensely secretive. In addition, Eakins's attitude toward the nude was not sexually liberated but puritanical, moralistic, and repressed, although in a fashion that was at odds with prevailing social standards.

This double pattern of secretiveness and puritanical attitudes is already evident in Eakins's early letters from Paris. For example, Eakins once insisted that his sister Frances should have nothing to do with a female friend of Emily Sartain. "I do not care to tell you my reasons but they are all sufficient," he wrote. When Frances, understandably annoyed, declared, "If you have got good reasons why let me know them," he answered, "These reasons . . . were medical and as such I do not consider a modest virgin the proper person with whom to enter upon an explanation even if she is my sister."[31]

Despite the odd nature of his behavior concerning the nude, Eakins insisted that he was innocent of any sort of misbehavior, while others were guilty of horrible transgressions. Indeed, Eakins's letters are filled with the same moral epithets that were thrown at him by his enemies—accusations of immorality, dishonesty, and so forth. He insisted, however, on inverting the usual attitudes about the appropriateness of nakedness.

Eakins declared that what other people thought was indecent—being undressed—in fact was moral, while wearing clothing was dishonest and deceitful. In describing his teachings at the Art Students League of New York, for example, Eakins defended his use of the nude model because it allowed him to follow the muscles to their exact source in the genital area. He went on to assert that for him to lecture from a model wearing a loin cloth was "trifling & undignified," and that "the smaller bag tied with tapes or thongs, hitherto used at the League is to my mind extremely indecent, and has been more than once a source of embarrassment and mischief."[32] What is peculiar here, of course, is the emotionally loaded language that Eakins used to describe what he pretends is a practical matter. Eakins mysteriously inverted the charges that were leveled against himself.

Any form of clothing or adornment was offensive to Eakins—even a bracelet incensed him, as reported in Walt Whitman's anecdote of how he tore off the bracelet of an otherwise nude model.[33] H. C. Cresson, who briefly served as president of the Philadelphia Art Students League, where Eakins designed and supervised the curriculum, set forth Eakins's position when he declared that it would be impossible "to give an *honest criticism* of the nude figure to his pupils" (the italics are in the original document) if the nude were covered at the loins. In other words, clothes were "dishonest" and nakedness was "honest."[34]

Those who opposed using nude models often implied that nude models were associated with immoral conduct. In the letter already cited from R. S. protesting Eakins's use of nude models, this issue was clearly delineated.

"Would you be willing to take a young daughter of your own into the Academy Life Class, to the study of the nude figure of a woman whom you should shudder to have sit and converse with your daughter?"[35] What distressed this writer was not simply the nudity of the model but the kind of woman who would be willing to pose in the nude—a prostitute.

During this period, many female artistic models were prostitutes, since "decent" women would not consider such work.[36] Eakins himself seized on this same issue, although from a different standpoint. Soon after he began teaching at the Pennsylvania Academy, Eakins proposed that the institution should desist from hiring prostitutes, since in his view they were "coarse, flabby, ill formed & unfit in every way for the requirements of the school." Instead, he asked to advertise for respectable ladies "among whom will be found beautiful ones with forms fit to be studied," and who might be "accompanied by their mothers or other female relatives. Terms $1 per hour."[37]

In an inversion of normal psychology, Eakins argued that it was less embarrassing for students to view the nakedness of people they knew well than to view strangers, although the violent reactions of his students and teaching staff, as well as the directors of the Academy, make it clear that this was not the case. For example, in describing the episode in which he removed his pants and showed his genitals to his student Amelia Van Buren, Eakins concluded, "There was not the slightest embarrassment or cause for embarrassment on her part or mine." He then added: "I think indeed [Van Buren] might have been embarrassed, if I had picked up a man on the street and endeavored to persuade him to undress before the lady for a quarter."[38]

To his contemporaries, the emphasis on using students rather than professionals as models was the most shocking aspect of Eakins's practice. Indeed, Elizabeth MacDowell Kenton (Susan Eakins's sister), singled out this point as the main issue of contention in a letter she wrote not long after the Academy scandal. As she declared: "Your mingling of personal and business relations I still consider to have been most unfortunate, and originated the trouble which ensued."[39]

To Eakins, however, such mingling of roles was essential. In fact, Eakins argued that it was immoral for an artist not to pose nude:

> I should have very little respect for any figure painter or sculptor man or woman who would be unwilling to undress himself if useful; yet by his presence in a life class would encourage a model to do it, holding it either a sin or degradation.[40]

Eakins pursued this line of thought in a way that most people found extremely peculiar. As Jennifer Doyle has noted:

> Eakins could with a straight face hand a photograph of himself naked to a colleague and ask her to study it closely, for the fine example of the nude; or invite a friend into his studio to meet a new model, opening the door to reveal a completely naked woman.[41]

Such behavior is not easy to explain as normal, but not because it was sexually aggressive in the usual meaning of that term. In fact, it was based on a denial that nakedness had sexual implications. While he was obsessed with the notion of male authority and fascinated by sexual differences, Eakins also tried to create a world in which sexual differences would be eliminated or repressed. Jennifer Doyle, for example, has noted that while Eakins was accused of "abusive relationships with female students," at the same time he "insisted the women participate in studio culture as equal partners," a practice that "attacked the male privilege that had long underwritten such art world contradictions as the idealization of the female nude as the supreme embodiment of aesthetic beauty and the exclusion of women themselves as artists from studio culture."[42] Eakins's approach was one that equalized men and women, since he denied that a woman's nudity should be a source of shame, and proposed that women should look at naked men and dissect cadavers just as men did. Astutely, Doyle has argued that the public was upset with the sexual politics of Eakins and his circle in part at least because it "favored treating men and women the same."[43]

"Art knows no sex," declared a Philadelphia newspaper, noting that Eakins "has pressed this always-disputed doctrine with much zeal and success."[44] Yet this phrase is disturbingly ambiguous. Initially it sounds like art somehow makes the sexes equal, but in fact it goes further. It proposes eliminating sex altogether.

The logic of this position was clearly drawn from some realm of personal fantasy that Eakins alluded to but never fully explained. Eakins's statements in his defense clearly show that his actions were part of a larger psychological pattern. For example, in 1886, when he was under attack at the Academy, Eakins turned to the metaphor of the surgeon to defend the righteousness of his position. As usual, his writing is difficult to follow because of its erratic grammar and punctuation, and the strange run of associations. At the same time, Eakins's skewed logic is what makes the passage fascinating. Rather than dealing with the matter at hand, it brings in additional elements, in a way that seems to reflect some powerful pattern of emotional associations. Eakins wrote:

> If for instance, I should be in a railroad accident, and escaping myself unhurt, should on looking around me, perceive a lady bleeding most dangerously from the lower extremity; then and there I should try to find the artery and compress it, perhaps tie it . . . and for this I might well receive both her gratitude and that of her folks.
>
> Now if years later, some evil person would run busily about and whisper that I had lifted up a lady's clothes in a public place, that on account of it, there was a great scandal at the time (when there was none) . . . I should have upon me at once more [accusations against me] than I might ever hope to contradict, except to a very few friends, and of my few friends, some would sympathize with me, but would wish I wouldn't do unconventional things, and some would tell me that it is always bad to have dealings with women anyhow; and others with much worldly wisdom [would say] that no motives can ever be understood by the public except lechery and money making, and as there was no money in the affair I should not have meddled, as if my chief care should be the applause of the vulgar.[45]

As Jennifer Doyle has noted, "the fable is a condensed version of Eakins's career."[46] Essentially, Eakins is railing against a social code that would chastise a man for saving a woman's life if it meant raising her skirt above her ankles. He imagines himself as the hero who plays this role. As Doyle notes, what Eakins is really doing is presenting a parallel to the scandal that his painting *The Gross Clinic* created nearly a decade earlier, in which Eakins revealed a similar gash-like wound to the public, and was roundly condemned for his efforts.[47]

Nonetheless, as Doyle observes:

> This does not seem to be quite the right story for Eakins to use to make his defense. The unavoidable gap between the story he tells about helping an injured woman in a train wreck and the path of his own career is that no one's life depended on Eakins's artistic practices. Try as he might to lend his project as sense of urgency, he was not a surgeon.[48]

Eakins's story presents a curious delusion of grandeur quite at odds with the actual facts. At the same time, Doyle perceptively notes that in psychological terms the choice of the injury in Eakins's story is exceedingly provocative:

"Not a broken bone, but a bleeding wound, almost as if he imagines treating her for being a (menstruating) woman." As Doyle concludes, "Eakins's fantasy of himself as an injured woman's savior makes us wonder what the difference is between imagining himself as this woman's healer and the fantasy of the injury that must precede it."[49]

There are several mysteries here, but the essential task is to determine why Eakins made this connection between posing figures in the nude and helping an injured, bleeding woman? Whereas most people would not even make such a connection, for Eakins it had some compelling emotional significance. One might also ask whether there is a connection between this image of a woman with a bleeding leg or vagina and the imagery of Eakins's most famous painting, *The Gross Clinic*, in which a doctor probes the thigh wound of an androgynous patient?

Eakins's Peculiarities

Because so much scandal surrounded Eakins, scholars have tended to focus on issues of scandal and sexual misconduct, and have failed to note that there were other peculiar things about his behavior. These often involved matters that were seemingly insignificant, but nonetheless extremely curious. Besides his deliberately shocking practices, contemporary observers noted other things about Eakins that were unusual, including his fondness for firearms, his habit of painting while seated on the floor, and his enormous consumption of milk.

While these traits in themselves are of small import, their strangeness makes them valuable as clues. Certainly it is worth considering that these small peculiarities might have some bearing on the other aberrations of Eakins's behavior. Let me say a word about each of these points.

Throughout his life, Eakins was entranced with guns. In listing his personal property, for example, Eakins listed "a gun, 2 rifles, and pistols" as almost the first items on the list, preceded only by his clothes and two watches.[50] For recreation, he rigged up a shooting gallery in his studio where visitors such as William Merritt Chase could practice target shooting with him during their visits.[51] During his trip out West in 1886, he acquired a number of guns. These included a .44-caliber Winchester, a double-barreled shotgun, and a .22-caliber squirrel rifle, all of which he eventually brought out to his sister's farm in Avondale.[52] Eakins's letters from the West boast of his prowess with guns, and revel in their messy, destructive power. "If we are out of deer meat," he wrote to Susan, with somewhat childish exaggeration, "I shoot their heads off with my rifle."[53]

Over the course of his career, Eakins regularly carried a pistol in his pocket. References to this fact can be found in various sources. Will Sartain reports, for example, that when Eakins was in Paris he was speaking of American mechanical skill when "to illustrate his point he pulled out from his pocket his Smith & Wesson revolver."[54] Sartain specifically mentioned that it was unusual to carry weapons. "I know of no other person in Paris who carried one!" Sartain stated."[55]

Adam Emory Albright also left an account of the guns that Eakins carried during his sojourn in France. According to Albright, when Eakins was being hazed in Gérôme's atelier, a group of French students called him down from an upper floor. Eakins came sliding down the banister with two revolvers, "yelling like an Indian." "There wasn't a Frenchman there when he landed with a Comanche yell," Albright reported.[56]

Eakins himself mentioned drawing his gun in a letter from Spain. When some porters expected extra payment from him, Eakins reported, "I clapped my hand on my pistol."[57]

Eakins was apparently still carrying a gun in his pocket twenty years later, when he strolled around Philadelphia. Gilbert Sunderland Parker reports that in the late 1880s the artist was walking across the Walnut Street bridge, when two toughs moved toward him in a threatening fashion. In response, Eakins cocked the revolver he was carrying in his pocket. The thieves then backed off and let him pass by.[58] Finally, Margaret McHenry reports that the Arctic explorer Admiral Melville was attending a prize fight with Eakins when he struck against something hard. "Melville asked what the devil was that and discovered Eakins always carried with him a big revolver. Melville declared he'd been in nearly every port in the world and he'd never carried a gun in all his life."[59]

Surely, an explanation of what was unusual about Eakins should deal with the question of why he carried a revolver in his pocket even in cities where such weapons were not necessary or customary.

Another notable point was Eakins's practice of sitting or lying on the floor, something that might still seem somewhat strange in certain contexts, but that was evidently quite unusual in nineteenth-century Philadelphia. One of the figures Lloyd Goodrich interviewed, James L. Wood, the son of Eakins's personal physician, stated (according to Goodrich's notes) that he thought it abnormal "that Eakins could sit on the floor and paint for a long times—says that some tribe of African savages do it." Certainly we should reject the racist thinking behind Wood's reference to "African savages," but Wood's testimony still makes clear that Eakins's practice was atypical. Children might sit on the floor, but grown men were expected to stand or sit on chairs.

Eakins's nephew Will Crowell also wrote about Eakins's sitting on the floor, and also found this practice to be somewhat exotic, although he compared Eakins's behavior not to the Africans but to the Japanese. Writing about his uncle's visit to the farm at Avondale, he wrote: "I think of him of an evening at the Farm sitting talking, sitting cross-legged on the floor like a Japanese, ultimately subsiding from the conversation and going to sleep still sitting cross-legged on the floor."[60]

Eakins's liking for floors is documented in a variety of sources. For example, contemporary accounts indicate that he sat on the floor while he was working on *The Agnew Clinic*, and would fall asleep on the floor while working on the project . Interestingly also, a posed photograph of Eakins with his class at the Pennsylvania Academy shows Eakins lying on the floor, while the other figures sit or stand. Finally, Samuel Murray's bronze of Eakins at work

Academy of the Fine Arts, Philadelphia. *Charles Bregler's Thomas Eakins Collection, purchased with the partial support of the Pew Memorial Trust.* **In a class photograph, Thomas Eakins is sprawled casually on the floor.**

shows him not standing but seated on the floor, with his brush and palette in his hand. (It appears that Murray chose this pose because he felt that it was in some way particularly memorable and distinctive.)

I will speculate later on the meaning of this. For the moment, all that we need note is that Eakins's habit of sitting, working, and sleeping on the floor was considered extraordinary not just by Philadelphia society as a whole, but even by his own students. His singularity in this respect merits an explanation.

Finally, there is Eakins's consumption of milk. Samuel Murray told Lloyd Goodrich that Eakins drank a quart of milk with every meal, hardly a standard practice. Goodrich, in reporting this fact, wondered whether it is physically possible to drink so much, although I think this objection can be dismissed.[61]

An account of Eakins that seeks to explore just what it was that made him so psychologically unusual should explain not only why he was fired from the

H. C. Phillips, Thomas Eakins at about Age Ten, *ca. 1854. Albumen carte-de-visite, courtesy of The Pennsylvania Academy of the Fine Arts, Philadelphia, purchased with funds donated by The Pennsylvania Academy Women's Committee.*

Pennsylvania Academy, why he urged women to undress and liked to undress in front of them, and why he was twice accused of incest by members of his own family, but also why he was so deeply attached to guns, why he chose to sit on the floor, and why he drank such great quantities of milk. In other words, a logical approach to understanding Eakins is not to begin by making moral judgments about either his guilt or innocence, but to gather facts about everything unusual in his behavior, and to see whether they can be organized into a coherent pattern.

One final clue should be mentioned. In photographs taken throughout his life, Eakins looks troubled. What is more, we find this troubled look in the earliest photographs of him, taken when he was about six or seven. Whatever it was that made Eakins's behavior unusual seems to have started very early.[62]

Circle of Thomas Eakins, Thomas Eakins at about Age Thirty-five, 1880.
*Albumen print, 4 ½ × 3 ¼ in., Bryn Mawr College Library, Seymour Adelman
Collection.*

Chapter 8

ANALYZING EAKINS

LET US NOW turn our attention to a second mystery, seemingly unrelated to the first: the mysterious power that Eakins's paintings have exercised over successive generations. Various theories have been advanced to explain this power: that his art is highly realistic, that it is very masculine, that it is thoroughly American, or that he portrayed things with acute precision by using careful measurements. None of these explanations seem very convincing. As we shall discover, Eakins often radically departed from the true appearance of his subjects, he had definite insecurities about his manhood, and his art was based on techniques acquired in France, and thus was American to only a limited degree. Measuring things with a ruler and placing them in proper perspective are the skills of an industrial draftsman, not an artist. Surely it is odd to base the reputation of "the greatest American painter" on a purely mechanical achievement.

The common denominator of all these traditional explanations is that they all seem to ignore precisely those aspects of Eakins's work that arrest our attention: his willingness to paint disturbing or embarrassing subjects, his preoccupation with unhappy states, and perhaps most of all, the air of psychological tension, of something emotionally significant, that he imparts even to seemingly ordinary scenes. My goal in what follows will be to explore these issues, and in doing so to propose a way of looking at Eakins's art often diametrically opposed to that of Lloyd Goodrich and those who have followed his approach up to the present day. I have drawn extensively, however, on the work of those revisionist scholars who, in recent years, have explored some of the dark undercurrents in Eakins's work.

In the broadest sense, I will be pursuing two avenues of inquiry. On the one hand I will be looking closely at Eakins's paintings to study their qualities of emotional unease. This entails comparing how Eakins treated themes with renditions by his contemporaries to reveal just what he did that was so fundamentally different. Most of all, it requires looking closely at his paintings and examining their details to discern elements that are unusual and provide clues to their real meaning.

In addition, I will ask whether there is some sort of connection between the subjects of Eakins's paintings and the events of his troubled personal and family life. To what extent do these two fields interact? Do the events of one world shed light on the nature of the other? Do they express parallel themes? Eakins often portrayed members of his family, and he included a likeness of himself in all his most ambitious paintings, suggesting that he was a direct witness to what he portrayed, or even a participant in the subject. The close connection between Eakins's art and life has often been noted in the literature on the artist. Sylvan Schendler, for example, once noted of Eakins, "His work, seemingly so objective, is closely connected with his personal life."[1] Like other Eakins scholars, however, Schendler pursued this insight only tentatively.

In fact, Eakins seems to have explored family relationships in two ways. First, many of his paintings portray members of his family and explore his relationship to them. Second, Eakins often seems to have transferred the patterns of his family relationships to his renderings of other subjects.

In exploring this process of transferring family patterns, many recent writers on Eakins have employed psychoanalytic concepts, particularly those of Sigmund Freud. These require a few words of explanation. Even a brief summary of Eakins's career raises issues of mental illness and sexual disturbance, the very issues on which Freud focused, and which his theories seek to explain. But Freud developed his concepts more than a century ago. His writings mix ideas that are widely accepted today with others that are no longer sustainable, and still others that remain unresolved and actively debated. Can we work our way through this minefield, and identify Freudian principles that we can employ with reasonable confidence that they are valid?

The first step toward this goal is to abandon unreasonable expectations. Freud was trained as a scientist, and he presented his ideas as if they were scientific. Yet Freud's ideas differ from science in a key respect. No one has ever worked out a viable way of effectively translating Freud's theories about the mind into measurable terms or reproducible experimental results. That Freud's ideas cannot be "proved" or quantified in this way, however, does not mean that they are not useful. It simply means that they belong to the humanities, rather than to the hard sciences, and like history or literary criticism, offer interpretations and plausible explanations rather than definite proofs. When we make use of Freud's ideas we should not pretend to be scientifically objective, but should freely confess that we are engaging in a form of humanistic inquiry.[2]

Furthermore, any reliance on Freud's theories presents a very practical difficulty. Should we present Freud's original formulation of his theories (often shown to be untrue in some respect)? Or should we use more recent clinical writings? If we pursue the latter course, how should we choose between the different camps of modern theory, which often differ significantly in their language and descriptive terminology and are sometimes diametrically opposed in their conclusions?

There is no simple answer to these questions. In the pages that follow I will draw on Freud's own writings as well as on those of contemporary clinicians. I should note, however, that very often in interpreting Eakins, Freud's writings have an interesting advantage: they were part of the same epoch. Freud's thinking was very much a reflection of the attitudes of his time, and by modern standards often seems strangely male chauvinist and paternalistic. The Eakins household, however, was organized along precisely such paternalistic, male chauvinist lines. Thus, the very aspects of Freudian theory that seem suspect in a modern environment are often remarkably useful for understanding Eakins.

To a large degree my use of Freud will be limited to a few key concepts. One is the concept of transference. Freud believed that the patterns and images that we absorb in early childhood form the basis of how we relate to the world later in life. In other words, in childhood we learn a basic pattern of human and sexual relationships, and we then transfer those patterns to the things we encounter later in life. Thus, for example, individuals who are sexually or psychologically abused as children, tend to be abusive to others when they become adults, and tend to have difficulty establishing positive relationships. While the ramifications of Freud's idea of transference can become complex and difficult to trace or understand, the basic concept is one that is now generally accepted, not simply by psychologists but by the general public.

A second useful concept is that of the unconscious. Freud established that behavior is often based not simply on conscious motives, but on feelings and desires that are deeply repressed, and not even accessible to the conscious mind. This is most evident in the case of individuals who are neurotic or mentally ill, who often behave in a fashion that seems highly illogical, but that

forms a logical expression of unconscious motives. Like the concept of transference, the notion of the unconscious is now generally accepted, although
many of Freud's proposals about precisely how the unconscious operates turn
out not to be right, and have been refined by new scientific evidence.

Closely connected with the concept of the unconscious is the idea of
repression. Freud believed that some desires are so embarrassing that we
block them from our conscious mind, although they continue to affect us at
an unconscious level. Such repressed desires are often connected with sexual
feelings, since such feelings are unacceptable to act out in public, or in many
instances, even to discuss. Freud used the concept of sex extremely broadly to
refer to a great variety of forms of sensual gratification, including not only
the act of sexual intercourse, but also other things that engage the genitals, or
which in some way mimic amorous activities, such as going to the bathroom
or sucking at a mother's nipple. One common denominator of these activities
is that it is embarrassing to discuss them in public—or even think about them.

In describing how transference and repression operate, Freud proposed
that family relationships, particularly a small child's contact with his father
and mother, play an enormously important role in human development.
Moreover, he proposed that what he termed "the Oedipus complex"—a boy's
conflict with his father—played an inevitable role in such relationships. I will
discuss the Oedipus complex in more detail in my conclusion. For present
purposes it is necessary to know only two things. First, Freud believed that
boys often fear castration, and think of women as castrated men. Second,
Freud believed that a child's conflict with his parents gives rise to a fear of castration. Freud's ideas about the Oedipus complex and castration have always
been somewhat controversial. But if nothing else, Freud's theories alert us to
the possibility that an obsessive concern with castration and emasculation
may signal some sort of conflict or trauma in a child's relationship with his
parents.

This is a highly simplified distillation of Freud's ideas, but the simplicity is
by intent. As Freud (and his followers) moved further and further from clinical
observations and tried to develop a more general theory of how the mind
operates, his concepts grew increasingly less accurate.[3]

In analyzing Eakins's art and life, we often encounter views that I personally
find offensive. Eakins firmly believed that women are mentally and physically
inferior to men. By combining basic Freudian concepts with an understanding
of the peculiar nature of Eakins's family experience, we can move toward an
understanding of why Eakins held this view, as well as other equally disturbing

opinions. I should make it clear, however, that in elucidating Eakins's vision of the world, I am not articulating my own views. My goal here is to explain Eakins, but not to excuse or defend him, nor to put forward my own philosophy of life.

I should also make it very clear that it is not necessary to believe Freud's theories to accept the fundamental argument of this book. Freud's theories, however, draw attention to patterns that we might otherwise disregard, and help us to discover connections between things that would otherwise seem unrelated. In many instances the interpretations I present are not ones that I developed myself but are summaries of the work of other scholars, such as Michael Fried and Whitney Davis. I myself initially found some aspects of these interpretations far-fetched, but was gradually won over, at least in large part, since I found that the patterns they observed in certain of Eakins's works were also evident in others, or surfaced in his behavior. Thus it may be helpful for the reader to suspend his or her disbelief until the full body of evidence has been presented.

One of the most disturbing aspects of Freud's theories is the suggestion that the boundaries between sanity and madness are often not clear-cut, and that we can learn to understand and empathize with those who are mentally ill by probing our own feelings. We tend to resist Freud's theories because to use them we need to analyze ourselves.

Freud's theories, of course, are simply one more tool to help us look closely at Eakins's paintings and to become sensitive to their emotional qualities. Paintings are often fascinating precisely because they do not have a single meaning, but rather suggest several meanings. Eakins seems to have been very aware of his fact. His paintings are often ambiguous. We often sense that something unusual is happening, or might happen, but cannot quite put a finger on what that might be.

I have always felt that Eakins's paintings are about both hiding a secret and about wishing to divulge it. Consequently, to understand them we need to look beyond their surface meanings and study the tensions that lie just beneath. While it is probably unorthodox to bring magic into the equation, what I mean by this is perhaps best explained with reference to a fairytale I read as a child, which deals with the whole question of secrets, and of how they are both hidden and disclosed.

The story told of a king of Lydia named Midas, who was born with goat's ears. Kings do not like to look ridiculous, so Midas hid his furry ears under a hat, and concealed the fact that he had them from everyone except his barber, who was told to keep quiet about what he knew or suffer the punishment of death. Understandably frightened, for a long time the barber kept the secret, but eventually the task of holding everything in became too much for him. Compelled to tell someone, he went out to a cluster of reeds by the riverbank and told them, thinking that since they could not speak that he would be able to unburden himself and no one would know. A few days later, however, a man came and cut one of the reeds to make a pipe; and when he played the pipe it kept repeating the same song—"King Midas has goat's ears"—over and over again. Before long, everyone knew the king's secret.

The moral of the story is that no one can truly keep a secret. At some point the compulsion to speak, to unburden oneself, to confess, will become too strong to suppress. And in the end no one we tell will be able to keep the secret either. Even if we tell it to a bunch of reeds, the news will eventually spread.

Perhaps Eakins and his paintings are like the barber and the cluster of reeds. On the one hand, Eakins probably did not wish to tell a truth that was embarrassing and shameful. He was surely trying to conceal something about himself and his life—perhaps trying to conceal it even from himself. On the other hand, he was clearly moved by an urge to speak out and to reveal what was hurting him. Perhaps if we study his paintings closely, they can communicate like music through the repetition of certain notes—through patterns repeated so insistently that we can sense they bear some significant meaning. These patterns contain the clues to Eakins's secret. They are like the tune played with the pipes cut from the reeds.

PART TWO

LIFE AND ART

Thomas Eakins Leaning against Building, 1870–1876.
Albumen print, 10 9/16 x 5 15/16 in., courtesy of The
Pennsylvania Academy of the Fine Arts, Philadelphia,
Charles Bregler's Thomas Eakins Collection, purchased
with the partial support of the Pew Memorial Trust.

Chapter 9

AN AMERICAN IN PARIS

AS ALREADY NOTED, an important first step toward understanding Eakins's life and art is to recognize that Goodrich twisted what actually occurred. This sets the stage for the second: to go through Eakins's life stage by stage, searching for clues, both in documents and paintings, which reveal what his life and art were really like.

In describing Eakins's early life, Goodrich imposed two false patterns, one on Eakins's family experience and the other on his artistic development. With regard to his family life, Goodrich insisted that Eakins was nurtured in an unusually warm and loving household, and that he had a "normal" American childhood.[1] In fact, the Eakins household contained powerful tensions and disturbances. Discovering what they were makes it possible to understand the scandals that surrounded Eakins as an adult, as well as the air of foreboding that pervades his art. Families generally are skillful at hiding their dark secrets, but by going through the primary sources systematically, we can tease out a picture bit by bit.

In addition, Goodrich presented Eakins as a figure whose exceptional technical skill and depth of insight into the nature of things was apparent from his earliest childhood. In fact, the evidence suggests a fundamentally different pattern. Eakins decided to become a painter relatively late, without having shown a particular inclination toward art as a boy. He seems to have taken this course not out of personal conviction but largely because of pressure from his father. As a student in Paris, he had unusual difficulty learning to make competent paintings, and he left France abruptly, with no honors or awards, seemingly at a midpoint of his training. At the time he returned from France, aside from studies of the model, he had produced only one finished painting, which

Photographer unknown, Benjamin Eakins, ca. 1880-90.
Photogravure, 5 ½ x 9 ⁹⁄₁₆ in., courtesy of The Pennsylvania
Academy of the Fine arts, Philadelphia, Charles Bregler's
Thomas Eakins Collection, purchased with the partial
support of the Pew Memorial Trust.

was much less than fully successful. Of the many artists who traveled to Paris in the decade following the Civil War, Eakins's stay was among the shortest. Moreover, unlike most of his contemporaries, he never returned to Europe. Far from being a story of solid success, Eakins's story is one of slow, awkward development and persistent technical difficulties. His later accomplishments should be assessed against this background.

Thomas Eakins's grandfather, Benjamin's father, was an immigrant from Ireland who spelled his name "Akens." He worked as a weaver and subsistence farmer in Chester County, Pennsylvania, but did not own his own land. His few possessions at the time of his death were worth only a few hundred dollars.

Benjamin Eakins, the artist's father, left farming behind and moved from Chester County to Philadelphia in the early 1840s. There he took up a skilled trade, that of writing master—one who penned official documents and diplomas. He soon became prosperous through contracts with local schools and civic organizations. In 1850 he won the contract to letter diplomas for the Medical College of the University of Pennsylvania.[2] The family assisted with this work. In the spring of 1868, for example, Eakins's sister Fanny wrote to him in Paris apologizing that she had not written:

> For the past week we have had our house filled with diplomas and have had so much to do that I could not find time or space to write your letter last Sunday. I think that space was the most important for I might have written in the afternoon if I could only have had a table."[3]

This early introduction to the discipline of finely executed writing clearly played a major role in forming Eakins's artistic outlook. His paintings frequently feature writing implements, documents, graffiti, and inscriptions of various sorts.

Benjamin Eakins's occupation drew him into the community of printers, engravers, publishers, craftsmen, and artists who were associated with publishing. The most influential member of Philadelphia's artistic community through much of the nineteenth century was the British-born mezzotint engraver and publisher John Sartain, who produced and published reproductive prints of popular paintings by both European and American artists, and worked as a magazine editor and publisher. He was also the administrator for the Pennsylvania Academy and the Fine Arts Section of the 1876 Centennial Exhibition, and an active figure in numerous local arts organizations. The Eakins children grew up with those of Sartain, and Eakins's first documented girlfriend was Sartain's daughter, Emily. John Sartain's success was a powerful force in persuading Benjamin Eakins to push his son toward an artistic career. Eakins's future wife, Susan, was part of this same social group. She was the daughter of William Macdowell, who engraved diplomas, certificates, invitations, and banknotes, and did the lettering on prints by others, including some by John Sartain.

Benjamin Eakins supplemented his income from writing by teaching girls at a Quaker school. He then shrewdly invested his earning in railroads and real estate. While never a member of Philadelphia's upper crust, by the end of his life Benjamin was a prosperous landlord, who owned eight buildings in working-class sections of Philadelphia. In making these purchases, he seems to have sniffed out bargains. The family home, for example, was purchased from a sheriff's sale when the first owner went bankrupt. While most writers on Eakins would probably blanch at such direct language, it is surely accurate to describe Benjamin Eakins as a slumlord. He also had thousands of dollars in the bank, and owned tens of thousands of dollars of railroad stocks.

Writers on Eakins have often presented him as the embodiment of working-class virtues and as one who identified with "the common man." The truth is more complex. While the Eakins family had working-class origins, Eakins worked for only six of his seventy-two years, and was always dependent on his father's wealth. According to the reports of those who knew him, Eakins dismissed "the common man" as a "nincompoop."[4] He was suspicious of democracy, preferring a government of experts, since he viewed the average man as too stupid to govern for himself.

Our knowledge of Benjamin's personality comes largely from circumstantial evidence, since Eakins destroyed his letters and papers except one or two that survived by happenstance. These are curt and formal and reveal little about their author. Lloyd Goodrich has claimed that Benjamin was "much loved" by his neighbors. Sylvan Schendler has lauded Benjamin's "strength," "self knowledge," "emotional stability," "mature sense of reality," and even his "imagination." But there is slight evidence to support these claims. In fact, what we know of Benjamin suggests a figure who was stingy, autocratic, and rather cold about emotional matters. One of the most curious and revealing facts about him is that he did not allow the family to talk at meals—the one time when family members converse and communicate with one another.[5]

We get a disturbing reflection of Benjamin's personality in Eakins's letters. Eakins's letters from Paris vary greatly in tone according to the recipient—providing a clear picture of the personality traits he associated with each. The letters to his mother and his mother's sister (Aunt Ella) are somewhat pedestrian, focusing on the arrangement of furniture in his room and women's fashions. His letters to his youngest sister, Caddie, are extremely childlike. His letters to his sister Frances contain the most passionate passages about painting and artistic issues. The oddest letters, however, are those to his father, which are full of extremely judgmental statements and often contain a strain of almost pathological violence. As William Innes Homer has perceptively suggested, their judgmental and often nasty tone, which differs markedly from the one he employed with other members of his family, suggests that he was echoing and mimicking some aspect of his father's personality. Thus, for example, while on a walking tour of Switzerland, Eakins wrote to his father of Zermatt:

> The people are all cretins or only half cretins with the goiter on their necks. They live in the filthiest manner possible the lower apartment being privy & barn combined & they breed by incest altogether. Consequently goiters and cretins only. If I was a military conqueror & they came in my way I would burn every hovel & spare nobody for fear they would contaminate the rest of the world.[6]

Most letters written by American artists of this period focus on the picturesque beauties of Europe. I can think of no other document from an American painter that is even remotely similar to Eakins's statement, which contemplates gratuitously slaughtering all the peaceful inhabitants of an entire city. The letter demonstrates that while Eakins himself was one who often crossed boundaries, he was highly moralistic and judgmental, even prudish, in his attitude towards others.

What is more, the letter has a suggestive relationship to the scandals that would plague him later in life. The young man who deplored incest and filth in the most extravagant language would be accused of indecent sexual activities himself, and would be described as filthy in his language and conduct. In this respect Eakins's letter from Switzerland provides a clue of some sort, though a paradoxical one. It establishes that for some reason the ideas of excrement, incest, and unnatural sexual practices were embedded, and linked together, in his mind at an early date. If we wish to seek deeper causes for Eakins's outburst of anger, the context of his remarks is intriguing. As has been noted, violent remarks of this sort appear particularly in letters to his father; it follows that these concerns may have been connected with their relationship.

Central High School

We know nothing significant about Thomas Eakins's childhood, and little about his adolescence except that he attended Central High School, which seems to have left a lasting mark on his artistic thinking. This unique institution was geared toward producing engineers, and possessed a curriculum quite as arduous and demanding as any college of the time. A key element of the program was a rigorous course in mechanical drawing that had been established years before by the first principal of the school, Alexander Dallas Bache, in partnership with the painter Rembrandt Peale. The four-year course, which used Peale's best-selling manual *Graphics* as a text, was based on the theory that anyone could learn to draw if provided with proper instruction. Indeed, Peale assured readers that drawing was as simple as "writing the forms of objects."[7] The goal of such drawing was primarily practical. As the educator Horace Mann insisted: "Every man should be able to plot a field, to sketch a road or river, to draw the outlines of a simple machine, a piece of household furniture, or a farming utensil, or to delineate the internal arrangement or construction of a house."[8] Although Peale himself was a painter, the intent of this instruction was not to produce artists but successful businessmen and engineers.

Eakins attended this class three times a week for all of the eight terms he was enrolled at Central, and gradually progressed from simple exercises in writing and outline drawing to more difficult challenges, such as constructing ellipses and cycloids. By the last term students were drawing complex three-dimensional shapes, such as the icosahedron, in precise three-dimensional perspective, and also rendering machines and architectural structures in the same fashion.

Eakins seems to have been strongly influenced by this training, which reinforced the teaching in calligraphy that he had already received from his father. In addition, it affected Eakins's attitude toward art. He came to believe that truth resulted from accurate calculation, and his approach to art stressed diligence rather than genius or intuition. As Elizabeth Johns has noted, "Many of his paintings seemed to his sitters—and to us—like research projects."[9]

Several of Eakins's mechanical drawings survive. Typical is a drawing now in the collection of the Hirshhorn Museum, which shows a lathe that is tilted into gentle perspective to reveal as much of the working mechanism as possible without distortion. Notations in the lower left corner indicate the angle of the object, the distance of the object from the viewer, and the placement of the vanishing point. With this data, it would have been possible to take measurements off the drawing to produce an exact working replica of the machine. From a technical standpoint, perhaps the most interesting of these drawings is a pen-and-ink rendering of Thomas Crawford's statue of *Freedom*, which adorns the dome of the U.S. Capitol in Washington. Like the drawing of the lathe, the measurements are precise, and the gradations of light and shade are handled with great skill. In their way, these early drawings are remarkable—although of course what they reveal is a mechanical skill, of the sort that is often disparaged in the work of other American artists. An odd departure from these careful renderings is marginal sketch, on a drawing of gears, which shows a figure bending over and exposing his buttocks to us.

Perspective of a Lathe, 1860. *Pen and ink and watercolor on paper, 16 5/16 x 22 in., Hirshhorn Museum and Sculpture Garden, Smithsonian Institution, gift of Joseph H. Hirshhorn, 1966.* Eakins's perspective drawing of a lathe, made when he was sixteen, shows exceptional precision and a complete mastery of perspective.

Less than a year after graduation, Eakins applied for the position of drawing master at Central High School.[10] Of the twenty problems presented to the applicants who took the test, nineteen were problems in geometry. The twentieth required drawing for three hours from a cast of the classical sculpture known as the Laocoön. Eakins came in second in the competition and did not obtain the job.[11]

Although he graduated in the summer of 1861, Eakins did not leave for Europe to study painting

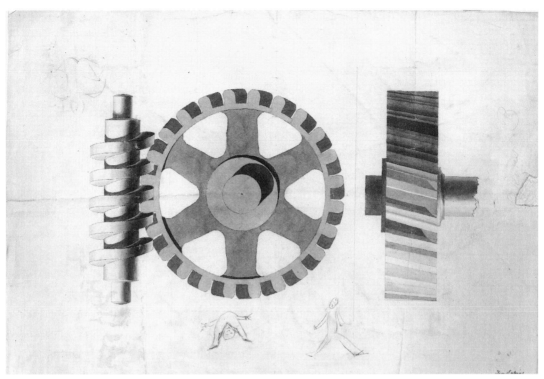

(Untitled) (Gears), ca. 1860. *Pen and ink, ink wash, and pencil on paper, 11 ⁷⁄₁₆ x 16 ⅞ in., Hirshhorn Museum and Sculpture Garden, Smithsonian Institution, gift of Joseph H. Hirshhorn, 1966.* Eakins adorned this drawing of gears with an odd sketch of a figure bending over and showing us his rear end.

until more than five years later, in September 1866. What he did in the interim is not well documented, but it appears that he was uncertain about what career he should pursue. In the Philadelphia Directory he is listed as a "teacher" and a "writing teacher," so it is likely he spent at least part of the time assisting his father with calligraphic projects.[12]

On October 7, 1862, Eakins enrolled in the Pennsylvania Academy to draw casts from the antique and attend lectures on anatomy. Five months later he was admitted to the life class.[13] Such training, however, was essentially informal. Aside from the anatomy lectures, there was no official teacher at the Academy to direct students until 1868. Many students supplemented their activities at the Academy with lessons and criticism from Philadelphia artists, such as Peter Rothermel and Christian Scheussele, although it is not clear whether Eakins did so. No life studies by Eakins survive from this period although we do have a portrait of him by Charles Fussell, showing him painting in the nude.[14]

Finally, we know that Eakins enrolled in an anatomy lecture course given by Dr. Joseph Pancoast and his son William at Jefferson Medical College. At this time medical training was still conducted through an apprenticeship system, and medical students learned their profession by attaching themselves to a physician rather than by attending a school. Eakins later told one of his sitters, Lucy Langdon, that he originally intended to become a doctor and did not begin painting until he went to Paris.[15] Most likely he was torn between art and medicine, and while he may have studied drawing, it appears that he did not work extensively in oil until he went to France. His wife told Lloyd Goodrich, when he asked her if Eakins had ever considered becoming a doctor, "He likely contemplated both professions."[16]

During this period most of Eakins's high school classmates enrolled in the Union Army, but Eakins did not: in August of 1864 he paid a fee to avoid conscription. Nonetheless, his sympathies appear to have been staunchly Unionist. (In a letter of 1866 from Paris he denounced a group of Copperheads—or Southern-sympathizing Democrats—as "ill-mannered blackguards.")[17] This avoidance may not have been Eakins's own preference. During this period Eakins seems to have dutifully followed his father's directives, and most likely Benjamin Eakins did not wish to risk losing his only son. Eakins's desire to avoid military service may account for his disappearance from the Philadelphia Directory in 1865, a time when his district was struggling to fulfill its quota of new recruits.[18]

Circumstantial evidence suggests that it was not Eakins himself, but his father who decided that he should go to Paris to receive professional training. John Sartain's success was surely a powerful force in persuading Benjamin to push his son toward an artistic career. Benjamin seems to have hoped that his son would pursue a vocation similar to his own, but to move a step higher in income and social status. Eakins himself seems to have been distressed to leave home, as is apparent from a somewhat melodramatic letter that he penned to Emily Sartain (and which he wrote in Spanish, a language they had studied together).

> Because I have a great need for consolation, I pray you, so that I may not die for lack of it, to have pity for my sorrow. I am departing not just from one friend, but from everyone. I am leaving my good father and my sweet mother, and shall go to some strange place . . . where there are no relatives, friends or friends of friends; and I go alone.[19]

Eakins's departure soon sparked an exclamation of surprise from an old family friend, Henry Huttner. "A few days since I received a letter bearing the post stamp of Paris," Huttner wrote to Benjamin Eakins. (Huttner was a German immigrant, and this is evident in his slightly awkward English.) "It aroused my curiosity very much, and when I opened it and found that my fellow correspondent was your Tom, I was so surprised that I could hardly believe my eyes." Huttner went on to recall, "How strong he always was opposed to going abroad before having seen thoroughly his native country."[20]

Away from Home

Paris was the logical place for an aspiring young American artist to go, since no school equivalent to the École des Beaux-Arts existed in the United States. Eakins or his father probably learned of the program through John Sartain, who had visited the École a few years earlier for guidance in reorganizing the Pennsylvania Academy, and cited the École as a model in his report. Eakins was relatively early in the flood of American artists to Paris, since foreign enrollment at the École des Beaux-Arts only became popular after the reform and reorganization of the school in 1863 by Count Nieuwerkerke. But Eakins was by no means unique or alone. In the year that Eakins embarked for Paris, four other students from Philadelphia did so also—Earl Shinn, Howard Roberts, Henry Bispham, and H. Humphrey Moore.

To enroll in the École he went through a considerable runaround with French bureaucrats, meeting successively with the secretary of the French School, Monsieur Lenoir; with the secretary of the American envoy, an obnoxious Colonel Hayes; and with the painter Jean-Léon Gérôme, who ceremoniously signed a letter allowing him to become a student. Yet the requisite paperwork did not appear allowing Eakins to start. Consequently (to quote the words of fellow student Earl Shinn) he pushed himself past "guard after guard with invincible determination and convenient misunderstanding of etiquette" until he finally gained entrance to the highest level of appeal, the office of the Minister of Fine Arts, Count Nieuwerkerke, who listened politely to his case."[21] Still not satisfied, he pushed his way in similar fashion into the offices of Monsieur Tournoi, a deputy minister of the Imperial Household, who notified Eakins that his admission papers had just been processed and that he had been accepted.

Shinn generously credited Eakins with gaining admission not only for him

Charles Reutlinger, Jean-Léon Gérôme, ca.
1867–1868. *Albumen carte-de-visite, Archives,
Pennsylvania Academy of the Fine Arts,
Philadelphia.* Eakins's teacher, Jean-Léon
Gérôme, specialized in precisely rendered
history paintings that often contain a
sadistic undercurrent.

but also for other American students, but in actual fact,
Eakins's brash maneuvers seem to have had no real
impact whatsoever. By the time he met with Count
Nieuwerkerke, the papers admitting the American students were already on their way, and if Eakins had simply
waited patiently the result would have been exactly the
same. Nonetheless, the episode brings out notable qualities of both stubbornness and subterfuge in Eakins's character. Eakins himself wrote home to his father that he felt
distressed by the deceptions he had employed, but that
"the end justified the means," and that "they were practiced on a hateful set of little vermin, uneducated except
in low cunning, who have all their lives perverted what little mind they had, [and] have not left one manly sentiment."[22]

While often cutting in his remarks about the people
he met, Eakins was also unusually susceptible to hero
worship. "I am delighted with Jerome," Eakins wrote to
his father on November 11, 1866, not yet having learned to
spell the master's name properly. "The often I see him the
more I like him."[23] In a later letter to his sister, Eakins
noted that Gérôme stood above other men "as man himself is raised above the swine." "He has made himself a
judge of men & insofar as a painter is a creator he creates new men or brings
back those you want to see . . . He makes people as they were as they are their
virtues their vices & the strongest characteristics of those he represents."[24]
"Who can paint men like my dear master, the living thinking acting men,
whose faces tell their life long story? Who ever has done so but him & who
will ever do it again like him."[25] Later in life, Eakins is said to have brought
Walt Whitman postcards of celebrated paintings by Gérôme, in order to eluci-
date the principles of great art.

Gérôme had started off as a leader of the Neo-Grecs, but soon came to
specialize in small-scale representations of ancient history or events from the
Near East. Many of his paintings contain a hint of sadism. For example, he
painted gladiators about to die in the arena, or Christians being thrown to the
lions (surrounded by the corpses of other martyrs, tied to stakes and covered
with pitch, who have just been burned to a frizzle). One of his most popular
paintings, *The Prisoner*, showed a shackled prisoner in a boat, being rowed to

prison or execution, tormented by his guards. At the time Eakins studied with him, Gérôme was at the peak of his success, and enjoyed the patronage of both the Empress Eugénie and the Princess Mathilde. His status was further enhanced by his marriage in 1863 to the daughter of Adolph Goupil, the most successful art dealer and publisher in the world, who turned his enterprise over to producing and distributing reproductions of Gérôme's paintings to a huge international audience.

Writers of the time referred repeatedly to the precision and science of Gérôme's pictures, and praised his extensive research. "The research for materials of a picture, which many find boring, interests Gérôme equally as much as the physical execution of a picture" wrote his pupil and biographer, Charles Moreau-Vauthier. "He often devotes months, even years to this pursuit. When he does not find what he wishes, he waits for it, with the patience of a hunter in his blind."[26] Gérôme's American biographer, Fanny Hering, also credited him with applying the methods of science to establish visual truth.[27]

Gérôme's icy clarity of color and design gave his work a dispassionate quality, to which he added a biting underlayer of irony and cynicism. He

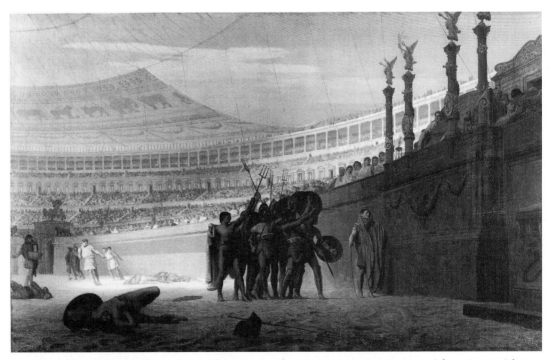

Jean-Léon Gérôme, Hail Caesar! We Who Are about to Die Salute You (Ave Caesar! Morituri te Salutant), 1859. Oil on canvas, 36 ⅝ x 57 ¼ in., Yale University Art Gallery, gift of Ruxton Love, Jr., B.A. 1925.

urged his students to pay close attention to the testimony of nature, *cette bonne mere,* and noted that too much attention to the old masters could stultify a young painter. When questioned about his rendition of *The Execution of Marshal Ney*, in which Ney's body lies face down in the mud in the foreground, Gérôme replied simply that he had endeavored to represent the episode "as I suppose it actually occurred."[28]

By all accounts, Gérôme was a patient and accommodating teacher, who was guarded in his compliments, but also led his students up slowly by degrees. "He constantly points out the truths of nature," one student observed, "and teaches that art can be attained only through increased perception and not through processes."[29]

Gérôme's teaching was entirely based on rendering the human figure. The students worked from the live model from eight o'clock until noon, five days a week. For the most part they worked from male models; female models were available only once every three or four weeks. The more advanced students sat closer to the model and were allowed to establish the pose. By the end of five days the student was expected to have a study, either drawn or painted, which was called an *academie* and which was judged by the master during his Saturday morning visits. Gérôme also visited the atelier on Wednesdays to view work in progress and make suggestions. The *academie* was judged on the basis of its precision and accuracy, which of course was difficult to achieve over a period of days, with a model whose pose was always slightly shifting.

Despite the elaborate regulations governing it, in practice the École was extremely informal, and the students learned to paint as much through trial and error as through instruction. Since Gérôme gave his critiques only once a week, the rest of the time there was a good deal of horseplay that made it difficult to concentrate. Indeed, Gerome's atelier was notoriously unruly and was "frequently closed for weeks at a time by the Administration in punishment for a disorder which became insufferable—hazing, singing, smashing easels, and other exhilarating exercises."[30] The painter Jean-Francois Raffaeilli, who became a friend of Degas and exhibited his work with the French Impressionists, later recalled that the other students were mostly "disgusting and vulgar."

> They chanted stupid obscenities. They invented ridiculous masquerades. Never in this gathering of men intending to become artists was there a discussion of art, a generous word, or an elevated idea. Never anything but stupid chatter, never anything but shit.[31]

Eakins, however, seems to have fit comfortably into this setting. In a letter home he observed that the other students were "an ill-mannered set when together, but easy to make friends with one at a time." One of Eakins's endearing traits is that he sometimes came to the defense of the unfortunate. At Gérôme's studio, for example, Eakins became the protector of his fellow student Humphrey Moore, a deaf mute from Philadelphia, and "begged [the students] not to amuse themselves at his expense."[32]

Eakins's Letters

The letters Eakins wrote from France provide important clues about his personality, since they are by far the largest body of his writing that exists. After he returned to the United States, he seldom wrote statements of more than a few paragraphs—generally only a few sentences. Thus, the French letters provide the only opportunity we have to "hear his voice," and to learn about the way he put thoughts together. In addition, the French letters often give his views on subjects, such as the goals of art, which Eakins never again discussed except in a perfunctory fashion. Over time his essential views changed surprisingly little, and thus the French letters provide clues to the thought process behind his artistic work, even later in his career.

The personality the letters reveal is an unusual one, at least for an artist. I have read many letters written by young American artists in France, and those by Eakins have an utterly different character and flavor than any other letters I have seen. What makes them unique is curiously difficult to articulate, but begins with their very grammar and diction, which in turn supplies clues to deeper levels of meaning. Eakins's letters do not have the literary or self-conscious quality that we find in the letters of other artists. They seem more like colloquial speech. A good many of the idioms seem to correspond to peculiarities of Pennsylvania speech, which gives the letters a regional, even provincial quality. While not written by a stupid man, the numerous errors of spelling and grammar are surprising from someone who had received an excellent education. (Appropriately, one of Eakins's few commercial illustrations, a design for *Scribner's Magazine*, showed a frustrated contestant at a spelling bee, who went berserk and murdered his rivals.)[33] Indeed, the colloquial idioms and grammatical mistakes suggest a conscious disregard for social niceties and an effort to stand apart from the leisure class.

Resentment toward upper-class swells surfaces quite frequently in Eakins's correspondence. On the trip over he noted that he avoided the first-class

"The Spelling Bee at Angell's," *Scribner's Magazine,* *November 1878.* **One of Eakins's rare magazine illustrations showed the frustrated loser of a spelling bee creating mayhem with his revolver.**

passengers, declaring, "A nastier looking set of young snobs I never saw in my life."[34] He described Howard Roberts, a fellow Philadelphian who was going to Paris to study sculpture, as "a rich disagreeable young man from Philadelphia."[35] When he met up in the summer of 1867 with a wealthy Philadelphian, Thomas L. Reese, he described him in a letter to his father as "the weakest minded stupidest little puke I ever saw in my life."[36]

On the other hand, Eakins often expressed admiration for people of lower-class origins who rudely elbowed their way to the top. For example, he expressed admiration for the sculptor Jean-Baptiste Carpeaux, who made a point of insulting upper-class people who crossed him. After mentioning the name of Carpeaux in one of his letters to his father, Eakins explained:

> He was the one that tapped the minister on the belly at the great dinner & motioned for the other boys not to fill themselves with the wine being given them, but ask for the bully little one he had in his glass. . . . He has an intense disgust for certain respects and proprieties. He was the man who called the Prince a damned little pig, because he wouldn't hold still while he was modeling him. But for all this he is in very high favor at court. . . . They can't afford to quarrel with such a man.[37]

Later, when Marianna Van Rensselaer, perhaps the most perceptive American art critic of the nineteenth century, who admired Eakins's work, visited him in Philadelphia, she was struck by his lack of sophistication about anything outside a narrow range of interests, and also by the lower-class quality of his manner and environment.

> He seems to understand his own aims and ideas & sort of work very well—as indeed, could hardly fail to be the case. But outside of that he is almost absurdly ignorant. He was not the clever man I had anticipated in any thing outside his immediate work. He & family were decidedly of the lower middle

class, I should say, & he himself a big ungainly young man, very untidy to say the least, in his dress—a man whom one would not be likely to ask to dinner, in spite of the respect one has for his work! [38]

Of course one can put this down to snobbery on Van Rensselaer's part, as some have done, but she was clearly responding to something different than mere background or degree of wealth. Augustus Saint-Gaudens, for example, was a shoemaker's son, but she had no qualms about inviting him to dinner, or admitting him into her inmost social circle. Saint-Gaudens, however, in the course of his study and work in Paris and New York, had developed a cosmopolitan and sophisticated outlook toward life. Eakins proudly clung to his lower-class origins and resisted new ideas and new influences.

Various explanations could be given for this narrow, self-satisfied outlook, but the simplest to my mind is that Eakins strongly identified with his father and with the framework of speech, manners, and outlook that dominated the family home. His father, while strikingly successful from a business standpoint, came from an extremely modest background. To put this in nineteenth-century language, he had risen from the lower class, and it appears that this was still reflected in his manner of speech and many aspects of his outlook. To an extraordinary degree, Eakins seems to have modeled himself on his father, rather than absorbing the mannerisms of his peers or the new social group in which he found himself. Physically, Eakins had traveled thousands of miles to Paris, but intellectually, he had never left home.

Indeed, this proud provincialism is echoed in the content of the letters themselves, which rate everything Eakins saw in Europe against what he knew in Philadelphia, generally judging it inferior. He made fun of the French for playing tennis, a game he had never seen, and which he considered "more stupid than cricket."[39] Even Lake Geneva struck him as inferior to its counterpart in Philadelphia. "Seneca Lake is better except that it has no Mont Blanc behind it."[40] "Things are all very different here from those at home more than anyone would suppose," he wrote shortly after his arrival. "The carriages, houses people animals, dresses everything. The ways of the people too are strange to me and so are those of the animals."[41]

He was largely unimpressed by the art that he saw. When he visited the Louvre he noted that while the marble statues "are much better than the miserable plaster imitations at Philadelphia," nonetheless, "I left right away. Statues make me shiver, they look so cold." He was equally unimpressed with the paintings. "There must have been half a mile of them, and I walked all the way from one end to the other, and I never in my life saw such funny old pictures." He concluded, with heavy-handed sarcasm: "I'm sure my taste has been much improved and to show it, I'll make it a point never to look hereafter on American Art except with disdain."[42]

On the other hand, when he saw American machinery at the Universal Exposition, it provided an occasion to discourse on the superiority of American things:

> The Locomotive is by far the finest there. I can't tell you how mean the best English, French and Belgian ones are alongside of it . . . One of the most amusing things in the American department is the soda water fountains. The foreigners above all the French have begun to taste the ice cream soda water and its fame has spread. No people will think of competing with the Americans for sewing machines.[43]

In fact, goings-on in Philadelphia continued to dominate Eakins's conversation throughout his stay in Paris. Earl Shinn reported that Eakins restricted his social conversation "pretty much to stories of the Schuylkill boating club."[44]

The Struggling Student

Contrary to the statements of most writers about him, Eakins was not an outstanding student. The French students at the École des Beaux-Arts competed in a series of *concours*, or competitions, leading up to the Prix de Rome, which awarded the winners four years of subsidized study at the French Academy in Rome. Foreign students were not eligible for the Prix de Rome, but all students were expected to participate. The task was to draw a study of the human figure in two six-hour sessions. Eakins seems to have competed just once in these contests, participating in the *concours des places* in March of 1867. He was not among the sixty-five students passed, although his friend Harry Moore placed fifty-ninth.[45] So far as is recorded, Eakins never took the examination again, although in theory students who did not do so after two years were supposed to be dismissed from the atelier. Despite his poor standing in the competition, not long after this examination Gérôme "at last told me I might get to painting and I commence Monday."[46] By April, Eakins was "working in color now and succeed in getting off some beastly things but hope to do better."[47]

By the end of Eakins's stay in France, most of the French students who had entered Gérôme's atelier when he did had already passed the *concours des places* and were competing for the Prix de Rome. Several of Eakins's American contemporaries, including Howard Helmick, Robert Wylie, Frederick Bridgman, and Mary Cassatt (who, being a woman, took private lessons from Gérôme) were beginning to show their work at the annual Salon. At this time, however, Eakins was still struggling to master the *ébauché*, a quick study of head and shoulders which was the first stage of learning to paint the model. While he struggled, Gérôme was patient but hardly effusive in praise. "The biggest compliment he ever paid me," Eakins wrote to his father, "was to say he saw a feeling for bigness in my modeling *(Il y a un sentiment de grandeur la dedans)* and sometimes he says 'There now, you are on the right track, now push.'"[48]

All of Eakins's surviving paintings from the *Ecole* fit into the category of *ébauché*. Eakins never seems to have developed the mastery to move to the final stage of student work, creating a careful full-length rendering of the model, in full color. Eakins's surviving sketchbook journal also suggests that he progressed only part way through the course of training. It focuses entirely on the painting and anatomy of the head and contains no comments on the painting of torso, limbs, arms, legs, hands, or feet.

Eakins was apparently self-conscious about his French work. He told Mrs. Van Rensselaer that he had destroyed all his academic studies, although this does not appear to have been the case.[49] Goodrich listed twelve paintings in his 1933 catalogue that he believed that Eakins had executed in Paris: two studies from the antique, a ram's head, and nine bust-length studies from male or female models. All these paintings were small, about eighteen by twelve inches in size. Five of these paintings have disappeared, including the ram's head and the antique studies, leaving seven *ébauchés*.

The painting by Eakins known as *The Strong Man* is typical of the group, and shows a model with his head in a three-quarter profile, holding a staff behind his head. Only the upper part of the torso has been finished. The palette is restricted to earth pigments. Because of the close cropping, there is little sense of the relationships among the different parts. The standard rule for these paint-

The Strong Man, ca. 1869. Oil on canvas, 21 ½ x 17 ⅝ in. *Philadelphia Museum of Art, gift of Mrs. Thomas Eakins and Miss Mary Adeline Williams.* **As a student in Paris, Eakins does not seem to have progressed to the point of making studies of the full figure. His surviving paintings show only details.**

ings was to paint shadows thinly and highlights thickly, giving each as much variety as possible. In the French method, one first blocked in the shadows and highlights, and then moved on to the halftones. Eakins's early stage in mastering this system is indicated by the fact that his painting displays strong contrasts of light and dark, but little in the way of halftones. What is striking about the piece is how broadly, indeed, how crudely, Eakins indicated the tonal relationships

Despite his admiration for his teacher, Eakins noted that the process of learning was essentially solitary:

> A teacher can do very little for a pupil and should only be thankful if he don't hinder him and the greater the master, mostly the less he can say. . . . Gérôme is too great to impose much, but aside his overthrowing completely the ideas I had got before at home, & then telling me one or two little things in drawing, he has never been able to assist me much & oftener bothered me by mistaking my troubles.[50]

One of Eakins's greatest problems seems to have been that his colors grew too muddy. Working harder on a painting only increased the problem. Toward the end of his stay in France, when felt he was making progress, he described his difficulties:

> How I suffered in my draftings & I would change again, make a fine drawing and rub weak sickly color on it & if my comrades or my teacher told me it was better, it almost drove me crazy & again I would go back to my old instinct & make frightful work again. It made me doubt of myself of my intelligence of everything & yet I thought things looked so beautiful & clean that I could not be mistaken. I think I tried every road possible. So, sometimes I took all advice, sometimes I shut my eyes & listened to none.[51]

As he explained:

> When you first commence painting everything is in a muddle. Even the commonest colors seem to have the devil in them. You see a thing more yellow, you put yellow in it, and it becomes only more gray when you tune it up. As you get on you get some difficulties out of the way, and what seems trying is that some of the things that gave you the greatest trouble were the easiest of all. As these difficulties decrease or are entirely put away, then you have more time to

look at the model and study, and your study becomes more regular and the works of other painters have an interest in showing you how they had the same troubles. I will push my study as far and as fast as I can, now I am sure if I can keep my health I will make better pictures than most in the exhibition.[52]

In a letter of September 1867 to his mother he noted that Gérôme had advised him to practice painting from brightly colored objects in order to learn color relationships. The strong contrasts made it easier to establish a scheme of color relationships.[53] Nonetheless, the handling of color continued to cause him difficulties. Even when Gérôme mixed colors for him in advance, Eakins found that he created "a devil of a muss and will get a good scolding tomorrow morning."[54] When Gérôme did see the result, however, he did not scold, but simply painted the head over, to Eakins's annoyance. "I am sure I would have learned more slathering around," he protested.[55]

In July and August 1868 Benjamin Eakins came to France with his daughter Frances. When they went to Eakins's studio both were surprised to discover that none of his paintings were "finished," although Eakins assured him that "that is lady's work." Frances reported "he thinks he understands something of color now, but says it was very discouraging at first, it was so hard to grasp."[56] Eakins's father was clearly distressed and wrote to his son in two letters. Eakins replied somewhat defensively in French:

> Indeed, I'm not yet a great painter. I've only been studying for two years. But I study with all the force and spirit which the good lord has given me and am making progress equal to the others.[57]

As he had with Frances, he tried to convince his father that finishing was not important. As he wrote:

> There's a common mistake made by those who do not know drawing & that is that one should have the habit of finishing studies. That is a great mistake. You work at a thing only to assure yourself of the principle you are working on & the moment you satisfy yourself you quit it for another . . . Gérôme tells us every day that finish is nothing that head work is all. . . . He calls finished needlework & embroidery and ladies work to deride us.[58]

Shortly after his father left, Eakins wrote that his studies were going well and that he was "able to paint from life better." He also announced that he planned "to give a great deal more of my time to composition, working only after nature during school hours."[59] After a brief walking tour of Switzerland in August of 1867, Eakins returned to Paris in early September and took a studio at 64 rue de l'Ouest near Montparnasse. "The studio will enable me to commence to practice composing & to paint out of school which I could not before. . . . As soon as I can get knowledge enough to enable me to paint quickly I will make pictures, but I have been only 4 months at the brush and can't do it yet."[60]

By January 1868, Eakins reported that he was "working from memory now and composing," although it is not clear what he meant by that. In fact, he still seems to have been focusing on studies of the nude model.

> When after painting a model I paint it from memory and then go back and do it again I see that the second time I would not have seen if I had staid at school painting on the same canvas all the week and maybe getting more and more tired . . . One consolation is that I am composing, it was hard to begin. I felt I ought to know more, but now I am hard at it and whatever I can gain in it, is straight towards making a selling picture.[61]

In many of these letters his desire to please his father surfaces, as well as his anxiety about whether he has been worthy of his father's financial sacrifices.

> God speed the day that I can stop my studies long enough to paint a good picture and relieve you of your share of an anxiety which should really all be mine, which in depression is harder than death to bear but which disappears in the joy of every progress felt or discovery made.[62]

When his father expressed disapproval, Eakins was devastated:

> Your last two letters though intended to encourage me to keep working could not but dispirit me a little by showing me you were fearing perhaps that I was not in the right path or had stopped working or some such idea. I am working as hard as I can & have always . . . I have made progress and can equal the work of some of the big painters done when they had only been studying as long as I have & as far as I have one I see in their work that they have had the same troubles that I had had & the troubles are not few in painting.[63]

A common theme is that he is learning to make paintings that will be salable, and that will justify his father's financial sacrifices.

If I live & keep my good health I am certain now of one thing that is to paint what I can see before me better than the namby pamby fashion painters. Whether or not I will afterwards find poetical subjects & compositions like Raphael remains to be seen, but Gérôme says the trade part must be learned first. But with or without that I will paint well enough to earn a good living & become even rich."[64]

In another letter he boasted:

One terrible anxiety is off my mind. I will never have to give up painting, for even now I could paint heads good enough to make a living anywhere in America. I hope not to be a drag on you a great while longer. I tried to make a long letter of this and it has been troubling me some time but I can't think of any more to say. All I can do is work.[65]

Or again, In March of 1868 Eakins wrote to his father:

I am less worried about my painting now than at one time last spring & consequently am in better order to study . . . I see color & think I am going to learn to put it on. I am getting on faster than many of my fellow students and could even now earn a respectable living I think in America painting heads.[66]

Eakins's reiteration of this theme is poignant, for he would never make enough income from his painting to support himself.

Along with painting, Eakins was interested in sculpture. (He particularly admired the work of Jean-Baptiste Carpeaux. In a letter home he declared that Carpeaux "probably models now better than any one in the world.")[67] In March 1868, when Gérôme was traveling in the Near East, Eakins officially transferred to the atelier of the sculptor Augustin Dumont. He probably studied with him only three months, since the spring semester ended in June, and by the next fall he was back with Gérôme. Dumont was then sixty-seven years old, and Eakins described him as "a stout old gentlemen, much older than Gérôme," adding that he was "like a father to us."[68]

Artistic Fathers

Curiously, Eakins's manner of paint handling never resembled that of Gérôme, the artist he seems to have most profoundly admired. Gérôme

Thomas Couture, The Little Confectioner (Petit Gille), *ca. 1878. Oil on canvas, 21 ½ x 25 ¾ in., Philadelphia Museum of Art, William L. Elkins Collection.* **While he studied with Gérôme, Eakins preferred the loose paint-handling he found in the work of Thomas Couture.**

worked down his canvas from the upper left hand corner, gradually stitching together the forms with fine, smooth brushstrokes. Eakins always worked more impulsively, almost randomly across the surface, with thick, crusted pigments. Eakins seems to have had two models for this approach: the work of Thomas Couture and that of Leon Bonnat.

In the 1840s, Couture burst into the French art world with a bold, spontaneous manner of paint handling, loosely based on that of the Venetians. Couture's trick was to work on a toned ground that he left bare as a middle tone. This allowed him to quickly lay in the lights and shadows with flickering brushstrokes. The method encouraged a sketchy approach since at whatever point one stopped the image looked finished. The signature of Couture's method is that he allowed some of the ground to show through in the finished picture—a trick that Eakins often employed.

Eakins praised Couture in several of his letters. One of the most passionate of Eakins's passages about painting concerned the work of Couture. "What a grand talent," he wrote. "He is the Phidias of painting & drawing. Who that has ever looked in a girl's eyes or run his fingers through her soft hair or smoothed her cheek with his hand or kissed her lips or their corners that plexus of all that is beautiful in modeling must love Couture for having shown us nature again & beauty on canvas."[69] On another occasion Eakins included Couture's name among those of the "greatest men in the world" whom he had been privileged to know.[70] In some fashion, Eakins seems to have conceived Couture as a counterbalance to Gérôme, whom he admired for his sense of solidity and structure, but not for his paint handling. In one of his notebooks, Eakins noted, somewhat curiously, "Gérôme always makes me think of Couture, they are so different."[71]

Eakins learned about Couture's methods not by studying directly with him but by purchasing his book. Soon after he arrived in Paris, Eakins acquired a copy of Couture's recently published manual, *Entretien sur l'atelier*, and he acquired a second copy early in 1868 for William Sartain, sending it to Philadelphia with the comment that the text was "curious & very interesting."[72]

Eakins was also influenced by the painter Léon Bonnat, who had made his debut at the Salon of 1857 when he was only twenty-four. Bonnat was raised in Spain and studied with Federico Madrazo in Madrid before moving to Paris. His work introduced Spanish effects into French art, such as broad brushwork and strong tonal contrasts. Bonnat executed paintings with a coarse, rough-hewn brushstroke and had no compunction about showing both saints and sinners at their most human. "He used a lot of paint," his student Edwin Blashfield recalled of Bonnat. "'Close your eyes' was his formula for shutting out unnecessary details of modeling."[73] Although a friend of Gérôme, Bonnat was considerably more liberal in his sympathies, and gently supported figures such as Courbet, Manet, and Degas.

During the summer of 1869, Eakins studied with Bonnat for about a month. Interestingly, he did not respond as powerfully to Bonnat as a person as he did to Gérôme, and never referred to him with the same kind of adulation. Eakins was frustrated that Bonnat seemed to have no system, and did not care if his pupils started with a drawing or simply began directly applying pigment to the canvas. "Bonnat is the most timid man I ever saw in my life & has trouble to join three words together. If you ask him the simplest question about what he thinks is the best way to do a thing, he won't tell you. He says to do it just as you like."[74] Nonetheless, while Eakins wrote admiringly of Gérôme and critically of Bonnat, his own paintings are much closer to the latter.[75]

Ferdinand Mulnier, Léon Bonnat, ca. 1868. Albumen carte-de-visite, collection of Daniel W. Dietrich II.

An Abrupt Return

Not long after his study with Bonnat, Eakins decided to return home, a decision he announced to his father in a letter of November 5, 1869. In this letter

Eakins declared, "what I have come to France for is accomplished." In another letter, written shortly afterward, he boasted "I am as strong as any of Gérôme's pupils and have nothing now to gain by remaining."[76] Essentially, Eakins seems to have decided that he had reached a point where he could progress most rapidly on his own. As he declared in a letter of autumn 1869:

> It is bad to stay at school after being advanced as far as I am. The French boys sometimes do and learn to make wonderful fine studies, but I notice those who make such studies seldom make good pictures, for to make these wonderful studies, they must make it their special trade, almost must stop learning and pay all their attention to what they are putting on the canvas rather than in their heads and their business becomes a different one from the painter who paints better even a study if he takes his time to it, than those who work in the schools to show off to catch a medal, to please a professor or catch the prize of Rome.[77]

Writers on Eakins's stay in Paris have not commented on the surprising fact that he decided to return to the United States at a point when his training was still incomplete. Nearly all American artists who went to Paris concluded their study by exhibiting at the Salon, and even many of the most modest talents won awards there before returning home. Eakins not only did not exhibit at the Salon but never passed an examination. His surviving French work suggests that he was at an early stage of study. If he had proceeded through the whole program of training, passing exams, learning to paint the full figure, and submitting a painting to the salon, Eakins would surely have needed to stay in France for another two or three years.

Why did he suddenly decide to come home at this juncture? Several reasons might be proposed: that he was homesick; that he felt guilty about being a financial burden to his father; or that he felt he'd had enough academic training. All might apply to some extent, but in addition, another even more compelling reason may be proposed. By this time Eakins had surely learned that his mother was seriously ill. By cutting short his study he could come home to assist his father and sisters in caring for her. It is true that Eakins did not rush home immediately, but spent several months in Spain before returning. This would make sense, however, if we suppose that he was eager to produce a finished painting for his father, to demonstrate that he had learned to paint with professional skill, and to justify the money that his father had invested in him.

The notion that Eakins may have returned from Paris to care for his mother may also explain a second mystery. When Lloyd Goodrich compiled his first monograph on Eakins, Susan Eakins did not allow him to view Eakins's letters from Paris. Instead, she laboriously copied long passages from them, word for word, and allowed him to use these transcriptions. Many of these passages were taken from letters that are no longer extant. No one has ever speculated about Susan's reasons for this procedure, but the logical deduction is that there was something in the letters that she did not wish Goodrich to see. What this could have been will never be known with certainty, but one possibility is that some of the letters discussed the mental illness of Eakins's mother, and that Susan did not want this information to come to light. This would reflect a consistent pattern of behavior on her part, since we know that she also withheld from Goodrich two other episodes of mental illness associated with Eakins's life—the madness of Lillian Hammitt and the mental breakdown and suicide of Ella Crowell.

Léon Bonnat, Mary Sears (later Mrs. Francis Shaw), *1878. Oil on canvas, 49 ¾ x 29 ½ in., Museum of Fine Arts, Boston, gift of Miss Clara Endicott Sears © Museum of Fine Arts, Boston.* **Eakins's mature portraits have many qualities in common with those of Léon Bonnat, who taught him free paint handling and introduced him to Spanish painting.**

A Spanish Interlude

Before returning to the United States, Eakins decided to make a trip to Spain, both to see Spanish painting and to make his first effort at a true figure composition. Remarkably, up to this point Eakins appears to have only made exercises, sketches, and studies, mostly of the human figure. He had never attempted to compose and create an original picture.[78]

The fact that Eakins chose Spain indicates that he was responding to a major shift in taste, away from the idealism of Ingres to the realism of Couture, Bonnat, and Courbet. Back in the 1840s, young artists came to Paris to learn to paint like the Italian masters—above all, Raphael. By the time Eakins finished his training in Paris, however, Spanish painting had begun to replace Italian art as the most important influence for young artists. Admiration for Spanish painting dated back to the time of Napoleon's occupation of the Spanish peninsula, but came to dominate advanced French painting only in the 1860s. Carolus-Duran, for example, spent two years, from 1866 to 1868, copying works in Spanish collections. In 1867 the young prodigy, Henri Regnault, cut short his residence at the French Academy in Rome to visit Madrid. John Singer Sargent, like Eakins, chose to mark the end of his student period with a trip to Spain. Edouard Manet began to emulate Spanish art at around this time. Just how and why Eakins became enamored of Spain is not entirely clear, since many influences could have pushed him in this direction, even Gérôme.[79] Most likely, however, Eakins learned about Spain through Bonnat, who was of Basque descent, was born in the Pyrenees, had studied in Madrid, and produced paintings that were strongly Spanish in effect and often directly echoed masters such as Velázquez and Ribera.[80]

In November 1869 Eakins informed his father that he was going to Spain and planned to look at pictures in Madrid and then proceed to Seville.[81] In Madrid he does not seem to have painted, but spent several weeks looking closely at the paintings in the Prado. He had never seen major Spanish paintings before and found the somber realism of the Spanish school very much to his liking. The day after arriving in Madrid, Eakins wrote home to his father:

> I have seen big painting here. When I look at all the paintings by all the masters I had known I could not help saying to myself all the time, its very pretty but its not all yet. It ought to be better, but now I have seen what I always thought ought to have been done and what did not seem to me impossible. O what a satisfaction it gave me to see the good Spanish work, so strong, so reasonable, so free of every affectation. It stands out like nature itself.[82]

This introduction to Spanish work reinforced his instinct that he should handle paint in a different fashion than Gérôme. As Eakins scribbled in his notebook:

> It made me decide to never paint like my master [Gérôme]. One could hardly hope to be stronger than him, and he is so far from painting like Ribera or Velasquez as he himself is above an amateur.[83]

From Madrid, Eakins went on to Seville, arriving on December 4 and spending the next five months there. In January he was joined by Harry Moore and William Sartain, for whom the interlude in Seville marked the real beginning of their professional careers. Both spent the rest of their lives painting picturesque Spanish scenes. Eakins never became so attached to Spanish subject matter, but for him also this marked a professional turning point: this was the first time that he had attempted to produce something more ambitious than a student exercise. Two works survive from this period: a study of a young model, Carmelita Requena, and a more ambitious composition of Carmelita and two other figures, performing music in front of a stucco wall.

Eakins's little portrait of Carmelita shows her silhouetted against a neutral brown background that is also used as the color for the shadows. While the picture is appealing, Eakins's struggle with technical matters is evident. The intense red and blue of Carmelita's jacket give no sense of its texture and contrasts abruptly with the careful, delicate blending of colors on her flesh. The shadows are muddy, and Eakins lost all sense of anatomy in the rendering of Carmelita's shoulder and chest. One would also never

Carmelita Requena, 1869. *Oil on canvas, 21 ¹⁄₁₆ x 17 ⅛ in., Metropolitan Museum of Art, bequest of Mary C. Fosburgh, 1978.* **Carmelita Requena was only seven but looks older in Eakins's portrait.**

guess that Carmelita was only seven years old. In Eakins's rendering she might be in her twenties.

Shortly after completing this piece, Eakins started a more ambitious figure composition. His difficulties with this painting are recorded in his letters. On Christmas of 1869 he announced that he was starting to paint:

Something unforeseen may occur & my pictures may be failures, these first ones. I cannot make a picture fast yet. I want experience in my calculations. Sometimes I do a thing too soon & I have to do it all over again. Sometimes it takes me longer to do a thing than I thought it would & that interferes with something ahead & I have a good many botherations but I am sure I am on the right road to good work & that is better than being far in a bad road. I am perfectly comfortable, have every facility for work, especially sunshine, roof & beautiful models, good-natured people desirous of pleasing me. If I get through with what I'm at, I want a few weeks of morning sunlight. Then I will make a bullfighter & maybe a gypsy one.[84]

On January 26, 1870, Eakins announced to his father that he had started "the most difficult kind of picture, making studies in sunlight." The proprietor of Eakins's pension had given him permission to work on the roof "where we can study right in the sun."[85] By March he was still laboring on the same painting.

> The trouble of making a picture for the first time is something frightful. You are thrown off the track by the most contemptible little things that you never thought of & then there are your calculations all to the devil & your paint is wet & it dries slow, just to spite you, in the spot where you are most hurried.[86]

In a subsequent letter he noted:

> If all the work I have put in my picture could have been straight work I could have had a hundred pictures at least, but I had to change & bother, paint in and out . . . Picture-making is new to me. There is the sun & gay colors & a hundred things you never see in a studio light and ever so many botherations that no one out of the trade could guess at.[87]

> My want of experience in picture making has made me lose weeks of time, but I am not in the least disheartened, as your last letter feared. I will know better how to go about another one.[88]

He worked on the painting for more than three months, from at least January 26 (by which time he had started it) until April 28, when he finally announced that it was finished. Eakins confessed that it was "an ordinary sort of picture" although he maintained that it contained "good things here and there so that a painter can see it is at least earnest clumsiness."[89] Eakins noted that he had "many more things to attend to" than in making an academic study. "Sometimes I have put down good steady work & then found it did not gee with something more important, & it all had to be painted over again & in painting every alteration you make does great harm."[90]

The models for the painting were Carmelita and her brother and sister. Eakins showed the three musicians against a wall: a young man, blowing a trumpet, a young woman banging a drum, and a small girl dancing with castanets. In the background, on the left, an older woman, with a small child in her arms, looks out from a barred window. At the lower left we can see the

A Street Scene in Seville, 1870. *Oil on canvas, 62 ¾ × 42 in., courtesy of Mr. and Mrs. Erving Wolf.*
Eakins struggled for months on his first painting. Three children perform on the street while
a mother and a baby look out a barred window on the left.

shadows of some invisible spectators. A graffito of a bullfight decorates the wall behind the performers. At the upper right we glimpse another house, blue sky, and a palm tree.

The general subject of the painting relates to renderings of street musicians by both Gérôme and Couture. Eakins's painting, however, again reveals serious technical difficulties. The drawing is weak and the composition unfocused. Eakins intended to spotlight the figures with strong sunlight. But as a result the background wall is completely in shadow and becomes a flat expanse into which the figures dissolve and disappear. At some point, Eakins substantially repainted the patch of sunlit blue sky and the yellow brick building beyond the wall, evidently attempting to balance to the accent of sunlight that falls on Carmelita. Unfortunately, however, this area is too bright, and in the end only adds to the spatial confusion of the design.

But for all its awkwardness—perhaps even because of its awkwardness—the painting conveys an odd sense of emotional urgency, strangely at odds with its rather conventional subject. It seems to be charged with some sort of personal message or meaning, though of a cryptic sort. In fact, this painting follows a pattern that, as we shall see, appears in much of Eakins's later work—namely that the subject seems to echo the dynamics of his own family. In this instance, the age, number, sex, and grouping of the figures closely match with Eakins and his siblings, around the time that he left for Europe. In other words, the young man can be seen as a stand-in for Eakins, the drumming girl for his sister Frances, and the dancing girl for his sister Margaret. The figures in the window correspond with Eakins's mother and his very much younger sister Caroline.

The setting, with its odd juxtaposition of levels, and its ambiguity about whether we are outside or within a courtyard, makes one think of the Eakins home. Specifically, it suggests the courtyard that runs alongside the house and connects with the street.

If we accept the idea that the painting alludes to Eakins's family, then two things become particularly intriguing—the position of the mother, and the absence of a father. The woman appears as a shut-in, imprisoned in the house, as seems to have been the case with Eakins's mother. The father is not visible, although he is indirectly evoked by the writing on the wall (he was, after all, a writing master). Eakins's father seems to have been an emotionally distant figure, who was preoccupied with his writing and the management of his rental properties, and spent much of his time out of the family's sight. What could be more appropriate than to represent him by the art form he practiced, rather than a physical presence? Is it going too far to note that the writing stands beside a graffito of a bullfight? Bulls, of course, are classic symbols of masculinity, both in martial and sexual terms. To place a bull that will be publicly slaughtered in this place thus hints at an element of Oedipal conflict.

An intriguing final element is the audience to the scene, who are represented only through their shadows on the left. The theme of an audience of spectators looking at something personal and intimate is a motif that appears in many of Eakins's later paintings, notably his representations of anatomical operations and boxing matches. The implied but unseen audience for the musicians provides a foreshadowing of this theme.

At the Piano (Frances and Margaret Eakins), ca. 1871. *Oil on canvas on masonite, 55.9 x 45.7 cm., Jack S. Blanton Museum of Art, the University of Texas at Austin, gift of Carolina Crowell, M.D., 1964.* Frances plays the piano while Eakins's second sister, Margaret, stands listening.

Chapter 10

ALL IN THE FAMILY

THE TRADITIONAL VIEW of Eakins portrays him as an artist who returned
to the United States as a "consummate draftsman" and master technician,
who had thoroughly absorbed the lessons of his French teachers. The opposite would be closer to the truth. At the time he returned to the United States
in June 1870, Eakins had not progressed far in his studies, had not impressed
his teachers, had not passed his exams, and had not shown in the Salon, as
most Americans did before they returned home.

The only finished painting he had made, *A Street Scene in Seville*, 1870, had
not come out as well as he had hoped. Eakins himself confessed, in a note to
himself, that it was "an ordinary sort of Picture" and "earnest clumsiness."[1]
Unfortunately, we have no record of what Eakins's father thought of the
piece—or what he thought of any of Eakins's works.[2] But the fact that Eakins
never exhibited the canvas suggests that he recognized that it was less than a
triumph.

What is remarkable is how quickly Eakins moved to a higher level of
accomplishment after his return to the United States. Within a year he had
completed one of his most complex works, *The Champion Single Sculls*, which
displays a level of skill in both drawing and paint handling that few American
artists have ever equaled.[3] Within five years he had painted *The Gross Clinic*,
one of the most complex figure compositions every executed in America.
Judged purely as a technical feat, it reveals an astonishing ability to portray the
human body from unusual angles. What lies between the Spanish painting
and these early masterpieces is a group of paintings of friends and family
members in which Eakins painfully pushed himself toward technical mastery.
As we trace the progression of these paintings, we can observe Eakins's

improvement step by step. In addition, for the first time we can begin to sense the enigmatic and ominous emotional qualities that make Eakins's paintings so unusual, and have established him as a unique and somewhat perplexing figure in nineteenth-century American art.

Eakins's first paintings after his return from Europe represented young women—his sisters, Frances, Margaret, and Caroline, as well as two family friends, Elizabeth and Kathrin Crowell. The Crowells were "almost family" because of impending relationships of marriage. Eakins was engaged to Kathrin, while his sister Frances, the eldest of his three sisters, was engaged to her brother Will, who had been Eakins's classmate at Central High School.

Eakins most likely began with two renderings of his sister Frances playing the piano. The one that seems to have come first, *Frances Eakins* shows Frances alone. The second, *At the Piano* shows Frances joined by Margaret, who stands beside the piano listening. Both paintings show Eakins struggling for depth of color without allowing the effect to grow muddy. For some reason, however, enlarging the design and adding a second figure caused difficulties, and the second painting is much more awkward than the first. Eakins probably then moved on to the most accomplished work of this piano-playing series, *Home Scene*, which was clearly made just afterward. In this case Frances does not appear. The painting shows Margaret at the piano, with the baby of the family, Caroline, lying on the floor.

Eakins's inexperience as a painter is very evident in these paintings, particularly the earlier ones, which sometimes are so dark that the figures merge with the background and become almost indistinguishable from it. No doubt Edward Hopper had some of these early works in mind when he commented of Eakins: "His paintings are so dark, it is a disadvantage."[4] If we follow Eakins's development from painting to painting, however, we can see how he gradually mastered this problem, achieving work

Frances Eakins, ca. 1870. *Oil on canvas, 24 x 20 in., The Nelson-Atkins Museum of Art, Kansas City, Missouri (Purchase: Nelson Trust).* **Eakins's first paintings after his return from France show his eldest sister Frances at the piano.**

that retains a rich sense of mystery in the darks but also allows us to make out the action of the figures.

While Eakins is generally described as a "realist," in many respects these paintings conjure up a world that is dreamlike and mysterious. They show figures in extremely dark interiors, whose features are defined by light that comes from nowhere—light that illuminates people and objects almost at random. Eakins's paint handling also has an arbitrary character. In *Home Scene*, for example, the music on the piano is rendered so carefully that we can read the individual notes, but a seemingly more important portion of the painting, Margaret's right hand and the kitten on her shoulder, are blurry smudges. To the extent that there is a pattern to these decisions, Eakins slurs over precisely those portions of a painting that most artists would make clear—those sections, that is, that clarify the interaction of figures, or that allow us to read the meaning of an expression.

As several writers have noted, Eakins's musical paintings focus on home and family. Music was an important accomplishment for Victorian women. It provided an emotional center for home life, and played a significant role in courtship. The instrument Eakins portrayed, the piano, had particularly strong familial connotations. Because it was expensive it was an important symbol of bourgeois prosperity. Because it was heavy and difficult to move, it effectively symbolized the stability and security of the home.

Yet Eakins's paintings seem to communicate something more complicated than that Eakins loved his family, as Lloyd Goodrich tells us, or that he loved music, as Elizabeth Johns documents. Something more troubling appears to be taking place, for these are not happy pictures. None of the figures smile. The curious darkness of these paintings, and the way the forms disappear into muddy, impenetrable shadows, gives them an anxious quality and hints that all is not right.

Several writers, in fact, have commented on the ominous mood of these painting, despite their ostensibly conventional and peaceful subject matter. Rodrigo Moynihan, for example, has declared that *Home Scene* exudes "a Balthus-like strangeness with a sense of something happening but not directly stated."[5] Similarly, James Fosburgh has described the same painting as "curiously disturbing and fascinating," and as "uncomfortable." He concludes: "What this young woman and this child may mean to each other, we may only hazard a guess, but the inner tensions—self-preoccupation and inevitable solitariness—are unmistakable."[6] He also observes that with Eakins, "The doctrines of significant form and formal analysis will not help us . . . Indeed,

J. G. Brown, The Music Lesson, 1870. *Oil on canvas, 24 x 20 in.,*
Metropolitan Museum of Art, gift of Colonel Charles A. Fowler,
1921. J. G. Brown's painting of a music lesson sums up what
19th-century viewers expected in the treatment of such a
subject and what Eakins did not deliver: sentimental
anecdote.

his composition has often been called
weak and even clumsy."[7] In other words,
Eakins's paintings seem to depend for their
power not simply on form but on a mysterious psychological quality.

The degree to which Eakins's portrayal
of his sisters diverged from conventional
imagery becomes apparent when we compare his early music paintings with a rendering of a musical scene by J. G. Brown,
painted in the very same year (1870) that
Eakins began his piano-playing series.
Brown's painting shows a well-dressed
young man and woman playing a flute in a
comfortable, well-furnished, middle-class
interior. Compared to Eakins's painting,
Brown's is clear and readable, both in the
way it portrays people and objects and in
the way in which these elements connect
with each other to tell a coherent story.
The room is clearly illuminated, so that
every element of middle-class prosperity,
from the lace curtains to the flower stand
and gold picture frames, can be savored and enjoyed. The figures are attractive—at least according to Victorian standards of taste, which favored figures
somewhat shorter and plumper than would be the ideal today. They are also
well dressed—the man with coat, tie, vest, and well-shined shoes, and the
young lady in a fashionable but not too flamboyant ruffled dress.

Perhaps most significantly, Brown's painting stresses the interaction of the
two figures, and the romantic feeling that is developing between them. The
young woman appears to have abandoned her harp (which rests to her left)
and has shifted her position to come closer to the flute player. In a gesture
that to a modern view is embarrassingly suggestive, she is blowing on the
mouthpiece of his flute while he fingers the keys to control the note. In fact,
Brown's original title stressed the element of collaboration between the figures. While known today as *The Music Lesson*, Brown titled the painting *A*
Game Two Can Play At.[8]

Brown's painting clearly fulfilled the expectations of a middle-class Victorian audience and provides a kind of inventory of everything that Eakins's paintings of music are not. Whereas Brown's figures are shown in the most flattering possible light, Eakins did not shrink from recording the physical oddities of the people he portrayed, whether his sister Frances's large nose, or the surprisingly masculine features of his sister Margaret. Whereas Brown's painting places the drama of the episode in the center of the painting, and the meaning of everything can be clearly understood, Eakins's paintings seem to hint at something that is happening that we do not fully understand. Whereas Brown's figures happily relate to each other, Eakins's figures seem pensive and isolated. Brown's painting is cheerful, almost sugary in feeling. Eakins's paintings are solemn, even tragic. In short, Eakins's paintings depart from the norm of nineteenth-century American genre painting, in ways that cry out for an explanation.

In mystery solving, clues can take the form of tangible evidence, such as a footprint or a fiber, but they also may take the form of something that one would expect to be present but which is not there—like the dog that didn't bark in the night, in the Sherlock Holmes story *Silver Blaze*. There are two ways in which we can move toward an understanding of Eakins's paintings. One is to ask what is missing from these images? The other is to ask what was happening in his life that would imbue simple paintings of his sisters playing the piano with such an ominous quality? Both questions lead to the same answer.

The missing element is Eakins's mother, and what was happening at this time is that she was going insane. Goodrich notes of Eakins's early canvases that "every picture was part of his daily life."[9] In exploring the meaning of these early works, however, he studiously avoided any mention of what was surely the most significant occurrence in Eakins's life at this time, his mother's mental illness and death. Once we take this into account, we come to a new understanding of Eakins's work of this period, and its enigmatic quality of sadness. Eakins repeatedly painted and photographed his sisters and his father, but one member of the family remains almost invisible—the one most central to generating a family in the first place. We have virtually no record of Eakins's mother. What little we do have is strangely unrevealing, as if screening something too painful to explore.

Eakins never made a single recorded statement about his mother. None of her letters survive, and Eakins's letters to her are emotionally distant and filled with descriptions of ordinary things—they might almost have been written to a stranger. Goodrich said almost nothing about her in his 1933 monograph,

A.P. Beecher, Caroline Cowperthwait Eakins, *1863–1869. Albumen carte-de-visite (before conservation), 3 x 4 in., courtesy of The Pennsylvania Academy of the Fine Arts, Philadelphia, Charles Bregler's Thomas Eakins Collection, purchased with the partial support of the Pew Memorial Trust.*

noting only that she had "a face full of character, in which one divines a capacity for strong feeling."[10] Like much of Goodrich's book, these phrases appear to have been a euphemism for a truth that he must have known was dark and uncomfortable.

Eakins's mother died on June 4, 1872, at the age of fifty-two, almost exactly two years after her son's return from Europe. Her death certificate declares that she died of "exhaustion" following "mania."[11] The attending physician was associated with the Philadelphia Hospital for the Insane. Despite the brevity of this statement, writers on Eakins, from Goodrich on, have all agreed that Eakins's mother suffered from bipolar disorder, or manic-depressive illness. The term "exhaustion" leaves some ambiguity about the actual cause of her death, which may have been due to heart failure, but which could have also been caused by dehydration or starvation, since severely depressed individuals often refuse to drink or eat.

The psychological impact of this situation was maximized by the fact that Eakins was his mother's primary caregiver—in other words his relationship with his mother was unusually close. Several sources indicate as much. Goodrich states that Eakins suffered from exhaustion after his mother's death because he had been caring for her night and day. A letter William Crowell wrote in Eakins's defense shortly after he was fired from the Pennsylvania Academy, noted Eakins's "unwearying gentleness and perfect skill as a nurse of the sick," a reference that almost certainly applies to his care of his sick mother, the one invalid in the household.[12] A letter of April 1871 from a neighbor, Rebecca Fussell, to her daughter, is the only contemporary mention of Caroline's illness. It mentions that Eakins needed to remain at home most of the time, since she became "worried" if he left.[13] Still another source, a family friend, Sally Shaw, stated that "Tom Eakins ruled his mother as well as the rest of the family," adding that he was "very domineering."[14]

The letter from Rebecca Fussell documents that Caroline had been emotionally troubled since the time of her son's return, on July 4, and quite probably for some time before that date. "Since her return home," she noted, "they never leave her a minute."[15] While cryptic, this reference suggests that Caroline had been taken somewhere outside the home, possibly a mental institution. One interpretation of Fussell's words is to suppose that Caroline Eakins had been hospitalized when Eakins was away in France, but was brought home when her son returned from Europe to care for her.

In women the symptoms of manic-depression are often exacerbated by menopause, since changes in hormone levels and body chemistry can intensify the symptoms. Eakins's mother, who died at the age of fifty-two, may have been experiencing menopause when her manic-depressive illness became fatal. She may also have been suffering from postpartum depression, since her youngest child, Caroline, was born in 1865, the year before Eakins left for Europe. Her depression may also have been connected with the absence of her eldest son, who appears to have been her principal caregiver.[16]

Caroline Cowperthwaite Eakins was the youngest of ten children. She came from a strict Quaker background, and she seems to have

Portrait of the Artist's Mother, ca. 1874. *Oil on canvas, 24 x 20 in., private collection, photograph courtesy of Gerold Wunderlich & Company, New York.* While Eakins's mother died of "exhaustion from mania," Eakins's portrait of her, which was copied from a photograph, is one of his few portraits of a woman that is completely neutral in expression.

accepted that fact that the Eakins household was paternalistic and domineering. Eakins's letters to her from Paris address topics that cater to feminine interests, such as fashion and household arrangements and, like most of his letters to women, have a somewhat condescending tone. Caroline Eakins's father is said to have been particularly strict about matters of female dress, and Eakins's portrait of his mother shows her demurely dressed, with a blouse that comes up to her neck.[17] Under "normal" circumstances, in short, Eakins's mother was evidently rather prudish and content to play a demure and "feminine" role.

During her manic and depressive phases, however, Caroline's behavior must have drastically changed. Both mania and depression lead to behavior that has disturbing sexual implications, as recorded by the standard guide on the subject, the *Diagnostic and Statistical Manual of Mental Disorders*. In a major depressive episode "the person may be unable to perform minimal self-care (e.g., feeding or clothing self)," and thus they often expose their bodies and disregard normal standards of decorum. During manic episodes, "increased sexual drive, fantasies and behavior are often present," as well as "sexual behavior unusual in the person."[18] Such behavior can become extravagant, as is suggested by the statement of one psychiatrist I spoke to:

> The husband of one of my patients would check her into a hotel when she was entering her manic phase. Then they would make love non-stop for two days straight. It was great. But after two days her behavior became so excessive that he needed to check her into a hospital.[19]

Mania may also lead to other forms of excessive behavior, such as compulsive talking, unrealistic projects, shopping or gambling.[20]

In its extreme phases, bipolar illness leads on to screaming, throwing things, and acts of violence. Kay Redfield Jamison, a leading expert on manic-depression, who herself was stricken with the disease, has written:

> Violence, especially if you are a woman, is not something spoken about with ease. Being wildly out of control—physically assaultive, screaming insanely at the top of one's lungs, running frenetically with no purpose or limit, or impulsively trying to leap from cars—is frightening to others and unspeakably terrifying to oneself. In blind manic rages I have done all of these things at one time or another, and some of them repeatedly.[21]

Presumably Eakins's mother did not attempt to jump out of cars (which had not been invented yet), but the rest of this litany surely describes the behavior compressed by Caroline's physician into a single word: "mania." Very likely at times she was suicidal as well as violent. Caroline's disregard of propriety when she was ill must have been all the more shocking because of her attention to such matters when she was in her normal state.

Bipolar illness has a strong genetic component.[22] Those who suffer from it generally have close relatives who are bipolar or suffer from other mood disorders. Most likely, Eakins's mother inherited her bipolar disorder from her father, Mark Cowperthwaite, who is said to have been violent and temperamental.[23] Some feminists would surely argue that the depression of Eakins's mother was the product of emotional abuse she received from her father, but it is equally logical to suppose that his violence (like hers) was a symptom of a genetically based disease.

Despite the emotional turmoil this illness must have caused, neither Eakins, his father, nor his siblings ever made any statements about Caroline Eakins's death. Such complete silence is surely a powerful statement of its own. Most likely Caroline's insanity was a source of distress and shame to them. In 1874, two years after her death, Eakins did produce a portrait of his mother—his only rendering of her—but this is interesting principally by virtue of what it is not. [24] The likeness was copied very faithfully, almost mechanically, from a photograph, and it is perhaps the only painting Eakins ever made of a woman that reveals no psychological tension, no emotion, and no hint of sorrow.

The attributes of Eakins's paintings of his sisters make sense if we imagine the strain that his mother's illness placed on the family, and recognize that he must have often been interrupted from working on these paintings in order to attend to her. Indeed, their musical theme may directly relate to her affliction, for music has been used to calm the mentally ill since the Middle Ages.

It is not surprising that Eakins's first paintings focused on his sister Frances. At the time he left for Paris she seems to have been his closest confidante in the family, and his longest letters home were written to her. In addition, as the eldest of the three sisters, Frances formed the most logical surrogate for Eakins's mother—the natural figure to take over as the female center of the household. The poignancy of Eakins's first two paintings *Frances Eakins* and *At the Piano* (both of 1870 or 1871) comes from the peculiar fashion in which Frances appears both present and absent. Music is a way of connecting with her audience, in this case probably her mother. But the way she has become absorbed in her music suggests a form of escape—a kind of extinction of consciousness—from painful thoughts and feelings. Paradoxically, music becomes at once a way of communicating with others who would otherwise be shut off and of disconnecting oneself from them.

After making these first two paintings, Eakins shifted his attention from Frances, to the next down in age, Margaret. In part this shift may have been because Frances became engaged to Will Crowell, whom she married in 1872. Thus, she may have had less time to pose for her brother. Margaret, however, seems to have deepened her affiliation with her brother to the point where their relationship came to possess many of the attributes of a marriage. At the time, aside from her relationship with her brother, Margaret was single and without romantic prospects.

All sources agree that Margaret's relationship with her brother was extremely close. Lloyd Goodrich has stated that there was "an unusual and deep affection between them."[25] As already noted, Eakins's brother-in-law Frank Stephens made the same assertion, but with a disturbing twist, claiming that she and Eakins engaged in incest. During this period Margaret began going on excursions with Eakins to the marshes and the beach; she posed for him; she did his housework; and she kept his account books. She even took spinning lessons so that she could assume an accurate pose for one of his spinning pictures. Given that Eakins pressed nearly all his models to pose for him in the nude, it seems possible that she did so, although no works of this type survive. One senses Eakins's special rapport with Margaret in his paintings of her, although they are not flattering by conventional standards.

Home Scene (circa 1870–1871), which focuses on Margaret, is the most complex of Eakins's early music paintings, as well as the most technically assured work in the series. Significantly, Eakins made Margaret look far older than her actual age. "The viewer realizes with a shock," Elizabeth Johns observes, "that at this time Margaret was only sixteen or seventeen years old."[26] In fact, Margaret's apparent age in the painting is about that of their mother at this time. Johns has perceptively described Margaret's look as "maternal," and in fact the whole point of the painting seems to be that she has assumed a role usually assigned to a mother, that of overseeing the education of a small child.

Eakins always seems to have been fascinated by subtle physical distinctions between men and women, and the painting plays on this issue. Margaret's face is curiously masculine.[27] It could even be that of a man. Indeed, many writers have noted that Eakins and Margaret resembled each other. Thus, the painting suggests a series of substitutions. Margaret takes on the role of the mother; then Eakins takes on the role of Margaret. Since Margeret's role is that of the mother, Eakins is also taking on the role of mother, in some sense.

An interesting detail is the bent position of Margaret's left wrist. To a modern viewer such a gesture appears feminine (or in a man effeminate—as in the slang term "limp-wristed"). However, Eakins assumed this very gesture in a photograph made at roughly the same time as this painting (shown on p. 124). Thus, this gesture linked Eakins with his sister, and also bridged the divide between masculine and feminine.

The youngest sister, Caroline, lies on the floor in front of Margaret. Caroline's attention to her writing slate clearly has an emotional significance, for Eakins's father was a writing master, and during particularly active periods the whole family helped him with his work. In learning to write, Caroline is learning to be like her father, and is affiliating herself with the family as a whole.

Eakins rendered the scene from an extremely low viewpoint, very close to the figure of Caroline. This produces two unusual effects. First, it makes Caroline seem very large. Since she was only seven at the time, one would expect her to be smaller than Margaret, but instead she is rendered at about the same scale. Second, it means that we look at Margaret from an odd angle. Rather than seeing her as an equal, we assume the perspective of a child, looking up

Home Scene, ca. late 1870–1871. Oil on canvas, 21 1/16 × 18 1/16 in., Brooklyn Museum of Art, gift of George A. Hearn, Frederick Loeser Art Fund, Dick S. Ramsay Fund, gift of Charles A. Schieren. Eakins's favorite sister, Margaret, nestles a kitten on her shoulder and looks down on the youngest child, Caroline, who is drawing on a slate. A mother cat arches its back in anger in the shadows at the left.

at a taller adult. Both effects give a quality of uneasiness to a seemingly straightforward relationship.

Finally, an almost invisible element illuminates the theme of the painting. On the floor, just to the left of Margaret, stands a barely discernible black cat with arched back. She looks up at her kitten, which Margaret is gripping in her hand. This cat underscores the theme of an emotionally volatile mother, who has forfeited her offspring to someone else's care.

In short, *Home Scene* explores a variety of themes related to Caroline Eakins's illness: the need of Margaret to take on a maternal role; the importance of activities such as music and writing for creating a sense of family identity; and looming over all, a sense of sorrow and disconnectedness that affected everyone in the household. Taken as a group, Eakins's paintings of his sisters comment on the disturbing gap created by the illness of his mother, and record the struggle of the siblings to maintain cohesion as a family.

Closely related to these paintings are three portraits of the Crowell sisters, Kathrin and Elizabeth. These can also be interpreted as attempts to find a woman to fill the gap created by his mother's illness. Like the paintings of his sisters, they contain strange psychological undercurrents.

Lloyd Goodrich has described Kathrin Crowell, Eakins's first fiancée, as a "dim and puzzling" figure in his life.[28] They became engaged shortly after he returned from Paris, when he was thirty and she twenty-three. There is no evidence that Eakins was in love with her. She was apparently chosen on the order of Eakins's father, who felt that his son was stirring up gossip by seeing too many girls. From surviving accounts, Kathrin was a quiet, undemonstrative girl. She possessed neither artistic nor musical talent. Eakins's letters to her have a condescending tone, as if he was writing to a small child. The courtship dragged on for years until Kathrin died of meningitis in 1879. Eakins never commented on her death, but was probably somewhat relieved by it. Legend has always maintained that Eakins was actually in love with Kathrin's more lively sister Elizabeth, and this is borne out by Eakins's paintings of the two. (Benjamin seems to have selected Kathrin for his son over her sister Elizabeth on the old-fashioned basis that she was the older of the two, and thus should be married first.)

While Eakins generally portrayed women engaged in thoughtful tasks, he chose to show Kathrin (1872) with a Japanese fan in her hand, playing silly games with her cat. Her face, seen at an odd angle, is distinctly plain. Indeed, the viewpoint brings out the coarseness of her features, and emphasizes her large nose and sloping forehead. The fluttering fan, a common emblem of flir-

tatiousness, brings out her "femininity," but not
in a fashion that is flattering. (Throughout
Eakins's oeuvre, anything Japanese seems to
have had a negative connotation.) Despite the
animation of Kathrin's pose, the overall effect is
not cheerful. She seems a diminutive figure,
swallowed up by the dark Victorian interior.

As many writers have noted, the painting
seems filled with tense sexual undercurrents.
Kathrin's fan appears to serve as an off-color
pun: as Linda Nochlin has noted, its shape
seems to allude to Kathrin's hidden triangle of
pubic hair.[29] The cat also suggests some sort of
sexual message. It is a traditional emblem of
female sexuality—a symbolism embedded in
our language through the double meaning of
the word "pussy."

Notably, a cat is also about the size of a
human baby at birth. Eakins shows Kathrin
with a cat turning in her lap and her legs awkwardly splayed apart. Since women were gener-

Kathrin, 1872. Oil on canvas, 62 ¾ x 48 ¼ in., Yale University
Art Gallery, bequest of Stephen Carlton Clark, B.A. 1903.
Eakins became engaged to Kathrin Crowell in 1874
at the insistence of his father.

ally encouraged to keep their legs pressed together, such a pose appears
"unfeminine," even impolite. It suggests something childish in Kathrin's character. In addition, the pose dramatizes the function of women in the crudest
of biological terms: it evokes sexual intercourse and how a cat-size baby
emerges at birth from between a woman's legs. Finally, the metaphor of a cat
is pursued in another fashion: Kathrin's hands are claw-like. While admittedly
her pose is less dramatic, her gesture anticipates that of the hysterical mother
with claw-like hands in *The Gross Clinic* (1875). As a rendering of a fiancée, the
painting is certainly odd. It does not emphasize beauty, or romance, or rapport with the painter. Instead, it suggests that Kathrin is clawed and dangerous, and that her principal role is as a machine for bearing children.

As every biographer of Eakins has observed, Eakins's portraits of Elizabeth appear more affectionate. Certainly, Eakins's portrait of Elizabeth, *Elizabeth Crowell and Her Dog* (circa 1872), exudes a sexual spark that is lacking from
the painting of her sister. The canvas shows Elizabeth seated on the floor,
making her poodle beg for a cookie balanced on its nose. We can infer that
she has just come home from school, for her coat has been hurriedly thrown

Elizabeth with a Dog, ca. 1871. *Oil on canvas, 13 ¾ x 17 in., San Diego Museum, purchase and a gift from Mr. and Mrs. Edwin S. Larsen.* **Several writers have speculated that Eakins was not in love with Kathrin, but with her sister Elizabeth.**

on a table in the background, and two schoolbooks still strapped together rest on the floor in front of her. As with the other painting, the pet appears to stand in for a person. It evokes a lover begging for affection. While Elizabeth is shown teasing and dominating a poodle, Eakins seems to imply that she did the same thing with men, and that in some slightly masochistic way they enjoyed it. While ostensibly an ordinary incident, the episode takes on a mysterious, even sinister, quality in the dark Victorian interior, whose furnishings are almost lost in the shadows. Even the girl's eyes are dark hollows, so that we cannot see their pupils. The only sparks of color come from Elizabeth's white hat and red blouse, and the red collar of her dog.

Some years later, Eakins painted the most romantic of his early works—perhaps the most romantic painting of his career—a second portrait of Elizabeth, *Elizabeth at the Piano* (1875; reproduced on page 9). This shows her at the keyboard, dressed in black, with a red rose in her hair. The pose relates closely to his first portrait of his sister Frances, but the handling is more delicate. Most of Elizabeth's figure is lost in shadow, but light comes in from the right hand side to shine on the music stand and to cast an indirect illumination on her attractive face. Her expression is gentle and absorbed, as if entranced by the music. Eakins evidently thought highly of the painting and showed it at the Centennial Exposition in Philadelphia. As late as 1887 he submitted it to an exhibition in Chicago and expressed regret to a friend that it had been rejected, supposedly because the organizers didn't want portraits. As has been noted, for years he hung this painting over the mantelpiece of the family home.[30]

These interior scenes, despite some technical awkwardness, are often moving. But to my way of thinking Eakins's first true masterpiece, and one of the greatest achievements of his career, was the astonishing portrait of his sister, *Margaret in Skating Costume*, of about 1871. Here Margaret stares blankly toward the viewer, but fails to make contact, because her eyes are unfocused.

Margaret was a tomboy, who was active in ice skating, rowing, sailing, and swimming, but had little interest in the feminine activities that women of her day were expected to pursue. Eakins's photographs of Margaret in indoor settings, wearing formal attire, show a woman who is sullen, ill at ease, and rather unattractive, with graceless posture and dull expression. In photographs taken outdoors she has a different presence: alert and alive. Although perhaps not a beauty in a traditional sense, she looks lovely and at one with her surroundings. Goodrich records the comment of a friend, who noted that Margaret carried herself "like an animal."[31]

Eakins's portrait of Margaret is strange in several respects. For one thing, her blank, uningratiating look is startling, almost rude. Unlike most nineteenth-century portraits, Margaret does not in any way acknowledge the presence of the viewer's gaze. While we are brought to an intimate distance, her eyes do not focus or look back at us, and her expression seems frozen and set. I can think of

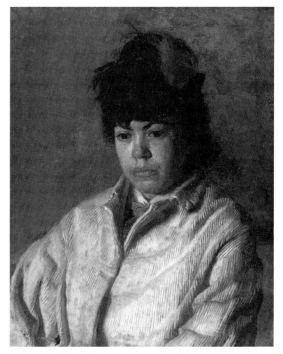

Margaret Eakins, ca. 1881. *Albumen print, 4 x 3 ¹⁵⁄₁₆ in., The Pennsylvania Academy of the Fine Arts, Charles Bregler's Thomas Eakins Collection, purchased with the partial support of the Pew Memorial Trust.* In Eakins's photographs of Margaret, she often looks morose.

Margaret in Skating Costume, 1871. *Oil on canvas, 24 x 20 ½ in., Philadelphia Museum of Art, gift of Mrs. Thomas Eakins and Miss Mary Adeline Williams.* Eakins's portrait of his sister Margaret breaks all the rules of sentimental portraiture, showing a woman who dresses like a man, looks depressed, and does not even engage the viewer.

no other nineteenth-century painter, not even Edgar Degas, who rendered a face so completely blank and unresponsive as Margaret's in this portrait.

Eakins may have been drawn to this approach through his interest in photography, for in the latter half of the century, photography revealed that human faces look different than had previously been supposed. Until then, painters recorded faces as filled with emotion and expression. It took photography to document that faces are often impassive. Early photographers tried to conceal this fact and make photographs that were more expressive and "artistic." Eakins, however, seems to have appreciated that an expressionless face had artistic possibilities of its own, and could communicate something profound about the human condition. Nonetheless, while Eakins may have been influenced by photography, his reasons for painting a woman with such a frozen expression were undoubtedly personal. The date of the painting provides a clue, for it was executed around the time of his mother's death, and it records the disconnected expression and general quality of lethargy that is characteristic of bipolar illness. In this sense, the likeness of another family member seems to serve in some way as a surrogate portrait of Eakins's mother, and attempts to come to terms with her illness.

Another thing about the painting is odd: the way it downplays overtly feminine elements, of the sort generally found in nineteenth-century American painting of women, and pushes masculine qualities to an extreme. Margaret's corduroy jacket might be a man's. Her hat, while somewhat more feminine, has a shape similar to that worn by boys, and Eakins emphasizes this resemblance through its dark color. While well-bred Victorian women avoided the sun, Margaret's skin looks leathery and brown, perhaps even sunburned, and her face lacks the "feminine delicacy" that is generally found in renderings of Victorian women. Only a few clues, such as the red feather in the cap (which seems to bleed like a gash) and the weakly articulated shoulders, convince us that we are not looking at a man. This element of gender reversal gives the painting a peculiar resonance, even today. But surely it would have been considerably more shocking to Eakins's contemporaries, who were accustomed to renderings of women that played up their "feminine" qualities.

The strangest thing about the painting is the degree to which Margaret resembles Eakins himself. As one writer noted: "The painting reveals, more than any other, the striking resemblance which Margaret bore to the artist."[32] Thus, in a sense, the painting is not simply a portrait of Margaret, but an image of Eakins as a woman. In psychological terms, it seems reasonable to propose that Eakins used his sister Margaret as a vehicle for getting into the mind of his mother, even for becoming his mother, a step that was psychically unsettling since it entailed both imagining himself as a woman and imagining himself as depressed to the point of insanity.

Far from a simple, objective record, the painting transforms reality to bring out themes that were of pressing concern to Eakins because of his mother's illness. In this regard, the painting serves as a useful Rosetta stone—a key to deciphering the meaning of Eakins's later paintings. For example, it introduces two key themes of his work: depression and gender reversal. It also suggests a possible reason for the changes in age and appearance that he often inflicted on his sitters—perhaps he was imagining them as his mother.

Outdoor Scenes

As with the home scenes, it is clear that Eakins had difficulty constructing his outdoor paintings, particularly the early ones. Having spent his time in France simply painting the nude, without attempting to create whole compositions, Eakins was often naive about how a painting should be organized. He thought that a painting could be made simply by putting together carefully studied pieces one by one, and it was hard for him to grasp that reality cannot go into a picture directly, without some rearrangement. His early paintings of boats provide evidence. *Sailboats Racing on the Delaware* (1874, Philadelphia Museum of Art), for example, is organized literally as a "slice of life," and attempts to duplicate what he actually saw, without any effort at aesthetic reorganization. As a consequence, the boat on the right is cut in half as it runs over the edge of the canvas, creating a jarring, abruptly truncated effect. Since framing is an artificial practice that does not correspond with what we see in nature, this edge looks arbitrary, and seems to disrupt the course of the race and the sense of movement without adequate logic or explanation.

After completing the picture, even Eakins seems to have recognized that this cropping looked very odd, and he decided to try the subject again in another way. But in doing so, he overcompensated. In his next boat painting, *Starting Out After Rail* he placed a boat at the center of the composition and made sure that no part of it was cut off, not even a small corner of the sail. This is less jarring, although the effect is still not entirely convincing, since in this case the composition is too centered and too obvious, and we feel that we are looking at a boat that is sitting on the floor of Eakins's studio rather than at one that exists in the context of real-life water and air.

Sailboats Racing, 1874. *Oil on canvas, 24 x 36 in., Philadelphia Museum of Art, gift of Mrs. Thomas Eakins and Miss Mary Adeline Williams.*

In fact, Eakins composed the painting by constructing separate pieces—boat, rippled water, sky, and so forth—and then assembling them. While the issues are sometimes subtle, in fact, various visual clues reveal that the painting was put together additively, rather than transcribed directly from the scene. Thus, for example, the faces of the men are strongly modeled in direct sunlight, with strong shadows. In real life, however, their faces would pick up scattered reflections from the water, as well as reflected highlights from the white sail (which would eliminate deep shadows from the faces the way a white screen does for a studio photographer).[33]

An early critic who described *Starting Out After Rail* pinpointed precisely these strengths and weaknesses of the artist's work. The viewer's pleasure in the painting, he noted, came from "the light touch of the hand of the man at the tiller, the stretch of his trousers across the seat, the shine of his companion's boots in the sun, the double-barreled shotgun in the bottom of the boat, the reflection and the shadows of the sails in the shoal water, the large boats making their way in the Delaware's channel, the blue haze of land through the gap."[34] The effect of the whole, however, was not well integrated. "The emptiness of the sky is perhaps disappointing, and that is where Eakins's weakness lies. His absorption with details often became so great that he frequently fails to organize them into a unified whole."[35]

The stiffness of Eakins's solution becomes apparent when we compare it with a contemporary painting of similar subject matter such as *Breezing Up*, by a master of composition, Winslow Homer, who knew how to lead the eye in toward the features of greatest dramatic interest. Yet it is just this slight sense of awkwardness and disjuncture that makes Eakins's paintings interesting. Although he quickly grew more skillful, even his most famous and successful paintings look as if they were pieced together from individual bits. When we look at them we mentally repeat something of the process by which Eakins put the parts together, and for this reason even seemingly straightforward, ordinary scenes take on a curious

Winslow Homer, Breezing Up (A Fair Wind), *1873–1875. Oil on canvas, 24 2/16 x 38 3/16 in., gift of the W. L. and May T. Mellon Foundation © Board of Trustees, National Gallery of Art, Washington, D.C.*

tension, one might even say a sense of anxiety. This is particularly noticeable in Eakins's outdoor paintings, which tend to look scattered. In indoor scenes

Starting Out after Rail, 1874. *Oil on canvas mounted on masonite, Museum of Fine Arts, Boston, The Hayden Collection, Charles Henry Haden Fund © 2004.* **The tilt of the boat and the configuration of the ripples were calculated in exact perspective.**

Eakins found that he could create a sense of unity by smothering almost everything in darkness, and focusing the attention on a few dramatically lit forms. Even here, however, the task of composing was clearly perplexing to him, and in the last phase of his career he either avoided multifigured compositions or closed in on single figures or individual heads.

Significantly, Eakins's early paintings contain an unusual mixture of rough passages and sections of microscopically precise detail. When one examines *Sailboats Racing on the Delaware*, for example, it becomes apparent that the figures in the boat at the far right and the boat in the center must be portraits of specific people rendered with remarkable exactitude (Kathleen Foster has identified one of the figures as Harry Lewis).[36] Other sections of the painting, however, such as the boats in the distance, are blurred and rendered with loose brushstrokes. Similarly, in Eakins's painting of *Pushing for Rail*, the marsh is rendered with a loose scumble of pigment, but the figures are rendered more precisely. The most remarkable figure is the one on the right, firing his gun. His shirt contains microscopically tiny criss-cross stripes, which must have been rendered with a brush that contained only one or two hairs. Details such as this are completely lost in the published reproductions of the paintings. For that matter, such details are not visible at a normal viewing distance—that is, the distance at which one can take in the whole composition. To see them clearly you need to move up to within a few inches of the canvas.

Many other painters, of course, have organized their compositions around

Pushing for Rail, 1874. *Oil on canvas, 13 x 30 ¹⁄₁₆ in., Metropolitan Museum of Art, Arthur H. Hearn Fund, 1916.* **Each of the hunters acts out a different stage of the hunt: shooting, pushing, and reloading.**

some passages that are clear and exact and others that are out of focus. (John Singer Sargent, for example, generally did this in his portraits.) Most often, however, this shift in focus corresponds to what the eye sees. We see the center of interest clearly, and the image becomes looser, brushier, less finished as we move away from this point. Two things are strange about Eakins's contrasts of clear and blurred areas. First, the points of sharp focus are scattered across the surface of the painting, with passages of blurred focus in between. Thus, they do not correspond with a single moment of vision. Second, the details are so minute that we cannot see them from a normal viewing distance. To make them out we need to move so close that we can no longer discern the composition as a whole. In psychological terms, this suggests a world of a peculiar nature. For Eakins, it seems that the world was either unusually blurred or unusually sharp, and that the difference between the two states was curiously arbitrary. Eakins's paintings are fascinating in part because it is hard work to read them. Just at the point when they seem chaotic and out of focus we discover passages of vivid detail. But when we try to establish the context for these details we often find that we are abruptly thrown into a world that is formless and confusing.

Father and Son

Eakins first portrayed his father in an outdoor painting, a scene of hunting for rail. A rail is a water bird that lurks in marsh grass. It can squeeze so tightly between stalks of grass that allegedly it has given rise to the expression "thin as a rail." Rail hunting was carried out at high tide when the flooded marshes provided no cover. A pusher would pole a boat through the marshes to come up close to the birds while a man at the bow would stand ready with a gun to shoot down the slow-flying game when it rose from cover. The sport required skillful teamwork between poler and shooter, since the poler needed to inch the boat forward while keeping it steady to provide a secure platform for accurate aiming. Perhaps the greatest challenge of rail shooting was not to hit the birds but to avoid mangling them. The rail do not take to the air until the boat comes within a foot or two of their hiding place, and shooting from that distance will so splatter them with shotgun pellets that they are virtually inedible. A skilled rail hunter will let the birds rise and come close to escaping before releasing his shot. He does not attempt a quick kill but sustains the bird's experience of fear and flight as long as possible.

In *The Artist and His Father Hunting Reed Birds,* Eakins showed himself in

The Artist and His Father Hunting Reed-Birds on the Cohansey Marshes, ca. 1874. *Oil on canvas laid on panel, 17 ⅛ × 26 ½ in., Virginia Museum of Fine Arts, Richmond, the Paul Mellon Collection.* **Eakins portrayed himself in silent companionship with his father, hunting reed birds in the marshes of New Jersey.**

the subordinate role, as the pusher, bent in an active position as he poles the boat forward. His father stands motionless in the bow, his gun ready. Although other figures are depicted, they are off in the distance, and play no role in what is happening between Eakins and his father. The landscape is amazingly bleak and featureless, and jumps abruptly from the foreground to the horizon. While this may seem logical in a rendition of a marsh, other nineteenth-century painters such as Joseph Meeker or Martin Johnson Heade did not present marshes so starkly, but used such devices as winding waterways to lead the eye artfully and gradually into the distance.

Eakins clearly intended the painting to celebrate the bonds of companionship between son and father, which must have helped to fill the emotional hole in their family life created by his mother's illness. Indeed, Eakins signed the painting on the bow of the boat with the words "Benjamin Eakins Filius Pinxit" ("The son of Benjamin Eakins painted this")—an inscription that subordinates his identity as a person to his position as his father's son. The fact that the painting takes place outside the home is no accident, because only outside the home, away from Eakins's mother, could this sort of male bonding take place. However, we notice that the father has his back turned to his son and no conversation or direct interaction occurs between them. The father's pose is uncommunicative, as he stands stiffly, with his gun poised at waist level. For Eakins the power of fatherhood seems associated with the power of a gun to kill—a gun that has a distinctly phallic aspect.

As so often in Eakins's work, what ought to be a relaxing pursuit takes place without evidence of pleasure. The figures are tense, and have grim expressions. Given the family's silence at meals, Eakins's relationship with his father probably involved little verbal communication. Here their companionship is silent, except for the sharp report of the gun when a bird is killed.

In fact, the visual message of the painting is ambiguous, since we can read its awkwardness as either humorous or threatening. Sylvan Schendler, for example, felt that the painting possessed an "almost comic" and "mock epic quality"—an effect largely due to the fact that "The artist is awkwardly off-balance as he poles his father toward some defenseless quarry."[37] At the same time, the relationship of son to father is menacing, while his father stands oblivious to the threat, with his back turned. In purely visual terms, whether or not this was intended, the paintings seems not so much to celebrate Eakins's relationship with his father as to express his Oedipal conflict with him.

Two years later, Eakins reworked this design in a more accomplished painting, *Rail Shooting on the Delaware*.[38] Here he substituted a family friend, Will Schuster, and an African-American pusher for the figures of his father and himself. One might conjecture, however, that the underlying significance of the painting is the same as that of the earlier work, and that at the deepest level this is still a painting about Eakins and his father, or at least about the sort of relationship they shared. The father figure, Will Schuster, appears even more powerful and lethal, since Eakins captured him as he is just about to shoot, with his whole body tensed. By making the pusher black, Eakins expressed his subordinate, filial position even more clearly. At the same time the rendering of this figure is more sensitive and makes the significance of his role even more evident. The black man's tense stance wonderfully captures the complex muscular effort required to maneuver the boat into position for the kill while keeping it perfectly balanced.

A Game of Chess

Eakins did not paint his father inside the family home until three years after his mother's death, when he created his most elaborate portrait of his father, *The Chess Players*, whose layers of meaning have been skillfully illuminated by

Martin Berger. While the painting postdates both his rowing pictures and *The Gross Clinic*, because of the way in which it illuminates Eakins's relationship with his father, it is convenient to consider it here.

The painting is set in a dark, wood-paneled room, often said to be the living room of the Eakins home, although Susan Eakins maintained that it was set elsewhere.[39] Eakins's father stands at the center of the composition, observing a chess game taking place between players on either side of him. The vanishing point of the painting is located at Benjamin's head. The exact center of the painting is located at his genitals. As if to underscore the issue of fatherhood, an engraving by Eakins's artistic "father," Jean-Léon Gérôme, showing a scene of gladiatorial combat, is located on the wall behind Benjamin's head. (The painting is *Hail Caesar, We Who Are About to Die Salute You*.) As he had with the painting of rail hunting, Eakins signed the canvas in Latin, in small red letters on the open drawer of the chess table, with the phrase "The son of Benjamin Eakins painted this." This time, however, Eakins himself is not visible. Still,

Will Schuster and Blackman Going Shooting, 1876. *Oil, 22 ⅛ x 30 ¼ in., Yale University Art Gallery, Bequest of Stephen Carlton Clark, B.A. 1903.*

since he made the painting, he is clearly located on the opposite side of the chessboard from Eakins's father (that is, he is where we are).

Seated on the left (Benjamin's right) is Bertrand Gardel, an elderly teacher of French. In a letter, with his usual fractured syntax, Eakins described him as a "poor good old man, a little, very little cunning but so very weak." On the right is George Holmes, a painting instructor and artist, who is somewhat younger. It seems to be late in the day and the game seems to be drawing to a close, as only a few pieces are left on the board. As a Victorian critic described the scene, it depicts "a game of chess that has lasted well into the twilight."[40]

The younger man, Holmes, is winning the game; the older man, Gardel, has lost his white queen, which is resting inside the chess drawer on the near side of the table. Holmes's black queen commands the center of the board. Gardel sits in a protective posture, and Holmes leans forward aggressively.

The Chess Players, 1876. *Oil on wood, 11 ¾ x 16 ¾ in., Metropolitan Museum of Art, gift of the artist, 1881.* **Eakins's father watches over a late-afternoon chess game between two friends, the elderly French teacher, Bertrand Gardel, on the left, and the somewhat young painter, George Holmes, on the right. Close study of the pieces reveals that Gardel has just lost his queen and that the younger man is winning the game.**

Thus, Eakins's father is watching youth defeat age. This, of course, is the same pattern that characterizes Benjamin's relationship with his son. We can imagine that another game is taking place across the opposite sides of the board, pitting Eakins against his father.[41] Eventually, Eakins's subordinate role will end and he will take his father's place.[42] As Martin Berger has stated: "Given the younger Holmes's attempt to kill the older man's king, and considering the cultural associations of chess with violence, it seems inevitable to read the work as one that grapples with Oedipal issues."

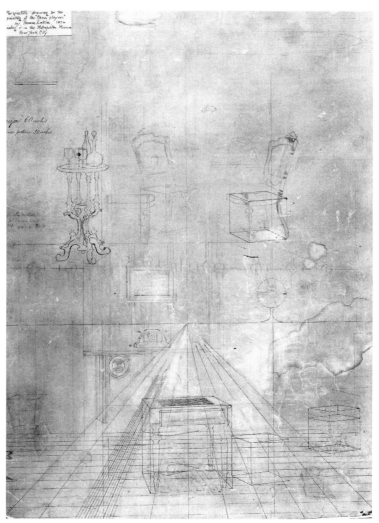

Perspective Drawing for the "Chess Players." *Pencil and ink on cardboard, 24 x 19 in., Metropolitan Museum of Art, Fletcher Fund, 1942.* **Eakins carefully plotted the perspective of every element in** *The Chess Players*, **although in the final painting his careful planning is almost completely obscured by the dark shadows.**

Significantly, Eakins painted his distinctly unplayful *Baby at Play* in the same year as *The Chess Players*, and this fact illuminates its meaning. Many of the strange features of Eakins's portrait of Ella Crowell seem to stem from the fact that Eakins wished to portray Ella as someone who closely resembled her grandfather. Ella's seriousness, her oddly masculine quality, her disinterest in toys, and her interest in writing blocks, are all qualities that Eakins admired in his father and imposed on Ella.

Gender Codes in Eakins's Early Work

As many scholars have observed, the first paintings that Eakins produced after his return from France are neatly divided between paintings of women inside a home and men engaged in activities outdoors. The female paintings show activities that Eakins seems to have conceived as "feminine," such as playing the piano or teasing a pet cat or poodle. Interestingly, however, over the entire course of his career, Eakins never portrayed a woman in a maternal role—the role favored by most artists. *The Gross Clinic* is the only painting in which he depicted a mother in the same picture with her child, and there the mother is in the corner, cowering.[43]

The male paintings are very different. They focus on sports, such as hunting, sailing, and rowing, and not only take place outside, but are generally set in a flat and featureless landscape such as the ocean, a river, or a salt water marsh. Thus, the spatial experience of these paintings is opposite to the female interiors. While the interiors are dark, oppressive, and claustrophobic, the outdoor scenes extend back to infinite, open, almost cloudless skies, and lack boundaries. In Eakins's family life there was a good deal of confusing crossover between the male and female spheres. From Eakins's letters, for example, we know that his sisters sailed, rowed, swam, and accompanied hunting expeditions, but none of his paintings of these activities includes a woman. Although the gender division of these paintings may partially have reflected Victorian mores, it was in large part a projection of Eakins himself.

In the work of his later career the distinction between male and female domains became less clear. He began to blur the two. But at the outset it was clearly important for Eakins to keep the two worlds separate. He started his career with a vision of reality that was selective and rigorously coded.

The Biglin Brothers Turning the Stake, 1873. *Oil on canvas, 40 x 59 ½ in., The Cleveland Museum of Art, Hinman B. Hurlbut Collection.* Eakins showed the Biglin brothers at the crucial moment of their race, when they were pushing their oars in opposite directions to turn the stake at the midpoint of the course. Eakins included himself seated in a scull in the distance on the left, firing a pistol into the air.

Chapter 11

TURNING THE STAKE

AROUND THE TIME of his mother's death, Eakins's subject matter began to change, perhaps in part because he became free to leave the family home. He ceased to paint his sisters and the Crowells, and family subject matter became less dominant in his work. He gradually began to take on other subjects, such as rowing scenes, medical operations, or artists working from the model. Nonetheless, one still feels a strong sense of autobiography, and of the pull of family relationships, in Eakins's subsequent work. For one thing, when he turned to subjects outside his family he often included himself in the background as a witness or participant in the scene. In addition, many of his later paintings continue to reflect the dynamics of the Eakins family.

Thus, the content of Eakins's paintings often has a double aspect. On the one hand there is the ostensible subject, and these subjects are often quite complex. Eakins often spent considerable time on research, pondering the meaning of every element and carefully studying seemingly insignificant details. Because of his attention to such matters, scholars have devoted enormous attention to anecdotal readings of his paintings. Such efforts, however, while valid in their way, often seem to have little or no connection with the deeper emotional qualities of Eakins's work, and too much attention to them has led to interpretations of Eakins's work that are unconvincing and trivial, such as the view that he was a great painter because he rendered the world accurately and could draw boats in correct perspective. In fact, what might be termed the "surface" subject, often seems to serve as a proxy for a deeper subject with emotions and meanings that have some other source.

In fact, Eakins's work provides a classic instance of the process that Sigmund Freud termed "transference." Eakins imposed the patterns of his family

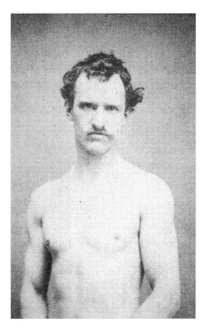

Schreiber and Son,
Max Schmitt, ca.
1871. Albumen carte-
de-visite, collection of
Daniel W. Dietrich II.

relationships, such as those with his father and mother, on society as a whole. To understand or "decode" Eakins's paintings, I would propose, we need to carry out this process in reverse. In other words, we need to recognize that the key figures in Eakins's paintings take on roles that resemble or recall members of Eakins's family. Thus, for example, the psychological tensions of *The Gross Clinic* make sense when we recognize that the stern, paternal figure of Dr. Gross serves in some sense as a surrogate for Eakins's father and the cowering, hysterical figure of the patient's mother has qualities that resemble Eakins's own mother. One of the peculiarities of Eakins's paintings is that he often included himself in the role of a bystander, and I take this as a sign that the scenes he recorded had some special personal significance.

Organizing the clues that lead us to one or another reading is often a complicated process, and some delicacy is required in deciding how far to push a particular interpretation. But the central insight, that Eakins transferred family patterns to the world at large, is logical and simple. That he did so to an unusual extent makes sense, since we know that over the course of his life he never fully broke out of the family home. In other words, Eakins's paintings of the later 1870s have many of the same emotional undercurrents, and explore many of the same issues, as the family paintings he created directly after returning from Paris. Seen in this way, Eakins's paintings have some of the qualities of a novel or a play. They are not simply pictorial exercises but stagings or restagings of emotionally significant scenes.

Eakins's rowing pictures form a transitional stage of this process of transferring family issues to the world at large. His first rowing picture, *The Champion Single Sculls* (1871), is fundamentally a self-portrait and a statement about his own ambitions, although somewhat slyly he placed himself in a secondary role, rather than as the main subject. The painting is still about Eakins's "family world," but shows this world and Eakins himself from a slightly different and more distanced standpoint. One of the peculiarities of the painting is that Eakins seems to have expressed his own feelings and ambitions not so much by means of how he showed himself (although he does appear in the painting), as through his representation of his friend Max Schmitt. In other words, while I do not wish to too narrowly limit the meanings of the piece, the painting is at least in part about roles and role playing.

The Champion

Eakins's rowing pictures, the earliest of which are concurrent with the later family pictures, mark the first instance in which he moved away from family subject matter. His father and sisters do not appear, although in the two most ambitious rowing pictures, including the first of the series, he portrayed himself in the background. While the best of the home scenes are superb, the rowing scenes surely mark a further advance in artistic achievement. Paintings such as *The Champion Single Sculls* move Eakins from the rank of a peculiar and intriguing young talent, a figure to watch, to the status of a major master.

Today we tend to forget how surprising the subject matter of Eakins's

The Champion Single Sculls (Max Schmitt in a Single Scull), 1871. *Oil on canvas, 32 ¼ x 46 ¼ in., Metropolitan Museum of Art, Alfred N. Punnett Endowment Fund and George D. Pratt Gift, 1934.* **While it was made to celebrate a victorious race, Eakins's painting of Max Schmitt is oddly pensive and elegiac in its mood. Eakins portrayed himself straining at the oars behind the champion.**

painting must have seemed at the time. To be sure, champion rowers were often featured in prints and magazine illustrations. Currier and Ives, for example, published their first rowing print in 1867.[1] However, while such sporting imagery was appropriate for popular images, it was a radical step to move it into an art gallery. Eakins seems to have been the first major painter to approach this theme, and when he exhibited his first rowing picture, in 1871, a critic described his choice of subject as "peculiar."[2] A few years later, in 1873, when Eakins sent a watercolor of a rower to his former teacher, Jean-Leon Gérôme, the French artist wrote back commenting that he was not sure if such a subject would be salable.[3]

Rowing was just coming into vogue at this time. Harvard, the first college in America to take up the sport, established rowing in 1846, and Yale took it up the next year. But the spread of rowing was slowed by the Civil War, and only after the conflict ended did it become popular. By the early 1870s, rowing clubs had sprouted in most major cities, totaling some 12,000 members and 2,000 boats.[4] Magazines such as *Harper's Weekly*, *Harper's Monthly*, and *Leslie's Illustrated Magazine* ran stories about races and regattas. They also energetically promoted amateur rowing, extolling its health benefits and moral discipline.[5]

Eakins mentioned rowing several times in his letters from Paris: asking his

James Hammill and Walter Brown, in Their Great Five Mile Rowing Match for $4,000 and the Championship of America, 1867. *Lithograph by Currier and Ives, collection of Thomas E. Weil, Jr.* Currier and Ives produced a few prints of rowing champions, but before Eakins no major painter had ever explored this subject.

mother if she had been on the river to witness the fall colors; suggesting that his sister Frances row on the river when she was depressed by her musical progress; and advising Frances and Margaret to learn to swim well, since they rowed so much. Several of Eakins's acquaintances at Central High also rowed, including Joseph Boggs, an artist/illustrator; his high school chemistry professor, Dr. Rand, whose portrait Eakins later painted; and Max Schmitt, a classmate.

Races took place on the Schuylkill River as early as the 1830s, but they matched heavy barges. Not until 1862 did a race take place in sculls, and Philadelphia was considered behind the times in racing until 1867, when the Schuylkill Navy began staging regattas, with well-trained rowers and radically streamlined racing sculls, which drew large crowds. Max Schmitt won the first regatta in 1867, and then alternately lost and won the next three competitions. Eakins returned from Paris in the summer of 1870, and probably witnessed the race of October 5th that year, which Schmitt won handily, leading the next boat by three lengths and finishing the three-mile course in the very fast time of twenty minutes. As Elizabeth Johns has proposed, Eakins's first painting of rowing, *The Champion Single Sculls* probably memorializes this race. Set in the autumn, in a section of the course, it shows the champion in the boat he raced, the *Josie*.

The setting is a turn in the Schuylkill River, and the exact location is defined by well-known landmarks: The Railroad Connection Bridge, with a train puffing across it from the right, and the Girard Avenue Bridge. On the right bank is Eaglesfield, a colonial mansion, at the brow of the hill, and on the shore just in front of the bridge, a stone boathouse, almost lost in shadow.[6]

Eakins filled the background with boats of various types. Three racing sculls are faintly visible in the distance. Near the left shore is a racing barge, of the sort from which modern racing sculls descend, with two rowers and a coxswain in old-fashioned Quaker dress. A little beyond the two bridges is a steamboat, giving off a puff of steam. Thus, Eakins suggests a series of contrasts and comparisons: old-fashioned rowboats versus modern rowboats, rowboats versus steamboats, and boats made for recreation versus boats made for work.[7] Perhaps half humorously, as a counterpart to these manmade forms of flotation, on the left at a bend in the shore Eakins included a family of ducks.

The mood of the painting is established by the figure of Schmitt, in the near middle ground, coming toward us, having relaxed his rowing to let the boat glide. He turns to look over his shoulder in our general direction, but casts his eyes downward toward the water, his face impassive. Schmitt was no Greek god. In photographs his hair is tousled and he looks slightly goofy. Eakins did nothing to idealize his appearance. In the painting his neck is crooked and his head is cocked at an odd angle, making him look like a hunchback. His receding hairline is evident. While presumably Schmitt was physically fit, all we see of his body is a white arm and the untidy wrinkles of his white shirt.

Beyond him we see Eakins in another boat. He has just rowed past Schmitt in the opposite direction. Unlike Schmitt, who is relaxing, Eakins is represented in mid stroke, with his shoulders bent, his arms extended. He appears to be grimacing, and is not engaged with his surroundings, but immersed in the exhilarating pain of his own physical effort. Thus, the painting portrays a contrast between thought and action, although curiously it is Schmitt, the athlete, who is shown thinking, and Eakins, the thinker and artist, who is shown in action. In different ways, however, both are completely self-absorbed. Indeed, one of the most striking features of the painting is the contrast between the rich scattering of details, which indicate things that are happening all over the pictorial surface, and the inwardness of both Schmitt and Eakins, who in different ways, seem lost in their own psyches and detached from the world around them.

The image is so tranquil that it seems frozen. The water is glassy smooth, the trees stand motionless, the clouds look pasted to the sky. Even the rowing figures in the background don't seem to be moving (there's no visible wake behind the boats). The light is very flat and evenly distributed, with little of the chiaroscuro seen in other Eakins paintings. There is almost the feeling of a moment preserved under glass.

Goodrich has described the scene as "photographically exact," but as Michael Leja has noted, Eakins's analytic methods produced something notably different from a direct rendering of the scene. Thus, for example, the marks produced by Eakins's oars, and the thirteen concentric rings produced by those of Schmitt, are much too regular, the clouds are not reflected in the water (nor are the red and white bridges), and the highlights on dramatically significant elements, such as Schmitt's shoulder, are more intense and expressive than optical reality (or a photograph). What is more, the paint textures tend to shift abruptly, from smooth to scumbled, in a fashion that corresponds with analytic distinctions rather than with visual reality.[8] While the process takes place largely unconsciously, the eye and mind note these divergences from real life. Moreover, all these divergences from reality have an expressive significance. For example, the too-precise ripples in the water communicate the progress of the boats and convey a precise sense of time; the absence of reflections plays up the affinities of shape between the boats and the cloud. In short, we take in the painting as a series of carefully analyzed, discrete, individual pieces at the same time that we appreciate that it has some sort of overall visual and expressive unity.

While no doubt Johns is right that the painting celebrates a race, as the celebration of a triumph the painting is strange. Schmitt is not shown racing, or as a victor, but in a lonely practice session. He is not shown rowing, but in a moment of relaxation and contemplation, when he lets his boat drift along on its own, and stares off into empty space. Even the season and time of day convey an elegiac mood and a sense of sadness. The season is autumn, when the leaves are changing color and winter is approaching. The time is late afternoon, when the light is beginning to fade

This all makes sense when we realize that the painting is not so much about Schmitt as about Eakins. Schmitt serves as a vehicle onto which Eakins projects his own anxieties and needs. Two facts about Eakins's life help explain the painting's solemn mood. One is that Eakins executed the canvas when he was engulfed in a family tragedy, his mother's mental illness, which he desperately wished to escape. The other is that he painted it at a time when he was intensely eager to become a champion like Schmitt, but had done nothing noteworthy enough to earn such a title.

For many months Eakins had been cooped up in the family home, tending to his mother's nervous ailments. She became distraught whenever he left. Only occasionally, when he was rowing, was he able to move outdoors, to the world of men and masculine pursuits. Seen in this light the painting has many powerful emotional undercurrents: Eakins's desire to escape the constricting family home by going outdoors, to leave his mother's feminine world behind and be a man, to dull the emotional anguish created by his mother's illness through physical exertion. At the deepest level the painting is about depression, both the depression of Eakins's mother and the depression he himself must have felt. At the same time, the painting is about an effort to recover from depression through outdoor activity. In particular, we now know that exercise releases substances known as endorphins, which have an effect similar to narcotics. These natural drugs produce an intensely pleasurable sensation, but it is a pleasure that can only be bought through pain.

The painting is also about champions—and Eakins's desire to be a champion. Indeed, it carries the title *The Champion Single Sculls*, which was bestowed by Eakins himself. This title, however, presents problems of accuracy. While Schmitt was a champion, and the painting can be read as a celebration of his victory, Eakins was not a rowing champion, and had never even competed in a public race. Elizabeth Johns, who realized this fact, assumed that punctuation was the problem, and added a comma, changing the title to *The Champion, Single Sculls.*[9] In a way this makes more sense. It makes it clear that the painting shows only one champion of single sculls, Schmitt, and transforms Eakins's self-portrait into an incidental element in the piece. Yet while thoroughly logical, this does not ring true to the feeling of the picture, which is clearly in good part a self-portrait and an assertion of how Eakins wanted to be seen. Admittedly, proper grammar and punctuation were never Eakins's strong suits, and his sloppiness on these points, compared with the neatness of his handwriting, is one of the jarring features of his letters home from Paris. Yet as we know from Eakins's public statements, he was quite skillful at playing with double meanings, and at seeming to say one thing while actually saying another. My guess is that he omitted the comma quite deliberately. The whole point of the painting was that Eakins wanted to be a champion like Schmitt. By the little trick of "forgetting" a comma, Eakins could transform that desire into an apparent fact.

At some level, however, Eakins clearly knew that he was not a champion. He focused on practice rather than victory, because the painting expresses his own condition—not Schmitt's. At this point in his life, Eakins was moving out of his artistic apprenticeship and gearing up for major achievements. Unlike Schmitt, however, he had never been a champion, although he was clearly eager to become one in the artistic sphere. Thus, the subject of the painting is Eakins's need to practice, to prepare, if he is to achieve the success that he desires, and that he has not yet reached. There is a double edge to this. One can read the painting as optimistic, since it proposes that Eakins, through effort and practice, will achieve greatness. But the painting also suggests that success, in any sphere, is very brief. To find satisfaction in life, we need to take pleasure not in success, but in the effort and practice that leads up to it. Eakins's painting, in fact, turns our attention away from success itself to focus on the deeper, more sober, more painful things that lie behind success, and form its foundation.

Later Rowing Scenes

Eakins exhibited *The Champion Single Sculls* only once, although it is one of his masterpieces. My own supposition is that he hoped to surpass it in more ambitious subsequent pictures, but that his effort failed, and that in the process of struggling with his failures he lost interest in rowing as a subject.

Eakins followed *The Champion Single Sculls* with three small paintings of rowers in a pair-oared shell. While all three of these paintings show evidence of much effort and required careful study of light and perspective, they feel like transitional works, and are considerably simpler in concept than the works that came both just before and just after. One of these paintings (National Gallery) shows the Biglin brothers racing. Their boat is placed parallel to the shore, and in the foreground, we can see the prow of the boat they are racing against, but no rowers. Two other paintings show rowers going under a bridge. The first (Philadelphia Museum) shows the Biglin brothers. The second (Yale University Art Gallery) is nearly identical in composition but shows the Schreiber brothers. Unlike the Biglins, the Schreibers were amateurs, who rowed for recreation rather than for sport, and Eakins's painting carefully records this fact. They are both rowing imperfectly, with the angle of their oars somewhat skewed.[10]

Eakins left a record of his dissatisfaction with these paintings in a letter of spring 1875 to Earl Shinn, describing his submissions to the annual exhibition at the National Academy of Design in New York. He explained that he did not

The Biglin Brothers Racing, 1872. *Oil on canvas, 24 ⅛ x 36 ¹/₁₆ in., gift of Mr. and Mrs. Cornelius Vanderbilt Whitney © Board of Trustees, National Gallery of Art, Washington, D.C.* In 1872 the Biglin Brothers became America's first national rowing champions in a race on the Schuylkill.

The Pair-Oared Shell, 1872. *Oil on canvas, 24 x 36 in., Philadelphia Museum of Art, Gift of Mrs. Thomas Eakins and Miss Mary Adeline Williams.*

wish to exhibit "those Biglin ones" because "they are clumsy & although pretty well drawn are wanting in distance and some other qualities." Instead, he planned to submit his painting of the Schreiber brothers. "The picture don't please me altogether," he noted. "I had it too long about I guess. The drawing of the boats & the figures . . . are all better expressed than I see any New Yorkers doing—but anyhow I am tired of it. I hope it will sell and I'll never see it again."[11]

Despite these self-deprecating comments, however, Eakins was incensed when the painting was rejected from the exhibition. "It is a much better figure picture than anyone in N.Y. can paint," he protested. "I conclude that those who judged it were incapable of judging or jealous of my work; or that there was no judgment at all on merit."[12]

All three of these paintings feel like studies or preludes to Eakins's largest rowing picture, *The Biglin Brothers Turning the Stake* of 1873, in which he was clearly trying to surpass his first rowing picture, *The Champion Single Sculls*, with a work that was larger, more complicated, and more emotionally intense. *The Biglin Brothers Turning the Stake* is in many ways the more ambitious of the two. It is much larger in scale, and has more rowers and hundreds of subsidiary figures. The subject reveals an attempt to capture more complicated forms of movement. But Eakins clearly had trouble handling the subject on such a large scale. Though he extensively reworked it at a later date, the

The Oarsmen (The Schreiber Brothers), 1874. *Oil on canvas, 15 x 22 in., Yale University Art Gallery, John Hay Whitney, B.A. 1926, M.A. (Hon.) 1956, Collection.* **Unlike the Biglin brothers, the Schreibers were amateurs, and Eakins portrayed them rowing imperfectly. Eakins confessed that "the picture don't please me altogether," but nonetheless was irate when it was rejected from an exhibition in New York.**

painting still feels less assured, less clear, less resolved than *The Champion Single Sculls.*

Like *The Champion Single Sculls*, the painting of the Biglin brothers celebrates a race on the Schuylkill River, held on May 20, 1872. Here we see the race in progress. Vying for the first national championship in rowing, the contestants were John and Barney Biglin of New York, racing against Henry Coulter and Lewis Cavitt of Pittsburgh. Because of a thunderstorm, the race was delayed for several hours. Finally, shortly after six o'clock, the weather cleared just enough to allow the race to go forward, and the Biglin brothers won by a handy margin.

Eakins shows the most exciting moment of the race when the rowers turned at the stake marking the halfway point of the contest and began pulling for the finish line. The Biglin brothers are already leading by at least two lengths: the dramatic tension of this moment becomes apparent only if we attempt to visualize the scene in motion. In fact, the boat of Coulter and Cavitt would be moving forward very rapidly, whereas that of the Biglin Brothers would be virtually stopped, since Eakins shows it at the moment when the brothers are making the turn.

Turning was the most difficult, the most critical single moment of the race—the one in which it is easiest to lose time or even capsize, the one that required the brothers to break the clockwork rhythm of their strokes and row against each other. John, in the bow, is digging his oar into the water and pushing backward, so that it acts as a fulcrum around which the boat turns. Barney is pulling forward, so that the boat will turn around the pivot provided by John's oar. In just a moment, however, when the boat has completed the turn, John must reverse the direction of his oars and start pulling forward. His timing at this moment must take two factors into account. First, he must reverse direction at just the moment when the turn is complete, so that the boat will be headed on course and will not lose time yawing off to the side. Moreover, when he shifts the direction of his stroke, he needs to do so in a way that will perfectly synchronize with his brother's movements, so that the oars will not hit each other.

All the rowers are exerting themselves to the full. Eakins celebrates a moment when their bodies and minds are utterly absorbed by this effort, so that the external world almost ceases to exist. Like his earlier rowing scene, the painting celebrates the extinction of consciousness.

Once again, Eakins included himself in the painting. According to a tradition that seems to go back to Susan Eakins, he is the faceless figure in a small boat (evidently a racing shell) in the distance at the left, who fires a pistol into the air to mark the moment when the Biglin brothers make the turn.[13] Thus, he signified his strong identification with the rowers, and indeed, their activity had many parallels with his own. Eakins himself was just turning a key marker at this point, for his apprenticeship was coming to an end and he was gearing up to go to work on *The Gross Clinic*, the painting that he intended to serve as his "masterpiece," and which he hoped would establish his reputation as the leading American figure painter. The rowers apparent lack of forward progress parallels Eakins's own situation at this time, since he also was at a critical moment of a race, but one in which there was no external evidence of forward movement. Thus, like *The Champion Single Sculls*, the essential subject of the painting revolves around Eakins and his dilemmas, even though he appears only as a background figure.

Despite the painting's aura of "realism," it contains several factual discrepancies. Coulter and Cavitt, for example, raced bare to the waist with no coverings on their closely shaved heads. Eakins showed them in white shirts and red headscarves. At the actual race, stake boats marked the turn. Eakins, however, realized that another boat would be too distracting, and simply showed stakes planted in the river bottom.

One could argue that in many respects *The Biglin Brothers* is superior to *The Champion Single Sculls*—larger, more elaborate, and in many respects more dramatic. Indeed, the painting was impressive enough to attract the attention of Mrs. Schuyler Van Rensselaer, who saw the painting in 1880 and immediately recognized it as something remarkable, and quite different from the work of other American artists. She was so tantalized that on the basis of seeing this single picture she made a special trip to Philadelphia to meet the artist.

Despite this token of success, however, the execution of the painting clearly caused Eakins anguish—in large part because of its scale. Areas that were convincing in the smaller works, such as the water in the foreground, failed to convey a credible illusion, becoming a flat expanse that resembles concrete pavement.

Evidently the sky also looked too flat. At some point Eakins completely repainted it. We do not know when he did this, but the rough execution of the sky resembles Eakins's work from the period after he was fired from the Pennsylvania Academy (that is, after 1886), and thus was probably executed at least six years after the painting was first exhibited. Cross-sections of the pigment show that Eakins's approach to paint application was messy, intuitive, and not very logical. He piled colors on top of each other in layers, apparently striving for density and solidity.[14]

In the end, he created a painting that communicates depth and distance in a manner analogous to a bas-relief. The thickest areas of pigment, however, are not where one would expect them to be. In the sky (the most distant area) he built up pigment thickly, so that it comes closer to the viewer, while in the water (in the foreground) he scraped away at the surface with a palette knife, making the physical surface recede. By the time he was through, Eakins had developed a surface richly worked in every part, and an overall effect of moodiness and emotional tension, but at the cost of the clarity he had achieved earlier in *The Champion Single Sculls*.

Eakins's last painting of rowers, *Oarsmen on Schuylkill*, was the least successful of the series: a rendition of a four-oared shell, possibly inspired by a competition of September 26, 1874, in which his friend Max Schmitt rowed in such a craft. Since the painting was never finished, the execution lacks sharpness and resolution. Moreover, the overall concept lacks drama. So many

Oarsmen on the Schuylkill, ca. 1874. *Oil on canvas, 27 ⅝ x 48 ¼ in., private collection, photograph courtesy of Hirschl and Adler Galleries, New York.* Eakins left his last rowing picture, unfinished. Oddly, while the rowers are dressed their reflections are nude.

rowers become repetitive, and the boat is awkwardly placed between the two shores of the river, seemingly going nowhere.[15] An odd feature of the piece is that while the men are clothed, their reflections appear nude. After this last effort, Eakins seems to have never again attempted a rowing subject.[16]

The Progression of the Rowing Pictures

Writers on Eakins's rowing scenes have generally focused on the specifics of each scene: who the rowers are, where they are placed on the Schuylkill River, and which race they are engaged in or preparing for. Pursuing such incidentals, however, can easily distract us from the task of exploring Eakins's deeper artistic intentions. In fact, if we disregard these details, and examine the general progression of Eakins's rowing pictures, several developments become apparent. One is that the paintings grow progressively less detailed and less finished—a pattern that was typical of Eakins when he worked and reworked a theme. The other is that the number of rowers and their relation to each other gradually changes. A list of the paintings runs as follows:

1871, *The Champion Single Sculls*: two rowers in two boats.
1872, *The Pair-Oared Shell*: two rowers in one boat.
1872, *The Biglin Brothers Racing*: two rowers in one boat.

1873, *The Biglin Brothers Turning the Stake*: four rowers in two boats.

1874, *Oarsmen on the Schuylkill*: four rowers in one boat.[17]

Two clear progressions are apparent: first, the number of rowers increases, and second, Eakins moved them from different boats into the same boat.

Just what this signifies is a little mysterious, but I think it begins to make sense if we consider that the whole point of his first rowing painting was Eakins's desire to identify with another man. By showing himself with Max Schmitt he asserted that they both were men, and that he was just as manly as his friend. Indeed, what ultimately fascinated him was the notion of men synchronizing with each other to the point where their individual identities are blurred and they become one entity. As he developed this theme, he moved the two rowers into the same boat, and ultimately, expanded the number of rowers once again, including four figures in the same boat. (The recurrence of brothers in these paintings is also an intriguing element, particularly since Eakins never had one.)

By the time he made the final four-man painting, however, the scene had lost its sense of reality. The men appear about to collide with the shore, or perhaps are just rowing nowhere. The nude reflections may express a desire to undress the men, but this impulse is expressed in a way that conflicts with the believability of the scene. The painting no longer seems to portray an actual moment. The theme of communal male bonding became so powerful that the credibility of the rest of the image became tenuous. Eakins seems to have been caught between his desire to create a realistic illusion and his need to express his underlying emotions about the subject. Reaching an impasse, unable to resolve the tension between the two, he left the painting unfinished.

Perspective

A striking aspect of Eakins's rowing scenes was his unusual use of perspective. Most artists use perspective in a casual way, simply ensuring that when objects recede into space they converge toward a single vanishing point. Eakins, however, used a strict system of perspective, like that employed for architecture or industrial design, in which the dimensions of every object are precisely accurate. To achieve this he made drawings in which every element of the composition was systematically plotted within a geometric grid. This provided him with an exact ground plan that indicated the location of the viewer, the vanishing point, and the precise dimensions of every object. To make such drawings, Eakins needed to carefully measure every object in his paintings. Conversely, in cases where Eakins's perspective drawings have survived, it is possible to use them to calculate the actual dimensions and position of each object.

Thus, for example, Eakins's drawing for *The Pair-Oared Shell* plots the plane of the water in a perspective grid, with each unit in the grid representing one square foot. By following his calculations the art historian and conservator Theodor Siegle has determined that the stern of the boat is 30.5 feet from the spectator, and 5.5 feet to the right of center, while the bow is 62 feet away and 4.5 feet to the left of center. The boat is 36 feet long and moving at an angle of 67 degrees away from the viewer. Even the reflections of the rowers were based on this system. Eakins assumed that each ripple was composed of three planes (parallel to the viewer, and slanting toward and away from him). For the two visible reflections, Eakins constructed two converging scales in the sky area and numbered them according to distance. By following the shadow line of the pier one can even calculate the time of the day in the painting: 7:20 P.M., in late spring or early summer.

Although simple in principle, carrying out such a system is quite confusing in practice. When he first developed this approach in his rowing paintings, Eakins drew grid lines on the floor of his studio so that he could place objects on the floor and see how they related to his perspective drawings. The rowing paintings provide a particularly obvious instance of this system, but Eakins seems to have used it subsequently for virtually every kind of subject—interiors, full-length portraits, rowers, hunters, and figures in motion. Interestingly, Eakins never departed from a one-point perspective method, with its clear, stage-like space and centralized point of focus. He never used the more dynamic two-point system, with dual vanishing points at left and right, although it was often employed by his teacher, Jean-Léon Gérôme.

Eakins's knowledge of perspective was clearly a source of pride in his dealings with other artists. In 1877, for example, while in the midst of disputes about his teaching at the Pennsylvania Academy, he wrote to the watercolorist William Trost Richards (who was eleven years older than he), enclosing a diagram of how to draw a yacht in perspective. Eakins's system was essentially to place the boat within a box, and calculate the tilt and angle of this cube. He would then divide the box up into a network of squares and chart the curves of the boat within the grid. While intellectually simple, the process was quite tedious, and required very accurate drawing. No doubt for this reason, there is no evidence that Richards ever used or even tried this method. Indeed, such a highly repetitive system had an obsessive-compulsive aspect. Eakins seems to have been the only nineteenth-century American artist who used such a laborious and detailed perspective system on a regular basis.[18]

Despite this immense effort, the perspective systems in Eakins's paintings are often not obvious. There are two reasons for this. First, unlike Renaissance painters, Eakins did not place objects within a clearly depicted ground plane, such as a checkerboard floor. Thus, the viewer has few reference points with which to gauge whether the perspective is accurate. Indeed, in many of the later portraits, Eakins provided no firm reference points. Thus, his application of his perspective system became a formal and intellectual exercise, which had limited bearing on the final visual outcome.

Second, Eakins often obscured the perspective system when he painted over it. This is particularly evident in his interior scenes such as *The Chess Players* (1876) in which the forms are so obscured by shadow that one can hardly tell whether or not they are rendered in true perspective. Other paintings also exhibit an expressive tension between the rigorously charted perspective system and the flowing paint laid on top of it.

Despite his reputation for "honesty" and exactitude, in many of his paintings, Eakins took liberties that impair the visual accuracy of his system. Frequently, after Eakins had plotted the elements of a composition in perspective, he found that the foreground objects looked too small. To compensate, he would slide the picture plane back, cropping out empty parts of the foreground on all sides. This creates a visual effect rather like a wide-angled lens. While still mathematically exact, the perspective in the painting no longer corresponds with optical reality. *The Biglin Brothers Turning the Stake* is one of many paintings in which Eakins moved the picture plane in this way.[19]

The artist also seems to have delighted in creating effects that were "correct" in perspective but that look unusual and strange. Perhaps the most notable instance of this is the way he often placed his signature in script so that it coincides with the floor plane without quite belonging to it. For example, in *Elizabeth Crowell at the Piano*, Eakins placed his signature so that it is misaligned with the carpet on which it appears to rest. Its inky color also seems to belong to another representational system. The result is an uneasy compromise that while technically "correct," creates a tension between different planes, making it seemingly impossible that they could exist in the same realm. [20]

Eakins's preoccupation with perspective clearly reflects the solid training in the subject he received at Central High School, but even more profoundly, it was related to his father's methods as a writing master. Consequently, for Eakins perspective seems to have been associated with things that he conceived as masculine, such as accuracy, reason, control, and discipline. His use of perspective tends to be most pronounced and elaborate in paintings that deal with "masculine" subject matter, such as the rowing scenes, or the chess game between his father's friends.[21] He was more likely to show women against murky and indeterminate backgrounds.

Elizabeth at the Piano (detail of signature and carpet below), 1875. *Oil on canvas, 72 ⅛ × 48 ³⁄₁₆ in., Addison Gallery of American Art, Phillips Academy, Andover, Massachusetts, gift of an anonymous donor.* Eakins's signature is in carefully calculated perspective, but it is misaligned with the carpet on which it rests.

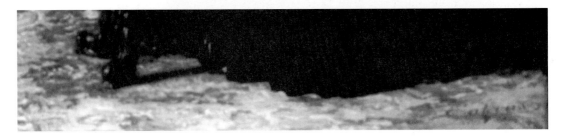

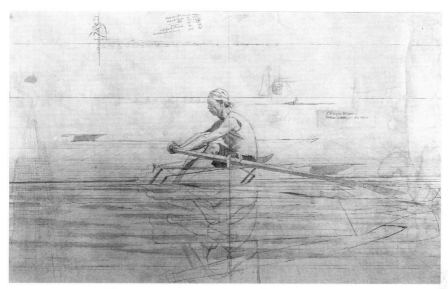

Perspective Studies for *John Biglin in a Single Scull*, ca. 1873. *Graphite, pen and wash on two sheets of buff paper joined together, 27 ⅜ x 45 ³⁄₁₆ in., Museum of Fine Arts, Boston, gift of Cornelius V. Whitney.* Eakins made a perspective study twice the size of the watercolor, in which he measured every object and worked out the placement of the reflections.

John Biglin in a Single Scull, 1873. *Watercolor on paper, 16 ⅞ x 23 ¹⁵⁄₁₆ in. (irregular), Yale University Art Gallery, gift of Paul Mellon.* In 1874 Eakins sent a watercolor, which is now lost, to win the approval of his former teacher, Jean-Léon Gérôme. When Gérôme criticized the pose of the rower, Eakins sent him this second painting, in which he corrected the faults. Gérôme pronounced the result "entirely good," adding "I am pleased to have in the New World a pupil such as you who does me honor."

Notably, Eakins's first explorations of perspective, in his rowing paintings, came at the time when his mother was dying. He seems to have found a kind of release from his worries by carrying out a system that was rigorously logical, highly repetitive, and which thus served as an antidote to the emotional chaos created by his mother's illness. As Kathleen Spies has noted, "It is interesting that it was around the time of his mother's death when he began his excessively detailed perspective studies for his series of paintings showing rowers on the Schuylkill, perhaps as a sort of obsessive need to control the uncontrollable—nature, woman, illness and death."[22]

Winning the Approval of Gérôme

Eakins scholars have tended to exaggerate the artist's talent as a student, thus obscuring the significance of one of the most poignant moments of his early professional life: in 1873, he sent one of his watercolors to his former master, Jean-Léon Gérôme, in a bid for sympathy and approval.

Eakins's choice of subject and medium was carefully calculated. The subject he chose was rowing, but rather than showing multiple figures, he took his oil of the two Biglin brothers racing and pared the design down to a single figure, placing the figure of John Biglin in a single scull against an expansive landscape. Thus, Eakins deliberately returned to the sort of rendering of the single male figure that had been the main focus of his work in Gérôme's atelier. Clearly he was interested in demonstrating that the single figure study, which he had failed to master in Paris, was now within his grasp.

Eakins shipped the watercolor to Gérôme in the spring of 1873, and Gérôme wrote back to him with his reactions on May 10. Though fierce toward his artistic rivals, Gérôme was impressively generous and patient toward his pupils. Nonetheless, the seemingly complimentary phrases in his letters to Eakins carry a double edge. "I am delighted that my counsels, however tardily applied, have at last borne fruit," Gérôme declared, adding "I will not conceal from you that formerly in the studio I was not without anxiety about your future as a painter, from the studies that I saw you make."[23] While obliquely stated, these phrases make it clear that Eakins's performance as a student in Paris had been less than fully satisfactory. Gérôme went on to note that the rower looked static, since Eakins had rendered him in midmotion. Gérôme proposed that it would work better to represent him either at the beginning or the end of the stroke.

So eager was Eakins to gain his master's approval that he produced an

entirely new watercolor, following this suggestion, which he sent to Gérôme
in May 1874. On September 18, Gérôme wrote back to Eakins pronouncing the
result "entirely good," except perhaps for a certain evenness of execution that
left the picture without dramatic focus.[24]

Eakins clearly took great pride in Gérôme's endorsement, and for the rest
of his life presented himself as one of his favorite pupils.[25] Yet Eakins's choice
of watercolor as a medium contained a strong element of duplicity. By this
time, when working in oil, Eakins had completely abandoned the smooth
paint handling that Gérôme favored, and employed pigment in a thick, crusty,
and expressive manner. Eakins's watercolor technique, however, was still tight
and "correct," according to Gérôme's standards. Indeed, in contrast to the
usual manner of handling the medium, he sometimes made oil studies for his
watercolors, to eliminate any element of spontaneity or guesswork.[26] Thus,
by sending a watercolor Eakins was able to conceal the fact that he had moved
very far from the principles of his teacher. Eakins must have known that
Gérôme's praise had been achieved through a ruse, and that Gérôme would
not have approved of the way Eakins painted in oil.

The Gross Clinic, 1875. *Oil on canvas, 96 x 78 in., Jefferson Medical College, Thomas Jefferson University, Philadelphia.* **The Gross Clinic was considered too shocking to show in the art pavilion of the Philadelphia Centennial Exposition and was hung instead in the medical section.**

Chapter 12

THE GROSS CLINIC

OVER THE SPACE of just five years—indeed, largely in the single year between 1870 and 1871—Eakins had transformed himself from a clumsy student to a virtuoso. But the battle was hard won. Eakins would never be a facile painter. Compared to most painters, his techniques were incredibly laborious, and when he did not have enormous amounts of time to work on a project the results were generally not impressive. Figures such as John Singer Sargent could produce a good painting in an afternoon and a nearly life-size portrait in a week. Eakins often took fifty, even a hundred times as long, sometimes requiring months to work out even a single detail, such as the way that water ripples against an oar or the tilt of a boat in proper perspective. Not surprisingly, Eakins often found it difficult to sustain the effort he needed to produce a major painting, as is evidenced by the gradual falling off in quality of his rowing pictures, which become progressively less finished and less resolved as he worked on the series.

Was this labor worth it? To us today the answer would be an emphatic "Yes." Critics and art historians today universally view the best of these early works as touchstones of American achievement, worthy to stand among the greatest paintings of the 19th century by masters from any country. During the period when Eakins produced these early masterworks, however, critical response was muted. Reviewers applauded the care Eakins put into his work but were put off by his odd subjects and the quality his painting had of being assembled from individual fragments, pasted together somewhat awkwardly. They said nothing about the curious emotional undercurrents of his work, which fascinate us today. One of the most extraordinary of Eakins's early works, *The Champion Single Sculls*, was exhibited only once and merited only a few casual lines of newspaper commentary. From the commercial standpoint Eakins was even more thoroughly repudiated: income from sales would not have kept him alive, even at a poverty level.

Given that Eakins's paintings were surely far better than most of the works beside them, Eakins must have been frustrated by the lack of response and must have felt that he must do something to draw attention to his work. In 1875, however, this situation changed from too little attention to too much with the exhibition of the most significant and controversial painting of his career, *The Gross Clinic*, which shows Dr. Samuel Gross conducting surgery in an amphitheater filled with students. The project was Eakins's most ambitious work to date, being more than ten times larger than any of his earlier paintings, and containing twenty-nine figures, most of them portraits. Eakins spent the better part of a year completing the canvas and clearly intended it to be his masterpiece—both in the old-fashioned sense of a work that demonstrated his move from journeyman to master, and also in the modern sense of a work that would astound people who saw it, and would earn him enduring artistic fame. Eakins had clearly been thinking about and planning this project for years. The mental effort he put into gearing up for this great effort, even before he started the actual work, may explain his increasing loss of interest in the rowing pictures and their consequent weakening in impact. When the painting was still only roughly blocked in he expressed the opinion that the painting would be "very far better than anything I have ever done."[1]

Rather than receiving critical acclaim, however, the final painting provoked controversy and was pointedly excluded from several major exhibitions. Along with the loin cloth incident, the "rejection" of *The Gross Clinic* has always played a central role in the mystique that has gathered around Eakins, establishing his credentials as an unjustly persecuted figure.

Eakins seems to have executed the painting specifically for the Centennial Exhibition, held in Philadelphia in May 1876. In April of that year, however, shortly before the show opened, the selection committee accepted five paintings but rejected *The Gross Clinic*. Eakins hurriedly arranged to show the painting at the Haseltine Galleries in Philadelphia, where it appeared just three weeks before the Centennial Exhibition opened. The picture received an extremely positive review from William Clark in the *Daily Evening Telegraph*, who declared, "We know of nothing in the line of portraiture that has ever been attempted in this city, or indeed in this country, that in any way approaches it. . . . This portrait of Dr. Gross is a great work—we know of nothing greater that has ever been executed in America."[2]

A notable feature of this review (the very first written about the painting)

THE GROSS CLINIC 217

is that despite the furor over the piece, it already proposes that Eakins's canvas should be singled out as the greatest painting ever made in America—a claim that has since been repeated by many later writers. Clark was one of the directors of the Pennsylvania Academy of the Fine Arts, the most important art institution in Philadelphia, so his editorial was not only a forceful piece of criticism but gave the painting some degree of official sanction.[3]

Shortly afterward, as a result of some behind-the-scenes maneuvering, the new painting was indeed shown at the Centennial—but not in the art exhibition. Instead it was shown in the U.S. Army Post Hospital, alongside hospital beds and medical equipment. Eakins's supporter Clark wrote a second review of the painting, suggesting that the painting had been exiled from the art exhibition not because of "squeamishness" but rather because of jealousy on the part of other artists.

In March 1879 Eakins showed the painting at the Society of American Artists in New York. It was noticed by all the major New York newspapers, as well as a number of magazines, including *The Art Journal*, *The Nation*, and *Scribner's Monthly*. Most of this press coverage was negative, condemning the painting as "horrible" and "morbid," although the extent of the coverage indicated that the painting had made a strong impression.

Some typical responses:

The Art Interchange: It ought never to have left the dissection room. . . . The scene is revolting to the last degree.[4]

The New York Times: This violent and bloody scene shows that . . . the artist had no conception of where to stop, or how to hint a horrible thing if it must be said, or what the limits are between the beauty of the nude and the indecency of the naked.[5]

The New York Daily Tribune: One of the most powerful, horrible and yet fascinating pictures that has been painted anywhere in this century . . . The more one praises it, the more one must condemn its admission to a gallery where men and women of weak nerves must be compelled to look at it. For not to look at it is impossible.[6]

A month later the exhibition traveled to the Pennsylvania Academy of the Fine Arts in Philadelphia. By this time Eakins was the most active teacher in the school, had exhibited in the Academy annuals for three years, and was even a member of the exhibition committee. Nonetheless, in the final hanging, Eakins's painting was separated from the rest of the show and hung in the East corridor at the opposite end of the building, in the company of the least significant pieces in the exhibition—watercolors, drawings, and student works. In the place of honor that would normally have been given to Eakins's canvas, the Academy installed a large, unexciting canvas by Thomas Moran, *Bringing Home the Cattle, Coast of Florida* (1879, Albright-Knox Art Gallery, Buffalo) which had been rejected from the New York show. Eakins composed a letter protesting what he took to be "a direct insult," and the exclusion of his painting was reported by newspapers in New York and Boston.[7]

After this, the painting was put on view at Jefferson Medical College, where few people saw it other than doctors. In 1893 it was in the World's Fair in Chicago (with a brief preliminary showing at the Pennsylvania Academy), and in 1904 it was in the Louisiana Purchase Exposition in St. Louis, where it received an award. These three showings, along with those of the 1870s, were the only ones in Eakins's lifetime. While occasionally mentioned in reviews, only after Eakins's death did the painting achieve its current canonical stature as a preeminent landmark of American art.[8]

What was it that caused so much controversy? We immediately grasp the essence of the drama—that is the contrast between the calm, godlike figure of Dr. Gross, with scalpel in hand, and the confusion of blood and limbs around the patient. It takes some time, however, to grasp the significance of every element. Details in *The Gross Clinic* are difficult to make out because of the dim light, the large number of figures, and the odd angle at which many of the elements are shown. I must confess that it took me years to make out the shadowy, headless assistant whose knee protrudes to the left of Dr. Gross, whose body wraps behind him, and whose one well-illuminated feature is a thumb holding a forceps just to the right of the doctor. I suspect that 99 percent of the people who look at the painting never notice this figure. Reproductions of the painting, because they greatly reduce its scale, make the painting look finished and meticulous when in fact it is executed roughly, with what seems like deliberate crudity. The head of Dr. Gross, for instance, was largely executed not with a brush but a palette knife. Many of the details of the painting are easier to make out in a pen-and-ink copy that Eakins made of the painting for reproduction, since it has darkened less than the actual canvas.

The setting is an amphitheater, with an audience of twenty-one students, including the son of Dr. Gross, who stands in the doorway, and Eakins himself, who sits hunched forward, immediately to the right of the entrance ramp, pencil and notebook in hand. At the left, a scribe (Dr. Franklin West) records the proceedings.

The focus of the painting is Dr. Gross. He stands just to the left of center, with light from a skylight illuminating his silvery hair like a halo. A bloody scalpel is in his right hand. He has paused and turned away from the operation, presumably because he is lecturing, although his mouth is not open.

To the right, on a table, is the patient—twisted in such an unusual posture that it is difficult to make sense of the arrangement of limbs. All that is visible are his naked buttocks, his twisted leg, and two feet. The feet are covered with blue-gray socks that dramatically enhance the sense of vulnerability and

The Gross Clinic, ca. 1875–1876. *India ink and watercolor on cardboard, 23 ¾ x 19 ¼ in., Metropolitan Museum of Art, Rogers Fund, 1923.* Eakins's ink and wash copy of *The Gross Clinic* shows details no longer visible in the oil, including a self-portrait of Eakins taking notes just to the right of the doorway.

nakedness. The patient's head and torso are largely hidden by gauze, which has been soaked in anesthetic and is being applied by an assistant (Dr. Joseph Hearn). A long bloody incision has been opened in his thigh.

Two assistants are preoccupied with attending to the incision. One (Dr. James M. Barton, Gross's chief of clinic) probes it with an implement, while another (Dr. Daniel Appel, a recent graduate of Jefferson Medical College) holds the wound open with a retractor. Another hand with a retractor is pulling on the wound from the opposite direction of Dr. Appel. The head of this figure is invisible, and, as has been noted, it takes very careful looking to realize that the legs of this figure are poking out from below the left side of Dr. Gross's coat. Still another figure (Dr. Charles S. Briggs) grips the patient's legs to hold them in position.

In this period, a relative of the patient was expected to attend the operation. This individual, an older woman, presumably the patient's mother, is seated just behind Dr. Gross, shielding her face from the operation with claw-like hands that evoke the talons of a bird of prey. Interestingly, while the spatial position of this figure is a little ambiguous, her scale is clearly too small—giving new meaning to the phrase "shrinking in horror."

A box of surgical instruments extends horizontally across the lower left of the composition. Beneath the table, where a box of sand was placed to catch the patient's blood, we catch a glimpse of red, indicating that blood has been spilled.

As with his music and rowing pictures, Eakins notably departed from the usual formula for portraying a surgeon. Indeed, the shock with which his painting was received makes it clear that this was the case. I know of no earlier American painting that deals in such fashion with a surgical operation, and most of the celebrated French academic paintings of such medical activities are later in date. One may well ask how an artist was expected to deal with such a medical theme. The probable answer is that he was supposed to avoid it. In portraying a surgeon he was expected to provide a portrait showing the individual standing or sitting in his best clothes, but not to draw attention to the gruesome nature of actual medical practices. Generally, such portraits featured a single figure, but it was also possible to employ essentially the same formula for a multifigured composition. Thus for example, the most celebrated painting by Christian Schuessele, the leading painter in Philadelphia during Eakins's childhood, was a work titled *Men of Progress* (1862) that portrayed a group of men of accomplishment and invention, such as Samuel Morse, the inventor of the telegraph, Charles Goodyear, the inventor of vulcanized rubber, Cyrus McCormick, the inventor of the mechanical reaper, and Samuel Colt, the inventor and manufacturer of the six-gun. In Schuessele's portrayal these figures are gathered together in their best clothes in a picturesque grouping, but nothing about their pose or setting provides a clue about what these individuals had accomplished.

Eakins's painting was clearly intended as a kind of rejoinder to paintings of this type. While shocking in its violations of decorum, it makes us conscious of Gross's actual activities and accomplishments. Rather than moving Gross into a genteel living room, it places him in the professional arena, and sets out, somewhat melodramatically, to illustrate the challenges he faced in attaining his reputation. In fact, Eakins's title for the painting, *Portrait of Professor Gross*, is revealing.[9] It makes it clear that he intended his portrait to be compared with the existing portraits of Philadelphia doctors and wanted the contrast between them and his work to be carefully noted.

The most popular interpretation of the painting is that of Elizabeth Johns, who argues that Eakins was celebrating a hero of modern life. So long as we do not look too closely at the painting itself, her proposal makes a certain sense, and in fact Eakins clearly designed the painting so that it could be read in this fashion.

Eakins surely took pride in the fact that Philadelphia was rivaled only by Boston as the major center of American medicine. Its most prestigious school was Jefferson Medical College, which was established in 1825 in rivalry with the University of Pennsylvania. Unlike the University of Pennsylvania, which was wedded to old-fashioned Scottish methods, Jefferson was modeled on more modern French schools. In addition, the college was more democratic than the University of Pennsylvania, allowing admission to all, without the need for "connections." In short, Jefferson Medical College fit neatly with those things that Eakins admired: it was in Philadelphia, it was modern, and it did not cater to rich snobs of the sort that Eakins despised.

Dr. Samuel Gross had long-standing connections with Jefferson Medical College, and in the 1870s was certainly the single most celebrated figure on its faculty. He had been one of the first students at the college, entering in 1826 and graduating two years later. Over the next twenty-five years he taught and practiced at medical colleges in Cincinnati, Louisville, and New York. He also translated medical texts, and published articles and books on pathological anatomy and the treatment of war wounds, particularly wounds to the intestines. In 1856 at the age of fifty-one, he was appointed to the professorship of surgery at Jefferson Medical College, where he taught for the next twenty-six years. In this role he continued to publish extensively, as well as to edit medical journals. His two-volume *System of Surgery* became a standard reference for the surgical profession.

Before the advent of anesthesia, surgery caused excruciating pain and it was often carried out by untrained individuals, such as barbers. The discovery of anesthesia in Boston in 1846 made possible intricate, time-consuming operations that would have been inconceivable before. In addition, the Civil War, with its many gunshot wounds, led to major improvements in surgical technique. By the 1870s, surgeons were at the forefront of new medical breakthroughs and stood at the head of the medical profession. Dr. Samuel Gross was a stunning example of this phenomenon. On his death a colleague wrote, "It is safe to say that no previous medical teacher or author on this continent exercised such a widespread and commanding influence as did Professor Gross."[10]

The operation Eakins depicted in *The Gross Clinic* was one particularly associated with Dr. Gross. It was the last stage of Gross's treatment for osteomyelitis, or bacterial infection of the bone. This problem was fairly common in the nineteenth century, although since the introduction of antibiotics in the 1930s it is now rare. The condition generally occurred in the larger bones of the body, such as the femur, tibia, and humerus, and most often afflicted patients between the ages of five and twenty-two. Until the late eighteenth century the problem was treated through amputation. In time, however, surgeons found that the infected bone would simply die, and then slowly separate itself from the bone shaft, allowing the shaft to regenerate itself. Unfortunately, as the bone broke away it generally caused damage to the surrounding flesh and often penetrated the skin. Thus, the process of healing could be speeded by cutting the diseased portion of bone away from the healthy shaft. Today, the operation, as Gordon Hendricks has noted, would be "as simple as a tooth extraction," but for nineteenth-century surgeons it presented significant challenges, since the pattern of decay was slightly different in each instance.[11] Often a series of operations were necessary, extending over a period of a year or more. Eakins's painting shows the last stage of Dr. Gross's treatment for this condition.

How we read *The Gross Clinic* depends in part on how we regard this operation. Elizabeth Johns presents Gross as a leader and a pioneer, as no doubt Eakins wished us to regard him. By the 1870s, however, many of his methods were reactionary and drastically outmoded. Thus, for example, Gross was a violent antagonist of British surgeon Joseph Lister's technique of antisepsis, which by that time had been widely accepted both in Europe and much of the

United States. In fact, Lister visited Philadelphia to promote his methods in 1876, the very year that Eakins's painting was exhibited.[12] Bombastically, and irrationally, Gross likened Lister's use of carbolic acid to sterilize the surgical arena to mesmerism and clairvoyance. Gross was also an ardent advocate of bleeding, a practice he defended with quotations from Galen and medieval medical treatises, although its value had by that time been rightly questioned by all progressive members of the medical profession.

Far from being put off by Gross's stubborn rejection of new methods, Eakins seems to have admired Gross's arrogance, which mirrored that of his own father, and also resembled the arbitrary, authoritarian rule that he himself imposed on the curriculum of the Pennsylvania Academy of the Fine Arts. Eakins surely relished Gross's stubborn unwillingness to yield to progress. Even visually, Eakins was strongly attracted to the aspects of Gross's procedure that were medical anachronisms. The dark clothing, which provides much of the visual drama of *The Gross Clinic*, had already been discarded by more progressive figures in favor of white surgical attire. Eakins's painting celebrates a reactionary figure, whose days of innovation lay in the past.

For Elizabeth Johns a key aspect of Eakins's painting is that it portrays "conservative surgery," which was less drastic than earlier methods, such as amputation.[13] In a technical sense this is correct, but visually the painting does not emphasize this fact. Instead, it maximizes the viewer's exposure to blood and to the horror of the scene.

In her extended essay on *The Gross Clinic*, Elizabeth Johns mentions "a noticeable awkwardness in his central grouping around the patient."[14] Of course, it is just this sense of confusion and indelicacy that lies at the heart of Eakins's message. The fundamental drama of the painting is expressed in the contrast between the two central figures: that of Dr. Gross, who is all head, brain, and hands, and that of the patient, who has no visible head or hands, but instead is only feet, leg, and buttocks. The first has his nakedness concealed with black clothes going up to his neck, leaving only his head and hand visible. The second is uncovered, except for the socks, and is exposed to our gaze. This sense of discomfort is emphasized by the public nature of the display. We join a crowd of more than twenty witnesses, themselves half-obscured by the darkness, who are intently watching the event.

Despite the efforts of generations of scholars to obscure this fact, contemporary viewers recognized immediately that the painting is distressing and violent—although also something luridly compelling and hard not to look at. Indeed, Michael Fried, who has written at length about the picture, has noted that if we disregard the precise operation being shown, and simply look at the painting as an interpersonal drama, it is a curiously strange and violent one, with many Freudian overtones.

Both Lloyd Goodrich and Elizabeth Johns have justified the confusion of Eakins's composition on the grounds that he was painting exactly what he saw, and was obliged to stay true to the facts. Thus, for example, after noting that there are bizarre elements in Eakins's presentation, Goodrich declares, "these enigmatic features of are part of Eakins' realism," and John argues, "the demands of a real situation took precedence over design, material over grace."[15]

As Michael Fried has pointed out, however, such an argument is fundamentally flawed, since it reverses the relationship of cause and effect. Our only evidence of what Eakins saw is the painting itself. Consequently, it is hardly logical to use an imagined reality as a justification for the painting. Moreover, even if we were to suppose that Eakins saw things in a way that was perfectly truthful and exact, in a sense analogous, let us say, to a documentary photograph of the scene, it still does not eliminate the element of

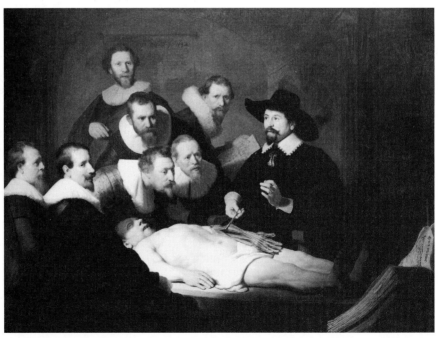

Rembrandt van Rijn, The Anatomy Lesson of Dr. Nicolaas Tulp, *1632. Royal Cabinet of Paintings, Mauritshuis, The Hague.* **Rembrandt's famous painting gave Eakins hints about how to organize his figures.**

artistic choice, since Eakins clearly put considerable thought into choosing a particular vantage point and a particular moment of the operation. In other words, he organized and selected from reality to express a particular kind of dramatic meaning.[16]

Indeed, the whole argument of "realism" constructed by Goodrich and Johns is logically unsatisfactory. If Eakins was simply presenting reality in a mechanical way, without altering what he saw, how could the result be so unusual and profoundly expressive that it has been termed "the greatest American painting"? Goodrich slides around this problem by suggesting that Eakins was presenting not simply things that were real but things that were "truly real"—that is, in some way different from the reality that most artists present. But he was not very clear about what makes "true realism" different from "realism," or about what procedure an artist should employ to obtain this mysterious quality.

In fact, it is apparent that when he painted *The Gross Clinic*, Eakins did not literally transcribe what he saw, but instead borrowed major elements of his composition from earlier paintings. The most famous painter before Eakins to deal with the subject of a surgeon was Rembrandt, and the composition of Eakins's painting is a synthesis of several well-known works by him. For example, in making a triangular composition that focuses on a lecturing surgeon, Eakins was clearly influenced by Rembrandt's *The Anatomy Lesson of Dr. Tulp* (1632), the first major painting of a surgeon teaching an anatomy lesson, and by far the most famous. In

TOP *Rembrandt van Rijn,* The Night Watch, *1642. Rijksmuseum, Amsterdam.* **Rembrandt's** *The Night Watch* **showed Eakins how to create a feeling of mystery by placing some figures in deep shadow.** BOTTOM *Rembrandt van Rijn,* The Anatomy Lesson of Dr. Deyman, *1656. Amsterdams Historisch Museum.* **Rembrandt's** *Anatomy Lesson* **probably inspired the dramatically foreshortened patient in Eakins's painting.**

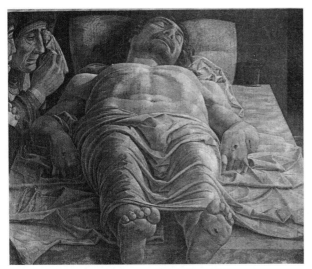

Andrea Mantegna, Dead Christ. *Brera Gallery, Milan, under license from Italian Ministry for Cultural Goods and Activities.* **Such dramatic foreshortening was ultimately based on Mantegna's famous** *Dead Christ.* BELOW *Diego Velásquez,* Las Meninas, *1656. Museo Nacional del Prado, Madrid.* **Eakins probably got the idea of silhouetting figures in a doorway from Velásquez's famous painting** *Las Meninas,* **which he had admired at the Prado.**

addition, the idea of representing some figures in bright light and others largely hidden by darkness was borrowed from Rembrandt's *The Night Watch* (1642), the first major painting to exploit this device in a multifigured composition. Previous writers have noted these parallels.

Curiously, earlier writers have never noted that Eakins's most important debt was to another painting by Rembrandt— *The Anatomy Lesson of Dr. Deyman* (1656), which shows the surgeon standing on the left and a strongly foreshortened corpse on the right. (Rembrandt, in turn, borrowed this foreshortened figure from Andrea Mantegna's *Dead Christ* (1506). In a general way, the scheme of Eakins's painting echoes that of Rembrandt. It shows a standing surgeon lecturing on the left and a strongly foreshortened, prostrate figure at the right. Eakins elaborated on his source, however, by altering poses and adding additional elements. Most notably, he twisted the pose of the foreshortened figure so that its head is not visible and its limbs form a pattern that is hardly recognizable as human. Eakins also added half a dozen medical assistants, in a visually compli-cated arrangement, and an amphitheater of spectators. His "recollection" of Rem-brandt's composition, in other words, is not simply a matter of direct copying. He isolated key dramatic principles and reconfigured them in a new way. Still, Eakins's debt to Rembrandt is plainly evident.

Not that Rembrandt was Eakins's

only source. As Michael Fried has noted, the backlit figures silhouetted in a doorway in the background recall Diego Velázquez's painting, *Las Meninas* (1656), which also employs this device. We know that Eakins was familiar with this source since he had carefully studied *Las Meninas* during his trip to Spain. As with his borrowing from Rembrandt, however, Eakins altered the poses and lighting just enough so that the borrowing is not too obvious.

Eakins's choice of Rembrandt as his major source may have possessed significance at a deeper level. Rembrandt was the classic instance of an abused and misunderstood artist, who painted works that were rejected by his contemporaries but hailed by posterity as masterpieces. At some level, perhaps an unconscious one, Eakins may well have wished to take on a similar role.[17]

Eakins's borrowings from the old masters make it clear that to a large degree he constructed his composition in the studio, rather than observing it. In fact, the spectators to the operation, to the extent that they have been identified, are not medical students but Eakins's pupils and helpers at the Pennsylvania Academy, including Hughie, the academy's janitor.[18]

Goodrich and Johns, in slightly different ways, construct an argument that negates the visual impact of the painting. They deny the element of shock and horror that was clearly central to Eakins's conception. Michael Fried has taken an entirely different approach. His argument is complex and not all of it is relevant here, but one aspect relates directly to the view of Eakins's paintings that I have proposed. Fried believes that we should read the painting in family terms, as an extrapolation of Eakins's relationship with his mother and father. Moreover, Fried explores this notion not only in literal terms, but more deeply. He marshals Freudian theories to argue that the painting forms an expression of deep-rooted psychological anxieties.

When I first encountered them, I must confess, I found some of Fried's interpretations quite far-fetched. Now I am not so sure. What makes them convincing is that the same disturbing undercurrents he claims to discover in *The Gross Clinic* seem to be also played out in other works, as well as in Eakins's behavior. Be that as it may, I ask the reader's indulgence in following Fried's argument to its conclusion. My summary of Fried's argument is in a different order than his, and mentions some elements that he omits. In its essentials, however, it recapitulates the same points.

Fried proposes that the drama being played out in *The Gross Clinic* involves what Freud termed a "family romance." Specifically, he proposes that the painting includes figures who are stand-ins for Eakins's father, his mother, and for Eakins himself. Eakins has cast Dr. Gross, Fried proposes, as a "glorified father figure."[19] Indeed, Eakins presented Dr. Gross in a fashion that is similar to the way in which he portrayed his father in *The Writing Master*. Fried notes that in both paintings, Eakins stressed a domed forehead framed by gray hair and seen under powerful spotlighting. The writing table stands at the same angle as the operating table. A speck of red at the end of Benjamin Eakins's quill in *The Writing Master* introduces an implication of violence that is echoed in the bloody scalpel of *The Gross Clinic*. In both renderings the eyes of the figures are hidden, and their expressions are firm but essentially inscrutable.

More generally, Fried notes that throughout his life, Eakins often seems to have formed relationships with older and elderly men who had a paternal quality, rather than with his own contemporaries. Thus, for example, Eakins revered his French master, Gérôme; had a close relationship with his father-in-law William Macdowell; established a relationship with Walt Whitman; and associated with elderly members of the Catholic clergy. In addition, he had many interactions with elderly and distinguished doctors and scientists, and often chose them as subjects for his pictures. The way Eakins signed his two portraits of his father also suggests a degree of filial devotion so intense as to be almost abnormal. In both cases, he omitted his own name, signing them (in Latin) with the words: "The son of Benjamin Eakins painted this."

The head of Dr. Gross has often been compared with the work of masters such as Rembrandt, and cited as a proof of Eakins's insight and profundity. But the devices that Eakins used to create this effect have not been clearly indicated. In fact, what is striking is that Eakins failed to satisfy the usual expectations of portraiture in this period. This becomes apparent when we compare Eakins's rendering of Gross to a more conventional portrait of him by Samuel Waugh.[20] Waugh threw bright light on Gross's face, and by accurately rendering every feature sought to reveal his personality and character. Eakins, on the contrary, cast much of Dr. Gross's head into deep shadow, and by concealing key elements, created an aura of mystery and psychological suspense. The eyes, the feature we look at most closely to discern what someone is thinking, are completely obscured

The Writing Master: Portrait of the Artist's Father, 1882. *Oil on canvas, 30 x 34 ¼ in., Metropolitan Museum of Art, Kennedy Fund, 1917.*

Samuel Waugh, Samuel Gross, 1874. *Oil on canvas, 30 x 25 in., Jefferson Medical College, Thomas Jefferson University.* **While a careful likeness, Waugh's rendering of Dr. Gross has none of the drama of Eakins's much sketchier image.** RIGHT Head of Dr. Gross, Detail of the Gross Clinic, 1875. *Oil on canvas, 96 x 78 in., Jefferson Medical College, Thomas Jefferson University, Philadelphia.*

by shadow, giving him a masked appearance. The one feature that is clearly visible, the mouth, is not expressive, but tightly drawn and straight, and consequently, as Sylvan Schendler has commented, Gross seems "almost lost to feeling."[21] In other words, the emotional power of the painting depends in large part on the fact that Eakins does not tell us much about Gross's character, but allows us to project our own personal readings.

Significantly, Waugh provides more visual information. If we were asked to identify Dr. Gross in a lineup, Waugh's likeness would be the more useful of the two. Eakins's likeness, however, is the more emotionally compelling. Eakins's paint handling adds to this sense of ambiguity. Whereas Waugh's head stands clearly in front of the background, Eakins's smeared paint surface seems to dissolve into it.

If Dr. Gross serves as a stand-in for Eakins's father, it is logical to suppose that the woman in the painting mirrors Eakins's mother. Indeed, her behavior resembles that of Eakins's mother: she plays an overly emotional, in fact hysterical role.[22] Other attributes of this figure also relate to Eakins's mother in intriguing ways. For instance, Eakins took the trouble to specify that the woman is or was married, since he included a gold wedding band on her finger. (Unfortunately, this is quite difficult to discern in reproductions.) In addition, the mother figure wears black mourning clothes, suggesting an association with death. As Fried notes, this mother figure does not appear in Eakins's initial sketch—at least not gesturing in such a dramatic fashion. Eakins's inclusion of her was based on what Fried terms a "logic of feeling" that "had nothing whatever to do with strictly realistic factors."[23]

If we read this figure as Eakins's mother, it strongly suggests that the patient is her son, that is, Eakins himself. Eakins, however, seems to have repeated the figure of the son in other guises as well. Thus, the figure of the scribe writing behind Dr. Gross plays a role like that of a dutiful son. In addition, Eakins included a portrait of Gross's own son as the nearer of the two figures visible in the doorway. Finally, as noted earlier, Eakins included himself to the right of the doorway, at the very edge of the painting, with notebook and pencil in hand.

An interesting subtheme of the painting is that of writing, an art that had a special significance in Eakins's life. Dr. Gross's scalpel seems to play a role similar to that of a writing instrument, and the doctor holds it like a pen. Eakins seems to be interested in creating a connection between it and the pen of the scribe behind him at the left, as well as with the writing implement that Eakins himself is holding. As it happens, in real life there was a strong association between Dr. Gross and writing, both because he was a voluminous author, and also because, like Eakins, he was the son of a writing master. In short, these variations on the theme of writing and cutting can be related to the Oedipal tension between father and son that lies at the heart of the painting.

Indeed, we can trace still another father–son connection between Dr. Gross and Eakins that relates to this cutting/writing theme. Along with suggesting a writing implement, Dr. Gross's scalpel, with its intense accent of color, suggests a painter's brush just dipped into a pot of paint. Thus, at some level, Eakins seems interested in equating Dr. Gross's scalpel with his own paintbrush, and Dr. Gross's surgery with his own controlled but brutal act of making the painting we are looking at. We might even imagine that another level of the Oedipal theme of the painting entails Eakins's confrontation with the overwhelming authority of his artistic predecessors as he seeks to surpass the artists from whom he borrowed, such as Rembrandt and Velázquez. He admires them but is also threatened by them, in a way that recapitulates his relationship with his father.

Turning to Eakins's presentation of the patient, Michael Fried has noted three significant points. First, while the position of the patient is hard to read, when we figure out what we are looking at it is hard not to be shocked, for we are staring directly at the buttocks of the prostrate figure. This is placed almost exactly at the horizon line of the painting—at eye level. (Dr. Gross stands above the level of the horizon, looking down at us.) At its simplest, this is a provocative assault on our sensibilities. Eakins has stripped away the normal protections of clothing to reduce the figure to a state of humiliation and helplessness—and through a process of empathy, to reduce us to the same state.

Second, the wound in the figure's leg is provocatively juxtaposed with the exposed buttocks, and Eakins emphasizes the painfulness of the incision. He draws attention to the glistening blood, carefully delineating the little drips and flecks, and uses spotlighting and intense color to heighten its impact. He also draws attention to the way in which the wound is pulled open by the almost invisible background figure, and the straining foreground figure with the retractor. Finally, he highlights the doctor's probe, which is exploring the incision. Although intellectually we may understand that the patient is chloroformed and unconscious, it is impossible to look at this section of the painting without imagining pain. Moreover, the general theme of savage penetration raises thoughts of penetration of various kinds.

Third, the genitals of the figure are not visible. While writers have generally assumed that the figure is an adolescent male, in fact it is not possible to tell whether it is male or female on the basis of the visual evidence. The fact that the figure is an adolescent makes the figure's sex ambiguous, since secondary sex characteristics, such as the larger hips and buttocks of women, are minimized. From a visual standpoint, the figure is androgynous.[24]

All these elements are then juxtaposed with the image of Dr. Gross's scalpel-bearing right hand, with wet, crimson blood on his fingers and on the instrument's blade. In addition, the emotions we feel of shame and helplessness are perversely emphasized by the large audience of spectators, who transform what seemingly should be a private experience into a public spectacle. Such seemingly minor details as the patient's socks accentuate the nakedness of the rest of his body, making the embarrassment more acute. None of the figures, however, seem to respond emotionally to what is taking place in front of them, with the exception of the mother, who overresponds. Her hands are the most dramatic element in the picture, and convey the sense that psychological violence is being done to her even more than to the patient.

The essence of this argument is that the painting is horrifying—not reassuring—something that most spectators would confirm. For example, an English art editor of my acquaintance has commented of the piece:

> I can still remember how disturbed I felt when I saw that painting. I don't think it was because I was shocked to see a medical operation. Something about the painting itself was disturbing.[25]

Indeed, if we respond to all these elements in visual and emotional terms, rather than on the basis of what we have been told about the subject of the painting and the operation it portrays, we find that we come to a very different set of conclusions about what the painting represents. Fried argues that the painting combines a number of basic psychological fears. The common denominator of these fears is that they are all assaults on manhood. On the one hand the emphasis on the buttocks (and on implements which probe and wound) seems to suggest anal penetration, and, in this case, because of the emphasis on the theme of father and son, of sexual possession and domination by the father. In addition, the proximity of the wound to the genitals seems to express a fantasy of castration. (Fried notes that Gross's bloody hand holding the scalpel "may be read not only as threatening castration but as having enacted it.")[26] Finally, the indeterminate sex of the patient suggests a confusion about the distinction between male and female. Freud postulated that boys suppose that females are really castrated males, and that the female genitals can be equated with a bleeding wound.[27] If we accept this idea, then the *Gross Clinic* can be seen as a vivid expression of a boy's fear that through castration he will be transformed into a woman. (Freud also noted that menstruation transforms the vulva into something resembling a bloody gash. Thus, the discovery of menstruation reinforces the fantasy that women are really castrated men.)

Of course, the painting explores these themes ambivalently, since Dr. Gross is at once a reassuring father figure and an agent of castration. Essentially, the painting presents two alternative enactments of the Oedipus complex, one that is positively resolved through the son's identification with his father, the other ending violently in castration and sexual abuse. Indeed, the painting reads like a classic statement of the Oedipal drama between father and son that stands at the heart of Freudian theory. The secondary elements of the composition all serve to illustrate key points of Freudian doctrine: fear of sexual domination by the father, fear of castration, and fear that women have suffered from castration and are physically incomplete.

These are fantasies of course, and they are hardly logical in commonsense terms. But there are two reasons for supposing that they may be valid. First, Freud elicited fantasies of precisely this sort from his emotionally disturbed patients. One of Freud's most notable case studies, the Schreber case, centers on precisely the same theme. Schreber developed the fantasy of being homosexually penetrated by his physician, whom Freud discovered was a surrogate for Schreber's father. Significantly, the threat of castration formed an integral part of Schreber's paranoid fantasy. Schreber imagined that his body was to be transformed through castration into a female body "with a view to sexual abuse."[28] While of course the parallel is not exact, Schreber's fantasy bears an intriguing resemblance to the psychodrama presented in *The Gross Clinic*.

Second, many of the themes that Fried reads into the painting seem to correspond with aspects of Eakins's behavior, and with the scandalous accusations made against him. For example, Eakins was accused of both incest and sodomy (a term most commonly applied to denote anal intercourse). In his anatomical teaching at the Pennsylvania Academy, he seemed inordinately interested in penises, and possibly also in castration. The theme of sexual crossover also seems to have been one that fascinated him, for the women with whom he was most scandalously involved, Ella Crowell and Lillian Hammitt, were both boyish and unfeminine. Fried's analysis of the painting, in short, seems to point with surprising accuracy to those aspects of Eakins's behavior that were disturbing and strange.

Significantly, Fried's interpretation suggests a link between seemingly disparate things, which might well appear puzzling if encountered on their own. Fried notes, for example, that the paranoid scenario of the Oedipus complex contains an element of "repressed homosexual desire." It would not be surprising to find Eakins exploring homosexual desire in certain paintings, as a theme by itself, quite possibly doing so in a fashion not so explicitly Oedipal as in this instance. To make sense of such occurrences, we would need to look at them within the context of Eakins's work as a whole. In fact, as we shall see, homosexual issues are explored in some of Eakins's later paintings, in a fashion that seems quite bewildering taken purely on its own terms.[29]

A notable peculiarity of *The Gross Clinic* is the strong emphasis on voyeurism—of figures looking down at nakedness and shocking acts. Eakins's presentation of this theme has a particularly ominous quality because while we know the figures in the audience are looking toward us, we cannot make them out clearly, and they do not clearly reveal their reactions. For Eakins this theme of voyeurism seems to have some connection with the issues of father and son, hysterical mother, and the psychological fear of castration. But just what these connections are remains to be explored more carefully.

Writers such as Goodrich and Johns have gone to great lengths to deny the element of violence in the painting, and to argue that Eakins was innocent of any such intent. Goodrich also reports that when Eakins's later painting of a medical operation, *The Agnew Clinic*, was similarly rejected, Eakins acted surprised, hurt, and betrayed. According to Goodrich, Eakins had tears in his eyes when he told a friend that he had been described as "a butcher" for making such a piece.[30]

In fact, however, Eakins seems to have been well aware of the shocking nature of his subject matter, as is indicated by a humorous photograph he staged with his students to parody *The Gross Clinic*—restaging it in a way that provocatively brings out its latent meanings. The photograph was probably taken in 1879, at the time when controversy about the painting was at its height. At least some and perhaps all of the students in this parody also posed for the painting.[31]

Dr. Gross wields an axe, and wears an expression that is ferocious rather than enlightened. Nearby, standing on a chair, is an assistant wielding a harpoon-like probe that, like the axe of Dr. Gross, is not so much an instrument of castration as a ridiculous, phallic toy. Meanwhile, an apparently deranged anesthesiologist holds a sack over the patient's head as if to smother him. At the foot of the table another man squats while he holds the patient's feet down, suggesting that he is engaged in a wrestling match with him. Finally, the hysterical mother who attends the operation becomes a man, and is moved into the light and in front of Dr. Gross, so that he effectively competes with the doctor for our attention. Interestingly, it is Eakins himself who poses in this role. Unlike the painting, in which he watches the operation, here his eyes are covered.

Associate of Thomas Eakins, Parody of The Gross Clinic, *1875–1876. Photograph, 10 x 8 in., Philadelphia Museum of Art, gift of George Barker.* Eakins staged a parody of *The Gross Clinic* with his students, placing himself in the role of the cringing mother.

The systematic way in which the photograph reverses and parodies the painting suggests that Eakins was very conscious of the shock value of every detail. Moreover, it is surely significant that Eakins chose to play the role of the emotionally unhinged female spectator. What this suggests is that the exaggerated masculinity of the painting might actually serve as a screen for deep-rooted anxieties that were both "feminine" and "hysterical."

The Agnew Clinic

Executed more than a decade later than *The Gross Clinic*, Eakins's other major medical painting, *The Agnew Clinic*, was the most ambitious painting of Eakins's middle years and the most important commission he ever received. It deals with themes that are very similar to those of *The Gross Clinic* but with interesting variations.

Eakins painted *The Agnew Clinic* when Dr. D. Hayes Agnew retired from the University of Pennsylvania School of Medicine, after serving as professor of surgery for twenty-six years. Like Samuel Gross, Dr. Agnew was a respected surgeon and teacher, as well as the author of a much esteemed textbook, the three-volume *Treatise on the Principles and Practice of Surgery*. When an assassin shot President Garfield in 1881, he served as the chief operating surgeon.

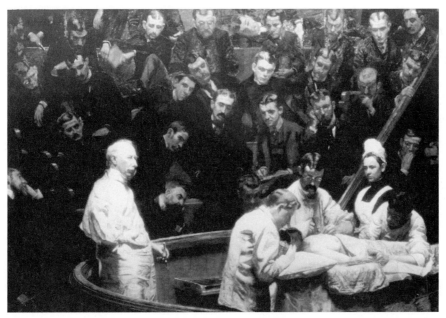

The Agnew Clinic, 1889. *74 ½ x 130 ½ in., courtesy of the University of Pennsylvania Art Collection, Philadelphia, Pennsylvania.* Dr. D. Hayes Agnew removes the breast of an unconscious woman. The painting repeats the main themes of *The Gross Clinic*, but focuses on a female rather than a male patient.

The fee of $750 that Eakins was offered for this commission would have been appropriate for a single-figure portrait. On his own initiative, however, Eakins decided to create a group composition, with six figures in the operating theater and an audience of twenty-five other figures watching them. All thirty-one figures in the painting are portraits, including likenesses of every student who contributed to the purchase.[32]

The time allotted to complete the painting was appropriate for a single figure, but extremely short for a multifigured composition. Eakins created the large painting, six by eleven feet in size, in just three months. Too large to go on an easel, the canvas was nailed to a stretcher and placed on the floor of Eakins's Chestnut Street Studio. Eakins sat on the floor to paint the lower figures. He often worked around the clock, even during a period when he was ill with grippe, and would often sleep on the floor in front of the painting.

The painting shows Dr. Agnew at the conclusion of an operation for breast cancer. Agnew holds the scalpel in his left hand (according to Lloyd Goodrich he was ambidextrous), while with his right he makes an explanatory gesture. The female patient, whose left breast has just been removed, reclines at some distance to the right. The feminist scholar Bridget Goodbody has proposed that at some subliminal level Agnew's relationship with the patient contains an "erotic" element. Specifically, despite the distance between Agnew and the patient, the movement of his right hand can be read as an affectionate, cupping motion toward the female breast. Thus, according to Goodbody, the painting explores the tension between cupping the female breast, an expression of intimacy, and using a scalpel to carve it out. [33]

At the right side of the painting, Dr. J. William White and two assistants, aided by Nurse Mary Clymer, stand beside the patient, finishing the surgery. Eakins used a beam of light to focus attention on Dr. Agnew and his second in command, Dr. White. This section of the painting, with attendants at the bedside of the prostrate figure, recalls a whole genre of nineteenth-century paintings that feature bystanders and patients who are about to die. (One of Picasso's first notable paintings, *Last Moments*, 1899, portrayed this theme.)[34] Elizabeth Johns has written that the horizontal format of the painting serves to emphasize "teamwork," but more importantly, it emphasizes the horizontality and mortality of the patient.

Like Agnew and White, Nurse Clymer plays a prominent role, but in a different way. She stands back a little and is not part of the group. Her face is expressionless and frozen; her role is to support the male doctors. Indeed, her rigidly upright stance strikes a relationship with that of the prostrate patient. Both are equally rigid; both are completely subservient to male control. In the background the audience watches the procedures with varying degrees of interest. Eakins also included a portrait of himself at the far right, peering in through the entrance (with Dr. Fred H. Milliken whispering in his ear). The likeness of Eakins was executed by his wife—the only instance in which she painted a figure in one of his works.

Along with *The Gross Clinic*, *The Agnew Clinic* has always been seen as one of Eakins's most important works. Sylvan Schendler, for example, enthusiastically praised it as a work "whose plain power of statement ranks with any ever painted."[35] At the same time, however, many writers have seen *The Agnew Clinic* as less gripping than *The Gross Clinic*, and as evidence of a lessening of artistic intensity. At the time of the Eakins memorial exhibition in 1917, for example, Henry McBride noted that *The Agnew Clinic* was not "so happily arranged" as the Gross painting, and lacked an overpowering climax.[36] One writer, Gordon Hendricks, has even gone so far as to declare that *The Agnew Clinic* is "not great" and that the "parts do not cohere into a successful whole."[37] As has been noted with the rowing pictures, such a falling-off in intensity was typical when Eakins repeated a theme. Nonetheless, his reworkings are often fascinating in terms of what they show about how he thought about his subjects. This is particularly true of *The Agnew Clinic*, since while it repeats the essential episode of *The Gross Clinic*, it inverts its sexual meaning.

In their essentials, *The Gross Clinic* and *The Agnew Clinic* are clearly variations on the same theme. Nonetheless, the differences between the two paintings are telling. Some of these differences are obvious on the surface. By this time, surgery had changed. The doctors wear antiseptic white rather than dark, everyday clothes; the surgical instruments are in a covered case; the anesthetist is holding an ether cone instead of a gauze; and there is a female nurse.

In addition, the painting differs from *The Gross Clinic* in its thematic emphasis. Here, women, are not thrust into the background, but are placed in the role of patient and assistant. In addition, this seems to be the only instance in which Eakins enlisted a woman—his wife—to actively contribute to his artistic activity and thus to implicitly endorse his artistic message.

This new emphasis on women may have had something to do with Dr. Agnew, since the most prominent controversy of Agnew's career involved his domineering and dismissive attitude toward women. In May 1871, Dr. Agnew resigned from the staff of attending surgeons at the Pennsylvania Hospital after refusing the request of its Board of Managers to lecture to the students of the Women's Medical College. One reason for this decision was squeamishness. He felt that women should not be exposed to the indelicate realities of medicine. As his biographer explained, "a modest-minded physician would naturally shrink" from the taste of exposing young women, perhaps seventeen or eighteen years old, to the "unpleasant sights and facts of venereal disease."[38] But Agnew also held that women had no place in the professional world. "A woman," he declared, "should be taught housekeeping, hygiene, and belles lettres." After that, he insisted, "The more *she knew* the worse off she was."[39] While not fully spelled out, Agnew's statement makes clear that he felt that women should concentrate solely on homemaking or on artistic and emotional pursuits such as literature, but were inherently lacking in intellect. Indeed, these attitudes formed an important part of his medical theories.

Unlike *The Gross Clinic*, which shows an operation that Gross had pioneered, *The Agnew Clinic* does not show a type of operation specifically associated with Dr. Agnew. The operation does, however, relate to the role of women, since breast cancer was believed to be a specifically female disease, somehow associated with the state of a woman's reproductive organs. Indeed, Dr. Agnew stated this not as opinion but as fact in his surgical guide, *Principles and Practices of Surgery*, published in 1883. As he wrote: "The sympathy which exists between the ovary, the uterus, and the mammae has a pathological as well as physiological importance."[40]

Specifically, doctors of the time thought that breast cancer was somehow associated both with menstruation, menopause, and the "nervous illnesses" of women. The first point was argued by Dr. Samuel Gross, son of the subject of Eakins's *The Gross Clinic*, who claimed that cancer was most frequently detected in menstruating women, which was then considered a woman's monthly disease. Agnew himself seems to have been particularly taken with the notion that breast cancer was somehow connected with menopause. As he wrote in his surgical manual:

> The connection between carcinoma and the diminution or loss of functions of certain organs in consequence of advancing age has very generally attracted the attention of writers. Thus, in cancer of the mammary gland and of the uterus the disease exhibits a singular partiality for developing about the period of menopause, oftener, perhaps, just before than after the important change referred to in the economy of these organs has taken place.[41]

As Agnew noted, the average age for a woman to develop breast cancer was forty-eight, when "the functional activity of the gland [was] on the decline, its work as a secreting organ over."

Agnew also proposed that nervousness or emotional imbalance could cause breast cancer. As he declared:

The influence of emotional causes, [such] as protracted grief, the nervous depression following loss of property, anxiety, worry, as predisposing factors in carcinoma, has been forcibly impressed on my mind for several years, especially with reference to cancer of the mammary gland.[42]

In other words, for Agnew, breast cancer was a kind of physical expression of the irrational qualities of women, and was specifically associated both with menopause and with emotional or mental illnesses such as manic depression. For Eakins, whose mother had died while suffering from bipolar disorder, around the time of menopause, this must have seemed significant, for it suggested that breast cancer was a kind of physical manifestation—a kind of objective correlative—of his mother's fatal mental illness. The implicit subject of the painting is what might be termed "the pathology of the feminine."

Surgery for breast cancer was a risky procedure. Between one in ten and one in six mastectomy patients died during surgery from loss of blood. In addition, the surgery did not cure the disease, since in this period, by the time breast cancer was detected, it had invariably spread too far to be completely removed. In his manual, Dr. Agnew wrote of the task of healing breast cancer, "this blessed achievement will, I believe, never be wrought by the knife of the surgeon." In psychological terms, this gave cancer surgery a particularly frustrating, brutal, somewhat pointlessly violent character. In his manual, for example, Agnew wrote that with breast cancer the surgeon's only recourse was to "go in and attack the cancer again and again with the knife."[43] Thus, in an important way, *The Agnew Clinic* differs from *The Gross Clinic*, for whereas *The Gross Clinic* portrays a presumably male patient who will probably live, *The Agnew Clinic* shows a female one who will probably die.

Eakins exposed and highlighted the woman's healthy breast, although as Nurse Clymer's class notes make clear, in an actual operation the healthy breast was carefully covered. Thus, Eakins must have had some expressive goal apart from pure naturalism. One possibility is that by showing a breast that is young and firm he wished to suggest that the doctor has the power to heal (although this was against the odds in this instance). In addition, the exposed breast gives the painting an implicitly sexual quality, since a woman's healthy naked body is being exposed for male inspection: Rachel Goodbody has declared that the exposed breast "lends a voyeuristic element to the painting."[44] Thus (at least according to this view), the painting deals with a dynamic of violence and domination of a woman who is both being carved with a knife and exposing her body for male control and pleasure.[45] Interestingly, however, Nurse Clymer, who serves as a kind of vertical surrogate of the patient, is desexualized. Her uniform covers her body up to her chin and even her hair is carefully concealed beneath her nurse's cap.

Symbolically, the operation has a striking and powerful significance, since removing a woman's breast removes the most obvious signal of her sexual nature. The nurse, who plays no active role, serves the role of a female witness to this act of male reconfiguration of the female body.

If we view both clinic paintings as statements of aggression against Eakins's parents, they thus form a neat pair: the first addressing his Oedipal relationship with his father, the second his even more troubled relationship with his mother. Whereas the first painting represents a symbolic act of male castration, the second portrays a kind of dismemberment that would turn a woman into something more similar to a man. In other words, at a fantasy level *The Agnew Clinic* can be read as an expression of Eakins's feelings of hostility and aggression against his emotionally disturbed mother, as well as his desire to change her into something less hysterical and feminine and more like a man. (As has been indicated, Eakins conceived women as inferior to men. I am not attempting to endorse this viewpoint.) As is typical of such fantasies, however, the painting also expresses another contradictory desire, which to some extent masks and screens the first. For it also projects a fantasy of healing.

It is unlikely that nineteenth-century viewers, unfamiliar with the theories of Freud, would have fully grasped the sexual and psychological undercurrents of the painting, but at some level they were clearly disturbed by it. Shortly after the painting was completed, Eakins became involved in the debate over whether it should be publicly exhibited. In 1891 a jury of Philadelphia artists invited Eakins to show several paintings at the Pennsylvania Academy, specifically requesting *The Agnew Clinic*. Shortly before the show opened, however, the directors of the Academy wrote asking them to eliminate the painting, and in deference to this request it was not hung. The affair led to a long correspondence between Eakins and Edward Horner Coates, the president of the Academy, who had acted as spokesman for the directors. Coates declared that the directors had simply made a "request" that the hanging committee could have declined, had they thought proper. Eakins protested that the pressure on the hanging committee had been exerted over time, in an increasingly forceful fashion. The jury had only given in during "a moment of weakness," after pressure had been exerted on them for several days. *The Agnew Clinic*, like *The Gross Clinic*, clearly disturbed viewers. The episode recapitulated the controversy of years before, when Eakins's *The Gross Clinic* had also been pointedly excluded from an exhibition at the Academy.

Eakins's letters often contain bewildering passages, but his correspondence with Coates is particularly intriguing in this regard. Eakins's copy of his letter to Coates contains a long postscript, in which he painstakingly copied a passage from Rabelais's sixteenth-century satire *Gargantua and Pantagruel*, which at first reading seems only remotely related to the matter at hand. Indeed, the passage stands so far afield from the issues of their dispute that it seems to have been included for some other reason.

The passage describes how a pregnant nun was brought to trial under the accusation of incest. The nun protested that she had been raped. When asked why she did not reveal the attack, the nun protested that she had not cried out because the rape occurred in a space in which she was enjoined to silence, but that she had signaled with her buttocks. No one, however, had paid attention. Moreover, she had "confessed to the father friar before he went out of the room, who, for my penance, enjoined me not to tell it, or reveal the matter unto any. It were a most enormous and horrid offence, detestable before God and the angels, to reveal a confession."[46]

The only connecting point between the episode by Rabelais and the rejection of Eakins's painting is that both episodes present instances in which people acted hypocritically. Surely, however, this point could have been made more succinctly. What was the point of copying the long passage from Rabelais, with its account of rape, incest, and forced silence? The obvious conclusion is that Eakins was preoccupied with these issues for some personal reason.

In fact, it is striking that the passage from Rabelais seems to touch in a powerful way on the themes that preoccupied Eakins. Signaling with one's buttocks, for example, like the raped nun, seems to be a central theme of many of Eakins's major paintings, including *The Gross Clinic, William Rush,* and *The Swimming Hole.* Moreover, *The Gross Clinic,* whose themes closely relate to *The Agnew Clinic,* seems to deal with the theme of sexual (in this case anal) penetration by a father figure. The passage from Rabelais tells a similar story with the additional element of a forced silence (it is quite striking that Rabelais specifically uses the word "incest"). The exact implications of these parallels are somewhat ambiguous, but at some level for Eakins, there was clearly a connection—if only one of subconscious free association—between *The Agnew Clinic* and the episode of rape, incest, and exposed buttocks from Rabelais. Moreover, both seem to point back toward something about Eakins's family experience that profoundly disturbed him.

William Rush Carving His Allegorical Figure of the Schuylkill River, A Study, 1876. *Oil on composition board, 20 ³⁄₁₆ x 24 in., Yale University Art Gallery, collection of Mary C. and James W. Fosburgh.* In the early studies for *William Rush*, Eakins's father posed for the figure of the sculptor, suggesting that the painting has some sort of family significance.

Chapter 13

WILLIAM RUSH AND HIS MODEL

GIVEN THAT *The Gross Clinic* has been so closely analyzed from a psychological standpoint, it seems curious that no writer has attempted such a reading of Eakins's next major painting, of *William Rush Carving His Allegorical Figure of the Schuylkill River* (1877), the artist's principal rendering of the female nude. Indeed, three things make it reasonable to suppose that the painting was charged with some particular psychological significance for Eakins.

First, *William Rush* is the only subject that Eakins returned to on his own initiative and repeated later in his career. Clearly there was something about this subject and its narrative implications that fascinated him.

Second, we know that the issue of the nude occupied a large and often scandalous place in Eakins's life, as well as in the mythology that has posthumously developed around his work. Thus, it seems logical to look closely at the painting in which he focused most intensely on this issue.

Third we know that in his first studies of the theme, Eakins made Rush closely resemble his father. Indeed, according to Theodore Siegl, Benjamin Eakins posed for the painting.[1] In the course of his work on the painting, however, he replaced this "father" with a likeness of himself, suggesting that the painting carries deeper psychological meanings, connected with the way a son takes on the guise of his father. This mode of reasoning further suggests that the drama of the painting—that of a woman undressing—carries some cryptic message about Eakins's family.

Eakins clearly considered the canvas a major effort. Although it is small, Eakins priced the canvas at $600, more than ten times what he asked for his least expensive pictures, and double what he asked for the painting of *The Biglin Brothers Turning the Stake*, which is considerably larger.[2] Without doubt, it is also one of his most emotionally compelling works. Along with *The Champion Single Sculls* and *The Gross Clinic, William Rush* is probably the most widely reproduced of Eakins's paintings.

William Rush represents Eakins's most significant venture away from modern life into so-called history painting—something Eakins could not have actually witnessed. Eakins showed Rush, a Philadelphia sculptor and ship's carver from the Federal period, hewing out an allegorical figure of the Schuylkill River, while a nude woman serves as his model. The painting provides striking evidence of Eakins's ability to give a veneer of realism and accuracy to an almost purely imaginary scene, with little relationship to any event that actually occurred.

William Rush was a woodcarver who apprenticed in Philadelphia with an English-trained ship carver and by 1779 had established his own workshop. For years Rush focused exclusively on figureheads and decorative carvings for ships. Around 1808, however, at a time when an economic depression had restricted the construction of new ships, Rush began to make public sculpture to ornament Philadelphia buildings. His commissions included decorations for the facade of a theater, crucifixes for churches, and figures that ornamented a triumphal arch honoring Lafayette. His finest creation was his *Allegorical Figure of the Schuylkill River*, also known as *Nymph with Bittern*, created for the newly constructed Philadelphia waterworks.[3]

The Philadelphia waterworks, designed by Benjamin Latrobe, brought water from the Schuylkill River to an engine house more than a mile from the river, in Central Square. From there the water was pumped by steam engine to users across the city. Rush's statue was created to glorify this engineering marvel and featured an allegorical representation of the river as a slender, lightly draped woman holding a bittern—a water bird often found along the marshy shores of the Schuylkill.

The statue was originally placed adjacent to the Central Square pump house, and served as the centerpiece of Philadelphia's first public fountain. (Rush designed it so that water from the Schuylkill spewed out from the beak of the bird.) In 1809, however, the pump house was abandoned. To replace it, a dam was constructed across the Schuylkill and an impressive neoclassical waterworks complex was created on the shore of the river, at the base of a natural acropolis on which the Philadelphia Museum of Art now stands. Rush was commissioned to create two new sculptures for this complex, and his *Water Nymph and Bittern* was also moved to this new site, where once again it served as the centerpiece of a fountain. Eakins would have been familiar with the statue from early childhood, since it is only a short walk from the family home.

The theme of a famous old master in his studio is a popular one treated by Ingres, Delacroix, Manet, Gérôme, and many other painters. Being a passionate booster of Philadelphia, Eakins, gave this theme a local twist. Rush was virtually unknown outside of Philadelphia, but in the city his work was viewed with considerable pride, and at the time of Eakins's painting it was experiencing a modest revival. Shortly before Eakins made his painting, Earl Shinn, Eakins's friend from Paris, praised Rush both in a book about Philadelphia, and also drew attention to early Philadelphia artists in a series of articles for *Lippincott's Magazine*.[4] Moreover, in 1872 the city of Philadelphia paid to have the very statue of the *Nymph and Bittern* that Eakins featured copied in the more durable material of bronze, and then erected as the centerpiece of a new fountain.

Thus, like Eakins's renderings of Max Schmitt and Dr. Samuel Gross, the painting of William Rush celebrates a local hero. Very likely Eakins's painting

William Rush Carving His Allegorical Figure of the Schuylkill River, 1876. *Oil on canvas, 20 ⅛ x 26 ½ in., Philadelphia Museum of art, gift of Mrs. Thomas Eakins and Mary Adeline Williams.* **Eakins showed Rush working from a nude model, although there is no evidence that he ever did so. In the final painting, Eakins shaped the nude woman quite differently than in his early studies.**

was originally conceived as a centennial tribute to one of Philadelphia's most distinguished colonial figures. Indeed, Eakins began sketching the subject of William Rush around 1876, about the same time that he was working on *The Gross Clinic*, but because of his painstaking working methods, it took him another two years to complete it.

Rush was one of the founders of the Pennsylvania Academy of the Fine Arts, where Eakins was then teaching. Thus it was natural for Eakins to present Rush as a kind of artistic father figure, and to use Rush's story as a guise for presenting his own artistic doctrines.

William Rush, Allegory of the Schuylkill River (Water Nymph and Bittern), *ca. 1854. Bronze cast of wooden original, Philadelphia Museum of Art, on loan to the Philadelphia Museum of Art from the Commissioners of Fairmount Park.* **Rush carved his figure of a woman with a marsh bird to ornament Benjamin Latrobe's ambitious Philadelphia waterworks.**

The picture shows Rush carving his figure from the nude model. We peer into a box-like room whose intense darkness recalls the shuttered interiors of the Eakins home. The space is illuminated only by flickering lights. The sculptor himself is almost lost in shadow at the far left, while he hammers away at his wooden statue with mallet and chisel, totally immersed in the physical effort of his work and seemingly unaware of the naked woman, though her presence is centrally important to his activity. Somewhat better lit, the woman stands on a log, with *Webster's* dictionary on her shoulder.[5] A small splotch of pink draws attention to her naked buttocks; but this point of interest seems dim compared with the brightly illuminated garments, including underclothes and silk stockings draped over the chair to the left, in a kind of still-life striptease. An old woman with her knitting, evidently a chaperon, is seated just behind the nude model to the right.

Anachronistically, two works that Rush carved after 1809 are visible in the background, a standing figure of *George Washington* that he carved in 1814, and an *Allegory of the Waterworks*, created for the new Fairmount site, that Rush carved in 1825.[6] In the left foreground are parts of two ship's scrolls. On the floor are chips of wood, on one of which Eakins signed the painting. Tools hang on the back wall and

William Rush, Allegory of the Waterworks (The Schuylkill Freed), *1825. Spanish cedar painted white, 39 ⅜ x 87 ⅟₁₆ x 26 ⅞₁₆ in., Philadelphia Museum of Art, on deposit from the Commissioners of Fairmount Park.*

rest on the bench along the right wall. Under the bench are two or three large books. Above the bench are various notations and a drawing of a scroll on the wall, which Eakins had carefully copied from a now lost notebook with drawings by Rush.[7]

The variety in the lighting and modes of paint handling suggest some sort of hierarchy, although imposed in an unexpected way. William Rush and his sculptures are the most shadowy figures. It is the model's underwear that is most prominently featured; next the nude model; and finally, the chaperon, who closely resembles the model in physique.

Eakins went to considerable trouble to perform research that would give his painting an aura of historical accuracy. He photographed Rush's works to serve as reference, and modeled the three sculptures by Rush that he included in the painting in wax. He also modeled a head of Rush in wax, drawn from Rush's self-portrait. To give the painting the correct period flavor, he studied a painting by John L. Krimmel of Central Square and made studies from it for the clothing of Rush, the model, and the older woman. He interviewed several elderly people who remembered Rush's workshop, which had burned down years before. ("The shop of William Rush," Eakins wrote, "was on Front Street just below Callow hill and I found several very old people who still remembered it and described it.")[8] Eakins also visited a modern carver's workshop and sketched the scene.[9]

Despite this research, which was clearly intended to make the painting seem authentic, the central premise of the painting, that Rush worked from a nude model, is purely imaginary. To be sure, history does record that Rush used an actual person as the model for his statue, a certain Miss Vanuxem, aged twenty-seven. She was the daughter of a prosperous Philadelphia merchant, James Vanuxem, who was on the committee that awarded Rush the commission. Her role in inspiring the piece was proudly recorded in genealogies penned by members of the Vanuxem family. There is no reason to suppose, however, that Miss Vanuxem posed nude, and it is nearly certain that she did not, since working from a nude model did not come into practice until

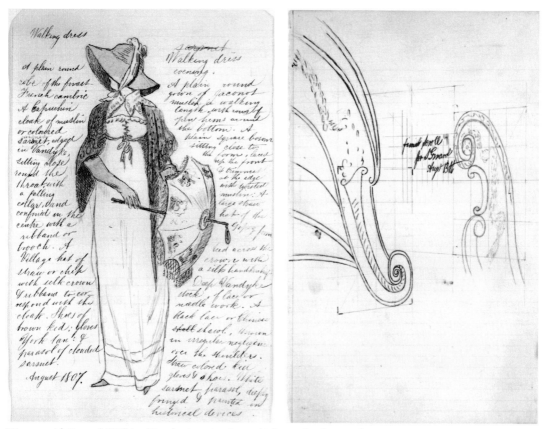

Woman with Parasol (Walking Dress), 1875–1876. Pen and ink, pencil and watercolor on paper, 7 ¼ x 4 1¹⁄₁₆ in., Hirshhorn Museum and Sculpture Garden, Smithsonian Institution, gift of Joseph H. Hirshhorn, 1966. **Eakins did careful research on female garments and undergarments of the period.** RIGHT Scrollwork, Foreshortened (Study for William Rush Carving His Allegorical Figure of the Schuylkill River), 1876–1877. Ink over graphite on paper, 12 ⁷⁄₁₆ x 7 ¹³⁄₁₆ in., courtesy of The Pennsylvania Academy of the Fine Arts, Philadelphia, Charles Bregler's Thomas Eakins Collection, purchased with the partial support of the Pew Memorial Trust and the John S. Phillips Fund. **The drawing of a scroll that appears on the wall of Eakins's painting was copied from one of Rush's notebooks.**

considerably later. Except for an aborted attempt by Charles Willson Peale to hold a life class in 1795, the first such sessions in Philadelphia were organized in 1813, and for the earlier part of the nineteenth century they occurred very irregularly, mostly with male models. Eakins's presentation of the nude, therefore, reflected his own preoccupations rather than any actual historical occurrence.[10]

Rather amusingly, as Elizabeth Johns has documented, Eakins's bizarre presentation of his fantasies came to be regarded as a record of a historical occurrence, and Rush's reputation and that of Eakins became confused and conflated. Shortly after Eakins was fired from the Pennsylvania Academy, writers about Rush began to assume that he had also been a scandalous figure in his time. In 1893, for example, a writer for *Lippincott's Magazine* claimed that Rush's water nymph was "denounced as immodest" when it was first shown, although there is no evidence that this was the case.[11] Five years later another writer declared with equal assurance that "many nice and fastidious persons were shocked" by Rush's female figure. By 1937 Henri Marceau, author of the first catalogue of the works of William Rush, wrote that it would be superfluous to air the scandal in detail.[12] In his 1933 biography of Eakins, Lloyd Goodrich confidently declared that Eakins admired Rush because he felt in harmony with the sculptor's practice of working from the nude, without stopping to question whether Rush had actually done so.[13] The realism of Eakins's presentation made viewers accept its truth, even when it was demonstrably contrary to the actual facts.

If Eakins invented his subject, it must have had an inner significance. What is the underlying meaning of this painting in psychological terms? As with the *Gross Clinic*, there are various clues that the figures are stand-ins for members of Eakins's family. Interestingly, in Eakins's early studies for the painting, he used his father as a model for William Rush. In the final version, however, the figure has a younger, slimmer build, resembling Eakins himself at the time. Interestingly also, in the later versions of *William Rush* the sculptor takes on an uncanny resemblance to Eakins himself—so much so that the figure can be viewed as a self-portrait.

Indeed, the parallels between Rush and Eakins are striking. Eakins liked to picture himself as a workman, and he worked in a space that was almost deliberately untidy, like Rush's studio. He once pointedly told his friends that whereas William Merritt Chase painted in an atelier, he himself painted in a workshop.[14] Like Rush, Eakins was from Philadelphia, and they were both closely associated with the Pennsylvania Academy of the Fine Arts. Both—at least in Eakins's presentation of the story—were fascinated with the nude. For as Earl Shinn noted in *The Nation* in 1878, when Eakins's painting was shown in New York, the canvas carried a strong didactic message. As Shinn declared, "The painter of the fountain seemed to have a lesson to deliver—the moral, namely, that good sculpture, even decorative sculpture, can only be produced by the most uncompromising, unconventional study and analysis from life."[15]

At the very time Eakins made the painting he was revamping the curriculum of the Pennsylvania Academy to eliminate such subjects as still life and landscape painting for concentration entirely on study of the nude. Moreover, in January 1877, Eakins addressed a letter to the Committee on Instruction, headed by John Sartain, proposing that they advertise for nude models. The letter—which will be discussed shortly—is interesting for its mix of brashness and prudery. It is thus possible that the painting is about Eakins's own relationship with the nude, an issue that was shortly to involve him in considerable scandal. Most writers on the painting have assumed that this is the case. The step they have not made, however, is to interpret this relationship to the nude in family terms.

When he started the project, Eakins used his father as the model for William Rush. As he developed the painting, he shifted this figure into one that closely resembled himself. In considering the deeper meaning of the painting, we can start from the premise that the artist is some kind of stand-in for both Eakins and his father. Eakins shows this person confronted with two women, one naked and one dressed. The naked woman is a young girl; the clothed woman is older. But we can guess that they represent different guises of the same woman since they both have the same very unusual proportions, with a high waist and legs that are much longer than normal. Except for their age, everything about the appearance of the figures is the same. Significantly, both figures appear calm. The elderly woman is not depressed or sullen but quietly absorbed in her knitting. The young girl stands gracefully.[16]

While other interpretations are possible, it is interesting to surmise that both these women represent aspects of Eakins's mother, and that the painting expresses a fantasy about his relationship with her, or is even a restaging, with some imaginative changes, of an actual incident. At first it seems curious that Eakins's sexiest painting is a historical scene set in a distant epoch. But this would make sense if we presume that Eakins's interest in sexuality was deeply related to his companionship with his mother, as he cared for her during her periodic illnesses throughout his childhood. Thus, his explorations into sex involved digging into the mind-set of an earlier generation. The painting is set at a time close to that of his mother's girlhood. The essence of the painting is that the woman is shown both clothed and nude. In fact undressing, rather than nakedness itself, seems in some way to be the real subject of the painting.

Every scholar who has written about this painting has assumed that the nude figure is the main subject of the painting. Visually, however, this is quite obviously not the case. The main feature of interest is the model's clothes on the chair. This is the area that is most brightly lit, and it is also the most visually complicated section of the painting—the one where Eakins's technical virtuosity is most apparent. By contrast, the nude is both more dimly lit and more summarily painted, while the sculptor himself is veiled in shadow.

As has been mentioned, Eakins was particularly fascinated with old-fashioned underwear, and even persuaded women to show him such underwear, in defiance of the usual Philadelphia standards of modesty. (He was also fascinated by old-fashioned dresses.) At its most literal level, *William Rush* is a study of old underwear, dating back to the time of his mother's childhood, or slightly earlier. Eakins's achievement is the more remarkable when we recognize that he had reconstructed the costume depicted in a painting by John Louis Krimmel, of which he had made a sketch. His reconstruction, however, had penetrated to the level of the undergarments that Krimmel did not picture.

Interestingly, the significance of the underwear seems to have been sensed by one of the earliest reviewers of the painting. In 1878 a reviewer for *The New York Times* commented that it was the underwear on the chair rather than the nude itself which "gives a shock" and which makes the painting "improper."[17] While this comment has been much ridiculed by recent scholars, in fact, it seems to me to point very directly toward the actual expressive intention of the canvas.

At first this focus on the clothes on the chair does not seem significant. Why does it matter that Eakins's interest rested not on the nude figure but on the clothes that she has removed, and that the painting is not so much a study of the nude as of old underwear? I will answer this question later, since a full answer draws in part on evidence we have not yet considered at this point. It seems clear, however, even at this stage, that this distinction is significant, and has led scholars to misconstrue the real meaning of the painting. Indeed, the quality of magic and mystery in the painting depends on the fact that Eakins's attitude toward the nude contains some element that is not straightforward or obvious. Something about the painting feels elusive.

By emphasizing the discarded clothes, Eakins was shifting emphasis from the nude as a beautiful or sexual object to the act of removing clothes.

Significantly, in his personal life, Eakins showed an obsessive interest in undressing. It is hardly unreasonable to suppose that in some way the discarded underwear featured so prominently in the painting relates to this obsession.

The historically inaccurate inclusion of the George Washington statue also seems related to this theme. In the shadowy setting, Washington is easily mistaken for a real person, and he seems to play a role of witness or voyeur to the event that is taking place.

The thrill of the painting seems to come from imagining the act of undressing, conceived almost as a substitute for sex. In key respects, Eakins's rendering is essentially unerotic. This becomes apparent when we compare the painting with a treatment of a very similar subject painted by his teacher Jean-Léon Gérôme, the myth of *Pygmalion*. Gérôme showed the moment at which the female statue comes to life. The lower half is still marble but the upper half (which blushes) bends to embrace the sculptor. Eakins, however, showed the opposite of Gérôme's fantasy of desire fulfilled. Instead he presents the nude woman who becomes immobile as a statue, so that desire is frozen or suspended. Rather than embracing the woman, the sculptor is preoccupied with his work, chiseling away at the side of a wooden ankle. Even the shapes of the two paintings contribute to their very different messages. Gérôme's painting is vertical and emphasizes the nude. Eakins's painting is horizontal and reflects the shape of the workplace. At some level, then, Eakins's painting is not about releasing sexual feeling, but about repressing it.

Leo Steinberg, following an avenue of interpretation first sketched out by Fairfield Porter, has proposed that Eakins's painting was an effort to invent a rationale for the nude that could stand up to the Puritanism and prudery of American society. "Eakins's *William Rush*," he writes, "is a manful attempt to silence the American objection to art and undress by assimilating both to the ethic of work. That is why everything in the picture is preoccupied."[18] Characteristically, this interpretation supposes that Eakins's social and artistic difficulties were due to the tension between his liberated attitudes and the repressed society of the time. But it is equally logical to speculate that this tension, this element of repression, reflected something about the psychological makeup of Eakins himself.

Indeed, there is a curious element of repression in the title of the painting itself: *William Rush Carving the Allegorical Figure of the Schuylkill River*, which is often shortened in discussion of the painting to *William Rush*. What is striking about this title is that it completely omits what is seemingly the subject of the painting, the female nude, and mentions only William Rush and his statue. To me this title suggests that despite his preoccupation with the subject, at some level Eakins shrunk back from a direct presentation of the female nude; and it also suggests that to understand the painting we should read it from a male viewpoint.

Why would this issue of a clothed and unclothed figure be significant to Eakins? We need not solve this mystery here. For the moment all that need concern us is the thought that possibly Eakins's compulsion with undressing was somehow connected with his relationship with his mother.

What of the nude itself? Recent writers have often described Eakins's nude as if his presentation was provocatively sensual. Schendler, for example, declares that the nude "lives fully, sensuously, with an identity and a beauty unequaled in American painting."[19] Leslie Katz writes of the painting in terms that

Jean-Léon Gérôme, Pygmalion and Galatea, *ca. 1890. Oil on canvas, 35 × 27 in., Metropolitan Museum of Art, gift of Louis C. Raegner, 1927.* **Unlike Eakins, Gérôme directly depicted an erotic connection between the sculptor and his model.**

might be part of a loss-of-virginity scene in a semipornographic romantic novel. "Her pose," he writes, "has the air of an initial or pioneer event. Her body is shown beautiful, infused by an unravished sensuousness, her flesh all white and gold in the dark, cluttered, barn-like studio . . . She is strong, even hearty, nothing pale or loath, modest but unashamed."[20] Lloyd Goodrich praises the figure's "roundness and sense of life," and notes "the discarded garments are a delightful invention."[21] Interestingly, however, contemporary critics thought Eakins's nude was ugly. One critic wrote that William Rush "was no judge of the 'human form divine.'"[22] Another declared, "If belles have such faults as these to hide, we counsel them to hide them."[23]

How can we explain these divergent responses? For one thing, they remind us that standards of female beauty have changed a good deal over the last century. Nineteenth-century taste favored an ideal of female beauty that was shorter, plumper, and more pear shaped than the one favored today, when slender, almost boyish proportions are in vogue. Most importantly, however, these responses alert us to the fact that the shape of this figure is loaded with some sort of meaning, although perhaps of an ambiguous kind. They encourage us to look at her shape more closely.

Eakins's model for the nude figure was a local beauty named Annie Williams, a schoolteacher in a home for wayward girls who was a friend of Eakins's sisters. Eakins later recommended her as a model to the sculptor George T. Morgan when he was designing coinage for the U.S. Government, and her features, slightly turned toward the Greek ideal, served for those of the Goddess of Liberty on American dimes, quarters, half-dollars, and golden eagles from 1872 well into the 1920s.[24]

Eakins accurately represented Miss Williams's attractive but somewhat stubby physique in his first studies of *William Rush*, such as the one that formerly belonged to the portrait painter James Fosburgh, now at Yale. When he created the final painting, however, something very odd occurred. Miss Williams's body changed proportions, becoming significantly more slender and boyish.

Why did Eakins so dramatically change the proportions of the figure? One possible reason is that Miss Williams was considerably shorter and squatter than the figure in Rush's statue. Thus, Eakins needed a slimmer figure to make his narrative convincing. This rationale, however, does not fully resolve the problem. For one thing, Eakins's figure still bears very little relation to the shape of the statue, an incongruity that Eakins largely concealed in his painting by placing the statue in such dim light that it is hard to focus on the figure and statue simultaneously. Some other impulse seems to be at work here, and in fact, if we look closely we discover that Eakins's figure is not a woman in the usual sense.

Years ago the art historian and museum director Peter Sutton, pointed out to me that the leg of the figure has the musculature not of a woman but of a man. While one could argue this point, I think that anyone who closely studies this section of the painting will at least agree that the legs of the figure are very "boyish" in character. To my eye the musculature is not possible in a woman's leg. Since Eakins has always been recognized as a master of anatomy, it is clear that this could not have been an accident. Indeed, it seems to me that his interest in studying dismembered parts of the human body may provide a clue to his creative process in this instance. In my opinion, Eakins was doing something quite strange with this figure, which deserves close examination.

Throughout his life, Eakins's seems to have been fascinated by women who were boyish, and he often complimented women for some boyish quality. At the time that Eakins was painting *William Rush* he was actively involved in anatomical dissection, and was making plaster casts and drawings of dismembered body parts, such as hands, arms, and legs. The nude woman in the final version of *William Rush* is a composite of male body parts that have been assembled to create a quasi-woman. The leg is that of a young man, being too firm and muscular to belong to a woman. The upper torso, with its diminutive arms, is that of a small boy. In other words, in this figure Eakins assembled pieces of boys and men to construct a woman, just as he had assembled his sailing and rowing pictures from separate pictorial studies. Conceivably the gender ambiguities of the figure were introduced unconsciously, although given Eakins's knowledge of anatomy, and his interest in dismembered body parts, they may well reflect a conscious process of manipulation.[25] Significantly, many other paintings by Eakins contain figures that are sexually ambiguous or androgynous, often as a central figure (such as the sexually ambiguous patient in *The Gross Clinic* or (to be discussed) the boy showing off his feminine rear end in *Swimming*.)

Notably, both *The Gross Clinic* and *William Rush*, in different ways, center the viewer's attention on a nude that conveys mixed messages about gender. It is interesting to speculate that, Eakins somehow imagined women as castrated or incomplete versions of men, and was at once disturbed and fascinated by this thought. We will explore the psychological meaning of Eakins's interest in androgynous figures later in this inquiry. Since Eakins also explored such ambiguities of gender in his later paintings and photographs, it is worth waiting until the evidence on this matter can be assembled in full. A hypothesis to hold in reserve, however, is that this issue of androgyny (and by implication castration) had some special significance for Eakins in family terms.[26]

If we compare *William Rush* with *The Gross Clinic* we discover that they appear to have a surprising number of themes in common: family relationships, particularly that of father and son; the disrobing of a rather androgynous figure to reveal its buttocks; and that of carving or slicing with a knife or chisel. From the standpoint of sexual fantasy, however, they operate in contrasting fashion. In *The Gross Clinic*, which features male figures, a fantasy of sexual assault is violently enacted. In *William Rush*, by contrast, male engagement with a naked woman is blocked or repressed, and the man's energy is transferred to another object, the statue that he carves. Indeed, even the sexual fantasy of the painting is no longer directed principally at the woman. The fantasy of sexual contact has been replaced by a focus on undergarments and underwear: sexual consummation has been supplanted by an obsessive focus on undressing.

Models for *William Rush Carving the Allegorical Figure of the Schuylkill River*, 1876–1877.
Plaster casts from wax models, ranging in height from 4 ½ x 9 ¾ inches high, Philadelphia Museum of Art, gift of Mrs. Thomas Eakins and Miss Mary Adeline Williams, 1930. As research for his painting, Eakins made copies of Rush's principal sculptures in wax.

Chapter 14

A FINE OLD ROW

THE YEARS 1871 to 1875 were uniquely productive ones for Eakins. They culminated in his most famous painting, *The Gross Clinic*, and included two other highlights of his career, *The Champion Single Sculls* and *William Rush*, which also rank among his greatest achievements. At no other period of Eakins's life did he paint so many masterworks in such a short span, or attempt such varied, complex, and emotionally charged subjects.

In the decade following the completion of *The Gross Clinic*, however, Eakins's productivity as a painter dropped significantly. Indeed, because of the decline in his production, he often pulled out older paintings and put them on exhibit. The emotional intensity of his work also diminished markedly in this period. For example, Eakins produced a number of historical pictures with such titles as *In Grandmother's Time, Young Girl Meditating, The Courtship, Retrospection, A Quiet Moment,* and *Spinning.* Writers on Eakins have noted that these share a repressed quality. Sylvan Schendler, for example, commented that although these "innocuous works" appear to have "found favor with the genteel," they demonstrate Eakins's "avoidance of the themes which were at the center of his consciousness" and suggest "the powerful personal and public repressions under which he labored." After noting that these paintings "lack the qualities of intensity which distinguished his greatest work," Schendler evoked the image of castration, writing, "They were works . . . of emasculation."[1]

No doubt many explanations could be provided for this lessening of Eakins's artistic prowess, not least the possibility that the technical and expressive challenges of producing *The Gross Clinic* may have left the artist physically and emotionally drained. One of the major reasons for this shift, however, was very simple. After 1876 Eakins became increasingly involved in teaching at the Pennsylvania Academy, and the various activities associated with this work left him with less time to paint.

Conflict at the Academy

Eakins's rise to the position of director of instruction at the Pennsylvania Academy of the Fine Arts occurred in a somewhat circuitous fashion and, like so many areas of the artist's life, seems to have involved conflicts, controversy, and seemingly contradictory behavior on all sides. In its governance, the Pennsylvania Academy was controlled by civic leaders, in contrast to the National Academy of Design, which was run by artists, or the Art Students League, which was run by students. Eakins's predecessor at the Pennsylvania Academy was the distinctly middlebrow genre and history painter Christian Schussele. Originally from Alsace, Schussele was trained by Paul Delaroche and Adolphe Yvon in Paris. In 1848 he settled in Philadelphia, and pursued a successful career producing storytelling pictures, several of which were engraved by John Sartain. In the mid-1860s, however, Schussele was stricken with palsy, which made it increasingly difficult for him to paint. Sartain saw this as an opportunity both to help his friend and to improve the quality of art teaching in Philadelphia. In 1868, with the approval of the trustees, Sartain transformed the art classes at the Pennsylvania Academy into a proper art school, with Schussele as professor of art.[2] In 1870 the school was suspended for six years while a new building for the Academy was constructed, although Schussele continued to teach in his home at 10 Northwest Penn Square. By the time the new building reopened in September 1876, Schussele was nearly paralyzed and had difficulty performing his duties. At this point Eakins entered the picture, volunteering to take over Schussele's evening life classes and serve as chief demonstrator for the lecturer on anatomy, Dr. William W. Keen. He performed both these activities without pay. Nonetheless, Eakins's arrival stirred up bad feelings. According to an article on the Academy by Earl Shinn, Schussele approved of his teaching, but Eakins immediately clashed with some of the trustees. This seems at least half plausible, since we know indirectly that Eakins had difficulties with the trustees. Still open to speculation, however, is whether he really got on well with Schusselle, since he seems to have openly repudiated Schussele's whole approach to teaching.

Along with Eakins's disparagement of Schussele's classroom methods, another touchy issue may have been his interest in the nude, which apparently offended local standards of propriety. Indeed, in January of 1877 Eakins addressed a letter to the Committee on Instruction, headed by John Sartain, which read as follows:

> Gentlemen, the Life Schools are in great need of good female models.
>
> I desire that an advertisement similar to the following be inserted in the Public Ledger.
>
> Wanted Female Models for the Life Schools of the Pennsylvania Academy of the Fine Arts.
>
> Apply to the Curator at the Academy Broad & Cherry at the Cherry St. entrance.
>
> Applicants should be of respectability and may on all occasions be accompanied by their mothers or other female relatives. Terms $1 per hour. John Sartain. Chairman of Com. On Instruction.
>
> The privilege of wearing a mask might also be conceded and advertised.
>
> The publicity thus given in a reputable newspaper at the instance of an institution like the Academy will insure in these times a great number of applicants among whom will be found beautiful ones with forms fit to be studied.
>
> The old plan was for the students or officers to visit low houses of prostitution & bargain with the inmates.
>
> This course was degrading & would be unworthy of the present academy & its result was models coarse, flabby, ill forms & unfit in every way for the requirements of a school, nor was there sufficient change of models for the successful study of form.[3]

Several things about the proposed advertisement are intriguing. One is that Eakins was interested in a constantly changing lineup of nude models. Another is that he encouraged models to come accompanied by their mothers or other close relatives. Still another is the element of sexual prudery in Eakins's letter. Much of Eakins's statement is devoted to a diatribe against the ugliness of prostitutes (although later in life, in pressing a stout, middle-aged woman to pose nude for him, he maintained that no nude body, however fat and wrinkled, is ugly). Interestingly, this element of prudery and moral self-righteousness surfaces almost without warning. In a pattern that also occurs in many other letters by Eakins, he abruptly shifts in tone, switching from cool, dispassionate, rather legalistic or bureaucratic language to emotionally violent statements. Finally, it is interesting that Eakins did not propose to sign this advertisement himself, but wished it to go out under the name of John Sartain.

These oddities follow patterns that resurface elsewhere in Eakins's art and life. The key point here, however, is simply that Eakins must have known that such a letter would be an affront to Philadelphia standards of propriety. Even Eakins's admiring biographer, Lloyd Goodrich, saw that Eakins's challenge to local mores is self-evident. As he states: "Needless to say, there is no record of any such letter appearing in the newspapers."[4]

Whatever the nature of the conflict, we can infer that Eakins's teaching was constrained in some respect, for in late March 1877 he started a new school with a group of male students, in a rented room on Juniper Street, under the aegis of the newly formed Philadelphia Society of Artists. The classes, known as The Art Students' Union, were carried out through the winter of 1877–1878. Eakins apparently was not paid for his activities.[5] Shortly after Eakins took up these new teaching duties in May 1877, the board of the Pennsylvania Academy wrote a letter instructing Schussele not to delegate any of his teaching responsibilities. This was an indirect way of dismissing Eakins from his post at the Academy, although he was not specifically named.

In November 1877, the secretary of the women's life class, Susan Macdowell, petitioned the trustees to initiate an additional life class, with Eakins as instructor. Two days later the Academy directors agreed to add an evening life class for women, but rather pointedly, Eakins was not appointed as its head.

By this time, however, Schussele's health was so tenuous that it was difficult for him to teach. In March 1878, the directors wrote to Schussele rescinding their earlier letter and authorizing him to make use of an assistant. Consequently, Eakins returned to his teaching post at the Academy—still serving without pay. This curiously roundabout way of handling the situation may have occurred because Eakins had never been paid. While the trustees wanted him back, they did not wish to offer him a salary.

In September 1879, William C. Brownell wrote an article for *Scribner's Magazine* on the teaching at the Academy in which he made it clear that Schussele and Eakins differed significantly in their approaches. According to Brownell, Professor Schussele was "a conservative" who "prefers a long apprenticeship in drawing." Eakins, conversely, was "a radical," who "prefers that a pupil should paint at once, and . . . thinks a long study of the antique detrimental."[6] Brownell's argument makes it clear that as soon as Eakins was put in place as a teacher he revised the curriculum and instituted a new approach. Brownell explicitly stated that Eakins had clashed with several of the trustees, although he maintained that the artist had remained on friendly terms with Christian Schussele.[7]

In fact, within three months of his return to the Academy, Eakins clashed heads with his old supporter, John Sartain, the father of his first girlfriend, Emily Sartain. On June 3, 1877, George Whitney, a trustee of the Pennsylvania Academy, wrote to the painter William Trost Richards reporting that Sartain had resigned from the Academy in the midst of a "high old row." Whitney promised Richards "particulars hereafter when I hear more." In his next letter of June 17 he provided more information. "Bemont told me that Eakins was the trouble at the Academy—would do things as he pleased, which did not please Sartain, & etc. etc.—I suppose Eakins was aching to be kin to a King and rule the realm! Until Sartain was dethroned or abdicated—Let them fight it out."[8]

Schussele died on August 21, 1879, and on September 9 the directors of the Academy appointed Eakins professor of drawing and painting, providing him with a salary of $600 a year—only half of Schussele's $1,200. Despite this rebuff, Eakins was elated by his victory over John Sartain. In a letter to Susan Macdowell, Eakins noted with glee that he was sure Sartain would have a fit when he learned of the appointment.[9]

In 1882, Eakins was promoted to director of instruction, and his salary was raised from $600 to $1,200 a year—four or five times that of an ordinary workman. At the time, the trustees agreed to double his salary again "as soon and as rapidly as the income of the school will permit." In 1885, after six years of teaching, Eakins wrote the trustees asking that his pay be raised, as they had promised, but they declined his application.[10]

This brief account tells everything that we know about Eakins's rise to power at the Pennsylvania Academy. We do not have enough information to understand fully what was going on, although many aspects of what occurred suggest disagreement and conflict. Over the course of about a year, the board of the Academy shifted from expelling Eakins from the rooms of the Academy, and declaring that he was not allowed to teach for free, to hiring him at a large salary for the most powerful position in the art school. They often carried out their actions in a sneaky way, issuing edicts that did not mention Eakins by name but were aimed specifically at him. Even from the surface facts it appears that Eakins gained his position not so much through a smooth and gradual rise to power as through a series of political flip-flops, which culminated in a takeover that may well have had something of the character of a coup d'état.

Eakins inspired emotions ranging from hatred to intense loyalty. Some of the board members clashed with Eakins from the first, and by the time he was appointed director of instruction he had become the violent enemy of his former supporter and old family friend, John Sartain. We also know that some of the students—such as his future wife, Susan Macdowell—passionately took up Eakins's cause, and that he had at least a few powerful supporters on the board, such as Fairman Rogers. The role of other figures is hard to determine. For example, Earl Shinn reports that Christian Schussele remained on friendly terms with Eakins, but this is hard to believe, since we know that Eakins immediately and openly repudiated Schussele's curriculum. Indeed, Eakins may have earned the enmity of John Sartain because of the way he had undercut Schussele's position.

Even with incomplete evidence, it is notable that, as in other instances throughout his life, Eakins seems to have polarized groups against each other, not only creating conflict between the Pennsylvania Academy and the Philadelphia Society of Artists, but also creating bands of both loyalists and enemies within the Pennsylvania Academy. While some of Eakins's changes to the curriculum seem logical, other actions by him seem puzzling. For example, the memo he wrote asking to advertise for nude models was not only clearly out of line with normal standards of Philadelphia propriety, but strangely intemperate in its language.

Some of Eakins's actions suggest a desire to court humiliation and play the role of martyr. For example, if Eakins was willing to teach for no salary both at the Pennsylvania Academy and the Philadelphia Society of Artists, why did he later insist on asking for a very significant pay raise from the Board of the Pennsylvania Academy, when he must have known that he had enemies there and was likely to be refused? Given Eakins's behavior on other occasions, it is at least worth asking if he might not have asked for this pay raise precisely because he knew that it would be rejected.

During Eakins's early years at the Academy, the institution was directed by Fairman Rogers, who supported his activities. Goodrich, and others who have followed him, have described Rogers as "a liberal" in his views, but this adjective is fundamentally misleading.[11] An engineer by training, Rogers was indeed interested in scientific progress, and was particularly fascinated by photography. But his social views seem to have been essentially conservative, as is suggested by his interest in the expensive and self-consciously old-fashioned hobby of coaching with a four-in-hand. This entailed keeping four horses, several servants, and an expensive coach and was just the sort of conspicuous

Eadweard Muybridge (1830–1904), Photograph of Edgarton Trottng, 1878–1879. *Free Library of Philadelphia.*

consumption that Thorstein Veblen was to satirize in his *Theory of the Leisure Class.* Rogers's support of Eakins was essentially a defense of entrenched hierarchy and male authority against criticism from outsiders or women.[12]

In fact, this authoritarian side of Rogers's personality may well have appealed to Eakins, who always seems to have admired strong-willed, somewhat autocratic figures, like his father or Dr. Gross. Eakins's painting of Fairman Rogers, *May Morning in the Park* (1879; Philadelphia Museum of Art) is chilling. The canvas shows Rogers riding in his coach with his small, submissive wife, two other couples, and two liveried black servants in top hats. No one smiles. While most of the faces are hidden in shadow, those that we can see are frozen in expression.[13] Rogers is at the front presiding over this cheerless undertaking. His face is in shadow but his control is effectively symbolized by his brightly lit hands, which are holding a switch.

The painting effectively contradicts Goodrich's contentions that Rogers was liberal or socially progressive in his leanings. Unfortunately, we have no evidence of his views on sexual morality, and he had left Philadelphia by the time Eakins became embroiled in the loin cloth scandal and its associated revelations. Would Rogers have sanctioned Eakins's behavior? To me it seems doubtful, and more likely that he would have joined the others on the board and asked Eakins for his resignation.[14]

Writers on Eakins invariably praise his accuracy and grasp of science, but Eakins's paintings often clash with visual reality, despite his laborious methods. *The Fairman Rogers Four-in-Hand* provides a striking instance of this. In order to render the gait of the animals with perfect veracity, Eakins based his painting on Eadweard Muybridge's photographs of horses in successive stages of movement, apparently also taking new photographs to serve as further documentation. But the challenge of evoking motion led Eakins into visual contradictions, as was described, with a touch of malice, by his pupil Joseph Pennell.

> The painter wished to show a drag coming along the road at a rapid trot. He drew and redrew, and photographed and rephotographed the horses until he had gotten their action approximately right. Their legs had been studied and painted in the most marvelous manner. He then put on the drag. He drew every spoke in the wheels, and the whole affair looked as if it had been instantaneously petrified or arrested. There was no action in it. He then blurred the spokes, giving the drag the appearance of motion. The result was that it seemed to be on the point of running over the horses, which were standing still.[15]

Furthermore, in order to indicate the complete succession of a horse's movement, Eakins rendered the full cycle of the trot, showing four consecu-

The Fairman Rogers Four-in-Hand (A May Morning in the Park), 1879–1880. *Oil on canvas, 23 ¾ x 36 in., Philadelphia Museum of Art, Gift of William Alexander Dick.* **In contradiction to actual fact, Eakins showed each of the four horses in a different stage of movement.**

tive positions. Horses in a four-in-hand, however, do not move this way. To move in harmony, their gaits need to be almost perfectly synchronized. In short, for all of Eakins's hard work on the painting—it was the product of a full year of research—the final result neither conveys a vivid sense of movement nor directly corresponds to reality in any sense.

Eakins's Teaching

Eakins's curriculum at the Pennsylvania Academy was unusually narrow, focusing entirely on learning to paint the nude human figure. This emphasis on the nude resembled the course of instruction he had received in France, but Eakins almost eliminated drawing from plaster casts, or indeed, drawing of any kind. Perhaps he felt that he had wasted too much time on such preliminaries before taking up a brush.

Classes in other subjects were redirected to focus on the nude. For example, Eakins transformed the modeling class from a preparation for a career in sculpture to still another class in which painters intensively studied the nude human figure. He insisted on anatomy classes for everyone, with dissection of human and animal cadavers for the more advanced students.

Eakins boasted of his program that "the course of study is believed to be more thorough than that of any other existing school."[16] But in fact, Eakins largely eliminated many of the staples of other art schools, such as classes in still life, landscape, or composition. When allowed, they were directed in some fashion toward the problems of rendering the nude. Eakins permitted a class in still life, for example, on the rationale that it taught students to develop skills in handling color and tone that could then be applied to the figure. The one exception to this complete devotion to the nude was that Eakins lectured on perspective, a subject that fascinated him.[17]

As has been noted, many of Eakins's contemporaries thought his behavior was strange. Rumors circulated that he had some sexual motive for being so fixated on the naked figure, and so interested in undressing his female students. But another aspect of Eakins's teaching does not conform readily with this interpretation of Eakins's motives—his unparalleled emphasis on anatomical dissection.

The training in anatomy was extremely thorough. The lectures were illustrated by a skeleton, a manikin, plaster models painted red, blue, and white to indicate muscles, tendons, and bones, and by live models. In some of his demonstrations, Eakins applied electric current to make the muscles jump,

Circle of Thomas Eakins, Women's Modeling Class with Cow in
Pennsylvania Academy Studio, *ca. 1882. Albumen copy print, 3 ¹¹⁄₁₆ x 4 ¹⁵⁄₁₆
in., The Pennsylvania Academy of the Fine Arts, Charles Bregler's Thomas
Eakins Collection, purchased with the partial support of the Pew Memorial
Trust.* **Women in Eakins's classes studied anatomy from a live cow,
which sometimes defecated in the classroom.**

applying it both to cadavers and
to Henry, the Academy's African
American janitor.[18] (In 1894
Eakins published an article in the
*Proceedings of the Academy of Nat-
ural Sciences of Philadelphia* on the
differential action of muscles.)

Eakins's requirement that all
his students, including women,
dissect cadavers had no counterpart in any art school anywhere
in the 1880s, whether in America
or Europe. (While students in
Paris were often encouraged to
do dissections, they did so in the
hospital or the morgue, not the
classroom.) The constant presence in the classrooms of corpses
and body parts, both animal and
human, created an atmosphere that was just the opposite of sexually stimulating. Eakins himself confessed that the process of dissection was often stomach turning.[19]

Since electric refrigeration did not exist, the bodies were pickled in brine.
One Christmas week, when the classrooms were largely deserted, Adam
Emory Albright witnessed the delivery of cadavers:

> An ugly hulk of a man opened the door and came in with a huge burlap
> wrapped bundle and dropped it onto the floor. Then another, and then a
> third, larger than the others, all closely wrapped. Seeing me he called, "Keep
> back." He opened a trap door in the front of our life class I had never noticed
> before, ripped off the burlap and dropped one human body after another in to
> the hole. "Pickles," he said, as I heard a splash. He closed the trap door, locked
> it, gathered up the burlap and drove away. "Pickles," he said again, as he
> closed the back door. A meaner looking man I had never seen. These were the
> cadavers we had in the dissecting room.[20]

Despite the pickling, the smell of decaying bodies must often have been
oppressive. Eakins not only supervised dissections but made casts of bodies

and body parts in various stages of dismemberment. In the process of these activities, body parts were scattered around the building and often played a role in practical jokes. Detached penises were a natural target of such fun. For example, Adam Emory Albright later recalled:

> To prepare a male stiff for the women's dissecting class, we removed the part that made a man a man. We all declared it was an accident that the part was found in some fellow's smock pocket as he took it down before leaving. Be that as it may, it had to be dodged several times and finally followed some one down the back stairs and into the washroom, landing in the flush toilet.[21]

Unfortunately, the dismembered penis clogged the drain, and a plumber needed to be summoned to remove it.

Body parts were also sometimes taken outside the building. Margaret McHenry has described an occasion when a paper sack being carried on a bus got wet and various grisly objects spilled out on the floor.[22] On another occasion, a raucous group of young men threw a dead horse over the balcony onto the landing of the grand staircase. It does not take much psychological insight to see that such "jokes" must have been an outlet for anxiety—anxiety about death, anxiety about castration—as well as a means for the young male jokesters to embarrass and assert their dominance over squeamish women. Certainly Eakins's insistence that women undertake the same dissections as the men was an assault on the Victorian notion that women were sensitive and delicate, and should live in a protected realm.

Goodrich has used words like "liberal" and "progressive" to describe Eakins's curriculum, but in fact he approached art as a technical and mechanical skill whose sole purpose was to represent things accurately. He completely disregarded issues such as emotional expression, paid little attention to aesthetics or art as formal design, and paid no heed to new stylistic tendencies.[23] Indeed, he boasted that he did not teach "picture making," which students were free to learn on their own.[24] As noted, the one "progressive" aspect of Eakins's

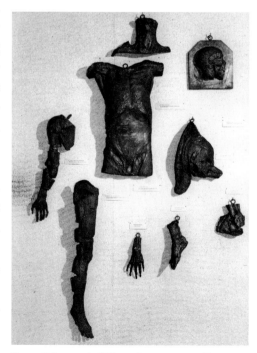

Casts of Anatomical Dissection, 1877–1880. *Bronze, cast 1930, Philadelphia Museum of Art, Gift of Mr. and Mrs. R. Sturgis Ingersoll.*

teaching was that he largely dispensed with drawing and with copying plaster casts, but encouraged his students to move directly to the model and to work with a brush. "There are no lines in nature," he remarked to the critic William Brownell, "there are only form and color."[25]

While his methods were rigorous and intense, Eakins eliminated awards and prizes, an action that might have been predicted from a letter he wrote to his father from Paris. "How childish the French people are with their prizes," he wrote. "Many a weak young man who might have been a good painter has been ruined wasting his time hunting prizes. If you consider the bottom of the thing you see that a prize is only to mask an injustice to endeavor to give a false position to some that don't deserve it."[26]

What of Eakins's performance in the classroom? Fortunately, we have a transcription of many of Eakins's actual statements, which were faithfully transcribed by his pupil Charles Bregler. From Bregler's notes we learn that you should "always think of the third dimension," that the model's feet should be planted on the floor, that one should think about the weight of the figure, and that one should get as much of the image as possible down at the beginning, before one tires.[27] Taken by themselves, statements such as these are not very stimulating, although possibly they were useful in their specific context. As Goodrich notes, Eakins made no attempt to inculcate wider artistic principles. His approach was purely naturalistic, concentrating on the task of representing the model.

The idiosyncratic nature of Eakins's curriculum becomes more striking when we consider that about half of the Academy's students were women who were largely interested in decorative arts, still life, and landscape. Eakins's program simply did not allow artists to develop these other interests. Even from the standpoint of figure painting, Eakins's curriculum was limited, since it simply taught students to render the individual figure, and did not in any way explore the problems of composition and figure organization. Not surprisingly, most of Eakins' students never mastered these basic and necessary skills. Indeed, the logic of Eakins's extraordinary emphasis on anatomy falls apart when we closely consider the matter. Many highly gifted figure draftsmen—the painter Paul Cadmus is a good example—know very little about anatomy and are not particularly interested in the subject. To argue that you need to know anatomy to draw the figure is as fallacious as to argue that you need to know plumbing and electric wiring to draw architecture. Moreover, most paintings show figures with clothes, which present very different challenges from a rendering of the nude and ones that Eakins's curriculum did not address. In short, Eakins's curriculum mirrored his own interests, but was not a very satisfactory way of training artists in general.

Eakins has been pictured as a great teacher, but this does not appear to have been the case. Goodrich declared in his monograph of 1933 that "Eakins was a born teacher," and he repeated this statement unchanged in his book of 1982.[28] At the same time, however, Goodrich implicitly confessed that Eakins had no significant students. He concludes his 1933 volume with the thought that "Eakins stands out as an isolated figure, belonging to no school, having few ancestors or descendants . . . Eakins' influence, like that of Ryder, would be difficult to trace."[29] Unlike his successor Thomas Anshutz, Eakins had no students who went on to become important painters in their own right.[30] The two most notable of the artists who studied with him, the illustrators Joseph Pennell and Arthur Burdett Frost, both spoke of him later in life with distaste and largely repudiated his teachings in their own work.[31]

Those students who responded to Eakins seem to have been impressed as much by the force and dogmatism with which he put forward his principles as by anything they actually learned from him. Indeed, one of the notable phenomena among Eakins's students is that those who were most devoted to him, such as Charles Bregler, produced wobbly, hesitant, indecisive work, seemingly at odds with the principles Eakins espoused. With the exception of Samuel Murray, who studied with him after he left the Pennsylvania Academy, none of Eakins's close associates produced work of any artistic distinction. While many of these figures studied with Eakins for years, it is now difficult to find even a trace of their artistic activities. Sylvan Schendler put the matter succinctly when he declared that Eakins "had no great students."[32] Perhaps, this is not surprising, since Eakins himself seems to have had difficulty learning from his teachers, despite his high respect for them.

Eakins seems to have spent very little of his time actually interacting with students. Adam Emory Albright, who studied with him, later recalled, "I doubt if Eakins ever spent more than thirty minutes in a review twice a week."[33] Much of Eakins's time seems to have been taken up with enterprises loosely associated with teaching, but somewhat apart from it, such as studies of anatomy, animal locomotion, and photography. These activities often took directions that were only very loosely related to the classes he taught, and became expressive ventures in their own right.

J. Laurie Wallace Nude, Playing Pipes, Facing Left, ca. 1883. *Copy negative from a dry-plate negative, 4 x 5 in., courtesy of The Pennsylvania Academy of the Fine Arts, Philadelphia, Charles Bregler's Thomas Eakins Collection, purchased with the partial support of the Pew Memorial Trust.*

Chapter 15

NAKED IN ARCADIA

EAKINS'S PHOTOGRAPHS are quite unlike those of any other nineteenth-century American artist. A great many of them portray nudes, and they do so in an unusual fashion. Eakins first took up the camera around 1880, shortly after he was appointed professor of drawing and painting at the Pennsylvania Academy. By June 1884, Thomas Anshutz noted in a letter that Eakins was experimenting with a photographic apparatus.[1] We do not know exactly what spurred Eakins in this direction, but Fairman Rogers, who served as the head of the committee on instruction at the Pennsylvania Academy, was an amateur photographer, and he may have encouraged Eakins to pursue this interest.[2]

Rogers was also a fanatical horseman, and helped subsidize Eadweard Muybridge's early motion photographs of horses. As mentioned, in 1879 Rogers commissioned Eakins to produce a painting of his four-in-hand, which would incorporate information from these new action photographs. While working on this project, Eakins became deeply involved in taking photographs of human and animal locomotion, and for a time worked alongside Muybridge at the University of Pennsylvania.

Born in England in 1852, Muybridge emigrated to the United States in 1852, and settled in San Francisco three years later. Variously known as Muggeridge (his birth name), Muygridge, and Maybridge, around 1866 he obliterated his former guises, occupations, and prior names, and at the age of thirty-six adopted a new name, took up photography, and quickly established a reputation as one of California's finest landscape photographers. Just six years later he was challenged to photograph a horse in motion by the immensely wealthy Californian railroad builder Leland Stanford, and began to use banks of cameras to record successive stages of animal and human movement.[3]

Muybridge murdered his wife's lover during the period when he produced his first motion study photographs in California. After his acquittal, he decided to move to a new location, and came to the University of Pennsylvania to pursue his experiments. In 1884 an outdoor studio for Muybridge's photographic experiments was built on the grounds of University Hospital. It contained a battery of twenty-four cameras, a track for the moving subject, and behind the track a long shed painted black inside, with a network of white threads for measurements. The moving figures were photographed in sunlight against this background. Muybridge began work in the late spring of 1884. That September, Eakins had a small shed built for his own photographic work.

Eakins later made false claims about his work with motion photography, as has been established by William Innes Homer and Lloyd Goodrich. [4] In the summer of 1887, Eakins wrote a statement about his work as a photographer, which he sent to Professor William D. Marks. The following year Marks published a report, based on Eakins's assertions, in which he declared that Eakins had invented a two-disc camera and had improved on the single revolving disc developed earlier by the French researcher, Etienne-Jules Marey.

This claim was not true. From the statements of Thomas Anshutz, who worked alongside Eakins in this period, we know that Muybridge was using a two-disc camera by June 1884, and that Eakins did not use a two-disc camera until five months later, in November of that year. Moreover, the notion of using a camera with multiple discs had already been explored and publicized by Marey, who invented a "photographic gun" in 1881 and published it in 1882. Thus, Eakins had not made a new invention, but at best had simply modified the apparatus of earlier researchers. [5]

Like all good lies, Eakins's statement probably contained an element of truth. Most likely he had developed a two-disc camera, but he was not forthright about stating that others had done so earlier. Eakins then confused matters further by enlisting someone else, William D. Marks, to publish his claims. This gave a spurious aura of objectivity to the product. It also complicated the task of contesting his statements, since errors might well be attributed not to Eakins but to the carelessness of his spokesperson. It drew others into the process of defending him, in order to maintain their own reputation. Goodrich, always eager to take Eakins's side, noted that the artist wrote his statement shortly after he had been fired from the Pennsylvania Academy. Consequently, "the trauma of his recent forced resignation" may have played a role in leading Eakins to make such exaggerated claims for his work. [6] This theory, however, is hardly reassuring, since it suggests that Eakins was a grudge holder, and that there was an undercurrent of anger and deceitfulness in his personality, which could surface unexpectedly in almost any context.

The Rediscovery of Eakins as a Photographer

The literature on Eakins's photographs provides a fascinating instance of how an artist's work can quite literally be reshaped to suit the dictates of current fashion. In the early twentieth century, artists who worked from photographs were viewed with disdain. As a consequence, Goodrich avoided mentioning Eakins's photographic work in his 1933 monograph on the artist. He noted only one small group of Eakins's photographs—the animal locomotion studies that were taken when Eakins was working alongside Muybridge. In discussing these photographs, Goodrich emphasized the intensity of the painter's study of anatomy and science, and he proposed that Eakins's experiments with cameras anticipated Thomas Edison's movie camera—a claim that has since been shown to be incorrect.[7] Goodrich specifically disparaged the notion that Eakins might have used photographs in any significant way in composing his paintings.[8]

As Alisa Luxenberg has shown, the coopting of photography into the Eakins mythology occurred quite abruptly, after photography had been validated as a fine art. This move took place in the 1970s, around the time that "photo-realism" made it acceptable for painters to work directly from photographs without attempting to conceal that fact.[9] The principle figure responsible for rediscovering Eakins's photographs was Gordon Hendricks, whose publications represented the first major challenge to Goodrich's position as the fundamental source of information on Eakins. The landmark event in this rediscovery was an exhibition organized by Hendricks in 1969 at the Pennsylvania Academy of the Fine Arts. Hendricks not only wrote the catalogue, but also owned most of the photographs that were included in the show.[10]

Hendricks's catalogue sparked a demand for Eakins's photographs that was quickly exploited by commercial galleries. In 1976 a group of twenty-one newly discovered prints were exhibited by the Olympia Galleries of Philadelphia, including several photographs of nudes, some in frontal views. The following year the Olympia Galleries put these photographs up for sale in New York at Sotheby Park Bernet. The catalogue opened by equating Eakins's photographs with his paintings. "The same fine and highly artistic vision which made Thomas Eakins one of America's greatest painters also made him a superb photographer. His finest photographs, like his finest paintings, are extraordinary works of art." In the subsequent sale one photograph of three female nudes set a record price for a photograph at auction.[11]

Four years later another large group of photographs attributed to Eakins surfaced at the Olympia Galleries. Containing mainly nudes, this collection had been discovered in the safe-deposit box of Edward Horner Coates, the president of Pennsylvania Academy, who had apparently confiscated them at the time that Eakins was fired from the institution. Again the Olympia Galleries published an exhibition catalogue, this time titled *Photographer Thomas Eakins* with an essay by another Eakins scholar, Ellwood C. Parry.[12] While this essay was full of the usual lavish praise of Eakins's genius, its most powerful statement was embedded in the title. It asserted that Eakins could and should be viewed as a major photographer, rather than as someone who practiced photography as a sideline, or as a support for other activities.

Thus, in a span of about fifteen years, Eakins changed from being an artist who did not use photographs at all to a major photographer whose prints set world sales records, and who was viewed as a pioneer in the use of photography as an art form.

Unusual Features of Eakins's Work as a Photographer

There are many ironies to this emergence of Eakins as a major photographer. For one thing, it appears that Eakins always viewed photography as subordinate to his activities as a painter and did not value photographs as independent works of art. With rare exceptions, he did not exhibit his photographs and he never kept detailed records of them, as he did for his paintings.[13] In an 1883 inventory of his personal belongings, Eakins noted that he owned a large number of photographs but did not bother to list them individually or to claim authorship.

In addition, Eakins clearly did not take all the photographs that have been grouped under the heading "Eakins photographs." Many of these images, for example, depict Eakins himself, often in the nude, making it clear that someone else snapped the shutter.[14] Moreover, the works grouped under Eakins's authorship employ a wide variety of materials and processes, including glass plate negatives and prints made with the cheap and functional cyanotype process as well as the more expensive platinum and wet collodion methods. The works also differ widely in framing, focus, and general effect.[15] These differences may reflect the work of various photographers and printers, for in some instances photographs once attributed to Eakins have been reassigned to others. Notably a group of photographs of Walt Whitman formerly ascribed to Eakins are now known to have been taken by Samuel Murray.[16]

To deal with this dilemma, writers on Eakins have answered the question, "Who was the author?" in interesting ways. Hendricks bluntly declares that since the photographs chronicle "the facts of [Eakins's] life" they are effectively by his hand.[17] Ellwood Parry explains them as the product of an artistic vision that did not require physical involvement. Parry notes that Eakins may have collaborated with students such as Samuel Murray and Thomas Anshutz, but declares: "Murray or Anshutz could have released the shutter. That does not really change the fact that the vision belonged to Eakins."[18]

Tracing Photographs

In his monograph of 1933, Lloyd Goodrich specifically dismissed the idea that Eakins's paintings might have been dependent on photographs. According to Goodrich, Eakins "never painted from photographs, except in a few cases of portraits of persons no longer living, a type of commission which he disliked to undertake."[19] Goodrich took pains, in fact, to make it clear that Eakins was not merely a "photographic painter," and that he never attempted to render appearances "like the camera."[20]

The obvious errors in these statements quickly became apparent when Hendricks made public a large body of Eakins's photographic work. Thus it was revealed that Eakins often used photographs to record poses and other information, as was the case, for example, with *Singing a Pathetic Song* (1881), in which the principal figure of the singer is closely based on photographs that were staged in Eakins's studio.[21] In addition, Eakins seems to have been interested in the optical qualities of the photograph. He not only based his painting *Mending the Net* (1881) on a photograph, but he also copied the photograph with nearly perfect exactitude—blurring the foreground and distance, and leaving the middle ground in sharpest focus, just as the photograph had recorded it.

Recently, Mark Tucker and Nica Gutman have established that for a brief period, around 1885–1886, Eakins traced his paintings from projected photographs. Study of Eakins's drawings revealed that in several instances he did not simply copy photographs, but traced them, apparently using either a magic lantern (which projects glass transparencies) or a catoptric lamp (which uses mirrors to project photographic prints) to transfer the image to the canvas.

Singing a Pathetic Song, 1881. *Oil on canvas, 45 × 32 ½ in., in the collection of the Corcoran Gallery of Art, Museum Purchase, Gallery Fund.* **Margaret Harrison sings while Eakins's future wife, Susan Macdowell, accompanies her at the piano.** RIGHT Margaret Harrison Posing for "The Pathetic Song," Painting Visible at Right, 1881. *Dry-plate negative, 4 × 5 in., courtesy of The Pennsylvania Academy of the Fine Arts, Philadelphia, Charles Bregler's Thomas Eakins Collection, purchased with the partial support of the Pew Memorial Trust.* **The painting does not record an actual concert but was based on photographs that Eakins staged in his studio.**

Shad Fishing at Gloucester on the Delaware River, 1881. *Oil on canvas, 12 ⅛ × 18 ⅛ in., Philadelphia Museum of Art, gift of Mrs. Thomas Eakins and Miss Mary Adeline Williams.* **Recent technical research has established that Eakins's** Shad Fishing at Gloucester on the Delaware River **was directly traced from projected photographs.**

The distinctive fashion in which Eakins drew whole contours without picking up the pencil clearly indicates that he was tracing images, rather than copying them freehand. Eakins also used guide marks to align his photographs, when he projected them onto the canvas.[22]

Throughout much of the nineteenth and twentieth century, such use of photographs was viewed as inherently antiartistic—even grounds for dismissal from a position as an art teacher.[23] Even today the discovery that Eakins did so has been greeted with such headlines as "Old Masters Cheated."[24] Because of the stigma attached to photography, Eakins took pains to conceal his methods. In his painting of *Swimming*, 1884–1885, for example, Eakins used a stylus to make marks that helped him exactly place photographic projections of each of the figures. In the final stage of his work, however, Eakins went back over the surface and added small dabs of pigment to hide these guideposts—concealing any sign that he might have worked from a photograph.[25]

Eakins's behavior contained elements of contradiction. His practice of using projected photographs appears to have been more arduous, more time-consuming, and more technically challenging than simply working freehand.

Three women, man, and dog near Delaware River, ca. 1881. *Copy negative from contact print, 4 × 5 in., Pennsylvania Academy of the Fine Arts, Philadelphia. Charles Bregler's Thomas Eakins Collections, purchased with the partial support of the Pew Memorial Trust.*

Benjamin Eakins Standing, and Man Sitting, under Tree Near Delaware River, ca. 1881. *Copy negative from contact print, 4 × 5 in., Pennsylvania Academy of the Fine Arts, Philadelphia, Charles Bregler's Thomas Eakins Collection, purchased with the partial support of the Pew Memorial Trust.*

Consequently, Eakins must have adopted it not to save time or effort, but to achieve a degree of exactitude not possible by other methods. By concealing his use of photographs, however, Eakins removed the evidence that his work was more "accurate" and more "realistic" than that of other painters. Few if any contemporary viewers looked closely enough to recognize that his work was any different in its technical qualities from that of everyone else.

Mending the Net, 1881. *Oil on canvas, 32 ¼ x 45 ¼ in., Philadelphia Museum of Art, gift of Mrs. Thomas Eakins and Miss Mary Adeline Williams.*

Two Fishermen Mending Nets, ca. 1881. *Dry-plate negative, 4 x 5 in., courtesy of The Pennsylvania Academy of the Fine Arts, Philadelphia, Charles Bregler's Thomas Eakins Collection, purchased with the partial support of the Pew Memorial Trust.*

Susan Eakins, who was trained as a photographer and is known to have made prints for her husband, was clearly well aware of her husband's techniques. Her claim to Lloyd Goodrich that Eakins did not use photographs was surely not only false but deliberately so.

Perhaps because the practice was so laborious, Eakins worked closely from photographs for only a relatively brief period, engaging in the practice from 1881 to 1885 (and possibly earlier). Eakins continued to take photographs after he was fired from the Pennsylvania Academy and moved on to the Philadelphia Art Students League. But he no longer traced them for his paintings, and used them in a more generalized way as a form of reference. After he abandoned teaching altogether, Eakins seems to have taken photographs less frequently and he abandoned the practice altogether after about 1900. The bulk of his photographic activity thus coincides with his years as a teacher.

Eakins's Emphasis on the Nude

In addition to his practice of tracing from photographs, one of the most unusual features of Eakins's photographic work—particularly in an American context—is its extraordinary emphasis on the nude. About one-third of the surviving photographs by Eakins portray nudes. The proportion was once higher, since, according to Seymour Adelman, large numbers of photographs of nudes were destroyed after Susan Eakins's death by a relative who was scandalized by their subject matter.[26]

From the beginning, Eakins's photographs of nudes have provoked particular interest. Thus, for example, at the 1977 sale from the Olympia Galleries, the nudes received higher estimates and bids than the clothed figures and portraits, and the record-breaking Eakins photograph was one that depicted three nudes.

Over the last few decades, in fact, probably more than half of the new articles and studies of Eakins's work have been devoted either to his photographs of the nude or to the paintings and sculptures that are related to them. Why so much attention? Artistic quality alone does not fully explain this phenomenon. While scholars do not always explain their motives, this attention seems to stem from the fact that Eakins's photographs are difficult to explain. They flout conventional standards of decorum and yet are not erotic in any conventional way.

In fact, photography has always been a particularly powerful medium for sexually charged subject matter. As Edward Lucie-Smith has noted, pornographic photographs are always more arousing than drawings, since what is presented actually occurred and was neither edited nor merely imagined. As he writes: "The painter recreates the world; the photographer spies on it. His excitement lies in preserving what should be ephemeral, in making public what is essentially private."[27]

Professional Needs

Recent writers have developed two explanations for Eakins's nude photographs, neither of which is convincing. The first is the notion that Eakins's photographs were entirely "professional," and were made for scientific and practical purposes. This explanation falls apart on several grounds.

For one thing, the concept of "professional use" quickly becomes so vague as to become nonsensical. When we endeavor to deduce what purpose Eakins's photographs served, we quickly encounter perplexing questions. Hendricks, for example, has proposed categorizing Eakins's photographs according to the degree to which they relate to his painting or to his teaching. Thus, he suggests a three-part division: those that Eakins made with the intention of using them in his work; those he made to help himself "understand his work better" (that is, to demonstrate some general principle of anatomy or artistic expression); and those that bear no apparent relationship to his paintings.[28]

This sounds like a sensible way of arranging things until we try to put it into practice, at which point these distinctions become murky. Some photographs, for example, have no relationship to existing works, but it is hard to tell whether Eakins made them because he intended to start a project but never did so. It is even more difficult to distinguish whether a photograph was made as an independent artistic statement, or to demonstrate some artistic or anatomical principle. Photographs that were made for a particular painting may also have been used as a teaching tool. In the end, Hendricks's categories are nearly useless.

Even in cases in which we can propose a professional purpose for which a photograph was made, Eakins's practice still stands out as peculiar. Thus, for example, Eakins made a very large body of "naked photographs" that show himself, his students, and other figures from front, back, and side. Allegedly these were made to demonstrate something about human posture, and Eakins even made tracings from some of them that allegedly were made with this purpose in mind. But Eakins does not seem to have used these photographs to make paintings, and while he may well have used them in his teaching, it is not clear why such photographs were necessary for Eakins but not for any other artist of the nineteenth century. The fact that he used such photographs for his teaching does not eliminate the possibility that they may have been made for some other reason, perhaps in response to a deeper impulse.[29]

Notably, the argument of "professional use" does not explain the most peculiar thing about Eakins's photographs: his insistence on recording himself in the nude, and in photographing not professional models but students and friends. This practice, which has no parallel in the work of any other nineteenth-century artist, whether American or European, was surely connected in some way with Eakins's motive for taking these photographs in the first place.

Indeed, even when Eakins's photographs did serve a "professional" role, we should not rule out the possibility that they may also have reflected some other personal or psychological motive. Interestingly, Elizabeth Johns, who at one point proposed that all Eakins's photographs were strictly professional in nature, has almost completely discarded this position in her recent writings on the subject. Essentially, she has argued that we should disregard whether the photographs had some practical purpose or not and consider the deeper question of what sort of narrative these photographs create in their own right. [30]

Were Eakins's Photographs Erotic?

The second explanation is that Eakins's photographs are erotic. Lincoln Kirstein, for example, who wrote most enthusiastically about these nude photographs, veiled his thoughts in somewhat flowery and ambiguous language, but essentially argued that Eakins's images were free-spirited, sensual, and sexual statements:

> The fullness and sweetness of his girls, the wholly unself-conscious frontal frankness of his boys and men, are illustrations of Walt Whitman's spirit. From these groupings one gains the image of a marvelous guru, guiding his dedicated adepts out of the miasma of Calvinist hypocrisy into a living arcadia, which, through his magic, leads into no resurrected Greece, but into a modern landscape where Attic values were declared openly.... In his photographs he is free, not only to pose models as he likes, but to play with them as he loves, surrounded, reassured, comforted by the warmest, most difficult subject available to any artist. He could take his train back to the deathly City of Brotherly Love, having for a few sunny hours basked in a truly heavenly hedonism.[31]

Coming from Kirstein, these words have a particular intensity. A bisexual (he married the sister of Paul Cadmus, but had many male lovers), Kirstein was an associate of the gay photographer George Platt Lynes, and made excursions to the beach with Paul Cadmus, Jared French and other artists, during which the friends took openly erotic photographs of nude sunbathing and other nude activities. Words like "Attic" in Kirstein's phraseology, not only allude to ancient Greece but also specify a culture open to the notion of physical love between men. Kirstein clearly viewed Eakins (and Whitman) as a forebear for his own physically uninhibited and often homosexual interest in the human body.

In major respects, Kirstein's interpretation is useful. His writing makes it clear that Eakins was presenting the nude in a way that violated conventional social norms, and that often seems to touch on "forbidden" sexual practices, such as homosexuality. Kirstein, however, clearly coopted Eakins's work to make it more in harmony with his own hedonistic views. This theory does not explain, however, why so many of Eakins's photographs show figures who are homely and ungraceful, and who seem uncomfortable and embarrassed. Nor does this view explain why Eakins was so interested in using his students as models, rather than professionals, and why it was so important that he undress himself.

Academic Nudes by Louis Igout, from *Album d'études-Poses,* ca. 1875–1880. *Albumen print.*
Artistic nudes by French photographers mimicked the poses of academic paintings.

The unusual nature of Eakins's photographs becomes apparent when we compare them with the work of his contemporaries. Photographs of nudes in the nineteenth century, most of which were French, tended to fit into one of three types. They might be medical (or scientific); they might be artistic—made for the use of artists—or pornographic—made for sexual titillation. Medical photographs tended to be the most straightforward, and often featured some deformity or disease. They made no effort to pose the model gracefully. "Artistic" photographs tended to feature muscular or good-looking models, at least according to nineteenth-century standards. The figures were generally placed in poses that echoed those of paintings or antique sculpture. Generally speaking, the models covered their pubic region and avoided direct eye contact. Eakins was clearly familiar with photographs that were either artistic or erotic, since his account book reveals that he purchased *photo femmes turques* in Paris.[32]

French, Pornographic Nude, ca. 1861–1863. *Albumen print (Archives de la préfecture de Police, Paris).* **Photographs that departed from the academic norm were considered pornographic and were often confiscated by the French police.** RIGHT Inherited Syphilis from Francis F. Maury and Louis A. Duhring, *Photographic Review of Medicine and Surgery I, 1870–1871. Albumen print, Historical Collections of the Library of the College of Physicians of Philadelphia.* **Photographs of naked people were socially condoned when they were used for a medical purpose.**

Because they were often confiscated by the police, we have a body of photographs that can be used to determine what was considered pornographic. Such photographs were often similar to "artistic" ones, but they were more likely to reveal pubic hair and often the model looked directly toward the spectator with a suggestive or inviting expression.

In practice, there was a gray area between these modes. Pornographic photographers tried to make their work look sufficiently "artistic" so that it could get past the government censors; and clearly many young men purchased "artistic" or even "medical" photographs of naked women because they found them titillating. Virtually all nineteenth-century French photographs of nudes, however, can be explained with reference to one or more of these three purposes.

Susan Macdowell Eakins Nude, Left Arm Resting on Neck of Thomas Eakins's Horse Billy, ca.1890. *Platinum print, 6 ⁷⁄₁₆ x 7 ½ in., courtesy of The Pennsylvania Academy of the Fine Arts, Philadelphia, Charles Bregler's Thomas Eakins Collection, purchased with the partial support of the Pew Memorial Trust.* **Eakins freely distributed photographs of himself and his wife in the nude. At some point, an owner of this print defaced Susan's face, presumably to conceal her identity.**

Eakins's work, however, overlaps each of these categories without fitting neatly into any of them. Some of his photographs, such as those that allegedly were made as studies of human posture, come close to the effect of "medical" photographs. But a large number of his images, such as those of naked boys wrestling, boxing, swimming, and playing tug-of-war, are not "scientific" in this way, so this category certainly does not suffice to describe his nude photographs as a whole.

Many of Eakins's photographs of the nude come close to the "artistic" type, but with a number of significant divergences from the French approach. Unlike French artistic photographs, Eakins's models are often unevenly lit, and he generally favored more slender models, both male and female, than was typical of his time. Eakins also was not interested in the studio settings that were employed by French photographers. Preferring to break down the barriers between the "artistic" nude and real life, he rarely used the arms-over-head pose that recurs in French photographs. He did not try to create stories or moods through facial expressions.

Finally, some of Eakins's photographs come close to the pornographic type in that they directly portray genitals and full frontal nudity, and they often seem to touch on issues of sexual fantasy. There is some evidence that Eakins's photographs were considered socially embarrassing. For example, one surviving photograph of Eakins with a naked woman was cut into two parts, to separate the figures and make their relationship less suggestive. In one of the photographs of Susan with Eakins's horse Billy, Susan's face was scratched out, presumably to make her unrecognizable. Unlike typical pornographic photographs, however, which tend to feature models with "come-hither" expression that directly engage the viewer, the models in Eakins's photographs tend to look away, as if ashamed. Only a nude on a Queen Anne chair and a young African-American child engage in direct eye contact with the viewer.[33]

Two Women in Classical Costume, with Eakins' "Arcadia" Relief at Left, ca. 1883. *Platinum print, 8 ⁵⁄₁₆ x 5 ¾ in., courtesy of The Pennsylvania Academy of the Fine Arts, Philadelphia, Charles Bregler's Thomas Eakins Collection, purchased with the partial support of the Pew Memorial Trust.*

Naked Students and Friends

For the most part, Eakins did not use professional models, but took photographs of his students, his friends, and himself. The statements made when Eakins was fired from the Academy indicate that he coerced his models into posing. Indeed, Eakins seems to have been interested in recording their offended expressions. In one such instance, he first photographed a female student wearing an eighteenth-century gown and then, after pulling the gown down to reveal more of her breasts, took two more pictures. These last two photographs are fascinating not so much because of what they reveal of the young woman's body, as because of the distress and humiliation on her face.

For the sake of argument, let us suppose that Eakins's motive in taking

Clara Mather Sitting in Carved Armchair, ca. 1891. *Dry-plate negative, 5 x 8 in., courtesy of The Pennsylvania Academy of the Fine Arts, Philadelphia, Charles Bregler's Thomas Eakins Collection, purchased with the partial support of the Pew Memorial Trust.* RIGHT   Clara Mather Sitting in Lyre-Back Chair, ca. 1891. *Dry-plate negative, 5 x 8 in., courtesy of The Pennsylvania Academy of the Fine Arts, Philadelphia, Charles Bregler's Thomas Eakins Collection, purchased with the partial support of the Pew Memorial Trust.* **Eakins's photographs often reveal increasing exposure of flesh and increasingly uncomfortable-looking models.**

such photographs was simply to get his students to undress. He must have gone about this process in stages. The first stage of this process would very likely have been the photographs that show students in Greek costumes. In the nineteenth century, Greek art was held up as a standard of artistic perfection, and consequently, anything that imitated Greek art had a certain social sanction. It was probably not hard to persuade students to pose in loose-fitting Greek gowns, often alongside completely naked Greek statues. Getting students into togas was a first step toward persuading them to discard their clothes entirely.

The photographs of models in costumes and togas seem to have been followed by nude studies, which Eakins was careful to give a clear didactic purpose. Essentially, these nude studies are of two types. One group closely resembles French art photographs of the period, showing students assuming standard academic poses. The major difference from the French photographs is that the models appear to be slightly embarrassed. They either avert their faces or wear masks. The other group, the "naked photographs," are not so much artistic as scientific in their approach. These are rather similar in character to

Thomas Eakins Nude and Female Nude, in University of Pennsylvania Photography Shed, 1885. *Dry-plate negative, 4 x 5 in., courtesy of The Pennsylvania Academy of the Fine Arts, Philadelphia, Charles Bregler's Thomas Eakins Collection, purchased with the partial support of the Pew Memorial Trust.* Around 1885 Eakins posed for a surprising group of photographs that show him naked, standing alongside an undressed woman and also carrying her in his arms.

police mug shots, except that they portray not only the face, but the entire naked figure, from the front, the back, and the side. Ostensibly, this was a way of recording posture and of indicating how every human figure has a slightly different stance, based on weight, length of limbs, musculature, and the curvature of bones. For practical purposes, however, it would have been just as easy to illustrate these points with a figure clothed in a loin cloth rather than entirely nude. Moreover, there was no necessity for using students as models rather than hiring professionals. In short, the anatomical and "scientific" purpose of these photographs seems to have been a screen for some other motivation.

A final group of photographs is more audacious and shows both Eakins and other people in provocative arrangements. Several photographs, for example, show Eakins and a female model in a shed that he built at the University of Pennsylvania in 1884 for his motion studies. In one photograph,

Thomas Eakins Nude, Holding Nude Female in His Arms, Looking at Camera, ca. 1885. *Dry-plate negative, 4 x 5 in., courtesy of The Pennsylvania Academy of the Fine Arts, Philadelphia, Charles Bregler's Thomas Eakins Collection, purchased with the partial support of the Pew Memorial Trust.* The pictures were taken in a photography shed at the University of Pennsylvania, where Eakins was working alongside Eadweard Muybridge. We do not know whether the woman was a student or a professional model.

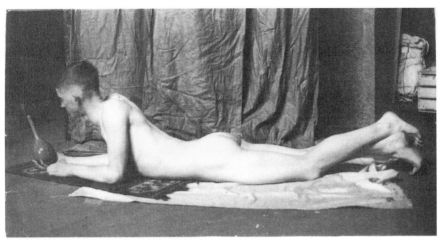

Bill Duckett Nude, Lying on Stomach, Holding Vase, ca. 1889. *Platinum print, 5 1⅟₁₆ x 11 in., courtesy of The Pennsylvania Academy of the Fine Arts, Philadelphia, Charles Bregler's Thomas Eakins Collection, purchased with the partial support of the Pew Memorial Trust.* **Eakins suggestively photographed Bill Duckett in the nude, holding a phallic object.**

Eakins and his model, both nude, stand side by side, as if consulting for the next pose. The photograph raises many questions about Eakins's practice, since we do not know who took it. Did Eakins alternate nude posing with standing behind the camera? If so, that would suggest that he himself was sometimes in the nude when he made photographs of naked figures.

Odder still are some photographs probably taken the same day, showing Eakins holding the nude model in his arms. Johns, who reads Eakins's expression as a smile, rhetorically asks whether these photographs were produced "in an atmosphere of high jinks," and suggests that they were taken in an atmosphere of "conspiratorial horseplay."[34] Eakins also occasionally made photographs of other individuals that show poses or props that seem sexually provocative. One photograph, for example, shows Walt

Photographer unknown, Walt Whitman and Bill Duckett, ca. 1886. Tintype, 4 ⅜ x 3 ⅞6 in., Rare Books and Manuscripts Division, The New York Public Library, Astor, Lenox and Tilden foundations, KLW Saunders 79.1. **Duckett was the lover and companion of Walt Whitman.**

Whitman's young male companion, Bill Duckett, lying prone on a rug with his buttocks prominently featured, holding a vase of distinctly phallic shape.[35] The boldest of these photographs were made at the Philadelphia Art Students League, where Eakins was not regulated by any higher authority.

Naked Excursions

Eakins also made at least two outdoor excursions, with friends, specifically for creating nude photographs. The first, which occurred around 1883, was to Manasquan Inlet at Point Pleasant, New Jersey, a popular tourist resort. The participants included Eakins, his student J. Laurie Wallace, and several of the Macdowell brothers and nephews. Against a backdrop of beach, inlet, sea oats, shrubbery, and trees, a cast of five men and at least one boy, accompanied by a man who remained clothed, assumed various classical poses.[36]

Eakins's photographs were carefully arranged, with many of them exploring variations of a motif. Several show nude figures in a contrapposto stance resembling classical statues of Apollo or the emperor Hadrian's male lover, Antinous. Several seem to reenact motion themes related to Greek sculpture, such as removing a thorn from a foot, or preparing to throw a rock. Eakins seems to have had difficulty persuading women to pose for pictures of this type, although he did take a few photographs of his wife outdoors, generally with her face averted from the camera.[37]

On an outing to Mill Creek, near Bryn Mawr in 1884, Eakins produced a second series of outdoor nude scenes, to which he would refer for his painting *Swimming*. Again, an older dressed man accompanied the group as a chaperon. The students engaged in swimming, boxing, playing tug-of-war, and similar activities. One photograph shows seven students posed on a rocky promontory. An image that shows Eakins himself climb-

Male Nude, Poised to Throw Rock, Facing Right, in Wooded Landscape, ca. 1883. *Albumen print, 11 x 18 ⅛ in., courtesy of The Pennsylvania Academy of the Fine Arts, Philadelphia, Charles Bregler's Thomas Eakins Collection, purchased with the partial support of the Pew Memorial Trust.* In 1883 Eakins took a group of photographs of friends and students in the nude during an excursion to Manasquan Inlet at Point Pleasant, New Jersey. Many of the poses were based on classical sculpture.

J. Laurie Wallace Nude, Playing Pipes, Facing Left, ca. 1883. *Copy negative from a dry-plate negative, 4 x 5 in., courtesy of The Pennsylvania Academy of the Fine Arts, Philadelphia, Charles Bregler's Thomas Eakins Collection, purchased with the partial support of the Pew Memorial Trust.*

ing out of the water seems to have been the favorite since it exists in four known enlargements. These photographs have often been described as evidence of a naturist *joie de vivre* on Eakins's part, but the figures frequently seem uncomfortable and look away from the photographer.

Unusual Themes: Androgyny

Three themes of Eakins's photographs have no close counterpart in the work of other nineteenth-century photographers: androgyny, exhibitionism, and voyeurism. French photographs favored models who were buxom and full-bodied. Eakins, on the contrary, preferred women who were boyish and slender in build. He also often photographed them in a way that brings out their androgynous characteristics. For example, a nude photograph he took of his wife Susan from the side could almost be taken for a photograph of a young man. Eakins also arranged young men in poses that are traditionally feminine, sometimes producing photographs of male and female figures that closely echo each other in appearance. Eakins's image of Bill Duckett, hold-

Hannah Susan Macdowell, ca. 1880–1882. *Albumen print on paper, 3 ³⁄₁₆ x 4 ⁷⁄₁₆ in., Hirshhorn Museum and Sculpture Garden, Smithsonian Institution, transferred from Hirshhorn Museum and Sculpture Garden Archives, 1983.*

ing a phallic vase, suggests a homosexual Duckett taking on the submissive "female" role.

Eakins had photographs taken of himself that feminize his features. Thus, for example, Eakins had a photograph taken at 1729 Mount Vernon Street that shows him naked, from the rear, in a half-reclining pose that makes his rear end look enormous and woman-like. (It would be particularly interesting to know who took this photograph—his wife Susan or another man.) The general pose of the photograph is strikingly similar to a rear view of a female nude that he took around the same time.

Of course, one can argue that these photographs were taken to emphasize some anatomical point, and this is probably true. But they also seem to express an emotional fantasy, that of transforming men into women or of turning women into men. Moreover, Eakins seems to have played with the idea of taking on the female role himself. The possibility of a professional purpose, in short, does not negate the notion that these images carry a deeper psychological meaning.

Thomas Eakins Nude, Semireclining on Couch, from Rear, ca. 1883. *Platinum print, 5 ⅜ x 7 ¼ in., courtesy of The Pennsylvania Academy of the Fine Arts, Philadelphia, Charles Bregler's Thomas Eakins Collection, purchased with the partial support of the Pew Memorial Trust.* **Eakins had himself photographed in the nude in a pose that looks distinctly feminine.**

Unusual Themes: Exhibitionism

One of the most interesting aspects of Eakins's nude photographs is that the models were generally identifiable and clearly intended to be recognized. Indeed, when he exhibited his painting *Swimming* at the Pennsylvania Academy, which showed five of his students in the nude, he also showed clothed portraits of two of the figures, leaving no doubt as to their identities.

Throughout his life, Eakins seems to have derived pleasure from the public display of images recording his own nudity and that of his students. A photograph taken at the Art Students' League of Philadelphia shows that Eakins exhibited several of his most provocative images on the back wall of the school, including a photograph of himself in the nude from Manasquan; a nude woman; photographs from swimming excursions; Eakins holding a nude woman; and his wife Susan in the nude. Pasted up alongside these photographs are a newspaper clipping and a printed program. Johns has suggested that the program may have come from an annual dinner at the Art Students League and the clipping might be an announcement of Eakins's forced resignation from the Pennsylvania Academy because of the loin cloth incident.[38] Taken as a group, these images represent a kind of exhibitionism.

In addition, along with his interest in undressing, Eakins seems to have enjoyed showing photographs of himself in the nude to visitors. For example, many years later, during a visit to his studio by Mr. and Mrs. James Mapes Dodge, Eakins showed the couple a photograph of himself carrying a nude woman (perhaps the very image that has already been mentioned), to their embarrassment and astonishment. ("I would have doubted this," Goodrich commented, "except that I saw one or more similar photographs in Mrs. Eakins' possession.")[39]

Unusual Themes: Intrusion and Voyeurism

Many of Eakins's photographs explore the theme of intrusion and voyeurism. Generally speaking, he did not place models in artful, contrived, or ideal settings, as is usually the case with French artistic photographs. Instead, the background of the working studio is introduced. What is more, very often we see other figures who are sketching or looking at the model. Thus, the model does not occupy a separate realm, but clearly contrasts with fully clothed figures, creating a tension that enhances a sense of indecency. An interesting case of this is a photograph of a nude woman viewed from the rear. If she were alone, against an empty backdrop, this might be taken as a typical "artistic" photograph. Instead, however, the backdrop of blanket and torn screen seems to be deliberately rough and makeshift, and she is juxtaposed with a man in the background at the left who is sketching her. Presuming, as seems likely, that a male also took the photograph, she is thus caught between two male viewers.

Photographs of male models are often similar, as for example, one that shows a standing man with a student (George Reynolds) at an easel behind him, and a cat stretched out on the floor. Eakins was also interested in capturing models in seemingly natural poses. In one, a male figure sits on a platform, apparently between formal posing sessions, toying with a small sculpture of a horse.

The confusion about the authorship of Eakins's photographs points toward what is unusual about them as a body of images—Eakins played a role not simply behind the camera but in front of it. The theme of spying on

Female Nude Semireclining, from Rear, ca. 1889. *Platinum print, 3 ⅞ x 5 ⅟₁₆ in., courtesy of The Pennsylvania Academy of the Fine Arts, Philadelphia, Charles Bregler's Thomas Eakins Collection, purchased with the partial support of the Pew Memorial Trust.* In contrast with typical artistic photographs of nudes, those by Eakins often show clothed bystanders staring at the model.

someone's nakedness and of having one's own nakedness spied on by someone else provides a constant undercurrent of these images. Even the photographs of clothed models take on a voyeuristic piquancy when we recognize that Eakins photographed most of these same models without their clothes, and very likely attempted to pose all of his models, willing or unwilling, in this fashion. In addition, the nude photographs take on a new meaning when we consider that the photographer, whom we cannot see, may have been just as nude as the subject. Once we recognize this, it also becomes apparent that these photographs document a process of sharing that probably has some psychological significance. The meaning seems to have been a sexual one, but not in the sense that sexual intercourse necessarily took place. Indeed, as has been mentioned, Eakins's photographs differ from "pornographic" photographs of this period precisely in that they do not record a "come-hither" glance that creates an interaction between subject and viewer. Nearly all the figures in Eakins's photographs look away.

The Crucifixion

Many of Eakins's most compelling paintings from this period also deal with the nude, but in an unorthodox way. Perhaps significantly, for his first nude he chose a subject that was inherently antierotic: the Crucifixion. In this phase of his career, Eakins seems to have been fascinated with the idea of taking a conventional academic subject and giving it an unusual twist. His *Crucifixion* provides a striking instance of this: it entirely eliminates the sort of spiritual or religious content usually associated with the subject. Modern viewers have often reacted negatively to this piece ("His single truly bad painting is a *Crucifixion*," Peter Schjeldahl wrote recently in the *New Yorker*.)[40] Eakins, however, seems to have valued the painting, since, as has been noted, he hung it in the front hall of the family home, where somewhat oddly, it faced the more romantic pictures he placed over the mantelpiece (first his portrait of Eliza-

Léon Bonnat, The Crucifixion, 1874. *Oil on canvas, 90 ⅛ × 63 in., Petit Palais, Musée des Beaux-Arts de la Ville de Paris.* Léon Bonnat was said to have based his Crucifixion on a corpse nailed to a cross on the roof of his studio.

beth Crowell at the piano, and later, *The Concert Singer*).

When Eakins first exhibited this painting, William Clark of the *Telegraph* noted that, "What he has done primarily has been to conceive the Crucifixion as an actual event."[41] Most contemporary viewers, however, were not pleased, since Eakins provided no suggestion that this event had religious significance. As a writer for the *Art Amateur* noted: "The mere presentation of a human body suspended from a cross and dying a slow death under an Eastern sun cannot do anybody any good, nor awaken thoughts that elevate the mind."[42] Indeed, Eakins seems to have exaggerated the mundane elements of the subject, to increase the sense of "realism." Thus, as the writer for the *Art Journal* observed: "When the feet are reached and one remarks the idiosyncrasies of the toenails, the ideal which everyone holds is degraded, and we realize that in an age tending so strongly toward realism, there are subjects which should be left untouched."[43]

In fact, there was a notable precedent for Eakins's design. His teacher
Léon Bonnat had painted a harrowing version of this subject, allegedly using
as a model a real cadaver nailed to a cross by a guardsman and hung up in the
courtyard of the Invalides.[44] Bonnat's painting, however, contains an element
of heroic melodrama, which makes it religiously compelling, despite its
impressive realism. Eakins's painting, on the contrary, seems to have been
intended to eliminate any spiritual or religious content.

One of the few who admired the painting was the New York art critic Mariana Griswold Van Rensselaer, who thought the painting powerfully expressed
the idea of sacrifice. As she wrote:

> I know there are some who see in the picture little but a most painful anatom-
> ical study; to me, however, it has an intensity of pathos touched with horror
> . . . It is extremely difficult to put into words the impression made by such a
> picture, so strong, so repulsive in some ways, yet so deeply pathetic, partly by
> reason, perhaps, of that very repulsiveness. I can only speak for myself when I
> say that after seeing a hundred crucifixions from modern hands this one
> seemed to me not only a quite original but a most impressive and haunted
> work.[45]

Goodrich noted that the painting contains "hardly a trace . . . of religious
feeling." But he concludes, "The irony is probably unconscious."[46] The first
statement is convincing. The second much less so. Indeed, while *The Crucifixion* stands out as something of an oddity in Eakins's oeuvre—it is his only religious subject—the painting provides a clue about his overall artistic strategy.
The picture is shocking not simply because of what is there but because of
what is not there. Eakins deliberately eschews the sort of sentiment or pathos
usually associated with the subject. Indeed, even the element of physical
agony is downplayed. The crucified figure is just limp, and the only expres-
sionistic element in the painting is the crudely rendered inscription above his
head.[47]

Pastoral Nakedness

Eakins's most ambitious renderings of the nude, however, were based on his
two photographic excursions, to Manasquan and Mill Creek, as well as one
nude photograph of his nieces and nephews that he took at his sister's farm at
Avondale. The first excursion led to several works that portray androgynous

figures outdoors, the second inspired his most ambitious painting of the male nude, *Swimming*.

The first project—which resulted in two paintings, a sculptural relief, and several oil studies—deals with a fantasy world, akin to ancient Greece, peopled by nude men and women outdoors. Today these works are generally known as the Arcadian Series, although the title is one that was provided in 1929 by Susan Eakins, and does not necessarily reflect Eakins's ideas about the subject. The one piece in the series that Eakins did name is the sculptural relief, which is listed in his records as *Pastoral Sculpture*.

Although Goodrich describes these works as "idyllic," their coloring is dreary, and none of the figures represents the typical Greek ideal of physical beauty, either as portrayed in Greek sculpture or in nineteenth-century academic painting.[48] The degree to which Eakins's pictures might be considered "ideal" is ambiguous, since the figures are all specific people whom Eakins had photographed, and the landscape is not an idealized setting, but the scrubby land around the farm owned by Eakins's sister at Avondale.

It might seem curious that Eakins would have chosen such a Greek subject, for when the topic of Greek art surfaced in his letters from Paris, it invariably released an explosion of hostile remarks. In one of his letters to his father, he criticized professors "who read Greek poetry for inspiration, talk classic & give out classic subjects & make a fellow draw antique."[49] As he continued, "If I went to Greece to live there twenty years I could not paint a Greek subject for my head would be full of classics the nasty besmeared wooden hard gloomy tragic figures of the great French school of the last few centuries and Ingres and the Greek letters I learned at High School with old Heaverstick and my mud marks of the ancient statues."[50] On still another occasion, Eakins declared: "I often wish now that I had never so much as seen a statue antique or modern till after I had been painting for some time."[51]

As usual, however, Eakins was not very consistent. To his students, he often spoke admiringly about the work of Phidias and other Greek sculptors, and he even started (but did not finish) a painting showing Phidias studying nude riders for his Parthenon frieze. In fact, his hostility seems to have largely been directed to artists who copied Greek art, rather than to Greek art itself. Significantly, Eakins seems to have viewed Greek sculptors as artists who, like himself, studied directly from life. "The Greeks did not study the antique," he once declared. "The Theseus and Illyssus and the draped figures in the Parthenon pediment were modeled from life undoubtedly."[52]

Perhaps most important, however, Greek art permitted Eakins to deal

Arcadia, ca. 1883. Oil on canvas, 38 ⅝ x 45 in., Metropolitan Museum of Art, bequest of Miss Adelaide Milton de Groot, 1967. **Eakins's two paintings of Arcadian subject make the difference between male and female highly ambiguous.**

with a subject that fascinated him, the nude. Indeed, in many respects, his references to Greek art and Greek subjects in this period seem to have been a ploy. Just as Greek costumes provided him with a pretext for beginning to undress his students, so Greek references made it possible for him to paint or sculpt subjects that would otherwise have been forbidden.[53]

Eakins's two paintings of this Arcadian, or pastoral, theme both show highly androgynous figures. The larger of the two, now generally known as *Arcadia* (1883, Metropolitan Museum of Art), shows two reclining figures on the left and a standing one on the right. All three have curiously feminized figures. The leftmost figure, probably a girl, shows her derriere in a feminine pose usually reserved for odalisques. The other young reclining boy hides his genitals in a manner that reminds us that small children of both sexes look very similar. The standing figure also looks feminine, except for the absence of breasts. Two of these children, however, hold pipes, which have distinctly

An Arcadian, probably 1883. *Oil, 14 x 18 in., private collection, photography courtesy of Spanierman Gallery, LLC.* Although the figure in *An Arcadian* looks male, it was based on a photograph of Eakins's wife, Susan.

phallic connotations. In particular, the standing figure holds an aulos or double-pipe, an instrument that in Greek art was associated with the god Pan, and with the erotic. Thus, in various ways the painting deals with revealing and concealing sexual identity. On the one hand, the penises of the male figures are hidden. On the other, the pipes draw attention to the fact that each has a penis. Moreover, the reclining female figure is staring directly at the penis of the standing figure, although it is hidden to the viewer of the painting.

In its present state the other, smaller painting, now known as *An Arcadian* (1883, formerly collection of Lloyd Goodrich), shows only a single figure. Many viewers interpret this figure as male, although in fact, it is female—it is based on photographs of Eakins's wife. The only clue to the female character of this figure, however, is the hairstyle, which has a small bun behind the head. When we compare this figure with its related photograph, it becomes clear that the photograph must have been deliberately staged with androgyny in mind. When Eakins made the painting, he made the gender of the figure even more ambiguous by arranging the drapery to make the female features even less obvious. Thus, like the other Arcadian paintings, the canvas explores gender ambiguity.

Susan Macdowell Eakins Nude, Sitting on Blanket, Looking over Right Shoulder, ca. 1883. *Cyanotype, 3 ¼ x 3 ¾ in., courtesy of The Pennsylvania Academy of the Fine Arts, Charles Bregler's Thomas Eakins Collection, purchased with partial support of the Pew Memorial Trust.*

An Arcadian was originally intended to portray two figures rather than one. Indeed, when Goodrich first saw the painting, Eakins's chalk drawing of the second figure was still visible on the surface. Mrs. Eakins, however, scrubbed this off at the time that she gave the painting to Goodrich, making the painting appear more "finished," but effectively destroying the meaning of Eakins's arrangement.[54] As Eakins conceived the scheme, the androgynous figure on the ground was looking toward a standing figure playing pipes at the right. Thus, as with the other painting, the relationship between the two figures, was somewhat suggestive. Again, the pipes can easily be construed as a metaphorical way of representing a phallus, and the glance of the figure on the ground was directed toward the piper's groin. In short, like the other canvas, the painting explores the issues both of what it means to have a penis and to be without one. Both paintings explore childhood as a time when boys are girlish, and girls can be confused with boys. Eakins seems to have been interested in capturing some presexual state, a time of gender freedom, in which boys and girls could coexist together in nakedness, like a family.

Arcadia, 1883. *Plaster, 12 x 25 x 2 ½ in., Yale University Art Gallery, gift of the H. J. Heinz II Charitable and Family Trust.*
In Eakins's *Arcadia* relief a naked figure displays his pipes to an audience of entranced spectators.

This is also the subject of Eakins's most significant treatment of this theme, a plaster relief, *Pastoral*, which seems to have had a deeply personal meaning for him. The relief is roughly finished, and its surface quality (to quote Johns) is "tentative, worked over, fragile: the artist's hand is practically still at work on it."[55] Nonetheless, Eakins hung the piece prominently in his studio, where it appears both in photographs and in his portrait *The Artist's Wife with His Setter Dog*.

The relief has never been well explained by writers on Eakins. For an Arcadian theme the figural types are homely. None of the figures exemplifies a classical ideal of beauty. The treatment of the figures is too sketchy to provide much anatomical information, and in fact the renderings are close to caricature. Most puzzling, the figures do not clearly portray any recognizable subject or theme, so attempts to see them in this light are clearly incongruous. Elizabeth Johns conjectured that the figures portray "the three ages of man," but in fact three of the female figures appear to be the same age, and that of the fourth is indeterminate.[56]

Pastoral shows five figures and a dog who are entranced as they listen to a seated nude figure who is playing the aulos. The first standing figure, at the right, is a lightly draped woman; then, at center, are two draped women, one embracing the other in friendship; next, toward the left, we see an old man leaning forward on a cane and cupping his ear; and last, at the far left, is a naked woman who glances downward. The middle figures are clothed, but the two outside figures are naked. Johns suggests that the figures at the far left and right, who frame the relief like parentheses, indicate a youth and his lover.[57]

If we read this in family terms we have a representation of Eakins's dog, his three sisters, his father, and finally, somewhat removed from the rest, his mother, the one figure whose glance is averted. The nude figure on the right is interpreted as a musician; but his aulos can also be seen as a metaphor for phallic exposure, an assertion of male dominance that fascinates his family audience, as well as the family dog. If Johns is correct about the special relationship between the end figures, then the ultimate subject of the piece might be Eakins's relationship with his mother. If so, surely it is intriguing that both Eakins and his mother are shown naked, whereas the other figures are dressed.

Like his painting, Eakins's photographs seem to contain subtexts. Why did Eakins insist on undressing his students rather than using professional models? Why did he stage scenes which are implicitly erotic, and at times homo-erotic, but do so in an anti-erotic fashion? Why did he juxtapose unclothed figures with clothed students and onlookers? What should we make of the sculpture and paintings based on these photographs, which explore the theme of sharing nakedness with figures of both sexes, and in some instances with members of one's own family?

The Swimming Hole, ca. 1883–1885. *Oil on canvas, 27 5/16 x 36 5/16 in., Amon Carter Museum, Fort Worth, Texas.* Five of Eakins's students display their nude bodies on a rocky ledge, while Eakins himself admires them from a vantage point in the water.

Chapter 16

SWIMMING

EAKINS'S SECOND photographic excursion, to Mill Creek, resulted in a more polished and ambitious creation, the painting that Eakins titled *Swimming*. It portrays six naked men, accompanied by a red setter dog, who are diving, pulling themselves from the water, or posing in different positions on a stone pier. Only one man is actually swimming, Eakins himself, which suggests that in some way the painting is about Eakins and his experience. In some way the painting clearly embodies Eakins's feelings about manhood, but very different explanations have been put forward about just what this profusion of male nakedness was meant to signify.

The painting focuses on a loophole in the armor of Victorian propriety and sexual inhibition. We think of Victorians as being more prudish than we are today, but an exception to this notion is the practice of swimming in the nude. Today we take it for granted that people should have appropriate costume for every form of sports or exercise, preferably with a designer label. In the nineteenth century, however, special attire for sports was a rarity, and for men and boys to swim without a bathing suit was not necessarily shocking or unusual. Even in the city, an utterly public setting, boys and men would unselfconsciously strip off their clothes to swim. Walt Whitman, for example, left an account of swimmers along the Harlem River in the 1880s: "A peculiar and pretty carnival—at its height a hundred lads or young men, very democratic, all decent behaving. . . . ranks of them naked, rose-color'd, with movements, postures ahead of any sculpture."[1]

Eakins's painting thus records one of the few occasions on which nudity was displayed in nineteenth-century life. Because no other nineteenth-century American painter focused on this theme, it is reasonable to ask why Eakins chose to do so. Gay men, such as Whitman, took special pleasure in this rare sight of naked male bodies, and Eakins's association with Whitman has encouraged the speculation that they may have shared a homosexual viewpoint.

In addition, however, *Swimming* seems to have a connection with other major paintings by Eakins. *Swimming* takes on a deeper significance when we note its repetition of an element that Eakins had dealt with before: exposed buttocks. Buttocks are a major point of interest in Eakins's three most ambitious figure compositions: *The Gross Clinic*, *William Rush*, and *Swimming*. In addition, while we conventionally assign a quality of masculinity or femininity to these buttocks, in all three paintings the sex of the naked figure is more than slightly ambiguous. In *The Gross Clinic* all distinctive sexual signs have been hidden; in *William Rush* the anatomy of the figure proves to be as much male as female; in *Swimming* the central figure is notably feminine, with exaggerated, rounded buttocks that are more like those of a woman than of a man. In the first two paintings Eakins pretended that the buttocks were a secondary element, and strongly highlighted something else—the head, hands and scalpel of Dr. Gross in *The Gross Clinic*, or the discarded clothes on the chair in *William Rush*. In both these paintings, however, the buttocks clearly have some strong connection with the painting's deepest level of meaning.

In *Swimming* this fascination is expressed more strongly. Here, a young man's bare buttocks provide the focal point of the composition, around which everything else revolves like the hands on a clock face. How can we explain Eakins's interest in this peculiar subject, or the fact that in all these paintings he seems to have included himself, either as a portrait or, by implication, as an actor in the scene?

In the years since the painting was produced, writers on Eakins have alternated between attempting to downplay the significance of Eakins's extraordinary focus on the nude and proposing that his emphasis on male nudity proves that he was homosexual. Lloyd Goodrich has noted that Susan Eakins was embarrassed by the scandals over the nude that surrounded her husband, and after his death she apparently attempted to divert attention from the nude in *Swimming* by giving the picture a more sentimental title.

During Eakins's lifetime the painting was first exhibited under the title *Swimming* and then later exhibited as *The Swimmers*. Susan Eakins, however, never used her husband's titles for the canvas. When she lent it to the painter's memorial exhibition at the Metropolitan Museum in New York in 1917, she changed the title to *The Swimming Hole*. Four years later, when she lent the painting to a show at Knoedler's, she altered the title again, calling the painting *The Old Swimming Hole*. Both of these posthumous titles clearly derive from James Whitcomb Riley's popular poem of 1883, which lamented the changes to the swimming hole of the author's childhood, because of the incursion of a railroad bridge and other modern "improvements." Thus, the new title—which is still the one favored by most writers on Eakins—essentially transformed the painting into a bit of Victorian nostalgia.[2]

Perhaps because they were misdirected by Susan's sentimental title, or perhaps because they did not choose to delve into matters that might be troubling, writers from the 1920s into the 1950s did not discuss any of the subversive undercurrents in the painting. Accounts from this period invariably describe *Swimming* as "lyrical" (or some roughly equivalent word), praise it for its mastery of anatomy and composition, and compare it with the work of Italian old masters such as Signorelli and Pollaiuolo.[3]

Eakins and American Queerness

But at an early date some viewers saw the work in a more provocative way. By the 1940s, and perhaps earlier, American homosexuals viewed Eakins as a forebear and role model, although they never came out and used the word "homosexual" in describing his work. Thus for example, the notion that *Swimming* might be homosexual in content was implicit in the long discussion of the picture in *American Renaissance*, published in 1941 by F. O. Matthiessen, himself a homosexual. In a lengthy passage, Matthiessen related the painting to a poem about naked swimmers by Whitman—who was already known to be homosexual—apparently as a covert way of asserting that the painting had homoerotic content.[4] Similarly, Lincoln Kirstein admired the painting for its homoerotic implications. While he never directly mentioned sex or sexual orientation, Kirstein's intense praise of the painting and feverish language ("the heroic pyramid of shining young men on their wet shelf of rock") suggest that the painting has provocative emotional and social implications.[5] At least one gay man of this generation, the composer Ned Rorem, wrote explicitly of his feelings of sexual desire for Eakins, although he did so late in life and in his private journal. In 1995, Rorem wrote regretfully:

> I can never meet and sniff and love, say, Thomas Eakins. Not his painting, but the finite trembling man. I long for his flesh, which was gone before I was born.[6]

The direct suggestion that Eakins might be homosexual finally made its way into print in print in 1974, when, curiously enough, three separate individuals raised the issue in slightly different contexts. Gordon Hendricks, in his biography of Eakins, noted that Eakins's sexuality seems to have been "ambiguous," and noted of Eakins's male photographs that "some have considered such photographs as evidence that Eakins, if not homosexual or bisexual, was at least homoerotic."[7] In the subsequent sentence, he drew back from this possibility, but later in his book he also seriously proposed that the relationship between Eakins and Samuel Murray might have been homosexual.[8] Donelson Hoopes, in the catalogue accompanying the exhibition *American Narrative Painting*, praised *Swimming* as "Eakins's paean to a liberated human sensuality."[9] Finally, and most explicitly, William Gerdts, in *The Great American Nude*, declared that there was "something very sexual" about Eakins's painting *Swimming*, and noted "such sexuality is lacking in Eakins's few treatments of the female figure."[10]

By the 1980s, as gay liberation gained momentum, this tentative suggestion was often magically transformed into a certainty, and Eakins was regularly included in accounts of homosexuality by both gay and straight writers. Emanuel Cooper in 1986 included Eakins in *Homosexuality in Art*, citing *Swimming* as evidence of his "homoerotic interests."[11] Michael Fried in his study of *The Gross Clinic* (1987) cited *Swimming* as "another major painting by Eakins in which homoerotic fantasy would appear to be in play."[12] Allen Ellensweig, in *The Homoerotic Photograph* (1992), cited Eakins's photographs for *Swimming* as evidence that Eakins's nature was homoerotic, "admiring of and drawn to male beauty, prowess and strength."[13] Michael Hatt (1993) in an essay on "The Male Body" concluded that Eakins's *Swimming* is "homoerotic" because it invites "the male gaze on the male body."[14] Adam Gopnik, writing in 1994, declared, "The homoerotic content of Eakins's work is evident."[15] Homoerotic desire also seems to be the subtext of a recent book by John Esten entirely devoted to Eakins's photographs and paintings of nude men, *Thomas Eakins: The Absolute Male*.[16]

Such views represented a complete about-face from early interpretations of Eakins by writers such as Lloyd Goodrich, who viewed the "masculinity" of Eakins as morally superior to the effeminate (homosexual) tendencies of less-masculine American or American expatriate painters such as John La Farge, John Singer Sargent, or James McNeill Whistler. Eakins was now linked with figures such as Walt Whitman, and presented as a model of American queerness, and many writers (such as Gopnik) viewed the gayness of his work as a given.

In 1999 Jennifer Doyle explicitly proposed that Eakins should be placed at the beginning of a queer tradition in American culture:

It is entirely possible to place Eakins and *The Swimming Hole*, for instance, near the beginning of a homoerotic (and even homosexual) visual tradition in American art. We could easily link Eakins and his work to, for instance, an artist like Robert Mapplethorpe and his meticulous portraits of naked black men, or Andy Warhol and his habit of taking Polaroids of the genitals of visitors to his studio, and Warhol films like *Lonesome Cowboys* or *My Hustler*, whose spirit of play suggest they are direct descendents of the photographs Eakins took of his students horsing around in the woods.[17]

Doyle's distinction between a "homoerotic" and "gay" viewpoint might be lost on a general audience, although in this context evidently a "homoerotic viewpoint" may be unconscious, lurking beneath the surface, whereas a "gay" viewpoint is more self-aware, and more likely to result in sexual acts. Significantly, Doyle is evasive on a key point—whether Eakins was or was not homosexual. But cleverly, Doyle argues that we do not need evidence that Eakins engaged in a gay lifestyle to read his work in this fashion or even to impute these motives to him at some subliminal level: "Do we really need to know anything about Eakins's sexuality to assert the homoeroticism, and even the gay component, of these works, and their relevance to a gay audience?"[18] Notably, Doyle's previous area of scholarship was the gay milieu of Andy Warhol, and her attraction to Eakins was clearly largely based not so much on a traditional admiration for the realism of his work as on his relevance to gay themes.

Up to the present, however, Eakins's major biographers have persistently denied that he was homosexual. Lloyd Goodrich, for example, included a long denial of Eakins's alleged homosexuality in his monograph of 1983. William Inness Homer (1992) has written, "There is no evidence that Eakins was gay."[19] Kathleen Foster has been a little more evasive, but has implied that the accusation is unlikely, on the ground that homosexuality is one of the very few sexual transgressions that Eakins was not accused of in his lifetime. (This is not entirely correct, however, since we know that James L. Wood thought that Eakins was "queer"—homosexual—a categorization that may have reflected the views of his father, Dr. Horatio Wood, who was Eakins's personal physician. Characteristically, Goodrich suppressed Wood's statement.)[20]

The divergence of views about Eakins's sexual orientation raises questions about the very discipline of art history as it is now practiced. What is intriguing is that based on exactly the same evidence—a painting of some naked men— some writers have concluded that Eakins was unquestionably homosexual and others that he could not possibly have been so. In both cases the writers have largely left out the reasons behind their conclusions, and we must conjecture what they must have been. Those arguing that he was homosexual were often homosexual themselves and seized on Eakins as a possible role model; or they may have been accustomed to the modern art world, where the prevalence of homosexuals is a given, and images of nude men generally carry a homosexual subtext. Those arguing against this conclusion have had more varied motives. Goodrich argues not very convincingly that homosexuality is fundamentally feminine and effeminate and therefore that Eakins's glorification of aggressively male qualities could not be homosexual. Foster glorifies Eakins's relationship with his wife and is thus unwilling to acknowledge the possibility of homosexual relationships which would undercut this glorious partnership. Homer seems to insist on firm documentation, of an incontrovertible sort, although surely the lack of such documentation does not say much, since in the nineteenth century homosexuality was an issue that was seldom openly discussed.

A final judgment on the matter is complicated by the fact that we know surprisingly little about the practice of homosexuality in nineteenth-century America, although it is clear that male friendship was viewed differently than today. Photographs of young men holding hands, for example, were viewed as natural expressions of friendship, whereas today they would carry homosexual implications. More profoundly, however, Eakins's imagery seems to move into a zone that is highly ambiguous, since he made no statements about it and there is no other nineteenth-century American painting of this subject. In this regard it is useful to remember that his behavior toward women and his interest in undressing them was also puzzling to his contemporaries, some seeing it as sexually motivated and others denying this altogether.

This raises the question of whether Eakins could have been both homosexual and not homosexual at the same time. In other words, his painting seems to challenge the usual boundaries between the heterosexual, the homosocial, the homoerotic, and the homosexual. According to this view, we might suppose that Eakins's sexual identity was unstable, and open to reconstitution and revision. Whitney Davis, for example, has worked his way around the question of the artist's orientation by ingeniously proposing that Eakins was "not not homosexual."[21] Such a view opens up still another set of questions. Defenders of Eakins, such as Kathleen Foster, have presented his sexual ideas as liberated. But Davis's verbal gyrations raise the possibility that he was tied in emotional knots and may well have been sexually repressed. In

John O'Brien Inman, Bathing Beauties on the Hudson. *Oil on panel, 12 x 18 in., courtesy Berry-Hill Galleries, New York.* **Paintings of multiple nudes were rare in America. Viewed as quite racy, and a bit low class, they often decorated saloons.**

short, perhaps what is interesting about Eakins's painting may well be its element of sexual confusion.

Naked Men Together

Both those who see Eakins as homosexual and those who do not draw almost all of their arguments from *Swimming* and the photographs related to it. But the clues that the paintings and photographs provide are strangely contradictory.

Significantly, there was no precedent in nineteenth-century American art for such a profusion of naked male figures. Representations of nude or nearly nude female figures did exist, but they seem to have been a low-class form, which existed as a type of popular art, but was not practiced by serious American painters. Typical of this genre is a painting by John O'Brien Inman showing *Bathing Beauties on the Hudson*, which is roughly contemporary with Eakins's painting. Anecdotal evidence suggests that this sort of painting often decorated saloons. Thus, Eakins was taking a low-class form and transforming it into a major statement, as well as taking a profusion of nudity considered appropriate only for risqué renderings of women, and applying it to men.[22]

Hendricks has argued that Eakins showed male figures in *Swimming* simply because he could not get female figures to pose. "The artist would undoubtedly have done the same thing with his women students if such a thing had been possible," he writes.[23] His assertion raises interesting questions, but is not entirely convincing. For example, Eakins's wife was clearly willing to pose for him in the nude, but Eakins seldom took advantage of this fact.

The few photographs of her in the nude apparently were taken early in their relationship, probably before their marriage. Susan looks stiff and uncomfortable, and rather than emphasizing her feminine qualities, Eakins arranged her to look like a young boy. In one photograph of her seated, in profile, for example, her breasts are almost entirely concealed by her arm and her long hair is lost in shadow, making it look as though her hair is cropped in male fashion. Only the shape of her thigh reveals that she is a woman, although since Susan was quite slender, the distinction between male and female is subtle. The one painting in which Susan appears nude is the painting *Arcadia*, in which she could easily be confused for a boy. After they had been married a few years, Susan does not appear to have posed for Eakins in the nude.[24] Making sense of Eakins's artistic practices is often difficult, but his choice of subject matter—male or female—was chiefly determined by his own volition, rather than by practical constraints.

Hendricks seems to evade addressing the issue at hand. Eakins *did* represent a profusion of male figures in his painting, and did so through conscious choice. Randall Griffin, for example, has noted that Eakins's painting sets "an obvious challenge to the late-nineteenth-century dominance of the female figure among nudes." Perceptively, he proposes that the painting "was Eakins's assertion . . . of the superiority of man as both principal maker of art and its ideal model."[25] In somewhat the same vein, Arthur Danto has declared that "The nakedness of Eakins's sporting men . . . is the mark of their being at play and away from work. . . . The men have left responsibility behind—as personified by the absent women."[26] Others, such as Whitney Davis, have asserted that the real text of the painting is that of men "setting aside care to become, once more, like carefree boys."[27] Several writers have suggested that Eakins had classical antiquity in mind, and that the painting, as Emanuel Cooper has written, "evokes the naked athletic comradeship of the Greek gymnasium."[28]

The paradox of Eakins's painting, however is that in seeking to assert the superiority of men over women, it actually undermines manhood by creating a situation in which women are completely absent and therefore men must play the female roles. He also does not seem to have grasped that most men are supposed to respond to male and female nudes in a different fashion; they are supposed to be sexually attracted to the beauty of female nudes but not men. In fact, he created this profusion of male nudity approximately a year after he married Susan Macdowell, at the point in their marriage when most sexually potent nineteenth-century couples were beginning to have children.[29]

Some seventeen years earlier, in May 1868, Eakins had written to his father from Paris proposing that a naked man was a superior artistic subject to a naked woman:

> When a man paints a naked woman he gives her less than poor Nature did. I can conceive of few circumstances when I would paint a woman naked, but if I did I would not mutilate her for double the money. She is the most beautiful thing there is—except a naked man, but I never yet saw a study of one exhibited. It would be a god send to see a fine man painted in a studio with bare walls, alongside the smiling, smirking goddesses of many complexions, amidst the delicious arsenic-green trees and the gentle wax flowers and purling streams a-running up and down hills, especially up. I hate affectation.[30]

This letter carries subtexts that resonate with the scandals that circulated around Eakins later. Eakins accuses the artists who paint the nude of doing something indecent—the very accusation that would be made later about his own work. Presumably by "he gives her less than nature did" he means that they left off the pubic hair—a standard nineteenth-century practice—although the force of the word suggests a kind of castration.[31]

Perhaps the oddest part of the statement is Eakins's abrupt jump from his discussion of representations of naked women to the idea of painting a naked man. He asserts that a naked man would be even more beautiful. Why this should be he does not explain. On other occasions Eakins made it clear that he considered men superior to women, and of course if this were true in all respects, then surely a naked man would be superior to a naked woman. In asserting this superiority of the naked man, however, Eakins went against a powerful social norm, for men are supposed to admire the opposite sex—"the fair sex," to use a Victorian locution. One possible explanation is that Eakins flouted this code because he was homosexual—whether consciously or unconsciously, openly or covertly. But another explanation is also possible—namely that he felt that the sexual connotations of the female nude were inherently bad, sinful, or embarrassing, and thus he preferred the male nude, where these connotations were less powerful.

The most puzzling aspect of *Swimming* is that Eakins presented such a profusion of naked male figures. What should be made of this fact? The multiplication of the figures sends an ambiguous message, for it both heightens the eroticism of the painting and effectively neutralizes it. Multiplication is a common theme of pornographic memoirs, such as those of Casanova, whose favorite fantasy seems to have been to spend the night cavorting with two or more nearly identical women, often sisters. The logic of this fantasy is clear. In Casanova's writings, the women are virtually indistinguishable from each other, but more women means more pleasure. For Eakins, multiplication may have had a similar significance. Eakins never attempted this approach to the nude with the female sex: he never showed more than one naked woman at a time. With men, however, he felt no such restraint. *Swimming* shows six naked men in an assortment of unusual postures. For most painters, one or two male nudes would have been quite sufficient. Eakins needed six to make his point.

Thus, Eakins's multiplication of naked young men suggests a form of erotic emphasis. Significantly, however, it simultaneously imposes sexual restraint, even prudery. For in real life a typical feature of most bands of young men is their strong hostility toward homosexuals. In groups of this sort the members generally tease each other, subtly or not so subtly, about being a "fairy," a "faggot," or a "queer," or of somehow failing to have adequate masculine qualities. If a member of the group is perceived as suspect in this regard, this generally inspires hostility, which can range from merciless teasing to physical violence or even murder.[32]

If there were just two nude figures in Eakins's painting, we might suppose that some sort of intimacy or coy sexual exploration would develop. But with six that possibility is considerably minimized. Indeed, in the actual "staging" of the painting we know that Eakins not only assembled a large group, but also brought along an elderly man, in clothes, who acted as "chaperon." Thus, in a paradoxical way, Eakins's multiplication of the nude figures is both erotic and antierotic. Like so much of Eakins's behavior, the painting seems to tease the viewer with possibilities of erotic or pornographic fulfillment, while at the same time effectively neutralizing the possibility that anything sexual will actually occur. (One might ask, of course, whether it was not precisely this confusing mixture of sexual and anti-sexual signals that was so destructive to many of the women in Eakins's life, such as Lillian Hammitt and Ella Crowell.)

Despite the title, Eakins and his dog are the only figures that are actually swimming. Eakins's position is a privileged one, since he plays the role of voyeur. His placement also suggests that he was the one who orchestrated the composition.

Indeed, a theme that earlier writers have not discussed, but which seems implicit in the painting, is the possibility that one of the young men might reveal some sort of sexual excitement (that is, an erection), and thus embarrass himself before the others. Significantly, the fact that the men are all concealing their genitals, not only indicates that they have something to conceal, and also leaves their state of arousal ambiguous, which is perhaps more provocative than resolving the question. (As early as 1967, Sylvan Schendler noted, "despite his absolute mastery of the human figure, Eakins could not permit himself to paint a male figure with his genitals showing.")[33]

While Eakins showed himself naked, the lower part of his body remains concealed under the water. Thus, he is in a position of power, in which he can flaunt his manhood but remain hidden, and in which he can look at the others but they cannot look at him. Viewers of the painting are encouraged to imagine him as sexually potent and in a dominant role, whether or not he actually was so.

Homosexual Currents

As Whitney Davis has noted, the painting's meaning takes on new overtones when we consider it in relation to the photographs that were made in preparation for the canvas, as well as to Eakins's preliminary oil study of the design.[34] Ten photographs survive that record Eakins's excursion to Mill Creek. Three of these show naked young men swimming and standing on the same stone pier that appears in the painting. Eakins himself, in the nude, is visible in one of these photographs. Seven other photographs show naked youths engaged in horseplay: wrestling, boxing, and playing tug-of-war. Throughout this second series the genitals of the figures are clearly shown. Close study of these photographs shows that the activities of these figures can be broken down into the interaction of four "couples," who relate to each other in each of the seven scenes. In other words, the photographs explicitly show genitals and present young men who are paired with each other, but set this theme in a context that is aggressive rather than explicitly sexual.

Eakins's oil study, which was loosely based on the swimming photographs, contains a number of differences that make the scene more sexually charged. Thus, for example, the standing figure in the center of the painting seems to be staring directly at the buttocks and genitals of the diver. The diver emerging from the water seems to pull himself directly toward the reclining figure. Even more remarkable, the figure at the far left, squatting on the ground,

Thomas Eakins or associate,
Male Nudes in a Seated Tug-
of-War, 1884. *Albumen print,*
3 ¾ x 4 ¾ in., The Detroit
Institute of Arts, Founders
Society Purchase, Robert H.
Tannahill Foundation Fund.

Seven Males, Nude, Two Boxing at Center, ca. 1883. *Dry-plate negative, 4 x 5 in., courtesy of The Penn-*
sylvania Academy of the Fine Arts, Philadelphia, Charles Bregler's Thomas Eakins Collection, purchased with the
partial support of the Pew Memorial Trust. In 1883 Eakins took an excursion to Mill Creek near Bryn
Mawr and took photographs of his students boxing, playing tug-of-war, and swimming in the nude.

Six Males, Nude, Wrestling, ca. 1883. *Dry-plate negative, 4 × 5 in., courtesy of The Pennsylvania Academy of the Fine Arts, Philadelphia, Charles Bregler's Thomas Eakins Collection, purchased with the partial support of the Pew Memorial Trust.*

Eakins's Students at the Site for "Swimming," ca. 1884. *Albumen print, 3 15/16 × 4 1/16 in., Princeton University Art Museum, Museum purchase, bequest of Mrs. John E. Long, in memory of John E. Long, Class of 1929.*

Thomas Eakins and Students, Swimming Nude, ca. 1883. *Dry-plate negative, 4 × 5 in., courtesy of The Pennsylvania Academy of the Fine Arts, Philadelphia, Charles Bregler's Thomas Eakins Collection, purchased with the partial support of the Pew Memorial Trust.*

Thomas Eakins and Students, Swimming Nude, ca. 1883. *Dry-plate negative, 4 × 5 in., courtesy of The Pennsylvania Academy of the Fine Arts, Philadelphia, Charles Bregler's Thomas Eakins Collection, purchased with the partial support of the Pew Memorial Trust.*

Study for *Swimming*, 1884. *Oil on fiberboard mounted on fiberboard, 8 ¾ x 10 ¾ in., Hirshhorn Museum and Sculpture Garden, Smithsonian Institution, gift of Joseph H. Hirshhorn, 1966.* Eakins's oil sketch for *Swimming* shows a boy at the far left touching the naked thigh of the reclining figure.

appears to be passing his hand over the upper thigh of the reclining figure, touching him just below the buttocks. In other words, although Eakins's theme is partially concealed by the looseness of his paint handling, the oil study seems to introduce the theme of one naked man touching another in an affectionate or amorous fashion. In Whitney Davis's view, Eakins "revised" his photographs according to a specifically homosexual point of view.

Eakins may have given the final painting a homosexual emphasis as well. The diver was difficult to paint, in part because of the way his body was inverted, so Eakins first modeled the figure in wax and then "put a spindle through the middle of the figure so that it could be turned upside down and hold the pose."[35] Whitney Davis argues that Eakins's treatment of his wax model could be interpreted as a kind of symbolic enactment of anal intercourse.[36]

Despite this sexually charged moment in the working process, however, Eakins's painting seems to eliminate the most overtly sexual elements of both the photographs and the oil study. It is more rigid, more self-conscious, more inhibited. In the final painting the figural arrangement was altered to conform to a triangular shape, reminiscent of the pediment of a Greek temple. While the painting pretends to be a "natural" outdoor scene, the light is curiously hard and studiolike. The effect is that of a tableau set against a studio back-drop.[37]

Most significantly, Eakins toned down the sense of sexual innuendo. The final design lacks the aggression and pairing of the photographs. In addition, Eakins not only eliminated the touching that is present in the sketch, but reworked each of the poses so that none of the figures directly interact with one another. The figure emerging from the water, for example, moves away from the reclining figure; and the standing male in the center no longer looks directly at the diver. All the figures look away from each other, with the possi-ble exception of Eakins, whose eyes are hidden, so that we cannot be certain of what he is looking at. All the figures ingeniously conceal their genitals.

Thus, Eakins revised his initial narrative of passionate bonding into a more general statement of casual male companionship. The introduction of the dog, which is not present in the sketch, also seems to emphasize a note of out-door play rather than sexual energy. The one element of possible erotic inter-action is presented as a fleeting illusion—namely that the diver's reflection is located only a few inches from Eakins's hand, which appears to reach toward it. In short, Eakins seems to have deliberately toned down the erotic implica-tions of the final painting, whether because of his own inhibitions or because of his knowledge of how his audience would react.

While it is certainly striking that Eakins represented the figures nude rather than clothed, several recent writers, such as Randall Griffin and Martin Berger, have chosen to describe Eakins not as "homosexual" but "homoso-cial."[38] That is, they have seen the painting as a celebration of male compan-ionship, which does not necessarily contain a sexual element.

Exhibitionism

In one major respect, however, the final painting contains an element of psy-chological tension that is more powerful than in the sketch. In the final oil, all the figures are explicitly identifiable as portraits and would have been known to most of the people who first saw the painting.

The reclining figure at the left, in the pose of an antique river god, is Talcott Williams, a well-known journalist and prominent figure in Philadelphia society. The diving figure to the right is George Reynolds, a veteran of the Civil War, who was one of Eakins's pupils, but a good deal older than his other students. The three remaining figures form an arc leading up to the apex of the compositional triangle. They are all somewhat younger men—boys in fact: Benjamin Fox, whose red hair provides a balance to the red hair of Harry, the dog; John Laurie Wallace, stretching his arm, who had posed for Eakins's *Crucifixion*; and finally Jesse Godley—the one whose rear end forms the dramatic climax of the picture—a boy of about twenty, who was serving at the time as Eakins's anatomy assistant. (Eakins commended Godley for his skill and energy in dissecting horses.) Eakins himself appears at the right—the only figure that is actually swimming. We do not know who snapped the shutter for the preparatory photographs, but very likely it was Eakins's assistant, Thomas Anshutz.[39]

Eakins seems to have envisaged the group portrayed here as a loyal gang of true believers in his teachings. Elizabeth Johns has even proposed that Eakins conceived the group as reenactors of Plato's Academy. Within a year, however, when Eakins was fired from the Pennsylvania Academy, the cohesion of the group was shattered. The older members of the group, river god Williams, arm-stretcher Wallace and diver Reynolds, all sided with Eakins. In fact Reynolds was a leader of the loyal secessionist group of students that left the Academy to gather around Eakins at the newly founded Philadelphia Art Students' League. The young Jesse Godley, however, whose rump Eakins focused on so intently, sided against Eakins. Around the time that Eakins was fired, Godley formed a business partnership with two of Eakins's archenemies, the painter Colin Campbell Cooper Jr., and Eakins's brother-in-law Frank Stephens. Thomas Anshutz, if he did indeed snap the shutter, was another figure who sided against Eakins in the Academy scandal.[40]

The loyalties of Benjamin Fox are not recorded, although he eventually seceded from the group for another reason. In 1892 he was admitted to the Lunatic Asylum of the Pennsylvania Hospital for acute mania. His fate is not known, but a few years after his release from the hospital his name disappeared from the Philadelphia directories.[41]

To underscore the fact that the painting showed specific people, not just anonymous models, Eakins showed clothed portraits of two of the figures, Wallace and Reynolds, alongside *Swimming*, when he first exhibited it at the Academy.

It is this element of "real life," not the mere fact that it shows naked people, that makes *Swimming* most intensely provocative. As Jennifer Doyle has written:

> How many of us . . . would really be comfortable hanging in our office, a painting like *The Swimming Hole*, executed by a colleague who appeared in the painting along with a number of his and our own students, all naked, of the same sex, and suggestively posed? With the cultural anxieties that swirl around sex and the workplace, not many would be inclined openly and unambivalently to support a project that involved, as did *The Swimming Hole*, a teacher spending an afternoon taking photographs of himself naked with students. Furthermore, how many of us can honestly say that we are sure enough of the boundary that protects student–teacher relationships to spend an afternoon naked with our students—and take pictures—and show them to our colleagues—and believe that we would keep our posts?"[42]

Along with embarrassing his models, Eakins also seems to have intended to embarrass the patron of the painting, Edward Horner Coates. An industrialist from an established Philadelphia Quaker family, Coates speculated shrewdly in a variety of businesses and was able to retire at the early age of forty-four. His wife was a poet who wrote sentimental verses scattered with classical allusions, which were once much admired but now seem quaint. After his retirement from commercial affairs, Coates's main interest became the Pennsylvania Academy. He was elected a trustee in 1877, and loyally served for years in a variety of roles—eventually becoming president, a post he held from 1890 to 1906. Over the years, Coates befriended and served as a modest patron for a series of painters associated with the Pennsylvania Academy, such as the landscapist William Trost Richards. He also collected paintings of the French Barbizon school, by figures such as Daubigny, Diaz, Dupré, Jacque, and Corot.

By temperament, Coates seems to have been a conciliator. (In his portrait by Robert Vonnoh, a bland, earnest, perhaps even poetic face is screened and protected from the world by an impressive halo of whiskers). Indeed, Coates's commission to Eakins, which in the end seems to have turned into a trial for both of them, began as a kindly gesture. Eakins had been promised a salary raise at the Academy in 1882 but the promised money had never appeared. Coates seems to have commissioned a painting from Eakins as a way to make up for this error. Throughout the episode in which Eakins was fired from the Academy, Coates seems to have struggled to keep up a cordial relationship with him. Shortly after Eakins was fired, when one of Eakins's patrons, James Scott, expressed displeasure with two decorative sculptures he had commissioned, *Spinning* and *Knitting*, Coates purchased them from Scott and then donated them to the Pennsylvania Academy. In a public address of 1890, Coates generously mentioned Eakins as one of the figures responsible for the success of the institution.[43]

In his letter outlining the commission, Coates specifically stated that he hoped for a painting that he could someday give to the Pennsylvania Academy, where, presumably, it would also serve to enhance Eakins's reputation. Eakins's choice of a subject, however, was clearly embarrassing to Coates. Although he allowed the painting to be shown under his name at the Academy's Annual, he wrote to Eakins in November 1885, while the painting was still on view in the exhibition, asking to exchange it for another work. Coates's letter is filled with words that evoke friendliness and intimacy, but underneath his politeness one can sense his discomfort:

Robert W. Vonnoh, Edward H. Coates, 1893. Oil on canvas, 50 ⅛ x 40 ⅛ in., courtesy of The Pennsylvania Academy of the Fine Arts, Philadelphia, gift of Mrs. Edward H. Coates (the Edward H. Coates Memorial Collection). **Edward Horner Coates, who served on the Board of The Pennsylvania Academy, struggled to be a conciliator, but Eakins made this role difficult.**

I want to make a proposal which may be a surprise to you but which I take the liberty of making relying on our kindly relations and knowing that we may talk frankly. The suggestion is that if you are willing you should allow me to make an arrangement to take something of your work which you have on hand instead of the "Swimming" picture . . . My reasons for this I would probably express better in person than by note. I would say, however, briefly and confidentially that as you will recall one of my chief ideas was to have from you a picture which might some day become part of the Academy collection. The present canvas is to me admirable in many ways but I am inclined to believe that some of the pictures you have are even more representative, and it has been suggested would be perhaps more acceptable for the purpose which I have always had in view. You must not suppose from this that I depreciate the present work—such is not the case.[44]

By December 8, Coates had paid Eakins $800, which was eventually applied to the purchase of a more conventional painting, *The Pathetic Song*. For whatever reason, Coates never donated that painting to the Pennsylvania Academy. The Corcoran Museum of Art eventually purchased it from him.

In addition to its element of sexual innuendo, the nudity in *Swimming* may have shocked Coates in another way. Eakins's letters from Paris tell us that he felt considerable resentment toward upper-class people, particularly if they acted the part of "swells." In nineteenth-century terms, the issue of nudity touched on the issue of social class in a way that was loaded with powerful meanings. On the one hand, working-class people, who engaged in physical labor, often stripped off their shirts when working outdoors, particularly in hot weather. When they wanted to cool off, they might even strip off their clothes entirely to swim. Upper-class people or supervisors, on the other hand, avoided physical activity of this sort, and even in hot weather were expected to maintain their ties, jackets, and hats, as signifiers of their superior social position.

Eakins's portrayal of naked young men thus represented a challenge to upper-class standards of behavior. It presented behavior associated with the working class as a kind of ideal, and as implicitly superior to upper-class standards. To lend credibility to this challenge, moreover, Eakins seems to have invoked the sanction of the classical antique. Indeed, the stiffness of his composition, although visually awkward, appears to have been deliberate, and a conscious invocation of the pediments of classical temples. (Eakins's poses also allude to famous classical statues. Talcott Williams, for example, is in a pose that resembles *The Dying Gaul*.) In short, Eakins's focus on the nude was a conscious affront to the sensibility of socially proper upper-class people such as Coates—the very gentleman who had instigated the commission.

When Eakins first exhibited *Swimming* at the Pennsylvania Academy, the press was ostentatiously silent about its expressive qualities, particularly given its unusual subject and the prominence of Eakins in the Philadelphia art world. A reviewer for the *Philadelphia Times* dismissed the painting as "not agreeable," but the only extended review, by Leslie Miller, avoided all mention of the naked figures and discussed the background instead—with a fervor that suggests that he was actually bothered by something else. Eakins's landscapes were invariably weak, Miller declared, and this one was "persistently and inexcusably bad." Eakins was creating "mischief," he noted, which was having a bad influence on the work of most of his older students. Notably, Miller did not clearly specify what sort of "mischief" Eakins was causing.[45]

In short, the painting seems to have been received with the mysterious, embarrassed silence that so often surrounds the subject of sex. Interestingly, an anonymous reviewer for *The Philadelphia Inquirer* noted that the painting was bound to "excite abundant criticism, both friendly and unfriendly."[46] What this criticism might be, the journalists did not wish to commit to print.

In fact, Eakins seems to have been interested in creating embarrassment at many levels. Surely it was embarrassing for his students to have their naked-ness on public view. Surely it was also embarrassing to his cautious patron to have his name associated with such a provocative image. Surely also, the shock that Eakins created with this picture was similar to the disruption he caused by asking people to undress for him, or by disrobing himself. As with Eakins's personal behavior, the affront was difficult to discuss. It does not sur-prise us that Coates was silent about what Eakins had done, or that journalists had little to say about the painting, for to admit that an affront had occurred required discussing unmentionable subjects, and violating accepted patterns of behavior. As with rape, the shame of the action became attached not only to the perpetrator, but to the victim.

Perhaps Eakins not only hoped to create embarrassment when he exhib-ited the painting, but also played with this issue when he created the work. From technical examination of the painting, we now know that Eakins must have relied on photographs of each of the figures naked. We know that Susan Eakins developed photographs for her husband. If she did so in this instance, it would suggest that Eakins wanted her to examine and touch these naked male bodies.

In *The Gross Clinic* and *William Rush* the story lines depicted tell us some-thing about how the different figures are relating to each other, but in *Swim-ming* the relationships are remarkably ambiguous. There is no real narrative—only the fact that the men are displaying their bodies.

The psychological undercurrents of the painting are also puzzling. Is this a painting about manhood or about men who do not feel like men, and who conceal their genital region because their genitals are missing? Is the painting homosexual in nature, or does it seek to deny homosexual impulses? How can we explain the way in which the men look away from one another, at the same time that the painting seems to be about some sort of voyeurism, and the pleasure of looking? Is this a painting about being sensually liberated or is it a painting about shame? How can we explain Eakins's fascination with prominently featured uncovered buttocks, a theme that also recurs elsewhere in his work? Are these various themes somehow connected, particularly since

Eakins repeated them on other occasions? Can we find some pattern that they share or some reminiscence that unifies them? In fact, the meaning of *Swimming* may not be entirely contained within the painting itself. Eakins's pleasure in creating it, for example, was evidently spurred by the thought of embarrassing his patron, Edward Horner Coates. Thus, the "narrative" of the painting extends out into the social sphere, and the best clues to its meaning may lie not within the canvas but in other aspects of Eakins's behavior.

A Wife and a Dog

The homosocial or homosexual qualities of *Swimming* become even more dramatic when we recognize that the painting is almost exactly contemporary with a remarkably unflattering portrait of Eakins's wife, *The Artist's Wife and His Setter Dog* (circa 1886). This canvas shows Susan slumped on a Queen Anne chair in Eakins's studio, looking out at the viewer with a dejected expression. At her feet, on a rumpled rug, lies Eakins's setter dog Harry, apparently dozing. While *Swimming* stresses the physical beauty and strength of men, the portrait of Susan Eakins is a study in ugliness and weakness.

Susan Eakins, ca. 1885. *Cyanotype, 2 ⁹⁄₁₆ x 2 ³⁄₁₆ in., The Pennsylvania Academy of the Fine Arts, Charles Bregler's Thomas Eakins Collection, purchased with the partial support of the Pew Memorial Trust.* At the time of the Academy scandal, Susan's brother William wrote to express worry about her worn appearance and to voice concern that she was headed toward "insanity or death."

According to Margaret McHenry, the portrait came about because Susan had "dressed herself in some gay bright costume to tempt her husband Tom to paint her."[47] Eakins took up her challenge, but handled it differently than Susan would have hoped. Instead of bright colors, he clothed her in an ugly blue dress with an extremely unflattering bodice and neckline. As McHenry noted: "The portrait is rather ruthless and not at all romantic, a decided contrast to the one Susan Hannah did of herself."[48] Susan's body slumps with fatigue or inherent frailty, and her physique is puny, with a shrunken frame that makes her head seem too large. Her head is tilted in a gesture of dejection. Her face is careworn and her eyes are so deeply lined that it looks as though she has been crying.

Eakins portrays his wife as a kind of defective man, with weak looking, shrunken shoulders and diminutive arms. The things that make women appear different from men, such as hips and breasts, are not emphasized. The brightest part of the painting is his wife's abdomen, locus of the womb—the source of children—and the reason for a woman's existence as a sexually separate creature. But Eakins's presentation of this part of her anatomy is not sexually enticing. We might speculate that when he made the picture he knew that her womb would be barren.

Significantly, the original form of the painting was less severe than the one we know today. In 1886, when the picture was reproduced in Mrs. Van Rensselaer's *Book of American Figure Painters*, Susan looked wistful but not quite so forlorn, since her expression could be read as slightly defiant rather than as completely broken. At some point shortly afterward, however, Eakins repainted the picture, making many alterations, but most noticeably repainting the head, giving a slight downturn to the mouth, adding lines to the eyes, and in general making his wife look older and more worn out. Susan is known to have become profoundly distressed at the time that her husband was fired from the Pennsylvania Academy, and the changes to the painting may have been made in response to this fact.[49] But as William Inness Homer has noted, even the first version of the painting was grimly unflattering, and Eakins's changes only underscored qualities that were already evident.

Eakins's depictions of his wife at this time generally paired her with an animal. One group of photographs, for example, shows his wife standing naked beside Billy the horse, in such a way that the similarity of their rib cages is apparent. In the portrait, Eakins showed his wife beside his dog, Harry, and portrayed Harry with his right leg protruding out, closely echoing Susan's own extended foot.

The painting can thus be seen as a study of the differences and similarities between woman and dog. To use a common slang phrase, this woman is "a dog." Overall, the woman comes off as second best. Recently William Inness Homer has commented, "It is telling that Eakins painted his dog with more warmth and sympathy than his bride."[50] In fact, the contrast in the treatment of the two was noted when the painting was first shown, when a critic for the *Art Amateur* noted that although the dog was rendered in accordance with a good theory of painting, the lady's figure was "unfortunate."[51]

An important clue to the meaning of the painting is provided by the book of Japanese prints on Susan's lap. Eakins's painting is really a parody of a voguish mode of painting at the time—the representation of women in Japanese costume, residing in a Never-Never Land of beauty and aestheticism. By the 1880s paintings of this sort were being churned out by a great number of

Portrait of a Lady with a Setter Dog (Mrs. Eakins), 1885. *Oil on canvas, 30 x 23 in., Metropolitan Museum of Art, Fletcher Fund, 1933.* William Inness Homer has commented that it is telling that Eakins painted his dog with more warmth and sympathy than his bride.

painters, both European and American, including James Tissot, Alfred Stevens, Thomas Dewing, and any number of less-talented figures. Most likely Eakins was thinking of the work of the most famous practitioner of this genre, James Abbott McNeill Whistler, who had largely invented the whole genre of women with Japanese objects. Whistler was also a particularly notable rival. Though he worked in Europe, Whistler was widely considered the greatest living American painter, a title that surely Eakins wished to gain for himself.

Eakins seems to have had a kind of love–hate relationship with Whistler, at once admiring his work and disdaining it. In later years, John Trask, secretary of the Pennsylvania Academy, found Eakins examining a painting of a

Lady with Setter Dog, ca. 1884–1888. Photogravure reproduction from Mariana Griswold van Rensselaer, *The Book of American Figure Painters*, 1886. Eakins's first version of the painting was slightly more flattering. He subsequently reworked it to make Susan look more careworn and her face more lined.

girl by Whistler, and asked him what he thought of the piece. Eakins "turned around on him" and said, "I think it a very cowardly way to paint."[52] On another occasion, when interviewed by the press, Eakins declared "Whistler was unquestionably a great painter, but there are many of his works for which I do not care."[53]

Eakins was probably thinking of a particular work by Whistler, *The Lange Lizzen of the Six Marks* (1864), which was Whistler's first painting in a Japanese style, and one that attracted exceptional interest when it was first exhibited. If we put Whistler's painting beside Eakins's portrait of Susan, the similarity of pose is very striking—at the same time that the overall effect of the two paintings is entirely different.[54] Whistler's painting shows a beautiful woman in

James A. McNeil Whistler, Lady of the Lijsen, *1864. Oil on canvas, 36 ¼ x 24 ¼ in., John G. Johnson Collection, Philadelphia Museum of Art.* Lady with Setter Dog *was probably in part a parody of Whistler's famous painting of a slender beauty decorating porcelain in a beautiful Japanese interior.*

Japanese costume, painting a blue-and-white vase. No crude realities of daily life intrude into the idyll. Being beautiful and creating beauty is her only concern. Given our present knowledge of Whistler's private life, there is definitely an ironic aspect to the serenity of his image, for Joanna Heffernan who posed for him was famously temperamental. In reality, she would have been as likely to throw a blue-and-white vase at Whistler's head as to demurely decorate it. Eakins, of course, did not need to know Whistler's private life to know that something was phony about the image. In his remake of Whistler's design he set out to show what he thought women are really like—physically frail and emotionally desperate.

As in Whistler's painting, the setting is artistic. In fact, the artist's studio as a fantasy retreat was a popular theme of this period, perhaps best exemplified in William Merritt Chase's renditions of his Tenth Street studio in New York, with its rich collection of Japanese and European bric-a-brac. Eakins's painting also seems to show a studio, and it is filled with artistic things, but the clutter and disorder of the room Eakins portrays is not particularly entrancing.[55]

At about the time that he completed this unusual painting, Eakins hung the larger of his two portraits of Elizabeth Crowell over the mantelpiece of the downstairs parlor of the family home, declaring to his wife that he was "satisfied with it."[56] Perhaps the most romantic of his paintings, this rendering of Elizabeth shows her playing the piano, clothed in a black dress and with a rose in her hair. The painting is subdued. Indeed, Elizabeth is almost lost in darkness except for her face, which is half lit and half washed with translucent shadows. Although only dimly visible, her profile is beautifully and sensitively rendered. Her dreamy expression shows that she is lost in the music, and her emergence from the darkness, with a face caressed by light, seems to express romantic longing. The upper-right portion of the painting glows with bright light that suggests movement toward emotional ecstasy.

In pictorial terms, the canvas stands as the closest Eakins ever came to an expression of love. Certainly the painting is far more flattering than the one of Susan. It is hard not to read Eakins's decision to hang it so prominently as a way of undercutting his wife's self-esteem, and of indicating to Susan that she was not the woman he loved most deeply.

Scholars on Eakins have always been hostile to those who rejected his portraits, viewing this as a failure of character on their part. Eakins's wife, however, clearly felt uneasy about his portrayal of her. When Bryson Burroughs organized the first retrospective of Eakins's work at the Metropolitan Museum of Art in 1917, Susan refused to lend the portrait to the exhibition.[57]

Eakins's followers have worked hard to deny the uncomplimentary nature of the painting. Samuel Murray, for example, noted Susan's worn expression, but explained this as an instance of Eakins's realism. According to Murray, the painting "was done under a skylight, which gave Sue's eyes shadows."[58] Writers such as Goodrich, Schendler, and Katz, have tried to find honeyed words to describe Eakins's portrayal of his wife. Even they, however, obliquely circle back to the fact that the picture is brutally harsh and that no other American artist of the nineteenth century depicted his wife in such an unflattering manner.

It is no accident that scholars have sought to deny the visual evidence in this instance. It is profoundly upsetting to suppose that Eakins would harbor such feelings about a woman who served him with a kind of desperate loyalty. Moreover, the painting challenges one of the fundamental premises of Eakins scholarship: the notion that Susan was an ideal wife and perfect helpmate to her husband.

Most writers have assumed that because Susan Macdowell was married to Thomas Eakins she understood his behavior and knew him well. Yet marriage does not necessarily bring true understanding. The essential loneliness of individuals—the ways their sorrows are utterly private—is, after all, one of the chief themes of Eakins's art. It is no surprise that he had inner secrets that he did not disclose. Certainly Eakins's portrait of his wife suggests that there were troubled undercurrents to their relationship that Susan always struggled to deny.

Portrait of Douglass Morgan Hall, ca. 1889. *Oil on canvas, 24 x 20 in.,
Philadelphia Museum of Art, gift of William E. Studdiford*. **Douglas Morgan Hall
died in the Pennsylvania Hospital for the Insane at the age of forty-four.**

Chapter 17

CONVERSATIONS WITH
THE DEAD

ASIDE FROM likenesses of family members, Eakins executed only a few portraits during the first phase of his career. His first portrait of someone outside his family showed his high school chemistry teacher, *Professor Benjamin H. Rand* (1874). He followed this with portraits of *Dr. George H. Brinton* (1876), a surgeon, and *Archbishop James Frederic Wood* (1877). In the spring of 1877 he was commissioned to make a portrait of President Rutherford B. Hayes. On the whole, however, until Eakins was fired from the Pennsylvania Academy, portraiture took second place to paintings of people carrying out activities such as surgery, rowing, or musical performances. To be sure, the figures in these genre paintings were also portraits, in the sense that they are specific, identifiable individuals. Yet the primary interest in these pictures lies not in the identities of the figures but in the activities being portrayed.

After Eakins was fired from the Pennsylvania Academy, portraiture began to dominate his painterly enterprise. In his later career, portraits vastly outnumber any other subject, and to an ever-increasing degree he tended to focus on the figure in isolation, making the background murky and ambiguous. Even in those increasingly uncommon paintings in which Eakins represented activities, such as wrestling or boxing, his compositions seem less unified than before. The pictures are no longer conceived as a unit, with a single light source, but are more like a collection of fragments. They tend to break apart into portraits of individual figures who seem isolated from one another, and occupy separate blocks of space, even when they are portrayed standing side by side.

It is appealing to believe that artists grow in insight as they develop and, therefore, that their later works are "richer" or "more profound" than their early work. In Eakins's case, however, it is clear that after he was fired from the Pennsylvania Academy he never again produced paintings as dramatic, as complex, or as artistically complete as some of his early masterworks such as *The Champion Single Sculls*, *The Gross Clinic*, *Swimming*, or his first version of *William Rush*. Indeed, he attempted few such compositions, for the most part focusing on portraits of single figures, which tend to become simpler and more reductive in their treatment as his career progressed. We can, if we wish, view Eakins's late paintings as "deeper" or "more mature" than his earlier work. But they are also more repetitive and more limited in subject matter—a stream of heads of suffering figures against dark backgrounds.

In the biographies that have been written thus far, the artist's early career has clear definition. His development has been smoothly traced from awkward student to technically confident master, a process that culminates in his controversial *Gross Clinic*. Eakins's later years, however, have never been fit into a coherent dramatic or narrative pattern, and developments become blurred.

Samuel Murray, Thomas Eakins in Three-Quarter View, in Chestnut Street Studio, *ca. 1891–1892. Dry-plate negative, 4 x 5 in., courtesy of The Pennsylvania Academy of the Fine Arts, Philadelphia, Charles Bregler's Thomas Eakins Collection, purchased with the partial support of the Pew Memorial Trust.*

Notably, Lloyd Goodrich, in his 1933 monograph, abandoned all attempt to present the artist's activities in chronological order after his association with the Academy ended, instead jumping from one theme to another, making no attempt to establish any logical sequence, either of theme or chronology. Nonetheless, Goodrich's comment that "Eakins' life in the middle years was quiet externally" becomes grimly ironic when we consider that these were the years of the insanity of Lillian Hammitt, the suicide of his niece Ella Crowell, and his break with his sister Frances and her husband.[1] One would expect such events to have some impact on Eakins's work, and indeed, this proves to be the case. The sadness of his art mirrors his personal sadness. As with his earlier production, his later work also often hints at something profoundly troubled about his early life and family experience.

By examining Eakins's work closely,

we can distinguish distinct episodes of development, which generally relate closely to the external events of his life. In addition, one of the interesting things about this period is that we have more testimony from people who knew Eakins and formed part of his circle than we do for the early years. Their often surprising testimony illuminates many aspects of the artist's character that are only hinted at in earlier accounts.

Nervous Breakdown

After losing his job at the Academy, Eakins moved back to the family home on Mount Vernon Street with his new bride—a move that surely saved money, but was also apparently made at the insistence of his father. Most writers have viewed this as a move of support, made to silence the rumors about his son's morality. But it is also possible that Benjamin recognized that his son's character was in some way unusual, and wished to monitor his behavior.[2] Eakins's return was accompanied by the ouster of his sister Caroline and her husband Frank Stephens.

After the death of his mother in 1872, Eakins became ill with exhaustion, and two years later he nearly died from an illness described as malaria, and was bedridden from fever for two months, coming close to death.[3] In 1887, after being fired from the Academy, he again became ill—this time suffering from what was then known as "nervousness," or what today we would call a nervous breakdown. To obtain relief, Eakins sought help from an expert in mental exhaustion, Dr. Horatio Wood. Women of the late nineteenth century were generally prescribed physical rest cures and directed to lie in bed. Men were assumed to be suffering from brain strain, and thus were advised to engage in a "camp cure," which would exercise their bodies and relax their brains.[4] In keeping with this pattern, Wood sent Eakins to recuperate at the B-T Ranch in the Dakota Territory (now North Dakota), near the town of Dickinson.

Dr. Horatio Wood, ca. 1886. *Oil on canvas, 63 ½ x 50 in., City of Detroit Purchase,* © 1995 *The Detroit Institute of Arts.* **After being fired from The Pennsylvania Academy, Eakins suffered a nervous breakdown and sought help from Dr. Horatio Wood, an expert on depression and mental illness.**

Eakins stayed in North Dakota from late July until early October 1887—his most extended sojourn away from home since his years abroad.[5] Theodore Roosevelt had described the landscape of the Dakota Territory as "a place of savage splendor that is not without an element of the terrible."[6] After his sufferings in Philadelphia, Eakins seems to have relished this bleakness. His letters to his wife make it clear that he enjoyed sharing the rugged, masculine life of the cowboys, eating and sleeping outdoors and taking part in the roundup. Significantly, these letters often stress violent episodes, such as the capture of a cattle thief, whom Eakins approvingly implies was hanged with summary frontier justice. His description of the incident bears a striking relationship to the climactic lynching scene of Owen Wister's famous Western novel, *The Virginian*. Eakins's letters also boast of blowing the heads off animals with his .44 Winchester.[7]

A League of Young Men

On his return to Philadelphia, Eakins again became involved in teaching. Some forty male students had protested Eakins's departure from the Academy. Of these, about thirty became involved in creating the Art Students League of Philadelphia, where Eakins taught without pay. Many of these young men, however, quickly lost enthusiasm for the project. By the time the school was actually operating the number of students had dropped to about sixteen. The journalist Frances Ziegler told Goodrich that even before Eakins was fired from the Academy, a group of students rejected his manner of teaching and formed their own group, the Art Students Union. Thus, for a brief period there were three groups: the Pennsylvania Academy, the Art Students Union and the Art Students League.[8]

    As with Eakins's curriculum at the Pennsylvania Academy, the sole subject of study at the Art Students League was the nude figure. But at the new organization, Eakins was free from supervision, and the atmosphere seems to have been considerably more bohemian and more raucous than at the Academy. The League's population was almost entirely male. Photographs show no women except for nude female models. Other than Eakins's wife, and his nieces Ella and Maggie Crowell, the only females associated with the place were an Ella Ahrens and a Miss White, both of whom appear to have stayed only a few weeks. Even most men seem to have found the atmosphere too unconventional. Enrollment continued to drop and for much of its history the student body comprised only about half a dozen students. While it existed in name for six or seven years, moving to a new location roughly every year, it seems to have ceased regular classes around 1889. For about three years, however, the League served as the major focus of Eakins's activities, both social and artistic.[9]

    The artists who studied with Eakins remain obscure; most vanished without a trace.[10] Eakins has been described as a natural leader, and in a sense this is correct, but this leadership clearly came at a cost. Strong-willed, self-reliant types had little interest in Eakins. Only one of his students—Samuel Murray—produced notable work, although he presents an unusual case, since Eakins shared a studio with him and directed his every move. In this sense, Murray's work seems less the production of an independent artist than that of a craftsman carrying out someone else's artistic program—rather like the Italian modeler Richard Guino, who produced sculpture in the style of Auguste Renoir under Renoir's careful supervision. Even then, Murray's work is interesting chiefly for its relationship to Eakins and his circle rather than for its own merits. His public sculpture is dry and uninspired. The "masterpiece" of his career was a small statuette of Eakins seated on the floor. While technically competent, the piece is of interest primarily because of its subject.

The Face of Despair

In the year after he was fired, 1886 and 1887, Eakins's artistic output dropped significantly. During the first six months of 1887 he did not produce a single canvas. In this period, however, he seems to have repainted major sections of several of his earlier canvases, making them muddier and rougher in paint handling. As noted, both *The Crucifixion* and *The Biglin Brothers Turning the Stake* originally had blue skies, but Eakins repainted them with thick layers of crusty pigment, applied in a chaotic manner. In addition, Eakins reworked *The Artist's Wife and His Setter Dog,* making Susan Eakins's posture more sagging, her face more lined, and her expression even more vacant. When he finally returned to original work, the character of his painting had changed.

Eakins's early portraits had tended to be crowded. His first major portrait, of Benjamin Rand (1874), who had been his chemistry teacher at Central High School, provides case in point. Eakins included dozens of objects on the desk, chair and floor that are meant to tell us about the sitter. Rand had just married and taken up a new position on the faculty of Jefferson Medical School. The portrait seems to allude to both these events. Scientific instruments, such as a microscope, beam balance, and test tubes, indicate his chemical expertise. A rose and a colored shawl evoke his recent marriage. The profusion of objects, however, and the dim light in which they are shown, creates a confusing effect. Early reviewers had varied reactions to the painting, one commenting that it is "a portrait which is made a picture by the many accessories introduced," and

Portrait of Benjamin H. Rand, 1874. *Oil on canvas,*
60 x 48 in., Jefferson Medical College, Thomas Jefferson
University, Philadelphia. Eakins cluttered his early
portrait of his chemistry teacher, Benjamin Rand,
with objects that evoke different aspects of the life
of the sitter.

another that it "is rather too elaborate for a portrait, and the eye is confused by the multitude of
objects that are introduced."[11]

Admittedly, the Rand portrait is particularly
crowded. In general, however, Eakins's early portraits tend to place his sitters in an activity or a context that reveals something about who they are.

After he was fired, Eakins adopted an entirely
different approach that eliminated accessories
almost entirely. He began to portray dreamy, lost-
looking young men, who are viewed from close up
and set against murky, ambiguous backgrounds.
Dark shadows eat away at their features, and their
expressions are somber.

Of the sixteen head-and-shoulder portraits that
Eakins created between 1885 and 1890, at least thirteen depict students from both the Academy and
the Art Students League. Many were inscribed "to
my friend," an inscription with charged implications, since during this period those who supported
Eakins were in open conflict with those who did
not.[12] These portraits served two obvious social purposes. First, they provided
him with patrons (although not patrons who could afford to pay). In addition,
when he exhibited them at the Pennsylvania Academy they served to promote
both Eakins and the students who still supported him. During this period he
painted very few women.

We can view these portraits in two ways. On the one hand, we can suppose
that they present a "realistic" record of the external world—a quasi-scientific
study of "types." Nicolai Cikovsky, for example, has noted that Eakins's fascination with cranial description began at just the time that the social sciences of
anthropology and sociology were being launched as "scientific" disciplines.
Eakins's interest in typological portraiture corresponds with the first attempts
to use physiognomic description for the identification of criminals, such as
Thomas Byrnes's *Professional Criminals of America* (1886), or Alphonse Bertillon's
Identification anthropometrique (1893). When he exhibited his portraits, Eakins
sometimes gave them titles that call attention to the sitter's social role, such as
Portrait of an Engineer, Portrait of a Poet, Portrait of an Artist, Portrait of a Student,
The Veteran, or *The Bohemian.* Viewed in this way, the portraits are studies of the

variety of the human species, as exhibited in a range of human professions and facial variations.[13] At the end of his life, when Eakins was asked to comment on the state of American art, he declared that "American art students and painters" should "study their own country and portray its life and types."[14]

On the other hand, we can regard these portraits as something more personal, an exploration of Eakins's emotional state. If we line them up side by side, they are extraordinarily repetitive, to the point where we might wonder whether they are portraits at all in the usual sense. An almost universal quality of the presentation is that the sitters appear depressed, with tilted heads, downcast or vacant glance, and red-rimmed or teary eyes. In addition, Eakins seems to have exaggerated the feminine qualities of his sitters. Spies has declared that the sitters are often "feminized and sexualized." She notes that these paintings tend to feature young men with boyish faces, curly hair, lush lashes, full curving lips, and bright pink bow ties.[15] Eakins played with these elements in numerous variations. In writing of these paintings, Sylvan Schendler used such adjectives as "romantic" and "sensual."[16]

At the time, Eakins was seeking medical help for his depression, and these paintings seem to explore this syndrome. Thus, Eakins was not simply recording faces, but also exploring something about his own mental condition. Whoever his sitter might be, he somehow managed to capture an aspect of their personality that was essentially a projection of his own.

In this period nervousness was considered a feminine quality. Thus, for example, Eakins's friend Dr. S. Weir Mitchell, who wrote extensively on nervous diseases, believed that, when nervous, "the strong man becomes like the average woman."[17] Contemporary medical studies often describe male neurasthenics as thin, anemic, and lacking manly musculature, as feminine, as coquettish and eccentric, and even as overtly homosexual.[18] Attitudes toward homosexuality were complex. In the nineteenth century, romantic—even passionate—friendships between young men were socially accepted. Married men, however, were expected to set aside the carefree play of youth and focus on the responsibilities of raising a family. Homosexuality between adults was considered a form of illness and was generally labeled as "perverted sexuality" or "sodomy."[19]

The Syphilitic Student

When we look into the lives of the figures whom Eakins portrayed, we often find that they were weak individuals, who were haunted by poverty, loss, and even insanity. An instance is that of Douglass Morgan Hall. The son of a prominent Philadelphia ophthalmologist, at age eighteen Hall enrolled at the Pennsylvania Academy of the Fine Arts, where he took the most elementary class in copying plaster casts. When Eakins was fired, Hall was not one of the loyalists who signed a petition to have him reinstated. In 1887, however, he enrolled in Eakins's Art Students League, where he stayed until about 1890. Despite such intensive study, Hall never pursued a professional artistic career, but depended throughout his life on the support of his father. Oddly, while Eakins's teachings focused exclusively on the human figure, Hall's surviving sketchbooks show an emphasis on landscapes, seascapes, and birds. Hall's aimless life ended in 1912, when he was forty-four, in the Pennsylvania Hospital for the Insane, where he is said to have died from syphilis.[20]

Eakins's portrait of Hall shows a young man staring blankly off into space with a dreamy, unfocused expression. His right arm is draped casually over the back of the chair, so we see him at an angle. Overall, Hall seems caught between the states of boy and man. His wispy mustache does not make him seem manly but emphasizes his boyishness. His shirt seems tight, as if he has grown too large for it. He has untidy hair and red-rimmed eyes. He appears weak, indecisive, and immature—an almost feminine figure quite unprepared for manhood. We might even say that the painting has a tragic quality—after looking at it, Hall's early death comes as no surprise. Nor is it surprising that Hall's family did not appreciate the portrait. Until the 1950s the canvas belonged to Hall's sister, who kept it in a closet, facing the back wall.

The Shell-Shocked Veteran

Failure or despair of a different sort is portrayed in Eakins's portrait of George Reynolds, the first curator of the Art Students League, who also appears as the nude diver in Eakins's *Swimming*. We know little about Reynolds's life but that little is tantalizing, for it suggests that he was idealistic, high-strung, and erratic. Reynolds was born in Ireland. He had arrived in the United States by 1861, at the beginning of the American Civil War, when he enrolled in the New York cavalry, listing his occupation as "gentleman." By early 1863 he had been arrested, court-martialed, demoted in rank, and sentenced to twelve months of hard labor at Fort Lyon, Virginia, for striking a superior officer. Within a year and a half, however, he had redeemed himself. In the fall of 1864 he was awarded the Congressional Medal of Honor for capturing the Virginia state flag during the Battle of Winchester on September 19, 1864.[21]

After the war, Reynolds worked as an artist in New York. In 1882, shortly after the death of his wife, he came to Philadelphia to study with Eakins. When the Academy fired Eakins, Reynolds was among those who signed the petition to have him reinstated and was also one of the loyalists who followed him to the Art Students League. By 1887, however, only about a year after the League was founded, Reynolds had moved back to New York City, where he died two years later. As with many of Eakins's students, there is little trace of Reynolds's artistic career. The largest body of work is a group of drawings of New York buildings, which were published posthumously. Despite Reynolds's close association with Eakins and his five years of study with him, the drawings are surprisingly undistinguished, both technically and artistically. They could easily be mistaken for the work of an amateur.

The Veteran, ca. 1885. Oil on canvas, 22 ¼ x 15 in Yale University Art Gallery, bequest of Stephen Carlton Clark, B.A. 1903. A veteran of bloody combat during the Civil War, George Reynolds came to study with Eakins after the death of his wife.

Charles Bregler remembered Reynolds as a figure "of serious demeanor."[22] This is borne out by his portrait, which Eakins titled *The Veteran*. In this ambiguous, unsettling image, only a few features are sufficiently visible to provide clues about the sitter's character and what he might be thinking. The entire right side of Reynolds's face is hidden in blackness, and since the lower part is largely hidden by a mustache and beard, we cannot read his expression fully. His mouth is tense. Is he angry or brooding? The most ominous aspect of the painting, however, is Reynolds's left eye—the only one visible. Strangely unfocused, this eye reflects a spark of light, which gives it a watery quality, as if Reynolds has just cried, or might begin crying. This eye suggests that Reynolds is both utterly withdrawn and profoundly unhappy. Its gleam eerily evokes something unspecified but terrible, such as madness or the frenzy of battle.

The picture's title suggests that Reynolds's brooding may be connected with the trauma of war. Indeed, the deep shadows in the painting seem to serve as a metaphor for the annihilation of death. Reynolds could be musing on the horrors he has witnessed, whether those of battle or those associated with the death of his wife, which occurred just before he went to study with Eakins. Whatever the cause, Eakins's portrait shows him as almost paralyzed, seemingly incapable of acting in the present.

As with the portrait of Douglass Hall, Eakins's portrait of Reynolds is essentially a painting of sadness and even helplessness, although with a slightly different nuance than the other painting, which turns on the differences of their personalities. Whereas Hall was young and inexperienced, Reynolds had seen a lot of life—enough to be damaged by it. Whereas Hall seems weak, Reynolds combines sorrow with a brooding quality that possibly verges on insanity.

The Bohemian Drifter

One of Eakins's favorite sitters was Franklin Schenck, who succeeded George Reynolds as the "curator" of the Art Students League. His duties were to obtain models, schedule classes, and care for the building. Schenck humorously called himself "Pythagoras" after the ancient Greek philosopher and geometer, who was the leader of a religious brotherhood.

Schenck never had any money, slept at the League, and, for sustenance, depended largely on Eakins, who brought him home for meals. The painter Frank Linton reported that as an artist Schenck "never seemed to progress much—not much will."[23] After Schenck left Philadelphia he settled in the country on Long Island. He built his own house, lived alone, raised his own

The Bohemian (Portrait of Franklin Louis Schenck), ca. 1890. *Oil on canvas, 23 ⅞ x 19 ¾ in., Philadelphia Museum of Art, gift of Mrs. Thomas Eakins and Miss Mary Adeline Williams.* **Always out of money, Franklin Schenck lived at the League and depended on Eakins for his meals.**

food, and is said to have painted romantic landscapes, rather like those of Ralph Albert Blakelock.[24] While a sympathetic, even fascinating, character, he never did anything with distinction and was a dropout and failure by the usual social standards. But of course, to Eakins, as his portrait series shows, failure could be complicated, fascinating, and even heroic.

In *The Bohemian*, Eakins painted Schenck facing toward the left, with a dreamy expression. As with the portrait of Reynolds, the right side of his face is completely lost in shadow. Writers often note how Eakins penetrated the depths of human personality, when in fact he did the opposite. Schenck's face is intriguing because it has no expression and betrays no emotion. Thus, we can read almost anything into it. Although we view him from an intimate distance, he seems completely unaware of our presence, as if lost in a trance.

The Special Companion: Samuel Murray

Less striking than the paintings just discussed, but fascinating as a biographical document, is a fourth portrait of this period. It portrays Samuel Murray,
with whom Eakins formed the deepest emotional attachment of his mature
life. Murray joined Eakins's orbit in November of 1886, when he was just seventeen. Of poor Irish background, he was the eleventh of twelve children, the
son of a stonecutter employed by Woodland Cemetery in Philadelphia.
Although twenty-five years separated them in age, the two almost immediately became inseparable companions. Within a year or so of their meeting,
Murray began to work alongside Eakins in the Chestnut Street studio, first as
an assistant, and then as a sculptor in his own right. They also relaxed
together, going out as a pair for dinner or social excursions, and swimming,
boating, cycling, and camping in the woods. Eakins's wife usually did not
accompany their frequent excursions, but remained at home, doing housework.

As Goodrich has phrased it, Murray soon "became like a son to the older
man"—or, if we to view the situation slightly differently, Murray became
attached to Eakins in a fashion strikingly similar to that in which young men
attached themselves to the poet Walt Whitman.[25]
Hendricks has noted of Eakins's relationship with
Murray: "We do not know whether their relationship was partly a sexual one, and it may be significant that Murray did not marry until a few months
before Eakins died, and neither had children."[26]
Whether or not their relationship was sexual, the
two men were devoted to one another. As has been
noted, Murray later claimed that during the artist's
final illness, he spent the last two weeks, day and
night, by his side, holding his hand, and that Eakins
would allow no one else to feed him, refusing to be
fed by his wife or Addie Williams.

Descriptions of Murray indicate that he was a
jokester and raconteur. Eakins's portrait, however,
shows him with a solemn expression, looking off to
the right. His dark coat blends into the dark background, but the pallor of his face is emphasized.
Only the loose purple tie, both flamboyant and
"artistic" by the standards of the period, provides

Portrait of Samuel Murray, 1889. *Oil on canvas, 24 ×
20 in., collection of the Mitchell Museum at Cedarhurst,
Mt. Vernon, Ill., gift of the John R. and Eleanor R.
Mitchell Foundation.* **Samuel Murray came to study
with Eakins at the age of seventeen, and soon
became his inseparable companion.**

a hint of his extroverted character. Schendler notes of Eakins's portrait of Murray, "Weakness contends with strength in that face . . . The promise of youth is undercut in a way by a softness, a lack of deeply defined intellectuality in the boy . . . The profound qualification of the romantic effect distinguished the portrait and accounts for its life."[27] As a portrait of a companion, even possibly a lover (a term that could mean a variety of things), the canvas is somewhat surprising, both because it is by no means flattering, and because it bears so little relationship to what we know from other sources about Murray's character and temperament.

Two Cowboys and a Black Cat

A more ambitious painting from this period, *Home Ranch* (1888, Philadelphia Museum of Art) comes closer to unlocking Eakins's inner feelings about Murray and about the significance of the friendship between the two men. The painting shows a singing, guitar-playing Franklin Schenck in an outfit of leather and fringe, part of the collection of cowboy costumes that Eakins brought back from his 1887 trip to the Dakotas (where he also acquired a horse, Billy, and a pony, Baldy). Goodrich has complained that the painting "has an air of masquerade" and that it shows Schenck, who was not a real cowboy, "dressed up as a cowboy."[28] To a postmodern sensibility, however, this element of pretense is precisely what makes the painting fascinating. Moreover, from our present-day perspective it is hard not to be influenced by the fact that such costumes have come to be a feature of gay culture, figuring prominently in films such as *Midnight Cowboy*, about a young stud's adventures in the night world of New York, or Andy Warhol's *Lonesome Cowboys*, about what lonely young men like to do with each other when they're out on the range. In fact, Eakins's painting is about both loneliness and the nature of attachments between men. Though not sexually explicit, it seems to carry a strong homosexual subtext.

Once again, Schenck stares off into space with an unfocused look. Schenck's manner suggests that his song is a sad one. His glance does not connect with anyone or anything, but he carries two phallic substitutes, his gun and his guitar, and significantly, the guitar points in the direction of an attractive young man seated at a table slightly in the background, holding a fork in his hand and gazing at Schenck with an expression of loneliness and longing. It seems no accident that this background figure is a portrait of Samuel Murray, the young man to whom Eakins was "romantically" attached.

Home Ranch. *Oil on canvas, 24 x 20 in., Philadelphia Museum of Art, gift of Mrs. Thomas Eakins and Miss Mary Adeline Williams.* **Samuel Murray and Franklin Schenck perform as lonesome cowboys, in costumes that Eakins brought back from the Dakotas.**

Between the figures, almost invisible, is a black cat, with its back arched in fright or anger. One can construe this humorously, as a hint that Schenk is caterwauling (early cowboy songs generally featured yodeling and falsetto). In addition, this cat brings to mind similar cats or references to cats in some of Eakins's other paintings, such as the distressed black cat in *Home Scene*, the cat in Eakins's portrait of *Kathrin*, and even the cat-like hands of the hysterical mother in *The Gross Clinic*. If we view the painting as a study of male friendship (or of something slightly more than just friendship—of male love that is felt but unfulfilled), the cat suggests a female presence that stands in the way of such connections.

Women in Pink

By 1892 the Philadelphia Art Students League had completely dissolved, and at about that time Eakins resigned from the Society of American Artists in New York, which had rejected his work from its last three exhibitions. Eakins continued to teach, lecturing on anatomy at the National Academy of Design from 1888 to 1895, at Cooper Union from 1891 to 1898, and for brief periods at the Art Students League of New York, the Art Students League of Washington, the Brooklyn Art Guild, and the Drexel Institute in Philadelphia. The early 1890s, however, was one of the most isolated periods of his career, when his paintings were regularly excluded from exhibitions, critics completely ignored him, and he had no organized body of students or followers.

It is probably no coincidence that Eakins began to take up portraits of women in a serious way shortly before 1890, for this was when the Art Students League began to fall apart. Like many artists, Eakins seems to have struggled for years to master certain themes that clearly had a deeper significance for him. One of the most evident is the theme of a woman in pink, with which he struggled for roughly twenty years. His five major renderings of this subject include some of the most celebrated and most emotionally gripping paintings of Eakins's late years, including *Amelia Van Buren*, *The Concert Singer*, and *The Actress*. (When the Eakins memorial exhibition came to Philadelphia in 1917, Helen Henderson hailed *The Concert Singer* as "without doubt the most purely beautiful thing that Eakins did.")[29] Analyzing these paintings as a group, exploring how they changed from one to the next, brings out themes and emotional nuances that are less clear if we simply examine them individually, and suggests reasons for the shifts in their emotional undercurrents.

Numerous clues suggest that these paintings related directly to Eakins's traumatic experiences with his mother. They all explore depression, and Eakins systematically altered his sitters to make them appear close to his mother's age at the time of her final illness.

From Blonde to Gray

The first of these paintings of women in pink is Eakins's portrait *Miss Amelia C. Van Buren*, executed just three or four years after he was fired from the

Pennsylvania Academy. With the exception of *The Agnew Clinic*, which is centered around a female patient, it may be the first major painting of a woman that Eakins undertook after his dismissal.[30]

Goodrich declared that Amelia Van Buren must have been a "complex personality," but we have few facts with which to support or reject this hypothesis.[31] Van Buren came from Detroit, and both her parents had died by the time she studied with Eakins at the Pennsylvania Academy, between 1884 and 1885. When he was dismissed in 1886, she was away in Detroit. Frank Stephens specifically mentioned her name in his campaign against Eakins, insisting both that she had posed in the nude and also that Eakins had taken her aside and "exposed himself" to her. Despite these allegations and the consequent rumors that circulated around her, she later returned to Philadelphia and stayed for long periods with Eakins and his wife. Given Eakins's preoccupation with the nude, and our knowledge that Van Buren undressed for him and that he undressed for her, it is puzzling that none of his surviving photographs or paintings record her naked form. His portrait presents her completely enveloped in clothing.

Amelia Van Buren Sitting with Cat On Shoulder, ca. 1891. *Platinum print, 3 ½ x 4 in., courtesy of The Pennsylvania Academy of the Fine Arts, Philadelphia, Charles Bregler's Thomas Eakins Collection, purchased with the partial support of the Pew Memorial Trust.* Amelia Van Buren was thirty-three in 1889. When he painted her, Eakins made her look much older. RIGHT Miss Amelia Van Buren, ca. 1891. *Oil on canvas, 45 x 32 in., The Phillips Collection, Washington D.C.* Van Buren suffered from an emotional illness, probably manic-depression like Eakins's mother.

There is little information about Van Buren's subsequent life and professional career. Periodically, she returned to Detroit to be treated for an illness, which appears to have been psychological in nature. A letter to Susan Eakins indicates that she was diagnosed as neurasthenic. She wrote: "I have at last discovered that the trouble with me is in my head it is exhausted by worry or something or other and I must just have patience until it is rested. . . . so provoking to have nothing the matter with you and yet be everlastingly ill." Presumably she suffered from depression or manic-depression, and thus aspects of her behavior must have resembled that of Eakins's mother. She never married and spent her later years in the Carolinas, where she lived with the photographer Eva Lawrence Watson.

No paintings by Van Buren survive, although she did exhibit photographs, so one can only guess what she was doing during her long years of artistic study. Perhaps she made paintings that were destroyed, but she did not pursue a professional career that led to sales or that can be traced through the records of public art exhibitions.[32] Nearly all we know about Amelia Van Buren is expressed in Eakins's portrait of her, and in some photographs made around the same time, which may or may not have been taken by Eakins. Van Buren was still alive when Goodrich wrote his monograph, but when he wrote to her asking for information she replied rather surprisingly that she had no particular reminiscences of Eakins.[33]

The portrait of Van Buren has always been regarded as one of Eakins's greatest works. Indeed, it was featured on the cover of the catalogue when a group of Eakins's paintings was shown at the National Portrait Gallery in London in 1993.[34] Yet previous scholarship does little to explain why the picture should be considered significant. Writers seem to circle around this question, leaving the central issue unexplored. William Inness Homer, for example, has written, "The quiet, yet dynamic integration of the volumes of Van Buren's head, arms, and torso brings the painting to life, without any hint of stiffness. Such a painting can hold its own against the best work of Eakins's contemporaries, no matter what their country of origin."[35] Such statements make it plain that the painting is a fine one, but do not clearly articulate why this is so.

The painting shows a woman of about fifty, with gray streaks in her hair, seated in an ornate dark wood chair with a fan in her right hand. The sense of scale is ambiguous; although Van Buren looks monumental, she is small in relation to the chair in which she sits. In photographs by Eakins the actual chair appears to be much smaller and less threatening. This chair, with its worn velvet upholstery, appears frequently in Eakins's portraits and seems to have had personal meaning for him. One cannot help wondering, however, whether it was simply a studio prop, or whether it was somehow connected with events in Eakins's life. Could this have been a chair in which Eakins's mother used, or even sat in during her final illness?[36]

The color scheme relies on a harmony of pink against brown, the pink consisting of the woman's dress, which is set off by the rich browns of the carved mahogany chair and the muddy dullness of its worn velvet upholstery.

The coherence of the pyramidal composition is belied by the sitter's slumped pose. She gazes vacantly to the side, looking into the picture's light source, the windows of Eakins's studio. Her eyes do not meet ours. Her tilted head rests on her bent left arm. She wears a pink dress, the front of which is covered with an apron-like attachment, decorated with a delicate floral pattern. It covers her lap, runs up her chest, and wraps tightly around her neck so that little flesh is visible. A feeling of despondency pervades the figure. Schendler describes her as "a small woman with a large brooding spirit . . . Miss Van Buren is graying, disappointed, her dress an elaborate and beautiful statement of unfulfillment."[37]

Van Buren's face is expressive through its very lack of animation. Her mouth is tight and straight, and her eyes are unfocused. Eakins provides hints that she may have been weeping. The edge of her right eye looks red, as if from crying. On the other side, a curious highlight just to the side of her mouth suggests the shape and location of a tear that has run down her cheek. Scholars have read the expression in a variety of ways: some read her expression as cynical, others see "resigned acceptance of unhappy realities."[38] But the consensus is that she is unhappy.

To Goodrich, Eakins simply recorded Van Buren as she was. He describes the painting as the "perfection of realistic representation."[39] But when we compare the portrait with surviving photographs of her (often attributed to Eakins but very likely taken by her companion, Eva Lawrence Watson) we can see that Eakins took great liberties with her appearance. The most obvious distinction is her age. Amelia Van Buren had blonde hair and was thirty-five when Eakins painted her. In Eakins's painting she has gray hair and looks as though she is in her early fifties. Eakins also made Van Buren look more melancholy than the photographs. To be sure, the photographs also have a moody quality, although not to the same extent.

For individuals who suffer from bipolar disorder, the aftermath of mania is lassitude, and that is how Van Buren is portrayed—slumped in the chair, exhausted. Yet although her pose is limp, it strongly implies the possibility of movement, because of the bent limbs and the fashion in which the bent fingers of the left hand come close to forming a fist. Thus, it suggests the possibility of manic behavior, either just before or just after the moment we witness.

Overall, it is apparent that Eakins emphasized those aspects of Van Buren's appearance and demeanor that most resembled those of his mother at the time of her death: he aged her and imparted to her qualities of bipolar illness.

Eakins also did something else that is curious: he made the figure androgynous. While the dress seems to assert that this is a woman, this fact is not very clear from the anatomy itself. The muscular arm and strongly emphasized shoulder appear rather masculine. The figure's breasts are not clearly defined and read like uncomfortable padding placed on top of this bony armature. Two prominent knobs on arms of the chair, however, seem to function in some peculiar way as breast substitutes. Indeed, everything feminine about the figure—the dress, the flower printed fabric, the slight suggestion of breasts, the oriental fan—seems detachable: we can easily imagine this as a rendering of a man in woman's clothes. Schendler seems to have sensed this androgynous quality. In an oddly male chauvinist phrase, he noted that Van Buren is "almost masculine in the quality of her understanding."[40]

Yet while in many ways the portrayal is manlike, in a sly pun, Eakins places the fan on Van Buren's lap in such a way that it refers to the thing women lack, that prevents them from being a man: a penis. It is surely no accident that this fan seems to be Japanese, for as was also apparent in the portrait of his wife, Eakins viewed the fashion for things Japanese as the epitome of feminine foolishness. In short, Eakins may have been intrigued by the fact that female and male traits are only marginally different, at the same time that he viewed women as defective, inferior versions of men, both from the physical and the emotional standpoint.

Interestingly, there is a doppelgänger to this portrait. Although Susan Eakins largely abandoned painting after her marriage, she did execute a portrait of her husband sitting in a chair very similar to the one in which he portrayed Amelia Van Buren, assuming a strikingly similar pose. The date of the painting is not certain, but it may well date from about the time that she also painted his likeness for *The Agnew Clinic*—1889. The painting seems to ask, what would it be like for Eakins to become Amelia Van Buren? Surely in some sense this is a rejoinder to the question posed by the Van Buren portrait— what would it be like for her to become a man? Since Van Buren was clearly a surrogate for Eakins's mother, both questions lead to a more disturbing one: what if Eakins was like his crazy mother?

Singing and Screaming

Eakins followed his portrait of Amelia Van Buren with a more ambitious painting of a woman in pink, *The Concert Singer*, a portrait of Weda Cook. Born in Camden, New Jersey, Cook made her debut at the Pennsylvania Academy of Music when she was only sixteen, and thereafter often performed in Philadelphia, including at Eakins's Philadelphia Art Students League. [41]

The painting shows Weda Cook during a performance, isolated on stage in a radiant rose pink gown. She is framed by the hand and baton of the conductor at the lower left, a single palm frond at the upper left, and a bouquet of roses lying at her feet at the lower right, as if just thrown from the audience.

Susan Macdowell Eakins, Portrait of Thomas Eakins, *possibly 1889, based on photograph of ca. 1889. Oil on canvas, 50 x 40 in., Philadelphia Museum of Art, gift of Charles Bregler.*

Weda Cook noted that Eakins's inspiration for the painting was a picture of the composer Jules Massenet (1842–1912) at the organ, accompanying his wife, who was shown with her mouth open in song. The open-mouthed pose fascinated Eakins, and he decided to make it the subject of a painting. So he portrayed Cook with her mouth open and throat muscles tense. Her head is tilted slightly upward and she gazes away from us, above the audience, completely absorbed in the music. She reported that at each posing session, Eakins had her sing the opening bars of "O Rest in the Lord" from Mendelssohn's *Elijah* oratorio. In the painting, the tension of her throat was intended to match this specific passage. Indeed, to make his intention plain, Eakins personally carved the opening notes of the song into the frame, declaring that to musicians this addition "emphasized the expression of the face and pose of the figure."[42] Hendricks has proposed that we can identify the specific word that she is singing, the "for" in the phrase "Wait patiently for him."[43] While her eyes are not so obviously red rimmed as those of many of Eakins's sitters, they are

The Concert Singer, 1892. Oil on canvas, 75 ⅜ x 54 ⅜ in.,
*Philadelphia Museum of Art, gift of Mrs. Thomas Eakins and Miss
Mary Adeline Williams.* Weda Cook posed for two years for
The Concert Singer but broke off seeing Eakins after the
suicide of Ella Crowell. Eakins completed the painting by
working from her empty dress and shoes.

surrounded by a flush of red and deep shadows that make it look as though she might be crying.

Eakins was even more obsessive than usual in devising the geometry and mechanics of this painting. He created a grid on the studio wall behind the sitter and marked it with little strips of cloth to make sure that she always stood in the same place and held exactly the same pose. Cook later recalled that he would look at her "as if through a microscope," and that if there was a wrinkle across her bodice he would put it in.[44] He worked with irritating slowness. Throughout the process, Eakins pressured Cook to undress, although she was unwilling to do so. He once got her down to her underwear. Cook found the whole procedure tiring and stressful, and felt relieved that Samuel Murray was always present, since she did not feel comfortable with Eakins alone.[45]

Stylistically *The Concert Singer* is unusual in Eakins's oeuvre, since it contains clear references to the work of European artists of the "feminine" and "modern" sort whom he usually ignored or spoke about disparagingly. The general subject and the device of the cut-off arm and palm tree clearly pay homage to the work of Edgar Degas, particularly to his paintings and pastels of café singers.[46] The placement of a full-length figure against an indeterminate, smoky background surely owes a debt to James Abbott McNeill Whistler and to his full-length renderings of musicians, such as the much publicized portrait of the Spanish violinist Pablo de Sarasate (1884, Carnegie Museum of Art, Pittsburgh).[47] The sensitively brushed flowers on the stage at the right resemble both the work of Henri Fantin-Latour, and the wreath paintings of John La Farge, which Eakins could easily have seen in New York.[48]

Indeed, in no other painting of his career did Eakins so downplay the masculine posturings that were usually a mannerism of his work, and perhaps in no other painting did he approach more closely the themes that frightened him most. For despite its stiff and frozen quality, the painting is simultaneously emotionally arresting and ominous. In this treatment of a seemingly innocuous subject, Eakins succeeded in communicating intense sorrow. No writer on Eakins, has offered more than formal description of the painting, or provided a convincing explanation for its emotional power, for the way it seems to touch on feelings that are profoundly tragic. But the picture's aura makes sense if we look at it as yet another attempt by Eakins to come to terms with his mother. As with Amelia Van Buren, Eakins aged his model. In 1890, when Cook posed for *The Concert Singer*, she was only twenty-three, although Eakins made her look considerably older—again, moving toward the age of his mother at the time of her death. He also portrayed her in a way that evokes bipolar illness. Singing, of course, is often very close to screaming. It seems likely that for Eakins, Weda Cook's notes are simply a more controlled, more orderly form of his mother's screams during her fits of mania.

The words of the song, "O Rest in the Lord," are clearly significant, since they allude to death and to the eventual, fatal outcome of his mother's illness. The disembodied hand of the conductor plays an important role in this fantasy. This seemingly unobtrusive element serves to maintain order, keeping the frightening chaos of female emotions under masculine control.[49]

Perhaps because of its emotional intensity, Eakins found it difficult to finish the painting. He worked on it for two full years, with Cook coming to pose for three or four days each week when she was not away on concert tours. Toward the end he insisted that she stand rigidly in position for long periods, while he looked at her and did nothing, or else he fiddled with details of her dress or slippers, making seemingly insignificant changes.[50] Schendler has commented, "The time he took for this very American masterpiece may hint of renewed psychic difficulty," although he did not speculate further about what this "psychic difficulty" might have been.[51]

In the end, the physical and emotional strain of sitting for Eakins exhausted Cook's patience. ("I got to loathe it," she later told Goodrich.")[52] According to some accounts, Cook stopped posing because she had heard scandalous stories about Eakins's relationship with Ella Crowell.[53] She may also have simply grown tired of the demands of posing, and Eakins's pressure for her to undress in front of him. In any event, she walked out just before the painting was completed, so Eakins was forced to finish the painting by hanging her dress over her shoes. Some years later she wrote to him, requesting to obtain the portrait, but when the artist wrote back he declared that he would not part with it, adding, "I have many memories of it, some happy, some sad."[54]

Eakins thought highly of the painting and hung it over the mantelpiece in the downstairs parlor of the family home, replacing the highly romantic portrait of Elizabeth Crowell that had hung there earlier as a kind of silent rebuke to his wife. *The Concert Singer* remained with him until his death, and was later given by his widow and Addie Williams to the Philadelphia Museum of Art.

The most notable difference between *Amelia Van Buren* and *The Concert Singer* is that *The Concert Singer* moves a step closer to the most frightening aspect of his mother's illness—her fits of hysteria—although through music the fear is softened, romanticized, and controlled. But there is another significant contrast between the two. Eakins showed Amelia Van Buren demurely clothed, in a dress that comes up to her chin. In contrast, he portrayed Weda Cook in a low-cut sleeveless dress, which reveals much of her shoulders, neck, and arms, and comes down nearly to her breasts. Moreover, not only does the likeness of Weda Cook reveal more flesh, but the handling of the painting is softer, more sensual, and more romantic, than the earlier picture. (As with the Van Buren portrait, however, the handling of the anatomy is somewhat strange. Despite the low-cut dress, there is no sign of cleavage. The slight bulge of the breasts could easily be padded fabric.) Overall, the second picture seems more tender, as though through the process of making these pictures Eakins was working through his psychological anxieties about his mother, and becoming more responsive to women.

The Rosebud

Eakins's next portrait of a woman in pink, a depiction of Weda Cook's cousin Maud, though much less ambitious in scale, in significant ways turns up the heat, for it is both more sensual and more intimate. Writers have described the work with words like "sensual," "invasive," and "erotic."[55] The art critic Peter Schjeldahl has even declared that the portrait of Maud Cook is "one of the most erotically charged pictures I have ever seen."[56] Eakins called the painting "a big rosebud," a phrase with an implicitly sexual significance, since roses are a traditional symbol of unravished virginity. Indeed, the sitter's pink blouse and pink undergarment look like the unfolding petals of a rose, which can be peeled back and opened up to reveal what is inside.

Like all Eakins's paintings of women, this portrait is serious in mood, but for once the overall effect is more wistful than tragic. The emotional quality

Maud Cook (Mrs. Robert C. Reid), 1895. *Oil on canvas, 24 x 20 in., Yale University Art Gallery, bequest of Stephen Carlton Clark, B.A. 1903.* Art critic Peter Scheldahl has termed Eakins's likenesss of Maud Cook "one of the most erotically charged pictures I have ever seen."

of the painting even suggests something maternal and comforting in Maud Cook's character. Of all Eakins's paintings of women this is the one that comes closest to the adjective "lyrical." In a passage noting that most of Eakins's portraits of women are unflattering, Darrel Sewell has commented, "*Maud Cook* is a rare example of Eakins's studying the physical beauty of a young woman."[57] Interestingly, for once Eakins offered the slight hint of a cleft between his model's breasts rather than treating her chest as an absolutely flat surface.

Ella's Death and the Rowland Portrait

From 1890 to 1895, Eakins's paintings of women in pink form a smooth progression, both visually and emotionally. In general, they move toward an increasingly gentle, romantic form of treatment, and they seem to express some sort of process of emotional healing. Around 1895, however, Eakins broke the rhythm of this series. In that year he abruptly dropped such romantic subject matter, and he did not revisit the theme of women in pink for eight years. Why did this series break off? Significantly, in 1895 Ella Crowell began to exhibit strange behavior and in 1897, at the age of twenty-four, she killed herself. Even before Ella's death her situation seems to have caused considerable tension between Eakins and his sister. After Ella's death, Frances and her husband broke off all relations with Eakins. The year of Ella's first breakdowns marks the point at which Eakins ceased painting his romantic pictures.

Eakins's first painting after Ella's death was a portrait of the physicist Henry Rowland, which he started about three weeks after the tragedy. Rowland was a physicist of genius, whose most famous invention was a machine for producing concave diffraction gratings to map the spectrum of solar light. This machine could engrave 14,400 lines into a five-inch plate. Its detail and accuracy made possible the new science of spectroscopy, and made it possible to solve such problems as the chemical composition of the sun's atmosphere.[58]

On several occasions, Eakins seems to have used mathematics and perspective as a way of retreating from emotional difficulties. At the time of his mother's death he began making his rowing pictures, his first paintings to be based on elaborate perspective studies. The portrait of Rowland seems to represent a similar response to Ella's death. The painting is one of his most extreme attempts to heroicize a male, scientific figure, and to express the world through perspective and scientific formulas.

Eakins portrayed Rowland seated in a chair with a diffraction grating in his hand. His engine for ruling sits just behind him and in the background his assistant, Mr. Schneider, works at his lathe. Eakins made a careful perspective drawing of Rowland's machine and in his painting he used reflections and highlights to evoke the way that the wheels moved. Moreover, not only did Eakins carefully represent Rowland's apparatus, but he inscribed the frame of the painting with diagrams and formulas representing Rowland's principal scientific contributions, such as his analysis of solar light, of electrical resistance, of the speed of light, of the mechanical value of heat, and of the sharpness of lines in the spectrum. Rowland seems to have provided much of this material, and the carvings on the frame imitate his handwriting. To most viewers, however, this material must have seemed completely esoteric, since even physicists have had difficulty making sense of the different formulas. At some level, in short, Eakins was both engaging in a game of one-upsmanship, and retreating into a private world of arithmetic and science oddly separate from observable visual reality.[59]

Despite all this, however, the painting is one of Eakins's most moody. Rowland emerges from a background of turbulent shadows. He appears both isolated and troubled, although we cannot tell whether his sorrow is simply the exhaustion of the dedicated scientist, or stems from some other cause.

The next year, in 1898, Eakins began producing large paintings of male sports, including *Taking the Count* (1898), *Salutat* (1898), *Between Rounds* (1899), and *Wrestlers* (1899). Although sometimes rather roughly executed, these are ambitious works. In fact, *Taking the Count* is Eakins's second largest painting, being a little smaller than *The Agnew Clinic* but larger than *The Gross Clinic*.[60] Eakins focused on such subjects for eight years.

Professor Henry A. Rowland, 1897. Oil on canvas, 80 ¼ x 54 in., © Addison Gallery of American Art, Phillips Academy, Andover, Massachusetts, all rights reserved, gift of Stephen C. Clark, Esq. Perspective, mathematics, and science dominate Eakins's portrait of Henry Rowland, which he started a few weeks after the suicide of Ella Crowell. Eakins even carved scientific formulas into his handmade frame.

Male Bodies on Display

Eakins is said to have been introduced to prizefighting by his companion Samuel Murray and the sportswriter Clarence Cranmer (who handled sales and correspondence for Susan Eakins after the artist's death). Eakins attended fights with Murray several times a week" and according to Cranmer saw some 300 rounds of fighting before he started the boxing paintings.[61] While he worked on the paintings, the fighters would come to Eakins's studio and use it as a workout place, and Eakins himself grew expert at mimicking boxing motions.[62] Pugilism," Goodrich notes, "was not yet a fashionable sport proper for gentleman and ladies to attend."[63] In fact, the world of boxing was entirely male, and this no doubt was one of the things about the sport that strongly appealed to Eakins at this time. Like *Swimming*, Eakins's boxing and wrestling pictures are about a world from which women are excluded. In this period, however, even the male world was not hospitable to Eakins, since he had no following and no critical support, and he was increasingly shut out of art organizations and exhibitions. Not surprisingly, therefore, in his pictures of this period, even the male world seems more violent and less friendly—a place not of harmonious male fellowship but of conflict.

Eakins strongly empathized with boxers, and saw their brutal profession as parallel to his own as a painter. Thus, when Sadakichi Hartmann praised Eakins in his *History of American Art*—the first time Eakins had ever been singled out in such a history as significant—Eakins rewarded him with the gift of the study for his painting *Salutat*, which shows a victorious boxer, raising his right arm in triumph. On the back, Eakins added an inscription: "He salutes the cheering crowd with his victorious right hand." Those words suggest a parallel between the boxer's triumph, achieved with his right hand, and Eakins's artistic victory, won by painting with his right hand.

Curiously, however, Eakins never pictured actual fighting. All the paintings portray a pause in the action, and the figures never make eye contact, as they would if they were actually engaged. As Carl Smith has noted, "Eakins's boxers are lonely and even reflective figures, [as] he recasts them as introspective artists like himself."[64] Many of his protagonists are not so much heroes as antiheroes. In casting Billy Smith as the victorious protagonist of *Salutat*, Eakins brought attention to a relatively little known featherweight fighter, who never won his class. In *Between Rounds* he recorded a documented fight at the Arena on April 22, 1898, that Smith went on to lose.[65]

The bouts that Eakins portrayed took place in the Arena, located on the northwest corner of Broad and Cherry Streets, diagonally across from the Pennsylvania Academy. (Interestingly, the building was constructed in 1886, the very year that Eakins was fired from the Academy.) Eakins was clearly fascinated by the contrast between the rough, low-class world of the Arena and the polite pretensions of the Academy, and through various details he emphasized its class distinctions. For example, in *Salutat* the contrast between the red of Billy Smith's head and neck and the pallor of the rest of his body indicates that he makes his living from weekday labor, and has picked up a sunburn from working outdoors. As a group, Eakins's fight pictures were clearly a conscious contrast to the moralizing and "feminine" paintings generally displayed in exhibitions at the Pennsylvania Academy.

Perhaps the most disturbing of these paintings is *Taking the Count*, an awkwardly resolved composition, which shows two boxers at the climax of a fight.[66] Kneeling at the right is Joe Mack, the younger of the two fighters, whose square jaw, callow good looks, and blank expression provide a kind of parody of the vacuous poster boys pictured by illustrators like Joseph Leydendecker and James Montgomery Flagg.[67] Mack

Taking the Count, 1898. Oil on canvas, 96 ⁵⁄₁₆ x 84 ⁵⁄₁₆ in., Yale University Art Gallery, Whitney Collections of Sporting Art, given in memory of Harry Payne Whitney, B.A. 1894, and Payne Whitney, B.A.. 1898, by Francis P. Garvan, B.A. 1897, M.A. (Hon.) 1922, June 2, 1932. Eakins included a portrait of himself under the crotch of the victorious boxer.

has clearly been brought down by a blow to the jaw. He rests on one knee, looking up at the crotch of his adversary, evidently deciding whether to rise and take more punishment. At the left, his triumphant antagonist, Charlie McKeever, whose face is older, more irregular, and more brutal, stands ready to sock Mack again if he attempts to get up. Between the two figures is the tuxedo-wearing referee, Henry Walter Schlichter, who is counting off seconds. His eyes do not engage either of the fighters, and his pose is stiff and awkward—one writer has compared him to a sleepwalker. Perhaps the most beautifully rendered passage is the boxing shorts of the older, victorious boxer, Charlie McKeever. Eakins lavished care

Taking the Count (detail), 1898. *Oil on canvas, 96 ⁵⁄₁₆ x 84 ⁵⁄₁₆ in., Yale University Art Gallery, Whitney Collections of Sporting Art, given in memory of Harry Payne Whitney, B.A. 1894, and Payne Whitney, B.A.. 1898, by Francis P. Garvan, B.A. 1897, M.A. (Hon.) 1922, June 2, 1932.*

on every stretch and seam, particularly in the groin area, which seems to bulge with triumph.

McKeever's shorts also draw attention to the oddest feature of the painting. Eakins included a self-portrait, as witness and voyeur, within the narrow wedge created by the boxer's legs, just below his crotch. The placement is sly—a kind of furtive joke that might easily pass undetected. Yet, once one notices it, the painting never looks quite the same. For surely it is no accident that Eakins juxtaposed himself with male genitals. After all, he was fired from the Academy for exposing male genitals to his classes. In some way Eakins clearly intended to associate himself and his identity as an artist with male genitals and their display.

The implications of McKeever's genitals become even more disturbing in the oil study for this painting, in which Eakins sketched the figures completely nude. Thus, it is clear that the glance of the downed boxer is directed toward the victor's penis. In addition, the gesture of the referee's hand seems like a

Taking the Count (study), 1898. *Oil, 18 x 16 ⅛ in., Hirshhorn Museum and Sculpture Garden, Smithsonian Institution, gift of Joseph H. Hirshhorn, 1966.* Eakins's study for *Taking the Count* shows the boxers with no clothes, although the referee is dressed. RIGHT Between Rounds, 1899. *Oil on canvas, 50 ¼ x 40 in., Philadelphia Museum of Art, gift of Mrs. Thomas Eakins and Miss Mary Adeline Williams.* The lightweight boxer Billy Smith rests between rounds in a fight that he lost on April 22, 1898.

continuation of the penis, shoving it toward the kneeling figure's face and mouth.

The other fight pictures also seem to devote inordinate attention to crotches and buttocks. In *Between Rounds* (1898–1889), for example, Billy Smith's bulging crotch is almost at the center of the painting, and is certainly the most brightly lit area of the composition.[68] In *The Wrestlers* (1899), the figures are locked in a quasi-erotic embrace, and the victorious figure has achieved "a crotch hold," in wrestling parlance. Eakins also showed two figures at the upper right hand corner—one clothed, the other in his boxing shorts—who are cut off at the waist so that our eyes focus on the groin area.

Salutat (1898) differs from the other paintings in the series in that the boxer's crotch is turned away from us, and turned toward the audience, which is staring at this area and applauding. Our view focuses on the buttocks of the victorious figure, which the water boy behind him is also staring at intently. Goodrich and other scholars have noted that the shorts of the boxer, which are shaped like underwear, are considerably scantier than what fighters actually

The Wrestlers, 1899. *Oil on canvas, 48 ⅜ × 60 in., Columbus Museum of Art, Columbus, Ohio, Museum Purchasse, Derby Fund.*

Study for *Salutat*, 1898. *Oil on canvas, 20 ⅛ × 16 ⅛ in., Carnegie Museum of Art, Pittsburgh, gift of Mr. and Mrs. James H. Beal.* Eakins gave this study to the art critic Sadakichi Hartman, who had praised him in his *History of American Art*. In his inscription Eakins noted that like the boxer, he had fought for victory with his right hand. RIGHT   *Salutat, 1898. Oil on canvas, 50 × 40 in., © Addison Gallery of American Art, Phillips Academy, Andover, Massachusetts, all rights reserved, gift of an anonymous donor.*

wore in the ring during this period, and the buttocks seem to bulge out of this inadequate covering.[69] The effect is arguably more provocative than if the fighter were completely nude.

A peculiar feature of the boxing paintings is the emphasis on the audience, a theme that seems to connect them with his paintings of surgical operations. Eakins seems interested not only in the fact that the nude or partially nude body is on display, but that an audience is looking at it, and that this audience includes identifiable individuals. This emphasis is particularly striking in *Salutat*.[70] Indeed, the writer of an article in *The Art Collector*, published in January 1899, felt that this element disrupted the painting, and that "the audience is too obtrusive."[71] Notably, all these figures were members of Eakins's immediate circle. From left to right they are his relative by marriage Louis Kenton, the reporter Clarence Cranmer, the painter David Wilson, the lithographer and photographer Louis Husson, the sculptor Samuel Murray, and the artist's father, Benjamin Eakins. (Eakins also made separate portraits of most of these figures.) Eakins's intention was clearly to portray a "family" of some sort, although the figures are oddly dissociated from each other, standing independently and not sharing the same light and space.[72]

Year of Reckoning: 1900

By the end of the 1890s, Eakins's interest in fight scenes had run its course and he turned back to portraiture, generally working on a small scale. Of particular interest are a group of six such portraits, portraying himself and the three people with whom he shared a home: his father, his wife, and Addie Williams. All six were produced around 1899–1900, when Eakins was sixty-five or sixty-six. They convey a sense of a summing up, even reckoning, as Eakins entered a new century, and moved into old age.

Eakins probably painted his father at this time because the man was in poor health and clearly did not have long to live. (The portrait is dated 1899, and Benjamin Eakins died on December 30 of that year.) The portrait shows Benjamin completely inactive, staring impassively into space. His large shoulders suggest that he was once a powerful figure, but now he is utterly still, and his body, with its dark coat, is almost absorbed into the dark background, which serves as a kind of metaphor for death. The whole point of the painting is the blankness of Benjamin's expression, his incomprehension of what he looks at. Thus, poignantly, the once powerful father figure is now seen as weak, helpless, and childlike—an empty shell that will soon be discarded, allowing his son to take his place. In his handling of the likeness, Eakins seems to play with the relationship between father and son. The upper part of the head resembles Eakins himself, and is nearly a self-portrait. As the life force within him is flickering and dying, Benjamin seems about to turn into his son.

Portrait of Benjamin Eakins, 1899. *Oil on canvas, 24 ⅛ x 20 in., Philadelphia Museum of Art, gift of Mrs. Thomas Eakins and Miss Mary Adeline Williams.* In 1899, a few months before his death, Eakins produced a last likeness of his father staring blankly into space.

Eakins's portrait of his wife (circa 1899) also explores the issues of lifelessness. Seen

Mrs. Thomas Eakins. *Platinum print, 6 ⅛ x 4 ⅛ in., Bryn Mawr College Library, Seymour Adelman Collection.* RIGHT   Mrs. Thomas Eakins, ca. 1899. *Oil on canvas, 28 ⅛ x 16 ⅛ in., Hirshhorn Museum and Sculpture Garden, Smithsonian Institution, gift of Joseph H. Hirshhorn, 1966.* **Eakins's portrait of his wife Susan shows her in close-up, but the expression provides no hint of intimacy.**

close up, she stares out at us—or at her husband—without recognition, withholding intimacy. It would be normal to find some sign of affection between husband and wife, but instead Eakins seems to take pleasure in showing a woman resigned to mistreatment.

Photographs show that Eakins took liberties with his wife's appearance: although by this time her hair was entirely gray, Eakins chose to represent it as almost completely dark, with a prominent gray forelock providing dramatic contrast. There were probably two reasons for this element.

First, it is likely that Eakins was taking an ironic jab at the aestheticism of Whistler. I have suggested earlier that Eakins's first portrait of his wife, *The Artist's Wife and His Setter Dog* was partially conceived as a parody of Whistler, and it seems to me that the late portrait may be such a parody also. Portraits of Whistler himself always featured a gray forelock that served as an emblem of his distinctiveness and eccentricity. Susan's forelock links her with Whistler's example, but also mocks Whistler's ideals, since her graying hair is not a badge of bohemianism, but a sad emblem of encroaching age.

Second, Eakins seems to have wished to show his wife not simply as old, but in the process of becoming old—that is, at a fateful turning point. At age forty-eight she was approaching fifty-two, the age of his mother when she died.[73]

Self Portrait, ca. 1902. *Oil on canvas mounted on fiberboard, 20 x 16 ⅛ in., Hirshhorn Museum and Sculpture Garden, Smithsonian Institution, gift of Joseph H. Hirshhorn, 1966.* In 1902 Eakins painted his self-portrait to gain membership in the National Academy of Design. In his first study, he looks menacing.

A few years later, in 1902, Eakins made a likeness of himself—doing so in response to the requirements of the National Academy of Design, which had just elected him a member. Although Eakins often included himself as an observer or background figure in narrative scenes, this portrait, and the study that he made for it, are the only paintings in which he focused on himself alone.

Comparing the finished portrait with its study reveals that Eakins's apparently honest and casual presentation of himself was carefully calculated for

Self-Portrait, 1902. *Oil on canvas, 30 x 25 in., National Academy of Design, New York.* **In the final painting Eakins appears as a more gentle man, embittered by persecution.**

dramatic effect. The study for this painting shows him in a closely cropped image, peering out at the viewer with down-turned mouth and cocked eyebrow. Kathleen Spies notes that these elements "give the work an overall sinister tone; the artist appears vengeful and angry, even mentally unsound."[74] Eakins clearly recognized that these features, while part of his romantic persona, could easily alienate viewers. Consequently, in the completed work, he made himself less threatening. He used a slightly larger format with his head tilted to one side and shoulder slightly turned, softening the confrontation with the viewer. Eakins showed himself with mussed hair, teary eyes, and a frowning mouth that is accentuated by the sloping lines of his mustache. His careworn appearance is combined with a hard, questioning gaze, however. As Spies notes: "The result is a painting that readily evokes sympathy from the viewer, yet also maintains the accusatory tone present in the first self-portrait."[75] Whereas the study is angry, the second is passive-aggressive. Thus, Eakins consciously promoted himself as the isolated, underappreciated genius.

A Model or a Mistress?

The most mysterious and debated relationship recorded in this series of intimate portraits is that between Eakins and Addie Williams, who also lived in the Eakins household. Addie had been the best friend of Eakins's favorite sister, Margaret. After his father died, Eakins and his wife invited Addie to live in the room which had formerly been occupied by his parents. Eighteen years earlier, after Maggie died, Addie had been invited to join the household but had declined. This time she accepted. She was forty-six.

Addie Williams was distantly related to Eakins, or at least connected by marriage. Margaret McHenry, in her biography of 1946, reported that the Eakinses and the Williamses were related, although Hendricks was unable to establish the connection.[76] Goodrich reports that Addie Williams was Will Crowell's second cousin.[77] Although this makes the relationship with Eakins somewhat remote, the connection is intriguing because of the prevalence with which the charge of "incest" recurs in Eakins's life. Perhaps Eakins was simply attracted to women who were in his house, and thus more easily available for his advances, whether personal or artistic, but we might also consider the possibility that Eakins was particularly attracted to women who were part of his "family." Addie Williams's role is particularly interesting since she was connected with, and thus may have served as a stand-in for, two deceased people of particular significance in Eakins's life: his sister Margaret (to whom she had been close) and his mother.

Shortly after Addie Williams moved in, Eakins painted successive portraits of her that exhibit a striking contrast in mood. As other writers have noted, the first (1899) epitomizes the concept of spinster. Its shows Addie with a chin-high collar, tight bun, tight lips, and stiff posture. She looks impassively to the right. The other (c. 1900) shows a different side of Addie, both literally and figuratively. This time she looks to the left. Her pose is more relaxed, even romantic; her clothes are more flowing. Her head is lowered to one side in a subtle gesture of acquiescence, submission, or thoughtfulness.

Scholars have suggested several reasons for the difference between these two pictures. Goodrich proposed that when the first portrait was painted, Addie was "worried," whereas at the time of the second painting she was "relaxed," since by then she was, in the alleged words of Susan Eakins, "a beloved companion in our house."[78] David Lubin has postulated that Eakins was consciously pairing different visual conventions and decided to cast Addie first as "the lonely old maid," and then as "the old maid in love."[79] Other writers, such as William Inness Homer, have suggested that Eakins had an affair with Addie Williams. Thus, the first painting would show her as sexually inhibited, the second as sexually fulfilled. As has been noted, many of those who knew the artist, including one of his nephews, Samuel Murray, Weda Cook, and Nicholas Douty, believed that Eakins and Addie were sexual partners.

An intriguing bit of evidence on this matter has been overlooked, namely that about eight years after making the two Addie Williams portraits, Eakins

Mary Adeline Williams, 1899. *Oil on canvas, 24 x 20 ¹⁄₁₆ in., Friends of American Art Collection,* © *The Art Institute of Chicago, all rights reserved.* Eakins's first portrait of Addie Williams looks spinster-like and sexually repressed. RIGHT Addie, 1899. *Oil on canvas, 24 ⅛ x 18 ¼ in., Philadelphia Museum of Art, gift of Mrs. Thomas Eakins and Miss Mary Adeline Williams.* In Eakins's second portrait of Addie the face has softened and filled with tender emotion. Some scholars have speculated that this may be because she had become sexually involved with the artist.

expressed a similar dichotomy in two new paintings on the theme of William Rush.

As has been noted, Eakins's reworking of subjects presents a pattern different from that of most artists. Rather than working toward a more complex and definitive treatment of a theme, he tended to progress in the opposite way, toward paintings that are less finished, less coherent, less complete, and less dramatically resolved. This process of deterioration can be observed in the rowing pictures, and perhaps somewhat less dramatically, in the contrast between Eakins's first medical painting, the emotionally arresting *Gross Clinic*, and the somewhat less compelling *Agnew Clinic*. Psychologically, however, the most suggestive instance of this phenomenon is the artist's return to the theme of William Rush at the very end of his artistic career, after an interlude of more than thirty years.

These paintings represent Eakins's last attempt at a subject other than portraiture. The more finished of these two paintings, *William Rush Carving His Allegorical Figure of the Schuylkill River* (Brooklyn Museum) is dated 1908. The other, *William Rush and His Model* (Honolulu Academy of Arts) is unfinished and unsigned. Most likely Eakins was working on it at the time he suffered the stroke that ended his painting career in 1910.

The first painting repeats the subject of Eakins version of 1876–1877, although the composition is less artful. In contrast to the complexly layered forms of the earlier version, the artist's sculptures and tools are spread regularly across the flat background, in a monotonous fashion. In contrast to the unified light of the earlier version, the light illuminates the individual objects, one by one, but does not unify the space as a whole. There are large empty areas and the paint handling is often so rough that one would judge the painting unfinished if it were not signed. As every writer on the painting, from Lloyd Goodrich on has noted, the figure of the sculptor resembles Eakins himself and the disorderly workspace resembles Eakins's own studio. Rather than a well-dressed white woman, the chaperon has become a middle-aged African American woman in contemporary clothes. This makes no sense in the eighteenth-century social context of William Rush, but probably corresponds to the workings of the Eakins household, where black servants, who were the cheapest to hire, probably did much of the cleaning, cooking, and household work. Overall, as Elizabeth Johns has noted, all sense of historical probability has been discarded. "The viewer does not peer into the past," Johns observes. Instead, we are looking at Eakins himself, in his studio.[80]

The second painting is indeterminate in setting, except for the model's tree

William Rush Carving His Allegorical Figure of the Schuylkill River, 1908. *Oil on canvas, 36 × 48 ⅞ in., Brooklyn Museum of Art, Dick S. Ramsay Fund.* **Eakins returned to the theme of William Rush late in two late paintings. The first shows the model standing stiffly, while the sculptor is preoccupied with his work.**

stump pedestal and two distinctly phallic scrolls in the foreground.[81] Once again the figure of William Rush strikingly resembles Eakins, and the setting, to the extent it is delineated, suggests his workshop.

Like the portraits of Addie, the two late versions of William Rush present a striking contrast of mood. In the first, the model has her back turned to us and stands almost ramrod straight. The scowling sculptor looks away from the model, focusing on his carving. The separateness of the two figures is very evident. In the second the treatment of the subject is entirely different. The sculptor, who bears an obvious resemblance to Eakins himself, bows slightly and takes the woman's hand with an almost courtly gesture, so that she can step down from the modeling stand. The model is turned toward us.

Thus, like the portraits of Addie Williams, these paintings form a pair that contrasts a frozen and a more responsive state: a spinsterish portrait and a more sensual and responsive one; a stiff, rigid nude and one that warmly engages the artist. Moreover, there is an interesting link that encourages us to consider the two pairs together, for Addie Williams appears to have posed not only for the portraits but for at least one of the two *William Rush* paintings—

the one that displays full frontal nudity. Along with her hairstyle, the model's large nose and receding chin closely correspond with the portraits of Addie Williams.[82]

The most remarkable thing about the second painting is that the model appears in full frontal nudity, including her pubic hair. This is the only painting of his career in which Eakins revealed the genitals of a woman or portrayed full frontal nudity.

This development clearly represents a psychological turning point of some sort. Most writers have maintained that this second version of the subject is sexually liberated, but I wonder whether this is the case. In fact, the relationship between sculptor and model is curiously formal and inhibited. Leslie Katz notes that the model is "gallantly and respectfully helped by Rush, who holds her hand."[83] Goodrich comments on Rush's gesture of "respect."[84] In short, what is peculiar about the painting is that while the woman fully

William Rush and His Model, 1907–1908. *Oil on canvas, 35 ½ x 47 ½ in., Honolulu Academy of Arts, gift of the Friends of the Academy, 1947.* In the artist's last painting of this theme, a figure who strikingly resembles Eakins takes the model's hand. She is turned toward him in full frontal nudity.

exposes her nudity to the man, they both behave as if this were not the case. William Rush, who is standing in for Eakins, acts as if the woman were fully clothed. Thus, the behavior of the figures seems to deny the very thing that is unusual about the painting.

The fact that Addie Williams posed for this painting clearly says something about Eakins's relationship with her. While it does not resolve whether she and Eakins had an affair, it suggests that she shared his nakedness with him. Given Eakins's behavior in other instances, it seems likely that he also exhibited his nakedness to her. The curious drama which is staged in the painting, however, raises questions about what this sharing of nakedness meant. The strangely formal attitudes of the figures seem to drain the painting of any sexual implications.

Past writers, in short, have oversimplified the mystery of the painting, which presents us with questions of two types. First, why did Eakins both affirm and deny the nudity of the figure, at once fully exposing the woman's body and presenting her in a relationship with another figure that implies she is not actually undressed? Second, why in his various version of William Rush, spread over a period of thirty-five years, did Eakins bring his own family and intimates into the story, including his father, himself, his mother, and Addie Williams? Putting together these two questions, even without coming to an answer to them, we can infer that the paintings of William Rush express something about Eakins's attitude toward the nude that was unusual, and that whatever this was, it was most likely connected with Eakins's family experience and with encounters that took place in the family home.

Seeing Through Clothes

Eakins's paintings of clothed female figures in this period also contain peculiar undercurrents. Lloyd Goodrich has noted that Eakins "liked feminine finery," although he handled it in a different way than most nineteenth-century portrait painters.[85] Whereas an artist like John Singer Sargent used satin dresses to reinforce the glamorous image of his sitters, Eakins used feminine clothing in a way that usually seems at odds with the awkward pose and frozen expression of his subject.

Eakins first portrayed a lonely woman in an evening dress in his portrait of *Letitia Wilson Jordon* (1888; Brooklyn Museum), which shows Jordon elegantly dressed with a fan in her hand, staring off into space with a pensive expression. He returned to this motif in his various paintings of women in pink. For example, Goodrich notes of *Amelia van Buren*, 1890, that "her fine dress does not seem altogether congruous with her melancholy air."[86]

This theme became particularly pronounced in the portraits of women Eakins made after 1900, in which the dresses become increasingly revealing, to the point of seeming incongruous. As Goodrich has noted, Eakins often asked his sitters to pose in low-necked sleeveless or short-sleeved gowns "that left bare the neck, shoulders, arms and upper bosom."[87] *Mrs. Mary Hallock Greenewalt* (1903) and *Miss Eleanor S. F. Pue* (1907) provide instances of this, as does the last major painting that he worked on, a portrait of Helen Montanverde Parker that is generally known as *The Old-Fashioned Dress* (1908).

The Old-Fashioned Dress shows Parker standing with one arm resting on a chair. As the title suggests, the dress is as much the subject of the painting as the sitter. As Helen Parker declared: "Thomas Eakins was not interested in my face—I have always felt a sense of being decapitated—but he was fascinated by my clavicles and the dress."[88] The dress, Parker recalled, was "my grandmother's old silk and pearls." Between sittings, she left the dress in the studio, and Eakins, Susan, and Addie Williams would "pore over it, examining every stitch."[89] The dress was a revealing one, which left much of the chest and shoulders exposed. In Eakins's painting this exposure is emphasized by the fact that it has been put on very much askew, and seems about to fall off the left shoulder.

The painting brings together three incongruous elements that Eakins had previously explored separately and had never combined in one work. First, the elegance of the dress contrasts with the sad but vacant expression of the sitter. Second, the dress hangs oddly on the body, and in fact, seems in danger of falling off. Third, the anatomy of the sitter blurs the distinction between male and female.

Mrs. Mary Hallock Greenewalt, 1903. *Oil on canvas, 36 ⅛ x 24 ⅛ in., The Roland P. Murdock Collection, Wichita Art Museum, Wichita, Kansas.* **The sensual implications of the low-cut dress are at odds with Mary Greenwalt's glassy-eyed expression and muscular stiffness.**

Miss Eleanor S. F. Pue, 1907. *Oil on canvas, 20 x 16 in., Virginia Museum of Fine Arts, Richmond, the State Operating Fund © Virginia Museum of Fine Arts.* **When it was exhibited at The Pennsylvania Academy, Pue's friends mockingly labeled her portrait "The Goddess of Murder."**

All these paintings expose flesh so drastically that they verge on striptease, but they are not erotic by any conventional standard. Indeed, one cannot help suspecting that their imagery is somehow connected with the numerous reports of Eakins's strange behavior—in particular, to the way in which he pressured women to pose for him in the nude, and to the fact that he liked to dress down or even undress in front of them.

Men Who Wear Dresses

In the last decade of his active career, Eakins turned to something new: portraits of the Catholic clergy. Two things prompted this development. One was that his young male companion, Samuel Murray, was Catholic, subsisted largely from portraits of Philadelphia's Catholic clergy, and liked to socialize with them. The other was the development of the bicycle. When the technology of the bicycle was perfected in the 1890s, America experienced a cycling craze. Eakins and Murray took up the new fad, which allowed Eakins, for the first time, to roam outside his immediate neighborhood. The St. Charles Seminary in Overbrook, a school for Catholic priests, made a natural destination for their excursions, being situated about six miles from Eakins's home, on the other side of Fairmount Park. Eakins and Murray would often pedal out there on Sunday morning, and stay for dinner. They would also often attend the late-afternoon Vespers service, during which the seminarians sang Latin chants. This seems to have appealed to both Eakins's interest in languages and his love of music.

In the years just after 1900 Eakins produced fourteen ecclesiastical portraits, representing thirteen people (in other words, he painted one of the clerics twice). One motive for these portraits was probably friendship. Eakins clearly enjoyed the company of the seminarians, and those who gathered around them, who were interesting, well-educated people. In most instances, the subjects he painted were not parish priests but individuals of intellect: teachers, scholars, writers, editors, and administrators, many of whom had studied in Rome or other centers of learning. Several of these individuals went on to outstandingly successful careers in the church hierarchy, including a cardinal, two archbishops, and two bishops. The sole woman he portrayed was a mother superior. They were also mostly of Irish descent, as was Eakins himself. Goodrich has noted that Eakins never painted a Protestant minister, an indication that they probably shunned his company. As Goodrich notes: "his preference for the Catholic clergy was perhaps linked to his alienation from the Wasp social establishment of Philadelphia."[90]

Nonetheless, there is a paradox in Eakins's choice of this subject matter, for as Schendler has noted, Eakins "was an atheist, with a profound distaste for supernatural religion."[91] In fact, Eakins's particular hostility to the Catholic faith is strongly stated in several of his letters from Paris. In a letter of April 1868, for example, Eakins wrote of "the contemptible catholic religion," adding, "when I see genuflexions and crossing & clap trap & wooden virgins gilt & statues in clay with gold crowns all jeweled on their heads I want to laugh always & I pity those who believe in them & I look down on them as my inferiors."[92] In another letter he declared, "Of all reli-

The Old-Fashioned Dress, 1908. Oil on canvas, 60 ⅜ x 40 ¼ in., Philadelphia Museum of Art, gift of Mrs. Thomas Eakins and Miss Mary Adeline Williams. Helen Parker commented that she felt "decapitated" by Eakins's likeness of her. Goodrich has noted that she looks "vacant, almost idiotic . . . half-witted."

gions the Christian is the most intolerant & inconsistent & no one without living here can know what a frightful war it wages against anything that is good."[93] In still another letter from Paris, Eakins also wrote approvingly of those who mocked the Catholic clergy, stating of the French author Rabelais that he was "a writer priest doctor of medicine and hater of priesthood. He wrote a very fine book which I bought and am reading."[94] Although these letters date from early in Eakins's life, his skepticism about Catholic doctrine late in life is also well documented. For example, Eakins told Cardinal Dougherty that he did not believe in the divinity of Christ. Similarly, James L. Wood wrote to Samuel Murray,

Photograph of Helen Parker, ca. 1906. *Private collection.* A contemporary photograph reveals the liberties Eakins took with the appearance of the sitter.

"Eakins used to smile superciliously when anyone spoke about future life, it was contrary to the knowledge of science he possessed."[95]

Thus, Eakins seems to have subverted the usual traditions of ecclesiastical portraiture, taking a portrait format that had traditionally been used to celebrate the church and its doctrines, and employing it to raise questions about the validity of supernatural belief. Eakins seems to have been fascinated by the idea that for all their intellect and finery, these men had dedicated their lives to something false, and were emotionally tortured by that fact. Schendler, for example, sees pain in the eyes of Patrick Garvey (1902), "something approaching anguish" in the expression of James Flaherty (1903), and "pain or anguish" in the portrait of the Right Reverend Denis Dougherty (1903).[96] A powerful sense of decay pervades these paintings, not only in the pathetically mortal figures, but also in the oppressive atmosphere surrounding them—a dull brown fog in which nothing is luminous.

In addition to ridiculing the spiritual hopes of these figures, Eakins seems to have been intrigued by the way that the clergy appeared to cross normal gender boundaries. Several writers have noted that Eakins must have been attracted to priests' clothing. As Schendler has noted: "By painting them in their vestments he could exploit possibilities of form and sometimes of color not available to him in the dark suits of Philadelphia businessmen."[97] In addition, however, these priestly clothes gave priests a sexually ambiguous quality. For example, if we place Eakins's portraits of *Archbishop William Henry Elder* (1903) next to his portrait of *Mrs. Frishmuth* (1900), it is hard to say which one seems more masculine, which one more feminine. The portrait of Elder emphasizes his dress-like alb and chasuble, his wide hips, and his almost feminine adornment with a ring and necklace. Indeed, in a general way, his face

Archbishop William Henry Elder of Cincinnati, 1903. *Oil on canvas, 66 ⅛ x 41 ⅛ in., Cincinnati Art Museum, Museum Purchase, Louise Belmont Family in memory of William F. Halstrick, bequest of Farny R. Wurlintzer, Edward Foote Hinkle Collection, and bequest of Frieda Hauck, by exchange.* **Although he was an atheist, Eakins made many portraits of the Catholic clergy.** RIGHT Antiquated Music (Portrait of Sarah Sagehorn Frishmuth), 1900. *Oil on canvas, 97 x 72 in. Philadelphia Museum of Art, gift of Mrs. Thomas Eakins and Miss Mary Adeline Williams.* **Mrs. Frishmuth posed with twenty instruments from her collection. "Eakins did not flatter her," Goodrich has commented.**

bears a definite resemblance to that of Eakins's mother, which had a similar large, sagging jaw and broad mouth, grimly shut (which in the case of Elder seems to have no teeth). The portrait of *Mrs. Frishmuth*, with her massive shoulders, homely face, rigid pose, and grim expression, is strikingly unfeminine—Goodrich terms her "a massive Rock of Gibraltar."[98] In short, Eakins seemingly enjoyed portraying men who appear on the verge of becoming women, and women who seem to be on the verge of becoming men.

An Actress in Pink

Eakins's series of women in pink halted in 1895, with his portrait of *Maud Cook*, and he did not return to the series until eight years later, after completing the last of his boxing pictures. When he finally returned to this subject in

1903, with *The Actress*, he handled the theme in a very different fashion. In contrast to *Maud Cook*, which has a romantic and gently sensual quality, *The Actress* smolders with undercurrents of violence and frustration. Perhaps for this reason, while it has often been reproduced, writers on Eakins have largely avoided discussing the picture. Homer, for example, employed it as the frontispiece of his book on Eakins, but did not discuss it in his text.

According to Murray, Santje needed "pursuing and pleading" before she consented to pose, and she seems to have stopped before the painting was fully finished, whether because the process was exhausting or because she was displeased with what Eakins did to her features and expression.[99] As in many other instances, Eakins's portrait seems to have born little resemblance to the way Santje really looked. An undated photograph of the actress, reproduced by Hendricks, shows a face with very different features and that also looks younger by some twenty years.

At first glance, in fact, the photograph and Eakins's portrait seem to show different people. More careful study, however, reveals that the hairstyle in the photograph and Eakins's portrait are nearly identical, suggesting that he may have used this photograph as a reference, and that it may well be roughly contemporary with the painting. Even if we suppose that the photograph was

The Actress, 1903. *Oil on canvas, 80 x 60 in., Philadelphia Museum of Art, gift of Mrs. Thomas Eakins and Mary Adeline Williams.* **The debris strewn around the actress suggests a fit of hysteria.**
RIGHT Photograph of Suzanne Santje, ca. 1900. *Private Collection.* **Judging from photographs, Eakins took great liberties with Santje's appearance.**

taken years earlier, it is clear that Eakins did not produce a good likeness. Despite its appearance of realism, his "portrait" of Santje was clearly largely an invention.

As with the portrait of Amelia Van Buren, the sitter is placed in Eakins's studio armchair. We see her from a very low viewpoint, like that of a frightened child. Santje morosely looks off to the right (her left), avoiding direct eye contact with the viewer. Her curiously masculine arms rest on the arms of the chair, and she grips the balls at the ends with her fingers, one hand rather tense, the other more relaxed. She looks as though she is upset, and a book, a letter, and other debris on the floor suggest that she has just had a tantrum, and has thrown them there. Harsh colors and rough textures contribute to the general effect of a moment that is emotionally out of balance. The brushwork is unusually disorderly and the phosphorescent pink of Santje's dress shrieks against the miasmic sewer colors of the muddy background.

This feminine chaos is balanced by a bit of male sobriety and order—a solemn portrait of her father on the background wall.[100] Thus, like many of Eakins's paintings, this one appears to contain a pairing of mother and father figures in a way that mirrors Eakins's own family: hysterical, emotionally vulnerable mother and stern, inscrutable father.

The book on the floor is labeled *Camille*, and from this fact and the title of the painting we can construct a simple narrative. The actress has just been reading a stormy passage from *Camille,* a drama about the sufferings of a "woman with a past." Presumably because she was dissatisfied with her performance, she has thrown down her book in frustration. Thus, the painting is about having hysterical fits, but distances this theme by making the hysteria a theatrical pretense, a game of "let's pretend," rather than the real thing. The layers of this implicit narrative, however, are complex, since the actress looks genuinely exhausted and annoyed. Moreover, we know that Eakins's mother went through phases when she was hysterical and insane. Thus, what the actress is doing as a game connects with something that was real and terrifying to Eakins in his early life.[101]

As with Eakins's other women in pink, Santje's clothing and anatomy are odd. Her dress is extremely peculiar, even given the strangeness of some Victorian fashions, with a long train and fully exposed arms, but without the usual décolletage, with the result that the breasts are not featured, and indeed, any sign of breast is completely hidden. Taken together, the strange dress, the muscular arms, the absence of breasts, and even the hard, square jaw of the sitter convey a persona that is not exactly feminine.

A Man in Pink

At this point Eakins's series of portraits of figures in pink went through a peculiar psychological shift. For his last creation in the series was not a woman but a man, *Monsignor Turner,* a member of the Catholic clergy. Except for his curious female portrait, *The Old-Fashioned Dress,* it appears to be the last large-scale project that Eakins completed before his stroke in 1910.

Popular tradition, repeated by Goodrich, asserts that Turner is shown officiating at a funeral mass. According to this interpretation, the painting of the Assumption in the background can be interpreted as a reference to death. Recent research, however, has cast doubts on this theory, since Turner's vestments are not those he would have worn at a funeral, and the fact that he wears a biretta indicates that he stands outside the altar sanctuary.[102] Still, whether or not he is officiating at a funeral, it is clear from Turner's frozen expression that he is suffering, and the surroundings suggest his thoughts are centered on mortality. Few paintings by Eakins, in fact, are so imbued with an atmosphere of death, and the feeling that life is a form of death.

Monsignor James P. Turner, ca. 1906. *Oil on canvas, 88 × 42 in., The Nelson-Atkins Museum of Art, Kansas City, Missouri, gift of the Enid and Crosby Kemper Foundation.*

What scholars have never noted is that in visual terms, Eakins's portrait of Monsignor Turner forms a natural sequel to *The Actress.* It is painted with the same shocking phosphorescent pinks set against the same sort of dark background. When we see it in this way, it is hard to avoid thinking that Eakins was exploring the idea of transforming a woman into a man. If we start from the premise that all the women in pink were surrogates for Eakins's mother and that the portrait series provided a means of exploring her manic-depressive illness, the Turner portrait forms a logical step in the sequence. Transforming this mother figure into a man was surely a step toward transforming this mother into Eakins himself, or vice versa. In other words, Eakins identified so strongly with his mother's suffering that he wished to picture himself in her role.

Monsignor Turner provided a logical vehicle for this game of changing sexual identities since priests were sexually ambiguous. Their vow of celibacy emasculated them, made them woman-like, and they wore an essentially feminine costume—a dress of sorts. The connection between priest and Eakins's mother was all the more striking because Eakins's mother dressed in a priest-like fashion: in the portrait he made of her she sports a clerical collar, or something very similar. As Eakins portrayed him, Turner's physiognomy has notable similarities to that of Eakins's mother, particularly in the prominent lips and protruding jaw. He is clearly depressed, even catatonic, as Eakins's mother often was because of her bipolar illness.

Monsignor James P. Turner (detail), ca. 1906. *Oil on canvas, 88 × 42 in., The Nelson-Atkins Museum of Art, Kansas City, Missouri, gift of the Enid and Crosby Kemper Foundation.*

Yet at the same time that he serves as a stand-in for Eakins's mother, Turner also serves as a stand-in for Eakins. Turner's withdrawn expression is very much the same expression we find in photographs of Eakins taken toward the end of his life.

Eakins's late work grows increasingly somber, claustrophobic, inward, and removed from a clear sense of setting or story. At times we have, as it were, the beginning of a narrative in a hint of romance; a glimpse of a woman on the verge of undress; or the spectacle of a powerful man, often nude or semi-nude, admired by other men. But isolated heads and faces dominate this late work, and as Eakins grew older they look increasingly unhappy or emotionally frozen, increasingly detached from an understandable context. Looking at Eakins's late canvases it seems as though the elaborate narratives and subjects of his early paintings have been eroded away to leave only a lingering feeling of sadness. What could have been the source of such an obsessive preoccupation with sorrow?

Unknown photographer, Thomas Eakins, *ca. 1900. Gelatin silver print from copy negative, Metropolitan Museum of Art, gift of Charles Bregler, 1961.*

Mrs. Edith Mahon, 1904. *Oil on canvas, 20 × 16 in., Smith College Museum of Art, Northampton, Massachusetts, purchased, Drayton Hillyer Fund, 1931.* **A piano teacher and accompanist, Mrs. Mahon posed for Eakins as a favor and did not like her portrait.**

Chapter 18

INFLICTING PAIN

EAKINS'S PREOCCUPATION with portraiture during the second half of his career raises questions fundamentally different from those raised by paintings of other subjects, such as still life or landscape. For looking at portraits engages instincts that go back to ancient needs and strategies for survival. We are accustomed to observing faces closely to get clues about what other people are thinking. As a consequence, we are more sensitive to variations in the configuration of the face than to any other form of visual information. Recent research has established that recognition of faces and facial expressions involves specialized parts of the brain, which have evolved to serve this specific function. In some way Eakins's paintings clearly deal with the issue of what people think and feel, what they are concealing or attempting to conceal, and how we relate to them.[1] The tension we feel when we look at Eakins's portraits suggests that something about our own existence is at stake.

For a century, writers on American art have recognized that Eakins's portraits possess a quality that is compelling and unique and have sought to explain the reason for their magic. These explanations, however, have often been unconvincing. Lloyd Goodrich claimed that Eakins's contribution was to make figures that were sculptural and solid.[2] By itself, however, the mere rendering of weight and volume seems an empty achievement. Moreover, it may be questioned whether Eakins fully succeeded in this task.

Although Eakins was obsessed with exactitude, he often left large areas of his canvases ambiguous. If we study a painting such as *The Thinker* (a full-length portrait of Eakins's brother-in-law Louis N. Kenton), it becomes apparent that the trousers and much of the rest of the costume are flat and indistinct, even though the figure appears to be standing in good light.[3] In other portraits key parts of the face are lost in shadow. While Goodrich maintains that Eakins captured "the underlying structure of bones and muscles," in fact, his paintings often obscure these features.[4]

Most of Eakins's paintings contain closely observed and carefully rendered details. But these are often balanced by equally significant elements that are withheld. In most of Eakins's paintings, the fall of light is almost arbitrary, since we never see its source. Thus, he used light to feature whatever element would make his point or create a sense of dramatic interest—and similarly, he used shadow in an equally arbitrary way, to obscure what we might normally expect to see. This spotlighting gives his paintings a concentrated emotional intensity. But it also narrows his point of view—and that of the viewer as well. In short, far from creating a clear sense of how figures stand in space, Eakins created a world that is rich in ambiguity.[5] Writers such as Goodrich have also extolled Eakins's understanding of character. Thus, Goodrich wrote:

> As a portraitist, Eakins was concerned above all with character. The basic form of the head, its bone structure, the unique personality of the features, the character shown in the hands, the shape of the body beneath the clothes—all the factors that make the sitter an individual like no one else in the world—he grasped with unerring sureness.[6]

Portrait of Louis N. Kenton, 1900. *Oil on canvas, 82 x 42 in., Metropolitan Museum of Art, New York, Kennedy Fund, 1917.* **Little is known about Louis Kenton, except that he was hen pecked by his wife.**

Once again, however, this explanation does not quite ring true. What Eakins actually did was more peculiar. The expressions of his figures are remarkably similar from one painting to another. They invariably look frozen; their eyes appear unfocused. In short, rather than responding to the individuality of his sitters, he seems to have imposed something on them. Moreover, as the art historian Patrick McCaughey noted many years ago in an essay in *Art News*, "intimacy is constantly denied" in Eakins's portraits, for Eakins refused to characterize his sitters "through gesture, accessories, context or whatever."[7] Thus, while Eakins brings us into a seemingly intimate relationship with his subjects, he denies us the information to understand who they are. They stare at us blankly, without engagement.

Indeed, the vacancy of the expression in many of Eakins's portraits has led to very disparate evaluations of their importance and what they are about. Sylvan Schendler saw Eakins's portrait of Talcott Williams (1890) as "entirely unequivocal in its implied admiration for the man."[8] Hendricks, however, suggested that the painting is essentially a satire in which "Talk-a-lot" Williams is portrayed with his mouth open wide enough to catch flies. Hendricks has argued that the portrait of the painter Louis Husson is more sympathetic than the likeness of his tight-lipped wife, and artistically far superior. Nicolai Cikovsky, however, has argued that Eakins's portrait of the wife is the better of the two. Examples such as this suggest that Eakins's portraits are remarkable not simply for what they reveal about the sitter, but because of what they withhold from us, and their sense of psychological ambiguity.

Louis Husson, 1899. *Oil on canvas, 24 x 20 ¹⁄₁₆ in., gift of Katharine Husson Horstick © Board of Trustees, National Gallery of Art, Washington, D.C.* A painter and photographer, Louis Husson served as pallbearer at Eakins's funeral.
RIGHT   Annie C. Lochrey Husson (Mrs. Louis Husson), ca. 1905. *Oil on canvas, 24 ¹⁄₁₆ x 20 ¹⁄₁₆ in., gift of Katharine Husson Horstick © Board of Trustees, National Gallery of Art, Washington, D.C.* On the basis of Eakins's portrait, Gordon Hendricks has concluded that Mrs. Husson was a "tight-lipped, narrow, small-souled woman."

For this reason, as McCaughey has rightly pointed out, Eakins's relationship to such figures as Rembrandt and Velázquez is "superficial." In Rembrandt's work, for example, "we are invited to know the character." Eakins, on the contrary, bars us from the inner life of his sitters.[9] In many instances, particularly with the unhappy, red-eyed women, this not only creates a sense of disquiet in the present, but a sense of apprehension about what they will do next.

Unlike John Singer Sargent, who produced some of his finest portraits when recording memorable personalities, such as Robert Louis Stevenson or Henry James, the opposite was true of Eakins. John Russell, the art critic for the *New York Times*, observed that Eakins's portrait of Walt Whitman (1887–1888) is one of the few paintings by him "that just doesn't ring true." For once, Russell noted, Eakins "allowed a histrionic element to intervene." Whitman's "huge vacuous grin" makes him look "like a summer-stock Falstaff."[10] Instead, many of Eakins's greatest portraits record individuals about whom virtually nothing is known.

Thus, while it is customary to state that Eakins penetrated the characters of his sitters, it appears that his most effective portraits are of individuals whose personality provided a relatively blank vehicle on which to project his own feelings. Oscar Wilde once stated, "Every portrait that is painted with feeling . . . is a portrait of the artist."[11] This aphorism seems particularly applicable to the work of Eakins. In the final analysis, his portraits are not so much about his sitters as about himself.

In a remarkable but telling oversight, writers like Goodrich (or his followers, including Elizabeth Johns or Kathleen Foster) have almost entirely avoided any discussion of the emotional component of Eakins's paintings, and above all the rather obvious point that his sitters almost invariably looked depressed. While the matter has never been stated directly, it is clear that those portraits considered Eakins's greatest are those in which the figure looks most reflective and most profoundly sad: paintings such as *Amelia Van Buren, The Concert Singer,* or the late portrait of his wife. Those paintings in which the figure looks most unhappy are generally viewed as superior. In the portrait of Mrs. Mahon (1904), generally regarded as the greatest of the late heads, the sitter looks even more distressed than the subjects of Eakins's other portraits, and seems to have been crying.[12] Almost without exception, Eakins's portraits are renderings of people in pain, or perhaps numbed by the pain they have experienced.

In several instances, Eakins's portraits have been singled out for praise because the figures look catatonic and virtually expressionless. Gordon Hendricks declares that the frozen figure of John B. Gest (1905), president of the Fidelity Insurance and Safe Deposit Company of Philadelphia "has scarcely been exceeded by the artist."[13] Similarly, "In his portrait of Mrs. Gilbert Lafayette Parker . . . with her marvelous rigidity and a face both expressive and consummately expressionless at the same time, he achieved one of the heights of his career."[14] According to this view, Eakins's portraits are profound because they show the emptiness of people's lives.

The issue of emptiness and ambiguity is key to much of modern art. From Whistler onward, artists have eliminated details and introduced large areas of near emptiness. There is, of course, a fundamental paradox to this. Works that are completely specific can be read in only one way; their meaning is limited. Works that are ambiguous can be read in several ways; therefore, the richest works of art are those without fixed meaning.[15]

Portrait of John B. Gest, 1905. *Oil on canvas, 40 x 30 in. The Museum of Fine Arts, Houston, Museum purchase with funds provided by the Agnes Cullen Arnold Endowment Fund.* Gest served as president of the Fidelity Trust Company in Philadelphia, which commissioned his portrait for $700.

If works are too empty, however, they are simply empty, and the distinction between emptiness that is "deep" and emptiness that is "meaningless" is often subtle. The blankness and deadness of expression in Eakins's portraits is often quite similar to the work of his academic contemporaries, who are typically considered minor artists, such as Leon Bonnat, or others even less well known. Patrick McCaughey has declared, "We recognize Eakins as Eakins and there is no confusing his "neutrality" with that of say, George Richmond's emptily academic manner."[16] (George Richmond was an English contemporary of Eakins, who produced expressionless academic portraits.) In fact, however, the deadness of Eakins's paintings often poses exactly this problem. Should we view them as profound or lifeless?

During his lifetime, many viewers thought that Eakins's portraits were boring and vacuous. Samuel Isham, in his *History of American Painting* of 1905, after describing Eakins's painstaking methods, declared, "The consequence was much tedium for the sitters and much woefully prosaic work."[17] In the last decade or so of the nineteenth century, however, when movements of social reform were gaining force, the more "advanced" and daring critics began to see these portraits as honest and morally profound precisely because of their uningratiating qualities.

In 1888, when Eakins's portrait of *George Barker* (1886) won the Thomas B. Clarke prize at the National Academy of Design, a writer for the *New York Sun* declared: "A more frank piece of realism, it would hardly be too much to say a more brutal piece of realism than Mr. Eakins's portrait of a Philadelphia professor it would be hard to imagine . . . The man is painted as though with a scalpel instead of a brush or palette knife." Similarly, the *New York Times* declared of the same picture: "it is not elaborated in a sort of winning style, but painted ruggedly, yet with the utmost truth to nature. We see the intent scholar, the Professor of Chemistry, careless of dress . . . It is a picture which may be readily overlooked, though it holds a place of honor, for it has no adventitious or picturesque details to attract the eye."[18] In commentary such as this, the very roughness of Eakins's treatment and the unflattering quality of the result is taken as proof of integrity and authenticity.

Ritter Fitzgerald expressed this same view in 1895 when he noted that Eakins painted his subjects as he found them, with "imperfections, blemishes, and all."[19] Similarly, a writer for the *Philadelphia Inquirer* (perhaps Helen Henderson) declared in 1896, "Mr. Eakins has the faculty of reproducing literally the characteristics of his sitters, with the result that his portraits are often brutally like his models."[20]

By the time of the Memorial Exhibition, this lack of flattery was seen as a unique aspect of Eakins's work. Gilbert Sunderland Parker noted in 1917, "When one compares most of the portraits of our time with an Eakins from Eakins's viewpoint they look weak and thin—the Eakins stands out full of life and character."[21]

Modern writers have tended to see the unflattering qualities of Eakins's portraits as a positive trait, although it is not entirely clear to me why this is the case. Linda Nochlin, for example, writes with icy contempt of the work of John Singer Sargent (who, ironically, was a friend of Eakins, and appears to have been the living painter whom Eakins most admired), declaring that Sargent's work celebrates precisely the qualities that made her, as a girl attending Vassar, feel insecure next to her aristocratic and good-looking classmates. As she writes:

> Sargent skillfully established a new iconography of elongated, fine-limbed, casually superior beauties, ancestors of those young women whose sheer physical confidence, not to speak of social self-assurance, were to give girls from

Brooklyn like me an inferiority complex at Vassar half a century later. That
there are no ugly members of the upper classes is the lesson these suavely
painted portraits teach, although admittedly, the artist seems to have had to
work harder deploying what Henry James referred to as his "pure tact of vision"
when the subjects were even slightly marginal—Jewish, for example . . .[22]

By contrast, she links the work of Eakins with that of Mary Cassatt
because "both artists seem resolutely to refuse to idealize or prettify their sitters"—adding that (presumably because of this unwillingness to idealize) both
artists "transformed American art from a provincial, rather limited pursuit
into a world-class enterprise."[23]

What is intriguing to me about Nochlin's discussion is the frankness with
which she brings in issues of class and race, making it clear that she sees Sargent as hostile to Jewish girls (or anyone else who is "marginal") and Eakins as
their ally. From what we know of the personal life of the two artists, the accuracy of this judgment is not clear. Sargent counted Jewish people among his
closest friends and socialized with them when he wanted to relax; Eakins
"didn't like Jews" according to one report.

The touchy issue of anti-Semitism, however, is something of a diversion,
for what attracts Nochlin to Eakins is clearly something about the paintings
themselves, quite apart from what the artists thought about race or the biographical data about them. She likes something about the viewpoint of
Eakins's paintings that is expressed within the paintings themselves. Quite cor-
rectly, Nochlin notes that Eakins's women differ from those of Sargent,
because they seem to be suffering:

> A common inner anxiety, an air of longsufferingness—or martyrdom, even—a
> veiled appeal tinged with self-withdrawal seem to characterize all of Eakins'
> female sitters.[24]

What is unclear to me is why Nochlin sees the element of suffering in
Eakins's paintings as a positive statement, rather than a misogynist one. Is she
pleased that Eakins seems to rip the mask of security from pampered WASP
women and portray them as helpless, vulnerable, and defeated? Does this feed
into her own sense of moral and intellectual superiority? Or does she see
Eakins as sympathetic to lonely, alienated outcasts, possibly including
thoughtful people like herself? Unfortunately, Nochlin's essay proceeds largely
by innuendo, so the exact logic of her argument is not clear. Somewhat

unconvincingly she proposes that Eakins may have been a feminist because "he seems to have encouraged some of his female students," but this direction of her argument seems weak.[25] Eakins's statements about the inferiority of women are quite straightforward, and his treatment of his wife shows that he was happy to put these principles into action.

On the face of it, Nochlin's reasoning inverts normal values. She asks us to believe that Eakins's paintings of women who look abused are a positive statement about women, whereas Sargent's paintings of healthy-looking women are a form of male imprisonment, and a deceitful sham. At one level, her reactions seem naive, since she never questions the innocent, idealistic sincerity of Eakins's intentions. While one would not contest Nochlin's right to admire Eakins's paintings, her explanation of her reasons for dong so feels incomplete. While her approach differs somewhat in flavor from that of Lloyd Goodrich, ultimately it shares the same weakness, that it does not directly confront the tragic, troubled quality of Eakins's work, nor broach the thought that something about his work feels not only not quite honest, but not very nice.

Interestingly, despite Nochlin's claim of Eakins's international stature, Europeans have never embraced Eakins as a major figure, and seem to view his work as simply bad academic painting. As Clement Greenberg has observed, Eakins's art resembles a wine that one cannot export.[26] Forbes Watson reports that when Eakins's paintings were shown in Venice in 1920, "Not once but innumerable times, I came upon groups of foreigners standing in front of the Eakins pictures roaring with laughter."[27] Recently, when Gary Tinterow, a curator at the Metropolitan Museum of Art, proposed adding some pictures by Eakins to an exhibition dominated by French work, he was greeted by his French colleagues with the reaction "ce n'est pas la peinture" ("It is not painting").[28]

Men and Women

A roster of Eakins's more notable portraits gives a sense of the range of professions he portrayed:

Samuel Gross: surgeon

D. Hayes Agnew: surgeon

Dr. John H. Brinton: surgeon

J. William White: surgeon

Horatio Wood: physician (nervous diseases)

J. M. Da Costa: physician

Dr. William Thomson: ophthalmologist

Dr. Charles Lester Leonard: X-ray pioneer

Dr. Edward A. Spitzka: brain specialist

Henry A. Rowland: physicist

Professor Benjamin Howard Rand: chemist

Professor William D. Marks: engineer

Frank Hamilton Cushing: ethnologist

Professor Stewart Culin: ethnologist

Monsignor Turner: cleric

Ritter Fizgerald: journalist

William Merritt Chase: painter

William O'Donovan: sculptor

As this list shows, Eakins tended to focus on men of intellectual and artistic accomplishment, including doctors, chemists, physicists, writers, artists, sculptors, clerics, and musicians. He painted doctors with particular frequency. He also went to considerable effort to portray these figures in their professional setting. For the portrait of the ethnologist Cushing, Eakins turned the Chestnut Street studio into a replica of a room in an Indian pueblo, even building an altar and fire on bricks on the floor to get an authentic effect of smoke. For the portrait of Henry Rowland he carefully rendered the apparatus in the chemist's laboratory. Professional women were fewer, but he portrayed several singers and musicians, as well as actresses, educators, and painters. As Goodrich notes: "The only types who hardly ever appeared in his work were the millionaire and the society lady, the chief support of the average portraitist. His sitters were intellectual and artistic workers."[29]

Eakins viewed women differently. He seldom showed men and women in the same painting, and when he did, in works such as *The Gross Clinic* and

Frank Hamilton Cushing, ca. 1894–1895. *Oil on canvas, 90 x 60 in., from the collection of Gilcrease Museum, Tulsa.* To get the setting right for his portrait of Cushing, Eakins constructed a kiva in his studio and lit the fire to get the authentic effect of smoke.

The Agnew Clinic, the men appear as thinkers and doers, the women as either passive or overly emotional, and most commonly detached from any setting or context. With men, he seems to have sometimes sought out people he had never seen, such as Rear Admiral George Melville (1904), the polar explorer, because he was interested in their achievements. With women, he would spot those whose appearance interested him, stare at them intensely, and invite them to pose.

In the nineteenth century, women were considered particularly susceptible to their emotions and disease-prone sex organs. Eakins's friend, the neurologist S. Weir Mitchell, claimed, "The man who does not know sick women does not know women."[30] In keeping with this attitude, Eakins's portraits of women tend to stress emotional vulnerability. As Schendler notes, women are portrayed as "more sensitive and more given to moody introspection than men."[31] Almost without exception, Eakins stressed three major symptoms of the psychological disorder known as neurasthenia, commonly diagnosed in women in his time: depression, physical exhaustion, and a tendency to cry.

Eakins liked to show women in a state of complete inactivity, with slouched, tired posture and heavy limbs. They often have weary, tilted heads and disheveled hair and clothes. Dark colors, harsh lighting, and downward sloping or jagged lines intensify the general tone of melancholy and emotional trauma. To stress elements of distress, such as a frozen expression or unfocused gaze, he often moved in close. Very often the women have red-rimmed eyes, as if they have been crying. Some writers have felt that Eakins was expressing some sort of sympathy for women through these works, and have even read them as a critique of patriarchy.[32] But in view of Eakins's repeated statements about the inferiority of women, this latter interpretation seems unlikely.

Many of the characteristics of these paintings point not simply toward unhappiness but toward emotional illness. The most striking of these is the vacant stare, which was thought to occur immediately before or after the hysterical fit, and was regarded as a sign of the neurasthenic's detachment from her surroundings.[33] This device was also used in other paintings of this period to communicate mental illness in visual terms, and was praised by critics when successfully deployed.[34] In fact, writers on Eakins have often noted this aspect of his portraits:

Letitia Wilson Jordon: "She is not looking at us and smiling but gazing in front of her."[35]

Jennie Dean Kershaw: "This thin intense woman stares wide-eyed at no corporeal object."[36]

Helen Parker: "She is gazing in front of her, not at us, with a vacant, almost idiotic stare; the poor girl looks half-witted."[37]

Eleanor Pue: "She looks sad and anxious, her eyes seem pleading."[38]

Suzan Eakins: "Although Mrs. Eakins looks out at the world, she does not appear to be seeing whatever her gaze rests upon, presumably the painter himself."[39]

In addition, muscular stiffness and rigidity are often cited as a symptom of neurasthenia. Such a frozen quality is typical of the facial muscles in Eakins's portraits, but is also evident in other areas of the anatomy, such as the notably stiff hands in the likeness of Mrs. Greenewalt (1903). Finally, signs of age, such as gray hair, had an association with neurasthenia, since menopause was considered a "disease-ridden time" in life, and neurasthenics were sometimes noted to have aged and grayed prematurely due to a high level of emotional distress.[40]

As Eakins grew older, his work grew more clinical in approach, and increasingly he tended to detach his sitters from any sort of background. The art historian Kathleen Spies comments that Eakins's paintings of women, ranging in date from about 1896 to 1900, abandon all pretext of external setting and take on the character of pathological studies. Specifically, she notes that Eakins increasingly favored a close-up bust format that accentuates the impression of categorization, while removing the figure from any sort of narrative context. In format the paintings are repetitive. Eakins almost always showed his sitters in a three-quarter view with a slight turn of the body, and with tilted heads and downcast or sidelong gazes. Unlike typical portraits of the period by John Singer Sargent and others, these images do not emphasize lush surfaces or material surroundings.[41]

Eakins alternated between showing his women with dresses that reveal a great deal of flesh, and even seem to be falling off, and dresses that completely cover them up to the next. Oddly, there is often a discrepancy between Eakins's manner of treatment and what we know about his relationship with the model. Amelia Van Buren had posed nude for Eakins, but he showed her smothered in clothes. Weda Cook would not undress (although Eakins pressured her to), but Eakins showed her largely bare. In fact, this seems to have been a general pattern in Eakins's portraits. Women such as Lillian Hammitt or his wife, who posed nude for him, he portrayed buttoned up to the chin. Women such as Weda Cook, Maud Cook, or Helen Parker, who would not do so, he portrayed in revealing gowns.

Biographers of Eakins have written so often about his supposedly remarkable knowledge of anatomy, that it has not occurred to them to question his rendering of the human figure. His rendering of female anatomy is generally quite far from correct and in many cases truly idiosyncratic. While the clavicles and chest area of his sitters fascinated him, he avoided representing the female breast. The gowns in his paintings often go very low, but we never get a trace of bulging or of cleavage between the breasts as we move down toward that area. Instead, the surface remains completely flat until it is broken off by a line of clothing—the women, whether they are young or old, appear flat-chested, like a boy.

Eakins's portrayal of Helen Parker in *The Old-Fashioned Dress* provides a good example. At the point where the flesh stops and the gown begins there is no roundness or bulge of any sort, no hint of indentation. The same peculiar flat-chested quality is evident in his portrait *Mary Hallock Greenewalt*, which is even stranger looking, since the costume and gesture seem to have been designed specifically to feature this area of the woman's figure. Even more grotesque is his rendering of the middle-aged singer *Mrs. Bowden* (The Art Museum, Princeton University), who seems to lack breasts altogether.

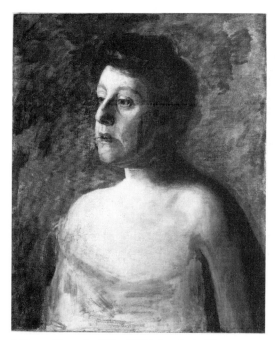

A Singer (Portrait of Mrs. W. H. Bowden). *Oil on canvas, 61.9 x 51.7 cm., The Art Museum, Princeton University, Museum purchase, Fowler McCormick, Class of 1921, Fund.* In a departure from normal female anatomy, Mrs. Bowden appears completely flat-chested.

Admittedly, Eakins did sometimes represent women with very large breasts, but in these instances he never directly indicated the flesh in this area. The breasts look like padding. Striking instances of this are his portraits of *Mrs. James Mapes Dodge* (1885) and *Anna Lewis* (c. 1898). Similarly, in both *Miss Amelia Van Buren* and *The Concert Singer*, it is easy to imagine that the figures have no breasts, but that the bulge is simply an attachment that has been sewn to their clothes.

Writers on Eakins disagree as to whether his male or female portraits are more successful. Hendricks declares that "Eakins generally had his greatest success with portraits of men rather than women," and he points to the Husson portraits as an instance of this. "Louis Husson," he declares, "was painted with much sympathy, while his wife appears to be a tight-lipped narrow, small-souled woman."[42] According to Hendricks, "Men were generally less

oppressed by the glacial conventions of the time, and this may be why, however conventional, rigid or shallow men sometimes are in Eakins' portraits,
the artist's conceptions of men are on the whole more ingratiating."[43]

Most other writers, however, have seen the matter differently, at least for
Eakins's late work. Generally speaking, the female portraits are viewed as
more emotional, more tragic, and more profound. From 1900 to 1910 Eakins
painted only about a third as many women as men. Nonetheless, portraits
such as *Mrs. Mahon* or the late portrait of his wife are generally considered the
high points of Eakins's later career.

This preference seems to reflect the belief that Eakins's female portraits
are particularly tragic. As Kathleen Spies observed, while nearly all Eakins's
sitters look fatigued, his portraits of men have been interpreted differently
than his depictions of women. Eakins's portraits of male doctors, scientists,
and musicians, have usually been viewed as essentially positive in their message—they are portraits of "endurance," in which "strength of character"
contends with "weariness of the flesh."[44] His insistence on having his sitters
wear old clothes, along with the general untidiness of the settings, has been

Miss Anna Lewis, ca. 1898. *Oil on canvas, 33 x 28 in., Hirshhorn Museum and Sculpture Garden, Smithsonian Institution,
gift of Joseph H. Hirshhorn, 1966.* RIGHT Mrs. James Mapes Dodge (Josephine Kern), 1896. *Oil on Canvas,
24 ⅛ x 20 ⅛ in., Philadelphia Museum of Art, gift of Mrs. James Mapes Dodge, 1951.* **Female breasts in Eakins's portraits
often look like padding strapped to a male figure. A vivacious extrovert, Anna Lewis was active in the feminist
movement.**

viewed as a way of expressing the "wear and tear" of hard work, as well as their disregard for material appearances while pursuing their intellectual creativity. His portraits of women, however, have been seen as records of emotional instability. Thus, for example, Eakins's portrait of the anthropologist Frank Hamilton Cushing has been seen as a "tribute to [Cushing's] daring and contributions to social science" and as a tribute to "the moral force of intellect."[45] While his portrait of the actress Susan Santje (1903) has been thought to represent "the mysterious beauty . . . of sadness," and to show the actress "In a state of near collapse."[46]

Painful Poses

The common belief that Eakins's likenesses were truthful depends on the assumption that his motives were straightforward. We generally assume that the portraitist sets out to flatter his sitters, and only brings out their negative qualities if they are forced on him. We do not expect an artist to present his sitters as flushed, fatigued, ugly, unhappy, or depressed unless they actually are. To think otherwise is to conclude that the artist is malicious. For this reason, the unflattering aspects of Eakins's portraits have almost always been taken as proof of his honesty and authenticity. Even the rejection of Eakins's work has been cited as evidence that it must have been truthful and accurate. As Goodrich notes, "Few persons are strong or broad enough to stand an unflattered version of themselves."[47] Consequently, when Eakins's work was rejected, Goodrich placed the blame not on the artist but on the supposed vanity of the sitter.

Artists usually make portraits as a way of earning income, and Eakins's letters from Paris note this fact. In one letter home he boasted, "I could even now earn a respectable living in America, I think, painting heads." In another letter he declared, "even now I could paint heads good enough to make a living anywhere in America."[48] Yet Eakins never realized even a modest income in America from his painting, let alone through portraiture. Eakins painted 246 portraits. Only twenty-five were commissioned, and in at least five of these cases the final painting was rejected or he had difficulty obtaining payment.

In most cases, Eakins chose the people he wanted to paint and coaxed them into posing for him. Eakins often protested to his sitters that his work was not simply a commercial matter. In 1900, after Mrs. Drexel broke off sitting for him because of the length of the sessions, Eakins declared, "I cannot bring myself to regard the affair in the light of a business transaction."[49] Thus, Eakins inverted the usual principles of portraiture. Rather than working for hire, for a patron, and producing work that satisfied his patron's requirements (as for example, John Singer Sargent did), he made portraits on his own initiative, which brought out those traits that interested him, often negative ones. Oddly, in those instances in which the sitters were willing to pay, Eakins seems to have made likenesses that were particularly unflattering. Schendler notes, "In general, he was kinder to friends than to the businessmen who paid or who objected to paying for his work."[50]

Indeed, the final product is only one part of what is odd about Eakins's paintings. The very process of making them caused considerable unhappiness and social disruption, both for the sitters and for the artist. To understand the meaning of Eakins's paintings we need to grasp his perplexing insistence on making himself and his sitters miserable at every step. When we examine Eakins's working method, we discover that nothing about his procedure followed normal principles. Everything about it, from the first pose to the final product, was calculated to cause distress to the sitter.

We can begin with posing. The astonishingly long sessions that Eakins demanded taxed the stamina and patience of his sitters, and in fact amounted to a kind of abuse. In 1876 Dr. Samuel Gross grew so tired of Eakins's demands during the six or nine months of work on *The Gross Clinic* that at one point he declared: "Eakins, I wish you were dead!"[51] The portrait of Dr. D. Hayes Agnew is said to have taken ninety-six hours, despite the doctors insistent refrain of "I can give you just one hour," every time he arrived in the studio.[52]

For a modest-size portrait, executed around 1890, Francis Ziegler posed from nine to five every day for a week. While the portrait showed only his head and shoulders, Eakins insisted that he pose standing. At the end of the day, Ziegler was so exhausted that he had to go to bed when he got home. "He never knew a knee could hurt as much as his did," Goodrich reported in his notes.

Harrison Morris, who posed in 1896, recalled that Eakins made him stand "day after day" and that "I posed on my feet for so many hours that I was seized of an irruption on my weary legs and had to go to a doctor for a remedy."[53]

Similarly, Samuel Myers, who posed in 1904, reported that although his portrait also showed only head and shoulders, on the first day Eakins made him stand from nine to five. "Says it was the worst day of his life," Goodrich recorded. "Thinks he must have posed 8 or 9 times more."

Adolph Burie, who posed in 1910, noted that Eakins was a "terrifically slow worker." He would pin ribbons on different parts of him and then line them up against the same colored ribbons in the background to make sure that he always held exactly the same pose. He would then shuffle away a few steps to a fixed position and then shuffle back and work on part of the picture. The painting was discontinued after Eakins became ill, and despite the long hours of posing the likeness is unfinished and most of the surrounding canvas is bare.

Eakins also demanded long poses of women. Mrs. James Mapes Dodge posed about forty hours for a simple head and shoulders portrait of 1896.[54] Mary Hallock Greenewalt, who posed for a portrait of 1903, wrote to Goodrich, "I gave Mr. Eakins forty sittings." Alice Kurtz (later Mrs. John B. Whiteman) noted, "Eakins spent a good part of the summer of 1903" working at her portrait.[55] Eleanor Pue (Mrs. Lavell), who sat for Eakins in 1907, told Goodrich that she posed sixty times for her portrait—a simple bust likeness that appears not completely finished. When Goodrich was incredulous, she confessed that this might be a slight exaggeration, but declared that she posed three or four mornings a week for an entire winter. Kate Parker, Helen Parker's mother, told McHenry that Helen "posed about thirty-five times, two or three hours at a time," for the The Old-Fashioned Dress (1908).[56]

Portraitists vary greatly in how quickly they work, but by any standard Eakins's demands were exceptional. John Singer Sargent painted *Lady Agnew of Lochnaw* (1893), one of his masterpieces, in just six days. Few professional portraitists require more than two weeks of posing. Eakins seems to have taken ten or twelve times as long as Sargent to finish much smaller paintings.

Why did it take so long? One reason was that Eakins was obsessed with measurements and mechanical exactitude, as Burie's account of the ribbons suggests. Even taking such procedures into account, however, Eakins seems to have worked slowly. Many of those who posed for him described his movements as lethargic. It is hard to avoid the impression that his torpid pace was deliberate, and that he was interested in tiring his sitters so that he could record their fatigue and psychological distress. Indeed, other aspects of sitting for Eakins were psychologically disturbing, particularly for women. His language was often crude. He told dirty jokes. He farted. He sometimes appeared for sessions in his underwear or in inappropriate clothes. He pressured his sitters to pose in the nude.

He also poked and fingered some sitters. Mrs. Dodge told Goodrich that Eakins executed her portrait in the parlor of the Dodge house in Germantown, facing a window from which Eakins had removed the shade and curtains to get the most light. At one point he came over and started to dig his fingers into her chest. She said, "Tom, for heaven's sake, what are you doing?" and he replied, "Feeling for bones." Similarly, when Mrs. Talcott Williams pulled in her stomach muscles, he prodded her in the belly and told her not to hold herself in.[57] As one of my students put it, "He drove his sitters crazy so that he could paint them that way."

Some sitters quit after Eakins manhandled or offended them. Mrs. Talcott Williams stopped posing after Eakins poked her. Elizabeth Duane Gillespie, a proud descendant of Benjamin Franklin, would not come back after Eakins received her dressed in his undershirt, and as a consequence, Eakins's 1901 portrait of her remains unfinished. As Leslie Miller reports:

> Mrs. Gillespie refused to go near him again after he received her one blistering hot day in his studio up three or four flights of stairs in the old Presbyterian Building on Chestnut Street dressed only in an old pair of trousers and an undershirt! He wanted her to give him one or two more sittings but she not only refused them, but wanted me to destroy the portrait after it came into my possession—which of course I didn't do."[58]

Many sitters found the long sessions of posing for Eakins burdensome and failed to show up.[59]

Going Beyond Honesty

Eakins himself maintained that his painstaking approach allowed him to capture reality. In a letter to Mrs. Drexel, who had broken off posing, Eakins declared that "a portrait of you that did not resemble you, would be false, have no historic value, and would not enhance my reputation."[60] Yet despite the supposed exactitude of his methods, Eakins frequently took dramatic liberties with the appearance of his sitters.

The most common of these was to exaggerate the effects of age or fatigue. For instance, Eakins presented Amelia Van Buren, a blonde woman of thirty-five, as a gray-haired matron of around fifty. The same process can be documented in many of Eakins's other portraits of women, including the late portrait of his wife. He did the same with men. Eakins asked the banker William B. Kurtz not to shave for twenty-four hours so that he would look more ragged and careworn. When painting Walter Copeland Bryant, he asked permission to represent him as a man of seventy rather than fifty.[61]

He also altered the scale and details of surrounding objects. An armchair from Eakins's studio appears in twelve pictures, and if we line them up side by side we realize the chair changes dramatically in scale, making the sitter seem larger or smaller. The chair is enormous, and its arms large and bulbous, in *Amelia Van Buren* (1890), but is smaller in scale and more slender in *The Old-Fashioned Dress* (1908).

Another idiosyncrasy was that Eakins liked to portray people in old clothes, even when they were inappropriate for the occasion he depicted. Thus, for example, Leslie Miller recalled:

Professor Leslie W. Miller, 1901. *Oil on canvas, 88 × 44 in., Philadelphia Museum of Art, gift in memory of Edgar Viguers Seeler by Martha Page Laughlin Seeler.* RIGHT *The Dean's Roll Call*, 1899. *Oil on canvas, 84 ⅛ × 42 in., A. Shuman Collection, courtesy of the Museum of Fine Arts, Boston, reproduced with permission, © 2000 Museum of Fine Arts, Boston, all rights reserved.* **Eakins asked the dean to pose in an old pair of shoes.**

When he painted my portrait [1901], he not only wanted me to wear some old clothes but insisted that I go and don a little old sack coat—hardly more than a blouse—that he remembered seeing me in, in my bicycle days, and which I certainly never would have worn facing an audience which the portrait represents me as doing. He did much the same thing with Dean Holland—see the picture "The Dean's Roll-call" [1899]. The Dean and I had lots of fun over his predilections in these cases. He made the poor Dean go, too, and put on a pair of old shoes that he kept to go fishing in, and painted him, as you know, shoed in this way, when he faced a distinguished audience on a very impressive occasion.[62]

Where photographs are available for comparison, it is often apparent that Eakins significantly altered the features of his sitters. In the case of *The Actress (Portrait of Suzanne Santje),* Eakins widened the face and thickened the nose of his sitter; in *The Old-Fashioned Dress,* Eakins made the slight nose of Helen Montanverde Parker prominent and bulbous.

The case of Ashbury Lee also provides an instructive example. Goodrich notes that Lee "was a builder, an organizer, a public-spirited denizen of his home town."[63] In Eakins's portrait of 1905, however, he "looks every inch the ruthless businessman: a predator, witch-burner and hanging judge." Eakins clearly imposed these characteristics since a Bachrach photograph records Lee sitting in the same pose as the portrait, and it differs significantly from Eakins's rendering. As Barbara Millhouse has noted:

Nothing about A. W. Lee supports Eakins's characterization of him. The difference between Lee's appearance and the Bachrach photograph shows that the artist converted a confidant, distinguished gentleman into a bitter, commonplace man. The expensive pressed suit in the photograph has been turned into a cheap, rumpled suit in the portrait.[64]

Very often, those who knew the sitter did not feel that Eakins produced a good likeness. A portrait of *Mrs. M. S. Stokes* (1903), who was the mother of one of Eakins's students, Frank W. Stokes, carries a label on the verso that reads "a good portrait but not an accurate likeness." Otto Wolf, a friend of the businessman Edward Schmidt, whom Eakins painted in 1906, wrote to Eakins that "Unfortunately, the expression of Mr. Schmidt's countenance as shown in your portrait, is so different form his usual one, that many of his friends who have seen the picture, have passed adverse criticisms upon the likeness; and

A. W. Bachrach, Photograph of Ashbury Lee, ca. 1905. RIGHT A.W. Lee, 1905. *Oil on canvas, 40 × 32 in., Reynolds House, Museum of American Art, Winston-Salem, North Carolina.* Eakins made Lee's suit look "cheap and rumpled" and "converted a confident gentleman into a bitter commonplace man."

you must concede that after all, it is intended as a portrait and not as an evidence of art only."[65]

Examples such as this make it difficult to credit Goodrich's statement that Eakins's portraits possess "complete honesty," or the claim by Barbara Weinberg, curator of American painting at the Metropolitan Museum of Art, that Eakins's portraits are "loving records of people to whom he was very close."[66] Nonetheless, the issue of "honesty" has always been stressed in evaluations of Eakins's work—even in describing instances in which he portrayed people differently than their actual appearance. Goodrich has noted that Eakins "sometimes he went beyond honesty, making his sitters homelier and more serious than they actually were."[67] The logic of this is dubious.

Realism or Slander?

The answer to this question goes to the heart of the significance and meaning of Eakins's work. For many viewers, both in his lifetime and today, Eakins created a fictional reality that seemed more intense, and in some sense more "truthful," than reality itself. William Clark, the strongest early advocate of Eakins's work, touched on this paradox in a review of a portrait of President Rutherford B. Hayes, one of the artist's most important early commissions.

The painting was exhibited at the Haseltine Galleries in Philadelphia in 1877, shortly after it was completed, and this provided the occasion for Clark's review. Sadly, the painting itself no longer survives, and it was never photographed, but this fact only intensifies what is odd about Clark's argument, since it encourages us to focus on the logic of his statements apart from visual distractions.

Clark began by noting, "This portrait is one of the most severely literal works that he has yet produced." He then added, "This portrait gives a very different idea of the President from that of any of the photographs of him or by any of the painted portraits that have yet come under our notice."[68] If we invert these statements, their logical absurdity becomes apparent. If the portrait did not resemble the other portraits and photographs of Hayes, by what standard was Clark describing it as a "severely literal" work? Clark did not know Hayes, and thus was not using the man himself as a touchstone. We can only conclude that the "severely literal" nature of the portrait was communicated by something in the artist's approach. In other words, Eakins's portrait had the look of verisimilitude, of literal realism, even if there was no standard against which to test whether it really resembled the subject.

How did Eakins create this sense of literal realism? In the case of the Hayes portrait, Clark's review lists some of the devices that Eakins used to make the portrait seem real. He showed the president "in his old alpaca office coat, with the stump of a lead pencil in his fingers, and with his sunburned face glistening with summer perspiration."[69] In other words, Eakins introduced elements that evoked physical and tactile qualities, as if the sitter existed in a world of heat, wear, and discomfort, like that we encounter in real life. American presidents are not usually pictured in this fashion, but this only made Eakins's approach more effective. For why would anyone seek to present a president in such an unflattering manner unless they were recording what they saw?

In ever varying forms, this tension runs through the literature on Eakins. On the one hand, those who knew the people Eakins painted often felt that he had not captured their personality or created an accurate likeness. On the other hand, these very same people often describe his paintings as intensely realistic.

It seems never to have occurred to most writers on Eakins that the artist may have invented rather than observed these elements. In the case of the Hayes portrait, however, we know that Eakins's likeness was not executed from life. Hayes was unwilling to consent to the long poses Eakins's method required. Hayes did agree to let Eakins into his office to observe him at work, but he moved about too much for Eakins to make proper sketches. Consequently, the portrait of Hayes was essentially an invention in which, to use his own expressive phrase, "I had to construct him as I would a little animal."[70]

Eakins's portrait was real in the sense that some characters in novels seem "real," but not real in the sense that it closely corresponded with an actual person. Those who knew Hayes, in fact, felt that Eakins had not created a satisfactory likeness. "This work of Eakins is such a caricature," wrote A. Loudon Snowden, who knew Hayes well, "that it gives no pleasure to any of your friends."[71]

In short, Eakins's alleged "realism" is of a peculiar sort, since his paintings do not closely resemble their subjects. Instead, the "realism" is communicated by the style of the painting itself, and does not require outside verification. Eakins's principal device for making things seem real was to undercut the notion that things could exist in a harmonious or ideal state. Introducing such qualities, however, often had disturbing implications, which were unacceptable to his patrons.

In the case of Hayes, Eakins did not take into account the political sensitivity of showing the president with a flushed face. Since Hayes was a well-known teetotaler, the act of depicting him with a flushed complexion, which suggested intoxication, immediately stirred up hostile commentary. Thus, the *Delaware County Republican* objected that the "rubicund countenance" in Eakins's portrait was a poor way to characterize "a temperate, not to say a temperance man." "As such a 'counterfeit presentiment' is likely to create erroneous impressions, prejudicial to our Chief Magistrate," the paper editorialized, "it is hoped that it will be either removed or 'turned to the wall,' at the earliest possible moment."[72] Paradoxically, the things that Eakins did to make his paintings appear "real" and "honest," also made them slanderous and untrue.

A still more acrimonious case of a disputed likeness concerned the business leader Robert C. Ogden. Once again the honesty and truthfulness of Eakins's likeness was disputed. When challenged, Eakins then behaved in a way at odds with the view that he was a man of integrity. The incident opens up multidimensional aspects of how Eakins handled the slippery issue of "truth" and "truthfulness."

The Ogden commission was arranged for Eakins by the painter Robert C. Stokes. Stokes had studied with Eakins, and during the summer of 1903 Eakins painted his portrait (later destroyed by Stokes's family, who thought that it was ugly and not a good likeness). During this process, Stokes suggested that Eakins could make money by painting portraits of New Yorkers. He then put Eakins in touch with Robert Curtis Ogden, who had grown up in Philadelphia but had made his fortune in New York, as head of Wanamaker's New York department store. A warmhearted, generous man, Ogden dispersed much of his wealth through philanthropy, focusing on education for African Americans in the South. He was a trustee and benefactor of both the Hampton Institute and the Tuskegee Institute.

Eakins started the portrait of Ogden early in 1904, probably in January, and had finished it by mid March. Stokes supplied his New York studio to Eakins free of charge while he worked on the project. Eakins's procedures were unusually elaborate, since he not only placed a grid on the wall behind Ogden and insisted that he hold an exact position against it, but drew a small square with diagonals on the opposite wall and insisted that Ogden keep his eyes fixed on this point. Ogden, however, disliked the portrait from the first, considering it a bad likeness. Stokes was also intensely critical. Even by the standard of the rest of his work, Eakins's portrait presents a man who seems cold and frozen. Ogden's expression does not seem to correspond in any way with what we know from other sources about his character.

Robert C. Ogden, 1904. *Oil on canvas, 72 ¼ x 48 ⅜ in., Hirshhorn Museum and Sculpture Garden, Smithsonian Institution, gift of the Joseph H. Hirshhorn Foundation, 1966.* Eakins tripled the price of his portrait of Ogden after the sitter protested that it was not a good likeness. Ogden was a generous philanthropist, particularly dedicated to the education of African Americans in the South.

Difference of opinion about the merit of the portrait soon escalated into a nasty dispute over its price. When he started the painting, Eakins declared that he was willing to make it without charge. At Stokes's insistence that Eakins be paid, he proposed a fee of $500. After both Ogden and Stokes complained about the finished painting, however, Eakins sent Ogden a bill for $1,500, three times the amount that he had stated.

Since Eakins usually made his portraits at no charge, it is hard to avoid the conclusion that he wished to retaliate against Stokes and Ogden for their low opinion of his work. Indeed, Eakins's letter to Ogden has a tone of personal animosity, attacking Stokes in forceful terms:

From the very beginning of my work, Mr. Stokes assumed towards me a
patronizing air and a spirit of criticism which his own accomplishments in art
do not warrant. He was quite angry that I did not exaggerate the length of
your upper lip, that I did not change the color of your hand and of your beard.
In his artistic ignorance he wanted me several times to change my whole composition and pointed out to me a hundred errors which I know existed only in
his untrained imagination. He was provoked that I consulted another than
himself as to where I should get a frame. Finally he criticized my price, which
comes with very ill grace from one who sold a color sketch for $5,000 which I
do not think would resell in any picture store in the world for ten dollars.[73]

Eakins went on to argue that such portraitists as Raimundo Madrazo and
Theobold Chartran received large sums for their work "and certainly do not
paint better than I do."[74] He also declared that it was customary for artists to
set the fee for their portraits when they completed the work—although this
was certainly not customary at the time. In a revealing aside, Eakins declared
that he should be treated with the same respect awarded by a gentleman to a
physician or a lawyer.

To avoid argument, Ogden was ready to pay the bill, but Stokes asked
Ogden to give him a check for $500 and visited Eakins at Mount Vernon Street
to deliver it. When he arrived, Eakins was working in the top-floor studio.
Eakins refused to come down, sending a reply through a servant that he was
too busy to see anyone. Stokes sent the servant back to tell the artist that it
was something important. Eakins replied via the servant that nothing that
Stokes could say could be important. Stokes then left the house without seeing him.

To settle the matter, Ogden paid the bill of $1,500. Not long afterwards,
Stokes spotted Eakins wheeling his bicycle down a street in Philadelphia.
Stokes stopped him and said, "That was a dirty trick you played." According
to Stokes, Eakins looked sheepish, but rode off without saying anything.[75]

By any reckoning, Eakins's demands over payment for his painting were
not only dishonest, but also vindictive and petty. Indeed, his behavior over the
payment raises question about his motives in making the painting itself, which
both Stokes and Ogden believed was not an accurate likeness. Why should we
believe that someone who behaved dishonestly in daily life produced art that
was absolutely truthful? Is it not reasonable to suppose that Eakins's art may
have been less than completely honest as well?

Negative Reactions

Because of their unflattering treatment, Eakins's portraits profoundly distressed many of his sitters and their friends. Mrs. Dodge did not like Eakins's
portrait of her (1896). One of her friends declared that it was "a bad likeness"
that made her look "like a fishwife." Frank Linton reported that Eakins's portrait of *Miss Eleanor Pue* (1907) did not resemble her, and that her mother wept
when she saw it. The sitter confirmed this when he interviewed her. "I don't
blame her in a way," Goodrich commented. "Eakins made it the Eakins
female with a long nose, tight lips, high cheek bones, a dusky complexion, and
a glassy, unhappy, injured beaten look—hurt. The face dark, with cold shadows, greenish—the neck startlingly white under the dark chin—as in 'The Old
Fashioned Dress.' She says her friends called it 'The Goddess of Murder' when
it was shown at the Academy as 'Portrait of a Lady.'"[76] Helen Parker noted
that Eakins portrait (*The Old-Fashioned Dress* of 1908) made her feel "decapitated," and wrote to Schendler that, "I cried the first time I saw it at the Academy."[77]

Since Eakins's portraits look so "real," the people Goodrich interviewed
often provided stories to explain why Eakins's sitters looked so unhappy.
Often they seemed apologetic about the fact that the person they knew was
not quite the same as the one portrayed with such apparent realism in the
Eakins portrait.

Mrs. Cryer, the widow of *Matthew H. Cryer* (1903), thought that Eakins's
likeness of her husband made him look too "tired," but then remarked that
her husband was "tired" at the time and that he later suffered from a nervous
illness. "He got to look more and more like it," she noted. Mrs. Montgomery,
the daughter of *Mrs. Helen McKnight* (circa 1903) noted that her mother was "a
dainty eater" and "a rather sad person," and that "Eakins brought it all out."
Mrs. Wilson Shaw Ward told Goodrich that she "was not well" when Eakins
made her portrait and that she was tired from having to climb three or four
flights of stairs to his studio. Also, her husband's business had just failed. She
noted that none of her children liked the portrait. "It has been in the cellar for
a number of years," she remarked.[78]

Miss Borie, whose father, the painter Adolph Borie, was painted by Eakins
in 1910, described the canvas as "a fine likeness," but noted that her father had
had an illness a while before—sunstroke—and that the portrait showed it.
Even less plausibly, Elizabeth Corless noted that Eakins's portrait of her
mother, *Mrs. George Morris* (1905), was painted during a thunderstorm, and

that consequently she looked distressed. ("Bunk," Goodrich noted, "because she said later that her mother posed a great many times for it—there couldn't have *always* been a thunderstorm.")[79]

In the same vein as the thunderstorm story, Elizabeth Corless also told Goodrich that Eakins's portrait of her father, *George Morris* (circa 1900), who had been a hunting and boating companion of Benjamin Eakins, was made at a time when her father's business partner was cheating him. Consequently Morris was anxious and was always gritting his teeth. She showed Goodrich photographs of her father as proof that Eakins's portrait was not a good likeness. "Certainly the portrait is of a much more grim and terrible looking individual than the photographs," Goodrich noted. "There is none of their joviality. The portrait seems to be a little caricatured."

More sophisticated individuals sometimes declared that Eakins had produced a bad portrait but a memorable image. Frank Linton reported that Eakins's portrait of his mother (1904) "is a very bad likeness, although beautiful painting."[80] Mrs. Harmstead, perhaps prodded by Goodrich, declared that Eakins's rendering of her father, the painter and collector Edward Taylor Snow, was "a masterpiece," but added, somewhat paradoxically, that it had none of her father's soul. "She showed me a photo of Snow," Goodrich noted. "He was more genial than Eakins made him. Eakins made him look rugged and homely—a little like an American merchant of the old school." Mrs. Cryer, as already noted, declared that Eakins made her husband look too tired, but added that she appreciated his portrait as a painting and thought it was like a Rembrandt.[81]

The prevalence of far-fetched stories about Eakins's canvases raises the question of whether the "facts" related about some of his sitters are truly facts, or stories made up to explain why the individual in question looks so sad or severe. One of the more fanciful stories is that told by Hendricks about the portrait of *John B. Gest* (1905), the head of the Fidelity Bank in Philadelphia. According to Hendricks, he "sits tensely and arrogantly, clutching in his hand the first nickel he ever made."[82] Hendricks gives no source for the claim that Gest has a nickel in his hands, and notably, Goodrich does not repeat this claim but simply states that Gest's hands are "tightly clenched, as if holding money bags."[83] In fact, even this may be questioned. Gest is actually grasping his right hand with his left, as if to prevent it from escaping. It seems fairly clear that the "first nickel" never really existed, and that the story was fabricated to explain the tense attitude of the sitter.[84]

The devastating harshness of Eakins's portraits made them dangerous, since it invited negative commentary on the person portrayed. While Richard Wood's brother felt that Eakins's likeness was "too severe" another acquaintance blamed this homeliness on the sitter. "To put it frankly," this gentleman wrote, "Mr. Eakins was given the task of painting a portrait of probably the ugliest man in Philadelphia, and has certainly succeeded."[85] Similarly, Bishop Henry Moellder wrote to Eakins with regard to his portrait of Archbishop Elder, noting, "some who have seen the picture do not like the Archbishop's expression, but that was not your fault. You gave the Archbishop the expression he had while you were doing the work."[86]

In such instances it remains open to question whether Eakins had accurately captured the appearance of the sitter. Nonetheless, in the literature on the artist the testimony of his portraits is generally viewed as infallible truth, without any need for additional corroboration. After noting that Mrs. Louis Husson (c. 1905) "appears to be a tight-lipped, narrow, small-souled woman," Hendricks declares, without citing any other evidence, that "there is no doubt that Mrs. Husson looked the way he painted her."[87] Similarly, Schendler described Helen Parker as "a sweet dull young woman who stares off in a kind of trance," without stopping to consider whether Helen Parker really was the sort of woman whom Eakins portrayed.[88]

A sitter's dislike of a painting has generally been viewed as a lapse of judgment on their part, and very likely a proof of vanity. Speaking of the unflattering likeness that the artist made of the Reverend Patrick J. Garvey (1902), Hendricks writes, "It was the hard eyes, according to legend, that Garvey did not like. But more than one of his seminarians agreed with Eakins that his eyes were hard."[89]

In many instances, like a good caricaturist, Eakins probably seized on some quality that actually existed in his sitter, and exaggerated it to dramatic effect. But the fact that these qualities were almost never flattering raises questions about his motives. The celebrated painter Edwin A. Abbey, on being asked why he did not sit for Eakins, humorously replied: "Because he would bring out all the traits of my character that I have been trying to hide from the public for years."[90]

Rejection and Destruction

Almost invariably, Eakins's portraits were poorly received. Four of Eakins's commissioned portraits were rejected. That of President Rutherford Hayes was destroyed.[91] In 1899 the colleagues of Dean James W. Holland objected to the dean's "tense almost haggard expression" and refused to pay for it. As Holland's son explained, Eakins, "having no general market at the time . . . as a friendly gesture gave the picture to my mother."[92] In two cases, those of Robert Ogden and Atwater Lee, the sitters agreed to pay Eakins's fee, but never displayed them; one returned the portrait to Eakins's studio.[93]

Most often, Eakins would simply give the portraits he had painted to the sitter or the sitter's family, often with an accompanying inscription. Many never bothered to pick up their portraits. Others destroyed the gift. Eakins painted both James and George Wood, the sons of his physician Dr. Horatio C. Wood, but both portraits have disappeared. George wrote to Goodrich: "He painted a portrait of me which was quite 'Eakineeze,' so much so that my family got it lost." In 1903 Eakins gave a portrait of his former pupil, Frank W. Stokes, to his family, who destroyed it. The same fate met his portrait of the pugilist Charlie McKeever, which Eakins gave to the fighter's mother. John Singer Sargent (or his family) misplaced or destroyed the portrait that Eakins gave him of their mutual friend Dr. J. William White. Similarly, the Buckley family destroyed the painting of Edward S. Buckley that Eakins painted in 1906. His daughter wrote: "It was so unsatisfactory that we destroyed it not wishing his descendants to think of their grandfather as resembling such a portrait."[94] Mary Waldon, the Superior of the Order of the Sisters of Mercy, did not like her portrait by Eakins and called in another painter, William Antrim, to paint one that was more pleasing. Antrim took the Eakins portrait off its stretcher and "tossed" it into the attic of his studio, where it was subsequently lost.[95]

Those paintings that do survive were often placed out of sight. Mrs. Dodge kept her portrait in an unused third-floor room. Patrick J. Garvey kept his portrait under his bed, and after his death the picture passed to his nephew, who kept it in a closet. Eakins's portrait of Douglass Morgan Hall was passed on to the sitter's sister, who stored it in the back of a closet, facing the wall. Because the commissions were never formal, it was often unclear who owned the paintings. Eakins loaned his portrait of Louis Kenton thirteen times. Four times it was listed as the property of Mrs. Kenton; twice as belonging to Kenton; and four times without an owner at all. Despite this, the painting remained at Mount Vernon Street after Eakins's death.[96] However, when a sitter did want a portrait, Eakins often appears to have been reluctant to part with it. He declined to give *The Concert Singer* to Weda Cook, even after she wrote to him requesting it.

At times, Eakins engaged in confrontations with owners about their appreciation of his portraits. In 1906 when he asked to borrow his portrait of Mrs. William D. Frishmuth (1904) from the Museum of Science and Art of the University of Pennsylvania, he was told that if he removed the picture from the walls he would not be permitted to return it to the museum. Consequently, Eakins borrowed the painting and kept it in his parlor until his death.[97]

When his work was criticized, Eakins responded with torrents of sarcasm. Rather than addressing the specific matter at hand, he tended to rely on his authority as an artistic professional. When the physician Dr. Jacob Mendez da Costa did not like his portrait, Eakins responded:

> I do not consider the picture a failure at all, or I should not have parted with it or consented to exhibit it. As to your friends, I have known some of them who I esteem greatly to give most injudicious art advice and to admire what is ignorant, ill constructed, vulgar, and bad; and as to the concurrent testimony of the newspapers, which I have not seen, I wonder at your mentioning them after our many conversations regarding them. I presume my position in art is not second to your own in medicine, and I can hardly imagine myself writing to you a letter like this: Dear Doctor, The concurrent testimony of the newspapers and of friends is that your treatment of my case has not been one of your successes. I therefore suggest that you treat me for a while with Mrs. Brown's Metaphysical Discovery.[98]

Like so much of Eakins's writing, the response is fascinating both for its tone and for the way it shifts the subject. He does not specifically address the merits or demerits of the painting itself. He does make it clear, however, that he is contemptuous of newspapers and popular taste and regards himself as an "expert," like a doctor, whose opinions should not be challenged. In his gratuitous reference to "Mrs Brown's Metaphysical Discovery," he again associates femininity with foolery.

Portrait of Dr. Jacob Mendez da Costa. *Courtesy of the Historic Collections of Pennsylvania Hospital, Philadelphia.* **When da Costa complained about his portrait, Eakins responded with sarcastic invective.**

While Eakins's sitters have been harshly criticized for destroying their portraits, Eakins and his wife engaged in the same practice. William Merritt Chase kept Eakins's portrait of him (circa 1899), but Eakins (or his wife) destroyed the one of Eakins by Chase, which was made around the same time.[99] Similarly, the sculptor William O'Donovan made a bust of Eakins that does not survive. Goodrich notes, "Susan Eakins had strong feelings about portraits of her husband, and she may not have liked it."[100]

While Eakins's interest in real life, and in engaging art with life, has often been noted, his paintings have generally been examined in essentially formal terms. When we probe more deeply into the process by which they were made, his art gains another dimension in ways that are often painful to admit.

PART THREE

THE CASE OF
THOMAS EAKINS

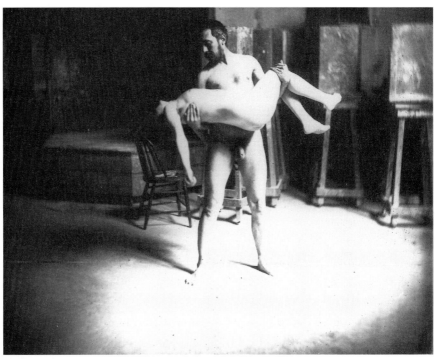

Thomas Eakins Nude, Holding Nude Female in His Arms, Looking Down, ca. 1885. *Dry-plate negative, 4 x 5 in., courtesy of The Pennsylvania Academy of the Fine Arts, Philadelphia, Charles Bregler's Thomas Eakins Collection, purchased with the partial support of the Pew Memorial Trust.*

Chapter 19

LOVE OF LOOKING

In seeking to understand Eakins and his work—above all to grasp the reasons for the scandals that surrounded him, and the reasons why his art is so compelling and memorable—we have looked so far at evidence of two distinct types: information about Eakins's life and information about his art. Both present challenges of interpretation.

The biographical data is often contradictory. Indeed, one of the recurrent themes of Eakins's biography is that he inspired strong argument and disagreement—his defenders maintaining that he was idealistic and high-minded, his attackers convinced that he was completely immoral. Given this inconsistency, and the degree of passion and anger on both sides, there is reason to suppose that both his defenders and attackers often misinterpreted what happened. Separating truth from falsehood, fact from supposition, is not easy.

The artistic evidence presents still more daunting challenges. Eakins's paintings have a powerful emotional quality and they often feel like confessions. We often feel that they communicate with a unique immediacy, since in his brushwork we encounter Eakins directly, rather than through the statements of some third party. But interpreting Eakins's paintings is by no means simple. They seem to elude simple readings. What is more, while it is tempting to study the paintings for psychological and biographical clues, the paintings clearly diverge from real life, albeit subtly. Eakins's "realism" often seems a form of deceptiveness, since it gives plausibility to things that were not true, for example, in his rendition of clothing and personality in his late portraits. On many occasions he seems to deliberately misrepresent and malign the character of his sitters. It is often difficult to tell whether Eakins's paintings narrate facts or give the guise of reality to psychological fantasies.

Yet even with these difficulties, to a striking degree the biographical data and the artistic material tell a similar story. They seem to shed light on each other. Similar themes, or patterns of behavior, are repeated in both. To grasp these connections it may be helpful to organize some of the repetitive elements of Eakins's life into lists, drawing both from biographical material and artistic evidence.[1]

First, we can take the issue of incest. I know of no other nineteenth-century American artist who was accused of incest, but in Eakins's life this issue surfaces repeatedly, both as a topic that preoccupied him and as an accusation against him. To cite a few examples:

1867   Eakins writes a letter to his father declaring that the inhabitants of Zermatt, Switzerland "breed by incest" and declaring that he would like to kill them.

1876   Eakins paints *The Gross Clinic*. Art historian Michael Fried has proposed that the painting expresses a fantasy of an anal sexual assault by a father figure.

1886   Frank Stephens, Eakins's brother-in-law, accuses him of incest with his recently deceased sister Margaret.

1888–1895   Lillian Hammitt becomes insane and declares that she is married to Eakins, after having described him as a "father."

1891   Eakins write a letter to Edward Coates, then president of the Pennsylvania Academy, protesting that his painting of *The Agnew Clinic* was excluded from an exhibition at the Academy. He concludes the letter with a long passage by Rabelais, describing a nun who is a victim of rape and incest.

1897   Eakins's niece, Ella Crowell, commits suicide after declaring that he sexually molested her.

1900–1910   Eakins's friends, relatives and associates, including Samuel Murray, suspect that he is having an affair with Addie Williams, who moved into the family home after his father's death. Addie is a relative of the Crowells, and thus related to Eakins by marriage.

This list is not necessarily complete, because other paintings by Eakins, such as the many versions of *William Rush*, seem to explore his relationship with his mother, and thus possibly touch on the theme of incest. Even in its brief form, however, two things about this list are compelling. First, the issue of incest pervades Eakins's life. It appears in his art, his letters, and his personal behavior. The second is a paradox. On the one hand, Eakins seems to be unusually repulsed by incest, to the point where it leads him to threats of violence. On the other hand, this accusation is repeatedly lodged against him.

It is tempting to suppose that this theme of incest is somehow connected with another major leitmotif of Eakins's career, his compulsive interest in disrobing—whether undressing himself or undressing his students and models. The instances are so numerous that I will not attempt to list them all, but even a summary list makes it clear that this preoccupation extended throughout the entirety of his career.

1865 (approx)   Shortly before Eakins leaves for Paris, Charles Fussell paints a portrait of him seated in the nude at his easel.

1872   Eakins's mother dies of exhaustion following mania. Severely depressed people may be unable to dress properly, while some patients with severe mania will throw off their clothes.

1883–1886   While teaching at the Pennsylvania Academy, Eakins takes a great many photographs of himself in the nude, poses in the nude, and sometimes undresses in front of his students. One set of photographs shows him in the nude carrying a nude woman in his arms.

Sometime between 1870 and 1882   Eakins repeatedly strolls with no pants on into a bedroom occupied by his sisters Margaret and Caroline and his aunt Ella. He frequently does so in the presence of a family friend Sallie Shaw. Caroline feels so uncomfortable that she moves to a more private bedroom in another part of the house.

Circa 1883   Eakins takes nude photographs of his wife and of other students, and uses them as the basis for his painting *Arcadia*.

1884–1885   Eakins paints *Swimming*, in which he shows himself in the nude with five other nude men. He had photographs taken of the group in the nude and also took separate nude photographs of each individual in the painting.

1886–1892   While teaching at the Philadelphia Art Students League, Eakins takes photographs of himself and his students in the nude. He posts some of these photographs on the walls of his classroom.

1890 (approx)   Eakins undresses in the next room and then walks into his studio naked while a woman is posing for his friend Samuel Murray. He comments that she had probably never seen a naked man before and that he thought she might like to see one.

1890 Ella Crowell tells her parents that Eakins forced her to pose for him in the nude and spanked her when she resisted. She also reports that he touched her genitals and made her touch his.

1887–1895 Lillian Hammitt poses for Eakins in the nude. She later becomes convinced that she is married to him. In the 1890s she is picked up on the street in Philadelphia, wearing a bathing suit and declaring that she is "Mrs. Thomas Eakins."

1892 (approx) While Francis Ziegler is privately posing for him in the nude, Eakins unexpectedly brings a woman into the room.

1890–1910 Eakins repeatedly asks women who sit for him to undress and pose for him in the nude.

1910 (approx) A group of photographs, show Eakins, then in his mid-sixties, swimming in the nude. One of these photographs shows full frontal nudity.

Eakins seems to have been particularly fascinated by exposed buttocks, and was interested in themes associated with buttocks, such as defecation and anal intercourse. Indeed, buttocks are the center of interest in his most ambitious paintings.

1865 (approx) When he is about sixteen, on the margin of a rendering of gears, Eakins sketches a figure bending over and exposing his buttocks.

1875 In a letter to his friend Earl Shinn, Eakins claims that his mother would give him vermifuge, an intestinal purge, to curb his outbursts of sentimental poetry in grammer school.

1876 Eakins's painting *The Gross Clinic* focuses on the exposed buttocks of a helpless patient, whose sex is ambiguous.

1883 Eakins's painting *William Rush* prominently features the buttocks of a model who is posing for the sculptor. The physique of the figure is androgynous.

1883 (approx) Eakins paints *Aracadia,* which features the buttocks of a reclining figure. Although it looks like a boy, this figure was derived from a photograph of Eakins's wife.

1883–1885 Eakins paints *The Swimming Hole,* whose center of interest is the feminized buttocks of his assistant, Jesse Godley, who was eighteen years old at the time.

1885 (approx) When a cow defecates in his classroom, in front of a group of female students, Eakins tells Thomas Anshutz to take a close-up photograph of the action.

1889 Eakins has photographs taken of himself in the nude, featuring his buttocks. He also takes photographs of a female model in a similar pose.

1889 Eakins takes photographs of Walt Whitman's companion, Bill Duckett, which feature his buttocks as well as objects that are strikingly phallic in shape.

1891 Eakins writes a letter to Edward Coates, with a postscript copied from Rabelais that describes a nun who signaled with her buttocks after being raped.

1898 Eakins paints *Salutat,* which focuses on the buttocks of a victorious boxer.

1908 Eakins returns to the theme of *William Rush* in a painting that shows the model facing away form the spectator, making her buttocks the main feature of interest.

Once again this list does not pretend to be complete. Throughout his life Eakins would have seen the bare buttocks of both male and female models. In addition, there are many instances in which Eakins undressed and presumably revealed his buttocks, as well as instances in which he showed photographs of his bare buttocks to visitors to his home or studio.

The motives for this compulsion do not seem straightforward or clear. Many writers have interpreted the prominent buttocks in both *William Rush* and *Swimming* as an indication of sexual attraction. In other instances, however, such as the prostrate patient in *The Gross Clinic,* Eakins's depiction of buttocks suggests revulsion, and he seems to have been abnormally interested in defecation, as suggested by the dirty jokes he told in his classroom, as well as by his desire to photograph a defecating cow. The theme of bending over and exposing buttocks suggests some element of hostility or embarrassment, or both.

A major theme of Eakins's life, which most writers on his work seem to have deliberately ignored, is that of family conflict.

1873–1877 (approx) Eakins feuds with his sister Caroline, because he killed her cat without consulting her.

1873–1877 (approx) Will Crowell, the fiancé of Eakins's sister Frances, threatens to kill him for an unspecified reason.

1886 Frank Stephens, the husband of Eakins's sister Caroline, accuses him of incest, bestiality, and immoral behavior with his students. Shortly after, both Frank and Caroline Stephens are expelled from the family home.

1886–1887 Elizabeth Macdowell, the sister of Eakins's wife, accuses him of improprieties with his students. Several years later, she recants her accusations.

1887 Charles Stephens, the cousin of Frank Stephens, accuses Eakins of improper behavior with his fiancé, Alice Barber.

1890 Eakins and his wife are outraged that his sister Frances and her husband, Will Crowell, have sent their son Benjamin to work with Eakins's accuser, Frank Stephens.

1895–1899 Ella Crowell, whose father had threatened to kill Eakins earlier, becomes mentally unbalanced and threatens Eakins (and others) with a revolver.

1897 Eakins's sister Frances and her husband break off all relations with Eakins because they believe that he shamed or molested their daughter Ella and brought about her suicide.

Also striking is the prevalence of mental illness both in Eakins's family and in his immediate circle.

1872 Eakins's mother dies of mania.

1872 Because of the strain of caring for his mother, Eakins suffers from "exhaustion"—presumably some form of nervous breakdown.

1886 After being fired from the Pennsylvania Academy, Eakins seeks medical help for nervous exhaustion.

1886 Susan Eakins also suffers from depression in this period. Her brother writes that he is worried by her worn appearance and fears that she is headed toward "insanity or death."

1886 Eakins's student Amelia Van Buren, who often stayed in his home, is diagnosed as suffering from neurasthenia and exhaustion from worry. "The trouble with me is in my head," she writes to Susan Eakins in May.

1887–1888 Eakins's student Lillian Hammitt goes insane and is committed to an asylum.

1892 Eakins's student Benjamin Fox, who posed for the painting *Swimming,* is admitted to the Lunatic Asylum of the Philadelphia Hospital for "acute mania."

1895 (approx) Eakins's aunt Ella, his mother's sister, becomes *non compos mentis.* Eakins devises a bell to warn the family when she wanders from her room.

1897 Eakins's niece Ella Crowell becomes emotionally unstable and is committed to a mental hospital in Philadelphia. After a short stay her parents bring her home to Avondale, where she commits suicide.

1912 Eakins's student Douglas Norman Hall, the subject of one of his major portraits, dies in the Philadelphia Hospital for the Insane.

The contradictory nature of Eakins's behavior is strikingly evident in his treatment of animals. Many accounts describe his fondness for animals. He kept a small menagerie in his home, including a dog Harry; a monkey Bobby; cats; a rabbit; tame rats; mice; and a turtle. (When Goodrich visited Mrs. Eakins in 1930, the turtle was still roaming around in the backyard.)[2] Eakins also brought a horse and an Indian pony home with him from the Dakotas. Nonetheless, Eakins was capable of acts of extreme violence against animals, such as shooting his sister's cat, or shooting the heads off deer when he was in the Dakotas. During his visits to Avondale he liked to kill small creatures, such as squirrels and rabbits, and then dissect them.[3] This violent side of Eakins's personality appears to have been somehow connected with his fascination with guns. Although most Americans did not regularly carry a gun, Eakins carried a revolver throughout his life and often used guns to make threats or to kill animals.

1866 To intimidate French students who are hazing him in Gérôme's atelier, Eakins threatens them with a revolver.

1867–1868 (approx)   Will Sartain comments that Eakins is the only person he knows in Paris who carries a revolver.

1870 While visiting Spain, Eakins threatens some porters with his revolver.

1874 Eakins paints a canvas of himself and his father hunting reed birds with a shotgun; he also portrays his father's friends shooting birds.

1875–1876 (approx)   Eakins shoots his sister Caroline's cat.

1876 Eakins portrays his father's friend Will Schuster shooting birds.

1876 Eakins illustrates "The Spelling Bee at Angell's" for *Scribner's Magazine* with a scene of a poor speller who eliminates his rivals with his six-shooter.

1880–1897 (approx)   Eakins shoots small animals at Avondale, the farm of his sister Frances, often dissecting the animals he has killed.

1886 In a letter to his wife from the Dakotas, Eakins boasts that he has been shooting the heads off of deer with his rifle.

1886 Eakins brings a .44 rifle, a .22 caliber rifle, and a double-barreled shotgun back with him from the Dakotas. He later gives some of these guns to the Crowell family.

1888 Eakins paints *Cowboys in the Badlands*, which shows two cowboys with guns.

1889 While strolling through Philadelphia at night, Eakins threatens a possible robber with his revolver.

1892 Eakins paints Franklin Schenck in cowboy costume, with a revolver strapped to his side.

1897 Ella Crowell threatens to kill both Eakins and Weda Cook with a revolver.

1898 Ella Crowell commits suicide—probably with a shotgun that Eakisn had given to the Crowell family.

1905 Admiral Melville brushes up against Eakins's revolver while they are attending a prize fight. He comments that unlike Eakins he has never carried a gun—even in more dangerous parts of the world.

This list suggests overlapping themes, since it includes not only Eakins's behavior, but that of his niece Ella Crowell. Ella's behavior seems to have some parallels with that of Eakins.

A great many of the odd and troubling things about Eakins can be grouped into two broad categories. The first is that he insisted on pressuring other people, both women and men, to disrobe in front of him, and also enjoyed displaying his own naked body to others. Very often he did this with a clear intent to shock, often using crude language, dirty jokes, or verbal insinuations for a similar effect.

The second is that Eakins's relationship with his siblings and close relatives was seriously out of order. On the one hand, we have siblings who acrimoniously broke off all contact with each other. In fact, by the end of his life Eakins had completely severed relations with all the surviving members of his immediate family. On the other hand, we have the reverse of this excessive distancing, in the form of two accusations of unnaturally close family contact: incest. While these accusations cannot be firmly proven, their very existence is remarkable. Public accusations of incest are rare. I ask the reader to consider: how many people do you know who have been publicly accused of incest? Previous writers have invariably dismissed the accusations of incest as incredible, but I think this is a mistake. Indeed, I believe these accusations point to the very crux of the Eakins enigma.

Exhibitionism

What was going on? Eakins's frequent episodes of disrobing, or pressuring others to do so, are characteristics of a well-known and often-described form of mental illness, that of the exhibitionist-voyeur—someone who likes to see others undress and to undress in front of them. In popular parlance, such individuals are known as peeping toms. A substantial body of literature documents this disorder, and peeping tom Eakins fits perfectly into the standard psychological profile.

The word "exhibitionism" has been used fairly frequently in the literature on Eakins. Jennifer Doyle has noted that Eakins's behavior "suggests a tendency toward exhibitionism."[4] Kathleen Foster has noted the Eakins displayed "an element of exhibitionism."[5] Jack Flam has even written that Eakins was a "daredevil exhibitionist."[6] While Goodrich did not use the word "exhibition-ism," he did declare that Eakins's interest in undressing was "an obsession," suggesting that this fixation had some psychologically abnormal quality.[7]

Nonetheless, it appears that no writer on Eakins's work has consulted the literature on such behavior, particularly that written from a Freudian perspective, although by the 1930s, when Goodrich wrote his first book on Eakins, Freud's theories were already avidly followed and discussed by many American intellectuals. No writer on Eakins even mentioned Sigmund Freud until 1987, when Michael Fried proposed that Eakins's paintings appear to exhibit Oedipal anxieties. Fried did not specifically address the issue of exhibitionism, nor have any subsequent writers on Eakins. But Fried did suggest that Eakins seems to have been preoccupied with castration—and according to Freudian theory, a fear of castration lies at the root of exhibitionist behavior.

Exhibitionism may be defined as the display of the male genitals to another person or persons outside an intimate relationship, and as a limited act without further progress toward assault or intercourse being intended or desired. Exhi-bitionism is closely related to voyeurism and the connection between the two has been recognized since the syndrome was first identified. Indeed, the pleas-ure of exhibitionism seems to stem in large part from imagining the experi-ence of a viewer. As the psychologist David Stafford-Clark has written:

> Perversions are forms of incomplete maturity of sexual object and aim, which prevent full union of any kind with another individual. Among them may be included voyeurism where looking at other people of the same or opposite sex naked, watching others having sexual intercourse, seeking to see the geni-talia of others, or watching them in the act of urination or defecation, takes the place of a more complete sexual aim. Exhibitionism, the desire to display and if possible to provoke a counter-display of the sexual organs, is the mirror image of voyeurism.[8]

Voyeurism can become openly aggressive when the victim is forced to undress. As I was completing this chapter, the local newspaper reported an instance of this type, in which a female postal worker was forced to disrobe and walk naked in front of her coworkers by a male colleague who threatened to kill her unless she complied.[9]

On the whole Eakins seems to have used gentler methods of persuasion than those employed in this Post Office episode, including seductive coaxing, but it is clear that in his role as teacher he often coerced students who did not wish to undress into doing so. In at least one instance, that of Ella Crowell, he apparently made use of physical force—a spanking—to persuade her to comply.[10]

Such behavior certainly has a sexual subtext, but seeks pleasure in a way quite different from actual sex. Indeed, for such actions to create a thrill it is clearly necessary that sex be seen as something shameful and indecent. The goal is not so much sexual pleasure as power—achieved by inflicting embarrassment on someone.

Literature on exhibitionism has been in existence for more than a century and predates Freud. Laseque first described the phenomenon in 1877, and descriptive studies were published by East (1924) and Ellis (1933).[11] Freud's writings provide the foundation for modern understanding of the inner dynamics of the disorder. Although many aspects of exhibitionism are still not well understood, certain common themes have been repeated in the literature about it for many decades.

In psychological terms, exhibitionism appears to be a uniquely male phenomenon. Women, such as strippers, sometimes engage in activities of exposing their bodies that appear to be somewhat analogous, but when interviewed they prove to have completely different motivations. Moreover, stripping is legal and exhibitionism is not. Exhibitionism accounts for about one-third of all sex offenses, and men are arrested for this behavior more often than for any other sexual offense.[12] Nonetheless, reports indicate that most episodes of exhibitionism are not reported. In many instances exhibitionists engage in hundreds of episodes of exhibitionist behavior before they are caught.

The disorder has many puzzling and paradoxical aspects. The behavior often dramatically contrasts with the "normal" behavior of the individual in question. Exhibitionists are usually not very open or revealing in daily life. They are often closed, guarded, hidden, secretive, noncommittal in interpersonal relations, and they tend to withhold their thoughts and feeling. (These traits fit well with what we know about Eakins.)[13] While the act itself appears to be aggressive, many studies suggest that exhibitionists are likely to be timid, and to feel inferior. Thus, the personality of exhibitionists often seems diametrically opposed to their behavior. Surveys consistently indicate that exhibitionists do not differ from the rest of the population with regard to intelligence, education level, or vocational interests. Most exhibitionists are married or have been married although some evidence suggests that they tend to marry late (as Eakins did).

Exhibitionism is often accompanied by extreme and bizarre forms of denial. One individual, for example, walked into a restaurant with his zipper open and fondled himself in front of a waitress. He was subsequently taken to police headquarters where his underpants were examined and seminal fluid was found. Nonetheless, this individual continued to deny both to the police and to his own lawyer that any sort of exposure had occurred. Macdonald (1973), who cites this case, also presents numerous additional examples of the elaborate and unconvincing explanations that exhibitionists give to authorities once they are apprehended. A typical instance is a man at a bus stop with his penis out who later sat down on a bench and held his penis in his hand. When apprehended he explained.

> I went to the corner to wait for the bus. I had trouble with my zipper and sometimes it comes unzipped. I don't think my penis was out. The next thing I know I was arrested.[14]

It seems possible that this denial is due to some sort of memory loss, similar to that associated with alcoholism.

The motives are often puzzling to the exhibitionist himself. Whether explaining their behavior in court or in a psychiatric interview, many exhibitionists express bewilderment, and describe being overtaken by the urge to expose. The phrase "something comes over me" is commonly employed. "At the time nothing else matters," one patient explained.[15]

Like alcoholism, exhibitionism blurs the distinction between rational, conscious decision making and uncontrollable compulsion. The exhibitionist's decision to expose himself is undertaken in a conscious state, when the individual is mentally lucid and seemingly able to make choices on a rational basis. But the behavior also has a compulsive aspect and, as mentioned, is often accompanied by extreme forms of denial or lack of memory. Thus, unconscious motives and mechanisms surely influence the syndrome. Recent research suggests that such behavior may have a genetic and chemical component since some forms of exhibitionism are curable or at least treatable with medication.

The sexual motivation for the behavior is ambiguous. Exhibitionists are not interested in sexual conquest since exhibitionism is in itself a goal that substitutes for sexual contact. Some exhibitionists experience erections when they exhibit, but others simply display their flaccid penis without masturbation or any sense of sexual arousal.[16] Eakins, for example, so far as we have documentation, seems to have been a limp exhibitionist. It is unclear what goal exhibitionists hope to achieve and whether their behavior should be considered hostile. When asked to describe their ideal response from a victim, some exhibitionists state that they would like to inspire fear, but in the majority of cases they indicate that they seek favorable, approving responses, such as a smile.[17]

As with many sexual disorders, exhibitionism is difficult to treat, since exhibitionists derive pleasure from their actions.[18] Eakins's stubborn intransigence, which has been perversely misread as a morally honorable quality, is characteristic of exhibitionist-voyeurs. In many instances, psychotherapy or medication, or the two in combination, seem to have positive results, but to date no universally effective form of treatment has been found. Moreover, gauging the effectiveness, or lack thereof, of different forms of treatment is extremely difficult because of the problems of gathering data about a representative group of exhibitionists, and defining the many variables involved. Many exhibitionists seem to cure themselves, whether because the shame of being caught acts as a deterrent, or because the process of growing older lessens their sexual drive, and thus reduces at least one of the factors that causes the behavior.

Many recent studies have attempted to quantify the variables in exhibitionism, but this has proved difficult, in part because establishing a satisfactory sample is not easy. Most such surveys are based on exhibitionists who have been imprisoned, but according to one survey only about 15 percent of incidents of exhibitionism are reported to the police. Studies suggest, in fact, that exhibitionists are generally only arrested when they expose themselves in public places, such as a bus stop or a restaurant.[19]

Exhibitionists who expose themselves at home or in other nonpublic places may shock people, and stir up scandal and commentary, but generally avoid arrest. Indeed, Eakins provides an instance of this game of crossing over social boundaries, but not too far, since he generally exposed himself either at home or in places where there was some kind of excuse for doing so, such as at the shore (nude swimming) or in an artist's studio (nude posing). Although exhibitionists most often expose themselves to young women and children, as Eakins seems to have done on occasion, apparently this does not indicate their sexual preference, but simply their belief that they are less likely to be caught.[20]

The onset of exhibitionistic behavior most frequently begins around either the ages of 11 to 15 or 21 to 25.[21] Eakins's exhibitionist tendencies surely had started by the time he was in his early twenties, since an early oil sketch by

Charles Fussell—made in about 1865, when Eakins was around twenty-one—shows him painting in the nude, surely not a common practice, particularly in Philadelphia.[22]

Goodrich has suggested that Eakins's difficulties in working with the nude created an obsession that became more exaggerated as he grew older—a view that has been echoed by Kathleen Foster.[23] But the many accounts of Eakins's exhibitionist behavior as an old man surely indicate that he behaved in this fashion as a young man as well. Typically, exhibitionism tends to grow less intense with age.

The relative lack of stories about such behavior when Eakins was young is probably due to a lack of documentation. Very few of those who witnessed Eakins's behavior ever set down their experiences in writing, and in some cases, such as the Academy scandal, the accusations against him were so potentially embarrassing to others that the records of the case seem to have been destroyed. Most of our knowledge of Eakins's exhibitionism is based on oral interviews undertaken by Goodrich, McHenry, and others, with people who knew him late in life. If we had such interviews from Eakins's earlier years, no doubt they would provide much fascinating material.

Exhibitionists have frequently been portrayed as self-centered and narcissistic.[24] They are typically passive-aggressive in their dealings with authority figures.[25] They have traditionally been viewed as shy and unassertive with women or as "lacking in masculinity," although it is not always clear how these characteristics should be measured or defined. Writings by Christoffel (1936), Karpman (1957), and Rickwels (1950) link exhibitionism to homosexuality, which they equate with feminine identification and passivity. (As has been noted, some acquaintances considered Eakins feminine in his manner.) This view has been questioned, however, by recent experts, some of whom have proposed that exhibitionists can be described as sexually ambivalent, but do not seem to possess a purely female identity.[26]

Hammer, who compared sex offenders with the rest of the prison population, reported differences in four areas. First, they suffered from "unequivocal, intense, and overwhelming castration anxiety." Second, their mothers were "particularly engulfing and sexually seductive toward their sons" and created "churning Oedipal conflicts." Third, they were characterized by a distinctly concrete, as opposed to an abstract mental structure, that reduced their capacity for the discharge of tension through fantasy or sublimation. Fourth, they reported more incest experiences in their childhoods.[27] All these qualities seem to apply to Eakins, as will be discussed.

As yet no unified theory has been developed that explains all aspects of exhibitionism, but significant advances have been made on several fronts. The most frequent and most persuasive explanation is that it results from castration anxiety.[28] Exhibitionism is an assertion that the individual does possess genitals and therefore has not been emasculated. A related explanation is that the exhibitionist is performing a "magical" gesture that says, "I am showing you what I wish you could show me." Exhibiting in this case is seen as a mask for latent voyeurism, and a wish that the person targeted will show a penis. (When the targeted person is a woman this wish relates to the fear that girls once had a penis but lost it through castration.)[29]

Other factors that may contribute to the exhibitionist urge include a masochistic need to be caught and punished by the authorities; a sadistic hatred or hostility toward women; overt or covert seduction by parental figures; and lack of privacy and modesty in the home during childhood. Some writers see exhibitionism as a form of "countershame." According to this theory, the motive is to overcome shame and feelings of inadequacy. Many writers have suggested that exhibitionists have an extremely low frustration tolerance. Douglas J. Smukler and Douglas Schiebel have noted: "Exhibiting seems to be a unique and very effective method of expressing and at the same time guarding against conscious awareness of aggression. It perhaps is a way of showing the world that they are potent and masculine men, without provoking the retaliatory response that more direct aggression might stimulate."[30]

Exhibitionism may also be due to a biochemical imbalance. One observation that occurs repeatedly in the literature is recognition of the compulsive quality of the act. In this way, it appears to have a relationship with other compulsive phenomena that have been traced to biochemical origins. In some cases, for example, exhibitionism seems to be linked with depressive irritability or depressive illness. Snaith, for example, cites a case study in which the onset coincided with the onset of depression and was successfully treated through medication.[31] Another study has linked exhibitionism with obsessive-compulsive disorder, which is also treatable with medication.[32]

Four Approaches to Exhibitionism

Loosely speaking, when we group these different theories, we come up with four different explanatory approaches, although to some extent these forms of explanation interlock.[33] One is the simple idea that disorders often mimic or mirror some form of trauma. For example, people who were beaten and abused as children often beat and abuse their own children. Various reasons have been proposed for this phenomenon, but what is most striking is that it largely holds true on an empirical basis and has been borne out by case studies. In the case of Eakins this simple principle allows us to work backwards, from symptom to cause. For example, we can conjecture that if Eakins exposed himself to other people, then at some point someone probably exposed himself to him—or did something that was emotionally equivalent to exposure.

The obvious problem with this approach is that we cannot assume that the stimulus and the disorder it caused are identical. While the disorder may have mirrored the stimulus, it did so imperfectly, and therefore, while the disorder provides clues about the cause, it does not replicate the cause exactly. Despite this reservation, the principle is a useful one, in part because it is so simple. Applying this principle allows us to bypass elaborate theories about the inner workings of the brain and periodically test our conclusions in a simple fashion.

The second mode of explanation is Freudian psychology. Essentially, Freud deduced a set of internal psychological mechanisms by which one impulse is converted to another—a sort of emotional algebra. Thus, for example, Freud proposed that a small boy will translate anxiety about punishment from his father into a fear of castration. Under extreme circumstances, he then develops various forms of unusual behavior that reflect this fear of castration, including exhibitionism. Viewed in the light of ordinary behavior, Freudian concepts of this sort appear strange. But, in fact, one of the premises of Freudian thinking is that these concepts *are* strange—and that because they are strange (and frightening) they are repressed, and operate at a largely unconscious level.

In many respects, Freud's theories are simply an elaboration of the concept of mimicking or mirroring a form of trauma. These theories, however, provide some understanding of the inner mechanisms of this process, and the way that one form of stimulus may be translated into a slightly different pattern of behavior. Thus, for example, Freud proposes that fear of one's father (or an unresolved relationship with one's father) may result in anxiety about castration. While initially this may seem far-fetched, in fact it is borne out by clinical studies. Freud's concepts are tricky to apply, in part because there is no consensus about exactly which are accurate under what circumstances. However, if we can persuade ourselves either to accept these concepts, or to suspend our disbelief momentarily, Eakins's behavior often falls into place according to Freudian theory, in textbook fashion.

The third approach is simply an extension of the second: Power Dynamics. Freud often seemed to set primary emphasis on issues of sexual pleasure (although his definition of sexual gratification was extremely broad). Very often, however, the behavior of exhibitionists seems to focus not so much on sexual pleasure as on a sense of power that is achieved through such weapons as humiliation and embarrassment. Since exhibitionism (and voyeurism) clearly focuses on things that are charged with sexual implications, a description of exhibitionism based on issues of power often overlaps significantly with a Freudian approach. Nonetheless, focusing on power rather than sex allows us to see exhibitionism in a slightly different light, and to weigh its components a little differently.

Finally, exhibitionism has been traced to biochemical factors, which presumably have a genetic basis. In recent years, dramatic advances have been made in understanding the biochemistry of the brain, and certain mental illnesses, including depression and exhibitionism, have become at least partly treatable through medication. Notably, on the whole such a biochemical approach does not so much contradict Freudian theories as reinforce and supplement them. Indeed, in today's clinical practice, the most effective form of treatment for such illnesses as depression is to combine psychoanalysis with medication, rather than using either psychoanalysis or medication alone.

In my analysis of Eakins, I will interweave and draw on all four of these approaches. Three of them—mirroring, power dynamics, and biochemistry—rest on intellectual foundations that are fairly easy to understand and do not require deeper grounding in fundamental principles. Freud's theories, however, are based on underlying assumptions that require some explanation.

Freudian Theories

While Freud dealt with exhibitionism only in passing, his theories provide a clear basis for interpreting the phenomenon. The issue of the penis and its possible loss plays a large role in Freud's explanations. As Elizabeth Young-Bruehl has observed:

> Freud understood that little boys value and take pleasure in their genitals, becoming quite anxious about any real or imagined threats of injury, punishment for masturbation, loss, and insufficiency in comparison with adult

males. Female genitals look to many boys like perfect pictures of loss: girls lack this wonderful thing, they have nothing. Or the "missing penis" idea may be so anxiety-producing that it cannot be entertained, and the boy fantasizes that females must have male genitals—perhaps tiny, hidden—or that he'll be fine if he equips his female baby-sitter with a sprinkler head from the back-yard. That way, nobody is castrated.[34]

There are two oppressive themes here—the notion of the male who is threatened by castration, and the belief that women are incomplete since they lack a penis and are therefore castrated. Both themes, it should be noted, are male fantasies, although Freud seems to have erred on one point, holding that girls feel "penis envy" toward boys. As Young-Bruehl notes:

> Freud assumed that girls similarly treasure the penis, thinking of themselves as lacking this wonderful thing when they see that boys have it. Left out of this account of "penis envy" are a little girl's experiences of herself independ-ent of, or prior to, any comparison with a male, or in comparison with her mother.[35]

Today most psychologists would agree that the view of women as cas-trated males is neither accurate nor adequate, and may even set the stage for emotional difficulties. Nonetheless, Freud's proposal that boys may some-times harbor this belief seems plausible, and is supported by many clinical studies.

Castration anxiety plays a key role in one of Freud's most challenging, fas-cinating, and debatable but fertile concepts—the Oedipal conflict, the tension between father and son. Freud's idea was that the child competes with the father for the mother's support and affection. Consequently, at some level, the child desires to murder the father and marry the mother. At a conscious level, however, this desire needs to be repressed, since murdering the father is socially unacceptable, and the desire to marry the mother conflicts with the taboo of incest.

Freud's presentation of the Oedipus complex was strongly paternalistic, and presupposed a basic dichotomy between male and female roles. This assessment may oversimplify the matter, although the pattern of dominating fathers and submissive but nurturing mothers appears to have been common in Victorian households (and is a pattern that was certainly pronounced in the Eakins family). We do not need to accept every aspect of Freud's formulation of the Oedipus complex to make use of it. The virtue of the proposal is that it encourages us to recognize that a boy's relationship with his parents is inevitably full of tension and violent feelings. When these feelings become repressed and enter the unconscious, they affect behavior in peculiar ways.

One cause of the Oedipus complex, Freud proposed, is that boys fantasize that their father will castrate them. (David Stafford-Clark has noted: "The Oedipus complex has to be conceived as the child's real but repressed fear that the father will castrate him in retaliation for the desire for exclusive possession of the mother.")[36] In other words, to put this in the broadest terms, Freud proposed that a poor relationship between a child and his father will give rise to sexual anxieties and consequent emotional difficulties.

Freud also implied that anxiety about castration can come from another source, the mother, in part because a too close relationship with the mother makes the father more threatening, in part because anxiety about incest short-circuits a boy's feelings of sexual desire and becomes emasculating. In short, the Oedipal conflict is best conceived as a three-way relationship between father, mother, and child.

This raises the possibility that the mother can become the key factor in this equation. Many psychologists emphasize the role of the mother in the development of exhibitionism, although they are not entirely consistent in specifying what the mother does to cause the disorder. Rickels, for example, blames exhibitionism on mothers who "make their sons overly dependent and overly involved with them, arousing incestuous wishes and exaggerated narcissism."[37] David Allen, on the other hand, has proposed that exhibitionism comes about when "gratification [from the mother] is traumatically disrupted or threatened." According to this view, the exhibitionist "is afraid of the mother, but also afraid of losing her, and he begins to identify with her in an attempt to resolve these fears of loss and merging."[38]

Most likely more than one pattern of relationship between mother and child can give rise to castration anxiety. The fundamental point is simply that if the mother behaves in a fashion that creates a fear of incest, this anxiety is then translated into the emotional equivalent of incest—a fear of castration.

In many instances exhibitionism appears to be triggered by some form or abuse or trauma—particularly some experience of embarrassment, shock, or sexually or emotionally provocative behavior in the exhibitionist's relationship with his father or mother. Indeed, a basic principle of such behavior is that the actor feels a compulsion to repeat a scenario that caused him (or her) unbearable anguish—whether out of an effort to release pent up anger toward someone else, to numb the pain that was caused through endless repetition, or to understand and analyze what happened by repeatedly reliving the event.

In Eakins's case, this means that the form of his aberrant behavior probably to some degree mimicked or mirrored things that were traumatic in his childhood. As a consequence, by studying Eakins's symptoms, to some degree we can deduce their cause. As a starting point we have two powerful clues: first, that exhibitionism often seems to be triggered by something troubled about a boy's relationship to his parents (whether father or mother); and second, that Eakins's mother was psychologically disturbed. In short, Eakins's family background fits with what we would expect to cause him to become an exhibitionist. The question then becomes, in what specific ways was Eakins's relationship with his mother traumatic and precisely how did his later behavior mirror or reflect these traumas? To answer these questions, at least in a tentative way, we need to review what we know of Eakins's relationship to his mother and of the nature of her illness.

Eakins's Mother

To a degree that seems almost willfully perverse, writers on Eakins have always discounted the bipolar illness of Eakins's mother, Caroline. When he wrote his first book on Eakins in the 1930s, Goodrich must have known that Eakins's mother suffered from mental illness, but he did not mention it, and the subject did not enter the literature on Eakins for another fifty years, when Goodrich devoted a paragraph to the matter in his two-volume study of the artist.[39] Neither Goodrich nor Hendricks, however, felt that the fact was particularly significant, and they both saw it as an isolated matter, without larger ramifications. Michael Fried is the only writer who has suggested that the illness of his mother had any psychological impact on Eakins, but his speculations on the matter have been quite limited. He simply proposed that the hysterical actions of the mother figure in *The Gross Clinic* may well have been inspired by the hysterical behavior of the artist's own mother.[40]

Both Hendricks and Goodrich seem to have supposed that the illness of Eakins's mother was a relatively brief episode. This seems highly unlikely. Manic-depression is generally a lifelong condition. The symptoms generally surface early in life (the average age of onset is eighteen) and then grow in intensity.[41] We can be virtually certain that Eakins's mother suffered from intermittent episodes of mania or depression and that her illness was one of the central experiences of her son's childhood. Our culture powerfully condemns violence by men against women, but tends to overlook that women are also capable of physical and emotional abuse. Until he reached his early teens, Eakins's mother was considerably larger than he was. Thus, he must often have feared not only for her safety, but for his own.

Significantly, neither Eakins nor any other member of his family ever left any verbal or written record of his mother's illness. We know about it only from her death certificate and the comments of neighbors. Most likely the matter was not even discussed within the family. A father who did not allow his family to speak at mealtimes was not the sort of parent to whom a boy could spill his troubles. From the psychological standpoint, however, this powerful element of repression probably made the experience even more devastating. Eakins's letters do contain frequent references to family secrets.

Direct evidence about Caroline's illness is scanty, but notably, the earliest photographs of Eakins, taken when he was about six, show a child who already looks unhappy and troubled.[42] One hint that Caroline Eakins may have been ill before her son left for Paris (in 1866) is the painting Eakins made in Seville in 1870 portraying street musicians. As has been noted, the ages and roles of the figures in this painting correspond with the members of Eakins's family, and the mother in the painting stands behind bars, as if she were incarcerated. While this kind of evidence is admittedly tenuous, the painting suggests the possibility that by this date Eakins's mother was already confined to the house, or even to an asylum. (Benjamin Eakins brought his daughter Frances to Europe, but not his wife. Possibly Caroline was too emotionally unstable to travel.)

We know that Eakins served as his mother's principal nurse during her final illness. Her intense distress when he left her even briefly suggests that she formed a closer emotional bond with him than with her husband. Most likely, Eakins took on these nursing responsibilities very early in life, since his father was preoccupied with business and writing activities, and thus would naturally have delegated care of his wife to his oldest son. Possibly Caroline's final emotional decline was even triggered in part by Eakins's separation from her when he was studying painting in Paris. Whatever the exact arrangement, it is clear that throughout his childhood Eakins must have spent long hours with his mother when she was in an emotionally troubled state.

This responsibility suggests a reason for one of the singularities of Eakins's art—his extraordinary preoccupation with doctors. If Eakins's mother was ill, surely doctors were consulted, and early in childhood Eakins seems to have developed the fantasy of becoming a powerful male figure, like a doctor, who could heal his mother's illness.

We have no verbal description of Caroline Eakins's behavior, but in his portraits of other women, Eakins seems to have explored the symptoms he had observed in his mother. As has been noted, the women Eakins painted invariably look distraught, whether or not they were so in real life. Indeed, his treatment of them when posing seems to have been calculated to bring out qualities of unhappiness and annoyance. What is more, Eakins's portraits of women often seem to bring out different aspects of manic-depressive illness. Thus, for example, if we consider his portraits of women in pink, we note that Amelia Van Buren looks lethargic and depressed, Weda Cook's singing seems to have an analogy to screaming, and Susan Santje's morose pose suggests an episode of mania that has left objects strewn around the room.

As has been noted, not only were Eakins's portraits unflattering, but his handling of his sitters was unkind, even perverse. To some extent, this may have mirrored his mother's treatment of him when he was a child. The one thing we know for sure about his mother's behavior during her illness is that she held Eakins prisoner, not allowing him to leave the house and becoming upset when he left. Eakins's treatment of his sitters followed a similar pattern, since he pressured his sitters into standing or sitting for long periods, and then became upset if they could not hold the pose properly, or abandoned the project.

Given her illness, and its typical manifestations, it is likely that Eakins's mother sometimes engaged in behavior that was disturbingly sexual, such as undressing, confiding intimate sexual matters, or even attempting to seduce him. Of these activities, the one that seems most directly mirrored in Eakins's paintings and personal behavior is that of disrobing. The act of being unclothed (or dressing improperly) plays a large role in Eakins's paintings. Many of his portraits of women expose a great deal of flesh. In several instances, such as *The Old-Fashioned Dress*, the clothing sits on the figure slightly askew, as it would on a woman who was too depressed to clothe herself properly. (Interestingly, the dress is an old-fashioned dress—it would have been new when Eakins's mother was a girl.) Eakins also devoted an important series of paintings, his representations of William Rush and his model, to the theme of a woman who undresses in front of a man. As he worked on this series the woman comes to look more and more maternal, and the sculptor comes to look more and more like Eakins. It is hard to escape the conclusion that these paintings in some way represent an emotionally charged episode or series of episodes of undressing that took place between Eakins and his mother and that profoundly embarrassed him.

Voyeurism also interested Eakins. It is tempting to suppose that Eakins's voyeuristic behavior mirrored in some way the actions of his mentally unbalanced mother. For example, if Eakins's mother embarrassed him by undressing during her fits of mania, he could invert this situation by forcing other women to undress, and embarrassing them.

Many of Eakins's paintings—notably his medical and boxing scenes, but other paintings as well—feature an audience of onlookers. One explanation for this preoccupation would be that looking at his naked mother caused Eakins emotional distress. Thus, the act of looking held particular importance for him. In addition, this theme may well have another autobiographical aspect. This is suggested by his Spanish painting—his first serious artistic effort—in which, as I have proposed, the street musicians and imprisoned mother and child seem to be stand-ins for the members of Eakins's own family. Notably, this painting contains an audience whose presence is revealed only by their shadows. In other words, the people on the street are staring in at Eakins's family.

The emotional significance of this becomes plain when we recognize that the illness of Eakins's mother undoubtedly resulted in embarrassing behavior, such as arguing, screaming, or undressing, which must have become known to the neighbors and even to strangers on the street. Throughout his child-hood Eakins must have suffered from the thought that neighbors, acquaintances and even strangers were looking at his family and judging it, and that he himself was an object of scrutiny.

Thus, Eakins's family situation was both privileged and abused. As the eldest child he was naturally favored, and since he was male he was allowed to rule over his mother and sisters. In his role as a surrogate father, however, Eakins was handed a responsibility that would be traumatic to any child, that of caring for an emotionally unstable person. Indeed, throughout his child-hood, Eakins appears to have taken on a partnership with his mother that was quite similar to that of a husband, a role with incestuous implications.

As psychiatrists like R. D. Laing have observed, to an extraordinary degree human beings develop their self-image from the way they are reflected back in the behavior of the people around them.[43] Tragically, Eakins's mirror was as bent and twisted as a fun-house mirror. When he looked into his own psyche he was confronted with the image of his mother's depression and moments of psychosis. Both Eakins's failure to control or cure his mother, and the embarrassingly sexual nature of her behavior, must have undercut his sense of masculine identity at the same time that it implanted a deep-rooted hostility toward women.

No doubt all men think about castration to some degree. But the question of whether one was male or female—in Freudian terms, whether one was or was not castrated—was particularly important for Eakins. In the Eakins family, which appears to have been unusually paternalistic even by nineteenth-century standards, being a boy—having a penis—gave him as role as the "boss" and leader of his family.[44] It allowed him to regulate the lives of his mothers and sister.

In addition, not having a penis—being a woman—was evidently connected in Eakins's mind with the bizarre behavior of his mother. Nineteenth-century medical literature strongly associated strange emotional outbursts with female qualities, and was a powerful undercurrent in the writings of doctors whom Eakins knew, such as D. Hayes Agnew and Horatio Wood, who associated diseases ranging from cancer to mental illness with the alleged weaknesses of female anatomy. No doubt Eakins's father also explained his mother's outbursts as a natural consequence of the fact that she was female. One aspect of this belief was to connect emotional outbursts with menstruation. This association has some validity in medical terms, since menstruation is connected with hormonal changes and physical pain, and thus is linked to shifts in mood. From a Freudian perspective, however, menstruation also had an association with castration, since it evokes the notion of the female vagina as a bleeding wound. (Eakins's odd letter to Coates describing himself as a doctor rescuing a woman wounded in the thigh seems to reflect this fantasy.)

Eakins's association between manic-depression and female qualities surely relates to his hostility toward anything feminine, and his belief that women were both mentally and physically inferior to men. While all these views were imbedded in nineteenth-century thinking, they were generally counterbalanced by other idealizing and romantic attitudes. Eakins's constant insistence that women were inferior to men, and should remain subordinate to them, seems misogynist even by nineteenth-century standards.

Finally, Eakins's anxiety about castration had still another source. As a caregiver for his mother—very likely, the primary caregiver—he was thrown into a relationship that was intimate and marriage-like. This triggered the fear of incest, which then expressed itself as a sense of emasculation and a fear of castration.

The Family

Eakins, then, was pulled in two directions. On the one hand, he felt contemptuous of women and viewed them as inferior, infirm, and hysterical. In his art and pronouncements he favored powerful, masculine father figures and scorned those he considered either "feminine" or henpecked. On the other hand, Eakins identified with his mother's anxiety and very likely empathized with her so deeply that he could imagine himself as a woman. To do so, however, must have been a fearful process, since it meant imagining himself as the victim of castration and sexual assault.

In his relationships with women, the crux of Eakins's psychological confusion was that his relationship with his mother was both like and unlike a marriage. Thus, it set a pattern in which Eakins compulsively created marriage-like relationships with inappropriate women, beginning with his mother, and moving on to his sister Margaret, his niece Ella Crowell, his pupil Lillian Hammitt, a family friend Addie Williams, and also, though to a lesser degree, with other female sitters and female students. Paradoxically, however, his relationship with his wife, Susan Macdowell Eakins, produced no children and was cold and distant, even by Victorian standards. Rumors circulated that they were not actually married. When Lillian Hammitt appeared at the doorstep claiming that she was "Mrs. Thomas Eakins," her behavior implicitly declared that Susan Eakins did not properly fill that role.

To some degree this confusion was caused by Eakins's inability to leave his father's home and develop an independent existence. Therefore, his wife did not have a true home, since she also lived in his father's house, which Eakins treated as his personal workplace, and where she was a subordinate and often an intruder. Yet when visitors came to his studio, they did not find a professional workplace in the usual sense, since Eakins insisted on prerogatives that are acceptable in the home but not in public, such as strolling around in his underwear or in the nude. Indeed, not only did Eakins indulge in such activities himself, but he also earnestly pressed his models and visitors to undress also, so that they, in certain respects, could take on the role of family members.

As this sort of behavior suggests, the issue of "family" relates to an issue of central importance to an exhibitionist, the issue of "clothes." While there is general agreement that one should wear clothes in public, within the realm of the family there seems to be no such firm standard. In my experience, there is a great range of behavior among outwardly "normal" families—ranging from children who have never seen their parents or siblings naked to families in which all the members, of both sexes, comfortably spend time together with no clothes on.[45]

Unfortunately, we have very little information about how nudity was viewed in Victorian families, and practices must have varied greatly, if only as a consequence of wealth. In poor families, five or six children of both sexes often slept in the same room, and in some cases parents and offspring slept in the same bed—with the obvious implication that the parents engaged in sex and conceived babies when they were in bed with their children. The wealthy, on the other hand, could afford more private and compartmentalized spaces, and in many cases, husbands and wives slept in separate bedrooms and appear to have seen each other's nakedness only by carefully negotiated prearrangement. Remarkably, as has been mentioned, Mrs. Dodge told Lloyd Goodrich that she had never seen a man completely naked until Eakins showed her a photograph of one, although by that time she had given birth to several children.

Clearly no single standard of behavior was enforced across the social spectrum. It does appear that Victorians were less conscious than people today of the possibility of inflicting sexual trauma on a child—in part, perhaps, because they viewed children as fundamentally innocent. For example, it seems to have been relatively common for children to sleep in their parents' bedroom. But the only thing that is clear is that social mores varied widely, and that the concept of "family" allowed latitude for a great variety of behavior.

This ambiguity about what constitutes "normal" or "acceptable" behavior is worth noting, if only to make it clear that for someone like Eakins, who was interested in flouting convention, one strategy for doing so was to present nudity as a family matter. That Eakins strolled around the house naked is indicated by Frank Stephens's complaints about this fact, as well as by the numerous accounts of sitters who came to the house and were greeted by Eakins in his underwear, or even more drastically undressed. Eakins also seems to have tried to persuade his students that they were "family," or that his role was that of a "father," and that consequently they could deal with the issue of undress in a way that fundamentally differed from behavior of a public sort.

The claim of Goodrich and many subsequent writers that Eakins was an innocent who was unaware of these social zones does not withstand examination, since he skillfully manipulated social barriers to fulfill his emotional needs. For example, he waited until he was alone with his female models to begin pleading with them to undress, softening his voice to endow it with an intimate and seductive quality. At the same time, he often hid behind the screen of professionalism or family. His letters during the Academy controversy are filled with complaints that students had revealed things that were true but which he felt were "professional," and thus should have been withheld from public scrutiny.

The claim that Eakins was inarticulate—which has become a staple of the literature on the artist—seems less than fully convincing given his great interest in languages. Rather, his slowness of speech and alleged difficulty with words feels like a ploy. Very early, Eakins seems to have recognized that his psychological needs could not be expressed directly. Consequently, he developed a pose of brusque, inarticulate awkwardness. Yet this inarticulateness and lack of charm would drop away at strategic moments. For example, when he wanted to see the underwear of some old ladies he was visiting, his customary taciturn manner dropped away and he became charming and witty. Or, when he wished to undress one of his female sitters, he suddenly ceased to be brusque, and became vulnerable, gentle, and intimate. Indeed, Eakins's written public statements, while spare, often reveal an artful use of ambiguity. Like those of a wily politician, his statements appear to say one thing, but when read carefully can be construed to mean something else entirely. In one of his most famous statements, for example, Eakins declared "For the public I believe my life is all in my work."[46] Scholars have always taken these words as an assertion that Eakins's art was separate from his life, but the statement can be read in a very different way. It also implies that his paintings constituted a record of his personal life, but that he did not wish to reveal this intimate process to the general public.

In short, Eakins skillfully manipulated the concept of family to serve his needs. Notably, however, those who attempted to become part of his intimate family—such as Lillian Hammitt, who wanted Eakins to become either her "father" or her "husband"—encountered disappointment. Habitually, Eakins retreated behind a barrier of professional conduct and resisted any attempt at real intimacy. Even Susan Eakins—a former student—seems to have hit this emotional wall. By marrying Eakins, she undoubtedly supposed that she could achieve a truly intimate family connection, but he seems to have kept her at a distance, carefully separating from her the most emotionally significant parts of his life, including the expression of his sexual desires.

Were Eakins's Motives Sexual?

A central question relevant to Eakins's behavior is whether his motives were sexual. Most recent writers have portrayed him as a sexually potent figure.[47] Jack Flam has declared that "Eakins seems to have been a very sensual man."[48] Kathleen Foster has described him as "intensely sexualized," and Elizabeth Johns has declared that "sexual energy echoes throughout much of Eakins' work" and has spoken of his "love for the . . . sexuality of the body."[49] At the time he was fired from the Pennsylvania Academy, several of Eakins's opponents assumed that he was seeking sexual favors from his students. The women whom Goodrich interviewed often mentioned Eakins's interest in undressing them. Some informants suggested that he engaged in sexual liaisons. For example, Dr. Wood, an old friend of the family, believed that Eakins's wife suffered because of his "affairs," and Samuel Murray, Eakins's favorite pupil, believed that the artist maintained a ménage à trois with his wife and Addie Williams.[50]

Both recent scholars and Eakins's contemporaries, however, may well have been misreading his behavior, since the paradox of exhibitionism is that while it appears to express an overcharged libido, it actually stems from deep-rooted feelings of inadequacy and impotence. The evidence about Eakins's sex life is highly ambiguous. He never conceived children out of wedlock, and he was never securely implicated in a sexual affair, despite the many "moral" scandals that circulated around him. While Eakins once boasted that he had "had" one of his models, it is hard to know whether this was fact or just talk. He also once maintained that "I never seduced a woman nor tried to," and he tended to react to accusations of sexual misconduct not only with outraged self-righteousness but also with a note of horrified prudery.[51]

According to Eakins's account books, in the winter of 1868, when he was in Paris, he made at least two visits to a house of prostitution. Foster has implied that this visit was for sexual purposes, but we do not know whether he engaged in sex or some other form of amusement.[52] In this period young men often visited brothels to drink beer and ogle the women, without actually engaging in sexual activities. Indeed, in a letter to his father, Eakins mentioned going to a house of prostitution and declared that his visit was purely educational.[53] A few years later, when Eakins was hiring models for the Pennsylvania Academy, he declared somewhat prudishly that he was firmly opposed to hiring prostitutes and considered their bodies flabby and ugly.[54]

We do not know why Eakins's marriage was childless. He and his wife may have practiced deliberate birth control, although this seems unlikely; his wife may have been infertile; or he himself may have been impotent. Lucy Langdon Wilson provided a clue when she reported to Goodrich that Eakins's wife was "not highly sexed."[55] Possibly this observation provides a clue about Eakins as well, since presumably she was responding to the degree of attention the two showed for each other.[56] Mrs. Lavell, who posed for Eakins, also had questions about the artist's sexual prowess. She told Goodrich that Eakins "had no sensual fire."[57] While other explanations are possible, the absence of offspring may well have been due to the artist's lack of sexual interest in his wife.[58]

Many of those who knew Eakins at the end of his life, including his confidant, Samuel Murray, believed that he was having an affair with Addie Williams.[59] Addie posed naked for Eakins, and must have dressed and undressed in his presence. Given his behavior with others, it seems likely that he exposed his nakedness to her while strolling around the home. Such activities would naturally have led visitors to suspect a sexual liaison between them. In fact Eakins may well have been indulging in exhibitionism for its own sake. It is quite plausible to suppose that no actual sexual activity occurred. As has been noted, Wilson believed that while Eakins made a show of sexual prowess, he was fundamentally timid about sex, and would always run away at the last minute.[60]

Eakins's extraordinary interest in guns take on significance in this light, for as Freud noted, guns (as well as other objects that we find in Eakins's paintings, such as poles, knives, and pens) can serve to symbolize the penis, and to serve as a substitute for it.[61] Eakins's fascination with revolvers thus was essentially an extension of his exhibitionism, and likewise reflected not a powerful sense of masculine identity but an inner fearfulness. Revolvers (and similar implements) provided a penis substitute, and thus masked his feeling that he was emasculated or castrated. Like his exhibitionism, his display of guns mimicked certain aspects of sexual behavior, but shifted the emphasis from sexual pleasure to issues of violence and dominance.

In the end, the issue of Eakins's sexual orientation and the degree of his sexual activity is difficult to resolve because of the insufficiency of clear evidence. Generally speaking, from the accounts of his behavior, Eakins seems to have belonged to a general category of individuals who are unfocussed in their sexual aim. Typically, such individuals have less sexual activity than most people but become involved with a variety of partners, as well as with unusual forms of sex, such as incest. Some therapists I have spoken to find it quite likely that Eakins had sex not only with both men and women but even with animals. But it would be misleading, they aver, to describe him as either homosexual or heterosexual since the main quality of his sexual behavior was its lack of focus. Freudian theory holds that individuals who exhibit such fundamental sexual confusion have suffered some sort of trauma or misdirection very early in life, and this belief is widely held although it is difficult to establish scientific proofs of this assumption.[62]

Eakins's Father

Throughout his life, Eakins seems to have taken contradictory positions regarding paternal figures, either assuming an attitude of excessive deference, as with his father, Jean-Léon Gérôme, or Dr. Gross, or challenging their authority in an almost childish way, as with John Sartain, Edward Coates and other authority figures at the Pennsylvania Academy. One way of reading this is to suppose that Eakins's relationship with his father was emotionally unresolved.

In his paintings and photographs, and in other ways, Eakins frequently voiced a set of very disturbing and seemingly interrelated themes: anal intercourse, castration, paternal assault, and incest. The idea of anal sex seems to be a subtext of many of Eakins's photographs (such as the ones of Bill Duckett) as well as of paintings such as *Swimming*. The theme of sexual abuse by a father, whether by anal assault or castration, seems to be powerfully expressed in his most ambitious and powerful painting, *The Gross Clinic*. The story of someone who has suffered incestuous rape, but has been sworn to silence, is the substance of the curious postscript that he appended to one of his letters to Edward Coates.[63] Finally, Eakins's paintings of his father, with their imagery of guns, hunting, or generational conflict, all contain an undercurrent of violence.

There are several ways of interpreting Eakins's fascination with these issues. The most literal is to suppose that he was sexually assaulted by his father. To my mind it is equally reasonable to suppose that Eakins's fixation with castration and sexual assault was simply a projection of his Oedipus conflict, in classically Freudian terms. In other words, it could have been a fantasy, though one based on very real family tensions.

A variant of this theory of sexual abuse is to suppose that Eakins was influenced by nineteenth-century forms of punishment. Early in the century, physical chastisement of children was standard practice, and the usual method was to pull down a child's pants and pummel the buttocks. (In England this embarrassing form of punishment was publicly administered in schools.) Interestingly, the image of a figure exposing his buttocks appears very early in Eakins's life. We first find it in the margin of a drawing of gears that Eakins made at the age of about sixteen. This humorous sketch shows a figure with his head between his legs who bends over to expose his rear end. If Eakins's father regularly punished his son in this way, perhaps it would explain why Eakins was so fixated with buttocks, and made them the focus of interest in his most ambitious paintings.[64]

Homosexuality

In recent years the issue of homosexuality has played a large role in the scholarship on Eakins, particularly in interpretations of his photographs and his painting *Swimming*, both of which have already been discussed. Moreover, the evidence seems strong that Eakins's relationship with Samuel Murray was a more intense emotional experience than his relationship with his wife. Significantly, there is a strong connection between exhibitionism and homosexuality. In fact, the issue of gender confusion is central to exhibitionism, since it is based on the notion that women are castrated men, and that men are at risk of becoming like women if their genitals are removed. Maleness thus becomes both unusually important and unusually fragile.[65]

Eakins's preoccupation with maleness made sense in the Eakins family, where a boy could achieve dominance over his sister because he was male. The illness of his mother, however, made this issue of gender an anxious one.

In his portraits, Eakins explored the theme of being female in ways that are simultaneously contemptuous and sympathetic. On the one hand, through his portrait of his sister Margaret, who resembled him, he imagined what it would be like to become a woman. On the other hand, he imagined his mother's illness projected on both male and female figures, and he often made the men feminine or the women curiously boy-like. In all these cases Eakins seems to have seen being female as a tragic condition, and feminine qualities as something that made men into pathetic figures as well.

Conversely, in his painting *Swimming*, Eakins expressed his belief in the superiority of men. Unfortunately, however, this resulted in a contradiction of sorts, since manly men are supposed to be interested in women rather than in other men. As has already been discussed, both *Swimming* and the studies for it seem to explore different aspects of homosexual desire, although this theme is invariably hinted at rather than directly expressed. In every instance, this desire was ultimately repressed or short-circuited. Indeed, with men as with women, Eakins seems to have been interested not in seduction, but in fostering discomfort. His treatment of Francis Zielger provides a revealing example of this. While Ziegler was posing naked in the studio, Eakins deliberately brought a woman into the room to look at him, and evidently took pleasure from Ziegler's embarrassment.[66] Like Eakins's relationships with women, his relationships with men seem to have been repressed and twisted in ways that blocked both love and sexual gratification.

Lillian Hammitt

One of the most notable patterns of Eakins's life is that he seems to have attracted and "collected" people who were weak or psychologically vulnerable, and then to have preyed upon those weaknesses. Several of his students, including Lillian Hammitt, Ella Crowell, Douglass Morgan Hall, and Benjamin Fox (who posed for *Swimming*) ended their lives in insanity. Others, such as George Reynolds, exhibited behavior that was emotionally erratic, and still others, such as Franklin Schenk, seem to have functioned only marginally in society. [67] Even for seemingly stable individuals, the stress of being with Eakins could be psychologically bruising. For example, shortly after Eakins was fired from the Pennsylvania Academy, Susan Eakins's brother wrote to her stating that he was troubled by her "worn appearance" and feared that she was headed toward "insanity or death."[68]

The most significant instances of this attraction to "insanity" are Lillian Hammitt and Ella Crowell, since in both cases their breakdown appears to have been directly connected with—and possibly even caused by—their association with Eakins. A key point is that neither woman appears to have been mentally ill before coming into contact with Eakins, suggesting that in both cases something he did served as a catalyst to their illness.

Let us first consider Lillian Hammitt. The most surprising thing about her letters is their complete lucidity. While at times they reveal an emotionally troubled individual, they are grammatical, well expressed, and thoroughly logical. Foster has described Hammitt's letters as "full . . . of self-deception," but this claim is based entirely on the fact that some of her statements were later contradicted by Eakins and his wife.[69] Taken on their own terms, Hammitt's statements are completely logical and coherent, and in fact we have no way of knowing for sure which account of events, hers or that of Eakins and his wife, was the true one. Surprisingly, Hammitt's letters are far more convincing and coherent than those of Susan Eakins, which contain logical contradictions as well as clear misrepresentations of fact.

In short, Hammitt's surviving letters reveal someone very different from the crazed woman who later appeared at Eakins's doorstep. What happened? Susan Eakins later declared that Lillian "went insane," but neither she nor any other writer has provided a clear diagnosis of what kind of insanity she suffered from or has suggested what might have caused it.[70]

Lillian's personality change at first suggests some form of schizophrenia, but for various reasons this explanation seems unlikely. For one thing, she was too old. Schizophrenia generally strikes in adolescence, and nearly always by the time a person has reached the age of twenty. Hammitt was born in 1865, and therefore was twenty-seven years old in 1892, when she had her first known breakdown. Moreover, while her behavior was delusional, Hammitt never exhibited the sort of incoherence we would expect in someone suffering from schizophrenia, and did not exhibit the characteristic symptoms of the disease such as hearing voices, having visions, or receiving directives or communications from a mysterious source. In other words, her fantasies do not seem to have been spurred by sudden change in chemistry, and they were not paranoid, as is most frequently the case with schizophrenics. Instead, they form a logical pattern, expressing unfulfilled emotional desires.

It seems most likely that Lillian Hammitt suffered from hysteria—now generally known as conversion syndrome—a condition whose etiology was just being unraveled by Freud at the time of these incidents. The first case of hysteria described by Freud was that of Anna O., who was treated by Joseph Breuer from December 1880 to June 1882. Freud's analysis of this case led to his theory of the sexual origin of this neurosis, as well as his theories about the operations of the unconscious.

Anna O. suffered from a variety of physical and mental aberrations, and she displayed two dramatically different personalities: one fairly normal; the other a naughty and troublesome child. Freud was able to demonstrate that the symptoms were caused by the acting out of repressed feelings through the unconscious, as a form of fantasy, similar to a state of hypnosis. Lillian Hammitt's behavior appears to fit neatly into this nineteenth-century pattern.[71]

One of the intriguing aspects of nineteenth-century hysteria was the ability of the unconscious to devise forms of expression that required exceptional mental and logical skills. For example, when in her normal phase, Anna O. would speak her native German. While in the other, however, she was unable to converse in German and spoke only in English. If confronted with a German text she could not make sense of it. Yet, if confronted with a text in French or Italian, she could read it swiftly and fluently—but translated into English.

In its specific manifestations the case of Lillian Hammitt was certainly different from that of Anna O. But the essential mechanism was the same. Like Anna O., Lillian dealt with the hopelessness of her situation by creating a double personality. Thus, the unfeminine, unattractive, impoverished, unmarried "old maid" of an art student, with little hope of a good marriage or a decent income, became the wife of Thomas Eakins, parading her erotic charms in her bathing suit. Her "mad" state was nothing more than the expression of the unconscious desires of her "sane" one.

Even Hammitt's most bizarre behavior followed logical patterns. For example, in her last breakdown she became an exhibitionist—she appeared on the streets of Philadelphia in a bathing costume. The wearing of improper attire for shock effect was similar to Eakins's technique of appearing at the door dressed in his underwear, of appearing at a formal event in cycling costume, or of unaccountably undressing before his students. In other words, her behavior, while irrational in conventional social terms, nonetheless logically mirrored that of Eakins himself. Moreover, like that of Eakins, her behavior was tailored to the conventions and expectations of nineteenth-century Philadelphia (both bathing suits and cycling costumes would have a different significance today).[72] As has been noted, sexually strange behavior is a common symptom of the manic phase of bipolar illness. Hammitt may well have been manic-depressive, like Eakins's mother, and her exhibitionist episode with the bathing suit may have been triggered by an outburst of mania, which is often associated with sexually exaggerated behavior.

Eakins's role in the affair is one that is difficult to reconstruct precisely, but we can guess that it followed a model of male control and female submission to male fantasy. An apt analogy can be found in nineteenth-century novels, such as George du Maurier's enormously popular best-seller *Trilby* (1894), in which a singer falls under the spell of the hypnotist Svengali, changing personality under his influence, and performing artistic feats that are not possible in her normal social guise. Indeed, when Svengali's spell is broken, she dies.

Eakins was clearly Hammitt's "Svengali." Whether Eakins slept with his female students is open to question, but clearly he was a master of psychological control and masculine domination. Whether conscious or unconscious, Hammitt's fantasy that she was his wife, along with her exhibitionist behavior, seems to have been provoked by Eakins, either directly or through some form of suggestion. Thus, the Hammitt episode provides a window into his mind, albeit a distorted one. Clearly something about his behavior led her to believe that he intended to marry her.

In this context, it is interesting that Hammitt's behavior and correspondence indicates her inability to distinguish between socially sanctioned matrimony and incest. In her state of "madness," she claimed that Eakins was her husband, but in one of her letters she speaks of him as a "father."[73] So, to the extent that these two levels of reality connected, she imagined herself sleeping with her father. If we view her behavior as a reflection of Eakin's influence, it becomes clear that there was something about his manner that was inherently confusing to women, since they could not determine whether it was fatherly or sexual. Thus, Hammitt's behavior touches on one of the most remarkable accusations made against Eakins, the claim that he engaged in incest.

Incest

Frank Stephen's charge that Eakins committed incest is so shocking that writers from Lloyd Goodrich to Kathleen Foster have not only rejected it, but have also attributed it to mania and delusion on Stephens's part.[74] Yet, as has already been noted, there is no evidence that Stephens was manic or delusional. In fact, he was the only member of the extended Eakins family who was ever able to successfully interact with the world at large and hold down a regular job. Just what Stephens meant by incest needs clearer definition, but surely his accusation pointed toward some form of behavior that appeared abhorrent and abnormal. Moreover, his accusation is paralleled by that of Ella Crowell just before she killed herself. The accusation is so unusual—no other nineteenth-century or early-twentieth-century American artist was ever accused of incest—that we need to consider this charge seriously.[75]

A remarkable number of the sexual scandals and romantic relationships in Eakins's life involved women who were in one or another fashion relatives, whether by blood or marriage. Margaret Eakins was his sister; Ella Crowell was his niece; Alice Barber was engaged to Charles Stephens, who was the cousin of Frank Stephens, who married Eakins's sister; Addie Williams was related to the Crowells. Those who were not actual relatives occupied a position close to that in psychological terms. For example, both Eakins's first girlfriend, Emily Sartain, and his wife, Susan Macdowell, were the daughters of engravers with whom his father did business, and thus belonged to his father's "business family"; the fiancée who died, Kathrin Crowell, was the sister of Will Crowell, the husband of Eakins's sister Frances. As already noted, even Lillian Hammitt seems to have become a relative in psychological terms, since she addressed Eakins as a "father."[76]

It seems possible that an element of family relationship made Eakins more eager to undress and share his nakedness with a woman. Eakins seems to have been confused about the nature of the boundary between the family and the outside world, and he seems to have been attracted to the notion that sharing nakedness was a kind of secret bond that held the members of a family together. Even in his teaching, he tended to create divisions between those

students who were "loyal" and part of his family, and those who were outsiders. Those who were part of his family were expected to undress for him
and view his nakedness in turn. The fact that family authority for Eakins was
based on being male seems to have formed part of this process. It made it
important for everyone to view the thing that made him male—his genitals.

In statistical surveys, exhibitionism has been strongly associated with
incest.[77] If we suppose that Eakins's psychological difficulties were rooted in
his troubled, marriage-like relationship with his mother, then anxiety about
incest was probably the crux of his psychological turmoil. While we have no
direct evidence on the subject, one psychologist I spoke to noted that on the
basis of Eakins's symptoms he felt that there was "an 85% chance that he was
the victim of some form of sexual abuse."[78]

Ella Crowell

The case of Ella Crowell is particularly informative because she left a fairly
detailed description of Eakins's sexual advances. But the case is also particularly complex because the tragic aspects of Ella's life fit into larger family patterns. Like Eakins, Ella had a marriage-like relationship with one of her
parents—in this case, a close relationship with her idle father, who was emotionally estranged from her mother and who confided his troubles to her. This
situation, a mirror image of Eakins's Oedipal predicaments, undoubtedly contributed to her emotional difficulties.

In addition, as the first grandchild of Benjamin Eakins, it appears that special pressures were placed on Ella to shun feminine frivolities, a theme that
Eakins explored in his painting *Baby at Play*. Notably, Ella became a tomboy,
lacking in feminine graces.

Ella's sense of insecurity, moreover, was clearly exacerbated by the tension
between her parents and Eakins and his wife. Though he had defended Eakins
at the time of the Academy scandal, Will Crowell clearly felt reservations
about his brother-in-law's character. He was even willing to send his son Benjamin to study with Eakins's single greatest enemy Frank Stephens, a move
that Eakins and his wife viewed as an act of treachery. As a result of these differences, Ella needed to behave differently in each household. At home, she
could not openly criticize her father and mother, whereas when she was with
Eakins and his wife she was expected to do so. When with the Eakins family
she could not protest against her uncle's violations of Victorian propriety,
although her parents expected her to report such matters. Given such a

divisive situation, Foster's claim that Ella was a liar probably has a measure of truth. As she moved from one household to the other, she must have vacillated between truths, omissions, half-truths, and outright lies.[79]

In his role as uncle, Eakins clearly felt that it was his duty to compensate for the inadequacies of her father, and give her a proper education. Thus he became a kind of father by default. But as an educator, he worked perversely, damaging Ella's self-esteem by at one moment expressing great hopes for her achievement as an artist, at the next setting impossible tasks for her and criticizing her accomplishment. Moreover, he emotionally manipulated her in other ways, with even more damaging consequences. When Frances Crowell wrote to her brother asking him not to pose Ella and her sister Maggie in the nude she clearly intended to protect them, but Eakins seems to have taken this statement as a challenge.[80]

Ella Crowell's accusations against Eakins have never been taken seriously by writers on Eakins. Goodrich, for example, concludes that she was "insane," and goes on to imply that her accusations had no basis in fact.[81] Foster has gone further, writing of "Ella's reputation as a liar," and labeling her not only as insane but dishonest, manipulative, and sexually devious.[82] But though no writer has ever pointed this out, unlike the case of Lillian Hammitt, it is by no means clear that Ella's behavior was ever truly delusional or crossed over into true psychosis.

The instances of odd behavior on her part—such as prescribing the wrong medication to a patient—are not in themselves unusual or atypical, except perhaps in the degree of anxiety that resulted. What is apparent is that she was emotionally distraught and felt a profound sense of shame and desperation. Even the act of threatening to kill people was not necessarily evidence of insanity. For example, we know that Ella's father once threatened to kill Eakins also.[83]

I have noted that much of Hammitt's "insane" behavior mirrored the actions of Eakins, and this applies to some of the "insane" behavior of Ella Crowell also. For example, Ella's act of threatening to kill Weda Cook and Eakins with a revolver directly mimicked Eakins's behavior, since he regularly carried a revolver and sometimes used it to threaten people. Her suicide also appears to have been linked with Eakins, since she appears to have used a gun that he had given to the family.

In fact, there are good reasons for believing that Ella's accusations against her uncle were accurate. She had no clear motive for making such statements unless they were true. They brought no benefit to her, except for the possible catharsis of revealing to her parents things that profoundly troubled her. In addition, Ella's accusations were somewhat unusual. They do not correspond with most accusations of sexual assault, nor did they correspond with the formulas of Victorian novels. They were odd, in a way that fits with the statements of other women who were mystified by Eakins's behavior.

Ella did not claim that she was raped, that Eakins engaged in a sexual act with her, or that he was sexually aroused. She did state that he touched her genitals, that he forced her to touch his, and that he spanked her to make her undress for him.[84] In short, the experience, while it embarrassed her, and left her feeling degraded, was sexually incomplete. Very likely, part of what was upsetting about the experience was that its motives were unclear. In a normal relationship, such touching of genitals would imply both sexual desire and emotional intimacy, but Eakins's behavior seemed to lack both these elements. As already noted, Lucy Langdon Wilson, in speaking of Eakins's overtures when she posed for him, said that she felt Eakins would retreat at the last minute, and Ella's account suggests just this sort of retreat from actual sexual engagement.[85]

Sexual perversion (which is now generally termed "paraphilia" in clinical practice) is often linked with both inflexibility and a fragile sense of masculine identity.[86] It often manifests itself in attacks on femininity. Eakins's behavior fits into this paradigm. In his dealings with women, he seems to have had difficulty accepting that women differ from men. He pushed women to be more like men, and was frustrated when they retained feminine qualities. As William Innes Homer has perceptively written:

> From the available accounts of Eakins's behavior it appears that he wanted to defeminize women, to make them like men. And by forcing women to become more like men Eakins was saying, in effect, that they were inadequate as they were. He thought that women, to survive as professionals, would have to shed their usual "feminine" inhibitions and deal with the unpleasant and often ugly realities of the world—and for women artists that required a detached and objective attitude toward the human body. He urged the women in the Academy to join equally with the men in the grisly work of the dissecting room, denigrating by contrast the common female occupation of china painting. There was no place in the Academy for such "feminine" concerns . . . Eakins's behavior toward women, especially compared to his relations with men, indicates an undeniable, if unconscious, hostility.[87]

In reconstructing how Eakins touched Ella we have three forms of evidence: those provided by her statements, by the typical behavior of exhibitionists, and by Eakins's behavior on other occasions. These provide three interesting clues. First, we have Ella's statements that Eakins not only touched her genitals, and had her touch his, but performed these acts in a way that she found degrading.[88] More than a century later, it is hard to know precisely what seemed "degrading" to a young Victorian girl, but it seems likely that Eakins was doing more than simply touching Ella's pubic hair. Her statements suggest that he was doing something more humiliating and invasive.

Second, we know that exhibitionists are fearfully concerned with the distinction between male and female genitals. If we accept Freudian theory, the fundamental motive of Eakins's behavior was to compare how male and female genitals area shaped, and most likely what he did fulfilled this goal.

Third, we know that Eakins had some sort of medical excuse for his behavior (he is said to have been preparing Ella for the rigors of being a nurse).[89] Given his training as an anatomist, it seems likely that he indicated to Ella the various parts of the female genitals—labia, clitoris, urethra, vagina, and so forth—and explained how these parts differ from or resemble the male member. (We know that he did something similar with Amelia Van Buren, when he dropped his trousers to explain the muscles of the leg and groin and to show that they are differently shaped in men and women.)[90]

In short, while our evidence is limited, all the evidence we have points toward the conclusion that Eakins explored the various parts of Ella's genitals with his fingers and probably penetrated her vagina. Very likely he had engaged in similar activities with animals (hence Frank Stephens's accusations of "bestiality") as well as with human corpses, both male and female, during his anatomical investigations.

This scenario fits with the diagnosis that Eakins was an exhibitionist: it is precisely the "display" and "counter-display" of genitals that David Stafford Clark describes.[91] Eakins's sexually incomplete behavior provides a perfect illustration of Freud's theories. By touching Ella, Eakins was confirming that the woman did not have a penis; by having Ella touch him he was asserting to the woman that he had one. In this instance, it seems to have been particularly upsetting to Eakins that Ella, Benjamin's first grandchild, was a woman rather than a man, and thus to his way of thinking, essentially castrated. Perhaps by having her touch his genitals he hoped to teach her about what she lacked. The most peculiar feature of Eakins's behavior—to the extent that we can reconstruct it—was that it had many of the features of a sexual advance with the motive of denying sex or the fact of sexual difference. All the evidence suggests that he did not engage in sexual intercourse. Indeed, his behavior was probably caused by a fundamental fear of sexual activity.

Eakins's behavior concerning Ella points toward what he did in other instances. Since Eakins's behavior was clearly repetitive, it seems quite possible that this same scenario of mutual touching of genitals was what occurred or what he was working toward in other instances in which he made advances on women or in which he was accused of incest or other improprieties. For example, if Eakins touched Ella Crowell's genitals and had her touch his, it raises the possibility that he did the same thing with Lillian Hammitt. It would have been quite natural for Lillian to suppose that this indicated sexual desire, even a desire for marriage. To Eakins, however, this touching signified something very different. Ultimately, in fact, it was some sort of reassurance that allayed his fears of castration; very likely it gave him no direct sexual stimulation.

Similarly, Frank Stephens charged that Eakins engaged in incest with his sister Margaret. While it is certainly possible that Eakins and Margaret slept with each other, it seems more plausible to suppose that Eakins engaged in some form of touching his sister that Stephens believed was indecent—presumably touching of genitals. If Eakins did this, we can imagine a scenario in which Stephens could honestly accuse Eakins of incest and Eakins could just as honestly deny it, though not without a bit of evasiveness.

Eakins seems to have particularly targeted women of a certain type. It is striking that his sister Margaret, Lillian Hammitt, and Ella Crowell were all somewhat homely, insecure women in their twenties with masculine characteristics. They all seem to have suffered from depression or bipolar illness.[92]

Definitions of incest differ, sometimes referring to sexual intercourse, sometimes to invasive acts of touching.[93] Similarly, definitions of rape vary greatly from state to state, and the meanings of the word go beyond the legal definitions. In some states "rape" requires penetration of a penis into a vagina; in other states digital penetration is an act of rape. Probably Eakins could honestly claim innocence from the charge of incest, or indeed of any form of sexual assault. No doubt he had plausible "professional" motives for what he was doing. But surely Ella Crowell felt herself the victim of incest. Her suicide provides evidence of how deeply she felt shamed.

Paradoxically, the fact that Eakins's advances were not truly sexual seems to have contributed to the psychological damage that he inflicted on women. Psychologists would agree that incest is abhorrent and injurious. Nonetheless, there are many instances of people who have engaged in incest without any obvious external ill effects. The English sculptor and designer Eric Gill, for example, maintained long-term sexual liaisons with both his sisters and also engaged in sex with his three daughters (as has been carefully documented by his biographer, Fiona McCarthy, based on Gill's own meticulous records).[94] Yet Gill's behavior, while certainly out of the ordinary, and quite probably emotionally damaging, does not seem to have had dramatic or catastrophic consequences in the lives of those who surrounded him. Sisters and daughters all married, had children, and led outwardly normal lives. What is striking about Eakins's behavior is the amount of human misery that it precipitated, and the strange aura of anxiety, depression, anger, family conflict, insanity, and suicide that surrounded him.

Depression in the Eakins Family

Bipolar illness has a strong genetic component. Children of bipolar parents are often bipolar or suffer from closely related mood disorders, such as depression. Thus it is logical to ask whether Caroline Eakins's illness descended to any of her children. In the case of Thomas the answer is clearly yes. In photographs taken throughout his lifetime, Eakins looks troubled or depressed; his odd behavior (he often seemed listless or withdrawn) fits with a diagnosis of depression; and we know that he sought medical guidance from S. Weir Mitchell and others on coping with depression. Oddly, this issue has never been discussed by any of Eakins's biographers, but it has not been missed by doctors: Kay Redfield Jamison's classic study of bipolar disorder, *Touched with Fire*, lists Eakins as a figure who probably suffered from this condition.[95] Recognizing this likelihood places both Eakins's life and art in a different light. It suggests that throughout his life, Eakins was troubled by the possibility that he would descend into his mother's insanity. Thus, the extraordinary emphasis on depressed people in his paintings had a personal significance for him. Through these works he was both exploring his mother's death and an illness with which he was also afflicted.[96]

Two other members of the family, Margaret and Frances, also appear to have suffered from depression, although so far as we know, they did not experience full-scale bipolar illness. Our chief source of information on this matter, admittedly a somewhat subjective form of evidence, is family photographs. In existing photographs, Margaret looks unhappy, and Frances looks fretful and sour. The accounts of Eakins's relationship with Frances also suggest that she was deeply unhappy. Frances's daughter, Ella, was probably bipolar like her grandmother, as is suggested both by her suicide and by numerous accounts indicating that she was unhappy, insecure and temperamental.

Caroline, the youngest, is the one child who seems to have been free of this affliction. The photographs taken of her convey a sense of life and vitality, and a range of emotion, that does not appear in images of other family members. In the literature on Eakins, Caroline has been vilified because she did not side with her brother, but ironically, she may well have been the most mentally healthy member of the family.

Two things are significant here. On the negative side, if several members of the family were bipolar, it must have given disputes within the family a particularly volatile quality since the causes of unhappiness and anger within the family were often not logical or reasonable. This situation in turn must have encouraged members of the family to become stubborn and intransigent, a pattern that they then transferred to relationships outside the family.[97] Eakins's tendency to become involved in feuds and disputes, and to be unreasonable in dealing with them, appears to have been based on patterns he learned from his family.

On the positive side, manic-depression is often associated with artists and highly creative individuals. As Jamison notes, "recent research strongly suggests that, compared with the general population, writers and artists show a vastly disproportionate rate of manic-depressive or depressive illness."[98] In many instances, this disease can also be traced in their ancestors and relatives. Thus, for example, the families of figures such as Byron, Tennyson, Melville, William and Henry James, Schumann, Coleridge, Van Gogh, Hemingway, and Virginia Woolf all show a high rate of manic-depression that runs through generations. As Jamison notes, "Manic-depressive illness, then, is a very strange disease—one that confers advantage, but often kills or destroys as it does so."[99]

The reason for this link between creativity and manic-depression is not fully understood, but two reasons may be proposed. The first is that the mood swings of manic-depression seem to create a more intense world of emotional experience, and this increase of feeling is translated into the creative product. While it does not follow a single pattern, manic-depression often swings individuals through a variety of mood states, from frenzied, expansive, bizarre, and seductive to reclusive, sluggish, and suicidal. Jamison has noted that the interaction, tension, and transition between changing mood states seems to spur creativity.

The other is that certain varieties of manic-depression seem to be linked to a special kind of intense, narrowly focused concentration. At least in certain instances, manic-depressive people appear to become more absorbed and more self-absorbed than most people in the process of creation. To depressed people, work seems to act as a kind of stimulant that makes them feel happier and more at ease. This type of concentration, however, appears to operate according to rules of its own, and often makes a person less interested in the matters that concern other people.

In Eakins's case, it is possible that bipolar disorder was associated with obsessive compulsive behavior, which is sometimes linked with manic-depression. As the name suggests, this term refers to a compulsive need to carry out repetitive tasks. In its extreme form it can lead to obsessive rituals of washing, organizing objects, checking locked doors, or similar activities, which are repetitively carried out for hours, and often so paralyze the individuals afflicted that they cannot function effectively. It is often associated with deeper feelings of psychological anxiety, and seems to function as a means of regaining emotional control. Eakins's behavior does not precisely fit the clinical description of obsessive-compulsive syndrome, since his compulsiveness was not so exaggerated, but it does seem to fit with a less extreme form of this general pattern, Obsessive-Compulsive Personality Disorder, which is a listed in the DSM as a Cluster C personality disorder. Eakins's fascination with the calculations of perspective may well fall into this category, as well as the elaborate produces he went through with his sitters, such as pinning ribbons to them and aligning these markers with a gridded background.

While writers have marveled about Eakins's brilliance in handling perspective, his methods were relatively simple, and surprisingly unvaried, but so repetitive that few artists were willing to undertake them. In short, what was unusual about Eakins was his willingness to compulsively carry out a highly repetitive task: to calculate curves that ran through hundreds of little boxes, and that required many hours of tedious work. Significantly, Eakins's interest in perspective first became evident at a time of great emotional anxiety: his first paintings of this type, his rowing paintings, were produced at the time of his mother's final illness. Later, he seems to have turned to perspective at times of particular stress, for example producing one of his most intricately plotted paintings, his portrait of Henry Rowland, shortly after the suicide of Ella Crowell.

The Chemistry of Depression

While Eakins's behavior falls very neatly into a psychoanalytic model, other forms of explanation also provide useful insights.[100] In recent years, psychotherapy has been profoundly influenced by the development of chemical treatments for depression. External clues often provide a misleading picture of the inner mechanisms of mental illnesses and disturbances, since many diseases exhibit identical symptoms. Mania, for example, may result from bipolar illness, schizophrenia, Alzheimer's disease, syphilis, and so forth. Depression may be due to many causes. In confusing cases the precise nature of a disease or disorder can often be precisely established by discovering whether it responds to one or another form of medication.[101]

Scientists have demonstrated that nerve cells in the brain communicate by releasing chemical substances—neurotransmitters—into the space or synapse between cells. The message is then terminated by a two-stage process. First the neurotransmitters are taken back up into the transmitting cell. Second, they are deactivated and broken down into other substances. Depression seems to result when this process does not occur smoothly and the signal is disrupted or incomplete.[102]

Newly developed drugs for depression allow the neurotransmitter to remain longer in the synapse, making it possible for prolonged transmission of the impulse to occur.[103] They can do so in two ways. The first is to inhibit the enzymes that digest the neurotransmitter. Iproniazid, for example, blocks the enzyme that digests the neurotransmitter, so that the process of transmission is not prematurely interrupted but continues for a longer period. The second is to block the reuptake of the released neurotransmitter back into the transmitting cell through the use of drugs that block the neurotransmitter transport protein.

Two types of neurotransmitters have been identified that seem to be most important to modulating depressive symptoms: norepinephrine and serotonin. Early drugs for depression such as imipramine, which are known as tricyclic antidepressants, affected the reuptake of both these substances. Over time, however, drugs were developed that target these neurotransmitters individually, temporarily blocking their reuptake. Desipramine, for example, is fifteen hundred times more active on the norepinephrine transporter than on the serotonin transporter. Fluoxetine hydrochloride (Prozac) targets the serotonin reuptake transporter and is known as a selective serotonin reuptake inhibitor (SSRI). Both drugs are useful for treating certain forms of depression, although no existing drug works in every instance, and some forms of depression do not respond to medication. While not universally effective, Prozac and other SSRIs such as Zoloft, which target serotonin, have been the most successful medications to date, in large part because they lack the side effects of the tricyclic antidepressants.

Why they work is not fully understood. While serotonin is a neurotransmitter, experiments suggest that its role in the transmission of thought and neural impulses is complex. It is possible to drastically decrease the amount of serotonin in the system through diet. This has no obvious impact on normal people, at least in the short term, but will send bipolar individuals into immediate depression.[104] Since normal people can mentally function without it, we can deduce that serotonin does not directly transmit neural impulses. Instead it must play some sort of modulatory or regulatory role on the neural circuits of the brain. Curiously, while SSRIs meliorate certain forms of depression, they do so only after a long delay. It usually takes four or five weeks for them to have an impact on depression, although they are distributed through the system in a few hours. While often useful for mild depression, SSRIs are less successful in treating major depression, and often have no effect.[105]

While the mechanism by which they function is not understood, perhaps what is most intriguing about Prozac and other SSRIs is that they affect a great variety of mental syndromes and illnesses. Unlike earlier medications for depression, SSRIs are relatively "clean" in their action. In other words, they do not affect body chemistry in a wide-ranging way but target a specific brain chemical, serotonin. Nonetheless, they have proved effective in treating not only depression but obsessive-compulsive disorder, panic anxiety, aggression and "impulse control," sensitivity to rejection, eating disorders, premenstrual syndrome, exhibitionism, substance abuse, attention-deficit disorder, and a number of other conditions.[106]

This has led researchers to rethink the fundamental nature of their medical categories. For example, obsessive-compulsive disorder and dysthymia (mild depression) are currently classified as discrete entities, one related to anxiety and the other to depression, but a current movement, based largely on observation of drug effects, views them as related disorders.[107] From external evidence there is no particular reason for linking exhibitionism with depression. But the fact that both phenomena frequently respond to SSRIs, suggests that they both have some link to serotonin, at least in some instances.

Indeed, drugs such as Prozac often challenge traditional concepts of mental disease. Many patients are not "diagnosable"—their symptoms do not fit the established criteria for mental illness. Nonetheless, when given drugs such as Prozac, their sense of well-being improves and they function more effectively. Such behavioral traits such as "obsessionality" and "compulsiveness" have traditionally been viewed as personal idiosyncrasies, as flukes of character. But because they respond to SSRIs it becomes tempting to view them as mild forms of mental illness. In some instances patients who can function normally nonetheless experience an enhanced sense of well-being when they take Prozac, becoming "better than well."

The relevance of this to Eakins is that most of the peculiarities of his personality—depression, obsessiveness, sensitivity to rejection, exhibitionism, and so forth—are disorders that have been successively treated with SSRIs, at least in some cases. While they were previously viewed as disconnected, it now appears likely that these syndromes bear a biochemical relationship to each other. Since Eakins is dead, we cannot put this theory to the test by giving him SSRIs and seeing if they alter his behavior and mental condition. But it seems quite possible that Eakins suffered from a deficit of serotonin neuromodulation and that many of the difficulties of his life were related to this fact.

Modern theory, in short, offers us two distinctly different models for describing Eakins's behavior, one based on Freudian theory, the other on biochemistry. To a large degree these theories stand apart from each other, and look at the problem of mental illness from seemingly opposite points of view. Nonetheless, in clinical practice it appears that when psychotherapy and chemical treatment are combined they are more effective than when either approach is carried out separately. At present, in practical terms, it is difficult to link these two models. We simply draw upon each as the occasion demands. In theory, however, it is certainly logical to suppose that thought and life experience, the raw data of psychiatry, must have an impact on body chemistry, as it is also evident that mental chemistry must have an impact upon thought. As our knowledge of brain chemistry becomes more sophisticated, very likely the two models will be reconciled.

Nineteenth-Century Treatments for Depression

During Eakins's lifetime, depression and related mental illnesses were poorly understood, but doctors were making first attempts both to describe and to treat these diseases. Several of Eakins's biographers have noted that he had a nervous breakdown of some sort after he was fired from the Pennsylvania Academy and that he sought treatment for his illness from the nationally known specialist on nervous diseases, S. Weir Mitchell. Eakins's excursion to the Dakotas was a "camp cure" that precisely followed Mitchell's directions. Writers have not noted, however, that Eakins also seems to have followed Mitchell's advice about diet and medication for nervous illness and depression.

Along with advocating rest and camp cures, Mitchell experimented with curing "nervousness" through diet. He wrote an entire book, *Fat and Blood*, outlining his ideas on this subject. His theory was that the fatigue and lethargy associated with the disorder was because of something wrong with the patient's blood, which consequently was not nourishing the brain in proper fashion. Specifically, he believed that the illness was associated with a loss of fat. Consequently, he believed that a diet high in fat would serve "to fatten and redden" the sufferer and lead to a cure. To achieve this end, he advised consuming quantities of milk. His treatment ordinarily began with a diet consisting entirely or nearly entirely of milk, and even when he added other food, he continued to press his patients to consume two quarts or more of milk on a daily basis.[108]

In the most extreme form of Mitchell's rest cure, the patient was prescribed bed rest for a month or longer, was not permitted visitors or permitted to read or write, and was spoon fed a diet of milk by a nurse. Eakins's consumption of milk was surely due to Mitchell's regimen.

One might even postulate that the large quantities of milk Eakins consumed can be taken as an indicator of the degree of his anxiety about his susceptibility to his mother's illness. In other words, attempting to cure himself may have become a compulsive act. Significantly, however, he does not seem to have confided his motives for drinking milk to anyone. Samuel Murray, his closest intimate, knew that he drank huge quantities of milk but did not know why. Eakins seems to have done his best to conceal his psychological anxieties even from those seemingly most intimate to him. But that Eakins consumed milk in such an extraordinary fashion suggests that he was secretly afraid that he suffered from his mother's illness and might lose his mind or die from it. The extent of his consumption may be taken as an indicator of the level of his anxiety.

Eakins's willingness to adopt this regimen may have also had deeper causes, since choices of food reflect deep-rooted emotional needs. Milk is a comfort food and one specifically associated with maternal love and with a mother's breast. Eakins's compulsive drinking of milk may suggest that in some fundamental way he felt deprived of maternal affection.

Ironically, Eakins's enormous consumption of milk, with its high-fat content, seems to have contributed to the health problems that plagued him in middle age, when he suffered from obesity and circulatory problems.[109]

Along with milk, one may ask whether Eakins took other medications. In the nineteenth century drugs such as cocaine, morphine, and laudanum were often given out to treat depression. Mitchell's writings indicate that he prescribed opium, morphine, and cannabis.[110] Harrison Morris and others who knew Eakins in the 1890s mentioned that he had a sagging lip and that he slobbered when he painted.[111] This may indicate that he was taking a narcotic in oral form and that it numbed his lip. Descriptions of Eakins strongly suggest that he may have been taking some form of narcotics. His glazed eyes, his slow speech, his shuffling gait, and even some of his strange behavior, such as his pattern of waddling after women at parties and staring at them intently, all fit with this supposition. In short, Eakins's peculiar behavior, while very likely largely due to depression and other biochemical imbalances, may well have been exacerbated by narcotic substances.

Photographer unknown, Thomas Eakins at about 65(?). *Samuel Murray Archival Collection, Hirshhorn Museum and Sculpture Garden, Smithsonian Institution.*

Chapter 20

THE GREATEST
AMERICAN ARTIST

IN RETROSPECT, the approach toward Eakins that has dominated the literature on his work for the last century seems inherently fantastical. As developed most completely by Lloyd Goodrich, this view proposed that Eakins's
art expressed a kind of perfect honesty and absolute realism—indeed, that
honesty was so fundamental to Eakins's character that even when his paintings obviously diverged from a realistic presentation of his subject or sitter,
that his art was nonetheless, as Goodrich expressed it, "more than real."

Even apart from its application to Eakins, the possibility of such a perfect
realism is hard to imagine. In fact, the overall tendency of twentieth-century
art and thought has been to move away from such a viewpoint. Surely, after
the cubism of Picasso and the abstraction of Kandinsky, after the atonal and
multitonal music of Charles Ives and Schoenberg, after the multilayered
wordplay of James Joyce and T. S. Eliot, after Kurt Goedel's proof of unprov-
ability in mathematical systems, and after Werner Heisenberg's proof of
uncertainty in physics, the notion of a fixed and absolute truth of the sort
attributed to Eakins, is hard to credit. Even in Eakins's lifetime, figures such as
the painter John La Farge eloquently and convincingly argued that no form of
realism is absolute, since all forms of representation entail choices of selection
and viewpoint.[1]

If we take the trouble to stop and consider the matter, the notion that
Eakins's art is not absolutely realistic, but must in some fashion contain personal choices and bias seems so obvious as to be self-evident. As Michael Fried
has pointed out, even if we imagine that a painting such as *The Gross Clinic*
represents exactly what Eakins witnessed, we should still ask ourselves why

Eakins chose that particular viewpoint and that particular moment to represent. When we closely examine paintings such as *The Gross Clinic,* or indeed any of Eakins's works, we soon discover that they were not exact transcriptions of what Eakins saw, in the operating theatre or anywhere, but were artistic fabrications—no doubt based in part upon reality, but differing from reality in significant ways.

Surely this element of manipulation on Eakins's part seems obvious, and if questioned, probably no living scholar of Eakins's work would question this fact. Nonetheless, in discussions of Eakins, writers have tended to focus on its truthfulness and accuracy at the expense of other qualities.

If we discard the notion that Eakins represents some sort of perfect honesty and perfect truthfulness, it allows us to wake up to the fact that much of Eakins's work is very strange. Simply taken on their own terms, for example, without even bothering to check them against photographs of the sitters, it is obvious that many of Eakins's late portraits (such as that of Eleanor Pue) are expressively distorted—so much so that they often bring to mind the work of twentieth-century modernists such as Picasso or Balthus. Similarly, if we discard the notion that Eakins was an expert anatomist, who represented things accurately, it becomes obvious that the anatomy in many of his paintings is thoroughly contrary to anatomical fact, for example in the way he represented women's breasts. Indeed, even the most "realistic" of Eakins's paintings handle the issue of focus in an odd way, which does not correspond with how the eye actually sees. Even when he made successive renderings of the same subject, such as rowing, Eakins's pictures vary greatly in finish and handling, one from another, in a fashion that seems to beg for an explanation.

Discarding the notion that Eakin's art is purely realistic from the visual standpoint, then leads us to the notion that it was probably expressively manipulative as well. For example, there is much evidence that Eakins's portraits often provide a false impression of the character of his sitters.

At the simplest level, this book is simply a plea that we should focus on the variations in Eakins's work and seek an explanation for these variations, rather than to suppose that he was always invariably following the same goal, and achieving perfect realism in every instance. It is then not a large step to suppose that there are reasons for these changes in and to explore what they might be. One logical approach is to suppose that Eakins was responding to events in his life, and that his paintings in some fashion reflect what was happening to him at that time. Thus, events such as the death of his mother or the death of Ella Crowell might have an influence on what he painted.

Another step is to suppose that his paintings, in many instances, may reflect deeper psychological motives.

Subversive Themes

The realization that Eakins was an exhibitionist-voyeur and that his behavior was somehow connected to his mother's illness not only explains much of the behavior that so puzzled his contemporaries, but also elucidates the meanings of his work, and brings out undercurrents of meaning that tie together seemingly disparate subjects. Sadly, the tendency of writers on Eakins to rush to his defense has led them to ignore clues that are lying out in plain sight, like the purloined letter of Edgar Allen Poe's famous story. In fact, the loin cloth incident, which has always stood at the center of the mythology that has developed around Eakins, in very striking fashion dramatizes the central features of Eakins's psychological disorder.

Eakins's paintings tend to deal with a few themes, to which he returned with continual variations. The most obvious is depression, an issue surely important to him because of his mother's illness, and quite likely also significant because he suffered from depression himself.

Eakins's preoccupation with individuals who appear depressed brings to mind a common phenomenon associated with the relatives and associates of manic-depressive individuals—hypervigilance. Bipolar individuals are normal most of the time, but can suddenly slip into extreme or bizarre forms of behavior. Those who live with manic-depressives often develop an exaggerated degree of vigilance toward any possible manifestation of their disease. Signs of unhappiness or irritation, which to most people would appear quite normal, take on a frightening character because they might escalate into mania. That Eakins was responsible for caring for his mother during his childhood and for being sensitive to her needs could well have exacerbated this problem. As David Milowitz and Michael J. Goldstein have noted, "Often one sees an over-identifying family member paired with a patient who is quite ill. Family members who over-identify with the illness are usually quite worried that the disorder will recur at any moment."[2]

Eakins's portraits, in fact, seem to focus on just this issue—the dividing line between reason and insanity, where normal unhappiness threatens to become full-scale mania or depression. He clearly was fascinated by the signs of depression in "normal" people and also seems to have been attracted to models who were depressive or emotionally unstable. The curious way that he "staged" his portraits, placing his sitters in exhausting poses and often doing other things to annoy or humiliate them, suggests that he wanted to make his sitters appear tired, worried, unhappy, distressed, worn down, or even mentally unbalanced. He depicted himself in similar fashion, for Eakins seems to have been fascinated by the thought, as well as fearful of the possibility, that he might lose his sanity. In his book *American Nervousness*, for example, Tom Lutz remarks that in his self-portrait of 1902, "Eakins turns a morbid eye upon himself and exaggerates his own debility." Far from creating an objective record, Eakins deliberately exaggerated symptoms of depression or of manic-depressive illness.

In addition to depression, Eakins was fascinated with undressing, as well as with wounding or penetration. Disrobing is the central theme of *William Rush* and *The Swimming Hole*, wounding or penetration that of *The Gross Clinic* and *The Agnew Clinic*. In exploring these ideas, Eakins shifted back and forth between a male and female viewpoint. Thus, *William Rush* examines the female nude, *The Swimming Hole* the male nude; *The Gross Clinic* records the cutting of a male patient, *The Agnew Clinic* the carving of a female one. While these issues of undressing and of wounding or penetrating sometimes push in opposite directions, they also often overlap. Thus, *The Gross Clinic* is not only a painting about cutting but about exposing the buttocks of the patient. At a less obvious level, a painting such as *The Swimming Hole* is not simply a painting about undressing, but about penetration, since it plays with the issue of homosexual desire.

If we accept some of Freud's fundamental principles, then it becomes clear that all these themes are fundamentally connected. Thus, Eakins's fear of being castrated, which is the subject of *The Gross Clinic*, is related to the fear that women are castrated and thus defective men, and should be reshaped. This theme is also a focus of *The Agnew Clinic,* as well as of many of his portraits of women, which seem to explore the concept of women who are almost—but not quite—men. In a less direct fashion, Eakins's concern with undressing expressed the same narrative, since its roots lay in his own fear of castration, and the fundamental goal of this undressing was to see whether or not a penis would become visible. In a somewhat different way, this issue of castration even underlies Eakins's portraits, which so often portray figures who are sexually androgynous—manlike women or womanlike men.

In short, the powerful and disturbing qualities of Eakins's paintings are to a large degree due to the fact that he combined three issues, which he saw as very similar to one another, if not quite identical—whether one was genitally intact or castrated, whether one was male or female, and whether one was sane and authoritative, or insane and hysterical. The very importance of these distinctions, however, made the issue of male and female more confusing. Could men be feminine and did this make them mad? Could women be masculine and did this make them sane? In fact, many of Eakins's paintings seem to explore situations in which this fundamental distinction between men and women becomes blurred and men are feminine or women almost but not quite like men. Indeed, Eakins's hostility toward women contained a paradox. When with his mother, he must have empathized with her, and at times he must have felt that he was mad or close to madness. Several of those who knew the artist noted that something about his personality was deeply "feminine," and in many of his paintings—notably the early portrait of his sister Margaret in skating costume—Eakins seems to project himself into the female role.

Eakins seems to have generalized this opposition between male and female, endowing objects and colors with a deeper symbolic significance. The color red, for example, seems to have had strong emotional connotations associated with wounds, menstruation, and female hysteria. Thus, for example, the red feather in his early portrait of his sister, *Margaret in Skating Costume*, reads as a red gash, and in some sense stands for the wound-like menstruating vagina that marks her as a woman (and that accounts for her depression), despite the otherwise masculine qualities of her appearance. More generally, the red dress of figures such as *The Actress* becomes a general metaphor for female hysteria and emotional unpredictability. Some of Eakins's most compelling paintings, such as *The Concert Singer* or his other late portraits of women, are effective precisely because they present this narrative in fragmentary or symbolic form, challenging the viewer to reconstruct the narrative from cryptic fragments.

The element of trauma in Eakins's childhood may explain not only the subject matter of the his most successful paintings, but the fundamental peculiarities of his artistic technique. One might propose that the basic duality of the carefully ruled, rational perspective grid and the impulsive, unpredictable overlay of pigment in Eakins's work reflects a slightly uncomfortable synthesis of the personalities of his two parents: his father the calligrapher, rigid, correct, and orderly; and his mother the manic-depressive, either lethargic or hysterically out of control. While Eakins's perspective grid evokes the carefully ruled lines of the calligrapher, extended from two to three dimensions, his loosely applied colors, with their careless splotches and drips, suggest his mother's emotional fluctuations.

Eakins's use of perspective is marked by an exceptional rigidity and lack of imagination, in keeping with what we know of his rigid and inflexible father. His use of color, however, evokes a great emotional range, from drabness and dullness to violence, anger, or hysteria. Eakins's favorite color choices—dull, dark brown, and, in contrast, shrieking pinks—seem to reflect his mother's emotional swings from apathetic torpor to shrieking hysteria. Thus, both the imagery of Eakins's paintings, and his fundamental technique, with its curious mixture of control and disorder, may well contain a deeply embedded symbolic system, integrally bound up with his family history.

The Pursuit of Happiness

The traditional literature on Eakins has pushed forward an obvious falsehood, that he was an individual of almost unparalleled honesty and virtue and that his art directly reflected the perfections of his character. While this was surely done to uplift Eakins's art, in the end it only undercuts its real significance. Eakins's paintings affect us as they do because they deal with powerful, tragic themes—depression, defeat, mental illness, loneliness, and anxieties of a truly horrible sort, such as castration and sexual assault. His life touches on a whole litany of psychological and social problems, including exhibitionism, obsessive compulsive syndrome, poor impulse control, misogyny, castration anxiety, sexual abuse, incest, and manic-depression. To conceal all this with sugary language, is to rob Eakins's paintings of their real meaning.

To be sure, when we recognize the degree to which Eakins was disturbed, his paintings take on extremely disturbing qualities. Linda Nochlin, for example, supposed that Eakins was sympathetic with the plight of nineteenth-century women, and that his paintings expressed some sort of advocacy for their needs. She proposes that his work is admirable from a feminist standpoint. This view is surely incorrect. Eakins's paintings surely mean something else, something more complicated, when we recognize that he considered women inferior to men, and that his women look suffering and abused because he mistreated them while they posed for him. Indeed, Eakins's career as a whole surely looks different when we balance his artistic achievement against the human havoc with which he was associated, such as the madness of Lillian Hammitt or the suicide of Ella Crowell. The degree to which we feel he was responsible for such episodes surely has some bearing on our overall assessment of his work and on the pleasure we take in looking at it.

Nonetheless, the notion that Eakins's art should be seen in moral rather than artistic terms has an element of truth. It points toward the fact that Eakins's work engages outside life to an unusual degree. A major theme of his art was to challenge the notion that art and life are separate, or that art should be judged purely in formal or decorative terms. In seeking to come to terms with Eakins and his art, one problem may be that our popular notion that art should be morally uplifting, while probably true in a certain sense, has often been construed in a way that is misleading. There is no particular reason to suppose that moral artists make more compelling paintings than immoral ones. The traditional view that the power of Eakins's work stems from qualities of honesty and incorruptible virtue is surely naïve. Indeed, aberrant behavior often sheds light on the mechanisms of normal life. One function of art, or of certain forms of art, may well be to bring us such insights.

Being moral, in fact, presents a curious paradox, well summarized by G. K. Chesterton's priest-detective Father Brown. To be moral we must recognize evil. To do so, we must, like Chesterton's detective, be able to fully identify with it. Father Brown solves crimes because he can imagine committing a murder. Behind his clerical collar and saintly demeanor lies a truly wicked imagination. His "empathy for evil" is the most important ingredient of his virtue. If he could not imagine evil, and in this sense become evil, he would not be able to discover evil and stamp it out.

Eakins presents a particular challenge in this regard. For most people the behavior of a figure like Eakins is difficult to imagine. As has been established by clinical studies, the disorder he suffered from, exhibitionism is distinctively male. Consequently, for women to imagine behaving in this way is fundamentally difficult if not impossible. Even for men to do so, presents a challenge, since it goes against habits—one might almost say instincts—that were ingrained in early childhood. How many of us would derive pleasure from dropping our pants in public in front of a female student?

For us to empathize with Eakins, even to a limited degree, requires going through a series of additional steps that retrace the conditions that impelled Eakins to behave in this way. We must go through the admittedly subjective exercise of trying to reconstruct his formative experiences. We must attempt to imagine the dark, claustrophobic house, which existed as a kind of universe of its own, sealed off from the world outside, or from any hope of outside assistance; the stern, distant, all powerful father, who allowed no conversation at meals and who shut down most expressions of emotional feeling; the frightened boy, dominant and domineering over his small sisters, but himself utterly subservient to his father's decisions, even on such matters as the choice of a wife or the choice of a career; and finally, the manic-depressive mother, who periodically went through periods of both depression and screaming hysteria, who sought from her eldest son a kind of marriage-like companionship that her husband did not provide, and who probably made strange sexual overtures to him.

Perhaps most important, we must remember that Eakins did not experience these things as a fully formed adult who could respond to them with an adult's understanding. Instead, he experienced them from earliest childhood, and they were the template on which his personality was shaped. Indeed, the strong element not only of Oedipal conflict in Eakins's work, but also of basic confusion over sexual and personal identity, suggests that traumas were inflicted on him at a very early age.

If some of the readings I have presented of Eakins's paintings seem bizarre, I nonetheless believe that no reader should dismiss these interpretations as unacceptable and alien who cannot imagine behaving in some of the strange ways that Eakins did—exposing himself and undressing in front of a woman, or inviting a woman to his home and then insisting that she undress. Exhibitionism, in fact, contains an inherent element of paradox, which we can extend not only to Eakins's life but to his art. An exhibitionist reveals in order to conceal. The act of seeming to disclose and to reveal is actually an exercise in hiding something.

A noted psychologist once told me that during his first visit with a patient he generally formulates a clear textbook diagnosis, but then, on every subsequent visit, he moves away from the clarity of that framework as the peculiarities of the individual case become apparent. With Eakins the same principle applies. On the one hand, understanding that Eakins was an exhibitionist clarifies much of what has always been puzzling about his behavior. On the other hand, the end result is to make his behavior and paintings even more mysterious, since it soon becomes clear that they are full of subtexts that are personal, even idiosyncratic, and tied to psychological needs and preoccupations that most people do not share.

Many elements in Eakins's paintings—such as the coy allusions to anuses and penises, or the portrayal of both hysteria and depression—mean something that was based on experiences that most of us have never had. I would argue that the real meaning of Eakins's paintings is not fully accessible to those who do not share his preoccupations as an exhibitionist-voyeur. Once we recognize this fact, we need to comb his paintings for clues with this in mind.

For example, clearly the childish question "Where is the penis?" had a powerful significance for Eakins, and we should look at all his paintings of figures, both nude and dressed, with this in mind. Given his disorder, we can suppose that it is probably significant that the vanishing point of his painting *The Chess Players* (1876) is placed precisely over his father's genital area. Similarly, in Eakins's first painting of *William Rush*, the sculptor holds a chisel at the level of his genitals, making it function as a substitute for a penis, or, alternatively, as an emphatic marker of where the penis is placed. Nothing about the painting particularly calls attention to this fact, but once we recognize that Eakins was preoccupied with the location of penises, this fact becomes significant, perhaps even a key to understanding the work. For Eakins, most likely, the whole drama of the painting resided in the fact that Rush has a penis and the woman does not.[3]

Even when such pointing to a penis does not occur, Eakins seems to have used surrogates, such as guns, scalpels, paint brushes, and conductor's batons, to serve the role of a performative phallus—assert the dominance and masculinity of the holder, and very often to embarrass women.[4]

Similarly, it takes a while to recognize that in his female portraits, Eakins often transformed the appearance of his sitters to recreate the symptoms of mental illness that he had witnessed in his mother, even adding gray hair and wrinkles to bring them to the age of his mother at the time of her death. Once we note this issue, it raises the possibility that Eakins also played up more subtle issues of resemblance. For example, if we place Eakins's second portrait of Addie Williams beside his portrait of his mother, we can see that there are similarities in the turn of the head, the set of the jaw, the wrinkles around the eyes, and many other equally subtle elements. Some of these same affinities can also be observed in other portraits. Very probably, in fact, every nuance of Eakins's portraits needs to be interpreted as in light of its similarity to or divergence from the appearance and behavior of his mother, and the entire meaning of this group of works is built out of this issue of resemblance. As with our search for penises, this issue is often not obvious or clearly articulated, but once we have extracted a general principle, we need to go back and give all of Eakins's paintings a careful second look.

Very likely, Eakins's subversive use of psychologically subversive themes explains why he has always been seen as a "modern" artist, despite his amazingly reactionary social views, and the old-fashioned nature of his technique. Attempting a comprehensive definition of modernism is therefore risky. But surely two key properties of modern art are first, that it often is an art of negation or of inverting the usual way of doing things, and second, that it plays with ambiguity, and with things that can be interpreted in different ways. While no doubt this could be said of all forms of art to some degree, it seems to be particularly true of art that has a modern aspect. Indeed, even when we are unable to clearly articulate the anxieties that preoccupied Eakins, we can often sense that they are there.

Eakins's likenesses are modern because they seem to reverse the usual purposes of portraiture and figural painting. Rather than affirming the self-worth and social station of his sitters, his paintings seem to undercut such certainties. Even Eakins's fascination with penises and castration touches on contemporary concerns. Much of Eakins's art seems to explore themes of the performative phallus that relate to the work of many contemporary artists. To cite just one example, Robert Morris's infamous I-box showed the artist in full frontal nudity, standing proudly in a box shaped like the letter I. Presumably Morris's piece was created ironically, to parody rather than to bluntly assert the rhetoric of male phallic dominance, but the parallels with Eakins's work are striking. Indeed, Eakins's anxiety about the body and gender roles seems to foreshadow a major tendency in both contemporary art and art criticism.

In the end, "explaining" Eakins makes him considerably more enigmatic than before. A solution to the riddles I have posed, while certainly a forward step, does not eliminate the mystery of Eakins's art, but opens up a whole new set of questions, and reveals that his art is considerably more mysterious than anyone has realized. For me to go back and reexamine all of Eakins's paintings here, given all that I have already said, would surely be tedious. But now that we have come to a new understanding of Eakins, I would encourage

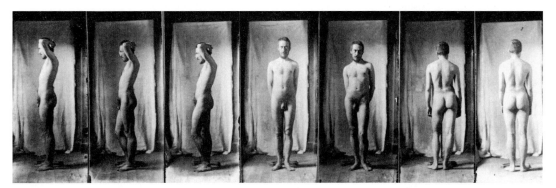

Naked Series: Thomas Eakins in Front of Cloth Backdrop, Pose 1, ca. 1883. *Dry-plate negative, 4 x 1 ¹¹/₁₆ in. each, courtesy of The Pennsylvania Academy of the Fine Arts, Philadelphia, Charles Bregler's Thomas Eakins Collection, purchased with the partial support of the Pew Memorial Trust.*

the reader to do so. Hopefully new meanings and messages will become apparent,
including some that I have missed. In a
sense we need to move backwards, and set
aside nearly a century of Eakins scholarship, so that we can look at Eakins's work
with the bewildered innocence of Bryson
Burroughs, who was ready to confess that
he found it "very puzzling."

The claim that Eakins was "the greatest American artist" has become a kind of
self-fulfilling prophecy, and indeed, has
been exploited as a device to avoid looking
to closely at his work. One may ask, however, whether there is any truth to this
belief—or at least to ask, what is it about
his work that is unique? Surely an honest
answer to this question would be almost
the opposite of the one provided by writers such as Lloyd Goodrich and Elizabeth
Johns. For Eakins, far from being the most

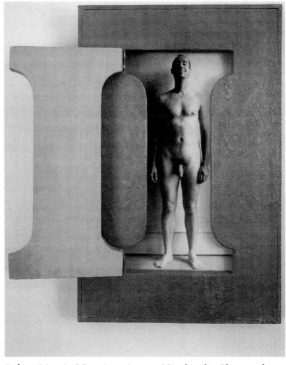

Robert Morris, I-Box (open), 1962. *Mixed media. Photograph
courtesy Leo Castella Gallery and the artist © Robert
Morris / Artists Rights Society (ARS), New York.*

moral of American artists, was surely one of the most profoundly confused,
even disturbed.[5] By making art out of the chaos, conflict, and scandal of his
own life, Eakins brought us more deeply into the world of sorrow, suffering,
and despair than any other American artist of the nineteenth century. By
some peculiar alchemy, he made his dark feelings beautiful, as anyone can
attest who has contemplated one of his major paintings. Their effect can only
be described as hypnotic.

I think it is naive to suppose that Eakins's artistic activity was purely liber-
ating, and thus was inherently good. His paintings often contained elements
that were deliberately designed to cause embarrassment or psychological discomfort. Yet if there is a redeeming aspect to his life and art, perhaps we can
find it in the notion that his art expresses a wish to heal himself. Although this
effort failed, what Eakins pursued in his art was in many respects similar to
the process that would be pursued by a psychoanalyst, seeking to probe back
into early half-conscious or unconscious memories to find the root of a psychological disturbance.

Because these memories were half conscious or unconscious, they were difficult to identify and locate. Consequently, Eakins's art often has a highly repetitive character, in which he pursued the same theme or issue over and over again, with slight but significant variations of treatment. In different guises, Eakins's art seems to probe back toward the family trauma that disrupted his emotional development and sense of masculine self-identity. His repeated portraits of depressed individuals, particularly women, seem to explore or reenact his mother's depression. His fixation with androgyny seems to explore the complex ways in which he identified with his mother. His paintings of William Rush seem to explore the embarrassment of encountering his mother's nakedness. His paintings *The Gross Clinic* and *The Agnew Clinic* apparently confront his fears of castration and incest—whether real or imagined. Even Eakins's coarse and often brutal treatment of his sitters—particularly the female ones—when its causes are fully understood, takes on the character of play-acting or a charade. For in fact, he was not really relating to them at all. He was simply carrying on a conversation with his mother—even after she had been dead for thirty years.

All human behavior comprises a mix of "normal" and "abnormal" impulses, as well as of both destructive and altruistic ones. To note that Eakins suffered from paraphilias (or perversions) does not mean that he did not also possess admirable qualities. It is tragic, of course, that the Eakins family broke apart in hatred and name-calling and finally in bitter and estranged silence, and tragic as well that Eakins's actions served in some way as a catalyst to madness and suicide. Yet his behavior was not entirely his fault, but was essentially a response to the abuse he must have suffered from his mother as a child, and perhaps also a reflection of the mental illness, manic-depression, that evidently afflicted them both.

The roots of exhibitionism seem to lie in childhood, and one way of seeing the disorder is as a kind of infantile regression. A feature of Eakins's behavior that was fairly regularly noted by his contemporaries was its childlikeness. Eakins's classmate in Paris, Earl Shinn, for example, declared that Eakins had "the manners of a boy." When he observed Eakins socializing with the members of Harry Moore's family, he noted "they fool with him and treat him like a little child."[6] His informal clothes looked childish to nineteenth-century eyes since they corresponded with what children wore and then abandoned when they became adults. Once, for example, when Eakins was sitting cross-legged on the lawn, wearing his sailor cap, sweater, and pants, James Dodge called his wife over with the words, "Josie, Josie, come here, see Tom. Doesn't he look just like a great big baby?"[7] Eakins's interests were also often curiously child-

Photographer unknown, Thomas Eakins at about 65(?) (detail). *Samuel Murray Archival Collection, Hirshhorn Museum and Sculpture Garden, Smithsonian Institution.*

like. He once arrived at the Dodge home with a little sailor cap on his head and three turtles in a paper bag.[8] Eakins's habit of sitting on the floor was essentially a way of mimicking childish behavior.

Eakins's pleasure in nakedness can also be seen in this light. Mrs. Dodge recalled that Eakins had a little niece and nephew who used to run around in the nude when she visited.[9] We can interpret this fact in different ways. Perhaps it reflects an unhealthy interest in children as sexual objects. On the other hand, little children enjoy throwing off their clothes. Perhaps Eakins's interest in nakedness was, at a deep level, sexually innocent, reflecting a desire to return to childhood, to the point where things went wrong, and to start over.

As David Stafford-Clark has written:

Prancing about naked is self-evidently satisfying and exciting for children. The antics which young children perform before getting into the bath, the mixture of coyness and self-assertion, the running away and being caught and brought back—the general gaiety and exuberance of this situation are evident to any parent with the capacity for calm, untroubled observation and an open mind. To see and to be seen are important parts of the emotional fulfillment and sexual excitation of children. They are not only not wrong, they are right; for they are at least a step along the way, and they will induce fixation at that stage only if further development is refused, denied, or repressed.[10]

The childish, regressive element of Eakins's behavior gives it a poignant quality. In most photographs, Eakins looks depressed and sad, if not haunted. Even in one in which he smiles (no doubt because Samuel Murray was mugging for him just off camera) the smile looks forced and not quite natural.

There is one striking exception to this look of anxiety and distress, however: a pair of photographs that show Eakins as an old man, round, pot-bellied, and entirely naked. The first shows him standing knee deep in water, happily facing the camera. The second shows him rushing farther into the creek, splashing the water like a child. As erotic enticements, these images are not exactly compelling, but they convey a need for attention and love that is quite affecting. Looking at these images one cannot but wish that all the misunderstandings of Eakins's public and family life had been handled a little differently; and one can see that in fundamental ways, much of Eakins's behavior was not so much malevolent as infantile. In these two photographs he resembles nothing more than a big, fat, naked baby, and for once in his life, Thomas Eakins looks truly happy.

Photographer unknown, Eakins at about 65(?) with Unidentified Man in Cohansy River at Eakins's Fish House in Fairton, NJ, ca. 1909. *Silver/gelatin developing out paper, 4 ¼ x 6 ¹⁄₁₆ in., Samuel Murray Archival Collection, Hirshhorn Museum and Sculpture Garden, Smithsonian Institution.*

ACKNOWLEDGMENTS

The thinking behind this book dates back many years, to my conversations with John Caldwell when we were both curators at the Carnegie Museum in Pittsburgh. While the Bregler Papers had not yet been discovered, Caldwell sensed, simply from looking at Eakins's paintings, that there was something dark and strange about Eakins's view of life and that he took cheap shots against women. In a subliminal way his intuitive insights, rather casually expressed, provided the groundwork for this book.

I owe an immense debt to Constance Bond, the former art editor of *Smithsonian Magazine*, who first stimulated me to write on Eakins, as well as to Don Moser, the chief editor of the magazine. With admirable courage, they dealt honestly with a difficult subject, even in a publication aimed at a family audience. Under their direction *Smithsonian* became one of the best magazines in the country, as well as one of the most popular.

That this book came into being is largely due to a casual meeting with Sandra Dijkstra, who immediately embraced the project and found a publisher for it. I am profoundly grateful for her support, her courage, her persistence, and her clear-headed advice. For additional assistance at the Dijkstra Agency I am grateful to the enterprise and alertness of Babette Sparr, as well as to the careful attention of Elizabeth James. Bernard Dod and David Anfam also provided encouragement to me at an early stage.

Three successive deans at Case Western Reserve University—John Bassett, Sam Savin, and Sandra Russ—have been wonderfully supportive. I am particularly grateful to John Bassett, who provided a W. P. Jones Presidential Faculty Development Fund Award of $1,500 to support a research trip to Philadelphia.

Peter Ginna at the Oxford University Press, the most intellectually probing editor I have ever worked with, unerringly spotted weak points, whether a nit-picking matter of wording or a dangerous flaw in the argument. Eager to confront Eakins first-hand, he even took the trouble to go through the Metropolitan Museum's exhibition of Eakins's work, and to study each painting with care. I stand in awe of his talent, and I found that I could follow his suggestions unhesitatingly. It is amazing to me that he continues to edit on a massive scale, while also supervising a large and complex business operation.

Peter's assistant, Furaha Norton, has also been attentive and wonderful, and has skillfully steered this project through the process of editing and production. My thanks to Mark McGarry of Texas Type & Book Works, whose design feels wonderfully clean and uncluttered despite the hundreds of illustrations. He perfectly realized my hopes for the look of the book. My deepest, most profound thanks to Helen B. Mules, who took charge of all the challenges of production, putting in an effort that went beyond the call of duty. Sensitive, diplomatic, skillful, and a master of detail, she also never lost sight of the larger goals. Grateful thanks go to Robert Swanson, who did a masterful job as indexer. Many others at Oxford also helped this book along, including Mary Ann Zissimos in publicity.

I have benefited from the help and guidance of two gifted editors in Cleveland. Katie Solender, the acting director of the Oberlin Art Museum, who has a long background in museum education, tactfully and sensitively reviewed the manuscript, making improvements to every page. B. J. Bradley, chief editor at the Cleveland Museum of Art, corrected flaws of spelling and usage, and sharpened and clarified the phrasing, with a skill honed by years of practice.

Darrell Sewell, curator of American Art at the Philadelphia Museum of Art, and Douglass Paschall, his research assistant, generously allowed me to consult research materials in the museum, including Lloyd Goodrich's unpublished notes on Eakins. Charles Ingersoll provided wonderful hospitality during my stay in Philadelphia; and my sister-in-law, Patricia Ingersoll Adams, provided lively accounts of the idiosyncrasies of the social elite in that city.

For guidance in sailing through the shark-infested waters of Eakins scholarship, I am indebted to a pair of the most gifted scholars of our time—Martin Berger, the author of a masterful book on Eakins and masculine identity, and Marc Simpson, who wrote five chapters of the monumental Eakins catalogue, published by the Philadelphia Museum in 1999. Marc Simpson's generosity was particularly noteworthy, since he disagrees with most of my argument but nonetheless gave the text a careful reading and caught many potentially embarrassing errors. Linnea Wren of Gustavus Adolphus College provided me with information on Dr. Gross at an early stage of this enterprise. Jennifer Hardin, whom I once worked with in Kansas City, generously shared with me a chapter on Eakins from her Princeton dissertation on depictions of the nude in nineteenth-century American art.

In an attempt to grasp the mysteries of psychoanalysis I have consulted a number of doctors, including Dr. Pedro Delgado, chief of psychiatry at University Hospital in Cleveland, Dr. Stanley Althoff, Dr. Stephen B. Levine, Dr. Michaela Kane Schaeffer, and Dr. Clay Whitehead. I also benefited from conversations with James Edmonson, Director of the Dittrick Medical Museum and Allen Medical Library in Cleveland, who kindly read through the manuscript from beginning to end. Dr. Lewis Obi of Jacksonville, Florida, perhaps this country's leading plastic surgeon, made many useful suggestions, particularly about Eakins's possible use of narcotics. Evan Deneris, in the Department of Neuroscience at the Case Western Reserve School of Medicine, shared with me his recent research on serotonin. A former art history student, Suzanne De Brosse, who is now attending the medical school at Case Western Reserve, gathered articles for me on medical subjects and helped me to make sense of them. I am grateful to Pedro Delgado for sharing with me the working draft of the chapter he is writing with Francisco A. Moreno on "Neurochemistry of Mood Disorders."

Genevieve Hill, who helped with this manuscript almost from its inception, has been the good angel of this project. She gathered research materials, ordered photographs, checked facts, and fixed problems with my computer and with my relationship with my computer. She also read over the text in many different stages. Most of all, I am grateful for her unwavering support of this somewhat unusual project, and her conviction that it would come to a happy conclusion. Katie Steiner, who first came to me as a high school intern, has been a solid rock of strength. A goddess of order, and thus something of a counterpoint to my own disorderly tendencies, she generously took on much of the gigantic task of gathering illustrations. She also read over the text many times, in many different stages, and suggested corrections and improvements.

I am grateful to another astute reader, Charles Yannopoulos, whose training as a lawyer provided the ideal background for grasping the different sides of a complex family argument. Kathleen McKeever, my former research assistant, read various drafts of this text and helped protect me from the darts and arrows of outrageous fortune when I was working at the Cleveland Museum of Art.

Three members of the Art History Department at Case Western Reserve, David Carrier, John Ciofalo, and Ellen Landau, read the entire manuscript and made valuable suggestions. Other readers include the architect Douglas Adams, the artist and calligrapher George Fitzpatrick, the art historian Linda Merrill, the art dealer Linda Hyman, the museum administrator Stephanie Stebich, and my students Kim Hyde, Karina Gobar, and Michael Weil. These are all amazing people and I am grateful to all of them. At a sluggish point in this venture, Natasha Staller visited Cleveland, and the hypnotic, dazzling conversation I had with her filled me with energy for months.

I have often introduced bits of my study of Eakins into my classes and am indebted to the response of my students, including Nickolaos Apostolides, Bradley Bailey, Laura Berick, Ellen Bortel, Siobhan Conaty, Suzanne DeBrosse, Justinya Drozdek, James Ellis, Deborah Freund, Kitty Heasley, Marcie Hocking, Linda Hulsman, Kim Hyde, Aimée Marcereau, Susan Martis, Shannon Masterson, Michelle May, Kathleen McKeever, May Schneider, Tiffany Washington, Catherine Watkins, Julie Worley, Charles Yannopoulos, and Molly Zillman.

Finally, I am indebted to Marianne Berardi, my most critical reader, and Thomas James Adams, who provided insight beyond his years.

BIOGRAPHICAL KEY

The Eakins Family

Benjamin Eakins, 1818–1899. Father of the artist. A writing master and speculator in slum real estate.

Caroline Cowperthwaite Eakins, 1820–1872. Mother of the artist. Suffered from manic-depression and died of manic-depressive illness shortly after Eakins returned from study in Paris.

Eliza Cowperthwaite, 1806–1899. The elder sister of Eakins's mother, lived in the Eakins home. Became non compos mentis by the 1890s.

Thomas Eakins, 1844–1916. Eldest child, celebrated American painter.

Frances Eakins, also known as **Fanny**, 1848–1940. Also listed under **The Crowell Family**. Eldest of the artist's sisters, four years younger than the artist. Married Will Crowell. Supported Eakins during the Academy scandal but turned against him later, when her daughter Ella committed suicide after asserting that Eakins had sexually molested her.

Margaret Eakins, also known as **Maggie** or **Maggy**, 1853–1882. Eakins's middle and favorite sister, eight years younger than he. Served as Eakins's companion, business manager and assistant. Did not marry and died of typhus at the age of twenty-nine. Eakins was accused of incest with her by his brother-in-law, Frank Stephens.

Caroline Eakins, also known as **Caddy**, 1865–1889. Eakins's youngest sister, twenty-one years younger than he, named after her mother. Disliked Eakins, feeling what one observer described as "an extravagance of hostility" toward him, and never forgave him for murdering her cat. Married Frank Stephens and in 1886 joined in the campaign to discredit Eakins, accusing him of various forms of sexual misconduct.

The Macdowell Family

William H. Macdowell, c. 1823–1906. An engraver and free-thinking atheist. Father of Eakins's wife and business associate of Eakins's father.

Susan Macdowell Eakins, 1851–1938. The fifth of eight children. Studied with Eakins at the Academy from 1876 to 1882 and married him in 1884, shortly after the death of his sister Margaret. Gave up her artistic career to keep house for Eakins and cook his meals. They had no children. An ardent defender of her husband, she became so distraught when he was fired from the Pennsylvania Academy that her brother feared for her sanity. Eakins made two portraits of her looking careworn, the first in about 1886, the second in about 1900.

William G. Macdowell, 1845–1926. Brother of Susan, provided Eakins with legal advice during the Academy scandal.

Walter Macdowell, 1854–1930. Brother of Susan. Regarded Eakins with distrust and warned his young daughter to steer clear of him, which she did.

Elizabeth Macdowell, later **Elizabeth Macdowell Kenton**, 1858–1953. Sister of Susan. Joined in the attacks against Eakins in 1886 but later apologized and often stayed in the Eakins home.

Louis Kenton. Married briefly to Elizabeth Macdowell. Is said to have been henpecked. Was the subject of Eakins's painting *The Thinker,* 1900.

The Crowell Family

William Crowell, 1844–1929. Eakins's high school classmate. Married Eakins's eldest sister, Frances, who bore him eleven children. Studied law but never worked. Retired to a farm in Avondale purchased by Benjamin Eakins, his wife's father. Once threatened to kill Eakins, then defended him during the Academy scandal, then turned against him after the suicide of his daughter, Ella.

Frances Eakins Crowell, 1848–1940. Also listed under **The Eakins Family**. Eakins's eldest sister. Supported Eakins during the Academy scandals of 1886 but broke off all relations with him after the suicide of her daughter Ella.

Kathrin Crowell, 1851–1879. Younger sister of Will Crowell. Was engaged to Eakins from 1874 to 1879, at the insistence of Eakins's father. She appears in an unflattering portrait by Eakins of 1872. They never married and she died of meningitis at the age of twenty-eight.

Elizabeth Crowell. Sister of Kathrin. Eakins is said to have been in love with her. Appears in several of Eakins's most romantic paintings, including *Elizabeth at the Piano,* 1875, which hung over the mantelpiece in the Eakins home.

Ella Crowell, 1873–1897. Eldest child of Will Crowell and Frances Eakins Crowell, and first grandchild of Benjamin Eakins. Pictured by Eakins at the age of three in *Baby at Play* of 1876. Studied painting with Eakins, then abruptly shifted to nursing. Threatened to kill Eakins and the singer Weda Cook with a revolver around 1895. Committed suicide at the age of twenty-four after claiming that Eakins sexually molested her.

Margaret Crowell, known as **Maggie** or **Maggy**, 1876–1920/24. Younger sister of Ella Crowell, named for Eakins's favorite sister. Often stayed in the Eakins home with Ella. Susan Eakins accused her of spreading rumors against Eakins, although she denied this.

Benjamin Crowell, known as **Ben**, 1877–1960. Brother of Ella Crowell, named for Eakins's father. Often stayed in the Eakins home, but went to work with Eakins's arch-enemy, Frank Stephens. Said to have accused Eakins of molesting his sister Ella.

The Stephens Family

George Frank Stephens, known as **Frank**, 1859–1935. Sometimes called "Kid Stephens" because he was four years younger than his cousin Charles. Married Eakins's sister Caroline. Was active in the campaign against Eakins when he was fired from the Pennsylvania Academy, accusing him of bestiality and incest.

Caroline Eakins, 1865–1889. Also listed under **The Eakins Family**. Eakins's youngest sister, named after her mother. Disliked her brother intensely and joined in her husband's campaign against him. In 1886, at the height of the controversy, she was ejected from the family home by her father, Benjamin Eakins, shortly after giving birth to her first child.

Charles H. Stephens, 1855–1931. First cousin of Frank Stephens. Painter of Native American subjects. Married to Alice Barber Stephens. Sided against Eakins in the Academy scandal.

Alice Barber Stephens, 1858–1932. Married to Charles Stephens. Studied with Eakins and became a successful magazine illustrator. Accused Eakins of indecent behavior at the time of the Academy scandal and imparted her accusations to her husband.

Directors and Staff at the Pennsylvania Academy

Christian Schussele, 1824–1879. An accomplished but conventional genre painter, trained in Alsace, who taught and served as head of instruction at the Pennsylvania Academy after palsy impeded his ability to support himself by making paintings. His worsening illness and eventual death made it possible for Eakins to rise to power at the Academy.

John Sartain, 1808–1897. The leading engraver in Philadelphia and for a time the most powerful figure in the Philadelphia art world. He moved in the same social circles as the Eakins family and was the father of Eakins's first girlfriend, Emily Sartain. He and Eakins fought bitterly, however, when Eakins took over at the Pennsylvania Academy, bringing in nude models and repudiating the methods of his predecessor, Christian Schussele. Sartain resigned soon after Eakins took charge.

Eadweard Muybridge, 1830–1904. Made the first photographs of animals in successive stages of movement under the patronage of the Californian millionaire Leland Stanford. After murdering his wife's lover, he left California, and moved to Philadelphia, where he continued his photographic work, sometimes in association with Eakins.

Fairman Rogers, 1833–1900. Served on the board of the Pennsylvania Academy, and defended Eakins on various occasions, one being when a group of male students threw a dead horse onto the landing of the grand staircase. An enthusiastic horseman, and author of a book on coaching, he commissioned a painting of his four-horse coach from Eakins in 1879. Resigned from the Academy in 1883 and moved to Paris.

Edward Horner Coates, 1846–1921. Chairman of the Committee of Instruction at the Pennsylvania Academy. Fired Eakins in February 1886, with the backing of the entire teaching faculty. Eakins painted *Swimming* for Coates in 1885 but Coates exchanged it for another painting, presumably because he felt uncomfortable with it's portrayal of Eakins and his students in the nude.

Thomas Anshutz, 1851–1912. Eakins's second-in-command at the Pennsylvania Academy. Sided against Eakins in 1885. Took over the life classes at the Academy until 1892, spent two years in Paris, and then resumed teaching at the Academy, becoming Director of the Academy's School in 1909. Became a major American painter but is even better known as one of the most influential art teachers of his generation. Was enormously admired by his students, many of whom became major figures in American art.

James P. Kelly, 1854–1893. Studied at the Academy and became Eakins's chief demonstrator of anatomy in 1881. Sided against Eakins in 1886. Taught at the Academy until 1892.

Mary Searle. Anatomy demonstrator at the Academy. Sided against Eakins in 1886.

Charlotte Connard. Anatomy demonstrator at the Academy. Sided against Eakins in 1886.

Jesse Godley, 1862–1889. Anatomy demonstrator at the Academy who appears in many of Eakins's motion photographs. Became an assistant in the decorating firm of George Frank Stephens and Colin Campbell Cooper Jr. Sided against Eakins in 1886.

Walter Dunk, 1855–. Studied at the Academy from 1876 to 1881 and was a member of the Sketch Club. Sided against Eakins in 1886.

Students of Eakins

Benjamin Fox, c. 1865–1900. Studied at the Academy in 1883, 1884, and 1888 and posed in the nude for Eakins's *Swimming*, 1885. Died at the age of twenty-seven in the Lunatic Asylum of the Philadelphia Hospital.

J. Laurie Wallace, 1864–1953. Studied at the Pennsylvania Academy from 1879 to 1882. Often appears in nude photographs by Eakins. Posed in the nude for Eakins's *Crucifixion*, 1880, and *Swimming*, 1885.

George Reynolds, c. 1839–1889. A traumatized Civil War veteran who posed in the nude for *Swimming*, 1885. Studied at the Pennsylvania Academy from 1882 to 1886, and helped form the Philadelphia Art Students League.

Franklin Schenck, 1855–1926. A bearded bohemian who studied with Eakins at the Art Students League and became the caretaker of its studio. Always out of money, he depended on Eakins for meals and handouts.

Douglass Morgan Hall, 1867–1912. Studied at the Academy in 1885–1886 and worked at Art Students League from 1887 to 1890. Painted by Eakins about 1889. Died in the Pennsylvania Hospital for the insane at the age of forty-four.

Samuel Murray, 1869–1941. The eleventh child of poor Irish immigrants. Came to study with Eakins as a boy of sixteen and established a uniquely close relationship with him. The two became virtually inseparable, working, socializing, and camping together.

Charles Bregler, 1864–1958. Student of Eakins both at the Pennsylvania Academy and the Arts Students League. Secretly removed thousands of documents and other items from the Eakins home after the death of Eakins's wife and kept them hidden until his death. They surfaced in the possession of his mentally disturbed common-law wife in 1985.

Female Students and Associates

Emily Sartain, 1841–1927. Eakins's first girlfriend, the daughter of the engraver John Sartain. Broke off with Eakins because of her distress over his "immorality" as an art student in Paris. Went on to become director of the Philadelphia School of Design for Women, where she became a pioneering advocate of advanced education for women.

Lillian Hamitt, 1865–. Student of Eakins. Posed for an unfinished portrait by Eakins. Became insane in 1888, believing that she was married to Eakins.

Amelia Van Buren, 1856–1942. A student of Eakins at the Academy in 1884 and 1885. Suffered from manic-depressive illness, like Eakins's mother. Often stayed at the Eakins home and was subject of a portrait by Eakins in 1890. Eventually established a "Boston marriage" with the photographer Eva Dawson Watson.

Weda Cook, 1867–1937. Singer and subject of the painting *The Concert Singer*, which Eakins worked on from 1890 to 1892. In 1895 Ella Crowell threatened to shoot her with a revolver. Married Stanley Addicks. Once declared that she "both loved and feared" Eakins.

Maud Cook. Cousin of Weda Cook. Eakins painted her in a low-cut dress in 1895, calling her his "rosebud."

Mary Adeline Williams, 1853–1941. Childhood friend of Eakins's sister Margaret. Moved into the Eakins home in 1900 and was rumored to be sexually involved with Eakins. Eakins painted two portraits of her around 1900.

NOTES

Preface

1. See Adams, 1991. I do not wish this statement to appear critical of the editors of *Smithsonian,* Connie Bond and Ed Moser, to whom I am profoundly grateful, as is indicated in my acknowledgments. They courageously dealt honesty with a difficult topic. In the end the project simply grew into a shape not suitable for a magazine such as *Smithsonian.*

2. See Lewis, 2001, pp. 27–32. With a prudery that contrasts, somewhat ironically, with the tough-minded objectivity traditionally associated with Eakins, on page 29 Lewis applauds "the exhibition's worthy decision to avoid slumming through Eakins's private life." Nonetheless, even Lewis notes that the result is intellectually superficial. "What is missing here," he writes, "is some sort of comprehensive assessment of Eakins's larger meaning in American culture as a whole," and he adds, "a certain discussion of psychology is essential to assessing his place."

Chapter 1

1. Eakins arrived in Paris in September 1866 and stayed there until June 1870, making one return trip to the United States, which occurred from December 1868 until March 1869. In total he spent about forty-two months in Europe.

2. Goodrich, 1982, vol. 2, p. 1; Milroy, 1986, p. 66, note 3. Eakins's longest excursion outside Philadelphia was a two month trip to the Badlands of North Dakota in 1886, when he was recovering from a nervous breakdown. He also visited New York to teach or see art exhibitions and Pittsburgh, to serve as juror for the Carnegie International Exhibition. Finally, he made occasional trips to paint portraits, such as a trip to Maine of about two weeks in 1897 to portray the physicist Henry Rowland.

3. Apparently the building where Eakins's downtown studio was located was condemned and he had to vacate the premises.

4. Goodrich, 1982, vol. 2, pp. 171, 258, 272.

5. Goodrich, 1933, p. 4.

6. McHenry, 1947, p. 60.

7. Just which paintings were set in this space is difficult to establish with certainty. Goodrich and other writers, for example, have stated that Eakins's painting *The Chess Players* of 1876 (Metropolitan Museum of Art) was set in the living room. But as noted by Simpson, Susan Eakins believed that this painting was set elsewhere. See Simpson in Sewell, 2001, p. 34. My own guess is that Susan's statement is misleading, as it is with so many of her assertions about her husband's work. Very likely the painting was based on the family living room, but did not follow it exactly.

8. Hendricks, 1969, p. 30.

9. McHenry, 1947, p. 125.

10. Goodrich, 1982, vol. 2, pp. 11–12.

Chapter 2

1. Flexner, 1956, unpaginated, text opposite plate 18.

2. Goodrich, 1982, vol. 2, p. 222.

3. Eakins also showed five works at the Pennsylvania Academy in 1891.

4. For a list of what Eakins exhibited see Milroy and Paschall, 1996. I should note that the degree to which Eakins was rejected during his lifetime forms a seesaw debate in Eakins scholarship, not unlike a discussion about whether a glass of water is half full or half empty. Goodrich and his followers probably overdramatized the rejection of Eakins as an artist. On the other hand, because of their sexual prudery, they probably failed to convey the intensity of the animosity toward him as a person.

5. Much of this summary is drawn from Goodrich, 1982, vol. 2, pp. 199–203, 262, 267.

6. Hartmann, 1902, vol. 1, pp. 189, 200–204. Nonetheless, Hartmann did not rate Homer and Eakins as the greatest masters of American art, reserving that place for George Fuller.

7. Caffin, 1907, pp. 230–233.

8. For Burroughs see Tomkins, 1970, pp. 230–235; Dreishpoon, 1984; Burke, 1980, pp. xvii–xviii; Mather, 1927; Owens, 1979; Field, 1919; Watson, 1935.

9. These included articles by Henry McBride, art critic of the *New York Sun*; Forbes Watson, editor of *The Arts*; Lloyd Goodrich, the managing editor of *The Arts*; Walter Pach, the former organizer of the Armory Show; Frank Jewett Mather, a professor at Princeton University; and Suzanne La Follete, who later wrote a survey of American art.

10. Burroughs, Alan, March 1923, December 1923, and June 1924.

11. These museums were the Fort Worth Art Association, the Addison Gallery in Andover, the Cleveland Museum of Art, the Yale Art Gallery, the Brooklyn Museum, and the Worcester Art Museum. For Marsh's purchase see Scott and Rutkoff, p. 186.

12. Mumford, 1931, reprint 1955, pp. 210–220.

13. Burroughs, 1937, pp. 403, 406.

14. Turano, 1988, p. 8.

15. Turano, 1988, p. 17.

16. Turano, 1988, p.10.

17. Cooper, 1996, p. 8.

18. For example, Bartlett, 1882 and Knowlton, 1899, wrote detailed and informative monographs that have turned out to be more accurate that Goodrich's biography of Eakins.

19. Goodrich, 1972, pp. 16–17.

20. Goodrich, 1930.

21. Phillips, 1980, pp. 3–18.

22. Among these articles are several noteworthy pieces, including Hopper's tribute to Burchfield, which might be taken as a manifesto of the realist approach of his generation, as well as Benton's seminal analysis of abstract composition, "Mechanics of Form Organization in Painting." See Hopper, 1928; Benton, 1926.

23. Two other art dealers of the period who handled modernist American work were William Macbeth and Charles Daniel.

24. Turano, 1988, p. 7.

25. Turano, 1988, p. 15.

26. Goodrich, 1982, vol. 1, p. 29.

27. Goodrich, 1982, vol. 1, p. 270.

28. Goodrich, 1933, p. 143.

29. Goodrich, 1933, p. 155.

30. Wilmerding terms it "very possibly the greatest picture ever painted by an American artist." See Wilmerding, 1976, p. 138. Thomas Hoving, former director of the Metropolitan Museum of Art, writes, "There is no disputing that the most moving American painting of the nineteenth century is Thomas Eakins's astonishingly candid masterpiece Gross Clinic." See Hoving, 1984.

31. Henri, 1960, p. 91.

32. Barr, 1930, p. 6.

33. Porter, 1959, pp. 26, 9, 17.

34. Katz, 1993, p. 6.

35. Schendler, 1967.

36. Johns, 1983, p. 169.

37. Russel, 1989. p. 108.

38. Hughes, 1991, p. 123.

39. Henri, 1960, p. 128. Bellows wrote of the Eakins retrospective at the Metropolitan Museum of Art (1917): "The Thomas Eakins exhibition proves him to be one of the best of all the world's masters. The greatest one man show I've ever seen and some of the very greatest pictures." See Morgan, 1965, p. 215.

40. Goodrich, 1982, vol. 1, pp. vii, x.

41. The picture might also be seen as a rejoinder to the famous photograph of "The Irascibles," as noted in *Life* magazine, which featured the abstract expressionists.

42. Soyer's painting, in fact, mimics the famous photograph "The Irascibles," which grouped together the major abstract expressionists. See Sandler, 1970, frontispiece.

43. Soyer, 1966, pp. 16, 117. According to Lloyd Goodrich, Eakins was Soyer's favorite painter. See Goodrich, 1968, p. 25.

44. "Just the Facts, Straight, The American Way," unsigned, *The New York Times,* September 1, 1996, p. 8.

45. Notably, however, there has been a recent reappraisal of Norman Rockwell's work, which was recently featured in a major exhibition at the Gugenheim Museum. In some way the new appreciation of Norman Rockwell seems to be associated with the new skepticism about Eakins. See Adams, October 2002.

46. Goodrich, 1982, vol. 2, p. 279; Schendler, 1967, p. 87; Katz, 1956, p. 21.

47. Johns, 1983.

48. Johns, 1983, and reprints of 1990, 1998.

49. Goodrich, 1933, p. 7.

50. Goodrich, 1933, p. 100.

51. Goodrich, 1982, vol. 2, p. 8; he used very similar language in Goodrich, 1933, p. 100.

52. Hendricks, 1974, p. 220.

53. Goodrich, 1982, vol. 2, p. 22.

54. These matters are recorded in Goodrich's unpublished interviews with Mrs. Addicks, Mrs. Doughty, Mrs. Lucy Langdale Wilson, Mrs. Lavell, James L. Wood and others. Some of this material is summarized in Goodrich, 1982, vol. 2, pp. 91, 94, 95.

55. Goodrich notes, Philadelphia Museum of Art.

56. Letter to Mr. Burroughs in Goodrich unpublished notes, signature cut off; Goodrich interview with Mrs. Addick and Adolph Burie.

57. Goodrich notes, interview with Mrs. Lavell.

58. Goodrich notes, interview with Mrs. Adicks.

59. Ironically, one of the figures who did most to create Eakins's high reputation was Seymour Adelman, a member of Philadelphia's Jewish community. Adelman never met Eakins himself, but was pulled into the Eakins orbit when his portrait was painted by Eakins's widow. I should note that nineteenth-century anti-Semitism was often filled with inconsistencies, and it would have been quite possible for Eakins to harbor anti-Semitic feelings and also have Jewish friends or acquaintances. A case in point would be his contemporary, the historian Henry Adams, whose letters often contain shockingly anti-Semitic gibes but who was also friendly with Bernard Berenson and introduced Berenson to people of power and wealth. See Levenson, 1994.

60. Goodrich, 1982, vol. 2, p. 35. See, for example, Goodrich's interview with Mrs.

Addicks, May 20, 1931, Goodrich papers, Philadelphia Museum of Art.

61. The obvious point is that people capable of strange or even profoundly evil actions may appear polite, charming and kind in most circumstances, even to people who know them well. Hitler and his close associates provide one of the most striking and chilling instances of this phenomenon. (See "Hitler seemed kind, says secretary," Gera, 2002, p. A4.) While I do not wish to directly compare Eakins to Hitler, his example powerfully illustrates the perplexing dualities of human nature and warns us that evil is not necessarily easy to recognize. The notion promulgated by writers on Eakins that he can be exonerated from the charges against him because he was generous or gentle in some other situation is not persuasive or psychologically convincing.

62. Goodrich, 1982, vol. 2, p. 212. Goodrich notes, interviews with Burie and Addicks.

63. Goodrich notes, interview with James L. Wood.

64. Goodrich notes, interview with Mr. and Mrs. Douty.

65. Lloyd Godrich's notes from his interview with Weda Cook seem to indicate that Mrs. Greenwalt thought that Susan was a "liar," but unfortunately the reference is cryptic and who was lying about what is not clear. At the least, this notation suggests the frequency with which accusations of duplicity and dishonesty circulated in the Eakins household and among members of Eakins's circle.

66. The notion that a man can be judged virtuous because he was supported and energetically defended by his virtuous wife is obviously questionable, as is illustrated by numerous historical examples. An extreme and fascinating case is the wife of the Marquis de Sade, who supported her husband through all his misdeeds, petitioning for his release from prison, supplying him with delicacies, overseeing his real estate holdings and paying him marital visits, one of which produced a child. See Eakin, 1998 and Gray, 1998.

67. Hendricks, 1974, p. 285.

68. Foster, 1989, p. 86.

69. Sewell, 2001, p. 351.

70. Homer, 1992, p. 41. Eakins's use of the word "Jersey" is ambiguous. Since the words "an Italian" refer to a European peasant, he was probably referring to the Isle of Jersey, and pairing peasant types from northern and southern Europe. But he may also have been referring to the State of New Jersey.

71. Goodrich, 1982, vol. 1, p. 222.

72. McHenry, 1947, p. 59.

73. McHenry, 1947, p. 58.

74. Goodrich, 1982, vol. 2, p. 3. Admittedly, Susan seems to have sometimes accompanied her husband, but close reading of contemporary statement suggests that often she stayed at home. Eakins's constant companion was Samuel Murray. It would be interesting to know whether Susan was present at the parties at which Eakins shuffled after women whose appearance appealed to him, staring at them. (See Goodrich, 1982, vol. 2, p. 67).

75. Goodrich, 1982, vol. 1, pp. 220, 223. Interestingly, Sylvan Schendler juxtaposes these two events in his text, but does not speculate on their relationship. See Schendler, 1967, p. x.

76. Hendricks, 1974, p. 275. Given the theme of male friendship that Murray expressed, it is interesting to note that McBride was homosexual.

77. For example by Hendricks, 1974, p. 275.

78. Goodrich, 1982, vol. 2, p. 334, note for p. 272.

79. For an instance of retitling, see the discussion of *Swimming* later in the text, as well as chapter 9, note 14. Mistakes such as this, while seemingly minor, have led to a significant misunderstandings of Eakins's artistic development.

80. Goodrich, 1982, vol. 2, p. 96.

81. In personal discussions such noted art historians as John Wilmdering, William Gerdts and the late Joshua Taylor have all expressed to me their intense dislike of Gordon Hendricks. His books undoubtedly contain many errors, some of them so obvious that they can be spotted by an attentive reader without any need for further background research. Nonetheless, Hendricks uncovered much valuable artistic and documentary material and provided the first real challenge to the dominance of Goodrich. While Goodrich has a reputation for greater accuracy, on balance it seems to me that they both made about the same number of factual mistakes.

82. For a review of this book see Johns, December 1983.

83. The fundamentally timid nature of Eakins scholarship in the late 1970s is vividly revealed by Elizabeth Johns's article "Thomas Eakins: A Case for Reassessment" (Johns, May 1979), which sums up the state of Eakins research at that time.

84. For an account of the discovery of the Bregler trove, see Foster, 1989, pp. 1–27, and Foster, 1986, pp. 1228–1237.

85. Foster, 1989, p. 14.

86. Foster, 1986, pp. 1231–1234.

87. For example, the Bregler collection contains a series of illustrations to a manual that Eakins wrote on perspective. The manual itself is owned by the Philadelphia Museum of Art. Perhaps someday the text and illustrations can be reunited and published for the first time.

88. Foster, 1989, pp. 4–5.

89. For further discussion, see the opening of the last chapter.

90. Wallach, 1984, pp. 21–24. On p. 24 he terms the book "a major achievement."

91. A panel on "The Forbidden Eakins: The Sexual Politics of Thomas Eakins and His Circle" was held on Monday, June 24, 2002 at the Humanities Institute, Stony Brook University, 401 Park Ave South, New York, NY. The participants were Martin Berger, SUNY Buffalo; Deborah Bright, Rhode Island School of Design; Jennifer Doyle, University of California, Riverside; Michael Hatt, University of Nottingham in England; Michael Moon, Johns Hopkins University; James Smalls, University of Maryland at Baltimore; Jonathan Weinberg, Senior

Fellow in residence, The Getty Museum, and Jonathan Katz, Stony Brook University.

92. Lubin, 2002, p. 510.

Chapter 3

1. Foster, 1989, p. 76.
2. McGill, 1986.
3. Goodrich, 1933, p. 87.
4. See Hendricks, 1974, p. 140, citing a clipping from the Philadelphia Press. See also, Foster, 1989, p. 75.
5. Goodrich, 1982, vol. 2, p. 284. Sorting out the different relationships of these figures makes a tangled web, for many of them were interlinked in complex ways, through kinship ties, social interaction, and business relationships. Jesse Godley, for example, Eakins's anatomy assistant (who just a year before had posed for and served as the centerpiece of Eakins's painting *Swimming*), was an employee of Frank Stephens's decorating firm (Bolger, 1996, p. 117). Godley sided against Eakins in the Academy scandal.
6. Hendricks, 1974, p. 137.
7. The degree to which posing nude ran against nineteenth-century American patterns of behavior is illustrated by an incident recorded by William Sartain. He recalled going out with Daniel Ridgeway Knight to get a male model for the life classes. When the man they brought back to the Academy discovered that he was expected to pose in the nude, he "squared off" at them. See Hendricks, 1974, p. 104.
8. Admittedly, it is unclear whether the models were always entirely nude, although Thomas Anshutz's work contains many representations of entirely naked figures, and he publicly exhibited many works of this type.
9. Foster, 1989, p. 76.
10. Letter addressed to "Dear Mr. Burroughs," signature cut off photocopy, Goodrich papers, Philadelphia Museum of Art.
11. This issue surfaces in Eakins's later correspondence with Edward Coates, and is discussed by Foster, 1989, p. 75. Foster's account suggests that Eakins had been specifically forbidden to use students as models but had continued to do so, defying the directives of the board. The chronology of the episodes she mentions, however, is not clear.
12. Goodrich, 1933, p. 86.
13. Goodrich, 1982, vol. 1, p. 284.
14. Hendricks, 1974, p. 142.
15. Foster, 1989, p. 76.
16. Foster, 1989, pp. 78, 238.
17. Parry, 1981; Bolger, 1996, pp. 40–41.
18. Foster, 1989, p. 77.

19. Goodrich, 1933, p. 86.
20. Goodrich, 1982, vol. 2, p. 96.
21. Goodrich, 1982, vol. 1, pp. 286, 247.
22. Goodrich, 1982, vol. 1, p. 290.
23. This statement, however, is hidden in a footnote. See Danly, 1994, p. 62, note 107.

Chapter 4

1. The original correspondence concerning the Sketch Club controversy was offered for sale by John F. Warren, pp. 55–56.
2. Foster, 1989, p. 228.
3. Foster, 1989, p. 84.
4. Foster, 1989, pp. 79–90.
5. Sellin, 2001, p. 48.
6. Foster, 1989, p. 86.
7. Foster, 1989, p. 229.
8. Foster, 1989, pp. 83, 89.
9. Sellin, 2001, p. 21. One indication that Eakins truly confused his contemporaries is that many of those who knew him well shifted their loyalty over time. Friend is often not easy to distinguish from foe. The social awkwardness of this situation seems to have been as painful to Eakins's accusers as to Eakins himself. Leslie W. Miller, who wrote negative criticism of Eakins's paintings early in his career, later became an intimate of the artist's household, and posed for one of his most important pictures. Weda Cook, who had been Eakins's friend and supporter for years, broke off her relationship with him in the middle of posing for *The Concert Singer*, only to change her mind once again, and restore her relations with Eakins. Thomas Anshutz, who played a major role in getting Eakins fired from the Pennsylvania Academy, presents a curious case. At the time of the Academy scandal, Anshutz lived very near Eakins, on Chestnut Street. The year after Eakins was fired Anshutz moved to a house directly facing the Eastern State Penitentiary. Presumably he made this move to get away from Eakins. While the distance is not great it would have prevented the two from encountering each other on a daily basis. By the early twentieth century, however, Anshutz had come to be seen by his own students, notably by the young painters of the Ashcan School, as someone who followed in the footsteps of Eakins. Interestingly, for example, Helen Henderson's guide of The Pennsylvania Academy of the Fine Arts (Henderson 1911) was "lovingly inscribed and dedicated to Thomas Anshsutz," who was her personal friend, but contains enthusiastic praise of Eakins. Moreover, on p. 137 she describes Anshutz as a student of Eakins. In her newspaper criticism, Henderson was one of the notable early boosters of Eakins. One would have thought that Anshutz would have taken steps to separate his reputation from that of the

man he had once so despised. But instead, he chose to remain silent, quietly allowing the notion to develop that he was a disciple of Eakins. And that, ironically, is how Anshutz is portrayed in most histories of American art. Griffin, 1994, p. 94, comments, "Probably Anshutz's greatest legacy was in conveying Eakins's teachings to the artists who later formed the core of the Ashcan School."

10. McHenry, 1947, p. 94.

11. Benjamin's character will be discussed in chapter 5. Eakins's eldest sister Frances, Mrs. William Crowell, told Lloyd Goodrich that Eakins's mother, Caroline Eakins, also had "decided ideas." See Goodrich unpublished interview with Mrs. Crowell.

12. Goodrich, 1982, vol. 1, p. 293.

13. Foster, 1989, p. 228.

14. Foster, 1989, p. 228. George Simenon has explored how the mistreatment and eventual killing of a cat can provide an outlet for family hatred. See Simenon, 1976.

15. Foster, 1989, p. 231.

16. Foster, 1989, pp. 84, 230.

17. Foster, 1989, p. 86.

18. Goodrich, 1982, vol. 1, p. 294.

19. Foster, 1989, p. 94. Eakins also taught anatomy at the Art Students League in New York from the fall of 1885 until the fall of 1888. There he also stirred up antagonism, although it never blew up into a major scandal. The minutes of the board of the League from December 1888 record "a letter from Mrs. J. H. Tyndale complaining of the method of conducting the anatomy lectures." In the spring of 1889, Eakins's lectures at the League were discontinued, either due to prudery of lack of interest. See Goodrich, 1982, vol. 1, p. 304.

20. Foster, 1989, p. 94.

Chapter 5

1. Hendricks, 1974, p. 75.

2. Hendricks, 1974, p. 75.

3. Foster, 1989, p. 110.

4. Goodrich, 1982, vol. 2, p. 169.

5. Foster, 1989, p. 106. In what I take to be a feeble attempt at humor, Hendricks notes that photographs of the family reveals a mood of "less than saturnalian hilarity" (Hendricks, 1974, p. 195).

6. Goodrich, 1982, vol. 2, p. 21; Homer, 1992, p. 202.

7. Foster, 1989, p. 107.

8. Foster, 1989, p. 296.

9. Goodrich unpublished interview with Mrs. Addicks.

10. Lloyd Goodrich interview with Mrs. Crowell.

11. Hendricks, 1974, p. 236; Goodrich, 1982, vol. 2, p. 136; Foster 1989, p. 118.

12. Homer, 1992, p. 209; Hendricks, 1974, p. 236. Eakins's defenders in the Academy scandal argued that if Eakins had offended his female students at the Academy through his obsession with the nude, then this was excusable because "it was intended for their benefit." Quite possibly Eakins had a similar justification for his behavior with Ella Crowell (Goodrich, 1982, vol. 1, p. 291).

13. Goodrich, 1982, vol. 2, p. 327, note 135:32. My wording closely follows that of Goodrich.

14. Foster, 1989, pp. 113–114. Schendler and Goodrich both state that Ella killed herself with a shotgun. Both spoke with siblings of Ella who heard the shot, although unfortunately they do not identify them (Schendler, 1967, p. xi; Goodrich, 1982, vol. 2, p. 136; Hendricks, 1974, p. 235). The various accounts of Ella's death are not 100 percent consistent, although they agree on the major points. For example, Foster states that Ella was kept in a locked room but Homer implies that she was not. Homer's account specifically states that Ella killed herself with a gun that Eakins had kept in his studio at Avondale. Foster's account implies that it was a gun that was in the house and belonged to the Crowells. In either case, it appears that Ella killed herself with a gun that was associated with Eakins.

15. Hendricks, 1974, p. 4, note 25 states: "The coroner's report from Chester County Archives is as follows: 'July 3, 1897 . . . Ella Crowell, daughter of William Crowell, Verdict, suicide by shooting herself in the head.' The Chester Valley Union, July 7, 1897 reported that Ella had killed herself on the previous Friday morning which would have been July 2."

16. Hendricks, 1972, p. 3 states: "The children came running from the fields to find that Ella, recently released from a mental institution, had gotten hold of a gun and killed herself." Schendler and Hendricks both state that they spoke with individuals who "heard the shot" but do not identify their informants. See Hendricks, 1974, p. 235, who spoke with "more than one relative who heard the shot" and Schendler, p. xi who spoke with an unidentified cousin.

17. Reik, 1960, p. 138.

18. Foster, 1989, p. 295.

19. Foster, 1989, p. 291.

20. Quite likely these complaints were largely accurate. According to Samuel Murray, Susan was a poor housekeeper and noted that Benjamin Eakins complained about her management of finances.

21. It is not clear from Susan's jumbled account whether the Crowells hoped to move into 1729 Mount Vernon Street, or whether they hoped that the house could be sold and the proceeds divided among the members of the family so that they could purchase a city house of their own. Susan also does not indicate whether this projected move would have entailed selling the farm at Avondale, although the implication is that the Crowells hoped to move from the country back into the city.

22. Foster, 1989, p. 293.

23. Foster, 1989, p. 293.

24. Susan's letter gives the date 1869 (Foster, 1989, p. 293), but from the context this is clearly a mistranscription of 1896, produced by inverting the last two numbers.

25. Foster, 1989, p. 294.

26. Foster, 1989, p. 295.

27. Foster, 1989, p. 298. To a twenty-first-century reader, some of the events that Susan narrates seem to reveal sexual undercurrents in Eakins's relationship with the two sisters that she does not explore. For example, she refers to the fact that Ella injured herself in a bicycle accident and afterward "sat on her Uncle Tom's lap that he might more closely examine the wound near her eye." She also describes another occasion in which "Maggy being chilled, Tom helped her to bed & rubbed her until she slept."

28. Foster, 1989, p. 294.

29. For the Rowland portrait, see Marc Simpson in Sewell, 2001, pp. 264–265.

30. McHenry, 1946, p. 100.

31. Fried in Wilmerding, 1993, p. 85. Fried has suggested that the numbers and letters on these blocks may have specific meanings. For example XVI are the last three numbers of the painting's date in Roman numerals. C may stand for Crowell and T could stand for Thomas.

32. In writing about this painting, I have drawn on a paper written by my student Marcie Hocking.

33. Lloyd Goodrich omitted all mention of Ella Crowell's suicide from his monograph of 1933. Schendler seems to have been the first to mention Ella's suicide in print, although he did not explore the circumstances of her death. See Schendler, 1967, p. xi. Mrs. Eakins never spoke of the Ella Crowell tragedy. Of Eakins's friends, only Weda Cook did, and Samuel Murray, briefly (Goodrich, 1982, vol. 2, p. 136). Goodrich did learn about the tragedy, however, when he interviewed Eakins's sister Frances not long before her death. Mrs. Crowell declined to talk about her brother and assured Goodrich that she had kept none of his letters (Milroy, 1986, p. 30). Despite Frances's statement to Goodrich that she had none of her brother's letters, after her death twenty-one of Eakins's letters to her were discovered by the family and eventually donated to the Archives of American Art.

34. Goodrich, 1982, vol. 2, p. 136.

Chapter 6

1. Foster, 1989, p. 98.

2. Foster, 1989, p. 245.

3. Foster, 1989, pp. 99–100.

4. Foster, 1989, pp. 100–101.

5. Foster, 1989, pp. 95–104.

6. Foster, 1989, p. 245. In his letter of March 2, 1888, to Lillian Hammitt, Eakins declared that "I have abandoned my portrait of you."

7. Foster, 1989, p. 98.

8. Foster, 1989, p. 99.

9. Emily Sartain to Thomas Eakins, July 8, 1868, Bregler collection; Milroy, 1986. p. 210.

10. Foster, 1989, p. 138, note 17.

11. Milroy, 1986, p. 210.

12. In a letter to his father of January 16, 1867, Eakins mentioned going to a house of prostitution and stated that his visit was purely educational. See Foster, 1989, p. 144.

13. Goodrich, 1982, vol. 2, p. 94.

14. Goodrich interview with James L. Wood.

15. Hendricks, 1974, p. 263; Goodrich, 1982, vol. 2, p. 95.

16. Goodrich, 1982, vol. 2, p. 91.

17. Goodrich, 1982, vol. 2, p. 96.

18. Goodrich, 1982, vol. 2, p. 94.

19. Goodrich, 1982, vol. 2, pp. 91, 94.

20. Goodrich, 1982, vol. 2, p. 94. Dunbar's experience is also mentioned by Margaret McHenry, who wrote: "In addition to the professional models whom Eakins paid to pose for him, he occasionally asked his personal friends to pose in the nude, which shocked them. For example, Elizabeth Dunbar, who was often at the Eakins house on Mt. Vernon Street, was asked several times by the painter to run upstairs to the studio and pose for a life study." See McHenry, 1946, pp. 128–129. Other individuals whom Eakins apparently asked to pose nude include Mrs. Whiteman, Mrs. Evans, and Rebecca Macdowell. According to Hendricks, Mrs. Whiteman told him that "Tom Eakins was somewhat hipped on nudes." Most likely Eakins requested her to pose in the nude. Hendricks also reports that "Mrs. Evans spoke to me of his having wanted her to pose nude." Eakins's interest in the nude extended to his own relatives. Susan's niece Rebecca Macdowell reported of Eakins that "He always wanted us to pose in the nude." See Hendricks, 1974, pp. 265, 263; Goodrich, 1982, vol. 2, p. 94.

21. Goodrich, 1982, vol. 2, p. 94.

22. Lloyd Goodrich interview with Mrs. Adicks, Philadelphia Museum of Art. In addition to Ella Crowell and Lillian Hammitt, she believed that Alice Baker and Maude Cook had all posed nude for Eakins.

23. Goodrich, 1982, vol. 2, p. 212.

24. Goodrich, 1982, vol. 2, p. 94.

25. Lloyd Goodrich interview with Mrs. Greenwalt.

26. Hendricks, 1974, p. 265.

27. Goodrich interview with Mrs. Dodge.

28. Goodrich, 1982, vol. 2, p. 96.

29. McHenry, 1946, p. 109.

30. McHenry, 1946, p. 126.

31. Goodrich, 1982, vol. 2, p. 96.

32. Goodrich, 1933, p. 153.

33. Goodrich, 1933, p. 109.

34. Goodrich, 1933, p. 110.

35. Lloyd Goodrich interview with Elizabeth M. Corless.

36. Goodrich, 1982, vol. 1, p. 145. Goodrich wrote of Eakins that, "He particularly enjoyed swimming, naked, regardless of an audience." It is hard to believe, however, that Eakins was truly "regardless of an audience." It seems that he enjoyed having one. Rather than caring little if others were shocked, he seems to have derived pleasure from inspiring this reaction.

37. Goodrich, 1982, vol. 2, p. 103.

38. Goodrich, 1982, vol. 1, p. 9. Hendricks, 1974, p. 29, fig. 31, and p. 288.

39. Foster, 1989, p. 225.

40. Lloyd Goodrich interview with James L. Wood; Hendricks, 1974, p. 228.

41. Goodrich interview with Mrs. Adicks.

42. Foster, 1989, p. 111.

43. Goodrich, 1982, vol. 1, p. 66.

44. Schendler, 1967, p. 218.

45. Goodrich, 1982, vol. 2, p. 7.

46. Homer, 1992, p. 179.

47. Goodrich interview with Mrs. Douty.

48. Goodrich interview with James L. Wood.

49. McCauley in Danly, 1994, p. 60.

50. Goodrich interview with James L. Wood.

51. Goodrich interview with Clarence Cramer and Frances Ziegler.

52. Lloyd Goodrich interview with Mrs. Addicks.

53. Hendricks, 1974, p. 244.

54. Goodrich, 1982, vol. 2, p. 97.

55. Foster, 1989, p. 76.

56. Goodrich, 1982, vol. 2, pp. 94, 224.

57. Goodrich, vol. 2, pp. 96, 224.

58. To make the meaning clear, I have placed Emily's statement in quotes, but Eakins's letter did not contain quotation marks.

59. Milroy, 1986, p. 213. Thomas Eakins to Frances Eakins, November 12, 1868, Archives of American Art.

60. Hendricks, 1974, pp. 36–37.

61. Milroy, 1986, p. 212; Thomas Eakins to Benjamin Eakins, October 29, 1868, Bregler Collection.

62. Letter to Fanny Eakins, July 1868, cited in Goodrich, 1982, vol. 1, p. 39.

63. Goodrich, 1982, vol. 2, p. 15.

64. Hendricks, 1974, p. 30.

65. Goodrich, 1982, vol. 1, p. 113. Vermifuge is a strong laxative, used to kill or expel worms from the intestine.

66. Hendricks, 1974, p. 68.

67. McHenry, 1946, p. 29.

68. Foster, 1989, p. 45.

Chapter 7

1. Sellin, 2001, p. 48.

2. Foster, 1989, p. 72.

3. Anshutz was Charles Demuth's favorite teacher at the Academy, as discussed by Farnham, 1971, pp. 52–53. Several other important modernists studied with Anshutz and remained friendly with him, including John Marin, Arthur B. Carles and Lyman Sayen. See Griffin, 1994, p. 98.

4. Griffin, 1994, p. 56.

5. Goodrich, 1982, vol. 2, p. 135.

6. Foster, 1989, pp. 104, 118.

7. Goodrich, 1982, vol. 1, p. 284. Will Crowell's letter defending Eakins notes that both Frank Stephens and his wife displayed "extravagance of hostility in their expressions concerning Mr. Eakins" in the summer of 1883, soon after they first became acquainted.

8. Foster, 1989, p. 228.

9. Foster, 1989, p. 133, note 15.

10. Goodrich, 1982, vol. 2, p. 298. For Sartain's accomplishments as an educator see Alice Carter, 2000, p. 18.

11. Goodrich, 1982, vol. 1, p. 44; Hendricks, 1974, pp. 36–37.

12. Carter, 2000, p. 21; as documented by a typewritten copy of the first draft of an article, possibly by Louise HIllyer Armstrong, mailed to Jessie Willcox Smith, January 31, 1927, Jessie Willcox Smith papers, Archives of American Art.

13. Goodrich, 1933, p. 87.

14. Foster, 1989, p. 103.

15. Hendricks, 1974, p. 226.

16. Hendricks, 1974, p. 173.

17. Doyle, 1999, p. 9.

18. Nude photographs do exist of Edvard Munch, Pierre Bonnard, Franz von Stuck, and a few others, although I think that comparison would show that these photographs are more conventional, and more in line with studio practice, than those of Eakins.

19. Goodrich, 1982, vol. 1, p. 304.

20. Goodrich, 1982, vol. 1, p. 308.

21. Jamison, 1993, p. 4.

22. Goodrich, 1982, vol. 2, p. 95.

23. Goodrich, 1982, vol. 2, p. 95.

24. The reasons for this obsession with female purity are complex, but were surely based on social and economic realities that are different today. Information about birth control was not easily available and the practice was widely viewed as immoral. Women were largely segregated from the male workplace, and had few opportunities for earning money other than sewing and doing laundry. A woman who bore children but had no husband represented a major social problem, which was all but certain to end in hardship or death for both mother and child. Society's strict code, while harsh by modern standards, was based on these facts. Women seem to have been treated with particular severity, but the code was strict for men as well. Thus, for example, the distinguished oriental curator Ernest Fenollosa was dismissed from his post at the Museum of Fine Arts in Boston after he divorced his wife and married his secretary. See White-hill, 1970, p. 125. For a history of sexuality in America, see De'Emilio, 1988, which has a discussion of birth control on pp. 60–61.

25. Homer, 1992, p. 186.

26. Anne McCauley in Danly, 1994, pp. 52–55.

27. Doyle, 1999, p. 8.

28. Doyle, 1999, p. 10.

29. Foster, 1989, p. 114.

30. Goodrich, 1982, vol. 1, p. 284.

31. Goodrich, 1982, vol. 1, p. 37.

32. Goodrich, 1982, vol. 1, p. 285.

33. Hendricks, 1974, p. 183.

34. Goodrich, 1982, vol. 1, p. 289.

35. Anonymous letter sent to J. L. Claghorn, the Academy President, 11 April 1882, printed in Schendler, 1967, pp. 90–92.

36. It does not appear that this generalization applied to men. At least we have no statements suggesting as much.

37. Eakins in a letter to the Committee on Instruction, January 8, 1876, para-phrased and cited in Foster, 1989, p. 343.

38. Letter from Eakins to Coates, 12 September 1886, in Foster, 1989, pp. 238–239.

39. Elizabeth McDowell Kenton to Eakins (late September 1894) in Foster, 1989, p. 179.

40. Letter to Edward Coates, September 11, 1886, in Foster, 1989, p. 238.

41. Doyle, 1999, p. 20.

42. Doyle, 1999, pp. 7, 18.

43. Doyle, 1999, p. 1.

44. Goodrich, 1982, vol. 1, p. 288.

45. Letter to Coates, 11 September 1886, in Foster, 1989, p. 235.

46. Doyle, 1999, p. 19.

47. Doyle, 1999, p. 20.

48. Doyle, 1999, pp. 19–20.

49. Doyle, 1999, p. 20.

50. Goodrich, 1982, vol. 1, p. 280.

51. Goodrich, 1933, p. 97.

52. Goodrich, 1982, vol. 2, p. 21.

53. Goodrich, 1982, vol. 2, p. 17.

54. Hendricks, 1974, p. 54.

55. Hendricks, 1974, p. 54. In a letter to his father of April 23, 1869, Eakins noted that he had no difficulty bringing his pistols into France. See Foster, 1989, p. 151.

56. Hendricks, 1974, pp. 32–33; Albright, 1947.

57. Foster, 1989, p. 154.

58. Gilbert Sunderland Parker, cited by Hendricks, 1974, p. 283.

59. McHenry, 1946, p. 119.

60. Goodrich, 1982, vol. 1, p. 229.

61. Goodrich, vol. 2, p. 223. Rather than exploring the psychological implications of this fact, Goodrich unconvincingly declared that such consumption "seems physically impossible." Many of my students felt that Eakins's fixation with milk was the single oddest thing about his behavior, and overshadowed his public scandals.

62. Hendricks, 1972, notes: "In fifty-two restless images there is scarcely a smile."

Chapter 8

1. Schendler, 1967, p. ix.

2. See Stone, 1997.

3. In part this occurred because, at the time Freud wrote, understanding of the chemistry and neurological configuration of the brain was at a primitive stage, and Freud drew on branches of science, such as thermodynamics, which provide only crude analogies with how brain mechanisms operate. Recent study of the biology and chemistry of the brain, for example, has not come up with entities that in any way correspond with Freud's principle divisions of human personality, such as the Ego, the Id, the Superego, and so forth. To some extent Freud's concepts are still useful as metaphors, much as the word "soul" is still useful in daily discourse, but we should be wary of supposing that these concepts match with concrete facts. To avoid using terms that are possibly misleading, I have avoided references to Freud's larger theories of mental operations, which are only marginally relevant in any case.

Chapter 9

1. Goodrich, 1933, p. 5.

2. Milroy, 1986, p. 35.

3. Frances Eakins to Thomas Eakins, February 25, 1868, Bregler collection (Milroy, 1986, pp. 35–36).

4. Goodrich, unpublished interview with Mrs. Addicks, the former Weda Cook.

5. McHenry, 1946, p. 125.

6. Homer, 1992, p. 33.

7. Milroy, 1986, p. 41; Peale, 1842, p. 13.

8. Mann, 1846, p. 66, cited by Marzio, p. 60; Milroy, 1986, p. 67; Johns, 1980, p. 141.

9. Milroy, 1986, p. 48.

10. Milroy, 1986, p. 45.

11. Johns, 1980, pp. 145–146. The winner of the competition was Joseph Boggs Beale (see Johns, 1980, p. 149).

12. Milroy, 1986, p. 57.

13. Milroy, 1986, p. 53.

14. The life drawing reproduced by Goodrich, 1933, plate 1, which he ascribed to "about 1855" based on Susan Eakins's statements, surely dates from the circa 1877, when it is known that Eakins was working from masked models at the Pennsylvania Academy. There is no evidence that Eakins drew from female models in Philadelphia in the 1860s and the style of the piece is entirely unlike Eakins's other early drawings. Foster, 1997, p. 26 continues this dating, basing her conclusions on the testimony of Susan, which she accepts throughout her account as an infallibly accurate source. I think it is obvious that this early dating is incorrect. I think Foster is right, however, in disputing Theodore Siegl's conclusions that the figure drawings of this group were made in different periods. While they vary in quality, they were clearly all made at the same time.

15. Goodrich, unpublished interview with Lucy Langdon W. Wilson.

16. Milroy, 1986, p. 73.

17. Milroy, 1986, p. 73.

18. Milroy, 1986, p. 64. While Eakins was not a practicing Quaker, his mother's Quaker background may also have encouraged a pacifist approach.

19. Milroy, 1986, p. 86; Thomas Eakins to Emily Sartain, September 18, 1866, Pennsylvania Academy of the Fine Arts.

20. Henry Huttner to Benjamin Eakins, January 29, 1867, Bregler collection.

21. Shinn, 1868, p. 294.

22. Thomas Eakins to Benjamin Eakins, October 26, 1866, Bregler collection; Milroy, 1986, p. 99.

23. Transcription by Susan Eakins, Goodrich papers, Whitney Museum of American Art; Milroy, 1986, p. 101.

24. Thomas Eakins to Frances Eakins, April 1, 1869, Archives of American Art, Smithsonian.

25. Thomas Eakins to Frances Eakins, June 24, 1869, Bregler collection; Milroy, 1986, p. 243.

26. Milroy, 1986, p. 106; Moreau-Vauthier, 1906, p. 66.

27. Milroy, 1986, p. 106; Hering, 1869, p. 21.

28. Milroy, 1986, p. 110; Masson, p. 183.

29. Julian Alden Weir to John F. Weir, not dated, January 1874, in Young, 1960, p. 28.

30. John Niamey, quoted in Hering, 1869, p. 635; see Milroy, 1986, p. 178.

31. Milroy, 1986, pp. 178–179, note 6; Crespelle, 1966, p. 41.

32. Thomas Eakins to Benjamin Eakins, November 1, 1866, Bregler collection; Milroy, 1986, p. 133.

33. Hendricks, 1974, p. 147.

34. Milroy, 1986, p. 88; Thomas Eakins to Caroline Cowperthwait Eakins, October 1, 1866, Bregler collection.

35. Milroy, 1986, p. 92; Thomas Eakins to Benjamin Eakins, October 13, 1866, Bregler collection.

36. Milroy, 1986, p. 155; Thomas Eakins to Benjamin Eakins, July 12, 1867, Bregler collection.

37. Milroy, 1986, p. 176; Thomas Eakins to Benjamin Eakins, September 28, 1869, transcribed by Susan Eakins, Goodrich papers, Philadelphia Museum of Art.

38. Goodrich, 1982, vol. 2, p. 197.

39. Milroy, 1986, p. 89; op. cit.

40. Milroy, 1986, p. 157; Thomas Eakins to Benjamin Eakins, September 20, 1867, Bregler collection.

41. Milroy, 1986, p. 89; Thomas Eakins to Caroline Cowperthwait Eakins, October 8, 1866, Bregler collection.

42. Milroy, 1986, pp. 138–139; Thomas Eakins to Frances Eakins, October 30, 1865, Bregler collection.

43. Goodrich, 1982, vol. 1, p. 30.

44. Earl Shinn to Elizabeth Shinn Haines, March 1867, November 10, 1866, Richard Cadbury papers, Friends' Historical Library, Swarthmore, Pennsylvania (Milroy, 1986, p. 29).

45. Milroy, 1986, p. 145.

46. Thomas Eakins to Benjamin Eakins, March 21, 1867, Bregler collection.

47. Milroy, 1986, p. 146; Thomas Eakins to Benjamin Eakins, April 5, 1867, transcript by Susan Eakins, Goodrich papers.

48. Thomas Eakins to Benjamin Eakins, March 12, 1867, excerpt transcribed by Susan Eakins, Goodrich papers; Milroy, 1986, p. 143.

49. Milroy, 1986, p. 218, note 4; Dinnerstein, 1979; letter of Marianna van Rensselaer to S. R. Kohler, S. R. Koehler papers, Archives of American Art, Smithsonian Institution.

50. Milroy, 1986, p. 249; Thomas Eakins to Benjamin Eakins, Autumn 1869, transcribed by Susan Eakins, Goodrich papers.

51. Thomas Eakins to Benjamin Eakins, Autumn 1869, transcribed by Susan Eakins, Goodrich papers; Milroy, 1986, p. 264.

52. Thomas Eakins to Benjamin Eakins, June 24, 1869, Bregler collection; Milroy, 1986, p. 247.

53. Milroy, 1986, p. 162; Thomas Eakins to Caroline Cowperthwait Eakins, September 21, 1867, excerpt transcribed by Susan Eakins, Goodrich collection.

54. Milroy, 1986, p. 164; Thomas Eakins to Benjamin Eakins, November 1867.

55. Milroy, 1986, p. 164; Thomas Eakins to Benjamin Eakins, November 1867, Bregler collection.

56. Frances Eakins to Caroline Cowperthwait Eakins, July 7, 1868, Archives of American Art, Philadelphia Museum of Art.

57. Thomas Eakins to Frances Eakins, October 29, 1868, transcribed by Susan Eakins, Goodrich papers.

58. Thomas Eakins to Benjamin Eakins, October 29, 1868, Archives of American Art.

59. Thomas Eakins to Benjamin Eakins, September 8, 1868, transcribed by Susan Eakins, Goodrich papers.

60. Milroy, 1986, p. 158; Thomas Eakins to Benjamin Eakins, September 20, 1867, Bregler collection.

61. Thomas Eakins to Benjamin Eakins, January 17, 1868, transcribed by Susan Eakins, Goodrich papers.

62. Thomas Eakins to Benjamin Eakins, October 29, 1868, Archives of American Art.

63. Thomas Eakins to Benjamin Eakins, October 29, 1868, Archives of American Art, Smithsonian Institution.

64. Thomas Eakins to Benjamin Eakins, October 29, 1868, Archives of American Art, Smithsonian Institution.

65. Thomas Eakins to Benjamin Eakins, June 24, 1869, Bregler collection; Milroy, 1986, p. 248.

66. Thomas Eakins to Benjamin Eakins, March 17, 1868, Bregler collection.

67. Milroy, 1986, p. 176.

68. Milroy, 1986, p. 164; Thomas Eakins to Benjamin Eakins, April 18, 1868 (Goodrich papers) and March 6, 1868 (Bregler papers).

69. Milroy, 1986, p. 246; Thomas Eakins to Frances Eakins, April 1, 1869, Archives of American Art, Smithsonian.

70. Milroy, 1986, p. 169; Thomas Eakins to Benjamin Eakins, October-November 1867, transcribed by Susan Eakins, Goodrich papers.

71. Milroy, 1986, p. 245.

72. Milroy, 1986, p. 168; Thomas Eakins to Benjamin Eakins, February 1868, Bregler collection.

73. Interview with Edwin H. Blashfield, conducted by deWitt Mcclellan Lockman, July 1927, New York Historical Society (unpublished); Milroy, 1986, p. 258.

74. Thomas Eakins to Benjamin Eakins, September 8, 1869, transcribed by Susan Eakins, Goodrich papers; Milroy, 1986, p. 260.

75. For an account of Eakins's study with Bonnat, see Milroy, pp. 254–261.

76. Thomas Eakins to Benjamin Eakins, November 5, 1869, Bregler collection; Thomas Eakins to Benjamin Eakins, Autumn 1869, transcription by Susan Eakins, Goodrich papers; Milroy, 1986, p. 262.

77. Thomas Eakins to Benjamin Eakins, Autumn 1869, transcribed by Susan Eakins, Goodrich papers; Milroy, 1986, pp. 251–252.

78. The most detailed account of Eakins's trip to Spain is Milroy, 1986, pp. 274–311.

79. Gérôme was strongly hostile to the Italian masters, and often engaged in diatribes against Michelangelo and Donatello. Milroy, 1986, p. 128, note 74, citing Dagnan-Bouveret.

80. See Milroy, 1986, pp. 276–285.

81. As early as September 1869, Eakins considered going to Algiers to work outdoors. "Open air painting is now important to me to strengthen my color and study of light." See Milroy, 1986, p. 274; Thomas Eakins to Benjamin Eakins, September 14, 1869, transcript by Susan Eakins, Goodrich papers.

82. Milroy, 1986, p. 286; Thomas Eakins to Benjamin Eakins, December 2, 1869, Bregler collection.

83. Milroy, 1986, p. 287; Spanish notebook, Bregler collection.

84. Thomas Eakins to Benjamin Eakins, Christmas 1869, transcribed by Susan Eakins, Goodrich papers; Milroy 1986, p. 300.

85. Goodrich, 1982, vol. 1, p. 55.

86. Thomas Eakins to Benjamin Eakins, March 14, 1870, transcribed by Susan Eakins, Goodrich papers; Milroy, 1986, p. 301.

87. Thomas Eakins to Benjamin Eakins, March 29, 1870, transcribed by Susan Eakins, Goodrich papers; Milroy, 1986, p. 58.

88. Thomas Eakins to Benjamin Eakins, April 28, 1870, transcribed by Susan Eakins, Goodrich papers; Milroy, 1986, p. 301.

89. Thomas Eakins to Benjamin Eakins, April 28, 1870, transcribed by Susan Eakins, Goodrich papers; Milroy, 1986, p. 302.

90. Thomas Eakins to Benjamin Eakins, April 28, 1870, transcribed by Susan Eakins, Goodrich papers; Milroy, 1986, p. 302.

Chapter 10

1. Goodrich, 1982, vol. 1, p. 57.

2. We have only one record of how Eakins's father responded to paintings by him. From Eakins's letters from Paris, cited in the text, we know that he was surprised by the rough and unfinished quality of the studies that his son made while studying with Gérôme. We have no record of what Benjamin Eakins thought about Eakins's mature work.

3. See Milroy, 1986, pp. 320–321.

4. Soyer, 1966, p. 19.

5. Moynihan, 1971, pp. 51–52.

6. Fosburgh, 1954, p. 17.

7. Fosburgh, 1954, p. 18.

8. Hoppin, 1989, p. 30, note 26.

9. Goodrich, 1933, p. 39.

10. Goodrich, 1982, vol. 1, p. 4.

11. Goodrich, 1982, vol. 1, pp. 76–77. Curiously, this key episode in Caroline's life is

not listed in the index of the book.

12. Foster, 1989, p. 233. Nineteenth-century medical descriptions are often somewhat misleading, and in fact "exhaustion," the cause of death listed on Caroline Eakins's death certificate, is not by itself a cause of death. The actual cause of her death must remain a matter of conjecture. Caroline Eakins could have died of a stroke or heart failure. She also may have died of starvation, since psychotically depressed individuals often refuse to eat. Possibly the word "exhaustion" was been used instead of "starvation" to remove the implication that she had suffered from family mistreatment or neglect.

13. Goodrich, 1982, vol. 1, p. 76.

14. McHenry, 1946, p. 29.

15. Goodrich, 1982, vol. 2, p. 76.

16. Typically, manic-depressive illness occurs at fairly regular intervals for many years and then begins to accelerate, a phenomenon known as "rapid cycling." For a discussion of recurrence of depression, see Jamison, 1992, pp. 15–17; Kramer, 1997, pp. 109–114; and Miklowitz and Goldstein, 1997, p. 20.

17. Goodrich, 1982, vol. 1, p. 4.

18. DSM-IV, p. 322.

19. Interview with Pedro Del Gado, chief of psychiatry, University Hospitals, Cleveland, June 26, 2003.

20. DSM-IV, pp. 322, 329.

21. Jamison, 1995, p. 120.

22. Jamison, 1993, contains family trees that chart the occurrence of manic-depression in highly creative families.

23. Goodrich, 1933, p. 4.

24. Hendricks, 1974, pp. 85–86.

25. Goodrich, 1933, p. 39.

26. Johns, 1983, p. 118.

27. Wilmerding, 1993, pp. 64 (by Margaret Rose Vandries) and 55 (by Martin Berger).

28. Goodrich, 1982, vol. 1, p. 79.

29. Nochlin 1994, p. 270.

30. Johns, 1983, p. 121, note 7; Schendler, 1967, p. 27; Sewell, 2001, p. 32; Wilmerding, 1993, pp. 85–86.

31. Goodrich, 1933, p. 39.

32. Margaret Rose Vandryes in Wilmerding, 1993, p. 65.

33. Leja, 2001, p. 482.

34. Schendler, 1967, p. 48.

35. Schendler, 1967, p. 48.

36. Foster, 1997, p. 371.

37. Schendler, 1967, p. 41.

38. The correct title is given by Foster, 1997, pp. 136–138.

39. Simpson in Sewell, 2001, p. 34.

40. "National Academy of Design Exhibition," 1878, p. 364; Berger, 2000, p. 82. My discussion of this picture is largely based on Berger's sensitive analysis.

41. The idea of intersecting dialogues was familiar to Eakins. To minimize postage, he wrote some of his letters from France cross-wise over each other. See Berger, 2000, pp. 77–79.

42. Berger, 2000, p. 76.

43. Marc Simpson informs me that Eakins exhibited a lost painting titled *The Mother at the Society of American Artists* but its appearance is not known.

Chapter 11

1. Johns, 1983, p. 31.

2. *Philadelphia Evening Bulletin*, April 27, 1871.

3. Johns, 1983, p. 34.

4. Johns, 1983, p. 28.

5. Johns, 1983, p. 30.

6. Johns identifies the mansion as Sweetbriar (Johns, 1983, p. 20), but Kathleen Foster has identified it as Eaglesfield (Foster, 1997, p. 296). Eakins presumably made numerous studies for the painting, although only two survive: a sketch of the Girard Avenue bridge and a sketch of an oar carefully inscribed, "left oar looking out to the blade." From the outlines that are still visible on the canvas it is evident that he precisely charted the contours of the bridge, of Schmitt's racing shell, and of the tree trunks and branches in the left middle ground. The other areas were painted free hand, without guidelines.

7. As rowing developed special boats were devised that served no practical purpose except to go fast. A major breakthrough was the development of the iron outrigger in the 1840s, which extended out from the side of a boat and increased the leverage of the oars. This made possible a thinner gunwale, which greatly reduced a boat's weight. A barge of the 1820s, constructed of sturdy planks of oak, weighed about 700 pounds, whereas a racing shell of about 1865, made of thinly sliced Spanish cedar, weighed only thirty-five pounds. The design of the boats was also streamlined. Barges were relatively broad, and held two rowers on each seat, which was fixed in place. Racing shells were pencil thin and held a single rower on a movable seat. See Johns, 1983, pp. 25–26.

8. Goodrich, 1982, vol. 1, p. 83; Leja, 2001, pp. 480–481.

9. The omission of the comma was first noted by Johns, 1983, p. 19, note 2.

10. In the discussion that follows I have largely drawn on Cooper, 1996.

11. Thomas Eakins to Earl Shinn, March 26, 1875, Friends Historical Library of Swarthmore College; Richard Tapper Cadbury Collection; Goodrich, 1982, vol. 1, p. 121; Cooper, 1996, pp. 64, 66.

12. See note 11.

13. Cooper, 1996, p. 52.

14. See Cooper, 1996, pp. 99 (diagram) and 100.

15. The figures are all portraits and can be specifically identified. Going from stern to bow they are John Lavens Jr., Max Schmitt, Frank Henderson, and Oscar West.

16. Elizabeth Johns has argued that Eakins abandoned rowing subjects because the sport changed in a way that did not appeal to him, becoming less genteel and shifting away from amateurs to professionals. Thus, it came to lack that special balance of being at once intellectual and physical that had initially drawn his attention, and no longer attracted figures such as Max Schmitt who achieved distinction in both spheres, as lawyer and athlete. This argument is clearly incorrect. For one thing, Eakins was not bothered by sports that were not genteel—witness his boxing pictures, in which he went out of his way to emphasize the sport's unsavory aspects. In addition, Eakins did make paintings of professional, lower-class rowers such as the Biglin brothers, whom he portrayed on a larger scale than his earlier rowing subjects. Something else must have turned Eakins away from rowing as a subject.

17. This sequence is slightly simplified, for in fact, Eakins made two more versions of rowers in a pair-oared shell, in 1873 and 1874, which are essentially reworkings of the painting of 1872. I am also leaving out the watercolors of rowers that Eakins sent to Jean-Léon Gérôme, which seem to have been conceived as a project separate from the oil paintings. Leaving out these distractions makes the development of Eakins's thinking more obvious.

18. Ferber, 1994, pp. 15–22.

19. For a discussion of the liberties that Eakins took with true perspective, see Amy B. Werbel's account in Cooper, 1996, pp. 87–89. Unfortunately, the book reproduces Eakins's drawings at such a small scale that it is near impossible to follow Werbel's description of Eakins's producers. Werbel's account also contains obvious inaccuracies. On page 82, for example, she equates Gaspard Monge's "descriptive geometry" with "an infinitely extended viewpoint," that is, with orthogonal perspective, which eliminates foreshortening. She then states that Eakins's teacher, Jean-Léon Gérôme, employed descriptive geometry, which would imply that his paintings contain orthogonal renderings. In fact, Gérôme did not employ orthogonal perspective, and orthogonal perspective is just one of many systems that fit under the general rubric of "descriptive geometry."

20. Fried, 1987, pp. 53–54.

21. The occasional instances in which Eakins used elaborate perspective systems in his portraits of women—such as his late portrait of Mrs. Frishmuth, executed in 1900, which portrays eighteen musical instruments carefully plotted in accurate perspective—generally deal with gender in a perversely ambiguous way. Mrs. Frishmuth, for example, looks strikingly masculine.

22. Spies, 1998, p. 94.

23. Goodrich, 1982, vol. 1, p. 114.

24. Goodrich, 1982, vol. 1, p. 116.
25. Goodrich, 1982, vol. 1, p. 118.
26. Hoopes, 1974, pp. 61–62; Hoopes, 1991, pp. 22–25.

Chapter 12

1. Goodrich, 1982, vol. 1, p. 123. For general information about the painting, see Berkowtiz, 1999, "Thomas Eakins as a Scientist and His Relationship with Jefferson Medical College," pp. 122–161, and "*The Gross Clinic* by Thomas Eakins," pp. 162–213.
2. Goodrich, 1982, vol. 1, p. 132.
3. Hendricks, 1974, p. 13.
4. Goodrich, 1982, vol. 1, p. 135.
5. Goodrich, 1982, vol. 1, p. 135.
6. Goodrich, 1982, vol. 1, p. 134.
7. Goodrich, 1982, vol. 1, pp. 137–138.
8. Goodrich, 1982, vol. 1, p. 138.
9. Hendricks, 1974, p. 71.
10. I. M. Hays, M.D., quoted in Johns, 1983, p. 62, note 32.
11. Hendricks, 1974, p. 90.
12. Guthrie, 1949, p. 87.
13. Johns, 1983, p. 75.
14. Johns, 1983, p. 51.
15. Goodrich, 1982, vol. 1, p. 124; Johns, 1983, pp. 51–52.
16. Fried, 1987, pp. 10–11.
17. Even Michael Fried has been so seduced by the "real-life" argument that he proposes that Eakins's compositional sketch for the painting was very likely executed from life (Fried, 1987, p. 56). However, the fact that key elements of this composition were borrowed from the old masters implies that, like the finished painting, it was a studio concoction.
18. Hendricks, 1974, p. 88.
19. Fried, 1985, p. 40.
20. See Gerdts, 1981, p. 62, who proposes that Eakins created *The Gross Clinic* in part as a rejoinder to Gross's portrait.
21. Schendler, 1967, p. 55.
22. Fried defensively notes that "no doubt it would be not just crude but misleading to construe the patient's mother was a figure for Caroline Cowperthwait Eakins," but he then proceeds to do exactly this. See Fried, 1985, p. 41.
23. Fried, 1985, p. 41.
24. Doyle, 1999, p. 21.
25. Conversation with Bernard Dod, Phaidon Press, London, May 20, 2002.
26. Fried, 1985, p. 66.
27. Jennifer Doyle has argued that the painting literalizes the moment in the oedi-

pal narrative when the sexual difference of a woman is interpreted as the absence of genitals. It is a visualization of the scene of castration. See Doyle, 1999, p. 22.

28. Freud, 1955, vol. 12, p. 44.

29. Fried, 1987, p. 69. Fried's analysis of *The Gross Clinic* forms a kind of sequel to his involvement in the criticism of contemporary art, an aspect of his career summarized by McQullan, 1970. Some of the twists of his argument suggest a desire to link the two ventures. A major theme in Fried's writing on Color Field Painting was an antagonism to storytelling art, and a preference for paintings that allegedly pose deep philosophical questions of a nonnarrative sort. His essay on the *Gross Clinic* also pays lip service to this viewpoint. In actual fact, however, despite some verbal smokescreens, Fried's reading of the *Gross Clinic* does not follow this formula. When we reflect on the matter, it is clear that his interpretation does not eliminate narrative elements but simply replaces anecdotal surface narrative with a deeper and more compelling Freudian one. Thus, his ultimate conclusion is that the painting is telling a dramatic story-and should be analyzed in dramatic terms. Fried's anxiety about the issue of storytelling, however, may account for his nervousness in tracing parallels between Eakins's personal life and his artistic products, even though the underlying intention of his article is clearly to do so.

Thus, for example, as has been noted, Fried states (p. 41) that it would be "crude and misleading" to construe the mother as a stand-in for Caroline Eakins, although this is one of the central elements of his interpretation. Perhaps because of nervousness about storytelling, in his concluding paragraphs Fried turns his argument away from Eakins's family life and psychological makeup and turns to issues of pictorial space and the relationship between painting and drawing. Nonetheless, even in this section, the importance of family factors in shaping Eakins's world view is a major undercurrent of Fried's argument.

30. Goodrich, 1982, vol. 2, p. 46.

31. Hendricks, 1974, p. 88. The photograph seems to have been made with Eakins's participation and collusion although as so often with photographs attributed to Eakins, it is difficult to determine his exact role in the project. Writers on this photograph universally identify the "mother" figure as Eakins himself. I accept this identification, and the physique of the figure perfectly matches that of Eakins at this time, although since the figure covers his face there is some room for doubt.

32. Goodrich, 1982, vol. 2, p. 39.

33. While expressed somewhat differently, this is the essence of Bridget Goodbody's discussion of the "erotics" of the painting. See Goodbody, 1994, p. 45.

34. In 1903, Picasso painted over *Last Moments* to create *La Vie,* now in the Cleveland Museum of Art. X rays reveal Picasso's earlier composition. See Richardson, 1991, p. 123.

35. Schendler, 1967, p. 106.
36. Hendricks, 1974, p. 280.
37. Hendricks, 1974, p. 184.
38. Schendler, 1967, p. 105.
39. Goodbody, 1994, p. 40.
40. Goodbody, 1994, p. 33.
41. Goodbody, 1994, p 38.
42. Goodbody, 1994, p. 35.
43. Goodbody, 1994, p. 44.
44. Goodbody, 1994, p. 45.
45. The eroticized sick woman often appears in nineteenth-century painting, for example, in Antoine Fleury's 1878 painting, *Penel Freeing the Madwomen*, in which the patients rip open their blouses to expose their breasts, kneel and kiss men's hands, and willingly allow men to examine their bodies.
46. Goodrich, 1982, vol. 2, pp. 48–49. Goodrich provides a full transcription of the passage by Rabelais.

Chapter 13

1. Johns, 1983, p. 91; Siegl, 1978, p. 102.
2. Goodrich, 1982, vol. 1, p. 165.
3. The historical background of the painting has been well summarized by Johns, 1983. The name Rush was also held by another distinguished figure of colonial Philadelphia, Benjamin Rush (1746–1813) who was a pioneer in the humane treatment of the insane. At a half-conscious level, Eakins may well have been attracted to this connotation of the last name.
4. Shinn, 1875, p. 4.
5. The book is identified as *Webster's Unabridged Dictionary,* 1947, p. 34.
6. Johns, 1983, pp. 88–89.
7. Simpson in Sewell, 2001, p. 37.
8. Goodrich, 1982, vol. 1, p. 146.
9. Goodrich, 1982, vol. 1, pp. 151, 153; Johns, 1983, p. 90. Johns states that Eakins took the photographs although he may have arranged to have them taken.
10. Rush's model turned down suitors for many years and only married at the age of thirty-five, which was elderly for the time. This fact seems to have inspired Eakins's companion painting to the *William Rush, Courtship*, showing the Annie Williams, the same model who posed for *William Rush*, sitting at a spinning wheel spurning the offers of a suitor. Significantly, Eakins himself was not married when he painted *Courtship*, and had long delayed doing so. He may well have projected his own uneasiness about marriage into the role of the female in the painting.
11. Gilliams, 1893, p. 251; Johns, 1983, p. 110.
12. Marceau, 1937, pp. 28–29.

13. Goodrich, 1933, pp. 59–60.

14. Goodrich, 1983, vol. 2, p. 8.

15. Sewell, 1982, p. 48.

16. Both Eakins's contemporary reviewers and his personal friends identified the chaperon as the model's mother. Historically, this was not accurate, since Miss Vanuxem's mother died before Rush's statue was started, but Eakins himself seems to have conceived the chaperon as a mother figure.

17. *New York Times*, March 13, 1878; Goodrich, 1983, vol. 1, p. 157. With characteristic lack of perception, Goodrich describes this comment as "the nadir of idiocy."

18. Steinberg, 1972, p. 34.

19. Schendler, 1967, p. 80.

20. Katz, 1956, p. 20.

21. Goodrich, 1982, vol. 1, p. 156.

22. Goodrich, 1982, vol. 1, p. 157.

23. Hendricks, 1974, p. 114, citing the *New York Herald Tribune*, March 9, 1878.

24. Goodrich, 1982, vol. 1, pp. 148, 150.

25. It is possible that in the final painting Eakins substituted a slimmer model for Annie Williams, although this would invalidate Goodrich's long account of the identity of the model. If so, the masculine qualities of the leg would have been due to an unconscious exaggeration of the figure's slender, boy-like qualities. I personally favor the view that Eakins referred to studies of male anatomy when he painted the final figure. The use of male models for female figures was common in the Italian Renaissance and accounts for the peculiarities of anatomy that we sometimes find in works by artists such as Michelangelo and Benvenuto Cellini.

26. As a continuation of this theme of androgyny, it seems to me possible that Eakins incorporated a hidden image in this work. It is striking that the bold brushwork defining the highlight just above the crack in the nude model's buttocks does not seem to correspond with the actual form of the human figure in this area. If we consider this "highlight" as an independent shape it is striking that its configuration is that of a flaccid penis.

Chapter 14

1. Schendler, 1967, p. 64.

2. Goodrich, 1982, vol. 1, pp. 167–173, summarizes Eakins's rise to power at the Pennsylvania Academy. For a short overview of the history of the academy see Toohey, spring 1988.

3. Goodrich, 1982, vol. 1, pp. 169–170.

4. Goodrich, 1982, vol. 1, p. 170.

5. Hendricks, 1974, pp. 105–106.

6. Brownell, 1879, p. 740; Hendricks, 1974, p. 125.

7. Brownell, 1879, p. 740, claimed there was "no conflict" between the figures.

8. Ferber, 1994, p. 21.

9. Hendricks, 1974, p. 124.

10. Hendricks, 1974, p. 136.

11. According to Goodrich, Rogers was "progressive and democratic" as well as "willing to entrust the guidance of affairs to professionals" (a fundamentally different process than that of being democratic!). With regard to Eakins, he notes that Rogers was "Always on his side, intelligent, urbane, smoothing out difficult spots... His successor, Edward Hornor Coates, was a less progressive person" (Goodrich, 1933, pp. 73, 85).

12. The principal incident in which Rogers supported Eakins was a minor scandal in which the male students in his anatomy class threw the carcass of a dead horse over the railing of the main staircase into the main lobby of the Academy building. Rogers's defense of Eakins at this time appears to have been not so much a matter of liberalism as of the notion that boys should be allowed to roughhouse and play pranks as part of the process of developing their manhood.

13. Schendler notes that "apart from the portraits of Rogers and his brother-in-law, there is nothing very engaging in the faces or attitudes of the others on the coach" (Schendler, 1967, p. 73).

14. For a discussion of this project, see Johns, 1981–1982.

15. Goodrich, 1983, p. 266.

16. Goodrich, 1982, vol. 1, p. 294.

17. Johns, 1998, p. 174

18. Goodrich, 1933, p. 77

19. Goodrich, 1982, vol. 1, pp. 178–179.

20. Albright, 1953, p. 62.

21. Albright, 1953, p. 62.

22. Hendricks, 1974, p. 132.

23. Goodrich, 1982, vol. 1, p. 186.

24. Hendricks, 1974, p. 135.

25. Brownell, 1879, p. 741; Goodrich, 1982, vol. 1, p. 175.

26. Milroy, 1986, p. 253.

27. Bregler, March 1931, pp. 384–386; Bregler, October 1931.

28. Goodrich, 1933, p. 73; Goodrich, 1982, p. 167.

29. Goodrich, 1933, p. 77.

30. Anshutz is chiefly remembered as the teacher of the leading figures of the Ash Can School, including Robert Henri, John Sloan, William Glackens, George Luks and Everitt Shinn. But he also taught notable modernists, such as Charles Demuth. His students universally remembered him with respect and affection, and Sloan made an etching showing one of his anatomy demonstrations.

31. Hendricks, 1974, p. 162.

32. Schendler, 1967, p. 237.

33. Hendricks, 1974, p. 146.

Chapter 15

1. Hendricks, 1974, p. 217.

2. Many of the figures in Eakins's artistic and social circle were engaged with photography. The Schreiber brothers, whom Eakins portrayed in one of his rowing pictures, were photographers. Eakins's wife, Susan, was one of the members of the Philadelphia Photographic Salon, as was her sister Elizabeth and two students of her husband, Alice Barber and Amelia Van Buren. Another member of this salon, Eva Watson Schutz (who became the partner of Amelia Van Buren) became a member of Alfred Stieglitz's circle. Susan Eakins submitted a photograph, *Child with Doll*, to the first Philadelphia Photographic Salon in 1898 at the Pennsylvania Academy. Charles Bregler recalled that Susan often helped her husband take photographs and that she did photographic processing for him. (See W. Douglas Paschall in Sewell, 2001, pp. 239–255; Hendricks, 1972, p. 4, no. 21; Luxenberg, 1995, p. 249.)

3. See Prodger, 1993; Hall, 2001.

4. Homer, 1963, pp. 194–216.

5. Goodrich, 1982, vol. 1, p. 277.

6. Goodrich, 1982, vol. 1, p. 277.

7. Goodrich, 1933, p. 70.

8. Goodrich, 1933, p. 45, states that "he never painted from photographs, except in a few cases of portraits of persons no longer living, a type of commission which he disliked to undertake."

9. Luxenberg, 1995.

10. In 1988, after Hendricks's death from cancer, the Pennsylvania Academy acquired about sixty of these photographs from his estate for its permanent collection.

11. *Philadelphia Inquirer*, October 23, 1977; Luxenberg, 1995, p. 248; Sotheby Parke-Bernet, Olympia Galleries, 1977.

12. Parry, 1981; Luxenberg, 1995, p. 248.

13. Hendricks, 1974, p. 205, claims that Eakins once exhibited a photograph, but gives no specifics. Eakins exhibited his *History of a Jump* photo in 1886, but as science rather than art. Two images of bathers by Eakins were exhibited during Eakins's lifetime, in 1899–1900, by Stieglitz at the Camera Club in New York. See Sewell, 2001, pp. 253, 352.

14. From the nature of many of these photographs, it is highly unlikely that Eakins used a time-release mechanism. For example, the photographs of him swimming nude with his students were taken from some distance and show figures who were carefully arranged into a composition, by someone who was looking through the view-finder. It would have been extremely difficult to set up such photographs through a time-release method. The fact that Eakins seems to have derived pleasure from being seen in the nude also suggests that a friend or student often snapped the shutter. Indeed, in several photographs he seems to be psychologically engaged with the person behind the camera. In

some cases, proposals have been made about who took certain photographs. For example, Thomas Anshutz has been proposed as the individual who took the swimming photographs, in part because he does not appear in any of the photographs himself.

15. Luxenberg, 1995, p. 249.

16. Homer, 1992, p. 214; Homer, February 1983; Homer, March 1983.

17. Luxenberg, 1995, p. 249.

18. Parry, 1981, n.p.; Luxenberg, 1995, pp. 248–249.

19. Goodrich, 1933, p. 46.

20. Goodrich, 1933, p. 148.

21. Hendricks, 1969, p. 13, noted that "Eakins sometimes went so far as to copy, brush stroke by brush stroke, from a photograph."

22. See Tucker and Gutman, "Photographs and the Making of Paintings," in Sewell, 2001, pp. 225–238. See also "The Camera Artist" by W. Douglass Paschall in the same volume, pp. 239–255. See also Woodward, October and November 2001.

23. For example, in 1940, one of the accusations made against Grant Wood by hostile faculty members at the University of Iowa was that his paintings were copied from photographs. The accusation stood at the center of a bitter struggle between Grant Wood and the rest of the art department. See Corn, 1983, p. 58.

24. "The Year in Ideas," *The New York Times Magazine*, December 9, 2001, section 6, p. 86.

25. Woodward, October 2001, pp. 58–66. Mark Tucker and Nica Gutman, in Sewell, 2001, pp. 225–238.

26. Johns in Danly, 1994, p. 65.

27. Kirstein, 1972, p. 632. Of course the notion that photographs provide an accurate, objective record of events has changed with the development of digital photography, which has made it much easier to manipulate images.

28. Hendricks, 1974, p. 201.

29. While these two explanations are essentially incompatible, writers have failed to address this fact, and some have even used both explanations in slightly different contexts to serve their immediate polemical purposes. Kathleen Foster, for example, has maintained that Eakins's photographs were purely professional when discussing the attacks against Eakins after he was fired from the Pennsylvania Academy, but has approvingly described them as sexually liberated in the context of Eakins's relationship with Walt Whitman.

30. Johns in Danly, 1994, p. 65.

31. Kirstein, 1972, p. 632.

32. Braddock, 1988, p. 142. For the context of Eakins's photographs, see Anne Mac-Cauley in Danly, 1994, pp. 23–63.

33. McCauley in Danly, 1994, p. 45.

34. Johns in Danly, 1994, p. 71.

35. As has been noted by Johns. See Danly, 1994, p. 78.

36. For an account of the excursions see Johns in Danly, 1994, pp. 80–88.

37. Eakins seems to have enjoyed circulating the photographs of Susan outdoors. The Pennsylvania Academy has three negatives and thirteen prints, two of which are enlargements.

38. Johns in Danly, 1994, p. 88.

39. Goodrich, 1982, vol. 2, p. 96.

40. Schjeldahl, 2001, p. 79.

41. Goodrich, 1982, vol. 1, p. 193.

42. Goodrich, 1982, vol. 1, p. 194.

43. Goodrich, 1982, vol. 1, pp. 193–194.

44. Hendricks, 1974, p. 158.

45. Goodrich, 1982, vol. 1, p. 196.

46. Goodrich, 1933, p. 105.

47. As noted by Schendler, 1967, p. 81.

48. Goodrich, 1982, vol. 1, p. 230.

49. Goodrich, 1982, vol. 1, p. 31.

50. Goodrich, 1982, vol. 1, p. 31.

51. Thomas Eakins to Benjamin Eakins and Caroline Cowperthwaite Eakins, November 1867, transcribed by Susan Eakins, Goodrich papers.

52. Goodrich, 1982, vol. 1, p. 173; Brownell, 1879, p. 742.

53. Sylvan Schendler, 1967, p. 81, has argued that the Arcadian paintings faced forces of social disapproval, and that this explains Eakins's failure to finish them. "Behind his failure to finish the painting or any of the other Arcadian studies," Schendler writes, "is the repressive force of a civilization . . . There was no place for an Arcadia of nudes in the imagination of a Philadelphian." Such an invocation of repressive Philadelphia, however, seems disingenuous. Surely the real source of the repressed feelings of these paintings—and their unfinished state—was the psyche of Eakins himself.

54. Goodrich, 1982, vol. 1, p. 233.

55. Johns, 1983, p. 130.

56. Johns, 1983, p. 129.

57. Marc Simpson has told me that he sees the figure at the far left as male but it seems to me that the arrangement of the hair in a bun establishes that it is female. Nonetheless, the androgyny of the figure is interesting since this is a recurrent theme in Eakins's work.

Chapter 16

1. Bolger and Cash, 1996, p. 49.

2. Kathleen A. Foster in Bolger, 1996, pp. 28–29.

3. Goodrich, 1933, p. 62.

4. Mathiessen, 1941, pp. 604–610. Johns in Bolger, 1996, pp. 66–79, draws many of

the same parallels between Eakins and Whitman although without crediting Mathiessen's account.

5. Kirstein, 1972, p. 632.
6. Ned Rorem, 2000, p. 265.
7. Hendricks, 1974, p. 160; see also Foster, 1989, p. 115.
8. Hendricks, 1974, p. 221.
9. Hoopes, 1974, p. 163.
10. Gerdts, 1974, pp. 122–123.
11. Cooper, 1986, p. 35.
12. Fried, 1987, p. 13.
13. Ellensweig, 1992, p. 25.
14. Hatt, 1993, pp. 19–20.
15. Gopnik, 1994, p. 87.
16. Esten, 2002.
17. Doyle, 1999, pp. 7–8.
18. Jennifer Doyle, 1999, p. 8.
19. Homer, 1992, p. 116.
20. Goodrich interview with James L. Wood.
21. Davis, 1994, p. 301; I am somewhat simplifying Davis's more complex formulation of this idea.
22. See Bruce Weber, 2004, pp. 64–66; Gerdts, 1974, p. 73.
23. Hendricks, 1974, p. 160.
24. The last nude photographs of Susan seem to be the ones that show her with the horrse Billy that Eakins brought back with him from the Dakotas. These photographs must have been made around 1888–1889.
25. Griffin, 1995, p. 70.
26. Danto, 1995, p. 95.
27. Davis, 1994, p. 330.
28. Cooper, 1986, pp. 33–34.
29. Because of birth control, and for cultural reasons, many modern married couples wait several years to have children, but in the nineteenth century it was most common to begin having children within a year or so of marriage, as was the case with Eakins's two sisters and his father.
30. Goodrich, 1982, vol. 1, p. 28.
31. Doyle, 1999, p. 13. In this letter Eakins went on to declare that he would "not mutilate" a woman for double the money—although of course as a teacher in Philadelphia, Eakins did exactly that, since he supervised dissections of female cadavers.
32. Indeed, even those involved in homosexual activities can behave according to this pattern. Jack Kerouac, for example, who engaged in homosexual relationships, included many derogatory references to "fags" in his book *On the Road,* including a scene of threatening a homosexual with a gun in a bar. See Kerouac, 1995.

33. Schendler, 1967, p. 86.

34. Claire M. Barry in Bolger, 1996, p. 108 notes that Eakins signed the painting 1885, not 1883 as had been assumed earlier. Thus, the date corresponds to the completion of the painting, not the date of the excursion, as some previous scholars had argued.

35. Albright, 1947, p. 139.

36. Davis, 1994, p. 326. While the evidence is circumstantial, it seems quite clear that this spindle went through the length of the figure. As Davis observes: "Perhaps the spindle went through the model's navel to its lower back, but this could easily break when turned. More likely, the spindle ran up the model's anus through its head. This way it could be 'turned upside down,' and its arms or legs moved around, to construct the form."

37. Kessler, 1962, p. 19, was apparently the first to declare that the painting "falls slightly short of complete success" because of the academic poses of the figures, the stiff and artificial triangular arrangement, and the incongruity between the supposed movement of the diver and the formality of the composition.

38. Griffin, 1995, p. 70; Berger, 2000, pp. 202–203.

39. Eakins's painting is set at Dove Lake in Bryn Mawr, several miles west of Philadelphia. The lake was relatively new, created in 1873 by damming Mill Creek, which flows into the Schuylkill River, to provide power for a copper rolling mill. The process of creating the new lake partially flooded the remnants of earlier structures. The jetty on which the swimmers posed was apparently the foundation of an earlier mill—possibly Dove Mill, built in 1748, which served first as a grist and fulling mill, and later became one of the first paper mills in the colonies. Writers have suggested that Eakins's patron, Edward Coates, swam in Dove Lake when he was a student at Haverford College, located just half a mile away. In fact, the lake did not exist when Coates was a college student, but he was probably familiar with the spot Eakins portrayed since, around the time of the painting, both he and his brother purchased land in the immediate vicinity.

40. See Cash, "'Friendly and Unfriendly': The Swimmer's of Dove Lake," in Bolger and Cash, pp. 49–65.

41. Bolger and Cash, 1996, p. 117.

42. Doyle, 1999, pp. 3–4.

43. Bolger and Cash, 1996, pp. 36–65.

44. Bolger, 1996, p. 44.

45. Bolger, 1996, pp. 123–124.

46. Bolger, 1996, p. 123.

47. McHenry, 1947, p. 59.

48. McHenry, 1947, p. 59.

49. Her brother William G. Macdowell wrote to Susan around this time stating: "Your own worn appearance tells the tale of worry and I grieve that you

announce a plan that means no end of trouble except insanity or death." See Foster, 1989, p. 88.

50. The relationship of woman and dog becomes even more disturbing when we remember that Eakins's brother-in-law, Frank Stephens, accused him of "bestiality" and suggested that his relationship with his pets was somehow unnatural. Homer, 1992, p. 127. Schendler also somewhat nervously notes the woman's relationship to the dog, declaring that the dog's engagement with the spectator "may be a parody of Susan's scrutiny." See Schendler, 1967, p. 89.

51. Hendricks, 1974, p. 174. The dog Harry originally belonged not to Eakins but to his sister Margaret. Indeed, Eakins photographed Margaret with Harry, in a pose that is strikingly similar to that seen in the portrait of his wife. In addition, a small oil study of Margaret appears on the wall in the background at the left. Thus, *Lady with Setter Dog* contrasts the painter's earlier "marriage" to his sister Margaret with his present marriage to Susan.

52. McHenry, 1946, p. 50.

53. Goodrich, 1982, vol. 2, p. 15.

54. Merrill, 2001, pp. 27–28 and 180–181, notes other instances in which Eakins made reference to Whistler, notably his portrait of *Frank Jay St. John* (1900, Fine Arts Museums of San Francisco), which alludes to Whistler's portrait of *Thomas Carlisle* (1873, Glasgow Museums), and his *Music* of 1904 (Albright–Knox Art Gallery, Buffalo), in which a reproduction of Whistler's portrait of *Pablo de Sarasate* (1884, Carnegie Museum of Art, Pittsburgh) hangs behind the violinist, Hedda van den Beemt.

55. Two of Eakins's own works of art are visible: on the left a small painting of a woman knitting, which has not survived, but resembles the figure of the chaperon in *William Rush*. As noted, his sister Margaret posed for this picture. To the right is a section of his relief *Arcadia* (circa 1883).

56. Schendler, 1967, p. 27.

57. Goodrich, 1982, vol. 2, p. 279. Oddly, six years later, she sold the painting to the Metropolitan Museum of Art.

58. McHenry, 1946, p. 42.

Chapter 17

1. Goodrich, 1933, p. 96.

2. For this thought I am indebted to Alice Carter, in a conversation of April 16, 2004.

3. Goodrich, 1982, vol. 1, p. 79; Sewell, 2001, p. xxviii. Eakins noted in a letter to Gérôme: "While waiting for the season that I represented in my picture I caught malaria pursuing this same hunt, and the fever took me badly. I was bedridden 8 weeks, senseless most of the time. They believed that I would die." A transcript of this letter is in the Bregler papers. See Sewell, p. 30.

4. Mitchell, 1871.

5. Johns, 1983, pp. 136, 160.

6. Hendricks, 1974, p. 176.

7. Homer, 1992, p. 200.

8. Goodrich, 1982, vol. 1, p. 288; Goodrich interview with Ziegler.

9. Chamberlin-Hellman, 1981, discusses the Art Students League, pp. 374–419, and provides a list of students in Appendix D, pp. 548–549.

10. Works by three figures particularly close to Eakins, Jesse Godley, George Reynolds, and J. Laurie Wallace, are reproduced in Bolger and Cash, pp. 119–120. With the exception of the portraits by Wallace it is surprisingly amateurish. See also Sellin, 2000.

11. *Evening Telegraph*, June 16, 1876; Berger, 2000, p. 59; McHenry, 1946, p. 31.

12. Berger, 2000, p. 109.

13. See Nikolai Cikovsky Jr., in Brown, 1989, pp. 126–130. On the other hand, Eakins may have chosen this approach simply because in Philadelphia the sitters were already known to a good part of his audience. When he sent the portrait of George Reynolds to Paris, he did not call it *The Veteran* but simply identified the sitter. See Berger, 2000, p. 110.

14. Cikovsy, 1989, p. 128.

15. Spies, 1998, pp. 98–99.

16. Schendler, 1967, p. 111. See also Martin Berger's essay on "Sentimental Realism in Thomas Eakins's Late Portraits" in Chapman and Hendler, 1999.

17. Spies, 1998; Mitchell, 1877, p. 179.

18. Spies, 1998, p. 100.

19. Spies, 1998, pp. 100, 101.

20. Wilmerding, 1993, p. 113. Goodrich, 1933, p. 180, says he died at the age of twenty–seven, but seems to have confused the date of Hall's death with the date of the portrait.

21. Bolger and Cash, 1996, p. 117.

22. Bolger, 1996, p. 118.

23. Goodrich interview with Frank B. A. Linton.

24. Goodrich, 1982, vol. 1, pp. 299–300.

25. Goodrich, 1982, vol. 1, p. 300; see also, Goodrich, 1933, p. 92.

26. Hendricks, 1974, p. 222.

27. Schendler, 1967, p. 111.

28. Goodrich, 1982, vol. 2, p. 26.

29. Hendricks, 1974, p. 281.

30. The painting has been given dates ranging from 1888 to 1891. It may well have been executed in 1888 when Van Buren stayed in the Eakins home for an extended period. It is not clear whether is precedes or comes after the painting of Letitia Wilson Jordan of 1888 in The Brooklyn Museum.

31. Goodrich, 1982, vol. 11, p. 72.

32. Conversation with Douglass Paschall, June 1999.

33. Goodrich, 1982, vol. 1, p. ix.

34. Wilmerding, 1993.
35. Homer, 1992, p. 231.
36. As Martin Berger has noted to me in an e-mail of March 18, 2004, the chair is Jacobian Revival in style and must date from the 1860s.
37. Schendler, 1967, pp. 124, 130.
38. Wilmerding, 1993, p. 121.
39. Goodrich, 1982, vol. 2, p. 72.
40. Schendler, 1967, p. 130.
41. Goodrich, 1982, vol. 2, p. 84.
42. Wilmerding, 1993, p. 117. For Eakins's frames, see Cannon-Brooks, 1993.
43. Hendricks, 1974, p. 193.
44. Goodrich, 1982, vol. 2, p. 84.
45. Goodrich interview with Mrs. Addicks (the former Weda Cook).
46. Eakins admired Degas. He once commented of Degas that "that fellow knew what he was about." (Bregler, March 1931, p. 385).
47. Merrill, 2003, p. 180.
48. Adams, 1987, p. 23. According to Goodrich, 1982, vol. 2, p. 84, the roses were given to Cook every day by Eakins's friend, the sculptor, William O'Donovan, who (in Cook's words) "fell in love with me, the old fool."
49. Fried, 1987, p. 168, note 32, mentions the interesting fact that the conductor originally held the baton like a paintbrush. Thus, the conductor's hand evoked the hand of the painter, painting. An interesting aspect of this connection is that it suggests that Eakins saw painting as a controlling activity—perhaps control over both the model and over the sometimes disturbing emotional implications of the enterprise.
50. Eakins's strange tendency to fuss over minor details was apparently not simply an effort to get every detail right. It seems to have had an emotional aspect, because his fussing often went on for months with no visible progress. No doubt at some level Eakins was interested in proving that his paintings were valid because so much work went into them. But in addition, this fussing allowed Eakins to linger over and savor the emotional twist of his paintings, which often had an allure that was different from the ostensible subject. He seems to have fussed particularly over details connected with bodices, undergarments, and other details of dress.
51. Schendler, 1967, p. 132.
52. Goodrich interview with Mrs. Addicks.
53. Wilmerding, 1993. p. 117.
54. Goodrich, 1982, vol. 11, p. 260.
55. See Johns in Bolger and Cash, 1996, p. 71.
56. Schjeldahl, 2001, p. 79. Patrick McCaughey has noted that "The portrait of Maud Cook is particularly distinguished for the rapidity with which light and dark alternate across the face. The inconsistency of the illumination, its uncertainty in the presence of lustrous shadows, achieves a striking ambiguity for

the sitter in which judgments about character and mood become impossible to assume (McCaughey, 1970, p. 61).

57. Sewell, 1982, p. 121.

58. Goodrich, 1982, vol. 2, p. 137.

59. Goodrich, 1982, vol II, pp. 137–144; Leja, 2001, pp. 487–490. Moore, 1982 provides an account of Rowland's career as well as a diagram and careful description of the "ruling engine" that Eakins portrayed. For information on Rowland I am indebted to my student Suzanne Debrosse, who has written an unpublished paper on the scientific formulas on Eakins's frame, which she was apparently the first to identify and decode.

60. The pace of Eakins's work had slowed around 1890. In 1891 there was only one dated painting, a portrait of Thomas B. Harned. Schendler notes that for Eakins much of the 1890s was a period of "creative impotence." However, his pace of production picked up again around 1895.

61. Goodrich, 1933, p. 103; Goodrich, 1982, vol. 2, p. 144.

62. Goodrich, 1982, vol. 2, p. 147.

63. Goodrich, 1933, p. 103.

64. Smith, 1979, p. 411.

65. Hendricks, 1974, p. 239.

66. Goodrich, 1982, vol. 2, p. 147.

67. The identification is provided by Goodrich, 1982, vol. 2, although it has been disputed.

68. In curiously heated language, Leslie Katz writes of *Between Rounds:* "The nude body of the boxer is like a white-hot coal, a thing of marvelously hard beauty and practical purity, a breathing incandescence" (Katz, 1956, p. 21).

69. Goodrich, 1982, vol. 2, p. 151.

70. David Wilson Jordan told Lloyd Goodrich that all the recognizable background figures in *Taking the Count* are portraits, but Goodrich does not identify them. See Goodrich, 1982, vol. 2, p. 147.

71. Goodrich, 1982, vol. 2, p. 155.

72. For a discussion of the composition of this audience and its significance see Berger, 2000, pp. 112–114.

73. If we study the two halves of Mrs. Eakins's face, it becomes apparent that they portray two different people. The lighted half is that of a woman still relatively young, whose mouth is resigned but not resentful. The shaded half is that of a much older woman, whose eyes are lined and whose mouth is turned down in bitterness.

74. Spies, 1998, p. 102.

75. Spies, 1998, p. 102.

76. Hendricks, 1974, p. 76.

77. Goodrich, 1982, vol. 2, p. 171.

78. Goodrich, 1982, vol. 2, p. 174.

79. Lubin in Wilmerding, 1993, p. 161.

80. Johns, 1983, p. 113.
81. Lloyd Goodrich writes of this scroll that "it is a striking form, with an Afrrican or South Pacific look, and a phallic suggestion. Its prominent position and its relation to the figures present an enigma (Goodrich, 1982, vol. 2, p. 249).
82. Hardin, 2000, p. 185, notes that Eakins used three different models for his late paintings of *William Rush,* which include several small studies I have not discussed. She also makes the very plausible suggestion (p. 181) that one of these models may have been Rebecca Macdowell, who was the niece of Eakins's wife.
83. Katz, 1956, p. 20.
84. Goodrich, 1933, p. 111.
85. Goodrich, 1982, vol. 2, p. 69.
86. Goodrich, 1982, vol. 2, p. 72.
87. Goodrich, 1982, vol. 2, p. 69.
88. Goodrich, 1982, vol. 2, p. 238.
89. Goodrich, 1982, vol. 2, p. 238.
90. Goodrich, 1982, vol. 2, p. 187.
91. Schendler, 1967, p. 197.
92. Hendricks, 1974, p. 48.
93. Hendricks, 1974, p. 48.
94. Goodrich, 1982, vol. 1, p. 36.
95. Hendricks, 1974, p. 160.
96. Schendler, 1967, p. 200. While James A. Flaherty was a layman, I think it is appropriate to consider him as part of this ecclesiastical series.
97. Schendler, 1967, p. 197.
98. Goodrich, 1982, vol. 2, p. 175.
99. Hendricks, 1974, p. 256.
100. Hendricks, 1974, p. 257.
101. The book originally was titled *Hamlet.* The most vivid female character in *Hamlet* is Ophelia, who, like Eakins's mother, went insane. Hendricks, 1974, p. 256.
102. Wilmerding, 1993, pp. 177–178; Foster 1997, pp. 215–219.

Chapter 18

1. For a popular account of this phenomenon see Sacks, 1985. In intuitive recognition of this fact, governments place engravings of faces on money, since they are particularly difficult to forge. Many forgeries have been detected because people noticed that there was "something wrong with the expression." If we stop to consider Eakins's achievement in a social context, it is interesting to note that the two other greatest American portraitists of the nineteenth century, John Singer Sargent and Mary Cassatt, both had their social roots in Philadelphia.

2. Goodrich, 1982, vol. 2, pp. 212, 69. He frequently concludes his discussion of a painting with comments such as "this is one of Eakins's most sculptural portrayals of the human figure," or that such-and-such a figure "exists physically."

3. Goodrich's belief that Eakins was a "realist" make is possible for him to see things that aren't there. Thus, for example, Goodrich declares of the portrait of Louis Kenton "every rumple of his unfashionable suit is precisely delineated" (Goodrich, 1982, vol. 2, p. 179).

4. Goodrich, 1982, vol. 2, p. 57.

5. Comparison of Eakins's paintings with related photographs shows that he "corrects" the casualness of the photograph and often manipulates elements.

6. Goodrich, 1982, vol. 2, pp. 55–56.

7. McCaughey, 1970, p. 61.

8. Schendler, 1967, p. 120.

9. McCaughey, 1970, p. 61.

10. Russell, 1989, p. 110.

11. Cited by Foster, 1997, p. 198.

12. Sylvan Schendler, one of the few to address this issue of emotional meaning, has written of Mrs. Mahon that her eyes "express personal injury and pain in a way that drives all comparisons out of mind . . . Restrained anguish and grief have never been more powerfully interpreted." See Schendler, 1967, p. 226.

13. Hendricks, 1974, p. 258.

14. Hendricks, 1974, p. 267.

15. This tendency, of course, has been pushed to an extreme by some of the most revered Abstract Expressionists, such as Ad Reinhart, Barnett Newman and Mark Rothko, who have produced near-empty canvases.

16. McCaughey, 1970, p. 61.

17. Goodrich, 1982, vol. 2, p. 204.

18. Hendricks, 1974, p. 179.

19. Hendricks, 1974, p. 233.

20. Goodrich, 1982, vol. 2, p. 165.

21. Hendricks, 1974, p. 282.

22. Nochlin, 2001, pp. 255–272, quotation p. 260. In strictly visual terms, Nochlin's analysis seems dubious, since Sargent's women often look intensely vulnerable behind their facades. It is interesting to note that while it has become customary to negatively compare Sargent's portraits with those of Eakins, Sargent seems to have been one of the few contemporary artists whom Eakins greatly admired, often speaking highly of his work to Samuel Murray and sending one of his own portraits to Sargent as a gift. See Goodrich, 1982, vol. 2, pp. 222–223.

23. Nochlin, 2001, p. 272.

24. Nochlin, 2001, p. 263.

25. Nochlin unconvincingly argues that Eakins's use of the nude model in female classes indicates his feminist stance. She writes: "He seems to have encouraged some of his female students and to have demanded greater availability of the

nude model in his classes." See Nochlin, 2001, p. 272.

26. Greenberg, 1961, p. 180.

27. Goodrich, 1982, vol. 2, p. 279.

28. Conversation with Gary Tinterow, Cleveland, May 1999.

29. Goodrich, 1933, p. 113.

30. Spies, 1998, p. 87, citing Mitchell, 1888, p. 10.

31. Schendler, 1967, p. 216.

32. Clark, 1991, pp. 6, 26.

33. Spies, 1998, p. 92; Smith-Rosenberg, 1985, pp. 190–191.

34. Spies, 1998, p. 92; Dijkstra, 1986, p. 43.

35. Goodrich, 1982, vol. 2, p. 69.

36. Schendler, 1967, p. 145.

37. Goodrich, 1982, vol. 2, p. 238.

38. Goodrich, 1982, vol. 2, p. 238.

39. McCaughey, 1970, p. 61.

40. Spies, 1998, p. 92; Smith-Rosenberg, 1985, p. 206.

41. Spies, 1998, pp. 87–94.

42. Hendricks, 1974, p. 267, 170.

43. Hendricks, 1974, p. 170.

44. Schendler, 1967, p. 69; 164.

45. Schendler, 1967, pp. 138, 145; Clark, 1991, pp. 17, 21.

46. Schendler, 1967, p. 145; Clark, 1991, p. 2.

47. Goodrich, 1933, p. 116.

48. Goodrich, 1933, p. 22.

49. Hendricks, 1974, p. 248.

50. Schendler, 1967, p. 180.

51. Hendricks, 1974, p. 90.

52. Hendricks, 1974, pp. 184, 186.

53. Morris, 1930, pp. 30–31.

54. Goodrich interview with Mrs. Dodge.

55. Hendricks, 1974, p. 263.

56. Hendricks, 1974, p. 262.

57. McHenry, 1946, p. 130.

58. Goodrich, 1982, vol. 2, p. 72.

59. Around 1900, Eakins began work on a portrait of Mrs. Joseph H. Drexel and her collection of fans. After a few sessions, however, Mrs. Drexel found the task of sitting for Eakins so wearisome that she sent her maid to sit, which caused Eakins to abandon the portrait. See Hendricks, 1974, p. 247.

60. Hendricks, 1974, p. 248.

61. Goodrich, 1982, vol. 2, p. 59.

62. Goodrich, 1982, vol. 2, p. 64. Letter from Leslie W. Miller, April 23, 1930. Even Eakins's frame had a humble look. In a letter to Henry Rowland, Eakins noted that, "My exhibition frames are mostly of plain chestnut gilded right upon the

wood and showing the grain." In 1899 Eakins wrote to John Beatty asking: "Is there in your institution a hard and fast rule that frames must be gold? I always protest against the barbaric splendor of new gold frames which injure all paintings. See Goodrich, 1982, vol. 2, pp. 9, 139.

63. Goodrich, 1982, vol. 2, p. 232.

64. I am quoting from the wall label at Reynolda House. The wording is similar to that found in Eldredge, 1990, p. 98. For the complex relationship understood by Victorians to exist between photographic portraits and a good likeness see Smith, 1999.

65. Goodrich, 1982, vol. 2, p. 236. Both Schendler and Goodrich declare that Eakins's portraits are never "satire." The frequency with which they repeat this claim, however, makes one wonder why they are so nervous about the issue, and makes one suspect that Eakins's portraits are indeed satire, though perhaps satire of an unusual sort.

66. Goodrich, 1982, vol. 2, p. 58. Weinberg's comment was made in the acoustaguide tour of the 2002 Eakins exhibition at the Metropolitan Museum of Art.

67. Goodrich, 1933, p. 114. "These late portraits of businessmen were, as always, uncompromisingly truth-telling, and hence, because of the men themselves, among the most devastating portraits he ever painted." See Goodrich, 1982, vol. 2, p. 236. His own account, however, makes it clear that Eakins's likenesses often did not closely correspond either with the appearance or the character of these men.

68. Goodrich, 1982, vol. 1, p. 143.

69. Goodrich, 1982, vol. 1, p. 143.

70. Goodrich, 1982, vol. 1, p. 142.

71. Goodrich, 1982, vol. 1, p. 144.

72. Hendricks, 1974, p. 118.

73. Goodrich, 1982, vol. 2, p. 230.

74. Goodrich, 1982, vol. 2, p. 230.

75. Goodrich, 1982, vol. 2, p. 229.

76. Goodrich unpublished notes, interview with Eleanor Pue.

77. Goodrich, 1982, vol. 2, p. 242. Even the boxer, Turkey Point Billy Smith, who posed for *Between Rounds* (1898–1899), was not flattered by how Eakins represented him. As he wrote to the art dealer Maynard Walker, who had just sold a portrait study of Smith to the Wichita Art Museum: "I recall while painting the portrait you just sold, I noticed a dark smear across my upper lip. I asked Mr. Eakins what it was, He said it was my mustache; I wanted it off; he said it was there, and there it stayed. You can see he was a Realist." See Hendricks, 1974, p. 236.

78. Goodrich unpublished interviews with Mrs. Cryer, Mrs. Montgomery and Mrs. Wilson Shaw Ward.

79. Goodrich unpublished interview with Miss Burie and Elizabeth Corless.

80. Curatorial files, Canajoharie Library.

81. Goodrich notes, interview with Mrs. Harmstead and Mrs. Cryer.

82. Hendricks, 1974, p. 258.

83. Goodrich, 1982, vol. 2, p. 61.

84. Susan Eakins reported that Signora Gomez d'Arza, whom Eakins painted in 1902, "had tragic experiences early in life. Similarly, she reported that Edith Mahon, whom Eakins painted in 1904, "had suffered great unkindness." In neither case did she provide any specifics, and it seems quite possible that she simply invented these claims based on the appearance of the portraits. See Goodrich, 1982, vol. 2, pp. 10–11; Wilmerding, 1993, p. 162.

85. Goodrich, 1982, vol. 2, p. 234.

86. Goodrich, 1982, vol. 2, p. 192.

87. Hendricks, 1974, p. 170.

88. Schendler, 1967, p. 226.

89. Hendricks, 1974, p. 253.

90. Goodrich, 1933, p. 116.

91. Not long after the editorial urging its removal, the members of the Union League Club followed this advice, despite the protests of Eakins's friends. They then sent to President Hayes, who apparently discarded it. Years later, when Eakins and his wife walked by the League, Mrs. Eakins went in to inquire about the portrait. She later wrote that she was sorry she had done so, for Eakins was in declining health at the time, and the news that no one knew anything about the fate of his painting seriously upset him.

92. Schendler, 1967, p. 189.

93. Goodrich, 1982, vol. 2, pp. 231–232, 234.

94. Goodrich, 1982, vol. 2, p. 234.

95. Hendricks, 1974, p. 255. In one instance, something about Eakins's likeness impelled a stranger to destroy one of his portraits. McHenry reports: "The portrait of Boulton (Edward W.) by Eakins was lent to the University Club for an exhibit, and a waiter ran amuck and slashed it up. Eakins patched up the picture and Boulton took it home, where the house caught on fire and the portrait burned up." See McHenry, 1947, p. 108.

96. Goodrich, 1982, vol. 2, p. 182.

97. Goodrich, 1982, vol. 2, p. 177.

98. Hendricks, 1974, p. 226.

99. Goodrich, 1982, vol. 2, pp. 220–221.

100. Goodrich, 1982, vol. 2, p. 125.

Chapter 19

1. To be sure, deciding what to include in such lists is somewhat subjective. Different individuals might organize lists around other categories, and certain facts can be listed under more than one category. Frank Stephens's accusation of

incest, for example, could be listed under the heading of "incest" or under that of "family conflict," and in fact it is useful to list it in both places. Just what belongs on a list in some instances might become a matter of dispute. For example, interpretations of paintings are often somewhat speculative—thus it is not always clear whether they belong on a list. Certainly information from a painting differs in many respects from information about an actual occurrence, and we should bear this in mind. Nonetheless, when we start compiling such lists, we quickly discover that Eakins's life and art contains patterns that are paralleled by no other figure in nineteenth-century American art. Indeed, they would stand out as unusual anywhere.

2. Goodrich, 1982, vol. 2, p. 11.

3. Interestingly, abuse of animals, such as Eakins's murder of his sister's cat, is more common among boys who have suffered physical punishment from their fathers or who have been sexually abused. Recent studies have shown that people who abuse animals are more likely to abuse people. They are more likely to commit violent crimes or to commit mass murder. For a popular summary of the issue of animal abuse see Snook, 2002, p. A4.

4. Doyle, 1999, p. 13.

5. Foster, 1989, p. 79.

6. Flam, 1991, p. 68.

7. Goodrich, 1982, vol. 2, p. 95. Goodrich seems to have borrowed this word from one of his informants, Mrs. Addicks, who knew Eakins well. See Goodrich, 1982, vol. 2, p. 91.

8. Stafford-Clark, 1997, p. 119. It is now standard practice for therapists to list exhibitionism as a specific disorder, and the DSM-IV-TR requires that exhibitionism and others paraphilias be listed separately. As J. Paul Federoff has pointed out, however, in some cases paraphilias can be difficult to categorize, or can be grouped together in highly unusual patterns. See Federoff, 2003, p. 349. While I think it is useful to think of exhibitionism as a specific disorder, we should also remain open to the notion that may be linked with other behavioral disorders or forms of biochemical imbalance. While current theories of exhibitionism are useful, and to my mind often quite convincing, they are still too general to be capable of predicting behavior with any degree of precision or for producing precise, repeatable results in therapeutic practice.

9. Farkas, 2003, p. 1.

10. Goodrich unpublished interview with Frances Eakins Crowell.

11. Blair, 1981, p. 439.

12. Jones, 1979, pp. 63–70; Huhasz, 1983, p. 55.

13. Zechnich, 1971, p. 72.

14. Singer, 1979, p. 526.

15. Jones, 1979, p. 65.

16. Smukler, 1975, p. 600.

17. Jones, 1979, p. 66.

18. Vlachs, 1993, argues that sex predators are generally incurable. This seems to me an extreme position, but at this point in time "cures" are highly unpredictable.

19. Cox, 1988, p. 228.

20. Wilson, 1987, p. 210.

21. Cox, 1988, p. 228.

22. Hendricks, 1974, p. 29.

23. Goodrich, 1982, vol. 2, p. 95; Foster, 1989, pp. 121–122 writes of Eakins: "Perhaps he felt liberated by age to do exactly as he pleased."

24. Karpman, 1957; Langevin, 1979.

25. Singer, 1979, p. 527.

26. Lang, 1987, p. 217.

27. Blair, 1981, p. 449.

28. This theory was solidly in place by the 1940s. Brown, 1940, p. 383, for example, states that "Psychoanalytically exhibitionism represents a denial of castration and an invitation for females to deny castration also."

29. Blair, 1981, pp. 448–449.

30. Smukler, 1975, p. 600.

31. Snaith, 1983, p. 233.

32. Abouesh and Clayton, 1999.

33. I do not claim that my summary is absolutely comprehensive, although it seems to me that most additional approaches can be encompassed within these schemas. A concept which has proved valuable for therapy is that of "courtship disorders"—the notion that an individual may become "fixated" on one stage of normal courtship. This theory has obvious value in therapy, since it focuses the patient toward "normal" forms of sexual fulfillment and makes it easier to discuss paraphilias. The approach has been eloquently developed by John Money, 1986.

34. Young-Bruehl in Stafford-Clark, 1997, p. xv.

35. Young-Bruehl in Stafford-Clark, p. xv.

36. Stafford-Clark, 1997, p. 112.

37. Rickles, 1950, p. 81; Rickles, 1942, pp. 11–17.

38. Allen, 1974.

39. Goodrich, 1982, vol. 1, pp. 76, 79.

40. Fried, 1987, pp. 41, 69.

41. Jamison, 1993, pp. 16–17.

42. Hendricks, 1974, p. 6.

43. Laing, 1965.

44. Eakins's nickname was "The boss." See Goodrich, 1933, p. 91.

45. For an interesting instance of disagreement about whether nudity is acceptable within a family see Van Buren, 2002, E8. Is it appropriate for a woman to have breakfast in the nude with her brother after his marriage?

46. Goodrich, 1933, p. 94.

47. Refreshingly, this has been challenged by some recent writers, notably by Martin A. Berger. See Berger, 2000.

48. Flam, 1991, p. 68.

49. Bolger and Cash, 1996, pp. 59, 69, 70.

50. Homer, 1992, p. 179; Goodrich, 1982, vol. 2, p. 91.

51. Foster, 1989, p. 76.

52. Foster, 1989, p. 138, note 17; Hendricks, 1974, p. 46.

53. Foster, 1989, p. 151.

54. Goodrich, 1982, vol. 1, p. 170.

55. Goodrich, unpublished interview with Mrs. Adicks, the former Weda Cook.

56. Homer, 1992, p. 182.

57. Goodrich unpublished interview with Mrs. Lavell.

58. Foster, 1989, p. 214.

59. Hendricks, 1974, p. 244; Goodrich, 1982, vol. 2, p. 174; Homer, 1992, p. 179.

60. In a perceptive on-line review of the 2003 Eakins show at the Metropolitan Museum, Francis O'Connor argued that it is more important that Eakins was a depressive than a homosexual, and went on to argue that his principal myth-maker and biographer, Lloyd Goodrich, was attracted to artists who were sexually inhibited. See FVOC@aol.com. The psychologists I have spoken with stress that Eakins's sexuality seems to have been unfocussed.

61. Stafford-Clark, 1997, p. 183.

62. Freud laid out his theories of progressive stages of infantile and adolescent sexual development in his *Three Essays on the Theory of Sexuality* of 1905.

63. Goodrich, 1982, vol. 2, pp. 48–49.

64. The psychological impact of spanking and caning is suggested by the effects of this practice in nineteenth-century English public schools, a setting in which homosexuality flourished. It is widely accepted that these punishments played a role in shaping sexual fantasies. It has been repeatedly stated, for example, that the homosexual poet Algernon Swinburne became fascinated by flogging and spanking as a result of his experiences as a schoolboy at Eton. See Henderson, 1974, pp. 17–19, 54, 267. Swinburne was also an enthusiastic reader of the Marquis de Sade. See Gray, 1998, p. 415.

65. The psychologist Allen, in fact, has proposed that exhibitionism reflects "unconscious homosexual submissiveness." See Cox, 1979, p. 63.

66. Goodrich, 1982, vol. 2, p. 96.

67. At least one of Eakins's students seems to have collected mentally unstable people, much as Eakins did. Charles Bregler, who idolized Eakins, married two successive women who were delusional and suffered from mental illness.

68. Foster, 1989, p. 88.

69. Foster, 1989, p. 101.

70. Foster, 1989, p. 97.

71. For Anna O. see Gay, 1988, pp. 63–67 and Freud, 1955, vol. 2, pp. 21–47. A word of caution should also be added. I will also use the word "hysteria," by itself, in

a somewhat different sense, to indicate behavior that was "hysterical" in its nature. The behavior of Eakins's mother, for example, seems to have often been "hysterical," although she did not suffer from the mental disease of "hysteria," as diagnosed and described by Freud.

72. While Hammitt mimicked Eakins's behavior, she did not mirror his motives, since her exhibitionism did not reflect a fear of castration.

73. Foster, 1989, p. 101.

74. Foster, 1989, p. 84; Goodrich, 1982, vol. 2, p. 294.

75. The only other case of incest-type behavior that I know involved the tonalist painter Bruce Crane. In 1904 Crane divorced his wife, Jean Burchard Brainerd, and married her daughter by a previous marriage, Anne Brainerd, by whom he subsequently had two children. Most of Crane's patrons were scandalized and deserted him after this episode. Crane's behavior, however, while it nominally involved a family member, did not involve an individual with whom he was genetically linked. See Clark, 1982.

76. Before the nineteenth century, marriages generally took place between people from the same neighborhood or village, and since families lived in the same area for centuries, they were often closely related. First and second cousins, as well as even closer relatives, often married and in fact such liaisons seem to have been considered desirable, as a way of holding land and property together and maintaining family solidarity. During this nineteenth century this pattern began to change, as people mixed more freely. Land became less significant as a source of wealth, patriarchal authority grew weaker, and it became more common for children to enter professions different from those of their parents. Individuals married more often for love and even crossed social boundaries in order to do so. Nonetheless, old patterns frequently remain in force even after the social reasons for them have disappeared. The Eakins family, seems to have exemplified the old-fashioned view of marriage as a kind of kinship alliance. Thus, Eakins did not question his father's insistence that he become engaged to Kathrin Crowell, whose family also provided a mate for his sister Frances. Later, after Kathrin died, Eakins married the daughter of an engraver, a woman from a social milieu very similar to his own.

77. Blair, 1981, p. 444.

78. Interview with Pedro Delgado, Head of Psychiatry, University Hospital, Cleveland, June 2003.

79. Foster, 1989, pp. 290–298.

80. Foster, 1989, pp. 110–111.

81. Goodrich, 1982, vol. 2, p. 136, writes that "there was general agreement that in Ella's last years she was insane."

82. Foster, 1989, p. 118.

83. Foster, 1989, p. 231.

84. Goodrich interview with Frances Eakins Crowell.

85. Goodrich, 1982, vol. 2, p. 97.

86. Therapists today generally refer to "paraphilia" rather than "perversion" because it is less jugmental. In clinical practice it is generally not useful to start off by informing a patient that he or she is a "pervert." The meaning of the two terms, however, is essentially the same. "Paraphilia" is constructed from two Greek words and literally means "To the side of love."

87. Homer, 1992, pp. 178–179.

88. For accounts of Eakins's advances see Foster, 1989, p. 118; Hendricks, 1974, p. 236; Homer 1992, p. 209; Goodrich, 1982, vol. 2, p. 136; and McHenry, 1946, p. 100.

89. Homer, 1992, p. 209.

90. Foster, 1989, pp. 238–239.

91. Stafford-Clark, 1997, p. 119.

92. Abusers generally target certain types, in part because they discover that these types are particularly vulnerable. Eakins may have been attracted to tomboys because he discovered that outdoor and masculine activities gave them a common interest and provided opportunities for disregarding usual standards of how men and women should behave in each other's presence. For example, Eakins is known to have gone on swimming excursions with his sister Margaret. It seems likely that they both removed their clothes and swam naked on these outings.

93. Whether such behavior should be interpreted as incest is a matter on which modern therapists do not agree, although the meaning of the term seems to be shifting, and in both clinical and popular understanding incest is defined more broadly than even a few decades ago. Thus, in 1991 a writer for *Time* magazine noted that whereas older definitions of incest refer to genital penetration, "During the past decade, the definition of incest has been broadened to include fondling, rubbing one's genitals against a child, and excessive or suggestive washing of a youngster's pubic area, among other sexual behaviors." Gorman, 1991, p. 46.

94. McCarthy, 1989, pp. 17, 104–105, 155–157, 204, 239, 282.

95. Jamison, 1993, pp. 236, 269.

96. Eakins's self portraits seem to dramatize his depressed state. As Tom Lutz has observed, "Eakins turns a morbid eye upon himself and exaggerates his own debility." See Lutz, 1991, p. 283.

97. See McHenry, 1946, p. 94.

98. Jamison, 1993, p. 5.

99. Jamison, 1993, p. 240.

100. My discussion of serotonin and SRIs is largely based on Kramer, 1997, particularly chapter 3. My thanks also to Suzanne DeBrosse, a medical student at Case Western Reserve, who coached me about this material and reviewed what I wrote. I have benefited from discussions with two pioneer researchers into the properties of serotonin, Pedro Delgado, head of psychiatry at University Hospital in Cleveland, and Evan Deneris, professor of neurosciences at the Medical

School at Case Western Reserve. Both kindly looked over a preliminary draft of this section and made corrections.

101. This process began in the 1950s. At the time American therapists tended to view bipolar illness and schizophrenia as variations of the same disease, and to trace the roots of both to "psychic conflict." As late as 1963 a leading American physician, Karl Menninger, declared that "we tend today to think of all mental illness as being essentially the same in quality, although differing quantitatively and in external appearance" (Kramer, 1997, pp. 43–43, note p. 341). When lithium was discovered, however, it proved effective for treating bipolar illness but not schizophrenia, and it became apparent that the two diseases are fundamentally different.

102. Diminished amount or function of the neurotransmitter has not been detected, and many studies now suggest that that cells that make up the brain circuits onto which the neurotransmitters are released may be "sick" or dysfunctional. Increasing serotonin makes them work better but may not be the root cause of the illness.

103. The first drugs to fight depression, such as lithium, essentially functioned as "mood uplifters." Anyone who takes them will experience a feeling of increased euphoria. More recently developed drugs, such as Prozac, function in a different way. They have no impact on the mood of normal people but do affect patients who are clinically depressed. This suggests that they more specifically target the chemical malfunction that causes depression.

104. Delgado and Charney, 1990.

105. Recently Evan Deneris, a researcher at Case Western Reverse University, has genetically manipulated mice so that they produce little serotonin during fetal development of the brain. While outwardly healthy, they show behavioral abnormalities, such as irregular breathing and an increased tendency toward aggression. This represents one of the first instances in which a specific gene has been shown to impact adult behavior through its control of embryonic serotonin production.

106   For the impact on exhibitionism see Zeltner, 2003, C3.

107   Obsessive-compulsive disorder may be due to a signal that has reached its destination but is not then reabsorbed into the transmitter cell. As a consequence, the message is not terminated, but continues to replay over and over again. Serotonin seems to put this process back into balance.

108. Mitchell, 1879, pp. 54, 76, 77. On page 91 he specifically mentions prescribing "two quarts of milk" to a male patient. See also Mitchell, 1885, p. 280.

109. According to Margaret McHenry, in 1911 Eakins was poisoned by milk that had been mixed with formaldehyde as a preservative. McHenry strongly implies that Eakins's death five years later was a consequence of this poisoning. It is hard to know how much credit to place in this account, since, while Eakins may well have been poisoned by bad milk, his final illness seems to have been progressive, and it is hard to believe that it was because of poison ingested five

years earlier. In his final years, Eakins was obese and suffered from circulatory problems and high blood pressure. These symptoms are consistent with a diet too high in fat—which in Eakins's case was probably largely milk fat.

110.   Mitchell, 1877, p. 183; Mitchell, 1879, pp. 19 and 77. In this period, cocaine was readily available, both as a medicine and as a mood enhancer. Freud experimented with cocaine, as did William James (and also the fictional character Sherlock Holmes). For a time cocaine was even an ingredient in the popular beverage, Coca Cola. My thanks to Dr. Lewis Obi, who suggested to me that Eakins may have been dependent on narcotics in an e-mail of January 19, 2003.

111.   Hendricks, 1974, p. 220.

Chapter 20

1.   La Farge, 1908.

2.   Miklowitz and Goldstein, 1997, p. 161.

3.   Significantly, however, Eakins made it uncertain whether the woman does or does not have a penis.

4.   For a discussion of the performative phallus and performative masculinity, see Jones, 1994, and Jones, 1995.

5.   This obviously touches on the question of whether madness plays a necessary role in great art, or whether artists are no more ill than other people. The classic debate over this issue occurred between Edmund Wilson and Lionel Trilling, Wilson suggesting that great art is associated with deep and unhealable psychic wounds and Trilling arguing that artists are only ill to the degree that "we are all ill." See Wilson, 1941; Trilling, 1950; and Kramer, December 1987, 1997, p. 276. It seems to me that generalizations are risky on this issue; it makes sense to examine the question case by case. A related question is whether by "curing" artists of their neuroses we would increase or decrease their ability as artists. For example, if it had been possible to give Eakins an SSRI and it had cured his exhibitionism, would this have increased his artistic ability or destroyed it? There is no simple answer to this conundrum, although Peter Kramer's book *Listening to Prozac* (Kramer, 1997) does a sensitive job of exploring this vexing question and others related to it.

6.   Goodrich, 1982, vol. 1, p. 21.

7.   Hendricks, 1974, p. 231.

8.   Hendricks, 1974, p. 229.

9.   Lloyd Goodrich interview with Mrs. Dodge.

10.   Stafford-Clark, 1997, p. 122.

BIBLIOGRAPHY

Bibliographical Note

Probably more has been written about Eakins than any other nineteenth-century American artist, but this literature is difficult to use. Several of the writers who had access to firsthand information, such as Margaret McHenry and Gordon Hendricks, were careless in their methods. Lloyd Goodrich, Eakins's most influential biographer, often willfully misrepresented facts because of his interpretive bias. There is no *catalogue raisonné* of Eakins's work. The most complete checklist of paintings is that in Goodrich's monograph of 1933, but most of the works are not reproduced; to find illustrations of these works, if they exist, one must thumb through multiple sources. There is no complete text of Eakins's letters, and different bits of the same letter may be cited in three or four different places, all of which need to be consulted and compared with each other. For years Lloyd Goodrich conveyed the illusion that the statements he made about Eakins were factual and accurate, but my impression is that much of what passes for fact in the literature on Eakins is far from certain. I have done my best to sort through the information available and to avoid factual errors, but some details will probably be overturned by new research. In this book I have cast my net broadly, but more research is needed on basic factual matters, such as the dates of Eakins's paintings, the places and activities they record, and the biographies of his sitters. As should be evident from my text, statements about Eakins, even of a seemingly straightforward and factual nature, have often been based on assumptions about his fine qualities as a person rather than on actual evidence.

My notes are intended to document my statements but not necessarily to indicate the first place where a given quotation or fact first appeared or to deal with the often vexing issue of who discovered what first. The most complete compilation of data on Eakins is Goodrich's plodding but useful monograph of 1982, and I have cited it frequently. Goodrich omitted some of the most interesting statements of those he interviewed, but fortunately I was able to consult his unpublished notes at the Philadelphia Museum of Art, where I found much useful material. It is also worth checking the sources he cited, since he often censored the most interesting passages. Gordon Hendricks and Margaret McHenry both compiled mounds of interesting source material, not very well digested. Kathleen Foster's compilation, *Writing About Eakins* (1989), lays out most of what is known about the scandals that surrounded the artist, and while I thoroughly disagree with her conclusions I have relied on it heavily. These books have served as my fundamental sources, but I have found surprising facts and useful insights widely scattered in the large body of articles on Eakins, which are specifically cited in my notes. As is indicated in the text, while I have not agreed on every point, I have been stimulated and inspired by the extraordinary insight of several revisionist writers on Eakins, such as Michael Fried, Whitney Davis, Marcia Pointon, and Martin Berger. For the general reader, William Inness Homer's monograph on Eakins (1992) provides the most balanced overview of Eakins as well as excellent illustrations.

Dealing with medical and psychological questions presented special challenges. There are many books about Freud and his theories. For me, David Stafford-Clark's *What Freud Really Said* was particularly helpful, and of course it was always stimulating to go back to Freud's own statements, the most salient of which have been collected in the Modern Library's anthology, *The Basic Writings of Sigmund Freud*. Kay Redfield Jamison has done a brilliant job of describing manic-depression, in writings that range from the popular to the technical. Thanks to her exemplary work, an individual writing about bipolar illness stands on solid ground. Our understanding of the biochemical causes of bipolar illness is rapidly changing, but Peter D. Kramer's *Listening to Prozac* provides an extremely useful account of the present state of our knowledge, as well as a sensitive exploration of some of the practical, ethical and philosophical issues that are raised by new forms of medication. Unfortunately, exhibitionism has not received equally satisfactory treatment, in part because the syndrome seems to elude a comprehensive explanatory model. Recent medical articles tend to be brief and narrowly focused. They also often do not clearly lay out their underlying assumptions, which seem to vary greatly from author to author. Earlier writings tend to be easier to follow and more comprehensive in their approach, but obviously do not reflect the most recent thinking on the subject. It seems to me that there is an opening here for a new synthesis of what to know about the disorder. While I have listed my principal sources on medical questions, anyone who wishes to explore these issues would be well advised to simply do a search on the Internet, which can quickly locate the most up-to-date publications.

I have not used the unpleasant and cumbersome *Chicago Manual of Style* system for my notes but have used the more sensible *Art Bulletin* method with some minor changes. I have given the short form of all citations in the notes and the full reference in the bibliography, regardless of how many times I have cited a work. I have indicated page numbers with the letter p. I have listed works by the same author chronologically.

Abouesh, Ahmed, and Anita Clayton, "Compulsive voyeurism and exhibitionism: A clinical response to paroxetine," *Archives of Sexual Behavior*, vol. 28, no. 1, 1999, pp. 23–30.

Ackerman, Gerald M., "Thomas Eakins and his Parisian masters, Gerome and Bonnat," *Gazette des Beaux-Arts*, April 1969, pp. 235–256.

Adams, Henry, "Thomas Eakins: The troubled life of an artist who became an outcast," *Smithsonian Magazine*, November 1991, pp. 52–69.

———, "Rediscovering Norman Rockwell," *American Artist*, October 1992, pp. 52–57, 75–76.

———, et al., *John La Farge*, Abbeville, New York, 1987.

Adler, Kathleen, and Marcia Pointon, *The Body Imaged: The Human Form and Visual Culture Since the Renaissance*, Cambridge University Press, Cambridge, 1993.

Albright, Adam Emory, "Memories of Thomas Eakins," *Harper's Bazaar*, August 1947, pp. 138–139, 184.

———, *For Art's Sake*, privately printed, Philadelphia, 1953.

Allen, David W., "The fear of looking—or scopophilic-exhibitionists conflicts," University Press of Virginia, Charlottesville, Va., 1974.

"A Portrait by Thomas Eakins," *The Minneapolis Institute of Arts*, February 3, 1940, pp. 22–25.

Aristotle, *Aristotle's Poetics*, Norton, New York, 1982.

Barchiesi, A., "Exhibitionism and ego states: A phenomenological account," *Transactional Analysis Journal*, vol. 6, no. 3, 1976, pp. 305–306.

Barchus, Agnes R., *Eliza R. Barchus, The Oregon Artist, 1857–1959*, Binford & Mort, Thomas Binford, Publisher, Portland, Oreg., 1974.

Barr, Alfred H., Jr., with an essay by Lloyd Goodrich, *Homer, Ryder, Eakins*, Museum of Modern Art, New York, May 1930.

Bartlett, Truman H., *The Art Life of William Rimmer*, J. R. Osgood, Boston, 1882.

Beard, George Miller, *American Nervousness*, G. P. Putnam's Sons, New York, 1881.

Beaux, Cecilia, *Background with Figures*, Houghton Mifflin Company, Boston, 1930.

Benton, Thomas Hart, "Mechanics of form organization in painting," *Arts*, November 1926, pp. 285–289; December 1926, pp. 340–342; January 1927, pp. 43–44; February 1927, pp. 95–96; March 1927, pp. 145–148.

Berger, Martin, *Determining Manhood: Constructions of Sexuality in the Art of Thomas Eakins*, doctoral dissertation, Yale University, UMI Dissertation Services, Ann Arbor, 1995.

———, "Modernity and Gender in Thomas Eakins's Swimming," *American Art*, Fall 1997, pp. 32–47.

———, *Man Made: Thomas Eakins and the Construction of Gilded Age Manhood*, University of California Press, Berkeley, California, 2000.

Bergman, Robert P., et al., *Thomas Eakins: Image of the Surgeon*, exhibition catalogue, Walters Art Gallery, Baltimore, 1989.

Berkowitz, Julie S., *Adorn The Halls: History of the Art Collection at Thomas Jefferson University*, Thomas Jefferson University, Philadelphia, Penn., 1999.

Berman, Avis, *Rebels on Eighth Street: Juliana Force and the Whitney Museum of American Art*, Atheneum, New York, 1990.

Bianchi, Michael D, "Fluoxetine treatment of exhibitionism," *American Journal of Psychiatry*, vol. 147, no. 8, 1990, pp. 1089–1090.

Bizouard, Elisabeth, "L'anonymat de l'exhibitionniste," *Revue Française de Psycho-analyse,* vol. 56, 1992, pp. 1721–1732.

Bjelajac, David, *American Art: A Cultural History,* Prentice Hall, New York, 2000.

Blair, C. David, and Richard I. Lanyon, "Exhibitionism: Etiology and Treatment," *Psychological Bulletin,* vol. 89, no. 3, 1981, pp. 439–463.

Boime, Albert, "American culture and the revival of the French academic tradition," *Arts Magazine,* May 1982, pp. 95–101.

Bolger, Doreen, and Sarah Cash, *Thomas Eakins and the Swimming Picture,* Amon Carter Museum, Fort Worth, 1996.

Boswell, Peyton, "Peyton Boswell comments: 900 percent Eakins preferred," *The Art Digest,* July 1, 1939, p. 3.

Bowman, Ruth, "Nature, the photograph and Thomas Eakins," *College Art Journal,* Fall 1973, pp. 35, 38.

Braddock, Alan C., "Eakins, race, and ethnographic ambivalence," *Winterthur Portfolio,* Summer–Autumn, 1988, p. 142.

Bregler, Charles, "The Brooklyn Memorial Arch: A note on its crowning group of sculpture," *Harper's Weekly,* January 1896, pp. 9, 15.

———, "Thomas Eakins as a teacher," *The Arts,* March 1931, pp. 378–386 (pp. 376–377, "Charles Bregler").

———, "Thomas Eakins as a teacher: Second article," *The Arts,* October 1931, pp. 28–42.

———, "Eakins' permanent palette," *The Art Digest,* November 15, 1940.

———, "Photos by Eakins: How the famous painter anticipated the modern movie camera," *American Magazine of Art* (later *Magazine of Art*), January 1943, pp. 28–29.

———, "A Tribute," in *A Loan Exhibition of the Works of Thomas Eakins, 1844–1944,* commemorating the centennial of his birth through June and July, 1944, M. Knoedler, New York, 1944.

Brown, J. Carter, et al., *American Paintings from the Manoogian Collection,* National Gallery of Art, Washington, D.C.–Detroit Institute of Arts, 1989.

Brown, J. F., *The Psychodynamics of Abnormal Behavior,* McGraw-Hill, New York, 1940.

Brown, Milton W., et al., *American Art,* Harry N. Abrams, New York, 1988.

Brown, Ron M., *The Art of Suicide,* Reaktion, London, 2001.

Brownell, William C., "The Arts Schools of Philadelphia," *Scribner's Monthly Illustrated Magazine,* September 1879, pp. 737–750.

———, "The younger painters of America," First Paper, *Scribner's Monthly,* May 1880, pp. 1–15.

Bryson Burroughs Memorial Exhibition, Metropolitan Museum of Art, New York, 1935.

Buki, Zoltan, and Suzanne Corlette, eds., *The Trenton Battle Monument, Eakins Bronzes,* New Jersey State Museum, Trenton, 1973.

Burke, Doreen Bolger, *American Paintings in the Metropolitan Museum of Art,* vol. 3, Metropolitan Museum of Art, New York, 1980.

Burroughs, Alan, "Thomas Eakins," *The Arts,* March 1923, pp. 185–189.

———, "Thomas Eakins, The Man," *The Arts,* December 1923, pp. 302–323.

————, "Catalogue of Work by Thomas Eakins (1869–1916)," *The Arts*, June 1924, pp. 328–333.

Burroughs, Bryson, "Drawings by Matisse," *Bulletin of the Metropolitan Museum of Art*, May 1910, p. 126.

————, "An Estimate of Thomas Eakins," *The Arts*, July 1937.

Buzov, Ivan, "Exhibitionism: The essential psychical conflict in manifest dream content," *American Journal of Psychoanalysis*, vol. 48, no. 2, 1998, pp. 180–183.

Byrd, Gibson, "The artist-teacher in America," *College Art Journal*, Winter 1963–1964, pp. 132–133.

Caffin, Charles, *The Story of American Painting*, Frederick A. Stokes, New York, 1907, pp. 230–233.

Canaday, John, "Familiar truths in clear and beautiful language," *Horizon,* Autumn 1964, pp. 88–105.

Cannon-Brookes, Peter, "Picture framing II: The frames of Thomas Eakins," *Museum Management and Curatorship*, December 1993, pp. 431–435.

Carlyle, Thomas, *Sartor Resartus and on Heroes and Hero Worship*, J.M. Dent & Sons, E. P. Dutton, London, 1908.

Carter, Alice A., *The Red Rose Girls: An Uncommon Story of Art and Love*, Harry N. Abrams, New York, 2000.

————, *The Essential Thomas Eakins*, Harry N. Abrams, New York, 2001.

Casals-Ariet, C., and Ken Cullen, "Exhibitionism treated with clompipramine," *American Journal of Psychiatry,* vol. 150, no. 8, 1993, pp. 1273–1274.

Casteras, Susan P., "Susan Macdowell Eakins 1851–1938," in *Susan Macdowell Eakins*, May 4–June 10, 1973, Pennsylvania Academy of the Fine Arts, Philadelphia, Penn., 1973.

Chamberlin-Hellmann, Maria, *Thomas Eakins as a Teacher*, doctoral dissertation, Columbia University, University Microfilms, Ann Arbor, 1981.

Chapman, Mary, and Glenn Hendler, eds., *Sentimental Men: Masculinity and the Politics of Affect in American Culture*, University of California Press, Berkeley, 1999.

Cikovsky, Nicolai, et al., *American Paintings from the Manoogian Collection*, National Gallery of Art–Detroit Institute of Arts, Washington, D.C.–Detroit, 1989.

Clark, Charles Teaze, "Bruce Crane, tonalist painter," *Magazine Antiques*, November 1982, pp. 1060–1067.

Clark, William J., "The Iconography of Gender in Thomas Eakins Portraiture, *American Studies*, Fall 1991, pp. 5–28.

Cooper, A. J., "Residual recidivism in sex offenders," *Canadian Journal of Psychiatry*, vol. 44, no. 1, 1999, p. 94.

Cooper, Emmanuel, *The Sexual Perspective: Homosexuality and Art in the Last One Hundred Years in the West*, Routledge & Kegan Paul, London, 1986.

Cooper, Helen A., et al., *Thomas Eakins: The Rowing Pictures*, Yale University Art Gallery, Yale University Press, New Haven, 1996.

Corn, Wanda, *Grant Wood: The Regionalist Vision*, Yale University Press, New Haven, 1983.

Costello, Charles, ed., *Symptoms of Psychopathology: A Handbook*, John Wiley, New York, 1970.

Cox, Daniel, "Incidence and nature of male genital exposure behavior as reported by college women," Brief Reports, *The Journal of Sex Research*, vol. 24, 1988, pp. 227–228.

Cox, Daniel, and Reid J. Daitzman, "Behavioral theory, research, and treatment of male exhibitionism," in *Progress in Behavior Modification*, eds. Michel Hersen, Richard Eisler, and Peter M. Miller, Academic Press, New York, 1979.

Cox, Daniel, J. K. Tsang, Alice Lee, "A cross cultural comparison of the incidence and nature of male exhibitionism among female college students," *Victimology*, vol. 7, nos. 1–4, 1982, pp. 231–234.

Craven, Wayne, *American Art: History and Culture*, Brown & Benchmark, New York, distributed by Harry N. Abrams, 1994.

Crespelle, J.-P., *Les maîtres de la Belle Epoque*, Hachette, Paris, 1966.

Cullen, Kevin, "British nudist walks free, clad in smile after his trial," *The Plain Dealer*, Cleveland, Ohio, January 14, 2001, 4A.

Danly, Susan, *Eakins and the Photograph: Works by Thomas Eakins and His Circle in the Collection of the Pennsylvania Academy of the Fine Arts,* ed. Susan Danly and Cheryl Leibold with essays by Elizabeth Johns, Anne McCauley and Mary Panzer, Pennsylvania Academy of the Fine Arts, Smithsonian Institution Press, Washington, D.C. 1994.

Danto, Arthur C., "Men Bathing, 1883: Eakins and Seurat," *ARTnews*, March 1995, p. 95.

Davenport-Hines, Richard, "Happy and gay," *The Times Literary Supplement*, London, January 9, 2004, pp. 9–10.

Davis, Whitney, "Erotic revision in Thomas Eakins's narratives of male nudity," *Art History*, September 1994, pp. 301–341.

DeFrancesco, David P., "Identifying differences among male sex offenders: Child molesters versus exhibitionists versus voyeurs," *Dissertation Abstracts International*, vol. 53, 9-A, 1993, p. 3146.

Delgado, Pedro L., and Dennis S. Charney, et al., "Serotonin function and the mechanism of antidepressant action: reversal of antidepressant-induced remission by rapid depletion of plasma tryptophan," *Archives of General Psychiatry*, vol. 47, 1990, pp. 411–418.

Delgado, Pedro L., M.D., and Francisco A. Moreno, M.D., "Neurochemistry of Mood Disorders," typescript of textbook chapter for *American Psychiatric Publishing Textbook of Mood Disorders*.

D'Emilio, John, and Estelle B. Freedman, *Intimate Matters: A History of Sexuality in America*, Harper & Row, New York, 1988.

Delteil, P., A. P. Baily-Salin, and F. Josselin, "Clinical and psychopathological aspects of exhibitionism," *Evolution Psychiatrique*, vol. 36, no. 1, 1971, pp. 13–30.

Diagnostic and Statistical Manual of Mental Disorders, 4th ed. (DSM-IV), American Psychiatric Association, Washington, D.C., 2002.

Dietz, Park Elliott, Daniel J. Cox, and Stephen Wegner, "Male genital exhibitionism," *Forensic Psychiatry and Psychology: Perspectives and Standards for Interdisciplinary Practice*, F. A. Davis, Philadelphia, 1986, pp. 363–385.

Dijkstra, Bram, *Idols of Perversity: Fantasies of Feminine Evil in Fin-de-Siecle Culture*, Oxford University Press, New York, 1986.

Dinnerstein, Lois, "Thomas Eakins's 'Crucifixion' as perceived by Mariana Griswold Van Rensselaer," *Arts Magazine*, 53, May 1979, pp. 140–145.

Domit, Moussa M., *The Sculpture of Thomas Eakins* [exhibition catalogue], The Cororan Gallery, Washington, D.C., May 3–June 10, 1969.

Donelson, F. Hoopes, *American Watercolor Painting*, Watson-Guptil, New York, 1977.

Doyle, Jennifer, "Sex, scandal, and Thomas Eakins' The Gross Clinic," *Representations*, Fall 1999.

Dreishpoon, Douglas, with a foreword by Stuart Feld and an appreciation by Lloyd Goodrich, *The Paintings of Bryson Burroughs*, 1869–1934, Hirshl & Adler Galleries, New York, 1984.

Drinka, Georg F., *The Birth of Neurosis*, Simon & Schuster, New York, 1984.

DuMaurier, George, *Trilby*, Harper and Bros., New York, 1894.

Dwyer, Margaretta, "Exhibitionism/voyeurism," *Journal of Social Work and Human Sexuality*, vol. 7, no. 1, 1988, pp. 101–112.

Eakin, Emily, "The pornographer and his wife," *The New York Times Book Review*, November 8, 1998, p. 8.

"Eakins cheated," in "The Year in Ideas," *The New York Times Magazine*, December 9, 2001, section 6, p. 86.

East, W. N., "Observations on exhibitionism," *Lancet*, vol. 2, 1924, pp. 370–375.

Eldredge, Charles, and Barbara Millhouse, *American Originals, Selections from the Reynolda House Museum of American Art*, Abbeville Press, The American Federation of Arts, New York, 1990.

Eliot, Alexander, *Three Hundred Years of American Painting*, Time Incorporated, New York, 1957.

Ellis, Havelock, *Psychology of Sex*, London, Heinemann, 1933.

Esten, John, *Thomas Eakins: The Absolute Male*, Universe, A Division of Rizzoli International Publications, New York, 2002.

Evans, D. R., "Exhibitionism," in C. G. Costello, ed., *Symptoms of Psychopathology*, Wiley, New York, 1970.

Eysenck, H. J., ed, *Handbook of Abnormal Psychology*, 2nd ed., Robert K. Knapp, San Diego, 1973.

Farkas, Karen, "Woman is made to walk naked before co-workers," *The Cleveland Plain Dealer*, Metro, January 28, 2003, section B, p. 1.

Farnham, Emily, *Charles Demuth: Behind a Laughing Mask*, University of Oklahoma Press, Norman, 1971.

Fedora, Orestes, John R. Reddon, and Lorne T. Yeudall, "Stimuli eliciting sexual arousal in genital exhibitionists: a possible clinical application," *Archives of Sexual Behavior*, vol. 15, no. 5, 1986, pp. 417–427.

Fedoroff, J. Paul, "The paraphilic world," in Stephen B. Levine et al., *Handbook of Clinical Sexuality for Mental Health Professionals*, Brunner-Routledge, New York, 2003, pp. 333–255.

Feldman, M. P., "Abnormal sexual behavior in males," in H. J. Eysenck, ed., *Handbook of Abnormal Psychology*, Pittman, London, 1973.

Ferber, Linda, "'My dear friend': A letter from Thomas Eakins to William T. Richards," *Archives of American Art Journal*, vol. 34, no. 1, 1994, pp. 15–22.

Field, Hamilton Easter, "Bryson Burroughs: The man and his work," *Arts and Decoration*, December 1919, p. 83.

Flam, Jack, "Eakins in light and shadow," *American Heritage*, September 1991, pp. 57–64, 66, 68.

Flexner, James, *Thomas Eakins, 1844–1916,* The Metropolitan Museum of Art in Miniatures, Book-of-the-Month Club, New York, 1956.

Flor-Henry, Pierre, "Cerebral aspects of sexual deviation," *Variant Sexuality: Research and Theory*, Johns Hopkins University Press, Baltimore, 1987, pp. 49–83.

Flor-Henry, P., Ruben A. Lang, Z. J. Koles, and Roy P. Frenzel, "Quantitative EEG investigations of genital exhibitionism," *Annals of Sex Research*, vol. 1, no. 1, 1988, pp. 49–62.

Forgac, Gregory, "Two types of male exhibitionists as seen in an outpatient forensic psychiatry clinic," *Dissertation Abstracts International*, vol. 41, 6-B, 1980, pp. 2318–2319.

Forgac, Gregory, and Edward J. Michaels, "Personality characteristics of two types of male exhibitionists," *Journal of Abnormal Psychology*, vol. 91, no. 4, 1982, pp. 287–293.

Fortunato, John Edward, "One exhibits, one gets high: A self-psychological analysis of similarities and differences in two clients with narcissistic behavior disorders," *Dissertation Abstracts International: Section B: The Sciences & Engineering*, vol. 56, 12-B, 1996, p. 7044.

Fosburgh, James, "Brooklyn's 'Home Scene' by Eakins," *ARTnews*, April 1954, pp. 60–61.

———, "Music and meaning: Eakins' progress," *ARTnews*, February 1958, pp. 24–27, 60, 61.

Foster, Kathleen A., "Philadelphia and Paris: Thomas Eakins and the Beaux Arts," Department Paper, History of Art Dept. Yale University Graduate School, May 1972.

———, "An important Eakins collection," *The Magazine Antiques,* December 1986.

———, and Cheryl Leibold, *Writing about Eakins: The Manuscripts in Charles Bregler's Thomas Eakins Collection*, Pennsylvania Academy of the Fine Arts, University of Philadelphia Press, Philadelphia, Pennsylvania, 1989.

———, *Thomas Eakins Rediscovered: Charles Bregler's Thomas Eakins Collection at the Pennsylvania Academy of the Fine Arts*, Yale University Press, New Haven, 1997.

Frankenstein, Alfred, (review of Gordon Hendricks), *The Life and Work of Thomas Eakins, ARTnews*, vol. 74, May 1975, pp. 48–49.

Freud, Sigmund, edited by James Strachey and Anna Freud, *The Standard Edition of the Complete Psychological Works of Sigmund Freud,* The Hogarth Press, London, 1955.

———, *The Basic Writings of Sigmund Freud,* translated and edited by Dr. A. A. Brill, Modern Library, New York, 1995.

Freund, Kurt, Michael C. Seto, and Michael Kuban, "Frotteurism: The theory of courtship disorder," *Sexual Deviance: Theory, Assessment and Treatment*, Guilford, New York, pp. 111–130.

Freund, Kurt, Robin Watson, and Doug Rienzo, "The value of self-reports in the study of voyeurism and exhibitionism," *Annals of Sex Research*, vol. 1, no. 2, 1988, pp. 243–262.

Fried, Michael, "Realism, writing and disfiguration in Thomas Eakins's *Gross Clinic*," *Representations,* Winter 1985, pp. 33, 104.

———, *Realism, Writing, Disfiguration: On Thomas Eakins and Stephen Crane,* University of Chicago Press, Chicago, 1987.

Fryer, Judith, "The body in pain in Thomas Eakins' Agnew Clinic," *Michigan Quarterly Review*, Winter 1991, pp. 191–209.

Fuerstein, Laura A., "A case of exhibitionism: Self-hatred beneath a mask," *Current Issues in Psychoanalytic Practice*, vol. 1, no. 3, 1984, pp. 69–81.

Gay, Peter, *Freud, A Life for Our Time*, Norton, New York, 1988.

Gera, Vanessa, "Hitler seemed kind, says secretary," *The Plain Dealer*, Cleveland, February 12, 2002, p. A4.

Gerdts, William H., *The Great American Nude*, Praeger, New York, 1974.

———, *The Art of Healing: Medicine and Science in American Art,* Birmingham Museum of Art, 1981.

Gilliams, E. Leslie, *Lippincott's Monthly Magazine,* August 1893, pp. 249–253.

Gittleson, N. L, S. E. Eacott, and B. M. Mehta, "Victims of indecent exposure," *British Journal of Psychiatry*, vol. 132, 1978, pp. 61–66.

Goodbody, Bridget, "'The present opprobrium of surgery,' The Agnew Clinic and Nineteenth-Century Representations of Cancerous Female Breasts," *American Art,* Winter 1994, pp. 33–51.

Goodrich, Lloyd, unpublished notes of interviews with individuals who knew Thomas Eakins, Philadelphia Museum of Art.

———, *Kenneth Hayes Miller,* The Arts Publishing Co., New York, 1930.

———, *Thomas Eakins, His Life and Work,* Whitney Museum of American Art, New York, 1933.

———, Introduction to *Thomas Eakins Centennial Exhibition, 1844–1944,* Dept. of Fine Arts, Carnegie Institute, Pittsburgh, 1944.

———, "Thomas Eakins today," *American Magazine of Art* (later *Magazine of Art*), vol. 37, May 1944, pp. 162–166.

———, "Realism and Romanticism in Homer, Eakins and Ryder," *The Art Quarterly,* Detroit, Winter 1949, pp. 17–29.

———, "Thomas Eakins," in *Thomas Eakins: A Retrospective Exhibition*, National Gallery of Art, Art Institute of Chicago, Philadelphia Museum of Art, 1961.

———, "What is American in American art?" in *Art in America: What is American in American Art,* edited by Jean Lipman, McGraw-Hill, 1963.

———, *Raphel Soyer*, Whitney Museum of American Art, New York, 1968.

———, *Reginald Marsh*, Harry N. Abrams, New York, 1972.

———, *Thomas Eakins*, 2 vols, National Gallery of Art and Harvard University Press, Cambridge, Massachusetts, 1982.

Review of Lloyd Goodrich, *Thomas Eakins*, The London Studio, London, June 1933, p. 365.

Goodwin, Frederick K., and Kay Redfield Jamison, *Manic-Depressive Illness*, Oxford University Press, New York, 1990.

Gopnik, Adam, "Eakins in the wilderness," *The New Yorker*, December 26, 1994–January 2, 1995, pp. 80–87.

Gorman, Christine, "Incest comes out of the dark," *Time,* October 7, 1991.

Gray, Francine de Plessix, *At Home with the Marquis de Sade*, Simon & Schuster, New York, 1998.

Green, David, "Adolescent exhibitionists: Theory and therapy," *Journal of Adolescence,* vol. 10, no. 1, 1987, pp. 45–56.

Greenberg, Clement, "Some advantages of provincialism," *The Art Digest*, January 1, 1954.

———, *Art and Culture, Critical Essays*, Beacon, Boston, 1969.

Griffin, Randall C., "Thomas Anshutz: A study of his art and teaching," doctoral dissertation, University of Delaware, Spring 1994.

———, *Thomas Anshutz, Artist and Teacher*, Hecksher Museum in association with the University of Washington, Seattle, 1994.

———, "Thomas Eakins' construction of the male body, or 'Men get to know each other across the space of time'," *Oxford Art Journal*, vol. 18, no. 2, 1995, pp. 70–79.

———, *Homer, Eakins & Anshutz: The Search for an American Identity in the Gilded Age*, Pennsylvania State University Press, University Park, 2004.

Gross, Samuel D., *A Discourse on Bloodletting Considered as a Therapeutic Agent,* American Medical Association, Philadelphia, 1875, offprint from *Transactions of the American Medical Association,* vol. 26, copy in the Library of Congress.

Guerisk, Ue, "The flasher," in Weldon, E. V., and C. Van Velsen, *A Practical Guide to Forensic Psychotherapy*, Jessica Kingsley, London, 1996, pp. 155–160.

Guthrie, Douglas, *Lord Lister: His Life and Doctrine*, E. & S. Livingstone, Edinburgh, 1949.

Haller, John S., Jr., "Neurasthenia: The medical profession and the 'new woman' of the late nineteenth century," *New York State Journal of Medicine,* vol. 71, 1971.

Hardin, Jennifer, *The Nude in the Era of the New Movement in American Art: Thomas Eakins, Kenyon Cox, and Augustus Saint-Gaudens*, doctoral dissertation, Princeton University, November 2000.

Hartmann, Sadakichi, *A History of American Art*, vol. 1, L. C. Page, Boston, 1902.

Hartmann, Terje, and Od Havik, "Exploring curiosity: A curiosity-exhibitionism inventory, and some empirical results," *Scandinavian Journal of Psychology*, vol. 21, no. 2, 1980, pp. 143–149.

Hatt, Michael, "The male body in another frame: Thomas Eakins' *The Swimming Hole* as homoerotic image," *Journal of Philosophy and the Visual Arts*, 1993, pp. 9–21.

———, "Muscles, morals, mind: The male body in Thomas Eakins's Salutat," in Kathleen Adler and Marcia Pointon, eds., *The Body Imaged: The Human Form and Visual Culture since the Renaissance,* Cambridge University Press, 1993, pp. 57–69.

Haughom, Synnove, "Thomas Eakins' portrait of Mrs. William D. Frishmuth, Collector," *Antiques*, November 1973, pp. 836–839.

———, "Thomas Eakins' *The Concert Singer*," *Antiques,* December 1975, pp. 1182–1184.

Henderson, Helen, *The Pennsylvania Academy of the Fine Arts and Other Collections of Philadelphia,* L. C. Page, Boston, 1911.

Henderson, Philip, *Swinburne: Portrait of a Poet*, Macmillan, New York, 1974.

Hendricks, Gordon, "Thomas Eakins's Gross Clinic," *Art Bulletin*, March 1969, pp. 57–64.

———, "The Eakins portrait of Rutherford B. Hayes," *The American Art Journal*, Spring 1969, pp. 104–114.

———, *Thomas Eakins, His Photographic Works*, Pennsylvania Academy of the Fine Arts, Philadelphia, 1969.

———, letter to the editor, *The American Art Journal*, Fall 1971, p. 103.

———, *The Life and Work of Thomas Eakins*, Grossman, New York, 1974.

———, "Gross dereliction," *Art in America*, May 1976, p. 5.

Henley, Robert J., "A study of certain personality characteristics and common personality variables of twenty-five exhibitionists," *Dissertation Abstracts International*, vol. 36, 10-A, 1976, p. 6473.

Henri, Robert, *The Art Spirit,* J.B. Lippincott, Philadelphia, 1960.

Hering, Fanny Field, *Gérôme: The Life and Work of Jean-Léon Gérôme*, Cassell, N.Y., 1982

Hill, Paul, *Edward Muybridge*, Phaidon, London, 2001.

Hills, Patricia, "Thomas Eakins's Agnew Clinic and John S. Sargent's Four Doctors: Sublimity, decorum and professionalism," *Prospects*, vol. 2, 1987, pp. 217–230.

Hollender, Marc H., "Genital exhibitionism in men and women," in *Sexual Dynamics of Anti-Social Behavior,* 2nd ed., Charles C. Thomas Publisher, Springfield, Ill., pp. 119–131.

Homer, William Innes, "Attributing and Reattributing Thomas Eakins's Photography," paper, College Art Association of America, February 13, 1983.

———, "Who took Eakins's photographs?" *ARTnews*, May 1983, pp. 112–119.

———, assisted by John Talbot, "Eakins, Muybridge and the motion process," *Art Quarterly*, Summer 1963, pp. 194–216.

———, *Thomas Eakins, His Life and Art*, Abbeville, N.Y., 1992.

Hoopes, Donelson F., *American Narrative Painting*, Los Angeles County Museum of Art, 1974.

———, *Eakins Watercolors*, Watson-Guptil Publications, N.Y., 1991.

Hopper, Edward, "Charles Burchfield—American," *The Arts*, July 28, 1928, pp. 5–12.

Hoppin, Martha J., *Country Paths and City Sidewalks: The Art of J.G. Brown*, George Walker Vincent Smith Art Museum, Springfield, Mass., 1989.

Horley, James, "Cognitive-behavioral therapy with an incarcerated exhibitionist," *International Journal of Offender Therapy and Comparative Criminology*, vol. 39, no. 4, 1995, pp. 335–339.

Hoving, Thomas, "Our best artworks," *Connoisseur*, July 1984.

Hughes, Robert, *Nothing If Not Critical: Selected Essays on Art and Artists*, Alfred A. Knopf, New York, 1991.

Huhasz, Anne M., "Exhibitionism," *Journal of Research and Development Education*, vol. 16, no. 2, 1983.

Hyman, Neil, "Eakins's *Gross Clinic* again," *Art Quarterly*, Summer 1972, pp. 158–164.

Jacobs, Douglas, *The Harvard Medical School Guide to Suicide Assessment and Intervention*, ed. Douglas G. Jacobs, Jossey-Bass, San Francisco, 1998.

Jamison, Kay Redfield, *Touched with Fire: Manic-Depressive Illness and the Artistic Temperament*, Simon & Schuster, New York, 1993.

———, *An Unquiet Mind, A Memoir of Moods and Madness,* Random House, New York, 1995.

Johns, Elizabeth, "Thomas Eakins: A case for reassessment," *Arts Magazine*, May 1979, pp. 130–133.

———, "Drawing Instruction at Central High School and Its Impact on Thomas Eakins," *Winterthur Portfolio*, Chicago, Summer 1980, pp. 139–149.

———, "I. A. Painter: Thomas Eakins at The Academy of Natural Sciences," *Annual of the Academy of Natural Sciences of Philadelphia*, vol. 3, 1981–1982, pp. 43–51.

———, *Thomas Eakins: The Heroism of Modern Life,* Princeton University Press, Princeton, N.J., 1983.

———, "Thomas Eakins and 'pure art' education," *Archives of American Art Journal,* vol. 23, no. 3, 1983; reprinted in *Archives of American Art Journal: A Retrospective Selection of Articles*, vol. 30, nos. 1–4, 1990, pp. 71–76; reprinted in Mary Ann Calo, ed., *Critical Issues in American Art: A Book of Readings,* Icon Editions, Westview Press, Boulder, Colo., 1998.

———, review of "Lloyd Goodrich, *Thomas Eakins,*" *The Art Bulletin*, December 1983, pp. 702–704.

———, *Thomas Eakins: Image of the Surgeon*, with essays by Elizabeth Johns, Jerome J. Byleby, and Gert H. Breiger, The Walters Art Gallery, The Johns Hopkins Medical Institutions, Baltimore, 1989.

Jones, Amelia, "Dis/playing the phallus: Male artists perform their masculinities," *Art History*, December 1994, pp. 546–584.

Jones, Amelia, "'Clothes make the man': The male artist as performative function," *The Oxford Art Journal*, vol. 18, no. 2, 1995, pp. 18–32.

Jones, Ernest, *The Life and Work of Sigmund Freud, vol 1, The Formative Years and the Great Discoveries 1856–1900*, Basic Books, New York, 1953.

———, *The Life and Work of Sigmund Freud 1901–1919, Years of Maturity*, vol. 2, Basic, New York, 1955.

Jones, Ivor H., and Dorothy Frei, "Exhibitionism: A biological hypothesis," *British Journal of Medical Psychology*, vol. 52, no. 1, 1979, pp. 63–70.

Karfft-Ebing, Richard von, *Psychopathia Sexualis*, F. A. Davis, Philadelphia, 1892.

Karpman, Benjamin, *The Sexual Offender and His Offenses: Etiology, Pathology, Psychodynamics and Treatment*, Julian Press, Washington, D.C., 1957.

Katz, Leslie, "Thomas Eakins now," *Arts*, December 1956.

———, "The Eakins Press Foundation," in *Message from the Interior, The Eakins Press Foundation* [Exhibition Catalogue], December 10, 1992–January 30, 1993, Zabriskie Gallery, 724 Fifth Avenue, New York.

Kerouac, Jack, *On the Road*, Penguin, New York, 1995; first published 1957.

Kessler, Charles, "The realism of Thomas Eakins," *Arts Magazine*, January 1962, pp. 16–22.

Kimmerle, Constance, *Thomas Eakins' Exploration of the Mechanism and Laws of Human Expression and Understanding of Mental Effort and Creative Activity*, Doctoral dissertation, UMI Dissertation Services, Ann Arbor, Mich., 1989.

Kirstein, Lincoln, "Aid and comfort to Eakins," *The Nation*, May 15, 1972, p. 632.

———, "Walt Whitman and Thomas Eakins: A poet's and a painter's camera-eye," *Aperture*, Millerton, N.Y., vol. 16, no. 3, 1972.

Klein, Julia M., "Thomas Eakins: Rigor mortis or arrogance," *The Chronicle of Higher Education*, December 21, 2001.

Kline, Paul, "Sexual deviation: Psychoanalytic research and theory," *Variant Sexuality: Research and Theory*, Johns Hopkins University Press, Baltimore, Md., 1987, pp. 150–175.

Knowlton, Helen, *William Morris Hunt*, Curtis and Cameron, Boston, 1899 (1915 edition).

Kolarsky, Ales, and Jaroslav Madlafousek, "The inverse role of preparatory erotic stimulation in exhibitionists: Phallometric studies," *Journal of Sexual Behavior*, vol. 12, no. 2, 1983, pp. 123–148.

Kolarsky, Ales, Jaraslov Madlafousek, and Vladimira, Novotna, "Stimuli eliciting sexual arousal in males who offend adult women: An experimental study," *Archives of Sexual Behavior*, vol. 7, no. 2, 1978, pp. 79–87.

Kramer, Peter D., "Heartbreak house," *Psychiatric Times*, December 1987, pp. 3ff.

———, *Listening to Prozac*, Penguin, New York, 1997.

La Farge, John, *Considerations on Painting*, Macmillan, New York, 1908.

Laing, R. D., *The Divided Self: An Existential Study in Society and Madness*, Penguin, Baltimore, 1965.

Lamontage, Yve, and Alain Lesage, "Private exposure and covert sensitization in the treatment of exhibitionism," *Journal of Behavior Therapy & Experimental Psychiatry*, vol. 17, no. 3, 1986, pp. 197–201.

Lang, Reuben A., et al., "Genital exhibitionism: Courtship disorder or narcissism?" *Canadian Journal of Behavioural Science*, vol. 19, no. 2, 1987, pp. 216–232.

———, et al., "Sex hormone profiles in genital exhibitionists," *Annals of Sex Research*, vol. 2, no. 1, 1989, pp. 67–75.

Langevin, Ron, "Experimental studies of the etiology of genital exhibitionism," *Archives of Sexual Behavior*, vol. 8, no. 4, 1979, pp. 307–331.

Langevin, Ron, and Reuben A. Lang, "The courtship disorders," *Variant Sexuality: Research and Theory*, Johns Hopkins University press, Baltimore Md., 1987, pp. 202–228.

Langevin, Ron, et al., "An examination of brain damage and dysfunction in genital exhibitionists," *Annals of Sex Research*, vol. 2, no. 1, 1989, pp. 77–87.

Lears Jackson, T.J., *No Place of Grace: Antimodernism and the Transformation of American Culture 1880–1920*, Pantheon, New York, 1981.

Leja, Michael, "Eakins and icons," *The Art Bulletin*, September 2001, pp. 479–497.

Leonard, Jonathan, "Dreamcatchers: Unleashing the genius in the sleeping mind," *Harvard Magazine*, May–June 1998, pp. 58–68.

Lester, D., *Unusual Sexual Behavior: The Standard Deviations*, Charles C. Thomas, Springfield, Ill., 1975.

Levenson, J. C., "The etiology of Israel Adams: The onset, waning and relevance of Henry Adams's anti-Semitism," *New Literary History*, vol. 25, 1994, pp. 569–600.

Levi-Strauss, Claude, *Structural Anthropology*, Doubleday, New York, 1967.

Levine, Stephen B., ed., *Handbook of Clinical Sexuality for Mental Health Professionals*, Brunner-Routledge, Hove, N.Y., 2003.

Lewis, Michael J., "The realism of Thomas Eakins," *The New Criterion,* December 2001, pp. 27–32.

Lifton, Norma, "Thomas Eakins and S. Weir Mitchell: Images and cures in the late nineteenth century," *Psychoanalytic Perspectives on Art 2*, 1987, pp. 247–274.

Lipson, L., "Of mind and meals," *Health Revelations*, May 1997.

Long, Diana, "Eakins' Anew Clinic: The medical world in transition," *Transactions and Studies of the College of Physicians and Surgeons*, 5th series, vol. 7, 1985, pp. 26–32.

———, "The medical world of the Agnew Clinic: A world we have lost," *Prospects*, 2, 1987, pp. 185–198.

"Louvre Accepts Portrait by Eakins," *ARTnews*, March 5, 1932, p. 14.

Lubin, David M., "The Agnew Clinic," in *Act of Portrayal: Eakins, Sargent, James*, Yale University Press, New Haven, 1985, pp. 27–82.

———, "Projecting an image: The contested cultural identity of Thomas Eakins," *The Art Bulletin*, September 2002, pp. 510–522.

Lutz, Tom, *American Nervousness, 1903: An Anecdotal History*, Cornell University Press, Ithaca, N.Y., 1991.

Luxenberg, Alisa, "Inventing Thomas Eakins the photographer," *History of Photography,* Autumn 1995, pp. 247–251.

Maas, Jeremy, *Victorian Painters*, Barrie and Rockliff, Crescent Press, London, 1969.

Maletzky, Barry M., "Exhibitionism: Assessment and treatment," in *Sexual Deviance: Theory, Assessment, and Treatment*, Guilford, New York, 1997, pp. 40–74.

Mann, Horace, *Report on an Educational Tour in Germany, France, Holland and Parts of Great Britain and Ireland*, Simpkin Marshall, London, 1846.

Marceau, William, *William Rush 1756–1833: The First American Sculptor*, Pennsylvania Museum of Art, Philadelphia, 1937, pp. 28–29.

Marshall, W. L., et al., "Exhibitionists: Sexual preferences for exposing," *Behavior Research & Therapy*, vol. 29, no. 1, 1991, pp. 37–40.

Marshall, W. L., A. Ecles, and H. E. Barbaree, "The treatment of exhibitionists: A focus on sexual deviance versus cognitive and relationship features," *Behaviour Research & Therapy*, vol. 29, no. 2, 1991, pp. 129–135.

Marzio, Peter, *The Art Crusade: An Analysis of American Drawing Manuals, 1820–1860*, Smithsonian Institution Press, Washington, D.C., 1976.

Masson, Frederic, *J. L. Gérôme et son oeuvre*, Paris, no date.

Mather, Frank Jewett Jr., "Bryson Burroughs," in *The American Spirit in Art*, Yale University Press, New Haven, 1927.

———, "Thomas Eakins," in *Estimates in Art*, Series 2, Scribner, New York, 1931, pp. 201–231, reprinted from *International Studio*, January 1930.

Matthiesen, F.O., *American Renaissance: Art and Expression in the Age of Emerson and Whitman*, Oxford University Press, New York, 1941.

Mayor, A. Hyatt, "Photographs by Eakins and Degas," *The Metropolitan Museum of Art*, New Series, Summer 1944, pp. 1–7.

———, "The photographic eye," *The Metropolitan Museum of Art*, new series, Summer 1956, pp. 15–26.

McBride, Henry, "Thomas Eakins I" (Nov. 4, 1917) and "Thomas Eakins II" (Nov. 11, 1917), *The Flow of Art: Essays and Criticisms of Henry McBride*, selected with an introduction by D. C. Rich, Atheneum, N.Y, 1995, pp. 130–136; 136–139.

McCarthy, Fiona, *Eric Gill: A Lover's Quest for Art and God*, E. P. Dutton, New York, 1989.

McCaughey, Patrick, "Thomas Eakins and the power of seeing," *ArtForum*, December 1970, pp. 56–61.

McCauley, Anne, "The most beautiful of nature's works: Thomas Eakins's photographic nudes in their French and American contexts," in *Eakins and the Photograph, Works by Thomas Eakins and His Circle in the Collection of the Pennsylvania Academy of the Fine Arts*, edited by Susan Danly and Cheryl Leibold, The Pennsylvania Academy of the Fine Arts, Smithsonian Institution Press, Washington, D.C., 1994.

McCreary, Charles P., "Personality profiles of persons convicted of indecent exposure," *Journal of Clinical Psychology*, vol. 31, no. 2, 1975, pp. 260–262.

McGill, Douglas C., "Collection of 1,000 Eakins works sold," *The New York Times*, June 18, 1986.

McHenry, Margaret, *Thomas Eakins Who Painted*, Oreland, Penn., privately printed, 1947.

McKinney, Roland, *Thomas Eakins*, Crown, New York, 1942.

McQuillan, Melissa, "The art criticism of Michael Fried," *Marsyas*, vol. 15, 1970–72, pp. 86–102.

Merrill, Linda, et al., *After Whistler* [exhibition catalogue], High Museum of Art, Atlanta, 2003.

Meyer, Walter J., Collier Cole, and Evangeline Emory, "Depo provera treatment for sex offending behavior: An evaluation of outcome," *Bulletin of the American Academy of Psychiatry & the Law*, vol. 20, no. 3, 1992, pp. 249–259.

Miklowitz, Michael J., and Michael Goldstein, *Bipolar Disorder: A Family-Focused Treatment Approach*, The Guilford Press, New York, 1997.

Milroy, Elizabeth, *Thomas Eakins' Artistic Training, 1860–1870*, doctoral dissertation, University of Pennsylvania, UMI Dissertation Services, Ann Arbor, Mich., 1986.

———, "'Consumatum Est': A reassessment of Thomas Eakins' Crucifixion of 1880," *Art Bulletin*, June 1989, pp. 270–284.

Miner, Michael H., and S. Margretta Dwyer, "The psychosocial development of sex offenders: Differences between exhibitionists, child molesters, and incest offenders," *International Journal of Offender Therapy and Comparative Criminology*, vol. 41, no. 1, 1997, pp. 36–44.

Mitchell, S. Weir, "Clinical nervousness in the male," *The Medical News and Library*, vol. 35, December 1877, pp. 177–184.

———, *Fat and Blood, and How to Make Them*, Lippincott, Philadelphia, 1878.

———, *Lectures on Diseases of the Nervous System, Especially in Women*, Lippincott, Philadelphia, 1881.

———, *Wear and Tear, or Hints for the Overworked*, Lippincott, Philadelphia, 1897.

Mohr, J. W, R. E. Turner, and M. B. Jerry, *Pedophilia & Exhibitionisim: A Handbook*, University of Toronto Press, Toronto, 1964.

Moncreiff, Manus, and Dennis Pearson, "Comparison of MMPI profiles of assaultive and non-assaultive exhibitionist and voyeurs," *Corrective & Social Psychiatry & Journal of Behavior Technology, Methods & Therapy*, vol. 25, no. 3, 1979, pp. 91–93.

Money, John, "Paraphilia and abuse martyrdom: Exhibitionism as a paradigm for reciprocal couple conseling combined with antiandrogen," *Journal of Sex & Marital Therapy*, vol. 7, no. 2, 1981, pp. 100–104.

———, *Lovemaps: Clinical Concepts of Sexual-Erotic Health and Pathology, Paraphilia and Gender Transposition in Childhood, Adolescence and Maturity*, Ardent Media, Irvington, N.Y., 1986.

Moore, A. D., "Henry A. Rowland," *Scientific American*, February 1982, pp. 150–161.

Moore, Frazier, "Analyzing the man behind psychoanalysis," *The Plain Dealer*, Cleveland, November 27, 2002, *Arts and Life*, E11.

Moreau-Vauthier, Charles, *Gérôme, peintre et sculpteur*, Hachette, Paris, 1906.

Morgan, Charles, *George Bellows: Painter of America*, Reynal and Company, New York, 1965.

Morris, Harrison, *Confessions in Art*, Sears, New York, 1930.

Moynihan, Rodrigo, "The odd American," *ARTnews*, January 1971, pp. 50–53.

Mumford, Lewis, *The Brown Decades, A Study of the Arts in America,1865–1895*, Dover Publications, New York, first published 1931, reprint 1955.

Myers, Robert G., and Ellen F. Berah, "Some features of Australian exhibitionists compared with pedophiles," *Archives of Sexual Behavior*, vol. 12, no. 6, 1983, pp. 541–547.

Myers, Wayne A., "The course of treatment of a case of photoexhibitionism in a homosexual male," *The Homosexualities and the Therapeutic Process*, International Universities Press, Madison, Conn., 1991, pp. 241–249.

"National Academy of Design Exhibition," *Nation*, May 30, 1878, p. 364.

Neumayer, Alfred, "Art history without value judgment: Some recent appraisals of nineteenth-century art," *College Art Journal*, Summer 1970, pp. 420–421.

New York Daily Tribune, March 8, 1879, p. 22.

Nochlin, Linda, *Realism*, Penguin, New York, 1971.

———, "Issues of gender in Cassatt and Eakins," in Stephen F. Eisenman et al. eds., *Nineteenth-Century Art: A Critical History*, Thames & Hudson, New York, 2001.

Novak, Barbara, *American Painting of the Nineteenth Century*, Praeger, New York, 1969.

Olfson M.C., Mark, "The Weir Mitchell rest cure," *Pharos*, vol. 51, 1989.

Onerato, Ronald J., "Photography and teaching: Eakins at the Academy," *American Art Review,* July–August 1976, pp. 127–140.

Ottervik, Kathleen Virgin, *Thomas Eakins and the Image of Women,* doctoral dissertation, UMI Dissertation Services, Ann Arbor, Mich., 1995.

Owens, Gewndolyn, "Pioneers in American museums: Bryson Burroughs," *Museum News,* May–June 1979, p. 51.

Pach, Walter, "A grand provincial," *Freeman,* April 11, 1923, pp. 112–114, reprinted in *The Freeman Book,* B. W. Huebsh, New York, 1924.

Paer, William E., "Punishment and reward seekers in activities associated with voyeurism (scoptophilia) and exhibitionism," *Dissertation Abstracts International,* vol. 36, 6-B, 1975, p. 3062.

Parry, Ellwood C., III, "Thomas Eakins and the Gross Clinic," *Jefferson Medical College Alumni Bulletin,* Summer 1967, pp. 373–391.

———, "The Gross Clinic as anatomy lesson and memorial portrait," *Art Quarterly,* Winter 1969, pp. 373–391.

———, "The Eakins portrait of Sue and Harry: or when did the artist change his mind?" *Arts Magazine,* May 1979, pp. 146–153.

———, "Photographer Thomas Eakins" catalogue notes by Dr. Robert Stubbs, Olympia Galleries, Philadelphia, 1981.

———, "Thomas Eakins' 'Naked Series' reconsidered: Another look at the standing nude photographs made for the Use of Eakins' students," *American Art Journal,* vol. 20, 1988, pp. 53–77.

Parry, Ellwood C., and Maria Chamberlin-Hellman, "Thomas Eakins as an illustrator," *The American Art Journal,* May 1973, pp. 20–45.

Peale, Rembrandt, *Graphics: A Popular System of Drawing and Writing,* 4th ed., C. Sherman, Philadelphia, 1842.

Pennell, Joseph, *The Adventures of an Illustrator,* Boston, 1925, pp. 50–52.

Philadelphia Evening Bulletin, April 27, 1871.

Phillips, Harland, "Lloyd Goodrich reminisces," interview with Lloyd Goodrich by Harland Phillips, 1962, *Archives of American Art Journal,* vol. 20, no. 3, 1980, pp. 3–18.

Pointon, Marcia, "Psychoanalysis and art history: Freud, Fried, and Eakins," in *Naked Authority: The Body in Western Painting 1830–1908,* Cambridge University Press, Cambridge, 1990, pp. 35–58.

Poirier, Suzanne, "The Weir Mitchell rest cure: Doctors and patients," *Women's Studies,* vol. 10, 1983.

Porter, Fairfield, *Thomas Eakins,* George Braziller, New York, 1959.

Price, Vincent, *The Vincent Price Treasury of American Art,* Country Beautiful Corporation, Waukesha, Wis., 1972.

Prodger, Phillip, *Time Stands Still: Muybridge and the Instantaneous Photography Movement,* Oxford University Press, N.Y., 1993.

Prown, Jules David, "Thomas Eakins' *Baby at Play,*" in *Studies in the History of Art,* Washington, D.C., National Gallery of Art, 1985, vol. 18, pp. 121–127.

Raboch, Jiri, and Jan Raboch, "Number of siblings and birth order of sexually dysfunctional males and sexual delinquents," *Journal of Sex & Marital Therapy*, vol. 12, no. 1, 1986, pp. 73–76.

Reik, Theodor, *Sex in Man and Woman: Its Emotional Variations*, The Noonday Press, New York, 1960.

Rhoads, John M, and Enrique P. Borjes, "The incidence of exhibitionism in Guatemala and the United States," *British Journal of Psychiatry*, vol. 139, 1981, pp. 242–244.

Richardson, John, *A Life of Picasso, Vol. 1, 1881–1906*, Random House, New York, 1991.

Rickles, N. K., "Exhibitionism," *Journal of Nervous and Mental Disease*, vol. 95, 1942, pp. 11–17.

———, *Exhibitionism,* Lippincott, Philadelphia, 1950.

Rob, Graham, *Strangers: Homosexual Love in the Nineteenth Century*, Picador, New York, 2004.

Rooth, Graham, "Exhibitionism outside Europe and America, *Archives of Sexual Behavior*, vol. 2, no. 4, 1973, pp. 351–363.

Rorem, Ned, *Lies: A Diary, 1986–1999*, Counterpoint, Washington, D.C., 2000.

Rosenzweig, Phyllis D., *The Thomas Eakins Collection of the Hirshorn Museum and Sculpture Garden,* Smithsonian Institution Press, Washington, D.C., 1977.

Rotundo, E. Anthony, *American Manhood: Transformations in Masculinity from the Revolution to the Modern Era*, Basic Books, New York, 1993.

Rousseau, Louis, et al., "Effect of combined androgen blockage with an LHRH agonist and flutamide in one severe case of male exhibitionism," *Canadian Journal of Psychiatry*, vol. 35, no. 4, 1990, pp. 338–341.

Rule, Henry B., "Whitman and Thomas Eakins: Variations on some common themes," *Texas Quarterly*, Winter 1974, pp. 7–57.

Russakoff, Dale, "Out of grief comes a legislative force: From Megan's Law to Jimmy's and Jenna's," *The Washington Post*, June 15, 1998, pp. 1, A10.

Russell, John, "Thomas Eakins," in *Reading Russell: Essays 1941–1988,* Harry N. Abrams, New York, 1989.

Sacks, Oliver, *The Man Who Mistook His Wife for a Hat and Other Clinical Tales*, Perennial Library, New York, 1985.

Sandler, Irving, *The Triumph of American Painting: A History of Abstract Expressionism*, Harper & Row, New York, 1970.

Sartain, William, "Thomas Eakins," *The Art World*, January 1918, pp. 291–293.

Schendler, Sylvan, *Eakins*, Little, Brown, Boston, 1967.

Schjeldahl, Peter, "The surgeon," *The New Yorker*, October 22, 2001, p. 79.

Schneider, Richard D., "Exhibitionism: An exclusively male deviation?" *International Journal of Offender Therapy and Comparative Criminology*, vol. 26, no. 2, 1982, pp. 173–176.

Scott, William B., and Peter M. Rutkoff, *New York Modern: The Arts and the City*, The Johns Hopkins University Press, Baltimore, 1999.

Sellin, David, *The First Pose 1876, Turning Point in American Art. Howard Roberts, Thomas Eakins, and a Century of Philadelphia Nudes*, Norton, New York, 1976.

———, "Eakins and the Macdowells and the Academy" in *Thomas Eakins, Susan*

Macdowell Eakins, Elizabeth Macdowell Kenton: An Exhibition of Paintings, Photographs and Artifacts, September 18–October 2, 1977, Progress Press, Roanoke, Va., 1977.

———, *Thomas Eakins and His Fellow Artists at the Philadelphia Sketch Club,* exhibition catalogue, October 21–November 25, 2001, The Philadelphia Sketch Club.

Sewell, Darrell, *Thomas Eakins: Artist of Philadelphia,* Philadelphia Museum of Art, Philadelphia, 1982.

———, *Thomas Eakins,* organized by Darrell Sewell with essays by Kathleen A. Foster, Nica Gutman, William Innes Homer, Elizabeth Milroy, W. Douglas Paschall, Darrell Sewell, Marc Simpson, Carol Troyen, Mark Tucker, H. Barbara Weinberg, Amy B. Werbel, Philadelphia Museum of Art, Philadelphia, 2001.

Shahn, Ben, *The Shape of Content,* Random House, New York, 1957.

Shawn, Michelle Smith, *American Archives: Gender, Race and Class in Visual Culture,* Princeton University Press, Princeton, New Jersey, 1999.

Shinn, Earl, "Art study at the Imperial School in Paris," *The Nation,* April 15, 1868.

———, *A Century After: Picturesque Glimpses of Philadelphia and Pennsylvania,* Allen, Land & Scott & J. W. Lauderbach, Philadelphia, 1875.

Sicherman, Barbara, "The uses of diagnosis: Doctors patients, and neurasthenia," *Journal of the History of Medicine and Allied Sciences,"* vol. 32, 1977.

———, "The paradox of prudence: Mental health in the Gilded Age," *Journal of American History,* vol. 62, 1976.

Siedman, Bonnie T., et al., "An examination of intimacy and loneliness in sex offenders," *Journal of Interpersonal Violence,* vol. 9, no. 4, 1994, pp. 518–534.

Siegl, Theodor, *The Thomas Eakins Collection,* introduction by Evan H. Turner, Philadelphia Museum of Art, Philadelphia, 1978.

Silverstein, Judith, "Exhibitionism as countershame," *Sexual Addiction and Compulsivity,* vol. 3, no. 1, 1996, pp. 33–42.

Simenon, Georges, *The Cat,* Harcourt Brace, New York, 1976.

Simpson, Marc, "Thomas Eakins and his Arcadian works," *Smithsonian Studies in American Art,* Fall 1987, pp. 71–95.

Singer, Barton, "Defensiveness in exhibitionists," *Journal of Personality Assessment,* vol. 43, no. 5, 1979, pp. 526–531.

Smith, Carl R., "The Boxing Paintings of Thomas Eakins," *Prospects: An Annual of American Cultural Studies,* ed. Jack Salzman, New York, 1979, vol. 4, p. 411.

Smith, Dinitia, "'Queer Theory' is entering the literary mainstream," *Arts & Ideas, The New York Times,* January 17, 1998, B9, B11.

Smith, Margaret Suplee, "The Agnew Clinic: 'Not cheerful for ladies to look at,'" *Prospects,* vol. 2, 1987, pp. 217–230.

Smith, Shawn Michelle, *American Archives: Gender, Race, and Class in Visual Culture,* Princeton University Press, Princeton, N.J., 1999.

Smith-Rosenberg, Carroll, *Disorderly Conduct: Visions of Gender in Victorian America,* Alfred A. Knopf, New York, 1985.

Smukler, Arthur J., and Douglas Sheiebel, "Personality characteristics of exhibitionists," *Diseases of the Nervous System,* November 1975, pp. 600–603.

Snaith, R. Philip, "Exhibitionism: A clinical conundrum," *British Journal of Psychiatry*, vol. 143, 1983, pp. 231–235.

Snook, Debbi, "Animal and human abuse linked, studies show," *The Plain Dealer*, Cleveland, January 7, 2002, A4.

Snyker, Elizabth C., "Treatment of exhibitionism in intensive short-term dynamic psychotherapy," *International Journal of Short-Term Psychotherapy*, vol. 7, no. 1, 1992, pp. 13–30.

Solomon, Maynard, *Beethoven*, Schirmer Books, New York, 1998.

Sontag, Susan, *On Photography*, Farrar, Straus & Giroux, New York, 1977.

Sotheby Parke-Bernet, *Olympia Galleries: Important Collection of Photographs by Thomas Eakins*, New York, November 10, 1977, n.p.

Soyer, Raphael, edited by Rebecca L. Soyer, *Hommage to Thomas Eakins*, A.S. Barnes and Company, Inc., Thomas Yoseloff Publisher, South Brunswick, N.J., 1966.

Soyer, Raphael, *Diary of an Artist*, New Republic Books, Washington, D.C., 1997.

Spies, Kathleen, "Figuring the neurasthenic: Thomas Eakins, nervous illness, and gender in Victorian America," *Nineteenth Century Studies*, vol. 12, 1998, pp. 84–109.

Stafford-Clark, David, *What Freud Really Said*, with a foreword by Elizabeth Young-Bruehl, Schocken Books, N.Y., 1965, reprinted 1997.

Steinberg, Leo, "Art/work: Eakins and Gérôme," *ARTnews*, February 1972, pp. 34–35.

Stone, Alan A., "Where will psychoanalysis survive," *Harvard Magazine*, January–February 1997, pp. 35–39.

Sutton, Peter, "Analogues in the modality of realism: The early works of Eakins and Whitman," unpublished paper, Yale University, 1976.

Taylor, Francis Henry, "Thomas Eakins—Positivist," *Parnassus*, March 1930, pp. 20–21, 43.

Tinterow, Gary, and Genevieve Lacombre, *Manet/Velasquez: The French Taste for Spanish Painting*, Metropolitan Museum of Art, New York, Yale University Press, New Haven, 2003.

Tomkins, Calvin, *Merchants and Masterpieces: The Story of the Metropolitan Museum of Art*, E. P. Dutton, New York, 1970.

Toohey, Jeanett M., "The Pennsylvania Academy of the Fine Arts: An idea and a symbol," *Pennsylvania Heritage*, Spring 1988, pp. 16–23.

Trilling, Lionel, "Art and neurosis," in *The Liberal Imagination: Essays on Literature and Society*, Viking, New York, 1950, pp. 160–180.

Truettner, William H., "Dressing the part: Thomas Eakins' portrait of Frank Hamilton Cushing," *American Art Journal*, Spring 1985, pp. 48–72.

Turano, Jan Van N., ed., "In honor of Lloyd Goodrich, 1897–1987," *American Art Journal,* vol. 20, no. 2, 1988, 14 pages, unpaginated.

Turner, Evan H., *Saint Charles Borromeo Seminary, Overbook*, catalogue of exhibition of portraits by Eakins, Philadelphia, April–May 1970.

———, "Thomas Eakins in Overbrook," *Records of the American Catholic Historical Society of Philadelphia*, December 1970, pp. 195–198.

Van Buren, Abigail, and Jeanne Phillips, "Nude sister-in-law needs modest rebuff," *The Plain Dealer*, Cleveland, January 7, 2002, p. E8.

Veenhuizen, A. M, D. C. Van Strien, and P. T. Cohen-Kettenis, "The combined psy-chotherapeutic and lithium carbonate treatment of an adolescent with exhibition-ism and indecent assault," *Journal of Psychology & Human Sexuality*, vol. 5, no. 3, 1992, pp. 53–64.

Vachss, Andrew, "Sex predators can't be saved," *The New York Times*, op-ed, January 5, 1993, A11.

Wagner, Edwin E., "Projective test data from two contrasted groups of exhibition-ists," *Perceptual & Motor Skills*, vol. 39, no. 1, 1974, pp. 131–140.

Wallach, Alan, "Elizabeth Johns, *Thomas Eakins: The Heroism of Modern Life*," *Archives of American Art Journal*, vol. 24, no. 4, 1984, pp. 21–24.

Walter, Marjorie Alison, *Fine Art and the Sweet Science, On Thomas Eakins, His Boxing Pictures, and Turn-of-the-Century Philadelphia*, doctoral dissertation, University of California, Berkeley, UMI Dissertation Services, Ann Arbor, Mich., 1995.

Warren, John F., *Art Books Catalogue 29*, 124 South 19th Street, Philadelphia, Pennsylvania.

Watson, Forbes, "Comment [on Eakins]," *The Arts*, March 1923, p. 225.

———, "About Thomas Eakins," *The Arts*, October 1931, p. 27.

———, "Bryson Burroughs," *Parnassus*, January 1935, p. 3.

Wawrose, Frederick E., and Timothy S.M. Sisto, "Clomipromine and a case of exhibi-tionism," *American Journal of Psychiatry*, vol. 149, no. 6, 1992, p. 843.

Weber, Bruce, *American Paintings XI*, Berry-Hill Galleries, New York, 2004.

Weidner, Irwin Ruth, "George Cochran Lambdin," in *George Cochran Lambdin, 1830–1896*, exhibition September 6–November 23, 1986, Brandywine River Museum, Chadds Ford, Penn., 1986.

Weigley, Russell F., ed., *Philadelphia: A 300-Year History*, Norton, New York, 1982.

Weinberg, Ephraim, "The Art School of the Pennsylvania Academy," *Antiques*, March 1982, pp. 690–693.

Weinberg, H. Barbara, *The American Pupils of Jean-Léon Gérôme*, Amon Carter Museum, Fort Worth, Tex. 1984.

———, *The Lure of Paris: Nineteenth-century American Painters and Their French Teachers*, Abbeville Press, New York, 1991.

———, with a contribution by Jeff L. Rosenheim, *Thomas Eakins and the Metropolitan Museum of Art*, *Metropolitan Museum of Art Bulletin*, vol. 52, no. 3, Winter 1994–1995.

Werbel, Amy Beth, *Perspective in the Life and Art of Thomas Eakins*, doctoral disserta-tion, UMI Dissertation Services, Ann Arbor, Mich., 1996.

Whelan, Richard, "Thomas Eakins: The enigma of the nude," *Christopher Street*, April 1979, pp. 15–18.

White, Nelson C., "Franklin L. Schenck," *Art in America*, February 1931, pp. 84–87.

Whitehill, Walter Muir, *Museum of Fine Arts, Boston, A Centennial History*, Harvard University Press, Cambridge, Mass., 1970.

Williams, Herman Warner Jr., *Mirror to the American Past: A Survey of American Genre Painting: 1750–1900*, New York Graphic Society, Greenwich, Conn., 1973.

Williams, Tommy Carroll, *The Teaching Philosophy of Thomas Eakins*, doctoral disserta-tion, University of Oklahoma, 1973.

Wilmerding, John, *American Art, The Pelican History of Art,* Penguin, New York, 1976.

———, review of Gordon Hendricks, *The Life and Works of Thomas Eakins, The Art Bulletin,* June 1976, pp. 311–312.

———, ed., *Thomas Eakins, 1844–1916, and the Heart of American Life,* exhibition catalogue, London, National Portrait Gallery, Smithsonian Press, Washington, D.C., 1993.

Wilson, Edmund, "Philocrates: The wound and the bow," in Edmund Wilson, *The Wound and the Bow: Seven Studies in Literature,* Houghton Mifflin, Cambridge, Mass., 1941, pp. 272–295.

Wilson, Glenn D., ed., *Variant Sexuality: Research and Theory,* Johns Hopkins University Press, Baltimore, 1987.

Wilson, Rob, "Sculling to the over-soul: Louis Simpson, American transcendentalism, and Thomas Eakins's *Max Schmitt in a Single Scull,*" *American Quarterly,* Fall 1987, pp. 410–430.

Winokur, George, Paula Clayton, and Theodore Reich, *Manic Depressive Illness,* C.V. Mosby Company, St. Louis, Mo., 1969.

Woodward, Richard B., "Doubting Thomas: A legendary painter's methods are finally exposed," *Lingua Franca,* October 2001, pp. 58–66.

———, "The truth is out: How realists could be so realistic," *The New York Times,* November 25, 2001, Art/Architecture, p. 34.

WPA Guide to Philadelphia: A Guide to the Nation's Birthplace, University of Philadelphia Press, Philadelphia, 1988.

Young, Dorothy Weir, *The Life and Letters of J. Alden Weir,* Yale University Press, New Haven, 1960.

Zalewski, Daniel, "Old masters cheated," The Year in Ideas, *The New York Times Magazine,* December 9, 2001, section 6, p. 86.

Zechnich, Robert, "Exhibitionism: Genesis, dynamics and treatment," *Psychiatric Quarterly,* vol. 45, no. 1, 1971, pp. 70–75.

Zeltner, Brian, "CWRU discovery opens paths in behavior research," *The Plain Dealer* Cleveland, February 24, 2003, p. C3.

Zohar, Joseph, Zeev Kaplan, and Jonathan Benjamin, "Compulsive exhibitionism successfully treated with fluvoxamine: A controlled case study," *Journal of Clinical Psychiatry,* vol. 55, no. 3, 1994, pp. 86–88.

INDEX

A. W. Lee (Eakins), 401, *402,* 410

Abbey, Edwin A., 409

Academic Nudes (Igout), *282*

Academy (Plato), 321

Act of Portrayal: Eakins, Sargent, James
(Lubin), 45

The Actress (Eakins), 346, 377, *378*
honesty of, 378–79, 401
parallels in, 435, 467
women's portrayal and, 396

Addie (Eakins), 367–69, *368,* 370–72
parallels in, 471

Addie Williams (Eakins), *98*

Adelman, Seymour, 4, 279

*African-American Girl Nude, Reclining on
Couch* (Eakins), *56,* 285

Agnew, D. Hayes, 390, 437
The Agnew Clinic and, 235–39, 397
background of, 235, 237–38

The Agnew Clinic (Eakins), 102, 121, *235*
content of, 235–37
Freudian analysis of, 240
Gross Clinic comparisons to, 237–40
interpretations of, 45, 239–41
rejection of, 13, 234, 240–41
themes of, 241, 466, 474
transference in, 240–41
voyeurism in, 239
women's portrayal in, 392

Ahrens, Ella, 336

Albright, Adam Emory, 120, 266–67, 269

*Allegorical Figure of the Schuylkill River
(Nymph with Bittern)* (Rush), 244–45,
246
models for, 248–49

Allegory of the Waterworks (Rush), 246,
247

Allen, David, 432

*Amelia Van Buren. See Miss Amelia Van
Buren*

*Amelia Van Buren Sitting with Cat On
Shoulder* (Eakins), *347*

American Art Society, 13

American Narrative Painting, 308

American Nervousness (Lutz), 466

American Renaissance, 307

The Anatomy Lesson of Dr. Deyman (Rembrandt), *225,* 226

The Anatomy Lesson of Dr. Nicolaas Tulp
(Rembrandt), *224,* 225

Annie C. Lochrey Husson (Eakins), 385, *385,*
409

Anshutz, Thomas, 51, *104,* 482
Eakins criticisms by, 61, 103, 104–5,
494n9
Eakins photography and, 271–72, 275,
321
legacy of, 269, 514n29

Antiquated Music (Portrait of Sarah Sage-horn Frishmuth) (Eakins), 376–77, *377*, 411

Antrim, William, 410

Arcadia (Eakins), *299*, 299–300, 312, 417
buttock representation in, 418

An Arcadian (Eakins), *300*, 300–301

Archbishop James Frederic Wood (Eakins), 333

Archbishop William Henry Elder (Eakins), 376–77, *377*, 409

Aristotle, xiv

Art Amateur, 296, 327

Art Bulletin, 47

Art Collector, 362

Art Interchange, 216

Art Journal, 216, 296

Art News, 384

Art Students League, 258, 321, 340
creation of, 336
dissolution of, 346
nudity and, 115, 293–94

Art Students Union, 260, 336

The Artist's Wife and His Setter Dog. See *Portrait of the Artist's Wife with a Setter Dog*

The Artist and His Father Hunting Reed Birds (Eakins), 185–87, *186*

The Arts, 16, 19

Artwork, Eakins. *See also* Interpretations (art); Paintings, Eakins; Perspective; Rowing portraits, Eakins; *specific artwork*
Casts of Anatomical Dissection, 267
construction of, 181–84
destruction of, 409–12
emotional components of, 386–90
exhibitions of, xiv, 14, 15–16, 28, 46–47
father paintings in, 185–91, 363, *363*
frames for, 526n62
gender codes in, 191
honesty of, 396–97, 399–402, 464–65
Knitting sculpture as, 323

men's portrayal in, 390–92, 394–95
modernism and, 471–72
mother paintings and, 171, *171*
negative reactions to, 13, 215–18, 234, 240–41, 407–12
outdoor scenes in, 181–87
Parisian catalogue of, 149
Pastoral sculpture as, *285*, 298, *302*, 302–3
perspective use in, 138, 207–12, 265, 352, 467–68
posing process for, 396–99, 466
preferred subjects for, 390–91, 396–97
realism v. slander in, 402–6
reproductions of, 244
sibling portraits in, *164*, 165–69, *166*, 173–76, *175*, 178–81, *179*, 467
Spinning sculpture as, 257, 323
style of, 154–55, 157–58, 167–69, 184–85
suffering in, 389–90
technique in, 467–68
themes, despair, in, 337–42
themes, repetitive, in, 306, 469, 473–74
themes, subversive, in, 465–68, 470–72
transference in, 193–95, 199–200, 204, 227–35, 240–41, 249–51, 253, 255, 380–81, 416, 473–74
uniqueness of, 383–90
wife paintings by, 8, 29–30, 326–31, *328*, *329*, 363–64, *364*
women's portrayal in, 191, 345–55, 377–79, 388–90, 391–96, 433, 471
work speed and, 397–98

At the Piano (Eakins), *166*, 166, 173

Avondale farm, 69, *70*

Baby at Play (Eakins), *81*, 81–82, 191
themes of, 449, 497n31

Bache, Alexander Dallas, 137

Bachrach, A. W., 402

Bacon, Peggy, 19

Balthus, 464

Barber, Alice, 91, 112, 419
  Eakins criticisms by, 51, 55, 64, 107, 448
Barnes, Albert, 13
Barr, Alfred H., Jr., 16, 25
Baskin, Leonard, 27
Bathing Beauties on the Hudson (Inman),
  311, *311*
Beaux, Cecilia, 100
Bellows, George, 26
Benjamin Eakins Standing, and Man Sitting, under Tree (Eakins), 277
Benton, Thomas Hart, 20
Berger, Martin A., 46, 93
  Chess Player interpretations by, 188, 190
  Eakins misogyny and, 108
  Eakins sexuality and, 320
Bertillon, Alphonse, 338
Between Rounds (Eakins), 357, 358, *360*,
  361
Biglin Brothers Racing (Eakins), 201, *201*,
  206
Biglin Brothers Turning the Stake (Eakins),
  192, 206–7
  alterations to, 337
  content of, 202–4
  discrepancies in, 204–5
  pricing of, 243
  transference in, 204
Bill Duckett Nude, Lying on Stomach, Holding Vase (Eakins), *289*, 289–90
Bishop, Isabel, 19
Blakelock, Ralph Albert, 342
Blashfield, Edwin, 155
Boggs, Joseph, 197
The Bohemian (Eakins), 338, 342, *342*
Bonnat, Leon, 154–55, *155*, 157
  The Crucifixion by, 296–97
  influence of, 158
  style of, 387
Book of American Figure Painters (Van
  Rensselaer), 327, 329
Borie, Adolph, 407
Bowden, Mrs. W. H., 394, *394*

Breezing Up (Homer), 183, *183*
Bregler, Charles, *43*, 483
  artwork of, 269
  Eakins biographies and, 36, 41
  Eakins memorabilia and, 42–43
  Eakins, Susan, and, 39
Bregler papers, 46
  discovery of, xiii
  Goodrich use of, 11–12
  history of, 42–45
Breuer, Joseph, 446
Bridgman, Frederick, 149
Bringing Home the Cattle, Coast of Florida
  (Moran), 217
Brinton, John H., 390
Brook, Alexander, 19
Brooklyn Art Guild, 346
Brown, J. G., 168
Brownell, William C., 260
The Brown Decades (Mumford), 16
Bruegel, Pieter, 15
Bryant, Walter Copeland, 399
B-T Ranch, Dakota Territory, 335–36
Buckley, Edward S., 410
Burchfield, Charles, 18, 20
Burie, Adolph, 35, 397
Burroughs, Alan, 16
Burroughs, Betty, 20
Burroughs, Bryson, 20, 331, 473
  background of, 14–15, 18
  influence of, 15–17
Burton, Elizabeth, 35, 91
Buttocks, 419
  Gross Clinic depiction of, 231–32, 241,
    418
  interpretations, Eakins fixation on,
    418–19, 443
  Swimming depiction of, 241, 306, 315–19,
    325, 418–19
  William Rush representation of, 241,
    306, 418
Byrnes, Thomas, 338
Byron, George, 455

Cadmus, Paul, 268, 282

Caffin, Charles, 14

Camille, 379

Candide (Voltaire), 103

Carmelita Requena (Eakins), 159

Carnegie International Exhibition, 13

Carpeaux, Jean-Baptiste, 146

Carville, Elizabeth, 91

Casanova, 314

Cassatt, Mary, 149, 389

Casts of Anatomical Dissection (Eakins), 266–67, 267

Centennial Exhibition, 23, 178, 215–16

Cézanne, Paul, 15

The Champion Single Sculls (Champion) (Eakins), 165, 195, 202, 206m, 215
  complexity of, 334
  content of, 197–99, 203, 205
  reproduction of, 244
  transference in, 194–95, 199–200, 204

Chartran, Theobold, 406

Chase, William Merritt, 119, 249
  art by, 330
  Eakins portrait by, 412
  Eakins portrait of, 391
  nudity and, 111

The Chess Players (Eakins), 187–91, 189, 190
  parallels of, 471
  perspective in, 209

Chesterton, G. K., 469

Cikovsky, Nicolai, 338, 385

Civil War, U.S., 140, 340

Claghorn, James, 52

Clara Mather Sitting in Carved Armchair (Eakins), 286

Clark, William, 215–16, 296, 402–3

Clymer, Mary, 236, 239–40

Coates, Edward Horner, 98, 323
  Agnew Clinic and, 240–41
  background of, 322–23, 482
  Eakins relations with, 322–26, 443
  nudity and, 55, 113, 274

Coleridge, Samuel Taylor, 455

Colt, Samuel, 220

Common Sense (Paine), 39

Comstock, Anthony, 14, 113

Comstock Law, 113

The Concert Singer (Eakins), 8, 37, 72, 352
  content of, 351–52, 393
  emotional components of, 386, 435
  making of, 90, 352–53
  ownership of, 410
  parallels in, 353, 354, 435, 467, 522n49
  perspective use in, 352
  success of, 346

Connard, Charlotte, 51, 482

Cook, Maud, 354–55, 355, 393, 484

Cook, Weda, 83, 87, 107. *See also The Concert Singer*
  background of, 351, 484
  Crowell, Ella, threat to, 72–73, 450
  Eakins nudity fixation and, 90, 91, 92, 110
  Eakins sexuality and, 98–99, 368
  portrait of, 72, 90, 351–54, 352, 393, 410, 435

Cooper, Colin Campbell, Jr., 51, 61, 321

Cooper, Emanuel, 308, 312

Cooper, Helen, 18, 28, 45, 108

Cooper Union, 346

Corcoran Museum of Art, 324

Corless, Elizabeth, 94, 407–8

The Courtship (Eakins), 257

Couture, Thomas, 154, 157, 162

Cowboys in the Badlands (Eakins), 421

Cowperthwaite, Eliza (Aunt Ella), 5–6, 39, 479

Cowperthwaite, Mark, 172

Cox, Kenyon, 111

Cranmer, Clarence, 357, 362, 362
  Eakins sexuality and, 97, 99

Crawford, Thomas, 138

Cresson, H. C., 115

Criticisms (of Eakins)
  Anshutz, 61, 103, 104–5, 494n9
  Barber, 51, 55, 64, 107, 448

critique of motivational, 114–19
critique of nudity, 110–13
critique of peculiarity, 119–23
critique of sodomy rhetoric in, 113–14
Crowell, Ella, 6–7, 72, 80–81, 105, 108,
    114, 353, 418, 448–54
Crowell, Frances Eakins, 74–77, 82–83,
    106
Crowell, William, Sr., 74–77, 82–83, 106,
    419
Foster responses to, 104–5, 108
Goodrich responses to, 105–12, 114,
    120–22
Hammitt, Lillian, 103, 105, 108
Sartain, Emily, 89–90
Smith, Jessie, 107
Stephens, Caroline, 61–64, 106–7
Stephens, Frank, 51, 61–66, 103, 106, 174,
    416, 419
truthfulness and, 108–9
women's perspective in, 106–8, 112
Crowell, Benjamin (Ben), 71, 77–79, 83,
    481
Crowell, Elizabeth, 480
    portraits of, 8, 9, 166, 176, 177–78, 330
Crowell, Ella, 5, 233, 481
    abuse reconstruction and, 452–53
    behavioral critique of, 450–51
    career shift by, 72–73
    death of, 6, 41, 69, 73, 334, 356, 416, 420
    Eakins portrait of, 81, 81–82
    Eakins studies with, 71–72
    Eakins, Susan, memorandum on,
        74–80, 114
    family influence on, 449–50
    interpretations, Eakins and, 449–54
    mental condition of, 72–74, 103, 105,
        108, 420, 445, 455
    molestation charges involving, 6–7, 72,
        80–81, 103, 105, 108, 114, 353, 418,
        448–54
    photographs of, 68, 71
    portraits of, 80–82, 81, 91, 191, 449

Crowell, Frances, 83
Crowell, Frances Eakins, 39, 71, 480
    daughter's suicide and, 69–80, 450
    Eakins accusations by, 74–77, 82–83, 106
    Eakins break with, 82–83, 334, 356, 420
    Eakins defense by, 64–66
    lifestyle of, 69–71
    mental health of, 454–55
Crowell, Kathrin, 8, 37–38, 44, 480
    background of, 448
    portrait of, 166, 176–77, 177, 345
Crowell, Margaret (Maggie), 5, 71, 481
    Eakins accusations by, 77–79, 114
Crowell, William, Jr., 65, 121
Crowell, William, Sr., 5–6, 39, 94, 480
    character of, 69–70
    daughter's suicide and, 69–80
    Eakins accusations by, 74–77, 82–83,
        106, 419
    Eakins break with, 82–83, 334, 356, 420
    Eakins defense by, 64–66, 170
    photographs of, 68, 71
The Crucifixion (Bonnat), 296, 297
The Crucifixion (Eakins), 8, 8, 9, 321
    alterations to, 337
    religious content in, 296–97
Cryer, Matthew H., 407
Culin, Stewart, 391
Currier and Ives, 196
Cushing, Frank Hamilton, 94, 391, 391,
    396

Da Costa, Jacob Mendez, 391, 411, 411
Daily Evening Telegraph, 215
Danto, Arthur, 312
Davis, Whitney, 46, 129, 310, 312
Dead Christ (Mantegna), 226, 226
The Dean's Roll Call (Eakins), 400, 401,
    409–10
Degas, Edgar, 144, 180, 352
Delacroix, Eugene, 21, 245
Delaroche, Paul, 258

Delaware County Republican, 404
Demuth, Charles, 104
Depression
  chemistry of, 457–59
  creativity link to, 455–56, 535n5
  Eakins family, 420, 445, 454–57
  exhibitionism link to, 458–59
  genetic components of, 172, 454–55
  interpretations, Eakins and, 454–61
  manic, 170–72, 507n16
  treatments for, 459–61
Dewing, Thomas, 328
*Diagnostic and Statistical Manual of Mental
    Disorders,* 171
Dickinson, Edwin, 27–28
Dobbs, John, 28
Dodge, Mrs. James Mapes, 394, 475
  Eakins peculiarities and, 92, 294
  portrait reception by, 407, 410
  posing process and, 92, 398–99
Dougherty, Denis, 376
Douty, Mrs. Nicholas, 91, 96
Douty, Nicholas, 368
Doyle, Jennifer, 46, 113, 117–19
  Eakins sexuality and, 308–9
  exhibitionism and, 422
  Swimming interpretation by, 322
Dr. George H. Brinton (Eakins), 333
Dr. Horatio Wood (Eakins), *335*
Drexel Institute, 13, 66, 346
Du Maurier, George, 447
Duckett, Bill, *289,* 289–90, 292–93, 419
Dumas, Alexandre, 112
Dumont, Augustin, 153
Dunbar, Elizabeth, 91
Dunk, Walter, 482

Eakins (Schendler), 25
Eakins, Benjamin, 3, 39, 99, *134,* 479
  background of, 134–36
  child punishment and, 443
  Eakins art and, 151–53

family quarrels and, 66, 69–70
  father-son relations and, 185–91, 443
  portraits of, 185–91, 362, *362, 363, 363*
Eakins, Caroline, 5, *60,* 95, 479. *See also*
    Stephens, Caroline Eakins
  portraits of, 166, 174–76, *175*
Eakins, Caroline Cowperthwait, *170, 171,*
    479
  background of, 171
  behavioral manifestations of, 435–36
  death of, 173, 507n12
  Eakins art parallels to, 350–51, 353–54,
    434–36, 466–67, 471, 473–74, 523n73
  Eakins interpretation of, 437–38
  mental health of, 169–73, 433–37
  portraits of, 171, *171*
Eakins, Frances, *70,* 151, 479. *See also*
    Crowell, Frances Eakins
  education of, 101
  home of, 5–6
  portraits of, *164,* 166, *166,* 169, 173
Eakins, Margaret, 5, *62,* 95, 367
  death of, 39–40
  incest charges regarding, 6, 64, 173–74,
    416, 448, 453
  mental health of, 454–55
  portraits of, 166, 173–76, *175,* 178–81, *179,*
    467
Eakins, Susan Macdowell, 4, 16, *37, 38,* 480
  background of, 135, 448
  bias of, 36, 40–41
  Bregler papers and, 42
  career of, 5–6, 101, 515n2
  Crowell, Ella, memorandum by, 73–80,
    114
  depression of, 420, 445
  Eakins paintings of, 8, 29–30, 302,
    326–31, *327, 328, 329, 337,* 363–64, *364,*
    393, 520nn50–51, 523n73
  Eakins photography and, 279, *284, 285,*
    291, 292, 301, 312, 326
  Eakins, Thomas, portraits by, 236–37,
    350, *351*

Hammitt scandal and, 85, 88

marital relations of, 37–40, 313, 331, 440, 532n76

sexuality of, 38, 98

Swimming titling by, 306–7

Eakins, Thomas, 479. *See also* Artwork, Eakins; Criticisms (of Eakins); Family, Eakins; Instruction, Eakins; Interpretations, Eakins; Literature (on Eakins); Parisian studies, Eakins; Photographs (of Eakins); Photography (by Eakins); Scandal(s), Eakins

Academy conflicts of, 3, 12, 23–24, 30, 50–59, 258–65

analysis, Freudian, of, 126–29, 227–34

animal treatment by, 420–21, 529n3

art instruction by, 259–61, 265–69, 336–37

artist-sitter boundaries and, 54–57

bronze of, *102*, 121–22, 337

Burrough, Bryson, influence on, 14–17

buttock representations by, 231–32, 241, 306, 315–19, 325, 418–19, 443

character, moral, of, 25–26, 30, 31, 113–14, 469

characteristics, personal, of, 29, 31–36

class attitudes by, 145–47, 324

clergy associations of, 374–77

coarse behavior by, 53–54, 96–97

Crowell, Ella, portraits by, 80–82

Crowell, Ella, suicide and, 69–80, 450

Crowells' break with, 82–83, 334, 356, 419–20

death of, 3, 40, 343, 534n109

drug use by, 461

education of, 137–42, 148–63

exhibitionism by, 293–94, 320–26, 422–28, 470

family background of, 134–37

family quarrels of, 51, 61–67, 69–70, 72, 74–77, 80–83, 103, 106–7, 174, 334, 356, 416, 419–20

father-son relations and, 185–91, 443

fidelity of, 97–99, 368, 372, 416, 442

fixation, floor, by, 120–22, 475

fixation, gun, by, 119–20, 421–22, 442

fixation, milk, by, 122–23, 460–61

fixation, nudity, by, 52–53, 90–94, 110–19, 417–18, 466

fixation, underclothing, by, 251–52, 372–73

Gérôme relations with, 142, 153–55, 188, 212–13, 228

Hammitt scandal and, 85–88, 440, 445–48, 453

home of, *2, 3–9,* 335

incest charges against, 6, 57, 64, 173–74, 416, 448, 453

marital relations of, 37–40, 313, 331, 532n76

mental health of, 335–36, 420, 454–56

molestation charges against, 6–7, 72, 80–81, 103, 105, 108, 114, 353, 418, 448

motivations of, 114–19

Murray's relationship with, 39–40, 308, 343, 444

paintings of, *95, 351, 365, 366, 412*

Parisian period of, 136–37

peculiarities of, 119–23

perception of families by, 437–40

perception of mother by, 437–38

photographs of, *xii, 9, 33, 38, 121, 122, 124, 132, 287–88, 334, 381, 414, 462, 472, 474, 475, 477*

revival of, 11–17

rise to glory by, 25–28

rivalries of, 328–29, 364

self-exposure by, 55–57, 94–99

sexual misconduct and, 6–7, 57–59, 72, 80–81

sexuality of, 97–99, 233, 307–11, 368, 372, 416, 440–44

Soyer tribute to, 26–28

spouse paintings by, 8, 29–30, 326–31, *328, 329,* 363–64, *364*

Eakins, Thomas (continued)
  student organizations and, 61, 66, 115,
      260, 336–37
  studios of, 3, 7, 7
  technique of, 467–68
  truthfulness of, 108–9
  Williams, Addie, relations with, 98,
      368, 372, 416, 448
  women's treatment by, 21, 99–101, 112,
      117–19, 128–29, 312–13, 388–94, 451,
      468
  work speed of, 397–98
East, W. N., 424
École des Beaux-Arts, 141, 148–49
Edward H. Coates (Vonnoh), *323*
Elder, Henry, 376–77, *377*, 409
Eliot, T. S., 463
Elizabeth at the Piano (Eakins), 8, *9*, *178*
  content of, 330–31
  perspective in, 209, *210*
Elizabeth Crowell and Her Dog (Eakins),
      177–78, *178*
Elizabeth Macdowell in Print Dress
      (Eakins), *63*
Ella Crowell (Eakins), *68*
Ellensweig, Allen, 308
Ellis, Havelock, 424
England Society for the Suppression of
      Vice, 113
Entretien sur l'atelier (Couture), 154
Esten, John, 308
The Execution of Marshal Ney (Gérôme),
      144
Exhibitionism. *See also* Freudian theory;
      Voyeurism
  approaches to, 428–30
  artwork, 293–94, 320–26, 470
  characteristics of, 424–25, 428
  childhood links to, 427–28, 431–37,
      474–76
  classification of, 529*n*8
  depression links to, 458–59
  Eakins, 293–94, 320–26, 422–28, 470

Freudian theories on, 424, 429–33,
      436–37
  goals of, 424
  homosexuality ties to, 444, 531*n*65
  incest ties to, 449, 452–53
  interpretations on Eakins, 422–28, 470
  motivations behind, 425–26, 429–30,
      441
  nudity and, 293–94
  offender identities in, 427
  treatment for, 426
  voyeurism connection to, 423, 435–36
Exposition Universelle, 13

*The Fairman Rogers Four-in-Hand (May
      Morning in the Park)* (Eakins), 37,
      263, 264, *264*
Family, Eakins
  background of, 134–37
  Crowell quarrels amongst, 6–7, 72–77,
      80–83, 106, 334, 356, 418–20, 449–50
  interpretations regarding, 419–20,
      433–40, 443
  Stephens quarrels amongst, 51, 61–66,
      72, 103, 106–7, 174, 416, 419
  transference involving, 193–95,
      199–200, 204, 227–35, 240–41, 249–51,
      253, 255, 380–81, 416
Fantin-Latour, Henri, 27, 352
Fat and Blood (Mitchell), 460
Female Nude Semireclining, from Rear
      (Eakins), *295*
Female Nude Sitting on Queen Anne Chair
      (Eakins), *56*
Fitzgerald, Ritter, 388, 391
Flagg, James Montgomery, 359
Flaherty, James, 376
Flam, Jack, 423, 440
Force, Juliana, 19, 20
Fosburgh, James, 167, 254
Foster, Kathleen, 36, 44, 61, 74
  Crowell, Ella, interpretation by, 450

Eakins criticism critiques by, 104–5, 108
Eakins sexuality and, 309–10, 440–41
exhibitionism and, 422–23, 427
Hammitt, Lillian, and, 445
Stephens, Frank, and, 448
Fox, Benjamin, 321, 420, 445, 483
France, 141–42, 148–63. *See also* Parisian
studies, Eakins
Frances Eakins (Eakins), *164*, 166, 173
Frank Hamilton Cushing (Eakins), 391, *391*,
396
Franklin, Benjamin, 399
Freedom (Crawford), 138
French, Jared, 282
Freud, Sigmund, 126–29, 193, 227–34, 240
hysteria and, 446, 531n71
Freudian theory. *See also* Transference
Agnew Clinic analysis using, 240
castration fear in, 429, 430–32, 436–37,
466
exhibitionism and, 423, 430–33
Gross Clinic analysis using, 227–34
Oedipal conflict in, 232–33, 240, 431–33,
443
transference in, 127–28
Fried, Michael, 45, 129, 423
Eakins, Caroline, and, 433
Eakins sexuality and, 308
Gross Clinic interpretations by, 45–46,
223–34, 416, 463–64, 511n29
Frishmuth, Sarah Sagehorn, 376–77, *377*,
411. *See also Antiquated Music*
Frost, Arthur Burdett, 269
Fry, Roger, 15
Fussell, Charles, 94, *95*, 139, 417
art by, 427
Fussell, Rebecca, 170–71

*A Game Two Can Play At. See The Music
Lesson*
Gardel, Bertrand, 189
Gargantua (Rabelais), 241

Garvey, Patrick J., 376, 409, 410
George Barker (Eakins), 388
George Morris (Eakins), 408
George Washington (Rush), 246
Gerdts, William, 18, 308
Gérôme, Jean-Léon, 22, 141, *142*, 196
art instruction by, 144–45
artwork of, 142–44, *143*, 153–54, 162, 245,
252–53
Eakins relations with, 142, 153–55, 188,
212–13, 228, 443
perspective use by, 208
Gest, John B., 387, *387*, 408
Gill, Eric, 454
Gillespie, Elizabeth Duane, 399
Girl in a Big Hat (Eakins), *84, 393*
Girl with a Cat-Kathrin (Eakins), 176–77,
177, 345
Godley, Jesse, 51, 321, 418, 482
Goedel, Kurt, 463
Goldstein, Michael J., 465
Goodbody, Bridget, 236, 239
Goodrich, Lloyd, 4, 8, 10, *10*, 448. *See also
Thomas Eakins, His Life and Work*
Amelia Van Buren interpretations by,
349
background of, 18–20
biography materials used by, 11–12
Crowell, Ella, and, 72–74, 450
The Crucifixion interpretation by, 297
Eakins biography by, 11–12, 18, 20–25,
46–47
Eakins, Caroline, and, 433
Eakins character use and, 384
Eakins clothing fixation and, 372–73
Eakins criticism critiques by, 105–12,
114, 120–22
Eakins homage and, 28, 473
Eakins honesty and, 401–2, 407–8, 463
Eakins nudity fixation and, 90–94, 423,
427
Eakins photography and, 272–73, 275
Eakins self-exposure and, 94–99

Goodrich, Lloyd (continued)
  Eakins sexuality and, 306, 308–10
  Eakins teaching and, 269
  essay by, 223
  falsifications, interview, by, 36–41
  falsifications, personality, by, 31–35, 133,
    249
  gender bias by, 107–8
  Gross Clinic interpretations by, 223–24,
    227
  musical painting interpretations by,
    167, 169
  perception of, 17–18
  Portrait of the Artist's Wife interpreta-
    tions by, 29–30, 331
  William Rush interpretations by, 249,
    253, 371
  Williams, Addie, portraits and, 367–68
Goodyear, Charles, 220
Gopnik, Adam, 308
Goupil, Adolph, 143
Graphics (Peale), 137
Grayson, Clifford, 67
The Great American Nude (Gerdts), 308
Greek art, 298–99
Greenberg, Clement, 390
Greenewalt, Mary Hallock
  parallels using, 393–94
  portrait of, *373*, 373–74
  posing by, 91, 398
Griffin, Randall, 46, 312, 320
Gross, Samuel, 23, 194, *229*, 390
  background of, 221–23, 238
  Eakins relationship with, 443
  The Gross Clinic and, 216, 218, 223,
    227–34, 397
The Gross Clinic (Eakins), 25, 27, 165, 177
  Agnew Clinic comparisons to, 237–40
  buttock exposure in, 231–32, 241, 418
  complexity of, 334
  content of, 215, 218–20, 227
  detail of, *229*
  Doyle interpretations of, 118–19
  elements borrowed in, 225–27

Freudian analysis of, 227–34
Fried interpretations of, 45–46, 223–34,
    416, 463–64
gender messages in, 255
Goodrich interpretations of, 223–24,
    227
ink and watercolor, *219*
Johns interpretations of, 221, 222–27
oil on canvas, *214*
parody of, *234*, 234–35
rejection of, 215–18, 240
reproduction of, *244*
themes of, 230, 241, 306, 325, 443, 466,
    474
transference in, 194, 227–35
voyeurism in, 233–34
women's representation in, 191, 345,
    391, 433
Guino, Richard, 337
Gutman, Nica, 275

Hail Caesar! (Gérôme), *143*
Hall, Douglass Morgan, *332*, *339*, 410, 483
  sanity of, 340, 420, 445
Hammitt, Charles, 86
Hammitt, Lillian, 6, *233*, 334, 418
  background of, 85–86, 483
  characteristics of, 88
  critiques of, 103, 105, 108
  diagnosis of, 445–47, 531n71
  Eakins influence on, 440, 447–48, 453
  interpretations on Eakins and, 445–48
  mental condition of, 86–87, 105, 108,
    416, 420
  portraits of, *84*, 91, *393*
Hannah Susan Macdowell (Eakins), 291,
    292
Harper's Monthly, 196
Harper's Weekly, 196
Harrison, Margaret, *276*
Hartmann, Sadakichi, 14, 358
Haseltine Galleries, 403
Hatt, Michael, 46, 308

Hayes, Rutherford B., 333, 402–4, 409
Heade, Martin Johnson, 186
Heffernan, Joanna, 330
Heisenberg, Werner, 463
Helmick, Howard, 149
Hemingway, Ernest, 455
Henderson, Helen, 14
Hendricks, Gordon, 41, 72, 90, 98
    Agnew Clinic interpretation by, 237
    Concert Singer interpretation by, 351
    Eakins, Caroline, and, 433
    Eakins photography and, 273, 275, 280
    Eakins sexuality and, 307–8, 343
    gender observations by, 394–95
    Husson interpretations by, 385, 409
    John B. Gest interpretation by, 387, 408
    scholarship accuracy of, 492n81
Henri, Robert, 25, 26
Hering, Fanny, 143
Hirshhorn Museum, 43, 138
History of American Art (Hartmann), 14, 358
History of American Painting (Isham), 387
The History of Impressionism (Rewald), 28
Holland, James W., 400, 401, 409–10
Holmes, George, 189
Holmes, Sherlock, 169
Homage to Eugene Delacroix (Fantin-
    Latour), 27
Homage to Thomas Eakins (Soyer), 27, 27–28
Home Ranch (Eakins), 344–46, 345
Home Scene (Eakins), 166–67, 174–76, 175
Homer, William Inness, 46, 108, 136, 183
    Amelia Van Buren interpretation by, 348
    Eakins photography and, 272
    Eakins sexuality and, 309–10, 368
    gender observations by, 451
    Portrait of the Artist's Wife interpreta-
        tion by, 327
Homer, Winslow, 14, 15–16
    Eakins comparisons to, 24, 111
The Homoerotic Photograph (Ellensweig),
    308
Homosexuality
    exhibitionism ties to, 444, 531n65

interpretations on Eakins and, 444
nineteenth century, 339
Swimming and, 307–11, 315–20, 444
Homosexuality in Art (Cooper), 308
Hoopes, Donelson, 308
Hopper, Edward, 18, 20, 26
    Eakins art and, 27, 166
Hughes, Robert, 26
Human Pool Tables (Marsh), 10
Huntington, David, 18
Husson, Annie C., 385, 385, 394, 409
Husson, Louis, 91, 362, 362, 385, 385, 394
Huttner, Henry, 141

I-Box (open) (Morris), 472, 473
Identification anthropometrique (Bertillon),
    338
Igout, Louis, 282
In Grandmother's Time (Eakins), 257
Incest
    bond establishment through, 448–49
    Crowell, Ella, and, 6–7, 72, 80–81, 103,
        105, 108, 114, 353, 418, 448–54
    definitions of, 453, 533n93
    Eakins, Margaret, and, 6, 64, 173–74,
        416, 448
    effects of, 453–54
    exhibitionism ties to, 449, 452–53
    interpretations on Eakins and, 416–17,
        448–54
    repetitive elements of, 416–17
Ingres, Jean-Auguste-Dominique, 157,
    245
Inherited Syphilis (Maury / Duhring), 283
Inman, John O'Brien, 311
Instruction, Eakins
    anatomy, 265–67
    constraints on, 260–61
    effectiveness of, 268–69
    nude studies in, 259, 265
    perspective, 265
    student organization, 336–37
    style of, 267–68

Interpretations (art), 470
  Agnew Clinic, 45, 236, 237, 239–41
  Amelia Van Buren, 348–50
  The Artist and His Father, 187
  Champion, 197, 199–200
  Chess Player, 188, 190
  Concert Singer, 351, 353
  The Crucifixion, 297
  Gross Clinic, 45–46, 118–19, 220, 222–34,
    416, 463–64, 511n29
  John B. Gest, 387, 408
  Old Fashioned Dress, 409
  Pastoral, 302
  Portrait of the Artist's Wife, 29–30,
    326–27, 331
  Portrait of Samuel Murray, 344
  Swimming, 306, 312–22, 324–26
  William Rush, 243–44, 249–55, 250, 253,
    369, 371
Interpretations, Eakins. See also Depres-
    sion; Exhibitionism
  compulsive nudity, 417–18
  Crowell, Ella and, 449–54
  depression and, 454–61
  exhibitionism, 422–33, 470
  familial conflict, 419–20
  family, 419–20, 433–40, 443
  father's influence, 443
  fixation, buttock, and, 418–19, 443
  fixation, guns, and, 421–22, 442
  Hammitt, Lillian and, 445–48
  homosexuality and, 444
  incest, 416–17, 448–54
  mental illnesses and, 420, 445
  mother's influence, 433–37
  reoccurring Eakins elements, 416–22
  sexual motivation, 440–43
Isham, Samuel, 387
Ives, Charles, 463

J. Laurie Wallace Nude, Playing Pipes, Fac-
    ing Left (Eakins), 270, 291

James Hammill and Walter Brown, in Their
    Great Five Mile Rowing Match (Cur-
    rier and Ives), 196
James, Henry, xv, 386, 455
James, William, 455
Jamison, Kay Redfield, 172, 454–55
Janvier, Catherine A., 96
Jefferson Medical College, 22, 25, 140, 221
  Eakins artwork at, 217
John Biglin in a Single Scull (Eakins), 211
Johns, Elizabeth, 108, 138
  Agnew Clinic interpretations by, 236
  Champion interpretations by, 197,
    199–200
  Eakins book by, 25–26, 28, 45
  Eakins essay by, 30–31, 223
  Eakins music paintings and, 167, 174
  Eakins photography and, 281
  Eakins representations by, 473
  Eakins sexuality and, 440
  Gross Clinic interpretations by, 220,
    223–24, 227
  Pastoral interpretation by, 302
  Swimming interpretation by, 321
  William Rush interpretations by,
    249–55, 369
Jordon, Letitia Wilson, 372, 392
Josie (boat), 197
Joyce, James, 463

Kandinsky, Wassily, 463
Karpman, Benjamin, 427
Katz, Leslie, 25, 30, 253, 331
  William Rush interpretations by, 371
Keen, William W., 258
Kelly, James P., 51, 61, 482
Kelly, William J., 44
Kenton, Elizabeth MacDowell, 42, 116
Kenton, Louis, 480. See also The Thinker
  portrait of, 362, 362, 383–84, 384, 410
Kershaw, Jennie Dean, 392
Kimball, Fiske, 16

Kirstein, Lincoln, 281–82, 307

Knitting (Eakins), 323

Koch, John, 27

Krimmel, John Louis, 247, 251

Kuniyoshi, Yasuo, 16

Kurosawa, Akira, xv

Kurtz, Alice, 91, 398

Kurtz, William B., 399

La Farge, John, 24, 111, 308, 352, 463

Lady Agnew of Lochnaw (Sargent), 398

Lady with a Setter Dog. See Portrait of the Artist's Wife with a Setter Dog

Laing, R. D., 436

The Lange Lizzen of the Six Marks (Lady of the Lijsen) (Whistler), 329–30, *330*

Latrobe, Benjamin, 244

Lee, Ashbury, 401, *402*, 410

Leibold, Cheryl, 44

Leja, Michael, 198

Leonard, Charles Lester, 391

Leslie's Illustrated Magazine, 196

Letitia Wilson Jordon (Eakins), 372

Levine, Jack, 27

Lewis, Anna, 394, *395*

Leydendecker, Joseph, 359

The Libyan Sibyl (Michelangelo), 15

The Life and Work of Thomas Eakins (Hendricks), 41

Linton, Frank, 342, 407, 408

Lippincott's Magazine, 245, 249

Lister, Joseph, 222–23

Literature (on Eakins)
    Bregler papers and, 42–45
    falsifications in, 31–35, 463, 468
    modern, 45–47
    oddities in, 28–31
    passive-aggressive figurem in, 35–36
    post-Goodrich, 41–45
    trustworthiness in, 36–41

The Little Confectioner (Couture), *154*

Loincloth scandal, 3

boundary issues and, 54–57

coarse behavior and, 53–54

Goodrich account of, 23–24, 51–52, 54–58

Johns account of, 30, 50

nude emphasis and, 12, 52–53

sexual misconduct and, 57–59

Lonesome Cowboys, 309, 344

Long Day's Journey Into Night, xiv

Louis Husson (Eakins), 385, *385*

Low, Will, 110

Lubin, David, 45, 47, 368

Lucie-Smith, Edward, 279–80

Lutz, Tom, 466

Luxenberg, Alisa, 273

Lynes, George Platt, 282

Macbeth, William, 36

MacDowell, Elizabeth, 51, 419, 480. *See also* Kenton, Elizabeth MacDowell

MacDowell, Susan, 3, *276*. *See also* Eakins, Susan Macdowell

Macdowell, Walter, 9, 64, 480

Macdowell, William G., 64, 480

Macdowell, William H., 39, 135, 480
    Eakins relations with, 228

Mack, Joe, 359, *359*

Madrazo, Federico, 155

Madrazo, Raimundo, 406

Mahon, Edith, *382*, 386, *395*

Male Nude, Poised to Throw Rock, Facing Right (Eakins), *290*

Male Nude Sitting on Modeling Stand, Holding Small Sculpture of Horse (Eakins), *56*

Male Nudes in a Seated Tug-of-War (Eakins), *316*

"The Male Body" (Hatt), 308

Manet, Edouard, 158, 245

Manic-depression disorder, 171–72, 507n16

Mann, Horace, 137

Mantegna, Andrea, 226

Mapplethorpe, Robert, 309

Marceau, Henri, 249

Marey, Etienne-Jules, 272

Margaret Eakins and Thomas Eakins's setter Harry (Eakins), 62

Margaret in Skating Costume (Eakins), 178–79, *179, 467*

Marks, William D., 272, 391

Marsh, Fred Dana, 19

Marsh, Reginald, 10, 18, 19
  art by, 20, 107
  Eakins support by, 16, 26, 27

Mary Adeline Williams (Eakins), 367–69, *368,* 370–72

Mary Sears (Bonnat), 157

Massenet, Jules, 351

Matthew H. Cryer (Eakins), 407

Matthiessen, F. O., 307

Maud Cook (Eakins), 354–55, *355,* 377–78, 393

May Morning in the Park. See *The Fairman Rogers Four-in-Hand*

McBride, Henry, 40, 237

McCarthy, Fiona, 454

McCaughey, Patrick, 384, 386, 387

McCormick, Cyrus, 220

McHenry, Margaret, 41, 65, 120, 367
  anatomy classes and, 267
  Eakins death and, 534n109
  Eakins nudity and, 92–94
  Portrait of the Artist's Wife and, 326

McKeever, Charlie, *359,* 359–60, 410

McKnight, Helen, 407

McMonnies, Frederick, 110

Meeker, Joseph, 186

Melville, George, 392

Melville, Herman, 455

Men of Progress (Schussele), 220

Mendelssohn, Felix, 351

Mending the Net (Eakins), 275, *278*

Las Meninas, 226, 227

Mental conditions. *See also* Depression; Exhibitionism

bipolar, 454–56

depression and, 170–72, 420, 445, 454–61, 459–61, 507n16

hysteria, 446–47

Interpretations on Eakins and, 420, 445

neurasthenia, 392–93

Obsessive-Compulsive Personality Disorder and, 456

Metropolitan Museum of Art
  Burrough collections at, 14–16
  Eakins artwork at, 14, 15–16, 46, 331

Michelangelo (Buonarroti), 15

Midnight Cowboy, 344

Miller, Kenneth Hayes, 19

Miller, Leslie, 324, *400,* 400–401

Millhouse, Barbara, 401

Milowitz, David, 465

Miss Amelia Van Buren (Eakins), 346, *347,* 354
  content of, 348–49, 373, 393
  emotional component of, 386, 435
  honesty of, 399–400
  parallels in, 350–51, 354

Miss Anna Lewis (Eakins), 394, *395*

Miss Eleanor S. F. Pue (Eakins), 373–74, *374,* 407

Mitchell, S. Weir, 339, 392, 454, 460–61

Moellder, Henry, 409

Monsignor James P. Turner (Eakins), *380,* 380–81, *381*

Moore, Humphrey (Harry), 145, 148, 158, 474

Moran, Thomas, 218

Moreau-Vauthier, Charles, 143

Morgan, George T., 254

Morris, George, 408

Morris, Harrison, 13, 96, 397, 461

Morris, Mrs. George, 407–8

Morris, Robert, 472, *473*

Morse, Samuel, 220

Motivations
  criticisms regarding Eakins, 114–19
  Eakins, 114–19

exhibitionist, 425–26, 429–30, 441
interpretations of sexual, 440–43
Moynihan, Rodrigo, 167
Mrs. Edith Mahon (Eakins), *382,* 386, 395
Mrs. Frishmuth. See Antiquated Music
Mrs. George Morris (Eakins), 407–8
Mrs. Helen McKnight (Eakins), 407
Mrs. James Mapes Dodge (Eakins), 394
Mrs. M. S. Stokes (Eakins), 401
Mrs. Mary Hallock Greenewalt (Eakins),
    373, 373–74, 393–94
Mrs. Thomas Eakins (Eakins), 363–64, *364*
    parallels in, 523n73
Mumford, Lewis, 16
Murray, Samuel, 36, 77, 94, 483
    art by, *102,* 110, 121–22, 334, 337
    background of, 343, 374
    Eakins peculiarities and, 121–22
    Eakins relationship with, 39–40, 308,
        343, 444
    photography and, 275
    portraits of, *343,* 343–44, *345,* 362, *362*
    success of, 269
    Williams, Addie, and, 368, 442
Musée d'Orsay, 46
Museum of Modern Art, 16
*The Music Lesson (A Game Two Can Play
    At)* (Brown), *168,* 168–69
Muybridge, Eadweard, 263, *264*
    background of, 271–72, 482
My Hustler, 309
Myers, Samuel, 397

Naked Series: Female Model (Eakins),
    48
Naked Series: John Laurie Wallace (Eakins),
    48
*Naked Series: Thomas Eakins in Front of
    Cloth Backdrop, Pose 1* (Eakins), *472*
The Nation, 216, 250
National Academy of Design, 13, 346
    exhibitions at, 201–2

membership at, 365
oversight of, 258
    Thomas B. Clarke prize at, 388
National Liberal League, 113
National Portrait Gallery, 348
Nelson, Mrs. L. B., 86
Neurasthenia, 392–93
New York Daily Tribune, 216
New York Society for the Suppression of
    Vice, 14
New York Sun, 388
New York Times, 26, 28, 216, 251, 386, 388
The Night Watch (Rembrandt), *225,* 226
Nochlin, Linda, 108, 388–90, 468
Novak, Barbara, 21
Nudity. *See also* Buttocks
    Academic Nudes and, 282
    androgyny and, 291–93
    eroticism and, 281–86
    exhibitionist, 293–94
    fixation, Eakins, on, 52–53, 90–94,
        110–19, 417–18
    friend and student, 286–90
    Inherited Syphilis and, 283
    interpretations, Eakins and, 417–18
    justifications for, 114–19
    loincloth scandal and, 12, 23–24, 30,
        52–53
    models and, 115–16, 250, 259–60
    morality ties to, 113
    outdoor excursion, 290–91, 324
    pastoral setting, 297–303
    photography, Eakins, use of, 279–303
    Pornographic Nude and, 283
    professional use of, 280–81
    sexual ties to, 117–19
    use, general, of, 104, 110–11, 248–49,
        500n18
    voyeuristic, 294–95
nudity
    Art Students League and, 115, 293–94
*Nymph with Bittern. See Allegorical Figure
    of the Schuylkill River*

"O Rest in the Lord" (Mendelssohn), 351, 353

Oarsmen on the Schuylkill (Eakins), 205–6, 206

The Oarsmen (Eakins), *203*

O'Doherty, Brian, 21

O'Donovan, William, 391, 412

Ogden, Robert Curtis, 404–6, *405*, 410

The Old Swimming Hole. See Swimming

The Old-Fashioned Dress (Eakins), 91, *375*, 380, 398

    content of, 373–74, 393–94

    honesty of, 400–401, 409

    parallels in, 435

    photograph for, 376

    reaction to, 407

Olympia Galleries (Philadelphia), 273, 279

O'Neill, Eugene, xiv

Paine, Thomas, 39

Painting Human Pool Tables (Marsh), *10*

Paintings, Eakins. *See also* Artwork, Eakins; Perspective; Photography (by Eakins); Rowing portraits, Eakins; *specific paintings*

    A. W. Lee, 401, *402*, 410

    The Actress, 346, 377–79, *378*, 380, 396, 401, 435, 467

    Addie, 367–69, *368*, 370–72, 471

    Addie Williams, 98

    The Agnew Clinic, 13, 45, 102, 121, 234, 235, 235–41, 392, 466, 474

    Annie C. Lochrey Husson, 385, *385*, 409

    Antiquated Music, 376–77, *377*, 411

    Arcadia, 299, 299–300, 312, 417, 418

    An Arcadian, 300, 300–301

    Archbishop James Frederic Wood, 333

    Archbishop William Henry Elder, 376–77, *377*, 409

    The Artist and His Father Hunting Reed Birds, 185–87, *186*

    At the Piano, 166, *166*, 173

    Baby at Play, *81*, 81–82, 191, 449, 497n31

    Between Rounds, 357, 358, *360*, 361

    Biglin Brothers Racing, 201, *201*, 206

    Biglin Brothers Turning the Stake, 192, 202–7, 243, 337

    The Bohemian, 338, 342, *342*

    Carmelita Requena, 159

    The Champion Single Sculls, 165, 194–95, 195, 197–201, 202–6, 244, 334

    The Chess Players, 187–91, *189*, 190, 209, 471

    The Concert Singer, 8, 37, 72, 90, 346, 351–54, *352*, 386, 393, 410, 435, 467, 522n49

    The Courtship, 257

    Cowboys in the Badlands, 421

    The Crucifixion, 8, *8*, 9, 296–97, 321, 337

    The Dean's Roll Call, 400, 401, 409–10

    Dr. George H. Brinton, 333

    Dr. Horatio Wood, *335*

    ecclesiastical, 374–77

    Elizabeth at the Piano, 8, 9, 178, 209, *210*, 330–31

    Elizabeth Crowell and Her Dog, 177–78, *178*

    The Fairman Rogers Four-in-Hand, 37, 263, *264*, 264

    feminine clothing's relevance in, 372–74

    Frances Eakins, 164, *166*, 173

    Frank Hamilton Cushing, 391, *391*, 396

    George Barker, 388

    George Morris, 408

    Girl in a Big Hat, 84, 393

    Girl with a Cat-Kathrin, 176–77, *177*, 345

    The Gross Clinic, 25, 27, 45–46, 118–19, 165, 177, 191, 194, 214, 215–41, 219, 244, 255, 306, 325, 334, 345, 391, 416, 418, 433, 443, 463–64, 466, 474

    Hayes, Rutherford, 333, 402–4, 409

    Home Ranch, 344–46, *345*

    Home Scene, 166–67, 174–76, *175*

    In Grandmother's Time, 257

    John Biglin in a Single Scull, 211

    Letitia Wilson Jordon, 372

Louis Husson, 385, *385*

Margaret in Skating Costume, 178–79, *179*, 467

Mary Adeline Williams, 367–69, *368*, 370–72

Matthew H. Cryer, 407

Maud Cook, 354–55, *355*, 377–78, 393

Mending the Net, 275, *278*

Miss Amelia Van Buren, 346–51, *347*, 354, 373, 386, 393, 399–400, 435

Miss Anna Lewis, 394, *395*

Miss Eleanor S. F. Pue, 373–74, *374*, 407

Monsignor James P. Turner, *380*, 380–81, *381*

Mrs. Edith Mahon, *382*, 386, 395

Mrs. George Morris, 407–8

Mrs. Helen McKnight, 407

Mrs. James Mapes Dodge, 394

Mrs. M. S. Stokes, 401

Mrs. Mary Hallock Greenewalt, *373*, 373–74, 393–94

Mrs. Thomas Eakins, 363–64, *364*, 523n73

Oarsmen on the Schuylkill, 205–6, *206*

The Oarsmen, 203

The Old-Fashioned Dress, 91, 373–74, *375*, *376*, 380, 393–94, 398, 400–401, 407, 409, 435

The Pair-Oared Shell, *202*, 206

Perspective of a Lathe, 138

Portrait of an Artist, 338

Portrait of the Artist's Wife with a Setter Dog, 29–30, 302, 326–31, 337, 364, 520nn50–51

Portrait of Benjamin Eakins, 363, *363*

Portrait of Douglass Morgan Hall, *332*, 339–40, 410

Portrait of Dr. Jacob Mendez da Costa (Eakins), 391, 411, *411*

Portrait of an Engineer, 338

Portrait of John B. Gest, 387, *387*, 408

Portrait of a Poet, 338

Portrait of Professor Benjamin H. Rand, 333, 337–38, *338*

Portrait of Samuel Murray, *343*, 343–44

Portrait of a Student, 338

Professor Henry A. Rowland, 356–57, *357*, 391, 456

Professor Leslie W. Miller, *400*, 400–401

Pushing for Rail, 184, *184*

A Quiet Moment, 257

Rail Shooting on the Delaware, 187, *188*

Retrospection, 257

Robert C. Odgen, 404–6, *405*, 410

Sailboats Racing on the Delaware, 181, *182*, 184

Salutat, 357, 358–59, 361–63, *362*, 419

Scrollwork, Foreshortened, 248

Shad Fishing at Gloucester, 276

A Singer, 394, *394*

Singing a Pathetic Song, 37, 275–76, *276*, 324

The Spelling Bee at Angell's, 146, 421

sports-orientated, 357–63

Starting Out After Rail, 181–83, *183*

A Street Scene in Seville, 160–62, *161*, 165, 434

The Strong Man, 149, 149–50

Swimming, 93, 241, 277, 290, 293, 304, 305–26, 334, 340, 358, 417, 418–19, 443–44, 466

Taking the Count, 357, 359, 359–60, *360*

The Thinker, 383–84, *384*, 410

Untitled (Gears), 138, *139*

The Veteran, 338, 340–42, *341*

William Rush and His Model, 369–72, *371*

William Rush Carving His Allegorical Figure of the Schuylkill River (1876), 241–55, *242*, *245*, 306, 325, 334, 416, 418, 435, 466, 471, 474, 513n25

William Rush Carving His Allegorical Figure of the Schuylkill River (1908), 369–70, *370*, 416, 419, 435, 466, 471, 474

Woman with Parasol, 248

women in pink era of, 346–55, 377–79

The Wrestlers, 357, 361, *361*

Paintings, Eakins (continued)
The Writing Master, 228, *228*
year of reckoning and, 363–72
Young Girl Meditating, 257
The Pair-Oared Shell (Eakins), *202, 206*
Pancoast, Joseph, 22, 140
Pancoast, William, 140
Pantagruel (Rabelais), 241
Parisian studies, Eakins
artistic fathers of, 153–55
completion of, 155–57
enrollment for, 141–42
Spanish interlude in, 157–63
struggles during, 148–53
written correspondences during, 140,
145–48, 150–53, 156–57
Parker, Gilbert Sunderland, 120, 388
Parker, Helen Montanverde, 393–94, 409.
See also The Old-Fashioned Dress
portrait of, *373, 375, 376,* 401, 407
posing by, 91
Parker, Kate, 398
Parker, Mrs. Gilbert Lafayette, 387
Parody of The Gross Clinic, 234, *234–35*
Parry, Ellwood C., 274–75
Pastoral (Arcadia Relief) (Eakins), 285, 298,
302, 302–3
*The Pathetic Song. See Singing a Pathetic
Song*
Peale, Charles Willson, 249
Peale, Rembrandt, 137
Pennell, Joseph, 264, 269
Pennsylvania Academy of the Fine Arts,
216–17. *See also* Instruction, Eakins;
Loincloth scandal
Bregler papers and, xiii, 44
class photograph at, *121*
Eakins artwork at, 14, 16, 273
instruction at, 259–61, 265–69
loincloth scandal at, 3, 12, 23–24, 30,
50–59
nude studies at, 53, 258–60, 493n8
oversight of, 258
staff of, 481–82

Perspective
The Concert Singer, 352
Eakins teaching on, 265
Eakins training on, 138
Gérôme use of, 208
grid drawings for, 207–8
John Biglin in a Single Scull, 211
liberties taken in, 209
The Pair-Oared Shell, 208
preoccupation with, 209–12,
467–68
Perspective of a Lathe (Eakins), *138*
Phidias (Greek sculptor), 298
Philadelphia Art Club, 61, 65
Philadelphia Inquirer, 14, 325, 388
Philadelphia Museum of Art, 244
Eakins artwork at, xiv, 16, 25, 46
Philadelphia Press, 91
Philadelphia Sketch Club, 61, 65
Philadelphia Society of Artists, 260, 262
Philadelphia Times, 324
Photograph of Edgarton Trotting (Muy-
bridge), *263, 264*
Photographs (of Eakins)
Academy of the Fine Arts, class photo, 121
*Age 35 to 40 in Heavy Wool Jacket, ca. 1882,
33*
Eakins at about 55, ca. 1900, 381
*Naked Series: Thomas Eakins in Front of
Cloth Backdrop, Pose 1, ca. 1883, 472*
Portrait of Eakins, xii
*Thomas Eakins and His Wife with a Dog,
1910–1914, 38*
Thomas Eakins at about 65, 462, 474
*Thomas Eakins at about 65, Nude, in
River, 475*
*Thomas Eakins at about 65, Nude, with
Unidentified Man in Cohansy River,
ca. 1909, 477*
*Thomas Eakins at about Age Ten, ca. 1854,
122*
*Thomas Eakins at about Age Thirty-Five,
1880, 124*
Thomas Eakins in Three-Quarter View, in

Chestnut Street Studio, ca. 1891–1892,
    334
Thomas Eakins Leaning against Building,
    1870–1876, 132
Thomas Eakins Nude and Female Nude,
    1885, 287
Thomas Eakins Nude, Holding Nude
    Female in His Arms, Looking at Cam-
    era, ca. 1885, 288
Thomas Eakins Nude, Holding Nude
    Female in His Arms, Looking Down,
    ca. 1885, 414
Thomas Eakins Nude, Semireclining on
    Couch, from Rear, ca. 1883, 293
Walter MacDowell, Thomas Eakins and J.
    Laurie Wallace Nude in Wooded Land-
    scape, ca. 1883, 9
The Photographs of Thomas Eakins (Hen-
    dricks), 41
Photography (by Eakins), 290. *See also*
    Artwork, Eakins; Paintings, Eakins;
    Perspective; *specific photographs*
    African American Girl Nude, Reclining on
        Couch, 56, 285
    Amelia Van Buren Sitting with Cat On
        Shoulder, 347
    androgyny in, 291–93
    authorship of, 274–75, 515n14
    Benjamin Eakins Standing, and Man Sit-
        ting, under Tree, 277
    Bill Duckett Nude, Lying on Stomach,
        Holding Vase, 289, 289–90
    Casts of Anatomical Dissection, 267
    Clara Mather Sitting in Carved Armchair,
        286
    Elizabeth Macdowell in Print Dress, 63
    Ella Crowell, 68
    eroticism of, 281–86
    exhibitionism in, 293–94
    exhibitions of, 273–74, 515n13
    false claims regarding, 272–73
    Female Nude Semireclining, from Rear, 295
    Female Nude Sitting on Queen Anne
        Chair, 56, 285

Hannah Susan Macdowell, 291, 292
J. Laurie Wallace Nude, Playing Pipes,
    Facing Left, 270, 291
Male Nude, Poised to Throw Rock, Facing
    Right, 290
Male Nude Sitting on Modeling Stand,
    Holding Small Sculpture of Horse, 56
Male Nudes in a Seated Tug-of-War, 316
Margaret Eakins and Thomas Eakins's
    setter Harry, 62
Naked Series: Female Model, 48
Naked Series: John Laurie Wallace, 48
Naked Series: Thomas Eakins in Front of
    Cloth Backdrop, Pose 1, 472
nude emphasis in, 279–303
outdoor excursions and, 290–91
pastoral, 297–303
The Pathetic Song study using, 275, *276*
professional needs and, 280–81
rediscovery through, 273–74
self-nudes in, 288, 288–89, 292, *293*
Seven Males, Nude, Two Boxing at Center,
    316
Six Males, Nude, Wrestling, 317
students and friends in, 286–90
Susan Macdowell Eakins Nude, Left Arm
    Resting on Neck of Thomas Eakins's
    Horse Billy, 284, 285
Susan Macdowell Eakins Nude, Sitting on
    Blanket, Looking over Right Shoulder,
    301
Thomas Eakins and Students, Swimming
    Nude, 318
Thomas Eakins Nude, holding Nude
    Female in His Arms, Looking at Cam-
    era, 288, 288–89
Thomas Eakins Nude, holding Nude
    Female in His Arms, Looking Down,
    414
Thomas Eakins Nude, Semireclining on
    Couch, from Rear, 292, 293
Three Crowell Boys Nude, in Creek, 75
Three Female Nudes, 56
Three women, man, and dog, 276

Photographs (of Eakins) (continued)
    tracing use in, 275–79
    Two Fishermen Mending Nets, 278
    Two Women in Classical Costume, 285
    voyeurism in, 294–95
    William G. Macdowell, Facing Left, 63
    William J. Crowell, 68
    Women's Modeling Class with Cow, 266
Picasso, Pablo, 21, 463–64
Picozzi, Mary Louise, 43–44
Plato, 321
Poe, Edgar Allen, 465
Poetics (Aristotle), xiv
Pointon, Marcia, 46
Poor, Henry Varnum, 27
Pornographic Nude (French photo), *283*
Porter, Fairfield, 25, 252
Portrait of an Artist (Eakins), 338
*Portrait of the Artist's Wife with a Setter
    Dog* (Eakins), 29–30, 302, 331
    alterations to, 327, 329, 337
    content of, 326
    influences on, 329–30, 364
    original, *328*
    parallels in, 327–28, 520nn50–51
    revised, *329*
Portrait of Benjamin Eakins (Eakins), 363,
    363
Portrait of Douglass Morgan Hall (Eakins),
    332, 339–40, 410
Portrait of Dr. Jacob Mendez da Costa
    (Eakins), 391, 411, *411*
Portrait of an Engineer (Eakins), 338
Portrait of John B. Gest (Eakins), 387, *387,*
    408
*Portrait of Louis N. Kenton. See The
    Thinker*
Portrait of a Poet (Eakins), 338
Portrait of Professor Benjamin H. Rand
    (Eakins), 333, 337–38, *338*
*Portrait of Professor Gross. See The Gross
    Clinic*
Portrait of Samuel Murray (Eakins), *343,*
    343–44

Portrait of a Student (Eakins), 338
Portrait of Thomas Eakins (Eakins, S.), 350,
    351
Principles and Practices of Surgery
    (Agnew), 238
The Prisoner (Gérôme), 142–43
*Proceedings of the Academy of Natural Sci-
    ences of Philadelphia,* 266
Professional Criminals of America (Byrnes),
    338
Professor Henry A. Rowland (Eakins),
    356–57, *357,* 391
    perspective in, 456
Professor Leslie W. Miller (Eakins), *400,*
    400–401
Pue, Eleanor S. F.
    portrait of, 373–74, *374,* 393, 407
    posing by, 90, *91,* 398
Pushing for Rail (Eakins), 184, *184*
Puvis de Chavannes, Pierre, 15
Pygmalion and Galatea (Gérôme), 252, *253*

A Quiet Moment (Eakins), 257

Rabelais, 241, 375, 416, 419
Raffaeilli, Jean-François, 144
Rail Shooting on the Delaware (Eakins),
    187, *188*
Rand, Benjamin, 391
    portrait of, 333, 337–38, *338*
Raphael, 157
Realism
    Eakins honesty as, 399–402, 463–65
    reactions to, 407–12
    slander v., 402–6
    subjectivity of, 463–64
Realism, Writing, Disfiguration (Fried), 45
Reese, Thomas L., 146
Regnault, Henri, 158
Rembrandt (van Rijn), 224–27, 228, 230,
    386
Renoir, Auguste, 337

Requena, Carmelita, *159,* 159–62

Retrospection (Eakins), 257

Rewald, John, 28

Reynolds, George, 321, 340–42, *341,* 483
  stability of, 445

Ribera, Juseppe de, 158

Richards, William Trost, 208, 261, 322

Richmond, George, 387

Riley, James Whitcomb, 307

Robert C. Odgen (Eakins), 404–6, *405,* 410

Roberts, Howard, 110, 146

Rockwell, Norman, 29

Rogers, Fairman, 262–63, 271, 482

Roosevelt, Theodore, 335

Rorem, Ned, 307

Rothermel, Peter, 139

Rowing portraits, Eakins
  Biglin Brothers Racing, 201, *201,* 206
  Biglin Brothers Turning the Stake, 192,
    202–7, 243, 337
  The Champion Single Sculls, 165, 194–95,
    195, 197–206, 334
  Gérôme and, 212–13
  Oarsmen on the Schuylkill, 205–6, *206*
  The Oarsmen, 203
  The Pair-Oared Shell, 202, 206
  perspective of, 207–12
  post-*Champion,* 200–206
  progression of, 206–7
  rowing's status and, 195–97
  timeline of, 206–7

Rowland, Henry, 79, 356–57, *357,* 391

Rush, William, 7, 41. *See also William
    Rush Carving His Allegorical Figure of
    the Schuylkill River (William Rush)
    (1876)* (Eakins)
  background of, 244–46, 249–50
  Eakins portraits of, 245–50, 369–72

Russell, John, 26, 386

Ryder, Albert Pinkham, 15–16, 24

Sailboats Racing on the Delaware (Eakins),
    181, *182,* 184

Saint-Gaudens, Augustus, 111, 147

Salutat (Eakins), 357, 361–63, *362*
  content of, 358–59, 419

Samuel Gross (Waugh), 229, *229*

Santje, Suzanne, *378,* 378–79, 396, 401, 435.
    See also The Actress

Sarasate, Pablo de, 352

Sargent, John Singer, 13, 15, 24, 158, 410
  art of, 372, 386, 388–90, 393, 398
  characteristics of, 29
  sexuality of, 308

Sartain, Emily, *89,* 99–100, 115
  background of, 135, 448, 483
  Eakins criticisms by, 89–90
  Eakins letters to, 140

Sartain, John, 39, 89
  background of, 135, 482
  Eakins clashes with, 261–62, 443
  Eakins studies and, 140–41
  nude models and, 250, 259–60

Sartain, William, 120, 155, 158

Scandal(s), Eakins, 49. *See also* Crowell,
    Ella; Hammitt, Lillian; Loincloth
    scandal
  Academy conflicts and, 258–62
  art club, 61–67
  Crowell, Ella, 6–7, 69–83, 103, 105, 108,
    114, 353, 418, 448–54
  Hammitt, Lillian, 85–101, 103, 105, 108,
    233, 440, 445–48, 453
  loincloth, 3, 12, 23–24, 30, 50–59
  loyalty shifts during, 494n9
  Parisian, 89–90
  Williams, Addie, 98, 367–68, 372, 416,
    442, 448

Schapiro, Meyer, 25

Schenck, Franklin, 483. *See also Home
    Ranch*
  portraits of, 342, *342,* 344–45, *345,*
    421
  stability of, 445

Schendler, Sylvan, 25, 96, 126, 257
  Amelia Van Buren interpretations by,
    349–50

Schendler, Sylvan (continued)
   The Artist and His Father interpretations by, 187
   Concert Singer interpretations by, 353
   Eakins teaching and, 269
   ecclesiastical interpretations by, 376
   gender portrayals and, 392
   Gross Clinic interpretations by, 229
   Old Fashioned Dress interpretations by, 409
   portrait meanings and, 385
   Portrait of the Artist's Wife interpretations by, 29–30, 331
   Portrait of Samuel Murray interpretations by, 344
   religious beliefs and, 375
   William Rush interpretations by, 253
Schiebel, Douglas, 428
Schjeldahl, Peter, 354
Schlichter, Henry Walter, 359
Schmidt, Edward, 401
Schmitt, Max. *See also The Champion Single Sculls (Champion)* (Eakins)
   background of, 197–98, 205
   portrait of, *194, 195,* 198–200, 207
Schoenberg, Arnold, 463
Schreiber brothers, 201–2
Schumann, Robert, 455
Schussele, Christian, 220–21, 481
   art instruction by, 23, 139, 258, 260–61
   background of, 258
   Eakins relations with, 258, 262
Schuster, Will, 187, 421
Scott, James, 323
Scribner's Magazine, 145, 216, 260, 421
Scrollwork, Foreshortened (Eakins), 248
Searle, Mary, 51, 482
Sears, Mary, 157
Self-Portrait (Eakins), *365,* 365–67, *366*
Sellin, David, 64
Seven Males, Nude, Two Boxing at Center (Eakins), *316*
Sewell, Darrell, 46, 355

Shad Fishing at Gloucester (Eakins), *276*
Shaw, Sallie, 95, 101, 170
Shinn, Earl, 245
   Eakins character and, 474
   Eakins letters to, 100, 148, 201, 418
   Eakins teaching and, 258, 262
   William Rush interpretation by, 250
Siegl, Theodore, 243
Silver Blaze (Holmes), 169
A Singer (Portrait of Mrs. W. H. Bowden) (Eakins), *394, 394*
Singing a Pathetic Song (Eakins), 37, 324
   photograph use in, 275–76, *276*
Six Males, Nude, Wrestling (Eakins), *317*
Sloan, John, 18
Smith, Billy, 358, *360,* 361
Smith, Carl, 358
Smith College Museum, 14
Smith, Jessie Willcox, 107, 108
Smithsonian, xiii–xiv
Smukler, Douglas J., 428
Snow, Edward Taylor, 408
Snowden, A. Loudon, 404
Society of American Artists, 13, 216, 346
Soyer, Moses, 27
Soyer, Raphael, 18, 20
   Eakins homage by, 27–28, 490n41
Spain, 157–63
The Spelling Bee at Angell's (Eakins), *146,* 421
Spies, Kathleen, 46, 339, 366–67
   gender observations by, 393, 395–96
Spinning (Eakins), 257, 323
Spitzka, Edward A., 391
Stafford-Clark, David, 423, 452, 475–76
Stanford, Leland, 271
Starting Out After Rail (Eakins), 181–83, *183*
Steinberg, Leo, 252
Stephens, Alice Barber, 481. *See also* Barber, Alice
Stephens, Caroline Eakins, 419, 481
   Eakins accusations by, 61–64, 106–7

family expulsion of, 66, 72

mental health of, 455

Stephens, Charles, 55, 61–64, 419, 481

Stephens, (George) Frank, 6, 75–76, 321, 481

  Eakins accusations by, 51, 61–66, 103, 106, 174, 416, 419

  family expulsion of, 66, 72

  mental health of, 64, 448

  photograph of, 60

Stevens, Alfred, 328

Stevenson, Robert Louis, 386

Stieglitz, Alfred, 20

Stokes, Frank W., 401, 410

Stokes, Mrs. M. S., 401

Stokes, Robert C., 404–6

Story of American Painting (Caffin), 14

A Street Scene in Seville (Eakins), 160–62, 161, 165, 434

The Strong Man (Eakins), 149, 149–50

Susan Macdowell Eakins Nude, Left Arm Resting on Neck of Thomas Eakins's Horse Billy (Eakins), 284, 285

Susan Macdowell Eakins Nude, Sitting on Blanket, Looking over Right Shoulder (Eakins), 301

Sutton, Peter, 254

Swimming (The Swimming Hole) (Eakins), 93, 290, 293, 340

  buttock prominence in, 241, 306, 315–19, 325, 418–19

  complexity of, 334

  content of, 305

  exhibitionism in, 320–26

  homosexuality and, 307–11, 315–20, 444

  interpretations of, 306, 312–20, 324–26

  male nudity and, 311–15, 417

  press reviews of, 324–25

  renaming of, 306–7

  site for, 317

  study for, 319

  themes of, 241, 306–16, 325–26, 358, 443, 466

  tracing of, 277

System of Surgery (Gross), 222

Taking the Count (Eakins), 357, 359, 359–60

  study of, 360

Tatham, David, 21

Telegraph, 296

Temple Gold Medal, 13

Tennyson, Alfred, 455

Theory of the Leisure Class (Veblen), 263

The Thinker (Portrait of Louis N. Kenton) (Eakins), 383–84, 384, 410

Thomas Eakins (Goodrich), 41

Thomas Eakins and Students, Swimming Nude (Eakins), 318

Thomas Eakins, His Life and Work (Goodrich), 11–12

  chapter breakdown of, 22–24

  style of, 21

  themes of, 21–22, 24–25

Thomas Eakins in Three-Quarter View (Murray), 334

Thomas Eakins Nude and Female Nude, 287, 288–89

Thomas Eakins Nude, holding Nude Female in His Arms, Looking at Camera (Eakins), 288, 288–89

Thomas Eakins Nude, holding Nude Female in His Arms, Looking Down (Eakins), 414

Thomas Eakins Nude, Semireclining on Couch, from Rear (Eakins), 292, 293

Thomas Eakins: The Absolute Male (Esten), 308

Thomas Eakins: The Heroism of Modern Life (Johns), 26, 28, 45

Thomas Eakins Who Painted (McHenry), 41

Thomson, William, 391

Three Crowell Boys Nude, in Creek (Eakins), 75

Three Female Nudes (Eakins), *56*
Three women, man, and dog (Eakins), *276*
Time, 26
Tinterow, Gary, 390
Tissot, James, 328
Touched with Fire (Jamison), 454
Transference
    The Agnew Clinic, 240–41
    Biglin Brothers Turning the Stake, 204
    The Champion Single Sculls, 194–95,
        199–200, 204
    Eakins family, 193–95, 199–200, 204,
        227–35, 240–41, 249–51, 253, 255,
        380–81, 416
    Freud theory of, 127–28
    The Gross Clinic, 194, 227–35
    William Rush, 249–51, 253, 255, 416
    woman-to-man, 240, 291–92, 380–81
Trask, John, 328
Treatise on the Principles and Practice of
    Surgery (Agnew), 235
Trilby (Du Maurier), 447
Tucker, Mark, 275
Turner, James P., 391
    portrait of, *380,* 380–81, *381*
Two Fishermen Mending Nets (Eakins), *278*
Two Women in Classical Costume (Eakins),
    285

Universal Exposition, 13
University of Pennsylvania, 271–72
Unkle, Maggie, 86
Untitled (Gears) (Eakins), 138, *139*

Van Buren, Amelia, 55, 116, 399
    background of, 347–48, 420, 483
    portraits of, 346–50, *347,* 393, 435
Van Gogh, Vincent, 21, 455
Van Rensselaer, Marianna, 146–47, 297,
    327, 329
Vanuxem, James, 248
Veblen, Thorstein, 263

Velázquez, Diego, 22, 158, 226–27, 230
    Eakins relationship to, 386
The Veteran (Eakins), 338, 340–42, *341*
The Virginian (Wister), 336
Voltaire, Francois M., 103
Vonnoh, Robert W., 323
Voyeurism
    The Agnew Clinic, 239
    Eakins photography, 294–95
    exhibitionism connection to, 423,
        435–36
    The Gross Clinic, 233–34

Waldon, Mary, 410
Wallace, J. Laurie, 483
    nudes of, *9,* 40, *270, 290, 291*
    Swimming and, 321
Wallach, Alan, 45
Ward, Mrs. Wilson Shaw, 407
Warhol, Andy, 309, 344
Washington, George, 26
Watson, Eva Lawrence, 348, 483
Watson, Forbes, 19, 390
Waugh, Samuel, 228–29
Webster's, 246
Weems, Parson, 26
Weinberg, Helene Barbara, 108, 402
Whistler, James McNeill, 24, 308, 352
    Eakins relations with, 328–29, 364
    paintings by, 329–30, *330*
White, J. William, 236, 390, 410
Whitman, Walt, 115, 142, 275
    Eakins portrait of, 386
    Eakins relations with, 228
    photographs of, *289,* 289–90
    sexuality of, 305–6, 307, 308, 343
Whitney, Gertrude Vanderbilt, 19
Whitney Museum, 18, 19
Wilcroft, J. R., 67
Wilde, Oscar, 386
William G. Macdowell, Facing Left (Eakins),
    63
William J. Crowell (Eakins), *68*

William Rush and His Model (Eakins),
369–72, *371*

*William Rush Carving His Allegorical Figure
of the Schuylkill River (1908)* (Eakins),
369–70, *370,* 416, 419
parallels in, 435, 471, 474
themes in, 466

*William Rush Carving His Allegorical Figure
of the Schuylkill River (William Rush)
(1876)* (Eakins), *245*
buttock representation in, 241, 306,
418
complexity of, 334
content of, 246–47
gender messages in, 254–55
Goodrich interpretations of, 249, 253
interpretations, general, of, 243–44,
249–55
Katz interpretation of, 253
misrepresentations of, 248–49
model for, 254, 513*n*25
parallels in, 435, 471, 474
Porter interpretation of, 252
pricing of, 243
reproduction of, 244
research for, 247–49
Schendler interpretation of, 253
Shinn interpretations of, 250
Steinberg interpretation of, 252
study of, *242*
themes of, 241, 306, 325, 466
transference in, 249–51, 253, 255, 416

Williams, Annie, 41, 254, 513*n*25

Williams, Mary Adeline (Addie), 5, 16, 40,
42, 85
background of, 367, 484
Eakins relations with, 98, 367–68, 372,
416, 442, 448
nude modeling by, 370–72
portraits of, *98,* 367–69, *368,* 370–72

Williams, Mrs. Talcott, 399

Williams, Talcott, 320–21, 385

Wilmerding, John, 18

Wilson, David, 362, *362*

Wilson, Lucy Langdon W., 38, 140
Eakins sexuality and, 98, 441–42, 451

Wister, Owen, 336

Wolf, Otto, 401

Woman with Parasol (Eakins), *248*

Women
The Actress portrayal of, 396
Agnew Clinic representation of, 392
criticism perspectives and, 106–8, 112
Eakins portrayal of, 191, 345–55, 377–79,
388–90, 391–96, 433, 471
Eakins treatment of, 21, 99–101, 112,
117–19, 128–29, 312–13, 388–94, 451,
468
Gross Clinic representation of, 191, 345,
391, 433
perceptions of, 392

Women's Modeling Class with Cow
(Eakins), *266*

Wood, George, 410

Wood, Horatio, 309, 335, *335,* 391
medical beliefs of, 437

Wood, James L., 35, 120, 375
Eakins crude behavior and, 95–96
Eakins sexuality and, 90, 97, 309
portrait of, 410

Wood, Richard, 409

Woolf, Virginia, 455

The Wrestlers (Eakins), 357, *361,* 361

Wright, John, 92

The Writing Master (Eakins), 228, *228*

Wyeth, Andrew, 29

Wylie, Robert, 149

Young Art Student (Fussell), *95*

Young Girl Meditating (Eakins), *257*

Young-Bruehl, Elizabeth, 430–31

Yvon, Adolphe, 258

Ziegler, Francis, 336
Hammitt, Lillian story by, 35, 109
posing by, 93, 397, 444